2yrs 3mon 2wks

THE THEORY OF RELATIONAL DATABASES

OTHER BOOKS OF INTEREST

Wayne Amsbury
Structured Basic and Beyond

Jean-Loup Baer
Computer Systems Architecture

Randal Bryant, editor
Proceedings of the Third Caltech Conference on VLSI

Peter Calingaert
Assemblers, Compliers and Program Translation

M. Carberry, H. Khalil, J. Leathrum, and L. Levy
Foundations of Computer Science

Shimon Even
Graph Algorithms

William Findlay and David Watt
Pascal: An Introduction to Methodical Programming, Second Edition

Owen Hanson
Design of Computer Data Files

Ellis Horowitz
Fundamentals of Programming Languages

Ellis Horowitz, editor
Programming Languages: A Grand Tour

Ellis Horowitz and Sartaj Sahni
Fundamentals of Computer Algorithms

Ellis Horowitz and Sartaj Sahni
Fundamentals of Data Structures

Yahiko Kambayashi
Database: A Bibliography

H. T. Kung, Guy Steele, and Robert Sproull, editors
VLSI Systems and Computations

Thomas Logsdon
Computers and Social Controversy

James J. McGregor and Alan H. Watt
Simple Pascal

Theo Pavlidis
Algorithms for Graphics and Image Processing

Gerald N. Pitts and Barry L. Bateman
Essentials of COBOL Programming

Ira Pohl and Alan Shaw
The Nature of Computation: An Introduction to Computer Science

Arto Salomaa
Jewels of Formal Language Theory

Donald D. Spencer
Computers in Number Theory

Jeffrey D. Ullman
Principles of Database Systems, ***Second Edition***

THE THEORY OF RELATIONAL DATABASES

DAVID MAIER
OREGON GRADUATE CENTER

COMPUTER SCIENCE PRESS

Printed in the United States of America.

Computer Science Press
11 Taft Court
Rockville, Maryland 20850

2 3 4 5 6 Printing Year 88 87 86 85

Library of Congress Cataloging in Publication Data

Maier, David, 1953-
The theory of relational databases.

(Computer software engineering series)
Bibliography: p.
Includes index.
1. Data base management. I. Title. II. Series.
QA76.9.D3M33 001.64 82-2518
ISBN 0-914894-42-0 AACR2

DEDICATION

For Rev. James P. Maier, 1899–1980,
and
Luke David Maier, 1982 and onward.
I wish they could have met.

TABLE OF CONTENTS

PREFACE

This book is a revision and extension of notes I wrote for a graduate seminar in relational database theory given at Stony Brook. The purpose of that course was to give students enough background in relational database theory to enable them to understand the current research being done in the field. I have not attempted to be exhaustive in covering all results in relational database theory—the field has already grown too large to cover everything. Instead, I have attempted to get within "one paper" of all current work: This book should give a student sufficient background to read recent papers in relational theory.

While most of the material presented here has been presented before, there is some new material, particularly on annular covers and in the chapter on database semantics. I have tried to bring material together that was available previously only in separate papers, and give some coherence to the results. That task has involved translating many of the results into standard notation, redoing some of the definitions, and constructing some new proofs for previously known theorems.

The book is aimed at a second course in databases, presumably at the graduate level, but possibly at the advanced undergraduate level. While an introductory course in database management systems is not an absolute prerequisite for this book, it is certainly desirable for some concrete motivation and intuition for the abstractions presented here. No specific course in mathematics is assumed, but there should be an acquaintance with set theory and the rudiments of formal logic. Some of the exercises require some sophisticated combinatorics, but those exercises are not central to the topic being developed—they are included for fun. Exercises that are deemed particularly difficult are marked with an asterisk.

Of course, I hope the book also will be a useful reference for researchers already working in the area. The bibliography is current through October 1981; some of the technical reports presumably have since appeared in journals and conference proceedings. I am grateful to Jeff Ullman for an advance copy of the bibliography to the second edition of *Principles of Database Systems*.

ACKNOWLEDGEMENTS

My interest in relational database theory came about in my final spring and summer as a graduate student at Princeton. I have since received much encouragement and many good ideas from the crowd I met there: Catriel Beeri, Peter Honeyman, Hank Korth, Alberto Mendelzon, Fereidoon Sadri, Yehoshua Sagiv, Ed Sciore, Mihalis Yannakakis, Jeff Ullman and, indirectly, Al Aho. My class at Stony Brook suffered bravely through the draft of the first eight chapters. Al Croker was the champion typo finder. Billie Goldstein kept at it for most of the rest of the manuscript. Ron Fagin also offered many suggestions, particularly on multivalued and join dependencies. Two classes have used the notes and relayed comments back to me—one at Penn State taught by Karen Chase, the other at Michigan taught by Joyce Friedman and Steve Tolken. Joyce also served as technical reader for the manuscript. I have also received much advice and amusement from the data semantics cadre here at Stony Brook: David Rozenshtein, Sharon Salveter, Jacob Stein and David Warren. Kaye VanValkenburg, my wife, has been encouraging and forebearing throughout. Finally, I feel immeasurable gratitude for Betty Knittweis, who typed and retyped the majority of the manuscript.

D.M.
Stony Brook
April 1982

Chapter 1

RELATIONS AND RELATION SCHEMES

One of the major advantages of the relational model is its uniformity. All data is viewed as being stored in tables, with each row in the table having the same format. Each row in the table summarizes some object or relationship in the real world. Whether the corresponding entities in the real world actually possess the uniformity the relational model ascribes to them is a question that the user of the model must answer. It is a question of the suitability of the model for the application at hand.

Whether or not the relational model is appropriate for a particular set of data shall not concern us. There are plenty of instances where the model is appropriate, and we always assume we are dealing with such instances.

1.1 BRASS TACKS

So much for philosophy. Let us consider an example. An airline schedule certainly exhibits regularity. Every flight listed has certain characteristics. It is a flight from an origin to a destination. It is scheduled to depart at a specific time and arrive at a later time. It has a flight number. Part of an airline schedule might appear as in Table 1.1.

What do we observe about this schedule? Each flight is summarized as a set of values, one in each column. There are restrictions on what information may appear in a given column. The FROM column contains names of airports served by the airline, the ARRIVES column contains times of day. The order of the columns is immaterial as far as information content is concerned. The DEPARTS and ARRIVES columns could be interchanged with no change in meaning. Finally, since each flight has a unique number, no flight is represented by more than one row.

The schedule in Table 1.1 is an example of a relation of type FLIGHTS. The format of the relation is determined by the set of column labels {NUMBER, FROM, TO, DEPARTS, ARRIVES}. These column names are

Table 1.1 FLIGHTS (airline schedule).

NUMBER	FROM	TO	DEPARTS	ARRIVES
83	JFK	O'Hare	11:30a	1:43p
84	O'Hare	JFK	3:00p	5:55p
109	JFK	Los Angeles	9:50p	2:52a
213	JFK	Boston	11:43a	12:45p
214	Boston	JFK	2:20p	3:12p

called attribute names. Corresponding to each attribute name is a set of permissible values for the associated column. This set is called the domain of the attribute name. The domain of NUMBER could be the set of all one-, two- or three-digit decimal integers. Each row in the relation is a set of values, one from the domain of each attribute name. The rows of this relation are called 5-tuples, or tuples in general. The tuples of a relation form a set, hence there are no duplicate rows. Finally, there is a subset of the attribute names with the property that tuples can be distinguished by looking only at values corresponding to attribute names in the subset. Such a subset is called a key for the relation. For the relation in Table 1.1, {NUMBER} is a key.

1.2 FORMALIZATION OF RELATIONS

We now formalize the definitions of the last section and add a couple of new ones. A *relation scheme* R is a finite set of *attribute names* $\{A_1, A_2, \ldots, A_n\}$. Corresponding to each attribute name A_i is a set D_i, $1 \leq i \leq n$, called the *domain* of A_i. We also denote the domain of A_i by $dom(A_i)$. Attribute names are sometimes called *attribute symbols* or simply *attributes*, particularly in the abstract. The domains are arbitrary, non-empty sets, finite or countably infinite. Let $\mathbf{D} = D_1 \cup D_2 \cup \cdots \cup D_n$. A *relation* r on relation scheme R is a finite set of mappings $\{t_1, t_2, \ldots, t_p\}$ from R to $\mathbf{D}$ with the restriction that for each mapping $t \in r$, $t(A_i)$ must be in D_i, $1 \leq i \leq n$. The mappings are called *tuples.*

Example 1.1 In Table 1.1 the relation scheme is FLIGHTS = {NUMBER, FROM, TO, DEPARTS, ARRIVES}. The domains for each attribute name might be:

1. dom(NUMBER) = the set of one-, two- or three-digit decimal numbers,

2. dom(FROM) = dom(TO) = {JFK, O'Hare, Los Angeles, Boston, Atlanta},
3. dom(DEPARTS) = dom(ARRIVES) = the set of times of day.

The relation in Table 1.1 has five tuples. One of them is t defined as t(NUMBER) = 84, t(FROM) = O'Hare, t(TO) = JFK, t(DEPARTS) = 3:00p, t(ARRIVES) = 5:55p.

Where did the mappings come from? What happened to tables and rows? We use mappings in our formalism to avoid any explicit ordering of the attribute names in the relation scheme. As we noted in the last section, such an ordering adds nothing to the information content of a relation. We do not want to restrict tuples to be sequences of values in a certain order. Rather, a tuple is a set of values, one for each attribute name in the relation scheme.* The mappings we defined are nothing more than correspondences of this type. Now that we have taken the trouble of avoiding any explicit ordering in relations, in nearly every case we shall denote our relations by writing the attributes in a certain order and the tuples as lists of values in the same order.

In either case, it makes sense, given a tuple t, to discuss the *value* of t on attribute A, alternatively called the A-*value* of t. Considering t as a mapping, the A-value of t is $t(A)$. Interpreting t as a row in a table, the A-value of t is the entry of t in the column headed by A. Since t is a mapping, we can restrict the domain of t. Let X be a subset of R. The usual notation for t restricted to X is $t_{|X}$. We, in our infinite knowledge, shall confuse the issue and write this restriction as $t(X)$ and call it the X-*value* of t. Technically, $t(A)$ and $t(\{A\})$ are different objects, but in keeping with the confusing customs of relational database theory, we often write A for the singleton set $\{A\}$. We also blur the distinction between $t(A)$ and $t(\{A\})$, even though one is just a value and the other is a mapping from A to this value. We assume there is some value λ such that $t(\emptyset) = \lambda$ for any tuple t. Thus $t_1(\emptyset) = t_2(\emptyset)$ for any tuples t_1 and t_2.

Example 1.2 Let t be the tuple defined in Example 1.1. The FROM-value of t is t(FROM) = O'Hare. The {FROM, TO}-value of t is the tuple t' defined by t'(FROM) = O'Hare, t'(TO) = JFK. We shall denote such a tuple as ⟨O'Hare:FROM JFK:TO⟩ or simply ⟨O'Hare JFK⟩ where the order of attributes is understood.

We have been treating relations as static objects. However, relations are supposed to abstract some portion of the real world, and this portion of the world may change with time. We consider that relations are time-varying, so that tuples may be added, deleted, or changed. In Table 1.1, flights may be added or dropped, or their times may be changed. We do assume, though,

*Actually, a tuple could be a multiset (a set with duplicates) of values, if domains for different attribute names intersect.

that the relation scheme is time-invariant. Henceforth, when dealing with a relation, we shall think of it as a sequence of relations in the sense already defined, or, in some cases, as potential sequences that the relation might follow, that is, possible states the relation may occupy. We shall discuss restrictions on the states a relation may assume, although nearly all of these restrictions will be *memoryless*: they will depend only on the current state of the relation and not on its history of previous states.

1.3 KEYS

A *key* of a relation r on relation scheme R is a subset $K = \{B_1, B_2, \ldots, B_m\}$ of R with the following property. For any two distinct tuples t_1 and t_2 in r, there is a $B \in K$ such that $t_1(B) \neq t_2(B)$. That is, no two tuples have the same value on all attributes in K. We could write this condition as $t_1(K) \neq t_2(K)$. Hence, it is sufficient to know the K-value of a tuple to identify the tuple uniquely.

Example 1.3 In Figure 1.1, {NUMBER} and {FROM, TO} are both keys.

Let us formulate some notation for relations, schemes, and keys. Our convention will be to use uppercase letters from the front of the alphabet for attribute symbols, uppercase letters from the back of the alphabet for relation schemes, and lowercase letters for relations. We denote a relation scheme $R = \{A_1, A_2, \ldots, A_n\}$ by $R[A_1A_2 \cdots A_n]$, or sometimes $A_1 A_2 \cdots A_n$ when we are not concerned with naming the scheme. (Another confusing custom of relational database theory is to use concatenation to stand for set union between sets of attributes.) A relation r on scheme R is written $r(R)$ or $r(A_1A_2 \cdots A_n)$. To denote the key of a relation, we underline the attribute names in the key. Relation r on scheme $ABCD$ with AC as a key is written $r(\underline{A}B\underline{C}D)$. We can also incorporate the key into the relation scheme: $R[\underline{A}B\underline{C}D]$. Any relation $r(R)$ is restricted to have AC as a key.

Example 1.4 We can write the relation scheme for the relation in Table 1.1 as FLIGHTS [<u>NUMBER</u> FROM TO DEPARTS ARRIVES].

If we wish to specify more than one key for a scheme or relation, we must list the keys separately, since the underline notation will not work. The keys explicitly listed with a relation scheme are called *designated keys*. There may be keys other than those listed; they are *implicit keys*. Sometimes we distinguish one of the designated keys as the *primary key*.

Our definition of key is actually a bit too broad. If relation $r(R)$ has key K', and $K' \subseteq K \subseteq R$, then K is also a key for R. For tuples t_1 and t_2 in r, if $t_1(K') \neq t_2(K')$, then surely $t_1(K) \neq t_2(K)$. We shall restrict our definition slightly.

Definition 1.1 A *key* of a relation $r(R)$ is a subset K of R such that for any distinct tuples t_1 and t_2 in r, $t_1(K) \neq t_2(K)$ and no proper subset K' of K shares this property. K is a *superkey* of r if K contains a key of r.

The new definition of superkey is the same as the former definition of key. We shall still use the old definition of key in designated key, that is, a designated key may be a superkey.

Example 1.5 In Table 1.1, {NUMBER} is a key (and a superkey), so {NUMBER, FROM} is a superkey but not a key.

There are some subtleties with keys. As we mentioned in the last section, we consider relations to be time-varying. For any given state of the relation, we can determine the keys and superkeys. Different states of the relation may have different keys. We consider relation schemes, though, to be time-invariant; we would like the keys specified with relation schemes not to vary either. Thus, in determining keys for a relation scheme, we look across all states a relation on the scheme may assume. Keys must remain keys for all permissible data.

Example 1.6 In Table 1.1, {FROM, TO} is a key for the relation. However, it is likely that there could be two flights between the same origin and destination, although they would undoubtedly leave at different times. Hence {FROM, TO, DEPARTS} is a key for the relation scheme FLIGHTS.

We shall mainly concern ourselves with keys and superkeys of relation schemes, thinking in terms of all permissible states of a relation on the scheme. What is and is not a key is ultimately a semantic question.

1.4 UPDATES TO RELATIONS

Now that we have relations, what can be done with them? As noted, the content of a relation varies with time, so we shall consider how to alter a relation. Suppose we wish to put more information into a relation. We perform an *add* operation on the relation. For a relation $r(A_1A_2 \cdots A_n)$, the add operation takes the form

$$\text{ADD}(r; A_1 = d_1, A_2 = d_2, \ldots, A_n = d_n).$$

Example 1.7 Call the relation in Table 1.1 *sched*. We might perform the update

ADD(*sched*; NUMBER = 117, FROM = Atlanta, TO = Boston,
DEPARTS = 10:05p, ARRIVES = 12:43a).

When there is an order assumed on the attribute names, the shorter version

$$\text{ADD}(r; d_1, d_2, \ldots, d_n)$$

suffices.

Example 1.8 The short version of Example 1.7 is

ADD(*sched*; 117, Atlanta, Boston, 10:05p, 12:43a).

The intent of the add operation is clear, to add the tuple described to the relation specified. The result of the operation might not agree with the intent for one of the following reasons:

1. The tuple described does not conform to the scheme of the specified relation.
2. Some values of the tuple do not belong to the appropriate domains.
3. The tuple described agrees on a key with a tuple already in the relation.

In any of these cases, we consider ADD(r; d_1, d_2, $\ldots$, d_n) to return r unchanged and in some manner indicate the error.

Example 1.9 If *sched* is the relation in Table 1.1, then

ADD(sched; NUMBER = 117, FROM = Atlanta, TO = Boston,
DATE = 4 March)

is disallowed for reason 1 above. The operation

$$\text{ADD}(sched;\ \text{NUMBER} = 84,\ \text{FROM} = \text{O'Hare},\ \text{TO} = \text{JFK},\ \text{DEPARTS} = 25{:}15\text{p},\ \text{ARRIVES} = 6{:}00\text{p})$$

is disallowed for both reasons 2 and 3. (Examine DEPARTS and NUMBER).

We must be able to undo what we do, which calls for a *delete* operation. On a relation r as above, the delete operation takes the form

$$\text{DEL}(r;\ A_1 = d_1, A_2 = d_2, \ldots, A_n = d_n).$$

Again, when there is an assumed order on the attribute names, we abbreviate to

$$\text{DEL}(r;\ d_1, d_2, \ldots, d_n).$$

Example 1.10 If *sched* is the relation in Table 1.1, we can have

$$\text{DEL}(sched;\ \text{NUMBER} = 83,\ \text{FROM} = \text{JFK},\ \text{TO} = \text{O'Hare},\ \text{DEPARTS} = 11{:}30\text{a},\ \text{ARRIVES} = 1{:}43\text{p}),$$

with short version

$$\text{DEL}(sched;\ 83,\ \text{JFK},\ \text{O'Hare},\ 11{:}30\text{a},\ 1{:}43\text{p}).$$

Actually, we do not need to give so much information to identify uniquely the tuple to be removed. Specifying the values on some key will suffice. If $K = \{B_1, B_2, \ldots, B_m\}$ is a key, then we may use the form

$$\text{DEL}(r;\ B_1 = e_1, B_2 = e_2, \ldots, B_m = e_m).$$

Example 1.11 A shorter version of the delete in Example 1.10 is

$$\text{DEL}(sched;\ \text{FROM} = \text{JFK},\ \text{TO} = \text{O'Hare},\ \text{DEPARTS} = 11{:}30).$$

If there is a primary designated key, such as {NUMBER}, we could even shorten this form to DEL(*sched*; 83).

The result of the delete operation is as expected. The specified tuple is removed from the relation, except when the tuple is not present in the relation. In this case, the relation is left unchanged and an error condition is signaled. There is no restriction on removing the last tuple from a relation; the empty relation is allowed.

Instead of adding or deleting an entire tuple, we may want to modify only part of a tuple. Modification is achieved with the *change* operation. For a relation r as before, with $\{C_1, C_2, \ldots, C_p\} \subseteq \{A_1, A_2, \ldots, A_n\}$, the change operation takes the form

$$\begin{aligned}\mathrm{CH}(r; A_1 = d_1, A_2 = d_2, \ldots, A_n = d_n;\\ C_1 = e_1, C_2 = e_2, \ldots, C_p = e_p).\end{aligned}$$

If $K = \{B_1, B_2, \ldots, B_m\}$ is a key, then we abbreviate to

$$\mathrm{CH}(r; B_1 = d_1, B_2 = d_2, \ldots, B_m = d_m; C_1 = e_1, C_2 = e_2, \ldots, C_p = e_p).$$

Example 1.12 For the relation *sched* in Table 1.1 we could have

CH(*sched*; NUMBER = 109, FROM = JFK, TO = Los Angeles,
DEPARTS = 9:50p, ARRIVES = 2:52a; DEPARTS = 9:40p,
ARRIVES = 2:42a),

with short version

CH(*sched*; NUMBER = 109; DEPARTS = 9:40p, ARRIVES = 2:42a).

The change operation is mainly a convenience. The same result can be obtained with a delete followed by an add. Therefore, all the possible errors for add and delete apply to the change operation: the specified tuple does not exist, the changes have the wrong format or use values outside the appropriate domain, or the changed tuple has the same key value as a tuple already in the relation.

Example 1.13 The effect of applying the operations

1. ADD(*sched*; 117, Atlanta, Boston, 10:05p, 12:43a),
2. DEL(*sched*; FROM = JFK, TO = O'Hare, DEPARTS = 11:30a), and
3. CH(*sched*; NUMBER = 109; DEPARTS = 9:40p, ARRIVES = 2:42a)

to Table 1.1 is shown by Table 1.2.

1.5 EXERCISES

1.1 (a) Let R be the relation scheme {EMPLOYEE, MANAGER, JOB, SALARY, YEARS-WORKED}, where EMPLOYEE and MANAGER

Table 1.2 New version of *sched*(FLIGHTS).

NUMBER	FROM	TO	DEPARTS	ARRIVES
84	O'Hare	JFK	3:00p	5:55p
109	JFK	Los Angeles	9:40p	2:42a
117	Atlanta	Boston	10:05p	12:43a
213	JFK	Boston	11:43a	12:45p
214	Boston	JFK	2:20p	3:12p

are names, JOB is a job title, SALARY is yearly salary, and YEARS-WORKED is the number of complete years the employee has been at the job. Construct a relation on R based on the following information.

i. Roberts, Ruskin, and Raphael are all ticket agents.
ii. Rayburn is a baggage handler.
iii. Rice is a flight mechanic.
iv. Price manages all ticket agents.
v. Powell manages Rayburn.
vi. Porter manages Rice, Price, Powell and himself.
vii. Powell is head of ground crews and Porter is chief of operations.
viii. Every employee receives a 10% raise for each complete year worked.
ix. Roberts, Ruskin, Raphael, and Rayburn all started at $12,000. Roberts just started work, Ruskin and Raphael have worked for a year and a half, and Rayburn has worked for 2 years.
x. Rice started at $18,000 and now makes $21,780.
xi. Price and Powell started at $16,000 and have both been working for three years.
xii. Porter started at $20,000 and has been around two years longer than anyone else.

(b) Give appropriate update operations for the following changes to the relation for part (a):

i. Ruskin and Raphael complete their second year.
ii. Rice quits.
iii. Powell quits. His duties are assumed by Porter.
iv. Randolph is hired as a ticket agent.

1.2 Consider the relation scheme R = {FLIGHT-NUMBER, DATE, GATE, TIME, DESTINATION}. A tuple $\langle d_1\, d_2\, d_3\, d_4\, d_5\rangle$ of $r(R)$ has the meaning "flight d_1 departs on date d_2 from gate d_3 at d_4 for d_5." What are the keys of R?

1.3 Let t be a tuple in $r(R)$ and let X and Y be subsets of R. When does the expression $t(X)(Y)$ make sense? When it does make sense, how can it be simplified?

1.4 (a) Can the union of two keys be a key?
(b) Is the intersection of two superkeys necessarily a key?

1.5* Given a relation scheme $R[A_1A_2 \cdots A_n]$, what is the maximum number of keys R can have? The maximum number of superkeys?

1.6 What can be said about a relation with a key $K = \emptyset$?

1.7 Let $K = \{B_1, B_2, \ldots, B_m\}$ be a key of the relation scheme $R[A_1A_2 \cdots A_n]$ and let r be a relation on R. Consider the operation

$$\text{CH}(r; A_1 = d_1, A_2 = d_2, \ldots, A_n = d_n; \\ B_1 = e_1, B_2 = e_2, \ldots, B_m = e_m).$$

Suppose that no tuple in r has K-value $\langle e_1\, e_2 \cdots e_m\rangle$, there is a tuple $\langle d_1\, d_2 \cdots d_n\rangle$ in r, and that $e_i \in \text{dom}(B_i)$, $1 \leq i \leq m$. Is this change operation necessarily legal?

1.8 Let Σ be a sequence of update operations to be applied to relation r. If the order of the operations is changed in Σ, will the result necessarily be the same when Σ consists of

(a) only add operations?
(b) only delete operations?
(c) add and delete operations?
(d) add and change operations?
(e) only change operations?

1.6 BIBLIOGRAPHY AND COMMENTS

The relational data model was originally expounded in a series of papers by Codd [1970, 1971a, 1971b, 1972a]. For background in database systems and the place of the relational model in the scheme of things, the reader is directed to the books by Cardenas [1979], Date [1981], Tsichritzis and Lochovsky [1977], Ullman [1980], and Wiederhold [1977].

Chapter 2

RELATIONAL OPERATORS

The update operations defined in the last chapter are not so much operations on relations as operations on tuples. In this chapter we shall consider operators that involve the entire relation. First, we see how the usual Boolean operations on sets apply to relations, and second, we consider three operators particular to relations: select, project, and join.

2.1 BOOLEAN OPERATIONS

Two relations on the same scheme can be considered sets over the same universe, the set of all possible tuples on the relation scheme. Thus, Boolean operations can be applied to two such relations. If r and s are relations on the scheme R, then $r \cap s$, $r \cup s$ and $r - s$ are all the obvious relations on R. The set $r \cap s$ is the relation $q(R)$ containing all tuples that are in both r and s, $r \cup s$ is the relation $q(R)$ containing all tuples that are in either r or s, and $r - s$ is the relation $q(R)$ containing those tuples that are in r but not in s. Note that intersection can be defined in terms of set difference: $r \cap s = r - (r - s)$.

Let $dom(R)$ be the set of all tuples over the attributes of R and their domains. We can define the *complement* of a relation $r(R)$ as $\bar{r} = dom(R) - r$. However, if any attribute A in R has an infinite domain, $\bar{r}$ will also be infinite and not a relation in our sense. We define a modified version of complementation that always yields a relation. If $r(A_1 A_2 \cdots A_n)$ is a relation and $D_i = dom(A_i)$, $1 \leq i \leq n$, the *active domain* of A_i relative to r is the set

$$adom(A_i, r) = \{d \in D_i \mid \text{there exists } t \in r \text{ with } t(A_i) = d\}.$$

Let $adom(R, r)$ be the set of all tuples over the attributes of R and their active domains relative to r. The *active complement* of r is $\tilde{r} = adom(R,r) - r$. Note that $\tilde{r}$ is always a relation.

Example 2.1 The following are two relations, r and s, on the scheme ABC:

r:

A	B	C
a_1	b_1	c_1
a_1	b_2	c_1
a_2	b_1	c_2

s:

A	B	C
a_1	b_2	c_1
a_2	b_2	c_1
a_2	b_2	c_2

The results of the operations $r \cap s$, $r \cup s$, and $r - s$ are shown below.

$r \cap s =$

A	B	C
a_1	b_2	c_1

$r \cup s =$

A	B	C
a_1	b_1	c_1
a_1	b_2	c_1
a_2	b_1	c_2
a_2	b_2	c_1
a_2	b_2	c_2

$r - s =$

A	B	C
a_1	b_1	c_1
a_2	b_1	c_2

Given $\{a_1, a_2\}$, $\{b_1, b_2, b_3\}$, and $\{c_1, c_2\}$ as the domains of A, B, and C, the domain of R and the complement of r derived from the domain of R are as shown:

$dom(R) =$

A	B	C
a_1	b_1	c_1
a_1	b_1	c_2
a_1	b_2	c_1
a_1	b_2	c_2
a_1	b_3	c_1
a_1	b_3	c_2
a_2	b_1	c_1
a_2	b_1	c_2
a_2	b_2	c_1
a_2	b_2	c_2
a_2	b_3	c_1
a_2	b_3	c_2

$\bar{r} = dom(R) - r =$

A	B	C
a_1	b_1	c_2
a_1	b_2	c_2
a_1	b_3	c_1
a_1	b_3	c_2
a_2	b_1	c_1
a_2	b_2	c_1
a_2	b_2	c_2
a_2	b_3	c_1
a_2	b_3	c_2

To derive the active complement of r (that is, $\tilde{r}$), note that the active domain of B in the relation r does not contain b_3. The active domain of r, and the active complement of r, are:

$adom(R) =$

A	B	C
a_1	b_1	c_1
a_1	b_1	c_2
a_1	b_2	c_1
a_1	b_2	c_2
a_2	b_1	c_1
a_2	b_1	c_2
a_2	b_2	c_1
a_2	b_2	c_2

$*r = adom(R) - r =$

A	B	C
a_1	b_1	c_2
a_1	b_2	c_2
a_2	b_1	c_1
a_2	b_2	c_1
a_2	b_2	c_2

It is difficult to imagine a natural situation where the complement of a relation would be meaningful, except perhaps for a unary (one-attribute) relation. Active complement might arise naturally. Suppose a company has a training program that has a group of employees working two weeks in each department. The information on who in the training program has completed time in which department could be stored in a relation *done*(EMPLOYEE TRAINED-IN). The relation $\widetilde{done}$ would tell who had not completed training in what department, provided every employee in the program and every department is mentioned in *done*. Active complement can also be used as a storage compression device, when the active complement of a relation has fewer tuples than the relation itself.

The set of all relations on a given scheme is closed under union, intersection, set difference, and active complement. However, not all these operations preserve keys (see Exercise 2.3).

2.2 THE SELECT OPERATOR

Select is a unary operator on relations. When applied to a relation r, it yields another relation that is the subset of tuples of r with a certain value on a specified attribute. Let r be a relation on scheme R, A an attribute in R, and a an element of $dom(A)$. Using mapping notation, $\sigma_{A=a}(r)$ ("select A equal to a on r") is the relation $r'(R) = \{t \in r | t(A) = a\}$.

Example 2.2 Table 2.1 duplicates the relation in Table 1.2.

Table 2.1 New version of *sched*(FLIGHTS).

sched(NUMBER	FROM	TO	DEPARTS	ARRIVES)
84	O'Hare	JFK	3:00p	5:55p
109	JFK	Los Angeles	9:40p	2:42a
117	Atlanta	Boston	10:05p	12:43a
213	JFK	Boston	11:43a	12:45p
214	Boston	JFK	2:20p	3:12p

Table 2.2 is the result of applying $\sigma_{\text{FROM}=\text{JFK}}$ to *sched*.

Table 2.2 Result of applying $\sigma_{\text{FROM}=\text{JFK}}$ to *sched*(FLIGHTS).

$\sigma_{\text{FROM}=\text{JFK}}(sched) =$	NUMBER	FROM	TO	DEPARTS	ARRIVES
	109	JFK	Los Angeles	9:40p	2:42a
	213	JFK	Boston	11:43a	12:45p

Select operators commute under composition. Let $r(R)$ be a relation and let A and B be attributes in R, with $a \in dom(A)$ and $b \in dom(B)$. The identity

$$\sigma_{A=a}(\sigma_{B=b}(r)) = \sigma_{B=b}(\sigma_{A=a}(r))$$

always holds. This property follows readily from the definition of select:

$$\sigma_{A=a}(\sigma_{B=b}(r)) = \sigma_{A=a}(\{t \in r \mid t(B) = b\}) =$$
$$\{t' \in \{t \in r \mid t(B) = b\} \mid t'(A) = a\} = \{t \in r \mid t(A) = a \text{ and } t(B) = b\} =$$
$$\{t' \in \{t \in r \mid t(A) = a\} \mid t'(B) = b\} = \sigma_{B=b}(\sigma_{A=a}(r)).$$

Since the order of selection is unimportant, we write $\sigma_{A=a} \circ \sigma_{B=b}$ as $\sigma_{A=a, B=b}$ and $\sigma_{A_1=a_1} \circ \sigma_{A_2=a_2} \circ \cdots \circ \sigma_{A_n=a_n}$ as $\sigma_{A_1=a_1, A_2=a_2, \ldots, A_n=a_n}$. (The A_i's need not be distinct. See Exercise 2.4.) If X is a set of attributes and x is an X-value, $\sigma_{X=x}$ is also legitimate notation, if we interpret x as a sequence of values rather than a mapping.

Select is distributive over the binary Boolean operations:

$$\sigma_{A=a}(r \gamma s) = \sigma_{A=a}(r) \gamma \sigma_{A=a}(s)$$

where $\gamma = \cap, \cup$, or $-$, and r and s are relations over the same scheme. We prove $\sigma_{A=a}(r \cap s) = \sigma_{A=a}(r) \cap \sigma_{A=a}(s)$:

$$\begin{aligned}&\sigma_{A=a}(r \cap s) = \sigma_{A=a}(\{t \mid t \in r \text{ and } t \in s\}) =\\&\{t' \in \{t \mid t \in r \text{ and } t \in s\} \mid t'(A) = a\} =\\&\{t \mid t \in r \text{ and } t(A) = a\} \cap \{t \mid t \in s \text{ and } t(A) = a\} =\\&\sigma_{A=a}(\{t \mid t \in r\}) \cap \sigma_{A=a}(\{t \mid t \in s\}) = \sigma_{A=a}(r) \cap \sigma_{A=a}(s).\end{aligned}$$

The order of selection and complementation does make a difference in the result (see Exercise 2.5).

2.3 THE PROJECT OPERATOR

Project is also a unary operator on relations. Where select chooses a subset of the rows in a relation, project chooses a subset of the columns. Let r be a relation on scheme R, and let X be a subset of R. The *projection of* r *onto* X, written $\pi_X(r)$, is the relation $r'(X)$ obtained by striking out columns corresponding to attributes in $R - X$ and removing duplicate tuples in what remains. In mapping notation, $\pi_X(r)$ is the relation $r'(X) = \{t(X) \mid t \in r\}$.

If two projections are performed in a row, the latter subsumes the former: If π_Y is applied to the result of applying π_X to r, the result is the same as if π_Y were applied directly to r, if the original application of π_Y was proper. More precisely, given $r(R)$ and $Y \subseteq X \subseteq R$, $\pi_Y(\pi_X(r)) = \pi_Y(r)$. Similarly, for a string of projections, only the outermost need be considered for evaluation. If $X_1 \subseteq X_2 \subseteq \cdots \subseteq X_m \subseteq R$, then

$$\pi_{X_1}(\pi_{X_2}(\cdots(\pi_{X_m}(r))\cdots)) = \pi_{X_1}(r).$$

Example 2.3 The following are the relations

1. $\pi_{\{\text{DEPARTS,ARRIVES}\}}(\textit{sched})$,
2. $\pi_{\text{DEPARTS}}(\pi_{\{\text{DEPARTS,ARRIVES}\}}(\textit{sched})) = \pi_{\text{DEPARTS}}(\textit{sched})$, and
3. $\pi_{\text{FROM}}(\textit{sched})$,

for the relation *sched* in Table 2.1.

1. $\pi_{\{\text{DEPARTS,ARRIVES}\}}(\textit{sched}) =$

(DEPARTS	ARRIVES)
3:00p	5:55p
9:40p	2:42a
10:05p	12:43a
11:43a	12:45p
2:20p	3:12p

2. $\pi_{\text{DEPARTS}}(sched) =$

DEPARTS
3:00p
9:40p
10:05p
11:43a
2:20p

3. $\pi_{\text{FROM}}(sched) =$

FROM
O'Hare
JFK
Atlanta
Boston

Projection commutes with selection when the attribute or attributes for selection are among the attributes in the set onto which the projection is taking place. If $A \in X$, $X \subseteq R$, and r is a relation on R, then

$$\pi_X(\sigma_{A=a}(r)) = \pi_X(\{t \in r | t(A) = a\}) = \{t'(X) | t' \in \{t \in r | t(A) = a\}\} = \{t(X)\ t \in r \text{ and } t(A) = a\} = \sigma_{A=a}(\{t(X) | t \in r\}) = \sigma_{A=a}(\pi_X(r)).$$

This identity does not hold when A is not an element of X (see Exercise 2.7).

The connection between projection and Boolean operations is treated in Exercises 2.8 and 2.9.

2.4 THE JOIN OPERATOR

Join is a binary operator for combining two relations. We illustrate its workings with an example. Suppose our imaginary airline maintains a list of which types of aircraft may be used on each flight and a list of the types of aircraft each pilot is certified to fly. These lists are stored as the relations *usable*(FLIGHT EQUIPMENT) and *certified*(PILOT EQUIPMENT). Table 2.3 shows sample states of these relations.

Table 2.3 Sample states of the relations *usable*(FLIGHT EQUIPMENT) and *certified*(PILOT EQUIPMENT).

usable(FLIGHT	EQUIPMENT)	*certified*(PILOT	EQUIPMENT)
83	727	Simmons	707
83	747	Simmons	727
84	727	Barth	747
84	747	Hill	727
109	707	Hill	747

We want a list showing which pilots can be used for each flight. We create a relation *options* on the scheme {FLIGHT, EQUIPMENT, PILOT} from the relations *usable* and *certified* by combining rows with the same value for EQUIPMENT. *Options* is shown in Table 2.4.

Once the relations are combined, if the EQUIPMENT values are no longer needed, we can compute $\pi_{\{\text{FLIGHT,PILOT}\}}(options)$, as shown in Table 2.5.

In general, join combines two relations on all their common attributes. Start with relations $r(R)$ and $s(S)$, with $RS = T$. The *join of* r *and* s, written $r \bowtie s$, is the relation $q(T)$ of all tuples t over T such that there are tuples $t_r \in r$ and $t_s \in s$ with $t_r = t(R)$ and $t_s = t(S)$. Since $R \cap S$ is a subset of both R and S, as a consequence of the definition $t_r(R \cap S) = t_s(R \cap S)$. Thus, every tuple in q is a combination of a tuple from r and a tuple from s with equal $(R \cap S)$-values.

Returning to Table 2.4, we see $options = usable \bowtie certified$. The definition of join does not require that R and S have a non-empty intersection. If $R \cap S = \emptyset$, then $r \bowtie s$ is the Cartesian product of r and s. Actually, the Cartesian product of two relations would be a set of ordered pairs of tuples.

Table 2.4 The relation *options* on the scheme {FLIGHT, EQUIPMENT, PILOT}.

options(FLIGHT	EQUIPMENT	PILOT)
83	727	Simmons
83	727	Hill
83	747	Barth
83	747	Hill
84	727	Simmons
84	727	Hill
84	747	Barth
84	747	Hill
109	707	Simmons

Table 2.5 Computation of $\pi_{\{\text{FLIGHT,PILOT}\}}$ (*options*).

$\pi_{\{\text{FLIGHT,PILOT}\}}(options) =$ (FLIGHT	PILOT)
83	Simmons
83	Hill
83	Barth
84	Simmons
84	Hill
84	Barth
109	Simmons

By Cartesian product we shall mean Cartesian product followed by the natural isomorphism from pairs of R-tuples and S-tuples to RS-tuples.

Example 2.4 Let r and s be as shown:

r(A	B)
a_1	b_1
a_2	b_1

s(C	D)
c_1	d_1
c_2	d_1
c_2	d_2

Then $r \bowtie s$ is seen to be:

$r \bowtie s =$

(A	B	C	D)
a_1	b_1	c_1	d_1
a_1	b_1	c_2	d_1
a_1	b_1	c_2	d_2
a_2	b_1	c_1	d_1
a_2	b_1	c_2	d_1
a_2	b_1	c_2	d_2

2.5 PROPERTIES OF JOIN

There are more properties of join than we have room to list. We shall give some of them here, use others for exercises, and leave the rest for the reader to discover.

The join operation can be used to simulate selection. Given $r(R)$, suppose we wish to find $\sigma_{A=a}(r)$. First define a new relation $s(A)$, with a single tuple t, such that $t(A) = a$. Then $r \bowtie s$ is the same as $\sigma_{A=a}(r)$. The intersection of R and A is A, so

$$r \bowtie s = \{t \mid \text{there exists } t_r \in r \text{ and } t_s \in s \text{ such that } t_r = t(R) \text{ and } t_s = t(A)\} = \{t \mid \text{there exists } t_r \in r \text{ with } t_r = t(R) \text{ and } t(A) = a\} = \{t \in r \mid t(A) = a\} = \sigma_{A=a}(r).$$

We can also manufacture a generalized select operation using join. Let $s(A)$ now be a relation with k tuples, $t_1, t_2, \ldots, t_k$, where $t_i(A) = a_i$ and $a_i \in dom(A)$, $1 \le i \le k$. Then

$$r \bowtie s = \sigma_{A=a_1}(r) \cup \sigma_{A=a_2}(r) \cup \cdots \cup \sigma_{A=a_k}(r).$$

If we choose two attributes A and B from R and let $s(AB)$ be the relation with the single tuple t such that $t(A) = a$ and $t(B) = b$, then

$$r \bowtie s = \sigma_{A=a, B=b}(r).$$

There are other variations of selection available by adding columns and tuples to s.

It can be seen that the join operator is commutative from the symmetry in its definition. It is also associative. Given relations q, r, and s,

$$(q \bowtie r) \bowtie s = q \bowtie (r \bowtie s)$$

(see Exercise 2.11). Hence, we can write an unparenthesized string of joins without ambiguity.

We introduce some notation for multiple joins. Let $s_1(S_1)$, $s_2(S_2)$, $\ldots$, $s_m(S_m)$ be relations, with $R = S_1 \cup S_2 \cup \cdots \cup S_m$ and let **S** be the sequence $S_1, S_2, \ldots, S_m$. Let $t_1, t_2, \ldots, t_m$ be a sequence of tuples with $t_i \in s_i$, $1 \leq i \leq m$. We say tuples $t_1, t_2, \ldots, t_m$ are *joinable on* **S** if there is a tuple t on R such that $t_i = t(S_i)$, $1 \leq i \leq m$. Tuple t is the *result* of joining $t_1, t_2, \ldots, t_m$ on **S**.

Example 2.5 Tuples $\langle a_1\ b_1 \rangle$, $\langle b_1\ c_2 \rangle$, and $\langle a_1\ c_2 \rangle$ from relations s_1, s_2, and s_3, as shown

s_1(A	B)
a_1	b_1
a_1	b_2
a_2	b_1

s_2(B	C)
b_1	c_2
b_2	c_1

s_3(A	C)
a_1	c_2
a_2	c_2

are joinable with result $\langle a_1\ b_1\ c_2 \rangle$, and tuples $\langle a_1\ b_1 \rangle$, $\langle b_1\ c_2 \rangle$, and $\langle a_2\ c_2 \rangle$ are joinable with result $\langle a_2\ b_1\ c_2 \rangle$:

$s_1 \bowtie s_2 \bowtie s_3 =$

(A	B	C)
a_1	b_1	c_2
a_2	b_1	c_2

If $m = 2$ in the definition above, then if tuples t_1 and t_2 are joinable on $\mathbf{S} = S_1, S_2$ with result t, then $t_1 = t(S_1)$ and $t_2 = t(S_2)$. From the definition of join, t must be in $s_1 \bowtie s_2$. Conversely, if t is a tuple in $s_1 \bowtie s_2$, then there must be tuples t_1 and t_2 in s_1 and s_2, respectively, with t_1, t_2 joinable on **S** with result t. Hence, $s_1 \bowtie s_2$ consists of those tuples t that are the result of joining two tuples t_1, t_2 that are joinable on $\mathbf{S}$.

Using the associativity of the join and induction, it is straightforward (but tedious) to prove the following result.

Lemma 2.1 The relation $s_1 \bowtie s_2 \bowtie \ldots \bowtie s_m$ consists of all tuples t that are the result of joining tuples $t_1, t_2, \ldots, t_m$ that are joinable on $\mathbf{S} = S_1, S_2, \ldots, S_m$.

Not every tuple of every relation may enter into the join. The relations $s_1, s_2, \ldots, s_m$ *join completely* if every tuple in each relation is a member of some list of tuples joinable on $\mathbf{S}$.

Example 2.6 Example 2.5 shows a three-way join where the relations do not join completely. Tuple $\langle a_1\, b_2 \rangle$ of s_1 and tuple $\langle b_2\, c_1 \rangle$ of s_2 are left out of the join, for instance. If tuple $\langle a_1\, c_1 \rangle$ is added to s_3, then the relations do join completely, as shown below.

$s_1(A$	$B)$
a_1	b_1
a_1	b_2
a_2	b_1

$s_2(B$	$C)$
b_1	c_2
b_2	c_1

$s_3(A$	$C)$
a_1	c_1
a_1	c_2
a_2	c_2

$s_1 \bowtie s_2 \bowtie s_3 =$

$(A$	B	$C)$
a_1	b_1	c_2
a_1	b_2	c_1
a_2	b_1	c_2

The join and project operators, though not inverses, do perform complementary functions. Let $r(R)$ and $s(S)$ be relations and let $q = r \bowtie s$. The scheme for q is RS. Let $r' = \pi_R(q)$. Is there any connection between r and r'? Yes, $r' \subseteq r$, since for any tuples t to be in q, $t(R)$ must be a tuple of r, and $r' = \{t(R) | t \in q\}$.

Example 2.7 The following shows that the containment is sometimes proper ($r' \subset r$).

$r(A\ \ B)$	$s(B\ \ C)$	$r \bowtie s = q(A\ \ B\ \ C)$
$a\ \ b$	$b\ \ c$	$a\ \ b\ \ c$
$a\ \ b'$		

$\pi_{AB}(q) = r'(A\ \ B)$
$a\ \ b$

Next is a case where equality holds ($r' = r$).

$r(A\ \ B)$	$s(B\ \ C)$	$r \bowtie s = q(A\ \ B\ \ C)$
$a\ \ b'$	$b\ \ c$	$a\ \ b\ \ c$
$a\ \ b'$	$b'\ \ c'$	$a\ \ b'\ \ c'$

$\pi_{AB}(q) = r'(A\ \ B)$
$a\ \ b$
$a\ \ b'$

The containment becomes equality when for each tuple $t_r \in r$ there is a tuple $t_s \in s$ with $t_r(R \cap S) = t_s(R \cap S)$. Containment can also become equality without r and s joining completely (see Exercise 2.14). However, if $s' = \pi_S(q)$, then the condition $r = r'$ and $s = s'$ is exactly the same as r and s joining completely. This result generalizes to more than two relations (see Exercise 2.15).

What happens when we reverse the order and project and then join? Let q be a relation on RS, with $r = \pi_R(q)$ and $s = \pi_S(q)$. Let $q' = r \bowtie s$. If t is a tuple of q, then $t(R)$ is in r and $t(S)$ is in s, so t is also in q'. Therefore, $q' \supseteq q$. If $q' = q$, we say relation q *decomposes losslessly* onto schemes R and S. Lossless decomposition for more than two relations is treated in Chapter 6.

Example 2.8 The relation q in the second part of Example 2.7 decomposes losslessly onto AB and BC.

We can go one step further. Let $r' = \pi_R(q')$, $s' = \pi_S(q')$ and $q'' = r' \bowtie s'$. We are performing the project-join procedure twice on q to get q''. Let T be the intersection of R and S. Then $\pi_T(r) = \pi_T(\pi_R(q)) = \pi_T(q) = \pi_T(\pi_S(q)) = \pi_T(s)$, so r and s join completely, since for any tuple t_r in r, there must be a tuple t_s in s with $t_r(T) = t_s(T)$, and vice versa. Hence $r = r'$ and $s = s'$, so q' and q'' must be the same. Thus, the project-join procedure is idempotent: the result of applying it once is the result of applying it twice. This project-join procedure will be treated in more detail in Chapter 8.

Finally, we examine join in connection with union. Let r and r' be relations on R and let s be a relation on S. We claim that $(r \cup r') \bowtie s = (r \bowtie s) \cup (r' \bowtie s)$. Call the left side of the equation q and the right side q'. Given a tuple $t \in q$, there must be tuples t_r and t_s that are joinable with result t, with t_r in r or r' and $t_s \in s$. If $t_r \in r$, then t is in $r \bowtie s$. Otherwise, t is in $r' \bowtie s$. We have shown $q \subseteq q'$. For the other containment, $q \supseteq q'$, if t is in q', then t is in $r \bowtie s$ or $r' \bowtie s$. In either case, t is in $(r \cup r') \bowtie s$.

2.6 EXERCISES

2.1 Let $r(ABC)$ and $s(BCD)$ be relations, with a in $dom(A)$ and b in $dom(B)$. Which of the following expressions are properly formed?

(a) $r \cup s$
(b) $\pi_B(r) - \pi_B(s)$
(c) $\sigma_{B=b}(r)$
(d) $\sigma_{A=a, B=b}(s)$
(e) $r \bowtie s$
(f) $\pi_A(r) \bowtie \pi_D(s)$.

2.2 Relations r and s are given below.

$r(A$	B	$C)$
a	b	c
a	b'	c'
a	b''	c'
a'	b'	c

$s(B$	C	$D)$
b'	c'	d
b''	c'	c'
b''	c	d

Compute the values of the following expressions.

(a) $\tilde{r}$
(b) $\tilde{s}$
(c) $\sigma_{A=a}(r)$
(d) all the properly formed expressions in Exercise 2.1.

2.3 Let r and s be relations on scheme R with key K. Which of the following relations must necessarily have key K?

(a) $r \cup s$
(b) $r \cap s$

(c) $r - s$
(d) $\overline{r}$, where $\overline{r}$ is a relation
(e) $\pi_K(r)$
(f) $r \bowtie s$.

2.4 Let $r(R)$ be a relation with $A \in R$ and let $a, a' \in dom(A)$. Prove

$$[\sigma_{A=a,A=a'}(r) = \emptyset \text{ or } \sigma_{A=a,A=a'}(r) = \sigma_{A=a}(r)].$$

2.5 Let r and s be relations on R with $A \in R$ and let $a \in dom(A)$. Prove or disprove the following.

(a) $\sigma_{A=a}(\tilde{r}) = \widetilde{\sigma_{A=a}(r)}$
(b) $\sigma_{A=a}(r \cap s) = \sigma_{A=a}(r) \cap s$.

2.6 Let r be a relation on $R[\underline{A}\ B\ C]$. What can be said about the size of $\sigma_{A=a}(r)$?

2.7 Let X be a subset of R, $A \in R$, $A \notin X$ and let r be a relation on R. Find a counterexample to

$$\pi_X(\sigma_{A=a}(r)) = \sigma_{A=a}(\pi_X(r)).$$

2.8 Let X be a subset of R and let r and s be relations on R. Prove or disprove the following equalities.

(a) $\pi_X(r \cap s) = \pi_X(r) \cap \pi_X(s)$
(b) $\pi_X(r \cup s) = \pi_X(r) \cup \pi_X(s)$
(c) $\pi_X(r - s) = \pi_X(r) - \pi_X(s)$
(d) $\pi_X(\overline{r}) = \overline{\pi_X(r)}$, where $\overline{r}$ is a relation.

2.9 For each of the disproved equalities in Exercise 2.8, try to prove containment in one direction.

2.10 Let A be an attribute in R, let $R' = R - A$ and let r be a relation on R. What relationships exist between the sizes of the relations r, $\sigma_{A=a}(r)$, $\pi_A(r)$, $\pi_{R'}(r)$ and $\sigma_{A=a}(\pi_A(r))$?

2.11 Given relations q, r and s, show

(a) $(q \bowtie r) \bowtie s = q \bowtie (r \bowtie s)$
(b) $q \bowtie q = q$
(c) $q \bowtie r = q \bowtie (q \bowtie r)$.

2.12 Let $r(R)$ and $s(S)$ be relations with $A \in R$. Prove

$$\sigma_{A=a}(r \bowtie s) = \sigma_{A=a}(r) \bowtie s.$$

2.13 Let r and r' be relations on R, and let s be a relation on S. Prove or disprove:

(a) $(r \cap r') \bowtie s = (r \bowtie s) \cap (r' \bowtie s)$
(b) $(r - r') \bowtie s = (r \bowtie s) - (r' \bowtie s)$
(c) $\tilde{r} \bowtie \tilde{s} = \widetilde{r \bowtie s}$.

2.14 Given relations $r(R)$, $s(S)$ and $q = r \bowtie s$, show that $\pi_R(q) = r$ can hold without r and s joining completely.

2.15* Let $s_1(S_1)$, $s_2(S_2)$, $\ldots$, $s_m(S_m)$ be relations and let $q = s_1 \bowtie s_2 \bowtie \cdots \bowtie s_m$. Prove that s_1, s_2, $\ldots$, s_m join completely if and only if $s_i = \pi_{S_i}(q)$, $1 \leq i \leq m$.

2.16 Let $q(R)$ be a relation and let S_i be a subset of R, $1 \leq i \leq m$. Define $s_i = \pi_{S_i}(q)$, $1 \leq i \leq m$. Prove s_1, s_2, $\ldots$, s_m join completely.

2.17 Let q be a relation on RS. Give an example of when the containment

$$q \subseteq \pi_R(q) \bowtie \pi_S(q)$$

is proper.

2.18 Given relations $r(R)$, $s(S)$ and $q = r \bowtie s$, define $r' = \pi_R(q)$ and $s' = \pi_S(q)$. Prove

$$q = r' \bowtie s'.$$

2.19* Given a relation $q(RS)$, find a sufficient condition for

$$q = \pi_R(q) \bowtie \pi_S(q).$$

Is your condition necessary?

2.7 BIBLIOGRAPHY AND COMMENTS

The relational operators select, project, and join in the form here were introduced by Codd [1970, 1972b], although analogs are given by Childs [1968] for a slightly different model. Join is sometimes called *natural join* to distinguish from other join-like operations, which we shall see in Chapter 3. In some sources, relations are treated in the traditional mathematical fashion, with ordered tuples and component denoted by number. We shall not make use of this treatment.

Chapter 3

MORE OPERATIONS ON RELATIONS

In this chapter we shall study some relational operators that are less elementary than those in Chapter 2. Some of the operators are generalizations of those in Chapter 2; others can be shown equivalent to a series of those operators. These operators, along with a set of relations and constants, will form a relational algebra. We shall see that we can restrict the set of operators and still retain the expressive power of relational algebra. Finally, we examine two operators that, while not part of the algebra, are sometimes useful in database implementations.

3.1 THE DIVIDE OPERATOR

The divide operator has a rather complex definition, but it does have some applications in natural situations.

Definition 3.1 Let $r(R)$ and $s(S)$ be relations, with $S \subseteq R$. Let $R' = R - S$. Then r *divided by* s, written $r \div s$, is the relation

$$r'(R') = \{t \mid \text{for every tuple } t_s \in s \text{ there is a tuple } t_r \in r \text{ with } t_r(R') = t \text{ and } t_r(S) = t_s\}.$$

Relation r' is the *quotient* of r divided by s. Another way to state the definition is that $r \div s$ is the maximal subset r' of $\pi_{R'}(r)$ such that $r' \bowtie s$ is contained in r. The join in this case is a Cartesian product. An example should clarify the definition.

Example 3.1 Table 3.1 is another instance of the relation *certified*(PILOT EQUIPMENT) given in Table 2.3. Suppose we want to find those pilots who can fly all the types of aircraft in some set. Let q(EQUIPMENT) and s(EQUIPMENT) be as follows:

q(EQUIPMENT)
707
727
747

s(EQUIPMENT)
707

Table 3.1 An instance of the relation *certified*(PILOT EQUIPMENT).

certified (PILOT	EQUIPMENT)
Desmond	707
Desmond	727
Desmond	747
Doyle	707
Doyle	727
Davis	707
Davis	727
Davis	747
Davis	1011
Dow	727

Division can then be used to garner information on what pilots can fly the types of aircraft in q, or to find what pilots can fly the aircraft in s.

certified $\div q = q'$(PILOT)
Desmond
Davis

certified $\div s = s'$(PILOT)
Desmond
Doyle
Davis

Division can be expressed in terms of the operators from Chapter 2 (see Exercise 3.3).

3.2 CONSTANT RELATIONS

In discussing join in the last chapter, we showed that the effect of select can be obtained by join with a constant relation. We have a notation for representing constant relations directly in expressions. If $A_1, A_2, \cdots, A_n$ are distinct attributes, and c_i is a constant from $dom(A_i)$ for $1 \leq i \leq n$, then

$$\langle c_1 : A_1 \; c_2 : A_2 \cdots c_n : A_n \rangle$$

represents the constant tuple $\langle c_1 \; c_2 \; \cdots \; c_n \rangle$ over scheme $A_1 \, A_2 \cdots A_n$. We represent a constant relation over scheme $A_1 \, A_2 \cdots A_n$ as a set of tuples. Let c_{ij} be a constant in $dom(A_i)$ for $1 \leq i \leq n$ and $1 \leq j \leq k$. Then

$$\{\langle c_{11} : A_1 \; c_{21} : A_2 \cdots c_{n1} : A_n \rangle, \\ \langle c_{12} : A_1 \; c_{22} : A_2 \cdots c_{n2} : A_n \rangle, \cdots \\ \langle c_{1k} : A_1 \; c_{2k} : A_2 \cdots c_{nk} : A_n \rangle\}$$

represents the relation we would normally write as

$(A_1$	A_2	$\cdots$	$A_n)$
c_{11}	c_{21}	$\cdots$	c_{n1}
c_{12}	c_{22}	$\cdots$	c_{n2}
$\vdots$	$\vdots$		$\vdots$
c_{1k}	c_{2k}	$\cdots$	c_{nk}.

In the case of a single-tuple constant relation, we shall sometimes omit the set brackets. For a single-attribute tuple, we shall sometimes omit the wickets ("⟨" and "⟩").

A constant relation of any number of tuples and any number of attributes can be built up from single-tuple, single-attribute constant relations through join and union.

Example 3.2 The relation shown below

(PILOT	EQUIPMENT)
Desmond	707
Davis	707

can be represented as

$$(\langle \text{Desmond:PILOT}\rangle \bowtie \langle 707\text{:EQUIPMENT}\rangle) \cup (\langle \text{Davis:PILOT}\rangle \bowtie \langle 707\text{:EQUIPMENT}\rangle).$$

3.3 RENAMING ATTRIBUTES

Consider the relation *usedfor* in Table 3.2, which tells what plane will be used for a given flight on a given day. Suppose we want to know all the pairs of flights that are scheduled to use the same plane on the same day. What we need is a join of *usedfor* with itself, but ignoring connections on the FLIGHT column. We can accomplish this join with a copy of *usedfor* where FLIGHT is renamed to, say, FLIGHT2.

To specify such a relation, we introduce a *renaming* operator δ. Let r be a relation on scheme R, where A is an attribute in R and B is an attribute not in $R - A$. Let $R' = (R - A)B$. Then r *with* A *renamed to* B, denoted $\delta_{A \leftarrow B}(r)$, is the relation

$$r'(R') = \{t' \mid \text{there is a tuple } t \in r \text{ with } t'(R - A) = t(R - A) \text{ and } t'(B) = t(A)\}.$$

We require that A and B have the same domain.

Table 3.2 The relation *usedfor*, telling what plane will be used for a given flight.

usedfor(FLIGHT	DATE	PLANENUM)
12	6 Jan	707-82
12	7 Jan	707-82
13	6 Jan	707-82
26	6 Jan	747-16
26	7 Jan	747-18
27	6 Jan	747-16
27	7 Jan	747-2
60	6 Jan	707-82
60	7 Jan	727-6

Example 3.3 An expression that denotes the relation with the desired pairs of flights is

$$s = \pi_{\{\text{FLIGHT},\text{FLIGHT2}\}}(\textit{usedfor} \bowtie \delta_{\text{FLIGHT} \leftarrow \text{FLIGHT2}}(\textit{usedfor})).$$

The value for s using *usedfor* as in Table 3.2 is given in Table 3.3. In Section 3.5.1 we shall see a generalization of the select operator that can be used to remove the redundancy in relation s (see Exercise 3.7).

Table 3.3 Relation s, showing what pairs of flights use the same plane.

s(FLIGHT	FLIGHT2)
12	13
13	12
12	60
60	12
13	60
60	13
12	12
13	13
60	60
26	27
27	26
26	26
27	27

Let r be a relation on R. Let $A_1, A_2, \ldots, A_k$ be distinct attributes in R and let $B_1, B_2, \ldots, B_k$ be distinct attributes not in $R - (A_1 A_2 \cdots A_k)$, where

$dom(A_i) = dom(B_i)$ for $1 \leq i \leq k$. We denote the simultaneous renaming of the attributes $A_1, A_2, \ldots, A_k$ to $B_1, B_2, \ldots, B_k$, respectively, in r by

$$\delta_{A_1, A_2, \ldots, A_k \leftarrow B_1, B_2, \ldots, B_k}(r).$$

Note that a simultaneous renaming sometimes cannot be written as a sequence of single-attribute renamings without introducing another attribute symbol. The renaming $\delta_{A,B \leftarrow B,A}$ is an example.

3.4 THE EQUIJOIN OPERATOR

As the join operator was defined in Chapter 2, relations may only be combined on identically named columns and must be combined on all such columns. In the last section we saw how to join on a subset of those columns. Relations can also be combined on columns with different attribute names but equal domains.

Example 3.4 Consider the relations *routes* and *based* in Table 3.4 and Table 3.5.

Table 3.4 The relation *routes*.

routes (NUMBER	FROM	TO)
84	O'Hare	JFK
109	JFK	Los Angeles
117	Atlanta	Boston
213	JFK	Boston
214	Boston	JFK

Table 3.5 The relation *based*.

based (PILOT	AIRPORT)
Terhune	JFK
Temple	Atlanta
Taylor	Atlanta
Tarbell	Boston
Todd	Los Angeles
Truman	O'Hare

Routes is a projection of the relation *sched* in Table 2.1. *Based* gives the home base for each pilot. Suppose we want to assign pilots to flights that originate at the pilots' home bases. We need a relation showing which pilots are based in the origin city of each flight. Table 3.6 shows such a relation.

Table 3.6 The relation *canfly*, showing which pilots live in the origin city of each flight.

canfly(NUMBER	FROM	TO	PILOT	AIRPORT)
84	O'Hare	JFK	Truman	O'Hare
109	JFK	Los Angeles	Terhune	JFK
117	Atlanta	Boston	Temple	Atlanta
117	Atlanta	Boston	Taylor	Atlanta
213	JFK	Boston	Terhune	JFK
214	Boston	JFK	Tarbell	Boston

We have taken an *equijoin* on the columns corresponding to attribute names FROM and AIRPORT.

We give a general description of equijoin. Let $r(R)$ and $s(S)$ be relations with $A_i \in R$, $B_i \in S$, and $dom(A_i) = dom(B_i)$, $1 \leq i \leq m$. The A_i's need not be distinct, nor need the B_i's. The equijoin of r and s on $A_1, A_2, \ldots, A_m$ and $B_1, B_2, \ldots, B_m$, written $r[A_1 = B_1, A_2 = B_2, \ldots, A_m = B_m]s$, is the relation

$$q(RS) = \{t \mid \text{there exists } t_r \in r \text{ and } t_s \in s \text{ with } t(R) = t_r \text{ and } t(S) = t_s \text{ and } t(A_i) = t(B_i),\ 1 \leq i \leq m\}.$$

Example 3.5 The relation *canfly* in Table 3.6 is

routes[FROM=AIRPORT]*based*.

This definition needs a little refinement. There could be an attribute A such that $A \in R$ and $A \in S$. In the equijoin of r and s, we want a column for each occurrence of A. We require that $R \cap S = \emptyset$ in the definition. This is not a great restriction, since if R and S do have a non-empty intersection, we can rename attributes in r or s to make the intersection of schemes empty. Note that there need not be any comparisons in the equijoin; m can be 0 in the definition. The equijoin $r[]s$ is simply the Cartesian product of r and s.

To emphasize the distinction between join as defined in Chapter 2 and equijoin, we sometimes call the former *natural join*. Equijoin is mainly a convenience, for it can be expressed in terms of renaming and natural join (see Exercise 3.5). Natural join can also be expressed using equijoin. For example, given relations $r(ABC)$ and $s(BCD)$ and attributes B' and C' with $dom(B) = dom(B')$ and $dom(C) = dom(C')$,

$$r \bowtie s = \pi_{ABCD}(r[B = B', C = C']\, \delta_{B,C \leftarrow B',C'}(s)).$$

The main difference between natural join and equijoin is that natural join does not repeat the connected columns.

3.5 EXTENSIONS FOR OTHER COMPARISONS ON DOMAINS

Up to this point, the only comparison between domain values we have been making is one for equality. We could also compare domain values using inequality. Often, domains are ordered, and in those cases, the comparisons $<$, $\leq$, $\geq$, and $>$ also make sense. For a general treatment of such comparisons, we posit a set Θ of *comparators*: binary relations (in the mathematical sense) over pairs of domains. If θ is a comparator in Θ, and A and B are attributes, we say A is *θ-comparable* with B if θ is over $dom(A) \times dom(B)$. We write "A is θ-comparable" to mean A is θ-comparable with itself. We assume every attribute A is equality-comparable and inequality-comparable.

We generally will only be concerned with the comparators $=$, $\neq$, $<$, $\leq$, $\geq$, and $>$ over a single domain. However, we use these symbols in a generic sense; for example, "$=$" actually represents different equality comparators for different domains. We shall use comparators to generalize selection and join to comparisons other than equality.

It is a somewhat artificial restriction to require that our comparators be binary relations. There are reasonable tests we might like to make that are represented by mathematical relations of degree other than two. For example, we might want the unary relation m, on the domain of times, where $h \in m$ means h is a morning time; or the ternary relation w on integers, where $w(i, j, k)$ means $i \leq j \leq k$. Any unary relation θ can be represented by a binary relation θ', where $\theta(a)$ if and only if $\theta'(a, a)$, and for no a, b where $a \neq b$ does $\theta'(a, b)$ hold. Some ternary and higher order relations, such as w, can be represented as the conjunction of binary relations, while others cannot (see Exercise 3.9). While the extension to comparisons based on relations other than binary is straightforward, the notation is messy, and we wish to keep our theorems neat.

3.5.1 Extending Selection

We extend our notation for the select operator to be $\sigma_{A\theta a}$, where θ is a comparator in Θ. If r is a relation on scheme R, and A an attribute of R, and a is a constant in $dom(B)$, where A and B are θ-comparable, then $\sigma_{A\theta a}(r) = \{t \in r | t(A)\ \theta\ a\}$. We use infix notation for comparators: $t(A)\theta a$ means $\theta(t(A), a)$.

Example 3.6 A relation *times*, which is a projection of the relation *sched* in Table 2.1, is shown below.

times

NUMBER	DEPARTS	ARRIVES
84	3:00p	5:55p
109	9:40p	2:42a
117	10:05p	12:43a
213	11:43a	12:45p
214	2:20p	3:12p

Relation $s = \sigma_{\text{ARRIVES} \leq 1\text{:00p}}(times)$, assuming $\leq$ orders the hours of the day from 12:01a to midnight, is as follows:

$\sigma_{\text{ARRIVES} \leq 1\text{:00p}}(times) = s$

NUMBER	DEPARTS	ARRIVES
109	9:49p	2:42a
117	10:05p	12:43a
213	11:43a	12:45p

It is a list of all flights and times that arrive at or before 1:00p.

Besides comparisons between an attribute and a constant, we also allow comparisons between two attributes. Let r be a relation on R, where A and B are attributes in R. Let $\theta \in \Theta$ be a comparator such that A and B are θ-comparable. Then $\sigma_{A\theta B}(r) = \{t \in r | t(A)\ \theta\ t(B)\}$.

Example 3.7 Let "$\ll$" be the comparator on times of day meaning "precedes by at least 2 hours." Then, for *times* as given in Example 3.6, $s = \sigma_{\text{DEPARTS} \ll \text{ARRIVES}}(times)$ is given below.

s

NUMBER	DEPARTS	ARRIVES
84	3:00p	5:55p
109	9:40p	2:42a
117	10:05p	12:43a

We let times of day wrap around midnight for $\ll$.

As before, we can abbreviate a series of selections. For example, $\sigma_{A \leq a}(\sigma_{B > D}(\sigma_{C = c}(r)))$ becomes $\sigma_{A \leq a, B > D, C = c}(r)$.

To give ourselves even more convenience, we allow the logical connectives $\wedge$, $\vee$, $\neg$ (and, or, not), and parentheses. For example, $\sigma_{((A = a) \vee (A > c)) \wedge (B \neq b)}(r)$.

The commas we used before were actually implicit ands. The logical connectives, while convenient, do not add any expressive power to our set of relational operators (see Exercise 3.10).

3.5.2 The Theta-Join Operator

The equijoin extends the join operator to handle comparisons between columns with different attribute names. With other comparators, we need not restrict ourselves merely to comparing for equality.

Example 3.8 Suppose we have a list of flights and times from city *a* to city *b*, and a similar list of flights and times from city *b* to city *c*. Table 3.7 and Table 3.8 show these lists, represented by two relations, *timesab* and *timesbc*.

Table 3.7 Flights between city *a* and city *b*.

timesab (NUMBER	DEPARTS	ARRIVES)
60	9:40a	11:45a
91	12:50p	2:47p
112	4:05p	6:15p
306	8:30p	10:25p
420	9:15p	11:11p

Table 3.8 Flights between city *b* and city *c*.

timesbc (NUMBER	DEPARTS	ARRIVES)
11	8:30a	9:52a
60	12:25p	1:43p
156	4:20p	5:40p
158	7:10p	8:35p

We want to know which flights from *a* to *b* connect with flights from *b* to *c*. We combine tuples from *timesab* and *timesbc* when the flight from *a* to *b* arrives at *b* before the flight from *b* to *c* departs from *b*. Table 3.9 shows the result, relation *connectac*. Note that we must first rename attributes in *timesbc*, and that we are not looking for connections over midnight.

Table 3.9 Flight connections between city a and city c at city b.

connectac (NUMBER	DEPARTS	ARRIVES	NUMBER′	DEPARTS′	ARRIVES′)
60	9:40a	11:45a	60	12:25p	1:43p
60	9:40a	11:45a	156	4:20p	5:40p
60	9:40a	11:45a	158	7:10p	8:35p
91	12:50p	2:47p	156	4:20p	5:40p
91	12:50p	2:47p	158	7:10p	8:35p
112	4:05p	6:15p	158	7:10p	8:35p

Let $r(R)$ and $s(S)$ be two relations we want to combine, where $R \cap S = \emptyset$. Let $A \in R$ and $B \in S$ be θ-comparable for θ in Θ. Then $r[A\theta B]s$ is the relation

$$q(RS) = \{t \mid \text{for some } t_r \in r \text{ and some } t_s \in s \text{ such that } t_r(A)\ \theta\ t_s(B),\ t(R) = t_r \text{ and } t(S) = t_s\}.$$

Example 3.9 For the relation in Table 3.9,

$$connectac = timesab\,[\text{ARRIVES} < \text{DEPARTS}']\,timesbc',$$

where

$$timesbc' = \delta_{\text{NUMBER, ARRIVES, DEPARTS} \leftarrow \text{NUMBER}', \text{ARRIVES}', \text{DEPARTS}'}(timesbc).$$

When we want a number of comparisons to take place, we write them all between the brackets. For example, $r[A_1 < B_1, A_2 = B_2, A_3 \geq B_2]s$. We call any such join a *theta-join*. Equijoin is a special case of theta-join.

3.6 RELATIONAL ALGEBRA

We refer to the operators union, intersection, difference, active complement, select, project, natural join, division, renaming, and theta-join, along with constant relations and regular relations, as the *relational algebra*. Any expression legally formed using these operators and relations is an *algebraic expression*. Given an algebraic expression E, and the current values of all the relations in E, we can evaluate E to yield a single relation. E represents a mapping from sets of relations to single relations.

Actually, the set of attributes, the domains, and the set of comparators we use limit the mappings we may define. In Chapter 10, where we compare the expressive power of relational algebra to other systems for operating on relations, these parameters will make a difference. In such cases, we must be a bit more formal.

Definition 3.2 Let $\mathbf{U}$ be a set of attributes, called the *universe*. Let $\mathfrak{D}$ be a set of domains, and let *dom* be a total function from $\mathbf{U}$ to $\mathfrak{D}$. Let $\boldsymbol{R} = \{R_1,$

$R_2, \ldots, R_p\}$ be a set of distinct relation schemes, where $R_i \subseteq \mathbf{U}$ for $1 \leq i \leq p$. Let $d = \{r_1, r_2, \ldots, r_p\}$ be a set of relations, such that r_i is a relation on R_i, $1 \leq i \leq p$. Let Θ be a set of comparators over domains in $\mathfrak{D}$, including at least the equality and inequality comparators for every domain. The *relational algebra over* **U**, $\mathfrak{D}$, dom, **R**, d, *and* Θ is the 7-tuple $\mathcal{R} = (\mathbf{U}, \mathfrak{D}, dom, \mathbf{R}, d, \Theta, O)$, where O is the set of operators union, intersect, difference, active complement, project, natural join, and divide, and renaming using attributes in $\mathbf{U}$, select using comparators in Θ, and logical connectives and theta-join using comparators in Θ. An *algebraic expression over* $\mathcal{R}$ is any expression formed legally (according to the restrictions on the operators) from the relations in d and constant relations over schemes in **U**, using the operators in O.

We allow parentheses in algebraic expressions, and assume no precedence of the binary operators, except for the usual precedence of $\cap$ over $\cup$. We also may omit parentheses for strings of relations connected by the same operator, if the operation is associative. Note that we do not allow two relations with the same scheme. We discuss this restriction again in Chapter 12.

The relation names $r_1, r_2, \ldots, r_p$ are analogous to program variables, where r_i ranges over relations on scheme R_i. Our notation is a bit ambiguous, in that we use r_i both as a relation name and to denote the current state of a relation. The same ambiguity arises when discussing variables in programs; this is the problem denotational semantics tries to address. The ambiguity only gets clumsy when we view an algebraic expression as a mapping.

3.6.1 Algebraic Expressions as Mappings

Since the result of every relational operation we use is a single relation, every algebraic expression defines a function that maps a set of relations to a single relation. The scheme of the single relation depends only on the schemes for the set of relations. Let the *scheme* of an algebraic expression E, denoted $sch(E)$, be the relation scheme of the relation.

We can define $sch(E)$ recursively according to the following rules.

1. If E is r_i, then $sch(E)$ is the relation scheme for r_i.
2. If E is a constant relation, $sch(E)$ is the scheme for the constant relation.
3. If $E = E_1 \cup E_2$, $E_1 \cap E_2$, $E_1 - E_2$, $\tilde{E}_1$, or $\sigma_C(E_1)$, where C is some set of conditions, then $sch(E) = sch(E_1)$.
4. If $E = \pi_X(E_1)$, then $sch(E) = X$.
5. If $E = E_1 \div E_2$, then $sch(E) = sch(E_1) - sch(E_2)$.

6. If $E = E_1 \bowtie E_2$ or $E_1[C]E_2$, for some set of conditions C, then $sch(E) = sch(E_1) \cup sch(E_2)$.
7. If $E = \delta_{A_1,A_2,\ldots,A_k \leftarrow B_1,B_2,\ldots,B_k}(E_1)$, then $sch(E) = (sch(E_1) - A_1A_2 \cdots A_k)\, B_1B_2 \cdots B_k$.

If E is an algebraic expression involving relation names $s_1, s_2, \ldots, s_q$, corresponding to schemes $S_1, S_2, \ldots, S_q$, then E is a mapping

$$E\colon Rel(S_1) \times Rel(S_2) \times \cdots \times Rel(S_q) \rightarrow Rel(sch(E)),$$

where $Rel(R)$ is the set of all relations with scheme R. We shall sometimes use $E(s_1, s_2, \ldots, s_q)$ to denote the value of E on the set of relations named by $s_1, s_1, \ldots, s_q$.

Sometimes we shall want to use the complement operator in expressions. If we add complement to our set of operators, we get a *relational algebra with complement.* An algebraic expression E involving complement potentially maps a set of relations to an infinite relation. We shall not use complement after this chapter until Chapter 10.

3.6.2 Restricting the Set of Operators

As we have seen numerous times, the relational operators are in no sense independent. There are restricted sets of operators that have all the power of the full set. One such set is given by the next theorem.

Theorem 3.1 Let E be an expression over relational algebra $\mathcal{R}$ that uses relation names $s_1, s_2, \ldots, s_q$. There is an expression E' over $\mathcal{R}$ that defines the same function of $s_1, s_2, \ldots, s_q$ and uses only single-attribute, single-tuple constant relations, select with a single comparison, natural join, project, union, difference, and renaming.

Proof By what we noted in Section 3.2, we can replace every constant relation in E by an expression involving union, join, and single-attribute, single-tuple constant relations. Exercise 3.13 shows that theta-join can be replaced by natural join and selection. Exercise 3.10 shows how to replace any generalized selection with an expression involving single-comparison selections and other relational operators, not including theta-join. Exercise 3.3a shows how to express division in terms of operators from Chapter 2.

In Section 2.1 we saw that intersection can be replaced by difference. The only operator left to replace in E to get E' is active complement. Active complement can be expressed with project, join, and difference. For example, suppose E_1 is an algebraic expression where $sch(E_1) = ABC$. Then $\tilde{E}_1$ is

$$(\pi_A(E_1) \bowtie \pi_B(E_1) \bowtie \pi_C(E_1)) - E_1.$$

Note that the joins are Cartesian products.

Corollary Let E be an expression over relational algebra $\mathcal{R}$ with complement that uses relation names $s_1, s_2, \ldots, s_q$. There is an expression E' over $\mathcal{R}$ that defines the same function of $s_1, s_2, \ldots, s_q$ and uses only single-attribute, single-tuple constant relations, select with a single comparison, natural join, project, union, complement, and renaming.

Proof By Theorem 3.1, the only operator that must be removed from E is difference. Note that $E_1 - E_2 = \overline{E_1 \cup E_2}$.

3.7 THE SPLIT OPERATOR

The split operator takes one relation as an argument and returns a pair of relations. We do not include it in relational algebra since we want the value of every expression in the algebra to be a single relation. Let r be a relation on scheme R and let $\beta(t)$ be a Boolean predicate on tuples over R. Then r *split on* β, written $\text{SPLIT}_\beta(r)$, is the pair of relations (s, s'), both with scheme R, where $s = \{t \in r \mid \beta(t)\}$ and $s' = \{t \in r \mid \text{not } \beta(t)\}$. Clearly, $s' = r - s$. We put no restrictions on what the predicate β may be, except that its value may only depend on tuple t and not on the state of r.

Example 3.10 The predicate, $\beta(t) =$ there exists t' in r with $t(A) \neq t'(A)$ would not be permissible, since it depends on other tuples in r.

Example 3.11 Consider the relation *certified* in Table 3.3. Let $\beta(t) = (t(\text{EQUIPMENT}) = 707$ or $t(\text{EQUIPMENT}) = 727)$. The relations s and s', where $\text{SPLIT}_\beta(\textit{certified}) = (s, s')$, are shown below.

s(PILOT	EQUIPMENT)
Desmond	707
Desmond	727
Doyle	707
Doyle	727
Davis	707
Davis	727
Dow	727

s'(PILOT	EQUIPMENT)
Desmond	747
Davis	747
Davis	1011

3.8 THE FACTOR OPERATOR

The *factor* operator takes one relation as an argument and generates two relations. The two relations, when joined, yield the original relation with an added column. We shall first demonstrate the factor operator by example.

Example 3.12 Consider a flight roster showing all the passengers booked on a flight, what class they are flying, and whether they are in the smoking or non-smoking section. We represent the flight roster as a relation *roster* on the scheme {PASSENGER, CLASS, SMOKING} as shown.

roster(PASSENGER CLASS SMOKING)

PASSENGER	CLASS	SMOKING
Salazar	first	yes
Schick	first	no
Shockley	coach	no
Stewart	first	yes
Sayers	coach	no
Sands	coach	no
Sachs	coach	yes

There are only four possible {CLASS, SMOKING}-values. We can represent the same information in less space by splitting off the CLASS and SMOKING columns, and creating a new column, LINK, as shown below.

roster1(PASSENGER LINK)

PASSENGER	LINK
Salazar	1
Schick	2
Shockley	4
Stewart	1
Sayers	4
Sands	4
Sachs	3

roster2(LINK CLASS SMOKING)

LINK	CLASS	SMOKING
1	first	yes
2	first	no
3	coach	yes
4	coach	no

It is easy to check that $roster = \pi_{\{\text{PASSENGER,CLASS,SMOKING}\}}(roster1 \bowtie roster2)$.

If r is a relation on scheme R and $B_1, B_2, \ldots, B_m$ are attributes of R, and L is an attribute not in R, we use the notation

$$\text{FACTOR}(r; B_1, B_2, \ldots, B_m; L)$$

to denote the operation of removing the columns corresponding to B_1, B_2,

$\ldots, B_m$ from r to form a new relation, and adding an extra column labeled L to r and the new relation on which to join. The relations *roster1* and *roster2* are the result of FACTOR(*roster*; CLASS, SMOKING; LINK).

We shall not specify the factor operator more formally. It main use is as a conceptual tool for finding efficient ways to store a relation. Again, we do not include this operator in the relational algebra, because it does not yield a single relation as its result.

3.9 EXERCISES

3.1 Let $r(R)$ and $s(S)$ be relations where $R \cap S = \emptyset$. Prove

$$(r \bowtie s) \div s = r.$$

3.2 Let r be a relation on scheme R and let s and s' be relations on scheme S, where $R \supseteq S$. Show that if $s \subseteq s'$, then

$$r \div s \supseteq r \div s'.$$

Show that the converse is false.

3.3* Let $r(R)$ and $s(S)$ be relations with $R \supseteq S$ and let $R' = R - S$. Prove the identities

a) $r \div s = \pi_{R'}(r) - \pi_{R'}((\pi_{R'}(r) \bowtie s) - r)$.
b) $r \div s = \bigcap_{t \in s} \pi_{R'}(\sigma_{S=t}(r))$.

3.4 For relation r with the scheme shown in Table 3.2, give an expression that, for a given flight f, evaluates to a relation on scheme FLIGHT giving all the flights that use the same plane as flight f on every date for flight f listed in r.

3.5 Show that any equijoin can be specified in terms of natural join and renaming, given sufficient extra attributes with the correct domains.

3.6 It is sometimes meaningful to equijoin a relation with itself. Compute relation $r = routes[\text{TO} = \text{FROM}']routes'$ where *routes* is the relation in Table 3.4, and *routes'* is *routes* with all attributes renamed to primed versions. Using r, compute the relation $s = \pi_{\{\text{FROM},\text{TO}'\}}(r)$. What meaning can be assigned to the tuples in s? Find an operation that will remove tuples such as ⟨JFK JFK⟩ from s.

3.7 In Example 3.3, let the domain of FLIGHT (and FLIGHT2) be $<$-comparable. Use selection as extended in Section 3.5.1 to give an expression that denotes s without the redundant information. That is, each pair should occur once, and pairs such as $\langle 12\ 12 \rangle$ should be removed.

3.8 Compute

$$\sigma_{(\text{DEPARTS} \geq 11{:}00\text{a} \wedge \text{ARRIVES} \leq 2{:}00\text{p}) \vee (\text{DEPARTS} \leq 5{:}00\text{p})}(\mathit{times})$$

for the relation *times* in Example 3.6.

3.9 Give a ternary relation (in the mathematical sense) that cannot be represented as the conjunction of binary relations without introducing new domains.

3.10 Show that the effect of any selection operation can be achieved using the select operator in the form $\sigma_{A\theta a}$ or $\sigma_{A\theta B}$ and the operators from Chapter 2 except for select. Do not assume the set of comparators Θ is closed under negation.

3.11 Compute

$$\sigma_{\text{ARRIVES}' \leq 2{:}00\text{p}}(\mathit{times}[\text{ARRIVES} < \text{DEPARTS}']\mathit{times}')$$

where *times* is the relation in Example 3.6 and *times'* is the same relation with all attributes renamed to primed versions. Assume time of day runs from 12:01a to midnight.

3.12 Compute

$$\mathit{sched}[\text{TO} = \text{FROM}', \text{ARRIVES} \lessdot \text{DEPARTS}']\mathit{sched}'$$

where *sched* is the relation in Table 2.1, *sched'* is *sched* with all attributes renamed to primed versions, and $\lessdot$ is the comparator "earlier by up to 3 hours" that wraps around midnight.

3.13 Show that any theta-join can be expressed using natural join and generalized selection.

3.14 Given relations $r(ABC)$ and $s(BCD)$, what is $sch(E)$ for

$$E = \pi_A(\sigma_{B=b}(\tilde{r})) \bowtie \pi_B(\pi_{BC}(r) - \pi_{BC}(s)).$$

3.15 Let $\mathcal{R}$ be the relational algebra

$$(\mathbf{U}, \mathfrak{D}, dom, \boldsymbol{R}, d, \Theta, O).$$

(a) Show that if Θ contains arbitrary comparators, then for no proper subset of the operations in Theorem 3.1 is the theorem true.
(b) Show that if Θ contains only equality and inequality comparators, then selection can be restricted to the form $\sigma_{A=B}$.

3.16 Show that if $\text{SPLIT}_\beta(r) = (s, s')$, then $r = s \cup s'$.

3.17 Let r and r' be relations on R. Let $s = r \cup r'$. Show that there does not necessarily exist a predicate β such that $\text{SPLIT}_\beta(s) = (r, r')$.

3.18 Let r be a relation on scheme R, let $\{B_1, B_2, \ldots, B_m\}$ be a subset of R, and let L be an attribute not in R. Let $p_i = |dom(B_i)|$, $1 \le i \le m$, and assume all the p_i's are finite. Suppose every value in a tuple of r requires one byte of storage and there are k tuples in r. Give an inequality involving m, k, and $p_1, p_2, \ldots, p_m$ that will indicate when the relations generated by $\text{FACTOR}(r; B_1, B_2, \ldots, B_m; L)$ will require less space than r.

3.10 BIBLIOGRAPHY AND COMMENTS

Codd [1972b] defines the relational algebra as given here, with the exception of renaming. Hall, Hitchcock, and Todd [1975] explore some generalizations of the algebraic operators. Beck [1978] discusses minimal sets of operators. The split operation is from Fagin [1980b].

Exercise 3.3b was suggested by Jon Shultis.

Chapter 4

FUNCTIONAL DEPENDENCIES

Two primary purposes of databases are to attenuate data redundancy and enhance data reliability. Any *a priori* knowledge of restrictions or constraints on permissible sets of data has considerable usefulness in reaching these goals, as we shall see. Data dependencies are one way to formulate such advance knowledge. In this chapter we shall cover one type of data dependency, the functional dependency. In Chapter 7 we cover two other types of data dependencies, the multivalued and join dependencies. Other general classes of data dependencies are treated in Chapter 14.

4.1 DEFINITIONS

We discussed keys in Chapter 1. Functional dependencies are a generalization. Table 4.1 depicts the relation *assign*(PILOT FLIGHT DATE DEPARTS). *Assign* tells which pilot flies a given flight on a given day, and what time the flight leaves. Not every combination of pilots, flights, dates, and times is allowable in *assign*. The following restrictions apply, among others.

1. For each flight there is exactly one time.
2. For any given pilot, date, and time, there is only one flight.
3. For a given flight and date, there is only one pilot.

These restrictions are examples of *functional dependencies*. Informally, a functional dependency occurs when the values of a tuple on one set of attributes uniquely determine the values on another set of attributes. Our restrictions can be phrased as

1. TIME functionally depends on FLIGHT,
2. FLIGHT functionally depends on {PILOT, DATE, TIME}, and
3. PILOT functionally depends on {FLIGHT, DATE}.

Table 4.1 The relation *assign*(PILOT FLIGHT DATE DEPARTS).

assign(PILOT	FLIGHT	DATE	DEPARTS)
Cushing	83	9 Aug	10:15a
Cushing	116	10 Aug	1:25p
Clark	281	8 Aug	5:50a
Clark	301	12 Aug	6:35p
Clark	83	11 Aug	10:15a
Chin	83	13 Aug	10:15a
Chin	116	12 Aug	1:25p
Copely	281	9 Aug	5:50a
Copely	281	13 Aug	5:50a
Copely	412	15 Aug	1:25p

We generally reverse the order of the two sets and write FLIGHT, DATE *functionally determines* PILOT, or {FLIGHT, DATE}→PILOT. (Recall that we let a single attribute A stand for $\{A\}$.)

We now state the notion formally using our relational operators. Let r be a relation on scheme R, with X and Y subsets of R. Relation r *satisfies* the *functional dependency* (FD) $X \to Y$ if for every X-value x, $\pi_Y(\sigma_{X=x}(r))$ has at most one tuple. One way to interpret this expression is to look at two tuples, t_1 and t_2, in r. If $t_1(X) = t_2(X)$, then $t_1(Y) = t_2(Y)$. In the FD $X \to Y$, X is called the *left side* and Y is called the *right side*.

This interpretation of functional dependency is the basis for the algorithm SATISFIES given below.

Algorithm 4.1 SATISFIES
Input: A relation r and an FD $X \to Y$.
Output: *true* if r satisfies $X \to Y$, *false* otherwise.
SATISFIES(r, $X \to Y$);

1. Sort the relation r on its X columns to bring tuples with equal X-values together.
2. If each set of tuples with equal X-values has equal Y-values, return *true*. Otherwise, return *false*.

SATISFIES tests if a relation r satisfies an FD $X \to Y$. Table 4.2 shows the result of running SATISFIES(*assign*, FLIGHT → DEPARTS) on the relation *assign* from Table 4.1. The dashed lines mark off sets of tuples with equal FLIGHT-values. The DEPARTS-values for each set are the same, so the FD is satisfied.

Table 4.2 The result of running the algorithm SATISFIES on the relation *assign* from Table 4.1.

assign(PILOT	FLIGHT	DATE	DEPARTS)
Cushing	83	9 Aug	10:15a
Clark	83	11 Aug	10:15a
Chin	83	13 Aug	10:15a
Cushing	116	10 Aug	1:25p
Chin	116	12 Aug	1:25p
Clark	281	8 Aug	5:50a
Copely	281	9 Aug	5:50a
Copely	281	13 Aug	5:50a
Clark	301	12 Aug	6:35p
Copely	412	15 Aug	1:25p

Table 4.3 shows the result of running SATISFIES(*assign*, DEPARTS → FLIGHT). There is a set of tuples with equal DEPARTS-values that does not have equal FLIGHT-values, so the FD is not satisfied by *assign*.

There are two extreme cases to consider, namely $X \rightarrow \emptyset$ and $\emptyset \rightarrow Y$. The FD $X \rightarrow \emptyset$ is trivially satisfied by any relation. The FD $\emptyset \rightarrow Y$ is satisfied by those relations in which every tuple has the same Y-value. In the sequel, we shall usually ignore FDs of these forms.

4.2 INFERENCE AXIOMS

For a relation $r(R)$, at any given moment there is some family of FDs F that r satisfies. We encounter the same problem we had with keys. One state of a relation may satisfy a certain FD, while another state does not. We want the family of FDs F that all permissible states of r satisfy. Finding F requires

Table 4.3 The result of running SATISFIES(*assign*, DEPARTS → FLIGHT)

assign(PILOT	FLIGHT	DATE	DEPARTS)
Clark	281	8 Aug	5:50a
Copely	281	9 Aug	5:50a
Copely	281	13 Aug	5:50a
Cushing	83	9 Aug	10:15a
Clark	83	11 Aug	10:15a
Chin	83	13 Aug	10:15a
Cushing	116	10 Aug	1:25p
Chin	116	12 Aug	1:25p
Copely	412	15 Aug	1:25p
Clark	301	12 Aug	6:35p

semantic knowledge of the relation r. We can also consider a family of FDs F applying to the relation scheme R. In this case, any relation $r(R)$ must satisfy all the FDs of F. It is not always clear which begets the other, the set of permissible states of a relation or the FDs on the relation scheme.

The number of FDs that can apply to a relation $r(R)$ is finite, since there is only a finite number of subsets of R. Thus it is always possible to find all the FDs that r satisfies, by trying all possibilities using the algorithm SATISFIES. This approach is time-consuming. Knowing some members of F, it is often possible to infer other members of F. A set F of FDs *implies* the FD $X \rightarrow Y$, written $F \models X \rightarrow Y$, if every relation that satisfies all the FDs in F also satisfies $X \rightarrow Y$. An *inference axiom* is a rule that states if a relation satisfies certain FDs, it must satisfy certain other FDs.

We now introduce six inference axioms for FDs. In the statement of the rules, r is a relation on R and W, X, Y, and Z are subsets of R.

F1. Reflexivity

The relation $\pi_X(\sigma_{X=x}(r))$ always has at most one tuple, so $X \rightarrow X$ always holds in r.

F2. Augmentation

This axiom deals with augmenting the left side of an FD. If r satisfies $X \rightarrow Y$, then $\pi_Y(\sigma_{X=x}(r))$ has at most one tuple for any X-value x. If Z is any subset of R, then $\sigma_{XZ=xz}(r) \subseteq \sigma_{X=x}(r)$ and hence

$$\pi_Y(\sigma_{XZ=xz}(r)) \subseteq \pi_Y(\sigma_{X=x}(r)).$$

Thus $\pi_Y(\sigma_{XZ=xz}(r))$ has at most one tuple and r must satisfy $X\,Z \rightarrow Y$.

Example 4.1 Consider relation r below. Relation r satisfies the FD $A \rightarrow B$,

$r(A$	B	C	$D)$
a_1	b_1	c_1	d_1
a_2	b_2	c_1	d_1
a_1	b_1	c_1	d_2
a_3	b_3	c_2	d_3

and hence the FDs $A\,B \rightarrow B$, $A\,C \rightarrow B$, $A\,D \rightarrow B$, $A\,B\,C \rightarrow B$, $A\,B\,D \rightarrow B$, $A\,C\,D \rightarrow B$, and $A\,B\,C\,D \rightarrow B$, by axiom F2.

F3. Additivity

This axiom allows us to combine two FDs with the same left sides. If r satisfies $X \rightarrow Y$ and $X \rightarrow Z$ then $\pi_Y(\sigma_{X=x}(r))$ and $\pi_Z(\sigma_{X=x}(r))$ both have at most one tuple for any X-value x. If $\pi_{YZ}(\sigma_{X=x}(r))$ had more than one tuple, then at least one of $\pi_Y(\sigma_{X=x}(r))$ and $\pi_Z(\sigma_{X=x}(r))$ would have more than one tuple. Thus, r satisfies $X \rightarrow Y\,Z$.

Example 4.2 In the relation of Example 4.1, r satisfies $A \rightarrow B$ and $A \rightarrow C$. By axiom F3, r must also satisfy $A \rightarrow B\,C$.

F4. Projectivity

This axiom is more or less the reverse of additivity. If r satisfies $X \rightarrow Y\,Z$, then $\pi_{YZ}(\sigma_{X=x}(r))$ has at most one tuple for any X-value x. Since $\pi_Y(\pi_{YZ}(\sigma_{X=x}(r))) = \pi_Y(\sigma_{X=x}(r))$, $\pi_Y(\sigma_{X=x}(r))$ can have at most one tuple. Hence r satisfies $X \rightarrow Y$.

Example 4.3 In the relation of Example 4.1, r satisfies $A \rightarrow B\,C$. By axiom F4, r must also satisfy $A \rightarrow B$ and $A \rightarrow C$.

F5. Transitivity
This axiom and the next are the most powerful of the inference axioms. Let r satisfy $X \rightarrow Y$ and $Y \rightarrow Z$. Consider tuples t_1 and t_2 in r. We know that if $t_1(X) = t_2(X)$, then $t_1(Y) = t_2(Y)$ and also if $t_1(Y) = t_2(Y)$, then $t_1(Z) = t_2(Z)$. Therefore, if $t_1(X) = t_2(X)$, then $t_1(Z) = t_2(Z)$, so r satisfies $X \rightarrow Z$.

Example 4.4 Relation r shown below satisfies the FDs $A \rightarrow B$ and $B \rightarrow C$. By axiom F5, r satisfies $A \rightarrow C$.

$r(A$	B	C	$D)$
a_1	b_1	c_2	d_1
a_2	b_2	c_1	d_2
a_3	b_1	c_2	d_1
a_4	b_1	c_2	d_3

F6. Pseudotransitivity
Let r satisfy the FDs $X \rightarrow Y$ and $Y Z \rightarrow W$ and let t_1 and t_2 be tuples in r. We know if $t_1(X) = t_2(X)$, then $t_1(Y) = t_2(Y)$ and also if $t_1(Y Z) = t_2(Y Z)$, then $t_1(W) = t_2(W)$. From $t_1(X Z) = t_2(X Z)$ we can deduce that $t_1(X) = t_2(X)$ and so $t_1(Y) = t_2(Y)$ and further $t_1(Y Z) = t_2(Y Z)$, which implies $t_1(W) = t_2(W)$. Thus r satisfies $X Z \rightarrow W$.

To summarize, if W, X, Y, and Z are subsets of R, for any relation r on R:

F1. Reflexivity: $X \rightarrow X$.
F2. Augmentation: $X \rightarrow Y$ implies $X Z \rightarrow Y$.
F3. Additivity: $X \rightarrow Y$ and $X \rightarrow Z$ imply $X \rightarrow Y Z$.
F4. Projectivity: $X \rightarrow Y Z$ implies $X \rightarrow Y$.
F5. Transitivity: $X \rightarrow Y$ and $Y \rightarrow Z$ imply $X \rightarrow Z$.
F6. Pseudotransitivity: $X \rightarrow Y$ and $Y Z \rightarrow W$ imply $X Z \rightarrow W$.

4.3 APPLYING THE INFERENCE AXIOMS

Using the axioms F1 to F6 it is possible to derive other inference rules for FDs.

Example 4.5 Let r be a relation on R with X and Y subsets of R. Axiom F1 says that r satisfies $Y \rightarrow Y$. Applying axiom F2 we get r satisfies $X Y \rightarrow Y$. Another way to state this rule is that for $Y \subseteq X \subseteq R$, r satisfies $X \rightarrow Y$.

Example 4.6 Let r be a relation on R with X, Y, and Z subsets of R. Suppose r satisfies $X\,Y \rightarrow Z$ and $X \rightarrow Y$. By axiom F6 we get r satisfies $X\,X \rightarrow Z$, which simplifies to $X \rightarrow Z$.

To disprove a conjecture about FDs, all we need to do is exhibit a relation where the conjecture does not hold.

Example 4.7 We want to disprove the conjecture $X\,Y \rightarrow Z\,W$ implies $X \rightarrow Z$. The relation r below satisfies $A\,B \rightarrow C\,D$, but $A \not\rightarrow C$.

r(A	B	C	D)
a	b	c	d
a	b'	c'	d

Some of the inference axioms can be derived from the others. For example, F5, transitivity, is a special case of F6, pseudotransitivity, where $Z = \emptyset$. F6 follows from F1, F2, F3, and F5: if $X \rightarrow Y$ and $Y\,Z \rightarrow W$, then by F1, $Z \rightarrow Z$. By F2, $X\,Z \rightarrow Y$, and $X\,Z \rightarrow Z$. Using F3, we get $X\,Z \rightarrow Y\,Z$. Finally, applying F5 we get $X\,Z \rightarrow W$.

We shall see in the next section that axioms F1 to F6 are complete; that is, every FD that is implied by a set F of FDs can be derived from the FDs in F by one or more applications of these axioms. We have shown that each axiom is correct, so applying the axioms to FDs in a set F can only yield FDs that are implied by F.

Given axioms F1, F2, and F6, we can prove the rest. We have just seen that F5 is a special case of F6. Given $X \rightarrow Y$ and $X \rightarrow Z$, we use F1 to get $Y\,Z \rightarrow Y\,Z$ and apply F6 twice, first to get $X\,Z \rightarrow Y\,Z$ and then to get $X \rightarrow Y\,Z$. Therefore, F3 follows from F1, F2, and F6. To prove F4, suppose $X \rightarrow Y\,Z$. By F1, $Y \rightarrow Y$, and by F2, $Y\,Z \rightarrow Y$. Applying F6 yields $X \rightarrow Y$. Thus axioms F1, F2, and F6 are a complete subset of F1 to F6. Axioms F1, F2, and F6 are also *independent*: no one of the axioms can be proved from the other two (see Exercise 4.5). These three axioms are sometimes called *Armstrong's axioms*, although they are not very similar to Armstrong's original axioms (but the name has a nice ring to it).

Let F be a set of FDs for a relation $r(R)$. The *closure* of F, written F^+, is the smallest set containing F such that Armstrong's axioms cannot be applied to the set to yield an FD not in the set. Since F^+ must be finite, we can compute it by starting with F, applying F1, F2, and F6, and adding the derived FDs to F until no new FDs can be derived. The closure of F depends on the scheme R. If $R = A\,B$, then F^+ will always contain $B \rightarrow B$, but if $R = A\,C$, F^+ never contains $B \to B$. When R is not explicitly defined, it is assumed to be the set of all attribute symbols used in the FDs of F.

The set F *derives* an FD $X \to Y$ if $X \to Y$ is in F^+. Since our inference axioms are correct, if F derives $X \to Y$, then F implies $X \to Y$. In the next section we prove the converse. Note that $F^+ = (F^+)^+$ (see Exercise 4.6).

Example 4.8 Let $F = \{A\,B \to C,\ C \to B\}$ be a set of FDs on $r(A\,B\,C)$. $F^+ = \{A \to A,\ A\,B \to A,\ A\,C \to A,\ A\,B\,C \to A,\ B \to B,\ A\,B \to B,\ B\,C \to B,\ A\,B\,C \to B,\ C \to C,\ A\,C \to C,\ B\,C \to C,\ A\,B\,C \to C,\ A\,B \to A\,B,\ A\,B\,C \to A\,B,\ A\,C \to A\,C,\ A\,B\,C \to A\,C,\ B\,C \to B\,C,\ A\,B\,C \to B\,C,\ A\,B\,C \to A\,B\,C,\ A\,B \to C,\ A\,B \to A\,C,\ A\,B \to B\,C,\ A\,B \to A\,B\,C,\ C \to B,\ C \to B\,C,\ A\,C \to B,\ A\,C \to A\,B\}$.

In Chapter 5 we shall see more succinct ways to express F^+.

4.4 COMPLETENESS OF THE INFERENCE AXIOMS

We wish to show that axioms F1 to F6 allow us to infer all the FDs implied by a set F of FDs.* That is, if F implies $X \to Y$, then F derives $X \to Y$. To prove this result, we shall show how to construct, for any F, a relation r that satisfies every FD in F^+ but no others.

Definition 4.1 $X \to Y$ is an FD *over* scheme R if X and Y are both subsets of R. F is a set of FDs *over* R if every FD in F is an FD *over* R.

Definition 4.2 If F is a set of FDs over R and G is the set of all possible FDs over R, then $F^- = G - F^+$. F^- is the *exterior* of F.

Definition 4.3 An FD $X \to Y$ is *trivial* if $X \supseteq Y$. If $X \to Y$ is a trivial FD over R, then any relation $r(R)$ satisfies $X \to Y$.

If F is a set of FDs over R and X is a subset of R, then there is an FD $X \to Y$ in F^+ such that Y is *maximal*: for any other FD $X \to Z$ in F^+, $Y \supseteq Z$. This result follows from additivity. The right side Y is called the *closure* of X and is denoted by X^+. The closure of X always contains X, by reflexivity.

---

*For the results of this section we must assume all domains are infinite in order to avoid unwanted combinatorial effects.

Example 4.9 Let $F = \{A \to D, A\,B \to D\,E, C\,E \to G, E \to H\}$. Then $(A\,B)^+ = A\,B\,D\,E\,H$.

Theorem 4.1 Inference axioms F1 to F6 are complete.

Proof Given a set F of FDs over scheme R, for any FD $X \to Y$ in F^- we shall exhibit a relation $r(R)$ that satisfies F^+ but not $X \to Y$. Hence we will know that there are no FDs implied by F that are not derived by F. Relation r will satisfy most of the FDs in F^+ vacuously: for an FD $W \to Z$ in F^+, there will be no distinct tuples in r with equal W-values.

Let $R = A_1\,A_2 \cdots A_n$ and let a_i and b_i be distinct elements of $dom(A_i)$, $1 \leq i \leq n$. There will be only two tuples in r, t, and t'. Tuple t will be $\langle a_1\,a_2 \cdots a_n \rangle$. Tuple t' is defined as

$$t'(A_i) = \begin{cases} a_i & \text{if } A_i \in X^+, \\ b_i & \text{otherwise.} \end{cases}$$

First we show that r does not satisfy $X \to Y$. From the definition of r, $t(X) = t'(X)$. Suppose $t(Y) = t'(Y)$. Then $t'(Y)$ must be all a's, and hence $Y \subseteq X^+$. But since $X \to X^+ \in F^+$, by projectivity, $X \to Y$ is in F^+, a contradiction to $X \to Y \in F^-$.

Now we show that r satisfies all the FDs in F^+. The only FDs we need worry about are those of the form $W \to Z$, where $W \subseteq X^+$. If $W \not\subseteq X^+$, then $t(W) \neq t'(W)$. Since $W \subseteq X^+$, by reflexivity and projectivity, $X^+ \to W$ is in F^+, and by two applications of transitivity, so is $X \to Z$. Hence $Z \subseteq X^+$ and $t(Z) = t'(Z)$. So r satisfies $W \to Z$.

Corollary For any set of FDs F over scheme R, there is a relation $r(R)$ satisfying F^+ and violating every FD in F^-. (Such an r is called an *Armstrong relation*.)

Proof For each FD $X \to Y$ in F^-, use Theorem 4.1 to construct a relation $r_{X,Y}(R)$ that satisfies F^+ but violates $X \to Y$. Rename the entries in each such relation so that no pair of relations share a common entry. Let

$$r = \bigcup_{X \to Y \in F^-} r_{X,Y}.$$

It is clear that r violates every FD in F^-. It is left to the reader to show that r satisfies F^+.

We see now that inference axioms F1 to F6 are consistent and complete. Thus $F \models X \rightarrow Y$ if and only if $X \rightarrow Y \in F^+$. From now on we use the terms implies and derives interchangeably when discussing FDs. We generally shall use only Armstrong's axioms or some other complete set of axioms for computing F^+.

4.5 DERIVATIONS AND DERIVATION DAGs

If $F \models X \rightarrow Y$, then either $X \rightarrow Y$ is in F, or a series of applications of the inference axioms to F will yield $X \rightarrow Y$. This sequence of axiom applications and resulting FDs is a *derivation* of $X \rightarrow Y$ from F. More formally, let F be a set of FDs over scheme R. A sequence P of FDs over R is a *derivation sequence on* F if every FD in P either

1. is a member of F, or
2. follows from previous FDs in P by an application of one of the inference axioms F1 to F6.

P is a derivation sequence for $X \rightarrow Y$ if $X \rightarrow Y$ is one of the FDs in P.

Example 4.10 Let $F = \{A\,B \rightarrow E, A\,G \rightarrow J, B\,E \rightarrow I, E \rightarrow G, G\,I \rightarrow H\}$. The following sequence is a derivation sequence for $A\,B \rightarrow G\,H$.

1.	$A\,B \rightarrow E$	(given)
2.	$A\,B \rightarrow A\,B$	(reflexivity)
3.	$A\,B \rightarrow B$	(projectivity from 2)
4.	$A\,B \rightarrow B\,E$	(additivity from 1 and 3)
5.	$B\,E \rightarrow I$	(given)
6.	$A\,B \rightarrow I$	(transitivity from 4 and 5)
7.	$E \rightarrow G$	(given)
8.	$A\,B \rightarrow G$	(transitivity from 1 and 7)
9.	$A\,B \rightarrow G\,I$	(additivity from 6 and 8)
10.	$G\,I \rightarrow H$	(given)
11.	$A\,B \rightarrow H$	(transitivity from 9 and 10)
12.	$G\,I \rightarrow G\,I$	(reflexivity)
13.	$G\,I \rightarrow I$	(projectivity from 12)
14.	$A\,B \rightarrow G\,H$	(additivity from 8 and 11)

This sequence contains unneeded FDs, such as 12 and 13, and is also a derivation sequence for other FDs, such as $A\,B \rightarrow G\,I$.

Definition 4.4 Let P be a derivation sequence on F. The *use set* of P is the set of all FDs in F that appear in P.

We have seen that some subsets of the axioms F1 to F6 are complete. Their completeness implies that if there is a derivation sequence P for $X \rightarrow Y$ using all the axioms F1 to F6, there is a derivation sequence P' for $X \rightarrow Y$ using only the axioms in the complete subset (see Exercise 4.10).

We shall be using a complete set of inference axioms that are not a subset of F1 to F6, called *B-axioms*. For a relation $r(R)$, with W, X, Y, and Z subsets of R, and C an attribute in R:

B1. Reflexivity: $X \rightarrow X$.
B2. Accumulation: $X \rightarrow YZ$ and $Z \rightarrow CW$ imply $X \rightarrow YZC$.
B3. Projectivity: $X \rightarrow YZ$ implies $X \rightarrow Y$.

The B-axioms are easily shown correct (see Exercise 4.11). We show the B-axioms derive Armstrong's axioms and hence are complete.

F1. Reflexivity: same as B1.
F2. Augmentation: if $X \rightarrow Y$, then by B1, $XZ \rightarrow XZ$ for any subset Z in R. By repeated application of B2, we get $XZ \rightarrow XYZ$, and B3 gives $XZ \rightarrow Y$.
F6. Pseudotransitivity: Let r satisfy $X \rightarrow Y$ and $YZ \rightarrow W$. By B1, $XZ \rightarrow XZ$. By repeated application of B2, $XZ \rightarrow XYZ$ and $XZ \rightarrow WXYZ$. One application of B3 yields $XZ \rightarrow W$.

Since the B-axioms are complete, we can always find a derivation sequence using the B-axioms if $F \models X \rightarrow Y$.

Example 4.11 Let F be the set of FDs in Example 4.10. Then

1.	$EI \rightarrow EI$	(reflexivity)
2.	$E \rightarrow G$	(given)
3.	$EI \rightarrow EGI$	(accumulation from 1 and 2)
4.	$EI \rightarrow GI$	(projectivity from 3)
5.	$GI \rightarrow H$	(given)
6.	$EI \rightarrow GHI$	(accumulation from 4 and 5)
7.	$EI \rightarrow GH$	(projectivity from 6)
8.	$AB \rightarrow AB$	(reflexivity)
9.	$AB \rightarrow E$	(given)
10.	$AB \rightarrow ABE$	(accumulation from 8 and 9)

11.	$B\ E \rightarrow I$	(given)
12.	$A\ B \rightarrow A\ B\ E\ I$	(accumulation from 10 and 11)
13.	$A\ B \rightarrow A\ B\ E\ G\ I$	(accumulation from 4 and 12)
14.	$A\ B \rightarrow A\ B\ E\ G\ H\ I$	(accumulation from 7 and 13)
15.	$A\ B \rightarrow G\ H$	(projectivity from 14)

is a derivation sequence for $A\ B \rightarrow G\ H$ using only the B-axioms.

4.5.1 RAP-Derivation Sequences

Consider derivation sequences for $X \rightarrow Y$ on a set of FDs F using the B-axioms that satisfy the following constraints:

1. The first FD is $X \rightarrow X$.
2. The last FD is $X \rightarrow Y$.
3. Every FD other than the first and last is either an FD in F or an FD of the form $X \rightarrow Z$ that was derived using axiom B2.

Such a derivation sequence is called a *RAP-derivation sequence*, for the order in which the axioms are used.

Example 4.12 Let F be the set of FDs in Example 4.10. Then

1.	$A\ B \rightarrow A\ B$	(B1)
2.	$A\ B \rightarrow E$	(given)
3.	$A\ B \rightarrow A\ B\ E$	(B2)
4.	$B\ E \rightarrow I$	(given)
5.	$A\ B \rightarrow A\ B\ E\ I$	(B2)
6.	$E \rightarrow G$	(given)
7.	$A\ B \rightarrow A\ B\ E\ G\ I$	(B2)
8.	$G\ I \rightarrow H$	(given)
9.	$A\ B \rightarrow A\ B\ E\ G\ H\ I$	(B2)
10.	$A\ B \rightarrow G\ H$	(B3)

is a RAP-derivation sequence on F for $A\ B \rightarrow G\ H$.

Theorem 4.2 Let F be a set of FDs. If there is a derivation sequence on F for $X \rightarrow Y$, then there is a RAP-derivation sequence on F for $X \rightarrow Y$.

Proof Let P be a derivation sequence on F for $X \rightarrow Y$ using the B-axioms, which must exist by our earlier remarks. Remove all the FDs in P past the first occurrence of $X \rightarrow Y$. P is still a derivation sequence for $X \rightarrow Y$. Insert $X \rightarrow X$ at the head of the sequence, if it is not already there.

We next show that we are able to get by without the FDs in P generated by B3, except for perhaps $X \rightarrow Y$. Let $Z \rightarrow W$ be an FD in P (other than the last) that was derived from $Z \rightarrow V\ W$ by B3. If $Z \rightarrow W$ is not used to derive any FD further along P, then simply remove $Z \rightarrow W$ from P.

If $Z \rightarrow W$ is used to derive an FD further on, it must be by an application of B2 or B3. If $Z \rightarrow W$ is used by B3, it must be to generate an FD $Z \rightarrow W'$ where $W' \subseteq W$. But $Z \rightarrow W'$ can be derived from $Z \rightarrow V\ W$ by B3, so $Z \rightarrow W$ can be removed from P. If $Z \rightarrow W$ is used by B2, it must be in one of two ways:

1. with an FD $W' \rightarrow C\ U$ to derive $Z \rightarrow C\ W$, where $W' \subseteq W$, or
2. with an FD $U \rightarrow Z'$ to derive $U \rightarrow B\ Z'$, where $Z' \supseteq Z$, and B is an attribute in W.

In case 1, use $Z \rightarrow V\ W$ in place of $Z \rightarrow W$ to derive $Z \rightarrow C\ V\ W$ instead of $Z \rightarrow C\ W$. In case 2, $Z \rightarrow V\ W$ can be used in place of $Z \rightarrow W$ to derive $U \rightarrow B\ Z'$. Remove $Z \rightarrow W$ from P in either case.

We have just shown that we can substitute an FD with a larger right side in a derivation using the B-axioms. The only effect is possibly to generate an FD with a larger right side than the FD originally generated, such as in case 1 above, where $Z \rightarrow C\ V\ W$ replaced $Z \rightarrow C\ W$. This change is just another substitution of an FD with a larger right side. Thus, the substitution of FDs with larger right sides can propagate down the derivation sequence.

The only problem that may arise from such substitutions is that $X \rightarrow Y'$, $Y' \supseteq Y$, might be generated as the last FD in P instead of $X \rightarrow Y$, if $X \rightarrow Y$ was derived using B2. In this case, add $X \rightarrow Y$ as the new last FD in P. $X \rightarrow Y$ can be derived from $X \rightarrow Y'$ using B3.

We now have P to the point where it starts with $X \rightarrow X$, ends with $X \rightarrow Y$, and has no FDs derived by B3 except possibly the last. The next step is to show that $X \rightarrow Y$ can be derived using only B2 (except for the first and last FDs in P) applied to FDs of the form $X \rightarrow Z\ W$ and $W \rightarrow C\ V$, where $W \rightarrow C\ V$ is in F. Thus any FDs in P derived by reflexivity are superfluous (except the first) and can be removed.

This portion of the proof is left to the reader and is illustrated only by example here. The gist of the proof is that if a new attribute is introduced into the right side of $X \rightarrow Z$ by B2, it can be introduced directly from some FD in F.

However, it may first be necessary to add other attributes to the right side. Consider the following piece of a derivation sequence, where A is introduced into the right side of $X \rightarrow V\,V'$

$\vdots$

10.	$X \rightarrow V\,V'$	
11.	$Z \rightarrow A\,W$	(given)
12.	$V \rightarrow U\,Z$	(given, by B1 or by B2)
13.	$V \rightarrow A\,U\,Z$	(from 11 and 12 by B2)
14.	$X \rightarrow A\,V\,V'$	(from 10 and 13 by B2)

$\vdots$

We want to get rid of $V \rightarrow A\,U\,Z$ and instead introduce A into the right side of some FD with left side X, using $Z \rightarrow A\,W$ directly. Let $Z = B_1\,B_2\,\ldots\,B_k$. We replace FDs 13 and 14 by

13.1	$X \rightarrow V\,V'\,B_1$	(from 10 and 12 by B2)
13.2	$X \rightarrow V\,V'\,B_1\,B_2$	(from 10 and 12 by B2)
13.3	$X \rightarrow V\,V'\,B_1\,B_2\,B_3$	(from 10 and 12 by B2)
	$\vdots$	
13.k	$X \rightarrow V\,V'\,B_1\,B_2 \cdots B_k$ $(= X \rightarrow V\,V'\,Z)$	(from 10 and 12 by B2)
14.	$X \rightarrow A\,V\,V'\,Z$	(from 11 and 13.k by B2)

This change gives us $X \rightarrow A\;V\;V'\;Z$ instead of $X \rightarrow A\;V\;V'$, but we have already seen that substitution of FDs with larger right sides poses no problems.

The basic idea of this part of the proof is to work backwards through P removing applications of B2 that yield FDs where the left side is not X, as shown in the example. Once this transformation is made, all applications of B1 (except the first) become superfluous and can be removed (see Exercise 4.14).

In the next section we shall introduce a pictorial means—a labeled DAG—to depict RAP-derivation sequences. We shall also show that every such graph models a derivation sequence.

4.5.2 Derivation DAGs

A directed acyclic graph (DAG) is a directed graph with no directed paths from any node to itself. A labeled DAG is a DAG with an element from some labeling set L associated with each node.

Definition 4.5 Let F be a set of FDs over scheme R. An F-*based derivation DAG* is a DAG labeled with attribute symbols from R constructed according to the following rules.

R1. Any set of unconnected nodes with labels from R is an F-based derivation DAG.

R2. Let H be an F-based derivation DAG that includes nodes $v_1, v_2, \ldots, v_k$ with labels $A_1, A_2, \ldots, A_k$ and let $A_1 A_2 \cdots A_k \rightarrow C Z$ be an FD in F. Form H' by adding a node u labeled C and edges (v_1, u), (v_2, u), $\ldots$, (v_k, u) to H. H' is an F-based derivation DAG.

R3. Nothing else is an F-based derivation DAG.

We abbreviate F-based derivation DAG to F-based DDAG.

Example 4.13 Let F be the set of FDs in Example 4.10, namely $\{AB \rightarrow E, AG \rightarrow J, BE \rightarrow I, E \rightarrow G, GI \rightarrow H\}$. Figure 4.1 shows various stages in the construction of an F-based DDAG.

Any F-based DDAG is built by one application of rule R1 and any number of applications of rule R2. R2 insures that the graph constructed is actually a DAG.

Definition 4.6 If H is an F-based DDAG, a node v in H is an *initial node* if v has no incoming edges. Any initial nodes must have been added to H by rule R1.

Definition 4.7 Let H be an F-based DDAG. H is a *DDAG for* $X \rightarrow Y$ if

D1. X is the set of labels of initial nodes.

D2. Every attribute in Y labels some node in H.

Definition 4.8 The *use set* of an F-based DDAG H, denoted $U(H)$, is the set of all FDs in F used in the application of rule R2 during the construction of the DDAG.*

---

*Use set is not quite well-defined, since for some sets F, there may be more than one way to construct H. We should really write *a* use set of H, but we won't.

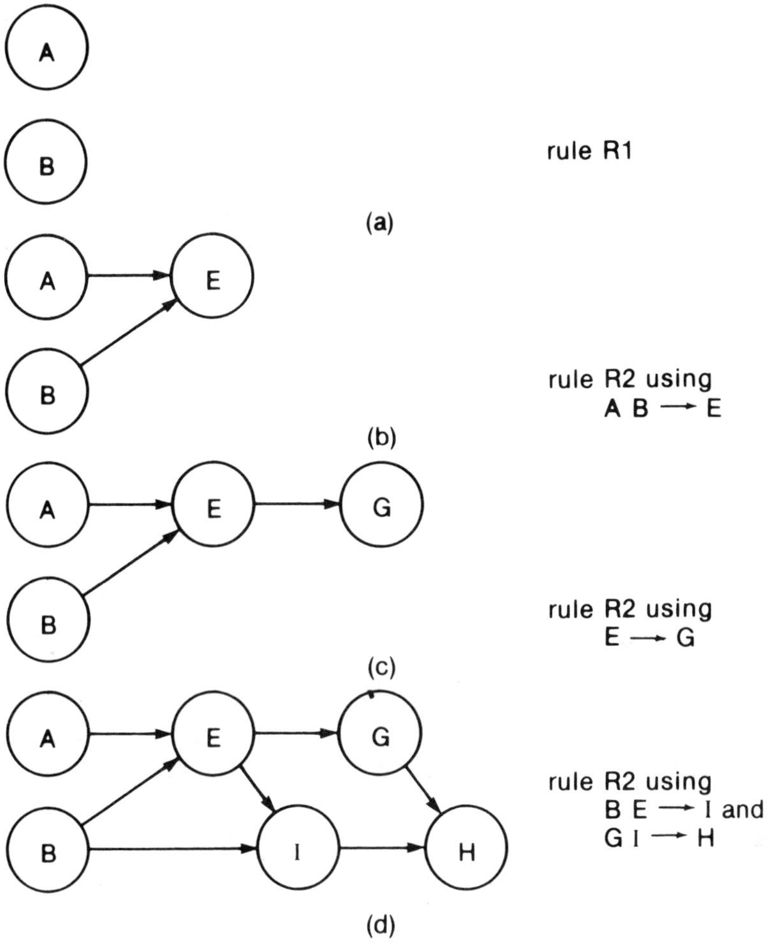

Figure 4.1

Example 4.14 The graph in Figure 4.1(d) is an F-based DDAG for $A\ B \rightarrow G\ H$. Its use set is $\{A\ B \rightarrow E,\ E \rightarrow G,\ B\ E \rightarrow I,\ G\ I \rightarrow H\}$. The initial nodes are the ones labeled A and B.

Example 4.15 Figure 4.2 shows a DDAG for $A\ B\ C \rightarrow A\ B\ C$ for any set of FDs over a scheme R containing A, B, and C. Its use set is $\emptyset$.

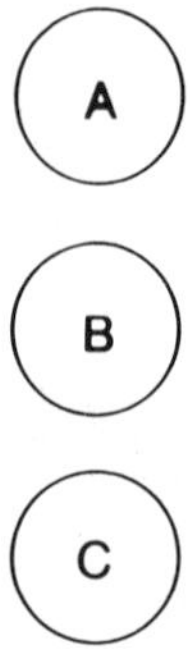

Figure 4.2

Observation Let H be an F-based DDAG with initial nodes labeled with exactly the attributes in some set X and all nodes in the graph labeled with exactly the attributes in some other set Y. If Y' is a subset of Y, then H is a DDAG for $X \rightarrow Y'$.

Theorem 4.3 Given a set of FDs F over R and an FD $X \rightarrow Y$, the following are equivalent.

1. $F \models X \rightarrow Y$.
2. There is a derivation sequence on F for $X \rightarrow Y$.
3. There is an F-based DDAG for $X \rightarrow Y$.

Proof We have already observed the equivalence of 1 and 2 from Theorem 4.1. Theorem 4.2 states that condition 2 is the same as there being a RAP-derivation sequence for $X \rightarrow Y$ on F. We shall show that we can construct an F-based DDAG for $X \rightarrow Y$ given a RAP-derivation sequence for $X \rightarrow Y$, and vice versa.

There is a natural correspondence between the B-axioms and the rules and conditions for an F-based DDAG for $X \rightarrow Y$. Axiom B1 corresponds to rule R1 for constructing DDAGs. Axiom B2 corresponds to rule R2. Axiom B3 is embodied in condition D2 of the definition of a DDAG for $X \rightarrow Y$.

Let P be a RAP-derivation sequence for $X \rightarrow Y$ on F. Let $X \rightarrow Z_1, X \rightarrow Z_2, \ldots, X \rightarrow Z_k$ be all the FDs in P, in order, that have X as the left side. We shall show inductively that we can construct a sequence of F-based DDAGs $H_1, H_2, \ldots, H_k$ such that H_i is obtained from H_{i-1} by the rules for constructing DDAGs, and H_i is a DDAG for $X \rightarrow Z_i$.

We know that $X \to Z_1$ must be $X \to X$. We use rule R1 to construct DDAG H_1 that consists of unconnected nodes labeled with the attributes from X. Suppose $H_1, H_2, \ldots, H_{i-1}$ are DDAGs for $X \to Z_1, X \to Z_2, \ldots, X \to Z_{i-1}$. Consider $X \to Z_i$. This FD could have come from one of three places:

1. from F,
2. from FDs $X \to Z_j$ and $Z \to C\,W$ by axiom B2. In this case $j < i$, $Z \to C\,W$ is in F, Z_j contains Z, and $Z_i = C\,Z_j$.
3. From an FD $X \to Z_j$ by axiom B3. In this case $j < i$, Z_j contains Z_i, and $Z_i = Y$.

In case 1, let $Z_i = B_1 B_2 \cdots B_m$. DDAG H_{i-1} contains DDAG H_1. Apply rule 2 once for each attribute in Z_i (m times) to H_{i-1} to add nodes labeled B_1, B_2, $\ldots$, B_m, and edges to these nodes from nodes labeled with the attributes of X. The result is H_i. In case 2, we know H_{i-1} contains H_j and H_j contains nodes labeled with the attributes in Z_j. Use rule 2 to add a node labeled C to H_{i-1} to form H_i. In case 3, H_j is already a DDAG for $X \to Z_i$ and so is H_{i-1}, since it contains H_j. Let $H_i = H_{i-1}$.

When the process of constructing the H_i's is completed, H_k will be an F-based DDAG for $X \to Y$.

Now let H be an F-based DDAG for $X \to Y$. We construct a RAP-derivation sequence from H. Let $H_1, H_2, \ldots, H_k$ be a sequence of F-based DDAGs such that H_i is constructed from H_{i-1} by rule R2, $2 \le i \le k$, and $H_k = H$. Let Z_i be the set of node labels in H_i. We shall construct a RAP-derivation sequence P with $X \to Z_1, X \to Z_2, \ldots, X \to Z_k$ as a subsequence.

Z_1 must be X and H_1 must be the DDAG with unconnected nodes labeled with the attributes in X. Let P begin with $X \to X = X \to Z_1$. Now look at H_i, $i \ge 2$. H_i comes from H_{i-1} by rule 2, using an FD $Z \to C\,W$ in F, where C is the label of the node added to H_{i-1} and Z_{i-1} contains Z. Thus $Z_i = C\,Z_{i-1}$. If $Z \to C\,W$ is not in P, add it to the end of P. Then add $X \to Z_i$ to the end of P. $X \to Z_i$ can be obtained by axiom B2, using $X \to Z_{i-1}$ and $Z \to C\,W$.

When this process terminates, we have a RAP-derivation sequence for $X \to Z_k$, where Z_k contains Y. Add $X \to Y$ to the end of P using axiom B3. P is now a RAP-derivation sequence for $X \to Y$.

Corollary There is an F-based DDAG H for $X \to Y$ with $U(H) = G$ only if there is a RAP-derivation sequence on F for $X \to Y$ with use set G.

Proof Immediate from the proof of Theorem 4.3. (Why is this corollary not if and only if?)

Example 4.16 The F-based DDAG in Figure 4.1(d) can be constructed from the RAP-derivation sequence in Example 4.12. The sequence of DDAGs in Figure 4.1(a)-(d) yields the RAP-derivation sequence

1. $A\,B \rightarrow A\,B$
2. $A\,B \rightarrow E$
3. $A\,B \rightarrow A\,B\,E$
4. $E \rightarrow G$
5. $A\,B \rightarrow A\,B\,E\,G$
6. $B\,E \rightarrow I$
7. $A\,B \rightarrow A\,B\,E\,G\,I$
8. $G\,I \rightarrow H$
9. $A\,B \rightarrow A\,B\,E\,G\,H\,I$
10. $A\,B \rightarrow G\,H$.

4.5.3 More about Derivation DAGs

Axiom B2 and rule R2 can both be strengthened in a similar manner. B2 can be strengthened to the following form, where V is also a subset of R.

B2′. $X \rightarrow Y\,Z$ and $Z \rightarrow V\,W$ imply $X \rightarrow V\,Y\,Z$.

The corresponding change in rule R2 is left to the reader (see Exercise 4.18).

Although the definition of DDAG allows multiple nodes with the same label, the freedom is not needed.

Lemma 4.1 Let H be an F-based DDAG for $X \rightarrow Y$. There is an F-based DDAG for $X \rightarrow Y$ wherein every node has a distinct label.

Proof Suppose H has two nodes with the same label, say v_1 and v_2 are both labeled C. In the construction of H, either v_1 and v_2 were added at the same time with rule R1, or one was added later than the other using rule R2. Assume v_2 was added to H at the same time as or later than v_1. There can be no directed path from v_2 to v_1 in H.

In the construction of H, any time rule R2 was applied using v_2, v_1 could have been used instead, as shown in Figure 4.3. Thus there is an F-based DDAG H' for $X \rightarrow Y$ that has the same nodes and labels as H, as well as the same set of initial nodes, but v_2 has no outgoing edges in H'. H' is still a DDAG for $X \rightarrow Y$ when v_2 and its incoming edges are removed, since the set of attributes labeling nodes does not change, and if v_2 is an initial node, so is v_1.

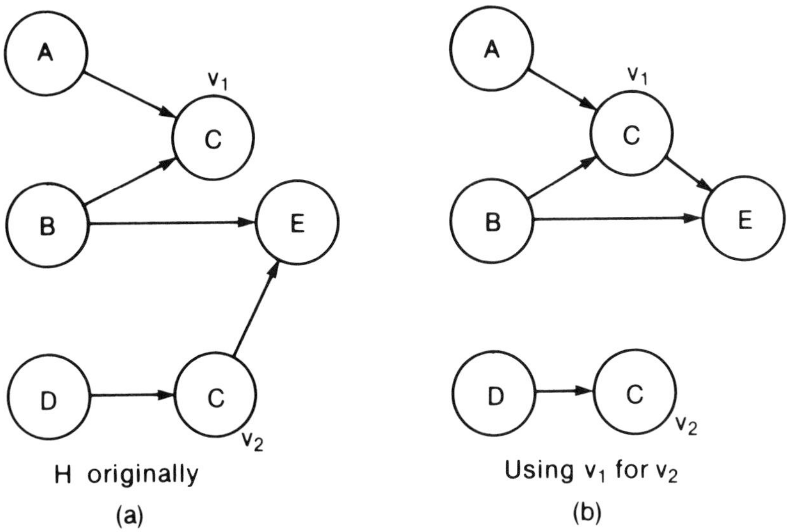

Figure 4.3

This transformation can be applied iteratively to all pairs of nodes with equal labels to remove all duplicate labels.

We have observed that if H is an F-based DDAG for $X \rightarrow Y$, then it is also an F-based DDAG for $X \rightarrow Y'$, where $Y \supseteq Y'$. Similarly, if $X \subseteq X'$, H is almost a DDAG for $X' \rightarrow Y$. The only problem is that not all the attributes in X' label some initial node in H. This problem can be solved by adding unconnected nodes to H with labels in $X' - X$.

Lemma 4.2 Let H and J be F-based DDAGs for $X \rightarrow Y$ and $Y \rightarrow Z$, respectively. There is an F-based DDAG K for $X \rightarrow Z$ with $U(K) \subseteq U(H) \cup U(J)$.

Proof We *splice* H and J together by overlapping the initial nodes of J with the same-labeled nodes of H. Figure 4.4 gives an example of the overlapping process where $F = \{A \rightarrow E, A\,B \rightarrow C, A\,C \rightarrow D, C\,D \rightarrow E, E \rightarrow I\}$. Notice that $U(H) = \{A \rightarrow E, A\,B \rightarrow C, A\,C \rightarrow D\}$, $U(J) = \{C\,D \rightarrow E, E \rightarrow I\}$, and $U(K) = F$.

Lemma 4.3 If H is an F-based DDAG for $X \rightarrow Y$, and $V \rightarrow W$ is in $U(H)$, then $F \models X \rightarrow V$.

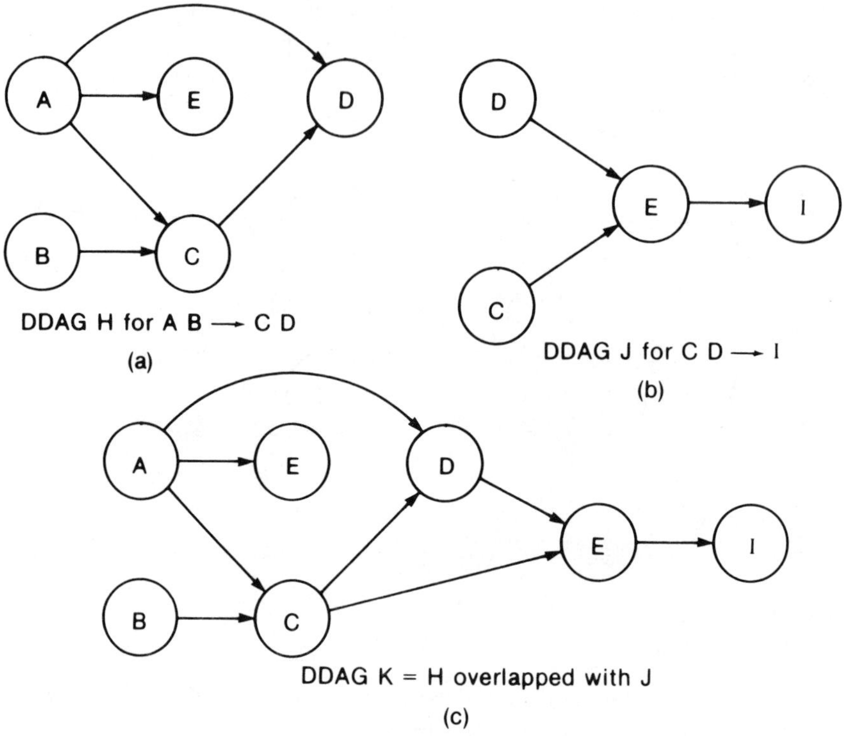

Figure 4.4

Proof For $V \rightarrow W$ to be used in constructing H, H must contain nodes with labels for every attribute in V. Hence H is an F-based DDAG for $X \rightarrow V$.

Corollary If H is an F-based DDAG for $X \rightarrow Y$ and $V \rightarrow W$ is in $U(H)$, there is an F-based DDAG for $X \rightarrow V$ that does not use $V \rightarrow W$.

Lemma 4.3 does not hold for derivation sequences, since $V \rightarrow W$ could be in the use set of a sequence without it being necessary to derive $X \rightarrow Y$.

4.6 TESTING MEMBERSHIP IN F^+

To determine if a set of FDs $F \models X \to Y$, we need only test if $X \to Y \in F^+$. However, as we saw in Example 4.8, F^+ can be considerably larger than F. We would like to find a means to test if $X \to Y$ is in F^+ without generating all of F^+. In this section we present such a membership algorithm. The core of the algorithm is a procedure that generates the closure of X under F. Once we have found X^+, we can test if F implies $X \to Y$.

We seek an algorithm for testing membership that is more efficient than generating all of F^+. One way to compare algorithms is to examine the maximum amount of time they consume for an input of a given size. The (worst-case) *time-complexity* of an algorithm is a function $T(n)$ that gives the maximum number of steps the algorithm will take on an input of size n. Naturally, $T(n)$ depends on what is counted as one step of computation. We shall use the RAM (random access machine) model as presented in Aho, Hopcroft, and Ullman as our model of computation. A RAM is basically a model of a simple digital computer with random access memory.

For a particular algorithm, $T(n)$ can be messy and complex, but often there is some "nice" function that approximates the behavior of $T(n)$. We write $T(n) = O(f(n))$ (read "$T(n)$ has order $f(n)$") if there are constants $c > 0$ and $n_1 \geq 0$ such that $T(n) \leq cf(n)$ for all $n \geq n_1$.

Example 4.17 $3n^2 + 2 \log_2 \log_2 n = O(n^2)$, since $3n^2 + 2 \log_2 \log_2 n \leq 4n^2$ for $n \geq 1$. Of course, $3n^2 + 2 \log_2 \log_2 n = O(n^3)$ as well, but we are more interested in the slower growing function, since it is a better approximation of $3n^2 + 2 \log_2 \log_2 n$.

For most algorithms, the time complexity $T(n)$ is at least $O(n)$, since most algorithms read all their input, which takes n steps. We first present a membership algorithm for FDs that is not $O(n)$, but is easy to understand. We then present a version of the algorithm that is more complex, but has $O(n)$ time complexity.

We start with the function CLOSURE given below. CLOSURE(X, F) returns X^+ under F, where X is a set of attributes and F is a set of FDs. *OLDDEP* and *NEWDEP* are variables for sets of attributes.

Algorithm 4.2 CLOSURE
Input: A set of attributes X and a set of FDs F.
Output: The closure of X under F.

```
CLOSURE(X, F)
begin
OLDDEP := ∅; NEWDEP := X;
while NEWDEP ≠ OLDDEP do begin
      OLDDEP := NEWDEP;
      for every FD W → Z in F do
          if NEWDEP ⊇ W then
          NEWDEP := NEWDEP ∪ Z
   end;
return(NEWDEP)
end.
```

Example 4.18 Let $F = \{A \to D, A\,B \to E, B\,I \to E, C\,D \to I, E \to C\}$. CLOSURE($AE$, F) begins with $NEWDEP = A\,E$. On the first pass through F, $A \to D$ is used to add D to $NEWDEP$, and $E \to C$ is used to add C to $NEWDEP$, so $NEWDEP = A\,C\,D\,E$ at the end of the **for** loop. The second time through F, $C\,D \to I$ is used to add I to $NEWDEP$, so $NEWDEP = A\,C\,D\,E\,I$ at the end of the **for** loop. The next pass through F causes no changes in $NEWDEP$, so $A\,C\,D\,E\,I$ is returned as $(A\,E)^+$.

The algorithm essentially constructs an F-based DDAG for $X \to X^+$, using a modified version of rule R2 in the definition of DDAG where more than one node is added at a time (see Exercise 4.18). We start with initial nodes labeled X and keep adding nodes to the DDAG until no new labels can be added. It is not necessary to record the edges of the DDAG, however, since whether or not we can use an FD $W \to Z$ depends only on there being nodes in the DDAG with labels for all the attributes in W. The value of X^+ does not depend on the edges in the DDAG either, just on the final set of node labels. Thus, it suffices to keep track of only the set of node labels in the DDAG during its construction. We keep track of the labels in *OLDDEP* and *NEWDEP*.

Since we are constructing an F-based DDAG with initial nodes labeled X, it follows that at any point in the execution of CLOSURE, $NEWDEP \subseteq X^+$. For any attribute A in X^+, A will eventually be added to *NEWDEP*. Since A is in X^+, $F \models X \to A$, and there must be an F-based DDAG H for $X \to A$. Any FD $W \to Z$ used in constructing H can eventually be used in the construction of the DDAG for the algorithm, and the DDAG in the algorithm will contain labels for every attribute in Z. Therefore A will be added to *NEWDEP* and we conclude that CLOSURE correctly computes X^+.

Using CLOSURE, it is simple to devise an algorithm to test membership in F^+. Algorithm 4.3 MEMBER performs this test.

Algorithm 4.3 MEMBER
Input: A set of FDs F and an FD $X \rightarrow Y$.
Output: *true* if $F \models X \rightarrow Y$, *false* otherwise.
MEMBER(F, $X \rightarrow Y$)
  begin
  if $Y \subseteq$ CLOSURE(X, F) **then return**(*true*) **else return**(*false*)
  end.

The time complexity for MEMBER is the same as the time complexity for CLOSURE, since CLOSURE makes up the body of MEMBER. The worst case for CLOSURE occurs when only one new right side of an FD is added to *NEWDEP* for each execution of the **for** loop. If $F = \{A_2 \rightarrow A_1, A_3 \rightarrow A_2, A_4 \rightarrow A_3, \ldots, A_m \rightarrow A_{m-1}\}$, in the computation for CLOSURE(A_m, F), only attribute A_{m-i}, is added to *NEWDEP* on the ith execution of the **for** loop. If a is the number of different attribute symbols in F and p is the number of FDs in F, then each execution of the **for** loop takes $O(ap)$ time, since a steps are required to test containment of two sets over a elements. The **while** loop can be executed p times before no changes occur to *NEWDEP*. Therefore, the time complexity of CLOSURE, and hence of MEMBER, is $O(ap^2)$. Note that the length of the input, n, is $O(ap)$ (see Exercise 4.21).

To see how the time complexity of CLOSURE can be improved, observe that during the execution of CLOSURE, if for some FD $W \rightarrow Z$, W is contained in *NEWDEP*, then Z is added to *NEWDEP* and $W \rightarrow Z$ is of no further use. At this point we could exclude $W \rightarrow Z$ from F and still compute the correct closure. By excluding FDs from F after their right sides are added to *NEWDEP*, we can reduce the number of FDs scanned during each execution of the **for** loop. We can save even more time if we also know which FDs in F currently have their left sides contained in *NEWDEP*. If such information is available we can consider an FD $W \rightarrow Z$ in F only when its left side is contained in *NEWDEP* and then remove it from subsequent consideration. Thus every FD in F would be considered only once. If each FD in F can be processed in time proportional to its length in attribute symbols, we would have an $O(n)$ membership algorithm, where n is the number of symbols required to represent F and $X \rightarrow Y$.

We accomplish these ends as follows. For each FD $W \rightarrow Z$ in F we shall keep track of the number of attributes in W that are not in *NEWDEP*. When this count becomes zero, it will be time to consider $W \rightarrow Z$. To decrement the count properly for each FD when a new attribute A is added to *NEWDEP*, it is necessary to access all FDs with attribute A on their left sides. We therefore maintain a series of lists, one for each attribute, consisting of all FDs in F with that attribute on the left side. Whenever an attribute is added to *NEWDEP*, the list for that attribute is traversed, and all FDs on the list have their counts decremented by 1. If some FD $W \rightarrow Z$ on the list has its count decremented to zero, then W is a subset of *NEWDEP* and Z is added to *NEWDEP*.

We must be careful when adding Z to *NEWDEP*. Suppose there is an attribute A in Z that is already in *NEWDEP*. If we traverse the list for A a second time, we get erroneous values for the counts of FDs on the list. To prevent this problem, we keep a set of attributes called *UPDATE* that is the subset of *NEWDEP* consisting of attributes that have not yet had their lists traversed. When an attribute is added to *NEWDEP* for the first time, it is also added to *UPDATE* until its list can be traversed. *UPDATE* allows us to do away with *OLDDEP*, since when *UPDATE* $= \emptyset$, there are no more FDs that can be used to add new attributes to *NEWDEP*.

In the algorithm LINCLOSURE, below, there is an array *COUNT* of integers containing the counts for each FD in F, and an array *LIST* of lists of FDs for each attribute symbol in F. While an FD may seem to occur in lists for more than one attribute, we actually store only one copy of the FD and have the various lists point to this copy.

Algorithm 4.4 The function LINCLOSURE
Input and Output: identical to CLOSURE in Algorithm 4.2
LINCLOSURE(X, F)

1. Initialization
   - **for** each FD $W \rightarrow Z$ in F **do begin**
     - $COUNT[W \rightarrow Z] := |W|$;
     - **for** each attribute A in W **do** add $W \rightarrow Z$ to $LIST[A]$
     - **end**;
   - $NEWDEP := X$; $UPDATE := X$.
2. Computation
   - **while** $UPDATE \neq \emptyset$ **do begin**
     - choose an A in *UPDATE*;
     - $UPDATE := UPDATE - A$;
     - **for** each FD $W \rightarrow Z$ in $LIST[A]$ **do begin**
       - $COUNT[W \rightarrow Z] := COUNT[W \rightarrow Z] - 1$;
       - **if** $COUNT[W \rightarrow Z] = 0$ **then begin**
         - $ADD := Z - NEWDEP$;
         - $NEWDEP := NEWDEP \cup ADD$;
         - $UPDATE := UPDATE \cup ADD$
         - **end**
       - **end**
     - **end**.
3. **return**(*NEWDEP*).

Example 4.19 Let F be as in Example 4.18. LINCLOSURE($A\ E$, F) initializes $NEWDEP$, $UPDATE$, $COUNT$, and $LIST$ as follows:

$NEWDEP = A\ E \qquad UPDATE = A\ E$

$LIST[A] = A \rightarrow D,\ A\ B \rightarrow E$	$COUNT[A \rightarrow D] = 1$
$LIST[B] = B\ I \rightarrow E,\ A\ B \rightarrow E$	$COUNT[A\ B \rightarrow E] = 2$
$LIST[C] = C\ D \rightarrow I$	$COUNT[B\ I \rightarrow E] = 2$
$LIST[D] = C\ D \rightarrow I$	$COUNT[C\ D \rightarrow I] = 2$
$LIST[E] = E \rightarrow C$	$COUNT[E \rightarrow C] = 1$
$LIST[I] = B\ I \rightarrow E$	

We select the A in $UPDATE$ and traverse $LIST[A]$. $COUNT[A \rightarrow D]$ goes to 0 and D is added to $NEWDEP$ and $UPDATE$. $COUNT[A\ B \rightarrow E]$ goes to 1. If we next select E from $UPDATE$ the result is

$NEWDEP = A\ C\ D\ E \qquad UPDATE = C\ D$
$COUNT[A \rightarrow D] = 0$
$COUNT[A\ B \rightarrow E] = 1$
$COUNT[B\ I \rightarrow E] = 2$
$COUNT[C\ D \rightarrow I] = 2$
$COUNT[E \rightarrow C] = 0.$

Traversing the lists for C and D leaves us with
$NEWDEP = A\ C\ D\ E\ I \qquad UPDATE = I$
$COUNT[A \rightarrow D] = 0$
$COUNT[A\ B \rightarrow E] = 1$
$COUNT[B\ I \rightarrow E] = 2$
$COUNT[C\ D \rightarrow I] = 0$
$COUNT[E \rightarrow C] = 0$

Traversing the list for I fails to reduce any counts to 0, so the algorithm returns $A\ C\ D\ E\ I$.

Let us review the workings of the computation step of LINCLOSURE. The **while** loop continues to execute while there are attributes in $NEWDEP$ whose lists have not been traversed. We choose one such attribute and traverse its list. For each FD $W \rightarrow Z$ in the list, we reduce $COUNT[W \rightarrow Z]$. If the count goes to 0, it is time to consider $W \rightarrow Z$. We compute the set of attributes in Z that are not already in $NEWDEP$ and add these attributes to both $NEWDEP$ and $UPDATE$. The **while** loop stops executing when there are no more FDs whose counts can be reduced.

Theorem 4.4 LINCLOSURE has time complexity $O(n)$ for input of length n.

Proof Computing $COUNT[W \rightarrow Z]$ in the initialization step takes time proportional to $|W|$ if W is represented as a list of attributes. Computing all the initial values for $COUNT$ therefore takes $O(n)$ time. Each FD $W \rightarrow Z$ in F gets inserted into $|W|$ lists in $LIST$. For an appropriate list representation, adding one FD to one list takes a constant amount of time. Thus, filling in $LIST$ takes $O(n)$ time. $NEWDEP$ and $UPDATE$ can also be initialized in $O(n)$ time.

In the computation step, each attribute is added to $UPDATE$ once, at most. For each attribute A added to $UPDATE$, one pass of the **while** loop is performed. For each pass of the **while** loop, an operation (decrement $COUNT$) is performed for each FD in $LIST[A]$. Since any FD $W \rightarrow Z$ appears in $|W|$ lists, the decrement operation is performed at most

$$\sum_{W \rightarrow Z \text{ in } F} |W|$$

times. Thus $O(n)$ time is spent decrementing COUNT.

For any FD $W \rightarrow Z$ in F, the predicate $COUNT[W \rightarrow Z] = 0$ evaluates to **true** at most once, since once $COUNT[W \rightarrow Z]$ reaches 0, all the attributes in W have been added to $NEWDEP$ and removed from $UPDATE$. Thus, $W \rightarrow Z$ does not appear in any attribute list remaining to be traversed. The computation involving ADD takes time proportional to $|Z|$ if $NEWDEP$ is represented as a bit vector. The total time spent with the statements involving ADD is proportional to

$$\sum_{W \rightarrow Z \text{ in } F} |Z|,$$

which is $O(n)$. Since no step of the algorithm takes more than $O(n)$ time, LINCLOSURE has time complexity $O(n)$.

Corollary Membership in F^+ can be tested in $O(n)$ time for inputs of length n.

Proof Substitute LINCLOSURE for CLOSURE in Algorithm 4.3. Henceforth we shall assume MEMBER uses LINCLOSURE.

4.7 EXERCISES

4.1 Consider the relation r below.

$r(A$	B	C	D	$E)$
a_1	b_1	c_1	d_1	e_1
a_1	b_2	c_2	d_2	d_1
a_2	b_1	c_3	d_3	e_1
a_2	b_1	c_4	d_3	e_1
a_3	b_2	c_5	d_1	e_1

Which of the following FDs does r satisfy?
$A \rightarrow D,\ A\,B \rightarrow D,\ C \rightarrow B\,D\,E,\ E \rightarrow A,\ A \rightarrow E$

4.2 Prove that r satisfies $X \rightarrow Y$ if and only if X is a key of $\pi_{XY}(r)$.

4.3 Let r be a relation on R, with X a subset of R. Show that if $\pi_X(r)$ has the same number of tuples as r, then r satisfies $X \rightarrow Y$ for any subset Y of R.

4.4 Prove or disprove the following inference rules for a relation $r(R)$ with W, X, Y, and Z subsets of R.
(a) $X \rightarrow Y$ and $Z \rightarrow W$ imply $X\,Z \rightarrow Y\,W$.
(b) $X\,Y \rightarrow Z$ and $Z \rightarrow X$ imply $Z \rightarrow Y$.
(c) $X \rightarrow Y$ and $Y \rightarrow Z$ imply $X \rightarrow Y\,Z$.
(d) $X \rightarrow Y$, $W \rightarrow Z$, and $Y \supseteq W$ imply $X \rightarrow Z$.

4.5 Prove that inference axioms F1, F2, and F6 are independent. That is, no one of them can be proved from the other two.

4.6 Show that for any set of FDs F, $F^+ = (F^+)^+$.

4.7 Suppose F is a set of FDs over scheme R. If $F = \emptyset$, what does F^+ look like?

4.8 For a set of FDs F, show that there is no relation satisfying all the FDs in F^- and no others.

4.9* Show inference axioms F1, F3, F4, and F5 are complete. Is this set of axioms independent?

4.10 Show that if there is a derivation sequence for $X \rightarrow Y$ using inference axioms F1 to F6, then there is a derivation sequence for $X \rightarrow Y$ using only Armstrong's axioms.

4.11 Prove the B-axioms are correct.

4.12 Find a set of two inference rules that is complete. The rules need not be a subset of axioms F1 to F6.

4.13 Let $F = \{A\,B \rightarrow C,\ B \rightarrow D,\ C\,D \rightarrow E,\ C\,E \rightarrow G\,H,\ G \rightarrow A\}$.
(a) Give a derivation sequence on F for $A\,B \rightarrow E$.
(b) Give a derivation sequence on F for $B\,G \rightarrow C$ using only Armstrong's axioms
(c) Give a RAP-derivation sequence on F for $A\,B \rightarrow G$.

4.14* Complete the proof of Theorem 4.2.

4.15 Let F be as in Exercise 4.13. Construct an F-based DDAG for $A\ B \rightarrow G$.

4.16 Prove that for sets F and G of FDs, if F contains G, then F^+ contains G^+.

4.17 Prove that an invalid inference rule can always be disproved with a two-tuple relation.

4.18 Modify rule R2 in the definition of DDAG to reflect the change from axiom B2 to B2′.

4.19 Let F and G be sets of FDs. Suppose for every FD $Z \rightarrow W$ in F there is a G-based DDAG for $Z \rightarrow W$. Prove that if $X \rightarrow Y$ has an F-based DDAG, it has a G-based DDAG.

4.20 Let F be a set of FDs over R. Find a bound on the size of F^+ in FDs, in terms of the number of attributes in R.

4.21 Let F be a set of FDs where a is the number of distinct attributes in F, p is the number of FDs in F, and n is the number of symbols required to write F. Compare ap^2 and n.

4.22 The algorithm MEMBER (Algorithm 4.3) computes more information than is necessary to ascertain if $F \models X \rightarrow Y$. Once Y is found to be in X^+, the rest of X^+ is immaterial. Modify MEMBER and LINCLOSURE to remove this unnecessary computation.

4.8 BIBLIOGRAPHY AND COMMENTS

FDs were present when Codd [1970] first introduced the relational model, in the form of keys. Codd [1972a] later introduced FDs that do not follow from keys, for the purpose of normalization (see Chapter 6). Delobel and Casey [1973] gave a set of inference axioms, which Armstrong [1974] showed were complete and correct. He also gave a method for constructing an Armstrong relation for a set of FDs. Beeri, Dowd, *et al.* [1980] explore the structure of Armstrong relations.

The LINCLOSURE algorithm is from Beeri and Bernstein [1979]. They used *derivation trees* in their proofs. Derivation trees were the precursor of DDAGs, introduced by Maier [1980b]. An exposition of the RAM model of computation is given by Aho, Hopcroft, and Ullman [1974].

Much work on the implication of FDs has focused on the discovery of keys and the structure of sets of keys; see the papers by Békéssy and Demetrovics [1979]; Békéssy, Demetrovics, *et al.* [1980]; Demetrovics [1978, 1979]; Forsyth and Fadous [1975]; and Lucchesi and Osborn [1978].

Chapter 5

COVERS FOR FUNCTIONAL DEPENDENCIES

In this chapter we shall explore methods to represent sets of FDs succinctly. For example, any FD implied by the set $F = \{A \rightarrow B, B \rightarrow C, A \rightarrow C, A\,B \rightarrow C, A \rightarrow B\,C\}$ is also implied by the set $G = \{A \rightarrow B, B \rightarrow C\}$, since all the FDs in F can be derived from FDs in G.

Why do we want shorter representations? We have already seen two algorithms, SATISFIES in Section 4.1 and MEMBER in Section 4.6, whose running times depend on the size of the set of FDs used as input. A smaller set of FDs guarantees faster execution. We shall see other algorithms with running times dependent upon the number of FDs in the input. FDs are used in database systems to help ensure consistency and correctness. Fewer FDs mean less storage space used and fewer tests to make when the database is modified.

5.1 COVERS AND EQUIVALENCE

Definition 5.1 Two sets of FDs F and G over scheme R are *equivalent*, written $F \equiv G$, if $F^+ = G^+$. If $F \equiv G$, then F is a *cover* for G.

The definition of cover makes no mention of the relative sizes of F and G. However, we shall soon consider restricted types of covers where F will be no larger than G in numbers of FDs.

If $F \equiv G$, then for every FD $X \rightarrow Y$ in G^+, $F \models X \rightarrow Y$, since $F^+ = G^+$. In particular, $F \models X \rightarrow Y$ for every FD $X \rightarrow Y$ in G. We extend our notation for implication to sets of FDs and write this last condition as $F \models G$. Since the definition of equivalent is symmetric in F and G, $F \equiv G$ also implies $G \models F$.

If $F \models G$, then $G \subseteq F^+$, since F^+ includes every FD $X \rightarrow Y$ such that $F \models X \rightarrow Y$. Taking the closure of both sides of the inequality, we get $G^+ \subseteq$

$(F^+)^+ = F^+$ (see Exercises 4.6 and 4.16). Similarly, $G \models F$ implies $G^+ \supseteq F^+$. We have proved the following result.

Lemma 5.1 Given sets of FDs F and G over scheme R, $F \equiv G$ if and only if $F \models G$ and $G \models F$.

Example 5.1 The sets $F = \{A \rightarrow B\,C,\ A \rightarrow D,\ C\,D \rightarrow E\}$ and $G = \{A \rightarrow B\,C\,E,\ A \rightarrow A\,B\,D,\ C\,D \rightarrow E\}$ are equivalent. F is not equivalent to the set $G' = \{A \rightarrow B\,C\,D\,E\}$ since $G' \not\models C\,D \rightarrow E$.

Lemma 5.1 provides a simple means to test equivalence for two sets of FDs. The function DERIVES in Algorithm 5.1 tests whether $F \models G$.

Algorithm 5.1 DERIVES
Input: Two sets of FDS F and G.
Output: *true* if $F \models G$, *false* otherwise.
DERIVES(F, G)
  begin
  v := *true*;
  for each FD $X \rightarrow Y$ in G **do**
    v := v **and** MEMBER(F, $X \rightarrow Y$);
  return(v)
  end.

The function EQUIV in Algorithm 5.2 tests the equivalence of two sets of FDs.

Algorithm 5.2 EQUIV
Input: Two sets of FDs F and G.
Output: *true* if $F \equiv G$, *false* otherwise.
EQUIV(F, G)
  begin
  v := DERIVES(F, G) **and** DERIVES(G, F);
  return(v)
  end.

5.2 NONREDUNDANT COVERS

Definition 5.2 A set F of FDs is *nonredundant* if there is no proper subset F' of F with $F' \equiv F$. If such an F' exists, F is redundant. F is a *nonredundant cover* for G if F is a cover for G and F is nonredundant.

Example 5.2 Let $G = \{AB \rightarrow C, A \rightarrow B, B \rightarrow C, A \rightarrow C\}$. $F = \{AB \rightarrow C, A \rightarrow B, B \rightarrow C\}$ is equivalent to G but redundant, since $F' = \{A \rightarrow B, B \rightarrow C\}$ is also a cover for G. F' is a nonredundant cover for G.

An alternative characterization of nonredundancy is that F is nonredundant if there is no FD $X \rightarrow Y$ in F such that $F - \{X \rightarrow Y\} \models X \rightarrow Y$ (see Exercise 5.3). Call an FD $X \rightarrow Y$ in F *redundant in* F if $F - \{X \rightarrow Y\} \models X \rightarrow Y$. This alternative characterization provides the basis for the redundancy test for F given in Algorithm 5.3.

Algorithm 5.3 REDUNDANT
Input: A set of FDs F.
Output: *true* if F is redundant, *false* otherwise.
REDUNDANT(F)

```
begin
v := false;
for each FD X → Y in F do
    if MEMBER(F − {X → Y}, X → Y) then v := true;
return(v)
end.
```

For any set of FDs G, there is some subset F of G such that F is a nonredundant cover for G. If G is nonredundant, $F = G$. If G is redundant, then there is an FD $X \rightarrow Y$ in G that is redundant in G. Let $G' = G - \{X \rightarrow Y\}$, and note $(G')^+ = G^+$. If G' is redundant, there is an FD $W \rightarrow Z$ that is redundant in G'. Let $G'' = G' - \{W \rightarrow Z\}$; $(G'')^+ = (G')^+ = G^+$. This process of removing redundant FDs must terminate eventually. The result is a nonredundant cover F for G. This process is the basis for the algorithm NONREDUN, Algorithm 5.4, which computes a nonredundant cover for a set of FDs.

Algorithm 5.4 NONREDUN
Input: A set G of FDs.
Output: A nonredundant cover for G.
NONREDUN(G)

```
begin
F := G;
for each FD X → Y in G do
    if MEMBER(F − {X → Y}, X → Y) then
        F := F − {X → Y};
return(F)
end.
```

Example 5.3 Let $G = \{A \to B, B \to A, B \to C, A \to C\}$. The result of NONREDUN(G) is $\{A \to B, B \to A, A \to C\}$. If G is presented in the order $\{A \to B, A \to C, B \to A, B \to C\}$, the result of NONREDUN(G) is $\{A \to B, B \to A, B \to C\}$.

Example 5.3 shows that a set G of FDs can contain more than one nonredundant cover. There can also be nonredundant covers for G that are not contained in G. $F = \{A \to B, B \to A, A\,B \to C\}$ is a nonredundant cover for the set G in Example 5.3.

5.3 EXTRANEOUS ATTRIBUTES

If F is a nonredundant set of FDs, there are no "extra" FDs in F, and in this sense F cannot be made smaller by removing FDs. Removing any FD from F would give a set of FDs that was not equivalent to F. However, it may be possible to reduce the size of F by removing attributes from FDs in F.

Definition 5.3 Let F be a set of FDs over scheme R and let $X \to Y$ be an FD in F. Attribute A in R is *extraneous in* X $\to$ Y with respect to F if

1. $X = A\,Z$, $X \neq Z$, and $(F - \{X \to Y\}) \cup \{Z \to Y\} \equiv F$, or
2. $Y = A\,W$, $Y \neq W$, and $(F - \{X \to Y\}) \cup \{X \to W\} \equiv F$.

The definition says that A is extraneous in $X \to Y$ if A can be removed from the left side or right side of $X \to Y$ without changing the closure of F.

Example 5.4 Let $G = \{A \to B\,C, B \to C, A\,B \to D\}$. Attribute C is extraneous in the right side of $A \to B\,C$ and attribute B is extraneous in the left side of $A\,B \to D$.

Definition 5.4 Let F be a set of FDs over scheme R and let $X \to Y$ be in F. $X \to Y$ is *left-reduced* if X contains no attribute A extraneous in $X \to Y$. $X \to Y$ is *right-reduced* if Y contains no attribute A extraneous in $X \to Y$. $X \to Y$ is *reduced* if it is left-reduced and right-reduced, and $Y \neq \emptyset$. A left-reduced FD is also called a *full* FD.

Definition 5.5 A set F of FDs is *left-reduced* (*right-reduced, reduced*) if every FD in F is left-reduced (respectively, right-reduced, reduced).

Example 5.5 The set $G = \{A \to B\,C, B \to C, A\,B \to D\}$ is neither left-reduced nor right-reduced. $G_1 = \{A \to B\,C, B \to C, A \to D\}$ is left-reduced but not right-reduced, while $G_2 = \{A \to B,\ B \to C,\ A\,B \to D\}$ is right-reduced but not left-reduced. The set $G_3 = \{A \to B,\ B \to C,\ A \to D\}$ is left- and right-reduced, hence reduced, since no right side is $\emptyset$.

We might imagine that we can compute reduced covers for a set G in a manner similar to NONREDUN: look for extraneous attributes and remove them. However, whether we reduce left sides or right sides of FDs first makes a difference. Reducing right sides first will not work. The set of FDs $G = \{B \to A,\ D \to A,\ B\,A \to D\}$ is right-reduced. Removing extraneous attributes from left sides yields the set $F = \{B \to A,\ D \to A,\ B \to D\}$, which is not right-reduced. Therefore, we will reduce left sides before right sides.

There is a problem, however, if G contains a redundant FD, say $X \to Y$. Every attribute in Y is extraneous, and eliminating them all leaves $X \to \emptyset$. It might seem we could save ourselves work if we first eliminate all redundant FDs from G before removing extraneous attributes. Unfortunately, even if we start with a nonredundant cover, we can run into the problem just described (see Exercise 5.7). Hence, as the last step in producing a reduced cover, we must remove any FD of the form $X \to \emptyset$.

Before we write an algorithm to find reduced covers, let us show that if we first remove all extraneous attributes from left sides of FDs and then from right sides of FDs, we are left with no extraneous attributes anywhere, as long as we discard FDs of the form $X \to \emptyset$.

Suppose we start with a nonredundant set of FDs G and produce an equivalent set of FDs F by removing extraneous attributes, first from left sides and then from the right sides of FDs in G. If F is not reduced, it can only be because there is an FD $X \to Y$ in F with $Y \neq \emptyset$ that is not left reduced. Assume A is an extraneous attribute in X. Let G' be G at the point immediately after all extraneous attributes were removed from left sides of FDs in the formation of F. Assume $X \to Y$ comes from $X \to YZ$ in G'. Let $X' = X - A$. Since A is extraneous in X in F, $F - \{X \to Y\} \cup \{X' \to Y\} \equiv F$, so $F \models X' \to Y$. Let H be an F-based DDAG for $X' \to Y$. If $X \to Y$ is not in $U(H)$, then $X \to Y$ is redundant in F and, specifically, $X \to Y$ is not right-reduced, since $Y \neq \emptyset$. Therefore $X \to Y$ is in $U(H)$ and $F = X' \to X$, by Lemma 4.3. Hence, $G' \models X' \to X$, since $F \equiv G'$. Clearly, $X' \to X$ can be derived from G' without using $X \to YZ$. It follows that $G' - \{X \to YZ\} \cup \{X' \to YZ\} \equiv G'$ and that G' was not left-reduced, a contradiction. We see that F is reduced if FDs of the form $X \to \emptyset$ are excluded.

Notice that $\{X \to Y\} \models X\,A \to Y$, for any FD $X\,A \to Y$. Whenever we remove an attribute from a left side in a set of FDs, the result is always a stronger set of FDs. That is, let $G = F \cup \{X A \to Y\}$ and $G' = F \cup \{X \to Y\}$. G' always implies G. To test $G' \equiv G$, we need only test $G \models G'$, which reduces to testing $G \models X \rightarrow Y$. The algorithm LEFTRED in Algorithm 5.5 uses this method to detect extraneous attributes on the left sides of FDs. If G is nonredundant, this test can be simplified to $G \models X \rightarrow XA$ or just $G \models X \rightarrow A$. (Why?)

Algorithm 5.5 LEFTRED
Input: A set of FDs G.
Output: A left-reduced cover for G.
LEFTRED(G)

```
begin
F := G;
for each FD X → Y in G do
   for each attribute A in X do
      if MEMBER(F, (X − A) → Y) then
         remove A from X in X → Y in F;
return(F)
end.
```

For removing extraneous attributes from the right sides of FDs, we note that if $G = F \cup \{X \rightarrow YA\}$ and $G' = F \cup \{X \rightarrow Y\}$, then G always implies G'. To test $G' \equiv G$, we only need to test $G' \models G$, which reduces to testing $G' \models X \rightarrow YA$. Since $X \rightarrow Y \in G'$, this test further reduces to $G' \models X \rightarrow A$. The algorithm for right-reduction is given as Algorithm 5.6.

Algorithm 5.6 RIGHTRED
Input: A set of FDs G.
Output: A right-reduced cover for G.
RIGHTRED(G)

```
begin
F := G;
for each FD X → Y in G do
   for each attribute A in Y do
      if MEMBER(F − {X → Y} ∪ {X → (Y − A)}, X → A) then
         remove A from Y in X → Y in F;
return(F)
end.
```

We can now easily obtain the algorithm for reduced covers shown as Algorithm 5.7.

Algorithm 5.7 REDUCE
Input: A set G of FDs.
Output: A reduced cover for G.
REDUCE(G)
  begin
  $F :=$ RIGHTRED(LEFTRED(G));
  remove all FDs of the form $X \rightarrow \emptyset$ from F;
  return(F)
  end.

Example 5.6 Let $G' = \{A \rightarrow C, A\,B \rightarrow D\,E, A\,B \rightarrow C\,D\,I, A\,C \rightarrow J\}$. LEFTRED($G'$) yields $G'' = \{A \rightarrow C, A\,B \rightarrow D\,E, A\,B \rightarrow C\,D\,I, A \rightarrow J\}$ and RIGHTRED(G'') yields $F = \{A \rightarrow C, A\,B \rightarrow E, A\,B \rightarrow DI, A \rightarrow J\}$, which is reduced.

Lemma 5.2 The time complexity of REDUCE is $O(n^2)$ for inputs of length n.

Proof Left to the reader (see Exercise 5.8).

5.4 CANONICAL COVERS

Definition 5.6 A set of FDs F is *canonical* if every FD in F is of the form $X \rightarrow A$ and F is left-reduced and nonredundant.

Since a canonical set of FDs is nonredundant and every FD has a single attribute on the right side, it is right-reduced. Since it is also left-reduced, it is reduced.

Example 5.7 The set $F = \{A \rightarrow B, A \rightarrow C, A \rightarrow D, A \rightarrow E, B\,I \rightarrow J\}$ is a canonical cover for $G = \{A \rightarrow B\,C\,E, A\,B \rightarrow D\,E, B\,I \rightarrow J\}$.

The following lemma relates reduced and canonical covers.

Lemma 5.3 Let F be a reduced cover. Form G by taking each FD $X \rightarrow A_1 A_2 \cdots A_m$ and splitting it into $X \rightarrow A_1$, $X \rightarrow A_2$, $\ldots$, $X \rightarrow A_m$. G is a canonical cover. Conversely, if G is a canonical cover, it is a reduced cover. If we form F by combining all FDs with equal left sides into a single FD, then F is also a reduced cover. In both cases, F and G are equivalent.

Proof Let G be derived from F by splitting FDs. If $X \rightarrow A_i$ is redundant, then A_i is extraneous in $X \rightarrow A_1 A_2 \cdots A_m$. If $X \rightarrow A_i$ has an extraneous attribute B on the left side, then $G \models (X - B) \rightarrow A_i$, which means that $G \models$

$(X - B) \to X$, since $X \to A_i$ is nonredundant. (See the discussion preceding LEFTRED.) It follows that $F \models (X - B) \to X$ and hence B is extraneous in the left side of $X \to A_1 A_2 \cdots A_m$ in F.

The remainder of the proof is left to the reader (see Exercise 5.9).

5.5 THE STRUCTURE OF NONREDUNDANT COVERS

What can be said about two nonredundant covers F and F' for a set G of FDs, other than $F \equiv F'$? The following definition and lemma will point us toward some similarities in structure between F and F'.

Definition 5.7 Two sets of attributes X and Y are *equivalent* under a set F of FDs, written $X \leftrightarrow Y$, if $F \models X \to Y$ and $F \models Y \to X$.

Lemma 5.4 Let F and G be equivalent, nonredundant sets of FDs over scheme R. Let $X \to Y$ be an FD in F. There is an FD $V \to W$ in G with $X \leftrightarrow V$ under F (hence under G).

Proof Consider a G-based DDAG H for $X \to Y$. Look at the FDs in $U(H)$. Each has an F-based DDAG. Some FD $V \to W$ in $U(H)$ must have an F-based DDAG J that uses $X \to Y$. If not, there is an $(F - \{X \to Y\})$-based DDAG for $X \to Y$ and so $X \to Y$ is redundant in F (see Exercise 4.19). Since J uses $X \to Y$, by Lemma 4.3, $F \models V \to X$. Since H uses $V \to W$, $G \models X \to V$, hence $F \models X \leftrightarrow V$.

We may restate Lemma 5.4 as follows. Given equivalent, nonredundant covers F and G, for every left side X of an FD in F, there is an equivalent left side V of an FD in G.

Example 5.8 Let $F = \{A \to B\,C, B \to A, A\,D \to E\}$ and $G = \{A \to A\,B\,C, B \to A, B\,D \to E\}$. F and G are nonredundant and equivalent to each other. Note that $A \leftrightarrow A$, $B \leftrightarrow B$, and $A\,D \leftrightarrow B\,D$.

For a set of FDs F over scheme R and a set $X \subseteq R$, let $E_F(X)$ be the set of FDs in F with left sides equivalent to X. Let $\bar{E}_F$ be the set

$$\{E_F(X) | X \subseteq R \text{ and } E_F(X) \neq \emptyset\}.$$

$E_F(X)$ is empty when no left side of any FD in F is equivalent to X. $\bar{E}_F$ is always a partition of F.

Given equivalent, nonredundant sets F and G, Lemma 5.4 implies that

$E_F(X)$ is non-empty exactly when $E_G(X)$ is. Therefore, the number of sets in $\bar{E}_F$ is the same as the number in $\bar{E}_G$.

Example 5.9 Let F and G be as in Example 5.8. Then $\bar{E}_F$ is

$$E_F(A) = \{A \rightarrow B\ C,\ B \rightarrow A\}$$
$$E_F(A\ D) = \{A\ D \rightarrow E\},$$

and $\bar{E}_G$ is

$$E_G(A) = \{A \rightarrow A\ B\ C,\ B \rightarrow A\}$$
$$E_G(A\ D) = \{B\ D \rightarrow E\}.$$

5.6 MINIMUM COVERS

A nonredundant cover of a set G of FDs does not necessarily have as few FDs as any cover for G (see Exercise 5.15). This fact prompts the following definition.

Definition 5.8 A set of FDs F is *minimum* if F has as few FDs as any equivalent set of FDs.

A minimum set of FDs can have no redundant FDs (why?), so it is also nonredundant.

Example 5.10 The set $G = \{A \rightarrow B\ C,\ B \rightarrow A,\ A\ D \rightarrow E,\ B\ D \rightarrow I\}$ is nonredundant but not minimum, since $F = \{A \rightarrow B\ C,\ B \rightarrow A,\ A\ D \rightarrow E\ I\}$ is equivalent to G but has fewer FDs. F is a minimum cover for G.

5.6.1 Direct Determination

Unlike nonredundant covers, the definition of minimum covers provides no guide for finding minimum covers or even for testing minimality. In this section we introduce a restricted form of functional determination that gives us the means to compute minimum covers.

Definition 5.9 Given a set of FDs G, X *directly determines* Y under G, written $X \stackrel{\cdot}{\rightarrow} Y$, if there is a nonredundant cover F for G with an F-based DDAG H for $X \rightarrow Y$ such that $U(H) \cap E_F(X) = \emptyset$.

In other words, we can find a nonredundant cover F for G in which $X \rightarrow Y$ can be derived using only FDs in $F - E_F(X)$. Observe that $X \stackrel{\cdot}{\rightarrow} X$ always holds, that $X \dot{\rightarrow} Y$ implies $X \rightarrow Y$, and that $E_F(X)$ can be empty. Also note that $A \dot{\rightarrow} B$ only when $A = B$.

Example 5.11 Let $G = F = \{A \rightarrow C\,D,\ A\,B \rightarrow E,\ B \rightarrow I,\ D\,I \rightarrow J\}$. Then $A\,B \dot{\rightarrow} J$ under G, as the DDAG H in Figure 5.1 shows.

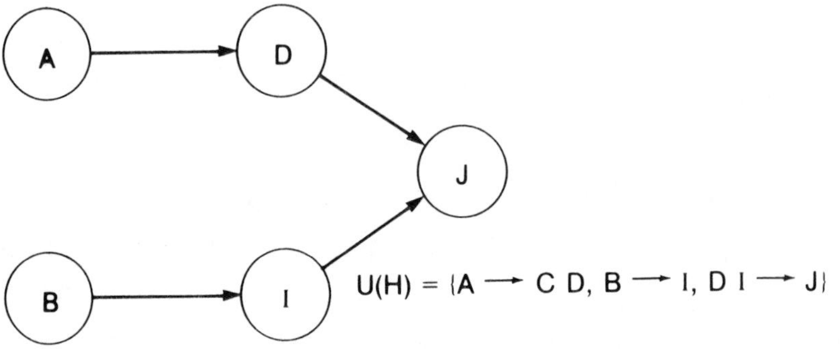

Figure 5.1

As the definition stands, it is not very useful. In order to test direct determination, we might have to find every nonredundant cover of G, which can be a lengthy task (see Exercise 5.11). The following lemma shows that life is not so hard.

Lemma 5.5 $X \dot{\rightarrow} Y$ under a set of FDs G if and only if for *every* nonredundant cover F for G there is an F-based DDAG H for $X \rightarrow Y$ with $U(H) \cap E_F(X) = \emptyset$.

Proof The if direction is trivial. We prove the only if direction. Let F be a nonredundant cover for G where there is an F-based DDAG H for $X \rightarrow Y$ using no FDs from $E_F(X)$. Let F' be any other nonredundant cover for G. For each FD $W \rightarrow Z$ in $U(H)$, we shall construct an F'-based DDAG using no FDs from $E_{F'}(X)$. We shall then splice these DDAGs together to get an F'-based DDAG for $X \rightarrow Y$ using no FDs in $E_{F'}(X)$, using Lemma 4.2.

If $W \rightarrow Z$ is in $U(H)$, then $F \models X \rightarrow W$ by Lemma 4.3. Suppose some F'-based DDAG for $W \rightarrow Z$ uses FD $U \rightarrow V$ from $E_{F'}(X)$. Again using Lemma 4.3, $F' \models W \rightarrow U$, hence $F \models W \rightarrow U$. But $U \leftrightarrow X$ under F' and F, hence $W \leftrightarrow X$ under F, so $W \rightarrow Z$ is in $E_F(X)$, contradicting the nature of H. Therefore every FD $W \rightarrow Z$ in $U(H)$ has an F'-based DDAG using no FDs from $E_{F'}(X)$ (see Exercise 5.19 for a slightly stronger version of Lemma 5.5).

Lemma 5.6 If $X \leftrightarrow Y$, $X \dot{\rightarrow} Y$, and $Y \dot{\rightarrow} Z$ under a set of G of FDs, then $X \dot{\rightarrow} Z$ under G.

Proof Left to the reader (see Exercise 5.20).

Definition 5.10 Let F be a set of FDs over scheme R. The set of all left sides in $E_F(X)$ is denoted by $e_F(X)$.

Lemma 5.7 Let F be a nonredundant set of FDs. Pick X, a left side of some FD in F, and any Y such that $X \leftrightarrow Y$ under F. There exists a Z in $e_F(X)$ such that $Y \dot{\rightarrow} Z$.

Proof If Y is in $e_F(X)$, then $Y \dot{\rightarrow} Y$ and we are done. Otherwise, since $Y \rightarrow Z$ for every Z in $e_F(X)$, there is an F-based DDAG for $Y \rightarrow Z$ for every Z in $e_F(X)$. Choose the Z in $e_F(X)$ which has a DDAG for $Y \rightarrow Z$ with the smallest number of nodes. Call this DDAG H. Suppose $U(H)$ contains $U \rightarrow V$ from $E_F(X)$. By Lemma 4.3 and its corollary, H is a DDAG for $Y \rightarrow U$, and furthermore, there is a node in H labeled by some attribute in V that can be removed from H and still leave a DDAG for $Y \rightarrow U$. Let H' be H with this node removed. H' has fewer nodes than H. Since U is in $e_F(X)$, the minimality of H is contradicted. There cannot be any FDs from $E_F(X)$ in $U(H)$, so $Y \dot{\rightarrow} Z$.

Example 5.12 Let $F = \{A \rightarrow B\,C,\ B\,C \rightarrow A,\ A\,D \rightarrow E,\ A\,D \rightarrow I,\ E \rightarrow B\}$. $B\,C\,D \leftrightarrow A\,D$, and Figure 5.2 shows an F-based DDAG for $B\,C\,D \rightarrow A\,D$ that uses no FDs from $E_F(A\,D)$.

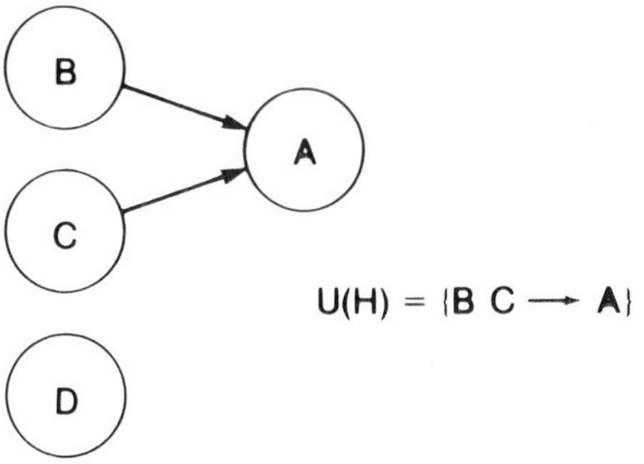

Figure 5.2

Lemma 5.8 Let F be a minimum set of FDs. There are no distinct FDs $Y \rightarrow U$ and $Z \rightarrow V$ in any $E_F(X)$ such that $Y \overset{\cdot}{\leftrightarrow} Z$.

Proof We shall show that if such FDs exist, we can find a set F' equivalent to F but with fewer FDs. Let H be an F-based DDAG for $Y \rightarrow Z$ that uses no FDs in $E_F(X)$ and let F' be F with $Y \rightarrow U$ and $Z \rightarrow V$ replaced by $Z \rightarrow U\,V$. Clearly, $F' \models Z \rightarrow V$. Since H is also an F'-based DDAG for $Y \rightarrow Z$ (it does not use $Y \rightarrow U$ or $Z \rightarrow V$), $F' \models Y \rightarrow Z$ and hence $F' \models Y \rightarrow U$. Every other FD in F is in F', so $F' \models F$. It is not difficult to show that $F \models F'$ and hence $F \equiv F'$. The minimality of F is contradicted.

Lemmas 5.7 and 5.8 are used to show the following result.

Theorem 5.1 Let F and G be equivalent, minimum sets of FDs. Then for any X, $|E_F(X)| = |E_G(X)|$.

Theorem 5.1 is stronger than Lemma 5.4. Not only does $|\bar{E}_F| = |\bar{E}_G|$ for minimum sets of FDs, but the sizes of corresponding equivalence classes are the same.

Proof Assume $E_F(X)$ and $E_G(X)$ are composed as follows, for m less than n.

$E_F(X)$	$E_G(X)$
$X_1 \rightarrow \bar{X}_1$	$Y_1 \rightarrow \bar{Y}_1$
$X_2 \rightarrow \bar{X}_2$	$Y_2 \rightarrow \bar{Y}_2$
$\vdots$	$\vdots$
$X_m \rightarrow \bar{X}_m$	$Y_n \rightarrow \bar{Y}_n$

Not all the Y_j's are the same as some X_i or else two Y_j's would be equal, contradicting Lemma 5.8. Thus there exists j such that $Y_j \neq X_i$, $1 \leq i \leq m$. By Lemma 5.7, there is a k such that $Y_j \overset{\cdot}{\leftrightarrow} X_k$. Renumber the FDs in $E_F(X)$ and $E_G(X)$ so that Y_j is Y_1 and X_k is X_1. In $E_G(X)$, replace $Y_1 \rightarrow \bar{Y}_1$ by $X_1 \rightarrow \bar{Y}_1$. Since $Y_1 \overset{\cdot}{\leftrightarrow} X_1$, $Y_1 \rightarrow \bar{Y}_1$ can still be derived in the modified G and the closure of G is unchanged. If $X_1 = Y_j$ for some j other than 1, combine $X_1 \rightarrow \bar{Y}_1$ and $Y_j \rightarrow \bar{Y}_j$ to get $X_1 \rightarrow \bar{Y}_1\,\bar{Y}_j$, which is a contradiction to the minimality of G.

Otherwise, $X_1 \neq Y_j$ for all j greater than 1, but the number of left sides in $e_G(X)$ that match left sides in $e_F(X)$ has increased by one. (We removed Y_1 and added X_1.) There must still be some Y_j not equal to any X_i in $e_F(X)$, by the remarks at the beginning of the proof. We return to the point in the proof where the renumbering took place.

If we never encounter a contradiction to the minimality of G, eventually every left side in $e_G(X)$ will be in $e_F(X)$, contradicting the observation that some Y_j must be different from every X_i. The assumption that m was less than n must be incorrect, and, in fact, $m = n$.

The correspondence between $E_F(X)$ and $E_G(X)$ goes further than there simply being the same number of FDs in each. Consider $E_F(X)$ and $E_G(X)$ again:

$E_F(X)$	$E_G(X)$
$X_1 \rightarrow \bar{X}_1$	$Y_1 \rightarrow \bar{Y}_1$
$X_2 \rightarrow \bar{X}_2$	$Y_2 \rightarrow \bar{Y}_2$
$\vdots$	$\vdots$
$X_m \rightarrow \bar{X}_m$	$Y_m \rightarrow \bar{Y}_m$

Choose any X_i in $e_F(X)$. There is some j such that $X_i \dot{\rightarrow} Y_j$, by Lemma 5.7. Also by Lemma 5.7, there must be a k such that $Y_j \dot{\rightarrow} X_k$. If $i \neq k$, then $X_i \dot{\rightarrow} X_k$ by Lemma 5.6, which is a contradiction to Lemma 5.8. Thus, $i = k$. We see that if $X_i \dot{\rightarrow} Y_j$, then $Y_j \dot{\rightarrow} X_i$.

Suppose $X_i \dot{\rightarrow} Y_j$ and $X_i \dot{\rightarrow} Y_h$, where $j \neq h$. By what we have just noted, $Y_j \dot{\rightarrow} X_i$, and by Lemma 5.6, $Y_j \dot{\rightarrow} Y_h$, again contradicting Lemma 5.8. We see there is a one-to-one correspondence between $e_F(X)$ and $e_G(X)$ induced by $\dot{\rightarrow}$. By the proof of Theorem 5.1, we see that X_i can be substituted for its corresponding Y_j in $E_G(X)$ without changing the closure of G.

Example 5.13 It is about time we got away from the As and Bs and got back to an example that resembles real life. Consider a relation *violations*(CAR-SERIAL# LICENSE# OWNER DATE TIME TICKET# OFFENSE) that holds a list of motor vehicle violations. One minimum cover for the set of FDs on this relation is $F =$

1. CAR-SERIAL# → LICENSE# OWNER
2. LICENSE# → CAR-SERIAL#
3. TICKET# → LICENSE# DATE TIME OFFENSE
4. LICENSE# DATE TIME → TICKET# OFFENSE.

An equivalent minimum set of FDs is

1. CAR-SERIAL# → LICENSE#

2. LICENSE# → CAR-SERIAL# OWNER
3. TICKET# → CAR-SERIAL# OWNER DATE TIME
4. CAR-SERIAL# DATE TIME → TICKET# OFFENSE.

E_F(LICENSE#) and E_G(LICENSE#) are composed of the first two FDs in each set, while E_F(TICKET#) and E_G(TICKET#) are composed of the last two FDs in each set. The FDs are arranged so that the left sides of same-numbered FDs directly determine each other. We can substitute CAR-SERIAL# DATE TIME for the left side of FD 4 in F without changing the closure of F. If we try to substitute where there is equivalence but not direct determination, such as LICENSE# for the left side of FD 1 in F, we change the closure.

The observations before the example indicate a means to combine equivalent minimum sets F and G to get an equivalent set of FDs with possibly fewer attribute symbols. Take $E_F(X)$ and $E_G(X)$ for some X and pair up the left sides using the correspondence induced by $\overset{\cdot}{\rightarrow}$. For each Y in $e_F(X)$ and the corresponding Z in $e_G(X)$, replace Y by Z if Z has fewer attributes than Y. If we can make such a substitution, the modified set F will have fewer attribute symbols than the original.

5.6.2 Computing Minimum Covers

The following Theorem will be our tool in developing an algorithm for minimum covers.

Theorem 5.2 Let G be a nonredundant set of FDs that is not minimum. There is some $E_G(X)$ containing distinct FDs $Y \rightarrow U$ and $Z \rightarrow V$ such that $Y \overset{\cdot}{\rightarrow} Z$.

This theorem is almost the converse of Lemma 5.8.

Proof Let F be a minimum cover for G. There must be some X such that $|E_F(X)| < |E_G(X)|$, by Theorem 5.1. Let $E_F(X)$ have FDs $X_1 \rightarrow \overline{X}_1$, $X_2 \rightarrow \overline{X}_2, \ldots, X_m \rightarrow \overline{X}_m$ and let $E_G(X)$ have FDs $Y_1 \rightarrow \overline{Y}_1$, $Y_2 \rightarrow \overline{Y}_2, \ldots, Y_n \rightarrow \overline{Y}_n$. For each Y_j in $e_G(X)$ there is an X_i in $e_F(X)$ with $Y_j \overset{\cdot}{\rightarrow} X_i$, by Lemma 5.7. Since m is less than n, there must be an i, j, and k such that $Y_j \overset{\cdot}{\rightarrow} X_i$ and $Y_k \overset{\cdot}{\rightarrow} X_i$, with $j \neq k$. In turn, $X_i \overset{\cdot}{\rightarrow} Y_h$ for some Y_h in $e_G(X)$. Either $h \neq j$ or $h \neq k$. If $h \neq j$, then by Lemma 5.6, $Y_j \overset{\cdot}{\rightarrow} Y_h$. Likewise, if $h \neq k$, $Y_k \overset{\cdot}{\rightarrow} Y_h$.

Theorem 5.2 says that if we have a nonredundant set G that is not minimum, we can find $Y \rightarrow U$ and $Z \rightarrow V$ in G with $Y \leftrightarrow Z$ and $Y \overset{\cdot}{\rightarrow} Z$ under G. Once we find these two FDs, we can replace them both by the single FD $Z \rightarrow U\ V$, as in the proof of Lemma 5.8. The result is an equivalent set with fewer FDs.

Algorithm 5.8 uses Theorem 5.2 in the manner just described and assumes a function DDERIVES that tests direct determination (see Exercise 5.18).

Algorithm 5.8 MINIMIZE
Input: A set of FDs G.
Output: A minimum cover for G.
MINIMIZE(G)

```
begin
F := NONREDUN(G);
Find the sets of Ē_F;
for each E_F(X) in Ē_F do
    for each Y → U in E_F(X) do
        for each Z → V ≠ Y → U in E_F(X) do
            if DDERIVES(F, Y → Z) then
                replace Y → U and Z → V by Z → U V in F;
return(F)
end.
```

Theorem 5.3 MINIMIZE can be implemented to have time complexity $O(np)$ on inputs of length n with p FDs.

Proof Finding F takes $O(np)$ time (see Exercise 5.8). Finding the sets in $\bar{E}_F$ might seem to require $O(np^2)$ time, but this much time is not necessary. We can use a modified version of LINCLOSURE to mark, for a given X, every FD $Y \rightarrow Z$ in F such that $F = X \rightarrow Y$. (The marked FDs are those with COUNT $= 0$.) In $O(np)$ time we can run this modified algorithm on the left side of every FD in F to produce a p by p Boolean matrix M with rows and columns indexed by FDs in F. The entry $M[X \rightarrow Y,\ W \rightarrow Z]$ is *true* if $F \models X \rightarrow W$ and *false* otherwise. From M it is possible to find all the sets in $\bar{E}_F$ in $O(p^2)$ time (see Exercise 5.23).

Now, for each $E_F(X)$ in $\bar{E}_F$, look at each FD $Y \rightarrow U$ in turn. Run the modified version of LINCLOSURE on Y and $F - E_F(X)$, but keep track of COUNT[$Z \rightarrow Y$] for each $Z \rightarrow V$ in $E_F(X)$. If the count reaches 0 for some $Z \rightarrow V$ when the algorithm finishes, we know $Y \overset{\cdot}{\rightarrow} Z$ and we make the proper substitution of FDs. The modified LINCLOSURE algorithm is run once for each FD in F, giving $O(np)$ time complexity for this stage. Hence, the entire algorithm takes $O(np)$ time.

Corollary A reduced minimum cover can be found for a set of FDs G in $O(n^2)$ time for inputs of length n.

Proof Apply REDUCE to the output of MINIMIZE(G) (see Exercise 5.8).

5.7 OPTIMAL COVERS

We have been measuring our covers in terms of the number of FDs they contain. We can also measure them by the number of attribute symbols required to express them. For example, $\{A\ B \rightarrow C,\ C\ D \rightarrow E,\ A\ C \rightarrow I\ J\}$ has size 10 under this measure.

Definition 5.11 A set of FDs F is *optimal* if there is no equivalent set of FDs with fewer attribute symbols than F.

Example 5.14 The set $F = \{E\ C \rightarrow D,\ A\ B \rightarrow E,\ E \rightarrow A\ B\}$ is an optimal cover for $G = \{A\ B\ C \rightarrow D,\ A\ B \rightarrow E,\ E \rightarrow A\ B\}$. Notice that G is reduced and minimum, but not optimal.

Lemma 5.9 If F is an optimal set of FDs, then F is reduced and minimum.

Proof If F has an extraneous attribute, it is clearly not optimal. MINIMIZE always decreases the number of attribute symbols in a cover whenever it makes a change. Thus MINIMIZE(F) must return F and hence F is minimum.

Unfortunately, there is probably no polynomial time algorithm for finding an optimal cover for a set of FDs. This problem belongs to the class of NP-complete problems, for which no one has yet found any polynomial time algorithms. Another NP-complete problem concerning covers is, what is the smallest set F contained in G that is a cover for G? Size in this case is measured in FDs.

5.8 ANNULAR COVERS AND COMPOUND FUNCTIONAL DEPENDENCIES

We have seen that FDs in a set F can be partitioned on the basis of equivalent left sides. It is possible to represent the information in an equivalence class by a single, generalized FD.

Definition 5.12 A *compound functional dependency* (CFD) has the form $(X_1, X_2, \ldots, X_k) \to Y$, where $X_1, X_2, \ldots, X_k$ are all distinct subsets of a scheme R and Y is also a subset of R. A relation $r(R)$ satisfies the CFD $(X_1, X_2, \ldots, X_k) \to Y$ if it satisfies the FDs $X_i \to X_j$ and $X_i \to Y$, $1 \leq i, j \leq k$. In this CFD, $(X_1, X_2, \ldots, X_k)$ is the *left side*, $X_1, X_2, \ldots, X_k$ are the *left sets* and Y is the *right side*.

A CFD is nothing more than a shorthand way of writing a set of FDs with equivalent left sides. We do make one slight departure from our conventions in allowing $Y = \emptyset$. In this case we write the CFD as $(X_1, X_2, \ldots, X_k)$.

Definition 5.13 Let G be a set of CFDs over R and let F be a set of FDs or CFDs over R. G is *equivalent* to F, written $G \equiv F$, if every relation $r(R)$ that satisfies G satisfies F and vice versa.

This definition is consistent with equivalence for sets of FDs.

Definition 5.14 F is a *cover* for G if $F \equiv G$, where F and G may be either sets of FDs, sets of CFDs, or one set of each.

Example 5.15 The set of CFDs $G = \{(A, B), (A\,C, B\,C) \to D\,E\}$ is equivalent to the set of FDs $F = \{A \to B, B \to A, A\,C \to D, B\,C \to E\}$.

Definition 5.15 A set of FDs F is a *characteristic set* for the CFD $(X_1, X_2, \ldots, X_k) \to Y$, if $F \equiv \{(X_1, X_2, \ldots, X_k) \to Y\}$. If F uses each left set in the CFD as the left side of an FD exactly once (that is, F looks like $\{X_1 \to Y_1, X_2 \to Y_2, \ldots, X_k \to Y_k\}$), then F is a *natural* characteristic set for the CFD.

The definition of CFD gives us one characteristic set for $(X_1, X_2, \ldots, X_k) \to Y$, but the set is not natural. Another characteristic set is $\{X_1 \to X_2, X_2 \to X_3, \ldots, X_{k-1} \to X_k, X_k \to X_1\,Y\}$. This characteristic set is natural, and is the source of the term annular. The left sets in the CFD can be visualized in a ring, as shown in Figure 5.3.

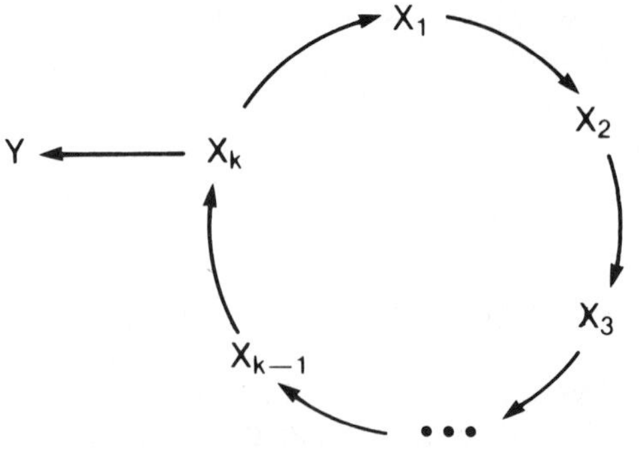

Figure 5.3

A set of CFDs can be treated as the union of characteristic sets for all the CFDs in the set. Treated as such, almost all the terminology from sets of FDs is applicable to sets of CFDs. In some cases we shall redefine our terms slightly for CFDs; when we do not, we use the corresponding definition for FDs. The only concept that does not carry over well is the closure of a set of CFDs. We shall interpret closure as the closure of an equivalent set of FDs.

Definition 5.16 A set F of CFDs is *annular* if there are no left sets X and Z in different left sides with $X \leftrightarrow Z$ under F.

Algorithm LINCLOSURE can be modified to run on sets of CFDs. Rather than keeping counts and lists for FDs, we keep them for left sets. When the count of some left set X_i in $(X_1, X_2, \ldots, X_k) \rightarrow Y$ reaches 0, we can add all the attributes in $X_1, X_2, \ldots, X_k$, and Y, to NEWDEP (see Exercise 5.24). MEMBER can therefore be modified to run on CFDs. DERIVES and EQUIV can be modified to work for a set of FDs and a set of CFDs or for two sets of CFDs by choosing characteristic sets for all the CFDs. The time complexity for all these algorithms remains the same (see Exercise 5.25).

Given a set of FDs G, it is possible to find an annular cover for G with no more than $|\overline{E}_F|$ CFDs, where F is a nonredundant cover for G. We combine all the FDs in one $E_F(X)$ into a single CFD. Every left side in $e_F(X)$ is a left set in the CFD, and the right side of the CFD is the union of all the right sides of FDs in $E_F(X)$.

Example 5.16 Let $G = F = \{A \rightarrow B\,C,\ B \rightarrow A\,D,\ A\,E \rightarrow I,\ B\,E \rightarrow J\,I\}$. An annular cover for G is the set $G' = \{(A,\ B) \rightarrow A\,B\,C\,D,\ (A\,E,\ B\,E) \rightarrow I\,J\}$.

The reverse process does not always work. If we have a nonredundant cover F for a set of FDs G and an annular cover G' for G with $|\bar{E}_F|$ CFDs, taking the union of natural characteristic sets for all the CFDs in G' does not necessarily yield a nonredundant cover for G.

Example 5.17 $G' = \{(A, AB, B) \to C D, (A E) \to I J\}$ is an annular cover for the set G in Example 5.16. When we form F' by combining natural characteristic sets, we can get $F' = \{A \to A B, A B \to B, B \to A C D, A E \to I J\}$. $A B \to B$ is redundant in F'.

Definition 5.17 Let G be a set of CFDs containing $(X_1, X_2, \ldots, X_k) \to Y$. Let X_i be one of the left sets and let A be an attribute in X_i. Attribute A is *shiftable* if A can be moved from X_i to Y while preserving equivalence. A left set X_i is *shiftable* if all the attributes in X_i are simultaneously shiftable.

Example 5.18 Let G' be as in Example 5.17. $A B$ in $(A, A B, B) \to C D$ is shiftable. The result of shifting it is $G'' = \{(A, B) \to A B C D, (A E) \to I J\}$. Note that A in $(A, AB, B) \to CD$ is not shiftable.

Definition 5.18 An annular set G is *nonredundant* if no CFDs can be removed from G without altering equivalence and no CFD in G contains a shiftable left set. Otherwise, G is redundant.

Example 5.19 The set G' in Example 5.17 is redundant, while G'' in Example 5.18 is nonredundant.

Lemma 5.10 Let G be a nonredundant annular set of CFDs. The union of natural characteristic sets for all the CFDs in G yields a nonredundant set of FDs equivalent to G. The proof is left to the reader (see Exercise 5.26).

We can also define the notions of reduced and minimum for annular covers.

Definition 5.19 Let G be a nonredundant annular set. A CFD $(X_1, X_2, \ldots, X_k) \to Y$ in G is *reduced* if no left set contains any shiftable attributes and the right side contains no extraneous attributes. The set G is *reduced* if every CFD in G is reduced.

Definition 5.20 Let G be a nonredundant annular set. G is minimum if it contains as few left sets as any equivalent annular set.

Example 5.20 $G = \{(A, B) \rightarrow C\,D, (A\,E) \rightarrow I\,J\}$ is a reduced, minimum annular cover for the set G' in Example 5.16.

LEFTRED and RIGHTRED can be modified to get a version of REDUCE for CFDs that runs in $O(n^2)$ time on input of length n. To aid in reduction, we can use the observation that $(X_1 \cup X_2 \cup \cdots \cup X_k) \cap Y = \emptyset$ for any reduced CFD$(X_1, X_2, \ldots, X_k) \rightarrow Y$ (see Exercise 5.27).

To find a minimum annular cover for a set G of FDs, we first find a minimum cover F for G. We then combine FDs with equivalent left sides into single CFDs. The question arises, is a reduced, minimum annular set really the same as a reduced minimum set of FDs? That is, can we get a reduced, minimum annular set by combining FDs from a reduced, minimum set of FDs? The answer is no, as the next example shows.

Example 5.21 Consider the set of FDs $F = \{B_1\,B_2 \rightarrow A,\ D_1\,D_2 \rightarrow B_1\,B_2,\ B_1 \rightarrow C_1,\ B_2 \rightarrow C_2,\ D_1 \rightarrow A,\ D_2 \rightarrow A,\ A\,B_1\,C_2 \rightarrow D_2,\ A\,B_2\,C_1 \rightarrow D_1\}$. F is minimum and reduced. The only equivalent left sides are $B_1\,B_2$ and $D_1\,D_2$. Let us combine FDs into CFDs to get $G = \{(B_1\,B_2, D_1\,D_2) \rightarrow A,\ (B_1) \rightarrow C_1,\ (B_2) \rightarrow C_2,\ (D_1) \rightarrow A,\ (D_2) \rightarrow A,\ (A\,B_1\,C_2) \rightarrow D_2,\ (A\,B_2\,C_1) \rightarrow D_1\}$. We have left $B_1\,B_2$ off the right side of the first CFD by the observation above that left sets and the right side should not intersect. Even so, the A on the right side of the first CFD is extraneous. It is not extraneous in $B_1\,B_2 \rightarrow A$ in F, since it is needed to prove $B_1\,B_2 \rightarrow D_1\,D_2$ (see Exercise 5.28).

We see that after converting from a reduced, minimum set of FDs to a minimum annular set, it is still necessary to perform a reduction step to get a reduced, minimum annular set.

We shall use annular covers again in Chapter 6, where we use them for synthesizing database schemes.

5.9 EXERCISES

5.1 Find a nonredundant cover for the set $G = \{A \rightarrow C,\ A\,B \rightarrow C,\ C \rightarrow D\,I,\ C\,D \rightarrow I,\ E\,C \rightarrow A\,B,\ E\,I \rightarrow C\}$.

5.2 Show how DERIVES (Algorithm 5.1) can be modified to run more quickly in some cases.

5.3 Show that a set of FDs F is redundant if and only if there is an FD $X \rightarrow Y$ in F such that $F - \{X \rightarrow Y\} \models X \rightarrow Y$.

5.4 Consider the following alternative to the algorithm NONREDUN (Algorithm 5.4).

```
REPUGNANT(G)
  begin
  F := ∅;
  for each FD X → Y in G do
     if MEMBER (G − {X → Y}, X → Y) then
        F := F ∪ {X → Y};
  return(G − F)
  end.
```

Does REPUGNANT correctly compute a nonredundant cover for G?

5.5 Give an example of a set of FDs that contains an FD $X \rightarrow Y$ with every attribute in X and Y extraneous.

5.6 Find sets of FDs F and G such that F is a nonredundant cover for G, but G has fewer FDs than F.

5.7 Show that starting with a nonredundant set of FDs, removing extraneous attributes from the left sides of FDs can yield a redundant set of FDs.

5.8 Prove that the algorithm NONREDUN (Algorithm 5.4) has time complexity $O(np)$ for inputs of length n with p FDs. Use this result to prove that the algorithm REDUCE (Algorithm 5.7) has time complexity $O(n^2)$ on input of length n.

5.9 Complete the proof of Lemma 5.3.

5.10 Let F be the set of all possible FDs over a relation scheme $R = A_1 A_2 \cdots A_n$, except those of the form $\emptyset \rightarrow Y$. Find a nonredundant cover for F.

5.11* What is the maximum number of nonredundant covers a set of n FDs may contain?

5.12 Show that an FD $X \rightarrow Y$ is redundant in F if and only if there is an F-based DDAG H for $X \rightarrow Y$ with $X \rightarrow Y$ not in $U(H)$.

5.13 Show that Lemma 5.4 can fail if F is redundant.

5.14 Show that for equivalent nonredundant sets of FDs F and G, it is possible that for some X, $E_F(X)$ has a different number of FDs than $E_G(X)$.

5.15 Find two equivalent nonredundant sets of FDs with different numbers of FDs.

5.16 Give a set of FDs G and sets of attributes X and Y such that $X \dot{\rightarrow} Y$ does not hold under G, but $X \rightarrow Y$ does.

5.17 Show that in a minimum set of FDs there cannot be two distinct FDs $X \rightarrow Y$ and $X \rightarrow Z$.

5.18* Find an algorithm to test direct determination.

5.19 Prove: If $X \dot{\rightarrow} Y$ under G, then for any cover F for G there is an F-based DDAG H for $X \rightarrow Y$ with $U(H) \cap E_F(X) = \emptyset$.

5.20 Prove Lemma 5.6.

5.21 Give an example of a set of FDs where some FD has two extraneous attributes, but only one can be removed if equivalence is to be preserved.

5.22 Prove that Theorem 5.1 does not hold if F and G are only nonredundant.

5.23 Given the p by p Boolean matrix M in the proof of Theorem 5.3, show how to find the sets of $\overline{E}_F$ in $O(p^2)$ time.

5.24 Let $(X_1, X_2, \ldots, X_k) \rightarrow Y$ be a CFD and let $S = X_1 \cup X_2 \cup \cdots \cup X_k \cup Y$. Show that $F = \{X_1 \rightarrow S, X_2 \rightarrow S, \ldots, X_k \rightarrow S\}$ is a natural characteristic set for the CFD.

5.25 Show that for any set of CFDs there is an equivalent set of FDs that uses no more than twice the number of attribute symbols.

5.26 Prove Lemma 5.10.

5.27 Show that in a reduced CFD $(X_1, X_2, \ldots, X_k) \rightarrow Y$, $(X_1 \cup X_2 \cup \cdots \cup X_k) \cap Y = \emptyset$.

5.28 Let F be the set of FDs in Example 5.21. Show that A is not extraneous in $B_1 B_2 \rightarrow A$.

5.29 Find a reduced, minimum annular cover for the set G in Exercise 5.1.

5.10 BIBLIOGRAPHY AND COMMENTS

Armstrong [1974] investigated equivalent sets of FDs and alternative representations for sets of FDs. Bernstein [1976b] demonstrated the usefulness of nonredundancy for database normalization (see Chapter 6). Canonical covers were introduced by Paredaens [1977]. Lewis, Sekino, and Ting [1977] examined a representation for all the nonredundant covers of a set of FDs. Lucchesi and Osborn [1978] present some NP-completeness results concerning covers and key finding. Beeri and Bernstein [1979] presented an efficient algorithm for computing a nonredundant cover, and also some NP-completeness results involving FDs. Direct determination and the algorithm MINIMIZE are from Maier [1980b], who also shows that finding optimal covers is NP-complete.

The reader is directed to Garey and Johnson [1979] for background on the theory of NP-complete problems.

Jou [1980] and Steiner [1981] give alternative formalisms for discussing covers and implications of FDs.

Chapter 6

DATABASES AND NORMAL FORMS

Before delving into relational databases, let us review keys and superkeys in light of what we know about FDs.

Recall: Given a relation scheme R, a key on R is a subset K of R such that for any permissible relation $r(R)$, there are no two distinct tuples t_1 and t_2 in r such that $t_1(K) = t_2(K)$, and no proper subset K' of K has this property. Remember that for some permissible relations on R, K' could be a key, but we are concerned with all permissible relations on R. A superkey is any set of attributes containing a key.

Example 6.1 In the relation *leaves* in Table 6.1 we have a list of departures from airports. At first, {FROM, DEPARTS} might seem to be a key for *leaves*, but when we consider that there can be two flights from the same city at the same time (say we add the tuple ⟨234 Denver 9:30p O'Hare⟩), we see that {FROM, DEPARTS, TO} is actually the key we want.

Table 6.1 The relation *leaves*.

leaves(FLIGHT	FROM	DEPARTS	TO)
16	JFK	9:10a	O'Hare
142	Denver	10:32a	O'Hare
146	Denver	9:30p	JFK
197	Atlanta	1:15p	Houston

In terms of FDs, a key for a scheme R is a subset K of R such that any permissible relation $r(R)$ satisfies $K \rightarrow R$, but no proper subset of K has this property. If K is a key for r, then there are no distinct tuples t_1 and t_2 in r such that t_1 and t_2 have the same K-values. Therefore, when testing the FD $K \rightarrow R$, if we ever have $t_1(K) = t_2(K)$, we must have $t_1 = t_2$, which is to say $t_1(R) = t_2(R)$. A superkey is a subset K of R such that $K \rightarrow R$, but there is no requirement for minimality.

6.1 DATABASES AND DATABASE SCHEMES

In what follows, we shall assume that a relation scheme R is composed of two parts, S and $\mathbf{K}$, where S is a set of attributes and $\mathbf{K}$ is a set of designated keys. (Remember that a designated key can be a superkey.) We write this situation as $R = (S, \mathbf{K})$. We shall sometimes still use R in place of S when discussing sets of attributes, such as using $X \subseteq R$ for $X \subseteq S$.

Definition 6.1 Let $\mathbf{U}$ be a set of attributes, each with an associated domain. A *relational database scheme* $\mathbf{R}$ *over* $\mathbf{U}$ is a collection of relation schemes $\{R_1, R_2, \ldots, R_p\}$, where $R_i = (S_i, \mathbf{K}_i)$, $1 \leq i \leq p$,

$$\bigcup_{i=1}^{p} S_i = \mathbf{U},$$

and $S_i \neq S_j$ if $i \neq j$.
A *relational database* d *on database scheme* $\mathbf{R}$ is a collection of relations $\{r_1, r_2, \ldots, r_p\}$ such that for each relation scheme $R = (S, \mathbf{K})$ in $\mathbf{R}$ there is a relation r in d such that r is a relation on S that satisfies every key in $\mathbf{K}$. We abuse set notation and always assume that r_i is the relation on S_i.

Example 6.2 Table 6.2 shows a database $d = \{$*flies, times*$\}$ on the database scheme $\mathbf{R} = \{$(PILOT FLIGHT DATE, {PILOT DATE}), (FLIGHT DEPARTS, {FLIGHT})$\}$. Relations *flies* and *times* are projections of the relation *assign* in Table 4.1.

Definition 6.2 A relation scheme $R = (S, \mathbf{K})$ *embodies* the FD $K \to R$ if K is a designated key in $\mathbf{K}$.

Notice that we are already using R for S.

Definition 6.3 A database scheme $\mathbf{R} = \{R_1, R_2, \ldots, R_p\}$ *represents* the set of FDs $G = \{X \to Y \mid \text{some } R_i \text{ in } \mathbf{R} \text{ embodies } X \to Y\}$. $\mathbf{R}$ *completely characterizes* a set of FDs F if $F \equiv G$.

Example 6.3 The database scheme $\mathbf{R}$ in Example 6.2 represents the set of FDs $G = \{$PILOT DATE $\to$ PILOT FLIGHT DATE, FLIGHT $\to$ FLIGHT DEPARTS$\}$. $\mathbf{R}$ completely characterizes the set $F = \{$PILOT DATE $\to$ FLIGHT DEPARTS, FLIGHT $\to$ DEPARTS$\}$.

Table 6.2 The relations *flies* and *times*, comprising a database.

flies(PILOT	FLIGHT	DATE)
Cushing	83	9 Aug
Cushing	116	10 Aug
Clark	281	8 Aug
Clark	301	12 Aug
Clark	83	11 Aug
Chin	83	13 Aug
Chin	116	12 Aug
Copley	281	9 Aug
Copley	281	13 Aug
Copley	412	15 Aug

times(FLIGHT	DEPARTS)
83	10:15a
116	1:25p
281	5:50a
301	6:35p
412	1:25p

We may wish to place constraints upon relations in our databases other than those imposed by the designated keys of the relation schemes. In some such cases we specify a set of FDs F that the relations in the database must satisfy. Not every FD in F will apply to every relation in the database. How could the FD $A\ B \rightarrow C$ apply to a relation $r(A\ C)$? We must modify the definition of satisfies to suit databases.

Definition 6.4 Let R be a relation scheme. The FD $X \rightarrow Y$ *applies* to R if $X \rightarrow Y$ is an FD over R.

Definition 6.5 Let $d = \{r_1, r_2, \ldots, r_p\}$ be a database on scheme $\mathbf{R} = \{R_1, R_2, \ldots, R_p\}$ over $\mathbf{U}$. Let F be a set of FDs over $\mathbf{U}$. Database d *satisfies* F if for every FD $X \rightarrow Y$ in F^+ and every R_i in $\mathbf{R}$, if $X \rightarrow Y$ applies to R_i, then r_i satisfies $X \rightarrow Y$. Let G be the set of all FDs in F^+ that apply to some scheme R_i in $\mathbf{R}$. Any FD in G^+ is said to be *enforceable* on $\mathbf{R}$; any FD in $F^+ - G^+$ is *unenforceable* on $\mathbf{R}$. The set F is *enforceable* on $\mathbf{R}$ if every FD in F^+ is enforceable on $\mathbf{R}$, that is, $G \equiv F$.

To show that a set F is enforceable on $\mathbf{R}$, it is sufficient to find a set $F' \equiv F$ such that every FD in F' applies to some scheme R in $\mathbf{R}$.

Definition 6.6 A database d on scheme $\mathbf{R}$ *obeys* a set of FDs F if F is enforceable on $\mathbf{R}$ and d satisfies F^+.

If F' is a set of FDs as described above, d obeys F if d satisfies F'.

Example 6.4 Let $\mathbf{R} = \{R_1, R_2, R_3\}$, where $R_1 = A\,B\,C$, $R_2 = B\,C\,D$, and $R_3 = D\,E$. Let $F = \{A \to B\,C,\ C \to A,\ A \to D,\ D \to E,\ A \to E\}$. FDs $A \to D$ and $A \to E$ do not apply to any relation scheme in **R**. However, F is enforceable on **R**, since $G = \{A \to B\,C,\ C \to A,\ C \to D,\ D \to E\}$ is equivalent to F and every FD in G applies to some relation scheme in **R**. The set $F' = \{A \to D\}$ is not enforceable on **R**.

6.2 NORMAL FORMS FOR DATABASES

We are about to define three normal forms for databases. A normal form is a restriction on the database scheme that presumably precludes certain undesirable properties from the database. Normal forms are first defined for a relation scheme in a database scheme, and are then extended to apply to the database scheme as a whole.

6.2.1 First Normal Form

A relation scheme R is in *first normal form* (1NF) if the values in $dom(A)$ are atomic for every attribute A in R. That is, the values in the domain are not lists or sets of values or composite values. A database scheme **R** is in *first normal form* if every relation scheme in **R** is in first normal form. All the examples we have seen thus far have been in 1NF. The definition of atomic is hazy; a value that is atomic in one application could be non-atomic in another. For a general guideline, a value is non-atomic if the application deals with only a part of the value.

Example 6.5 Shown below is a relation *born* that lists birthdays.

born (

NAME	BIRTHDATE
Allen	June 7, 1949
Alfred	March 21, 1933
Alphonse	April 30, 1959
Alice	December 12, 1963

)

If we are ever interested only in the month or year a person was born, the relation *born* is not in 1NF, since we are dealing with part of a value. To be in 1NF in this case, the attribute BIRTHDATE should be broken up as shown below.

born (NAME BMONTH BDAY BYEAR)

NAME	BMONTH	BDAY	BYEAR
Allen	June	7	1949
Alfred	March	21	1933
Alphonse	April	30	1959
Alice	December	12	1963

Example 6.6 The relation *gender*, shown below, is not in 1NF because it contains values that are sets of atomic values.

gender (NAME SEX)

NAME	SEX
{John, Jean, Ivan}	male
{Mary, Marie}	female

To be in 1NF, *gender* should be stored like this:

gender (NAME SEX)

NAME	SEX
John	male
Jean	male
Ivan	male
Mary	female
Marie	female

What is the advantage of 1NF? It may not be possible to express FDs in as great detail as we would like without 1NF. Suppose we want to add an attribute SIGN that gives the astrological sign of the person to the first relation *born* in Example 6.5. SIGN is functionally dependent only on the month and day of birth, and not on the year of birth. However, the best we can do the first relation of Example 6.5 is BIRTHDATE → SIGN, which would allow two people born on the same day in different years to have different signs. In the second relation *born*, there is no problem. We can write the FD BMONTH BDAY → SIGN, which prevents the problem with the previous FD.

Updates can also be a problem if a scheme is not in 1NF. Suppose we want to process the update CH(*gender*; Jean, male; SEX = female). The result of this update is ambiguous in the first relation gender in Example 6.6. Do we move Jean from one set to the other or do we change male to female? The update is unambiguous when applied to the second version of *gender* in Example 6.6.

6.2.2 Anomalies and Data Redundancy

Second and third normal forms arise from trying to avoid anomalies when updating relations and data redundancy in relations. An update anomaly is an unwanted side effect that results from changing a relation.

Consider the relation *assign* in Table 6.3.

Table 6.3 The relation *assign*

assign (FLIGHT	DAY	PILOT	GATE)
112	6 June	Bosley	7
112	7 June	Brooks	7
203	9 June	Bosley	12

FLIGHT DAY is a key for *assign*, and the relation must also satisfy the FD FLIGHT → GATE. We would like to update the relation by specifying values for the key and then giving values for the remaining attributes. However, if we perform

CH(*assign*; 112, 6 June; PILOT = Bosley, GATE = 8),

the relation will violate the FD FLIGHT → GATE. To avoid violating the FD, every time an update is made, we have to scan the relation and update the gate number every place the flight number appears. We wanted to change only one tuple. Furthermore, the flight number-gate number information is duplicated in the relation, thus making the data redundant.

We are better off, with respect to updates and redundancy, if we represent the same information as a database of two relations, *passign* and *gassign*, as shown below.

passign (FLIGHT	DAY	PILOT)
112	6 June	Bosley
112	7 June	Brooks
203	9 June	Bosley

gassign (FLIGHT	GATE)
112	7
203	12

We can reconstruct the original relation *assign* by taking *passign* $\bowtie$ *gassign*. The update anomaly no longer exists, since only one tuple needs to be altered to change a gate assignment. We have also removed some data redundancy, since flight number–gate number pairs are only recorded once.

6.2.3 Second Normal Form

Definition 6.7 Given a set of FDs F and an FD $X \rightarrow Y$ in F^+, Y is *partially dependent* upon X under F if $X \rightarrow Y$ is not left-reduced. That is, there is a proper subset X' of X such that $X' \rightarrow Y$ is in F^+. If $X \rightarrow Y$ is left-reduced, then Y is *fully dependent* on X.

Example 6.7 Let F = {FLIGHT DAY → PILOT GATE, FLIGHT → GATE}. GATE is partially dependent upon FLIGHT DAY, while PILOT is fully dependent upon FLIGHT DAY.

Definition 6.8 Given a relation scheme R, an attribute A in R, and a set of FDs F over R, attribute A is *prime* in R with respect to F if A is contained in some key of R. Otherwise A is *nonprime* in R.

Caveat Lector: Do not confuse the keys in the definition of prime with designated keys for R, as the latter may actually be superkeys. Also, there may be keys for R that are not designated.

Example 6.8 Let R = FLIGHT DAY PILOT GATE and let F be as in Example 6.7. FLIGHT and DAY are prime, PILOT and GATE are nonprime. (We allow the possibility that a pilot can have two flights in one day, so PILOT DAY is not a key.)

Definition 6.9 A relation scheme R is in *second normal form* (2NF) with respect to a set of FDs F if it is in 1NF and every nonprime attribute is fully dependent on every key of R. A database scheme **R** is in *second normal form* with respect to F if every relation scheme R in **R** is in 2NF with respect to F.

Example 6.9 Let R and F be as in Example 6.8 and let **R** = {R}. **R** is not in 2NF because in R, GATE is partially dependent on FLIGHT DAY. If we let **R** = {FLIGHT DAY PILOT, FLIGHT GATE}, then **R** is in 2NF. FLIGHT is now a key for the relation scheme FLIGHT GATE.

6.2.4 Third Normal Form

Consider the relation *assign* in Table 6.4. It is similar to the relation *assign* in Table 6.3. We again assume *assign* has the key FLIGHT DAY and further satisfies the FDs PILOT-ID → NAME and NAME → PILOT-ID.

Table 6.4 The relation *assign*

assign (FLIGHT	DAY	PILOT-ID	NAME)
112	6 June	31174	Bosley
112	7 June	30046	Brooks
203	9 June	31174	Bosley

If we make the update

CH(*assign*; 112, 6 June; PILOT-ID = 31039, NAME = Bosley),

we violate the FD NAME → PILOT-ID. We also have redundant pilot identification-pilot name pairs. The cause of the problem here is not a partially dependent nonprime attribute, although the solution is the same. We represent the relation as a database, as shown below.

passign (FLIGHT	DAY	PILOT-ID)
112	6 June	31174
112	7 June	30046
203	9 June	31174

ident (PILOT-ID	NAME)
31174	Bosley
30046	Brooks

We can still retrieve the original relation through a join.

Definition 6.10 Given a relation scheme R, a subset X of R, an attribute A in R, and a set of FDs F, A is *transitively dependent* upon X in R if there is a subset Y of R with $X \rightarrow Y$, $Y \not\rightarrow X$, and $Y \rightarrow A$ under F and $A \notin X\,Y$.

Example 6.10 Let R = FLIGHT DAY PILOT-ID NAME and let F = {FLIGHT DAY → PILOT-ID NAME, PILOT-ID → NAME, NAME → PILOT-ID}. NAME is transitively dependent upon FLIGHT DAY, since FLIGHT DAY → PILOT-ID, PILOT-ID $\not\rightarrow$ FLIGHT DAY, and PILOT-ID → NAME. PILOT-ID fills the role of Y in the definition.

Definition 6.11 A relation scheme R is in *third normal form* (3NF) with respect to a set of FDs F if it is in 1NF and no nonprime attribute in R is transitively dependent upon a key of R. A database scheme $\mathbf{R}$ is in *third normal form* with respect to F if every relation scheme R in $\mathbf{R}$ is in third normal form with respect to F.

Example 6.11 Let R and F be as in Example 6.10 and let $\mathbf{R} = \{R\}$. $\mathbf{R}$ is not in 3NF with respect to F because of the transitive dependency of NAME on FLIGHT DAY. If $\mathbf{R} = \{$FLIGHT DAY PILOT-ID, PILOT-ID NAME$\}$, then $\mathbf{R}$ is in 3NF with respect to F.

Lemma 6.1 Any relation scheme R that is in 3NF with respect to F is in 2NF with respect to F.

Proof We show that a partial dependency implies a transitive dependency. Suppose nonprime attribute A in R is partially dependent upon key $K \subseteq R$. Then there is a proper subset K' of K such that $F \models K' \rightarrow A$. $K' \not\rightarrow K$, since then K' would be a key for R, and keys cannot properly contain keys. Also, $A \notin K$, since K is a key and A is nonprime. So $K \rightarrow K'$, $K' \not\rightarrow K$, $K' \rightarrow A$, and $A \notin K\,K' = K$. Therefore A is transitively dependent upon K.

6.3 NORMALIZATION THROUGH DECOMPOSITION

It is always possible to start with any relation scheme R that is not in 3NF with respect to a set of FDs F and decompose it into a database scheme that is in 3NF with respect to F. Decomposing a relation scheme means breaking the relation scheme into a pair of relation schemes R_1 and R_2 (possibly intersecting) such that any relation $r(R)$ that satisfies F decomposes losslessly onto R_1 and R_2. That is, $\pi_{R_1}(r) \bowtie \pi_{R_2}(r) = r$. We may have to repeat the decomposition process on R_1 and R_2 if either of them is not in 3NF. We keep decomposing until all the relations we have are in 3NF with respect to F.

Suppose we have a transitive dependency upon a key in R. We have a key $K \subseteq R$, a set $Y \subseteq R$, and a nonprime attribute A in R with $K \rightarrow Y$, $Y \not\rightarrow K$, $Y \rightarrow A$ under F and $A \notin K\,Y$. Let $R_1 = R - A$ and $R_2 = YA$. If we have designated keys for our relation scheme, say $R = (S, \mathbf{K})$, then let $\mathbf{K}$ be the set of designated keys for R_1 and let $\{Y\}$ be the set of designated keys for R_2. It is possible that some designated key K in $\mathbf{K}$ contains A. If so, K is a superkey for R. Let $K' = K - A$. K' is still a superkey for R, since A cannot be part of any key for R. Replace K by K' in $\mathbf{K}$.

We have removed one transitive dependency from R, and for any $r(R)$ satisfying F, $r = \pi_{R_1}(r) \bowtie \pi_{R_2}(r)$ (see Exercise 6.4).

We can decompose again if any transitive dependencies remain in R_1 or R_2. We do not go on decomposing relation schemes forever, though. Every time we decompose a relation scheme, the two resultant relation schemes are smaller, and there can be no transitive dependencies in a relation scheme with only two attributes (see Exercise 6.5).

The decomposition process can be speeded up by checking if there are any other nonprime attributes in $R - (K\,Y)$ that are dependent upon Y. If such attributes exist, they are also transitively dependent upon K and can be removed at the same time. Suppose $A_1, A_2, \ldots, A_m$ are in $R - (K\ Y)$ and are dependent on Y. We then let $R_1 = R - (A_1\ A_2 \cdots A_m)$ and $R_2 = Y\ A_1\ A_2 \cdots A_m$. Again, any relation $r(R)$ that satisfies F decomposes losslessly onto R_1 and R_2.

Example 6.12 Let $R =$

FLIGHT FROM TO DEPARTS ARRIVES DURATION PLANE-TYPE FIRST-CLASS COACH TOTAL-SEATS #MEALS,

where FIRST-CLASS and COACH are the number of seats available in each section. Let the set of designated keys be

K = {FLIGHT, FROM TO DEPARTS, FROM TO ARRIVES}.

We are assuming there cannot be two flights from the same source to the same destination arriving or departing at the same time. Let all the designated keys be actual keys, and suppose we also have the following FDs in our set F.

PLANE-TYPE → FIRST-CLASS COACH TOTAL-SEATS
DEPARTS DURATION → #MEALS
ARRIVES DURATION → #MEALS
FIRST-CLASS COACH → TOTAL-SEATS
FIRST-CLASS TOTAL-SEATS → COACH
COACH TOTAL-SEATS → FIRST-CLASS

It might seem that ARRIVES DEPARTS → DURATION should also be an FD, but the times for ARRIVES and DEPARTS are assumed to be local times, so DURATION depends also on the time zones for the source and destination cities.

We first remove the transitive dependency of #MEALS upon FLIGHT via DEPARTS DURATION. We get the relation scheme

R_1 = FLIGHT FROM TO DEPARTS ARRIVES DURATION PLANE-TYPE FIRST-CLASS COACH TOTAL-SEATS

with designated keys

$\mathbf{K}_1$ = {FLIGHT, FROM TO DEPARTS, FROM TO ARRIVES}

and the relation scheme

$$R_2 = \text{DEPARTS DURATION \#MEALS}$$

with designated key

$$\mathbf{K}_2 = \{\text{DEPARTS DURATION}\}.$$

Scheme R_2 is in 3NF; scheme R_1 is not, since FIRST-CLASS, COACH, and TOTAL-SEATS are all transitively dependent upon FLIGHT via PLANE-TYPE. We decompose R_1 into schemes

$$R_{11} = \text{FLIGHT FROM TO DEPARTS ARRIVES DURATION PLANE-TYPE}$$

with designated keys

$$\mathbf{K}_{11} = \{\text{FLIGHT, FROM TO DEPARTS, FROM TO ARRIVES}\}$$

and

$$R_{12} = \text{PLANE-TYPE FIRST-CLASS COACH TOTAL-SEATS}$$

with designated key

$$\mathbf{K}_{12} = \{\text{PLANE-TYPE}\}.$$

Relation scheme R_{11} is now in 3NF with respect to F, but R_{12} is not, since TOTAL-SEATS is transitively dependent upon PLANE-TYPE via FIRST-CLASS COACH. We decompose R_{12} into

$$R_{121} = \text{PLANE-TYPE FIRST-CLASS COACH}$$

with designated key

$$\mathbf{K}_{121} = \{\text{PLANE-TYPE}\}$$

and relation scheme

$$R_{122} = \text{FIRST-CLASS COACH TOTAL-SEATS}$$

with designated key

$$\mathbf{K}_{122} = \{\text{FIRST-CLASS COACH}\}.$$

We have now decomposed R to the point where every relation scheme is in 3NF with respect to F. Hence, the database scheme

$$\mathbf{R} = \{R_{11}, R_{121}, R_{122}, R_2\}$$

is in 3NF. Furthermore, we can faithfully represent any relation $r(R)$ that satisfies the FDs in F by its projections onto the relation schemes in $\mathbf{R}$, since

$$r = (\pi_{R_{11}}(r) \bowtie (\pi_{R_{121}}(r) \bowtie \pi_{R_{122}}(r))) \bowtie \pi_{R_2}(r).$$

The parentheses are not necessary, since join is commutative and associative. They only serve to point out the stages by which r was losslessly decomposed. If the order of taking the joins is changed, however, the intermediate results may not be meaningful. For example,

$$\pi_{R_{122}}(r) \bowtie \pi_{R_2}(r) \neq \pi_{R_{122}R_2}(r).$$

If the evaluation is done according to the parentheses, every intermediate result is a projection of r.

Database scheme $\mathbf{R}$ is not unique. There are points at which we had a choice of ways to decompose a relation to remove a transitively dependent attribute. At the first step, we could have chosen

$$R_2 = \text{ARRIVES DURATION \#MEALS},$$

since #MEALS is also transitively dependent upon FLIGHT via ARRIVES DURATION. There are three choices for decomposing R_{12} at the third step. (What are they?) Some keys for relation schemes are not picked up as designated keys, such as FIRST-CLASS TOTAL-SEATS and COACH TOTAL-SEATS for R_{122}.

6.4 SHORTCOMINGS OF NORMALIZATION THROUGH DECOMPOSITION

Several problems can arise when normalizing a relation scheme by decomposition. First, the time complexity of the process is probably not polynomially bounded. There can be an exponential number of keys for a relation scheme in terms of the size of the relation scheme and the governing set of FDs (see Exercise 6.8). Also, deciding if an attribute is nonprime in a scheme is an NP-complete problem.

A second problem is that we may end up producing more relation schemes than we really need for 3NF.

Example 6.13 Let relation scheme $R = A\ B\ C\ D\ E$ and let $F = \{A\ B \rightarrow C\ D\ E, A\ C \rightarrow B\ D\ E, B \rightarrow C, C \rightarrow B, C \rightarrow D, B \rightarrow E\}$. The keys for R under F are $A\ B$ and $A\ C$. Using the transitive dependency of D on $A\ B$ via C, we decompose to

$$R_1 = A\ B\ C\ E \qquad \mathbf{K}_1 = \{A\ B,\ A\ C\}$$
$$R_2 = C\ D \qquad \mathbf{K}_2 = \{C\}.$$

We then use the transitive dependency of E on $A\ B$ via B in R_1 to get

$$R_{11} = A\ B\ C \qquad \mathbf{K}_{11} = \{A\ B,\ A\ C\}$$
$$R_{12} = B\ E \qquad \mathbf{K}_{12} = \{B\}.$$

The final 3NF database scheme is

$$\mathbf{R} = \{R_{11}, R_{12}, R_2\}.$$

There is a 3NF decomposition of R into only two relation schemes, namely

$$R_1 = A\ B\ C \qquad \mathbf{K}_1 = \{A\ B,\ A\ C\}$$
$$R_2 = B\ D\ E \qquad \mathbf{K}_2 = \{B\}.$$

A third problem is that we can introduce partial dependencies into a relation scheme through decomposition. The partial dependencies can cause more relation schemes to appear in the final database scheme than are actually needed.

Example 6.14 Let relation scheme $R = A\ B\ C\ D$ and let $F = \{A \rightarrow B\ C\ D, C \rightarrow D\}$. A is the only key for R under F. D is transitively dependent upon A via $B\ C$. Decomposing, we get

$$R_1 = A\ B\ C \qquad \mathbf{K}_1 = \{A\}$$
$$R_2 = B\ C\ D \qquad \mathbf{K}_2 = \{B\ C\}.$$

$B\ C$ is an actual key of R_2, but D is partially dependent upon it. Hence D is transitively dependent upon $B\ C$. Scheme R_2 must be decomposed into

$$R_{21} = B\ C \qquad \mathbf{K}_{21} = \{B\ C\}$$
$$R_{22} = C\ D \qquad \mathbf{K}_{22} = \{C\}.$$

R_1, R_{21} and R_{22} form a 3NF database scheme for R. However, the two relation schemes R_1 and R_{22} also form a 3NF database scheme for R.

This problem can be avoided if we are careful that the intermediary set of attributes in the transitive dependency we decompose with is minimal. In Example 6.14 above, we had D transitively dependent on A via $B\ C$, but $B\ C$ is not minimal. D is transitively dependent upon A via C only.

A fourth problem is that we may create a database scheme on which the set of FDs involved is not enforceable.

Example 6.15 Let relation scheme $R = A\ B\ C\ D\ E$ and let $F = \{A \rightarrow B\ C\ D\ E,\ C\ D \rightarrow E,\ E\ C \rightarrow B\}$. If we eliminate the transitive dependency of E upon A via $C\ D$, we get

$$R_1 = A\ B\ C\ D \qquad \mathbf{K}_1 = \{A\}$$
$$R_2 = C\ D\ E \qquad \mathbf{K}_2 = \{C\ D\}.$$

F is not enforceable on the database scheme $\mathbf{R} = \{R_1, R_2\}$, since $E\ C \rightarrow B$ is not implied by the FDs in F^+ that apply to R_1 or R_2. (This statement must be checked by generating F^+.)

Finally, we can produce relation schemes with "hidden" transitive dependencies through decomposition.

Example 6.16 Let relation scheme $R = A\ B\ C\ D$ and let $F = \{\mathrm{A} \rightarrow B,\ B \rightarrow C\}$. $A\ D$ is a key for F and B is partially dependent on $A\ D$. Decomposing, we get

$$R_1 = A\ C\ D \qquad \mathbf{K}_1 = \{A\ D\}$$
$$R_2 = A\ B \qquad \mathbf{K}_2 = \{A\}.$$

Although R_1 and R_2 are both technically in 3NF, there is still a "hidden" transitive dependency of C on $A\ D$ in R_1.

6.5 NORMALIZATION THROUGH SYNTHESIS

In this section we present another means for achieving third normal form, which avoids the problems associated with decomposition cited in the previous section.

The basic problem we address is finding a 3NF database scheme to represent a relation scheme that is not in 3NF. We assume our input to be a relation scheme R and a set F of FDs over R. With this input, we wish to create a database scheme $\mathbf{R} = \{R_1, R_2, \ldots, R_p\}$ over R with the following four properties:

1. F is completely characterized by $\mathbf{R}$. That is,

$$F \equiv \{K \rightarrow R_i \mid R_i \text{ is in } \mathbf{R} \text{ and } K \text{ is a designated key of } R_i\}.$$

2. Every relation scheme R_i in $\mathbf{R}$ is in 3NF with respect to F.
3. There is no database scheme with fewer relation schemes than $\mathbf{R}$ satisfying properties 1 and 2.
4. For any relation $r(R)$ that satisfies F,

$$r = \pi_{R_1}(r) \bowtie \pi_{R_2}(r) \bowtie \cdots \bowtie \pi_{R_p}(r).$$

We call any database scheme R satisfying properties 1 to 3 above a *complete* database scheme for F.

Let us discuss the reasons for these requirements. Property 1 ensures that F is enforceable on $\mathbf{R}$ and that we know how to enforce it without computing F^+. Property 1 also guarantees that the only FDs we must enforce to make $\mathbf{R}$ obey F are the ones that derive from designated keys. The reasons behind property 2 have already been discussed. Property 3 prevents data redundancy. Property 4 allows us to represent a relation on scheme R faithfully by its projections onto the schemes in $\mathbf{R}$.

We first develop an algorithm using annular covers that produces a complete database scheme for F. We call this algorithm a *synthesis* algorithm, since it constructs the database scheme directly from the FDs in F. We then point out some other useful properties the database schemes synthesized by our algorithm possess. We shall then modify the algorithm so that its output satisfies property 4 and also show how to make some further refinements to the algorithm.

The synthesis algorithm we develop will have polynomial time complexity, since the hardest part of the algorithm is computing a reduced, minimum annular cover for the input set of FDs. Therefore, we avoid the first problem mentioned in the previous section. The second and third problems are avoided by property 3. The fourth problem mentioned is prevented by property 1 and the fifth problem is avoided by properties 1 and 3 together.

6.5.1 Preliminary Results for the Synthesis Algorithm

Lemma 6.2 If **R** is a database scheme representing the set of FDs G, then there are at least $|\bar{E}_G|$ relation schemes in **R**. That is, there are at least as many relation schemes in **R** as there are equivalence classes in $\bar{E}_G$.

Proof All the FDs embodied by a single relation scheme R in **R** must have equivalent left sides. If K_1 and K_2 are designated keys for R, then $K_1 \to R$ and $K_2 \to R$, hence $K_1 \to K_2$ and $K_2 \to K_1$. Therefore, each relation scheme in R can embody FDs from at most one equivalence class in $\bar{E}_G$. To represent all the FDs in G, we need at least $|\bar{E}_G|$ relation schemes in **R**.

Corollary Let F be a set of FDs. Any database scheme **R** that completely characterizes F must have at least $|\bar{E}_{F'}|$ relation schemes, where F' is a nonredundant cover for F.

Proof By Lemma 6.2, we know if G is the set of FDs represented by **R**, then $|\bar{E}_G| \geq |\bar{E}_{F'}|$, since $G \equiv F \equiv F'$ and F' is nonredundant.

6.5.2 Developing the Synthesis Algorithm

The corollary to Lemma 6.2 suggests a way to synthesize a complete database scheme for a set F of FDs. We find a nonredundant cover F' for F and compute the equivalence classes in $\bar{E}_{F'}$. For each $E_{F'}(X)$ in $\bar{E}_{F'}$, we construct a relation scheme R consisting of all attributes appearing in any FDs of $E_{F'}(X)$. We let $e_{F'}(X)$ be the set of designated keys for R. The database scheme **R** consists of all relation schemes so synthesized. **R** certainly has the minimum possible number of relation schemes, by the corollary to Lemma 6.2. It is also possible to show that **R** completely characterizes F (see Exercise 6.11). However, the relation schemes may not be in 3NF with respect to F, as the next example shows.

Example 6.17 Let $F = F' = \{A \to B\ C,\ B \to C\}$ and let $R = A\ B\ C$. The procedure outlined above gives relation scheme

$$R_1 = A\ B\ C \quad \text{with designated key } \mathbf{K}_1 = \{A\}$$

and relation scheme

$$R_2 = B\ C \quad \text{with designated key } \mathbf{K}_2 = \{B\}.$$

Relation R_1 is not in 3NF with respect to F. (Why?)

The problem in Example 6.17 arises from F not being reduced. The next example shows that even with a reduced set of FDs, we are not guaranteed a 3NF database scheme.

Example 6.18 Let F be the FDs

$B_1\ B_2 \to A$	$D_1\ D_2 \to B_1\ B_2$
$B_1 \to C_1$	$B_2 \to C_2$
$D_1 \to A$	$D_2 \to A$
$A\ B_1\ C_2 \to D_2$	$A\ B_2\ C_1 \to D_1$

and let $R = A\ B_1\ B_2\ C_1\ C_2\ D_1\ D_2$. This is the same set of FDs as in Example 5.21. The only two FDs that are in an equivalence class together are $B_1\ B_2 \to A$ and $D_1\ D_2 \to B_1\ B_2$. The relation scheme produced from this equivalence class is

$$R = A\ B_1\ B_2\ D_1\ D_2, \quad \text{with designated keys } \mathbf{K} = \{B_1\ B_2,\ D_1\ D_2\}.$$

R is not in 3NF, since A is transitively dependent upon $B_1\ B_2$ via D_1.

Finding a minimum cover for F does not help the situation, as the set F in Example 6.18 is minimum. Attribute A is the problem here just as it was in Example 5.21. If we use annular covers, as before, our problems are solved. A synthesis algorithm using annular covers is given as Algorithm 6.1.

Algorithm 6.1 SYNTHESIZE
Input: A set of FDs F over $\mathbf{U}$.
Output: A complete database scheme for F.
SYNTHESIZE(F)

1. Find a reduced, minimum annular cover G for F.
2. For each CFD $(X_1, X_2, \ldots, X_k) \to Y$ in G, construct a relation scheme $R = X_1\ X_2 \cdots X_k\ Y$ with designated keys $\mathbf{K} = \{X_1, X_2, \ldots, X_k\}$.
3. Return the set of relation schemes constructed in step 2.

Example 6.19 Let F be the set of FDs

$$
\begin{array}{lll}
A \rightarrow B_1\, B_2\, C_1\, C_2\, D\, E\, I_1\, I_2\, I_3\, J & & \\
B_1\, B_2\, C_1 \rightarrow A\, C_2\, D\, E\, I_1\, I_2\, I_3\, J & & \\
B_1\, B_2\, C_2 \rightarrow A\, C_1\, D\, E\, I_1\, I_2\, I_3\, J & & \\
E \rightarrow I_1\, I_2\, I_3 & & \\
C_1\, D \rightarrow J & C_2\, D \rightarrow J & \\
I_1\, I_2 \rightarrow I_3 & I_2\, I_3 \rightarrow I_1 & I_1\, I_3 \rightarrow I_2
\end{array}
$$

and let $R = A\, B_1\, B_2\, C_1\, C_2\, D\, E\, I_1\, I_2\, I_3\, J$.

We are using the same FDs as in Example 6.12; we have only renamed the attributes. Set F is minimum, but not reduced. Reducing F we get $F' =$

$$
\begin{array}{lll}
\{A \rightarrow B_1\, B_2\, C_1\, C_2\, D\, E & & E \rightarrow I_1\, I_2 \\
\;B_1\, B_2\, C_1 \rightarrow A & & B_1\, B_2\, C_2 \rightarrow A \\
\;C_1\, D \rightarrow J & & C_2\, D \rightarrow J \\
\;I_1\, I_2 \rightarrow I_3 & I_2\, I_3 \rightarrow I_1 & I_1\, I_3 \rightarrow I_2\}.
\end{array}
$$

Converting to an annular cover and making the obvious reductions we get $G =$

$$
\begin{array}{ll}
\{(A,\, B_1\, B_2\, C_1,\, B_1\, B_2\, C_2) \rightarrow D\, E & \\
\;(E) \rightarrow I_1\, I_2 & \\
\;(C_1\, D) \rightarrow J & (C_2\, D) \rightarrow J \\
\;(I_1\, I_2,\, I_2\, I_3,\, I_1\, I_3)\}. &
\end{array}
$$

Converting each CFD to a relation scheme with designated keys we get

$$
\begin{array}{ll}
R_1 = A\, B_1\, B_2\, C_1\, C_2\, D\, E & \mathbf{K}_1 = \{A,\, B_1\, B_2\, C_1,\, B_1\, B_2\, C_2\} \\
R_2 = E\, I_1\, I_2 & \mathbf{K}_2 = \{E\} \\
R_3 = C_1\, D\, J & \mathbf{K}_3 = \{C_1\, D\} \\
R_4 = C_2\, D\, J & \mathbf{K}_4 = \{C_2\, D\} \\
R_5 = I_1\, I_2\, I_3 & \mathbf{K}_5 = \{I_1\, I_2,\, I_2\, I_3,\, I_1\, I_3\}.
\end{array}
$$

The final database scheme is $\mathbf{R} = \{R_1,\ R_2, R_3, R_4, R_5\}$.

6.5.3 Correctness and Other Properties of the Synthesis Algorithm

Lemma 6.3 Let $\mathbf{R}$ be a database scheme produced by SYNTHESIZE from a set of FDs F. For any relation scheme R_i in $\mathbf{R}$, every designated key of R_i is a key.

Proof Let $(X_1, X_2, \ldots, X_k) \rightarrow Y$ be the CFD from which R_i was synthesized. Let K be a designated key for R_i that is not a key. $K = X_j$ for some X_j in the left side of the CFD. Since K is not a key, X_j contains a shiftable attribute. Hence, $(X_1, X_2, \ldots, X_k) \rightarrow Y$ is not reduced, a contradiction.

Theorem 6.1 SYNTHESIZE constructs a complete database scheme for a set of FDs F in $O(n^2)$ time on inputs of length n.

Proof First, we show the time complexity of SYNTHESIZE is $O(n^2)$. The time spent in steps 2 and 3 of the algorithm is dominated by the time spent in step 1. From the observations in Section 5.8, we know that step 1 can be implemented to run in $O(n^2)$ time.

Let **R** be the result of SYNTHESIZE(F). **R** completely characterizes F, since the set of embodied FDs for any relation scheme R in **R** is a characteristic set for the CFD from which R was synthesized (see Exercise 5.24). From Lemma 5.10 and the corollary to Lemma 6.2, we see that **R** has a minimum number of relation schemes among all database schemes that completely characterize F.

All that remains to be proved is that all the relation schemes in **R** are in 3NF with respect to F. Consider a relation R_i in **R**, with designated keys $K_i = \{X_1, X_2, \ldots, X_i\}$, that was synthesized from the CFD $(X_1, X_2, \ldots, X_k) \rightarrow Y$. If attribute A is nonprime in R_i, then A is in Y, since every X_j in K_i is a key for R_i, by Lemma 6.3. Let X be a key for R_i (not necessarily a designated key). Suppose there is a subset Z of R_i such that F implies $X \rightarrow Z$ and $Z \rightarrow A$, F does not imply $Z \rightarrow X$, and $A \notin X Z$. Form F' from the set G of CFDs in SYNTHESIZE by taking natural characteristic sets for every CFD in G. Consider an F'-based DDAG H for $Z \rightarrow A$. $U(H)$ can contain no FDs from $E_{F'}(X)$, which is the natural characteristic set for $(X_1, X_2, \ldots, X_k) \rightarrow Y$. If it did, we would have $Z \rightarrow X$ under F. Thus, if we remove A from Y, we still can prove $Z \rightarrow A$ from F', hence $(X_1, X_2, \ldots, X_k) \rightarrow Y$ is not reduced.

The proof of Theorem 6.1 uses both conditions for a reduced CFD: no shiftable attributes on the left side and no extraneous attributes on the right side. We cannot simplify SYNTHESIZE by leaving out either part of the reduction step. The proof of Theorem 6.1 actually demonstrates a slightly stronger result than the statement of the theorem, namely, that no attribute in a relation scheme produced by the synthesis algorithm is transitively dependent upon a key unless it is contained in a designated key. The next example shows it is possible to have a 3NF database scheme where this stronger condition does not hold.

Example 6.20 Let $R = A\,B\,C\,D\,E$ and let $F = \{A \rightarrow B,\ B \rightarrow A\,E,\ A\,C \rightarrow D\}$. Consider the database scheme **R** for F consisting of the relation schemes

$$\begin{array}{ll} R_1 = A\,B\,C\,D & \text{with designated key } \mathbf{K}_1 = \{A\,C\}, \text{ and} \\ R_2 = A\,B\,E & \text{with designated keys } \mathbf{K}_2 = \{A,\ B\}. \end{array}$$

R_1 is in 3NF since B is prime ($B\,C$ is a key), although B is partially dependent upon $A\,C$.

There are two other properties we can prove about database schemes produced by SYNTHESIZE.

Lemma 6.4 Let **R** be the database scheme constructed by SYNTHESIZE from a set of FDs F. There is no complete database scheme for F with fewer designated keys.

Proof Left to the reader (see Exercise 6.15).

Consider the 3NF database scheme **R** consisting of relation schemes

$$\begin{aligned} R_1 &= \underline{A\,B}\,D \\ R_2 &= \underline{A\,C} \\ R_3 &= \underline{B\,C}\,D \end{aligned}$$

where the underlined attributes are designated and actual keys and there are no other FDs. Notice that $A\,B \rightarrow B\,C$, $B\,C \not\rightarrow A\,B$, and $B\,C \rightarrow D$. R_1 is in 3NF, since $B\,C \not\subseteq R_1$. However, D can be removed from R_1 without changing the closure of the set of FDs represented by **R**.

Definition 6.12 Let R be a relation scheme in database scheme **R** over **U** and let F be a set of FDs. Let $X \subseteq R$ and $A \in R$. A is *externally dependent* upon X under F if there is a subset Y of **U** such that Y is not a subset of R and $X \rightarrow Y$, $Y \not\rightarrow X$, and $Y \rightarrow A$ under F and $A \notin X\,Y$.

An external dependency is what we were calling a hidden transitive dependency in Example 6.16. External dependencies cannot always be avoided in 3NF database schemes.

Example 6.21 Let **R** be the database scheme composed of the relation schemes

$$\begin{array}{ll} R_1 = A\,B & \text{with designated key } \mathbf{K}_1 = \{A\}, \text{ and} \\ R_2 = B\,C & \text{with designated keys } \mathbf{K}_2 = \{B,\ C\}. \end{array}$$

Let F be the set of FDs represented by **R**. B is externally dependent upon A under F, since $A \rightarrow C$, $C \not\rightarrow A$, and $C \rightarrow B$, but B cannot be removed from R_1 without changing the closure of the set of FDs **R** represents.

Let **R** be a 3NF database scheme over **U**. Let G be the set of FDs that **R** represents and let R be a relation scheme in **R**. Suppose attribute A in R is externally dependent upon key K of R via a set $Y \subseteq \mathbf{U}$, where $Y \not\subseteq R$. Unless $K' \rightarrow A$ is necessary to derive $K \rightarrow Y$, for some designated key K' of R, A can be removed from R without changing the closure of G, since G still would imply $K \rightarrow Y$ and $Y \rightarrow A$. $Y \rightarrow A$ still holds because any G-based DDAG H for $Y \rightarrow A$ cannot use any FD in $E_G(K)$, or else $Y \rightarrow K$.

Definition 6.13 Let **R** be a 3NF database scheme over **U** and let G be the set of FDs that **R** represents. Let R be a relation scheme in **R**. Attribute A in R is *removable* in R if removing A from R does not change the closure of G. (Removing A implies removing any designated key of R containing A.)

Complete 3NF database schemes derived by decomposition do not contain removable attributes (see Exercise 6.17). The same holds for synthesized database schemes.

Lemma 6.5 If **R** is the database scheme produced by SYNTHESIZE from a set of FDs F, then no relation scheme R in **R** contains a removable attribute.

Proof Suppose R contains a removable attribute A. Let $(X_1, X_2, \ldots, X_k) \rightarrow Y$ be the CFD from which R was synthesized. A cannot be in any X_i in the left side of the CFD. If A were in some X_i, since A is removable, either X_i is not a key, contradicting Lemma 6.3, or X_i can be removed completely from $(X_1, X_2, \ldots, X_k) \rightarrow Y$, contradicting Lemma 6.4. We conclude A is in Y. Therefore, $(X_1, X_2, \ldots, X_k) \rightarrow Y$ is not reduced, since A is extraneous in Y. Hence, A does not appear in $(X_1, X_2, \ldots, X_k) \rightarrow Y$, contradicting the construction of R.

6.5.4 Refinements of the Synthesis Algorithm

Although synthesis solves the problems associated with decomposition listed in Section 6.4, there is one shortcoming of synthesis that is not shared by decomposition. In a 3NF database scheme **R**, obtained from a single relation scheme R and a set of FDs F by decomposition, we know that any relation $r(R)$ satisfying F decomposes losslessly onto the relation schemes in **R**. The same is not true if **R** is obtained by synthesis.

Example 6.22 Let $F = \{A \to C, B \to C\}$. SYNTHESIZE(F) produces the relation schemes

$$R_1 = \underline{A}\,C \quad \text{and} \quad R_2 = \underline{B}\,C,$$

where the underlined attributes are the designated keys. However, the relation r shown below does not decompose losslessly onto R_1 and R_2.

$r(A$	B	$C)$
a	b	c
a'	b'	c

Definition 6.14 A database scheme **R** over **U** has the *lossless join property* with respect to a set of FDs F if any relation $r(\mathbf{U})$ that satisfies F decomposes losslessly onto the relation schemes of **R**.

Property 4 at the beginning of Section 6.5 says that the database scheme **R** we synthesize must have the lossless join property with respect to the set of FDs **R** represents. Example 6.22 shows that a database scheme produced by synthesis does not necessarily have the lossless join property. There is a related problem involving attributes in **R** that are not mentioned in the dependencies of F. They do not show up in the database scheme synthesized from F. However, a minor modification of SYNTHESIZE will solve both problems.

Definition 6.15 Let **R** be a database scheme over **U** and let G be the set of FDs that **R** represents. A subset X of **U** is a *universal key* for R if $G \models X \to \mathbf{U}$. We make no requirement for the minimality of X.

We shall see in Chapter 8 that if some relation scheme in a database scheme R contains a universal key, then **R** has the lossless join property with respect to the set of represented FDs, and conversely. The problem with the synthesis algorithm is that there may be no relation scheme in **R** containing a universal key. Such is the case in Example 6.22. The problem can be remedied by adding a relation scheme consisting solely of the attributes in some universal key. This addition technically violates the minimality constraint on R, but we shall look the other way during such transgressions.

The modification to SYNTHESIZE is to add the FD $\mathbf{U} \to C$ to F as the first step, where C is an attribute not contained in **U**. In finding the annular cover G for F, $\mathbf{U} \to C$ will not be eliminated as redundant, since no other FD in F has C on the right side. $\mathbf{U} \to C$ may be combined with the FD $X \to Y$

when finding a minimum cover for F, but then $X \leftrightarrow \mathbf{U}$ and X must be a universal key. During the reduction stage of finding G, $\mathbf{U}$ may be reduced to $\mathbf{U}'$ by removing shiftable attributes (or X reduced to X' in the same way), but $\mathbf{U}' \rightarrow \mathbf{U}$ holds, so $\mathbf{U}'$ is a universal key.

Some relation scheme R_i is synthesized from the CFD containing $\mathbf{U}'$ as a left set, and hence $\mathbf{U}$ will have a universal key in one of its relation schemes and the lossless join property with respect to F. At the end of the algorithm, attribute C can be removed from the relation scheme in which it appears. (It will only appear in one.)

Example 6.23 Let $F = \{A \rightarrow C, B \rightarrow C\}$. We add $A\ B\ C \rightarrow D$ to F, convert to an annular cover, and reduce, to get $G = \{(A) \rightarrow C, (B) \rightarrow C, (A\ B) \rightarrow D\}$. The CFD $(A\ B) \rightarrow D$ is used to synthesize the relation scheme $R_1 = A\ B\ D$ with designated key $\mathbf{K}_1 = \{A\ B\}$. R_1 contains the universal key $A\ B$. D can be removed from R_1.

6.6 AVOIDABLE ATTRIBUTES

We have seen that SYNTHESIZE(F) produces a complete database scheme $\mathbf{R}$ for F with no removable attributes. It may still be possible to remove an attribute from a relation scheme R in $\mathbf{R}$ by changing the set of designated keys.

Example 6.24 Let $F = \{A \rightarrow B, B \rightarrow A, A\ C \rightarrow D\ E, B\ D \rightarrow C\}$. SYNTHESIZE($F$) produces a database scheme $\mathbf{R}$ containing the relation schemes $R_1 = A\ B$ with designated keys $\mathbf{K}_1 = \{A, B\}$ and $R_2 = A\ B\ C\ D\ E$ with designated keys $\mathbf{K}_2 = \{A\ C, B\ D\}$. B is not removable from R_2, since it belongs to a designated key. If K_2 is changed to $\{A\ C, A\ D\}$, $\mathbf{R}$ still completely characterizes F and B becomes removable.

Definition 6.16 Let $\mathbf{R}$ be a complete database scheme for a set of FDs F. Let R_i be a relation scheme in $\mathbf{R}$, and let B be an attribute in R_i. B is *avoidable* in R_i if changing the designated keys of R_i makes B removable in R_i.

An avoidable attribute in a database scheme produced by SYNTHESIZE must belong to a designated key of some relation scheme, otherwise it is removable. It might seem as if finding an alternative set of designated keys for a relation scheme R that preserves the enforceability of F is as hard as finding all the keys of R. If R was generated by SYNTHESIZE, it is possible to find a set of alternative keys, if one exists, without generating every key or set of keys for R. The designated keys in R correspond to the left sides of FDs in a single equivalence class in a minimum cover of F, and we know a great deal about the structure of minimum covers.

Suppose relation scheme R in database scheme $\mathbf{R}$ was synthesized from the CFD $(X_1, X_2, \ldots, X_k) \rightarrow Y$ in a minimum, reduced annular cover G for F. Thus, the set of designated keys for R is $\mathbf{K} = \{X_1, X_2, \ldots, X_k\}$. $X_1, X_2, \ldots, X_k$ are left sides of FDs in a single equivalence class $E_{F'}(X)$ for some minimum cover F' for F. Therefore, we know that any alternative set of keys $\mathbf{K}' = \{Z_1, Z_2, \ldots, Z_m\}$ must have $m \geq k$, if the enforceability of F is to be preserved. If $m > k$, then $Z_i \dot{\rightarrow} Z_j$ for some i and j. Z_i can be removed from $\mathbf{K}'$ without changing the closure of the set of FDs represented by $\mathbf{R}$. Therefore we shall assume that any alternative set of keys we seek will have exactly k members.

Let $\mathbf{K}' = \{Z_1, Z_2, \ldots, Z_k\}$ be an alternative set of designated keys for R. We know direct determination induces a one-to-one correspondence between the elements of $\mathbf{K}$ and $\mathbf{K}'$, since they both can be used as left sides for an equivalence class in some minimum cover for F. Assume $Z_1, Z_2, \ldots, Z_k$ are numbered so $X_i \dot{\rightarrow} Z_i$ and $Z_i \dot{\rightarrow} X_i$, $1 \leq i \leq k$, under F.

Let us try to remember where we are headed. We are trying to detect if some attribute B in R is avoidable by finding a replacement set of designated keys for R that does not use B. We assume that $\mathbf{K}'$ above is such a set. We may further assume that $X_i = Z_i$ if $B \notin X_i$. If not, since $Z_i \dot{\rightarrow} X_i$, we can replace Z_i by X_i in $\mathbf{K}'$ without reintroducing B and still keep $\mathbf{R}$ a complete database scheme for F.

We have narrowed the problem down considerably. Starting with the set $\mathbf{K} = \{X_1, X_2, \ldots, X_k\}$ of designated keys for R, for each X_i in $\mathbf{K}$ containing B, we are looking for a replacement key Z_i not containing B with $X_i \dot{\rightarrow} Z_i$ and $Z_i \dot{\rightarrow} X_i$ under F. Note that Z_i must be contained in R, or we cannot use it as a replacement key for X_i. AVOID in Algorithm 6.2 finds an alternative set of designated keys for R not containing B, if such exists. AVOID assumes a procedure DCLOSURE(X, F) that returns the maximum set X' such that $X \dot{\rightarrow} X'$ under F.

Algorithm 6.2 AVOID
Input: A relation scheme R produced by SYNTHESIZE(F), with designated keys $\mathbf{K}$, and an attribute B in R, and the set F of FDs.
Output: An alternative set of designated keys for R not containing B, if such a set exists; $\emptyset$ otherwise.

AVOID(R, B, F)
  begin
  $\mathbf{K}' := \mathbf{K}$; fail := *false*;
  for each X_i in **K** **do**
    if $B \in X_i$ **then begin**
      $M :=$ DCLOSURE(X_i, F);
      $M' := (M \cap R) - B$;
      if DCLOSURE(M', F) $\supseteq X_i$ **then**
        replace X_i in $\mathbf{K}'$ by a minimal subset Z of M' such that $Z \dot{\rightarrow} X_i$
        else fail := *true*
      end;
  if fail = *false* **then**
    return($\mathbf{K}'$)
    else return($\emptyset$)
  end.

Example 6.25 Let F, R_1, and R_2 be as in Example 6.24. AVOID(R_2, B, F) will only consider BD in $\mathbf{K}_2$ for replacement. M will be ABD and M' will be $A\,D$. $A\,D \dot{\rightarrow} B\,D$ under F, so $A\,D$ can replace $B\,D$ in $\mathbf{K}_2$.

We shall not spend more time with AVOID to derive its time complexity, which is polynomial, or prove its correctness (see Exercise 6.20). We can use AVOID to eliminate avoidable attributes from a relation scheme R in a database scheme **R** produced by SYNTHESIZE(F). For each attribute B in R, we run AVOID(R, B, F). If AVOID returns something other than $\emptyset$, we replace the set of designated keys for R by the alternative set provided by AVOID. We know that if such a set of keys exists, B must be removable when the set of keys is used. $R - B \rightarrow B$ can be derived from the new set of FDs represented by **R**, since there must be a new designated key K for R with $K \dot{\rightarrow} B$. (K is one of the replacement keys found by AVOID. See Exercises 6.21 and 6.22.)

A complete database scheme with no avoidable attributes is in *LTK normal form* (for Ling, Tompa, and Kameda). Exercise 6.23 gives another characterization of LTK normal form.

6.7 BOYCE-CODD NORMAL FORM

We saw that our synthesis algorithm yielded relation schemes that were in a form slightly stronger than 3NF in that any attribute in a designated key was not transitively dependent upon any key. We now ask the question, is it possible to remove all transitive dependencies? The answer is a qualified yes. Starting with a relation scheme R with FDs F, we can find a database scheme $\mathbf{R}$ for R with no transitive dependencies, but F may be unenforceable on $\mathbf{R}$.

First, let us see why we might want to remove a prime attribute that is transitively dependent upon a key.

Example 6.26 Consider a relation *billto* on the relation scheme AIRPORT COMPANY OFFICE. The meaning of a tuple $\langle a\ c\ f \rangle$ in *billto* is that if someone from company c charges a ticket at airport a, the bill should be sent to office f of the company. We thus have the two FDs AIRPORT COMPANY $\rightarrow$ OFFICE and OFFICE $\rightarrow$ COMPANY. AIRPORT OFFICE is a key for the relation scheme, and COMPANY is partially, hence transitively, dependent upon AIRPORT OFFICE. Although COMPANY is a prime attribute, it is still desirable to remove it from the relation scheme, since there is a duplication of COMPANY-OFFICE pairs.

Definition 6.17 A relation scheme R is in *Boyce-Codd normal form* (BCNF) with respect to a set of FDs F if it is in 1NF and no attribute in R is transitively dependent upon any key of R. A database scheme $\mathbf{R}$ is in *Boyce-Codd normal form* with respect to a set of FDs F if every relation scheme R in $\mathbf{R}$ is in Boyce-Codd normal form with respect to F.

BCNF implies 3NF (see Exercise 6.24). The relation scheme AIRPORT COMPANY OFFICE in Example 6.26 is not in BCNF. The following is an alternative definition of BCNF (see Exercise 6.25).

Definition 6.18 A relation scheme R is in *Boyce-Codd normal form* with respect to a set of FDs F if for every subset Y of R and for every attribute $A \in R - Y$, if $Y \rightarrow A$, then $Y \rightarrow R$ under F. That is, if Y non-trivially determines any attribute of R, then Y is a superkey for R.

We can always use decomposition to find a BCNF database scheme for a relation scheme that is not in BCNF. If $Y \rightarrow A$ under F for relation scheme R with $Y \subseteq R$ and $A \in R - Y$, and if Y is not a key for R, then decompose R into $R_1 = R - A$ and $R_2 = YA$. The designated keys for R_1 and R_2 are produced in the same manner as for 3NF database schemes.

Example 6.27 Let relation scheme R = AIRPORT COMPANY OFFICE with the FDs given in Example 6.26. Using the FD OFFICE $\rightarrow$ COMPANY, we decompose R into

$R_1 =$ AIRPORT OFFICE with designated key $\mathbf{K}_1 = \{$AIRPORT OFFICE$\}$

and

$R_2 =$ COMPANY OFFICE with designated key $\mathbf{K}_2 = \{$OFFICE$\}$.

Unfortunately, the synthesis approach does not guarantee BCNF.

Example 6.28 Let $R = A\ B\ C\ D\ E$ and let $F = \{A \rightarrow B\ C,\ B\ C \rightarrow A,\ B\ C\ D \rightarrow E,\ E \rightarrow C\}$. The annular cover for F produced by SYNTHESIZE is

$$G = \{(A,\ B\ C),\ (B\ C\ D) \rightarrow E,\ (E) \rightarrow C\}.$$

The second CFD in G yields the relation scheme

$$R_2 = B\ C\ D\ E \quad \text{with designated key } \mathbf{K}_2 = \{B\ C\ D\}.$$

R_2 is not in BCNF since $E \rightarrow C$ and E is not a key of R_2. Choosing an equivalent annular cover

$$G' = \{(A,\ B\ C),\ (A\ D) \rightarrow E,\ (E) \rightarrow C\}$$

will produce a database scheme in BCNF.

6.7.1 Problems with Boyce-Codd Normal Form

We have seen that given a set of FDs F over R, it is possible to find a 3NF database scheme that completely characterizes F. The same is not true for BCNF. Exhaustive consideration of Example 6.26 will show there is no BCNF database scheme completely characterizing the given set of FDs. We are faced with a choice of BCNF or enforceable FDs.

Not only is it possible for a set of FDs not to have a complete BCNF database scheme, it is NP-complete to decide if a given database scheme is in BCNF.

6.8 EXERCISES

6.1* Assume we restrict database schemes over $\mathbf{U}$ so that for any two relation schemes R_1 and R_2 in a database scheme, $R_1 \not\subseteq R_2$. Let $\mathbf{U}$ contain

n attributes. How many database schemes of p relation schemes are there over **U** (ignoring keys)?

6.2 Let database scheme $\mathbf{R} = \{A\,B\,C,\ A\,D\,E,\ C\,E\}$. Prove that the set of FDs $F = \{A\,B \rightarrow C,\ C \rightarrow E,\ E \rightarrow C,\ C \rightarrow D,\ A\,B \rightarrow E\}$ is enforceable on **R**.

6.3 Give an example of a relation in 3NF that has some prime attribute transitively dependent upon a key.

6.4 Let R_1 and R_2 be relation schemes with $R_1 \cap R_2 = X$. Show that for any relation $r(R_1\,R_2)$ that satisfies $X \rightarrow R_2$,

$$r = \pi_{R_1}(r) \bowtie \pi_{R_2}(r).$$

6.5 Let F be a set of FDs containing no FDs of the form $\emptyset \rightarrow Y$. Show that any relation scheme R with two attributes can have no transitive dependencies under F.

6.6 Let R = STUDENT# NAME BIRTHDAY AGE ADVISOR DEPARTMENT SEMESTER COURSE GRADE, with key STUDENT# SEMESTER COURSE and FDs STUDENT# $\rightarrow$ NAME BIRTHDAY AGE ADVISOR DEPARTMENT, BIRTHDAY $\rightarrow$ AGE, and ADVISOR $\rightarrow$ DEPARTMENT. Find a 3NF database scheme for R.

6.7 Find a relation $r(R)$ such that r decomposes losslessly onto some set of three relation schemes, but r does not decompose losslessly onto any pair of relation schemes. In both cases assume no relation scheme is the same as R.

6.8 (a) Show that a set of $2n$ FDs can induce 2^n keys on a relation scheme with $2n$ attributes.

(b) Try to generalize the result of part a) to sets of m FDs on relation schemes with n attributes.

6.9 Let $\mathbf{R} = \{R_1, R_2, \ldots, R_p\}$ be a database scheme over **U** where $R_1 \subseteq R_2$. Show that if a relation $r(\mathbf{U})$ decomposes losslessly onto the schemes in **R**, then r decomposes losslessly onto the relation schemes in $\mathbf{R}' = \{R_2, R_3, \ldots, R_p\}$, and conversely.

6.10 Give a set of FDs F and a database scheme **R** completely characterizing F, such that **R** has more than $|\bar{E}_F|$ relation schemes, yet no relation scheme can be removed from **R** and still have **R** completely characterize F.

6.11 Show that the method for producing a database scheme **R** from a set of FDs F by using a nonredundant cover F' for F (as outlined at the beginning of Section 6.5.2) guarantees that **R** completely characterizes F.

6.12 Compare the database schemes produced by decomposition and synthesis in Examples 6.12 and 6.19.

6.13 Show that SYNTHESIZE may not work correctly if some CFD in the annular cover G contains either shiftable or extraneous attributes.

6.14 Use both synthesis and decomposition to obtain a 3NF database scheme for the set of FDs in Example 5.13.

6.15 Prove Lemma 6.4.

6.16 Give an example of a relation scheme R in a database scheme $\mathbf{R}$ with an external dependency $K \rightarrow Y$, $Y \nrightarrow K$, $Y \rightarrow A$, where K is a key of R, $A \nrightarrow Y$, but A is not removable in R.

6.17* Prove that any complete database scheme $\mathbf{R}$ for a set of FDs F produced by decomposition from a single relation scheme R does not contain any removable attributes.

Definition 6.19 Let F be a set of FDs, let $\mathbf{R} = \{R_1, R_2, \ldots, R_p\}$ be a database scheme, and let G be the set of FDs in F^+ that apply to relation schemes in $\mathbf{R}$. F is *indirectly enforceable* on $\mathbf{R}$ if $\mathbf{R}$ has the lossless join property with respect to G.

6.18* Prove that for any database scheme $\mathbf{R}$ produced by decomposition from a relation scheme R and a set of FDs F, F is indirectly enforceable on $\mathbf{R}$.

6.19 Consider the algorithm SYNTHESIZE as modified in Section 6.5.4. Show that adding $R \rightarrow C$ to F does not produce an extra designated key unless it produces an extra relation scheme. Show that $R \rightarrow C$ does not produce an extra relation scheme if there is an FD $X \rightarrow Y$ in F with $X \rightarrow R$ under F.

6.20 Find the complexity of Algorithm 6.2 in Section 6.6. You may assume that information calculated by SYNTHESIZE is available to AVOID.

6.21 Let R be a relation scheme in a complete database scheme $\mathbf{R}$. Show that if B is not avoidable in R, then B is not avoidable in any relation scheme R' obtained by changing the designated keys of R and removing removable attributes.

6.22 Give an algorithm to put a complete database scheme produced by SYNTHESIZE into LTK normal form.

6.23* Let $\mathbf{R}$ be a complete BCNF database scheme for the set of FDs F and let R be a relation scheme in $\mathbf{R}$. Let B be an attribute in R. Let $\mathbf{R}'$ be the database scheme obtained by removing B from R in $\mathbf{R}$. Let F' be the subset of F^+ that applies to some relation scheme in $\mathbf{R}'$. Prove that B is avoidable in $\mathbf{R}$ if and only if $F \equiv F'$.

6.24 Show that BCNF implies 3NF.

6.25 Prove the equivalence of the two definitions of BCNF in Section 6.7.

6.26 Exhibit a database scheme that is in BCNF but not LTK normal form and vice versa.

6.9 BIBLIOGRAPHY AND COMMENTS

Second and third normal forms were introduced by Codd [1971b, 1972a], who showed how to achieve them through normalization. Kent [1973] provides an introduction to normal forms. Early proposals for synthesis algorithms were given by Delobel and Casey [1973] and Wang and Wedekind [1975], but they contained some imperfections. Bernstein [1976b] was the first to give a synthesis algorithm for a complete database scheme for a set of FDs. Osborn [1977], Dayal and Bernstein [1978a], and Biskup, Dayal, and Bernstein [1979] discuss 3NF database schemes that meet the lossless join condition. Other algorithms for 3NF schemes are given by Beeri and Bernstein [1979] and Pichat and Delobel [1979]. Avoidable attributes were introduced by Ling, Tompa, and Kameda [1981], who propose an algorithm for their removal. BCNF was introduced by Codd [1974].

Fagin [1977] compares decomposition and synthesis for achieving normal form schemes. Beeri, Bernstein, and Goodman [1978] discuss the goals of normalization. Heath [1971] attempts to classify update anomalies by their severity. They also point out that there can be many normalized schemes for a given set of dependencies, and there is no clear criterion for which is the "best". Bernstein and Goodman [1980b] raise questions about how well BCNF avoids update anomalies.

Lucchesi and Osborn [1978] show that several problems connected with normalization, such as finding nonprime attributes and minimum keys, are NP-complete. Beeri and Bernstein [1979] use those results to show that determining if a given database scheme is in BCNF and determining whether a set of FDs has a complete BCNF scheme are NP-complete problems. Osborn [1979a] and LeDoux and Parker [1980] give algorithms for determining if a set of FDs has a complete BCNF scheme, although both can use exponential time in the worst case. Tsou and Fischer [1980] give a polynomial-time algorithm for finding a BCNF database scheme for a set of FDs with the lossless join property, but the scheme may not be complete. Jou [1980] and Tsou [1980] both examine complexity issues related to normalization.

Chapter 7

MULTIVALUED DEPENDENCIES, JOIN DEPENDENCIES AND FURTHER NORMAL FORMS

We saw in Chapter 6 that the presence of certain functional dependencies in a relation scheme means that the scheme can be decomposed to eliminate redundancy while preserving information. However, it is not necessary that an FD hold before such a decomposition may take place. Consider the instance of relation *service* in Table 7.1.

Table 7.1 The relation *service*.

service(FLIGHT	DAY-OF-WEEK	PLANE-TYPE)
106	Monday	747
106	Thursday	747
106	Monday	1011
106	Thursday	1011
204	Wednesday	707
204	Wednesday	727

A tuple $\langle f\ d\ p \rangle$ in relation *service* means that flight number f flies on day d and can use plane type p on that day. There is no functional dependency FLIGHT → DAY-OF-WEEK or FLIGHT → PLANE-TYPE in *service*, yet *service* decomposes losslessly onto FLIGHT DAY-OF-WEEK and FLIGHT PLANE-TYPE, as shown in Table 7.2.

Table 7.2 The relation *service* decomposes losslessly into the relations *servday* and *servtype*.

servday(FLIGHT	DAY OF WEEK)
106	Monday
106	Thursday
204	Wednesday

servtype(FLIGHT	PLANE-TYPE)
106	747
106	1011
204	707
204	727

Now consider another instance of the relation *service*, as given in Table 7.3.

Table 7.3 A second instance of the relation *service*.

service(FLIGHT	DAY-OF-WEEK	PLANE-TYPE)
106	Monday	747
106	Thursday	747
106	Thursday	1011
204	Wednesday	707
204	Wednesday	727

If we decompose this instance of service onto FLIGHT DAY-OF-WEEK and FLIGHT PLANE-TYPE, we also get the projections shown in Table 7.2. Therefore, when we join the two projections, we do not get back our original relation.

7.1 MULTIVALUED DEPENDENCIES

What property of the first instance of *service* that the second instance lacks allows the lossless decomposition? In the first instance, if a certain plane type can be used for a flight on one day it flies, that plane type can be used on any day the flight flies. This property fails for the second instance of *service*, since flight 106 can use a 1011 on Thursday but not on Monday. The first instance of *service* should be decomposed, since once we know a flight number, DAY-OF-WEEK gives us no information about PLANE-TYPE, and vice versa.

We can state this property another way. If we have tuples $\langle f\ d\ p \rangle$ and $\langle f\ d'\ p' \rangle$ in relation *service*, then we must also have tuple $\langle f\ d'\ p \rangle$. We define this concept formally.

Definition 7.1 Let R be a relation scheme, let X and Y be disjoint subsets of R, and let $Z = R - (X\ Y)$. A relation $r(R)$ satisfies the *multivalued dependency* (MVD) $X \twoheadrightarrow Y$ if, for any two tuples t_1 and t_2 in r with $t_1(X) = t_2(X)$, there exists a tuple t_3 in r with $t_3(X) = t_1(X)$, $t_3(Y) = t_1(Y)$, and $t_3(Z) = t_2(Z)$.

The symmetry of t_1 and t_2 in this definition implies there is also a tuple t_4 in r with $t_4(X) = t_1(X)$, $t_4(Y) = t_2(Y)$ and $t_4(Z) = t_1(Z)$.

Example 7.1 The MVD FLIGHT $\twoheadrightarrow$ DAY-OF-WEEK holds on the instance of *service* in Table 7.1, but not on the instance in Table 7.3. The instance in Table 7.1 also satisfies the MVD FLIGHT $\twoheadrightarrow$ PLANE-TYPE.

It is not a coincidence that the instance of *service* in Table 7.1 satisfies two MVDs, as the following lemma shows.

Lemma 7.1 If relation r on scheme R satisfies the MVD $X \twoheadrightarrow Y$ and $Z = R - (X\ Y)$, then r satisfies $X \twoheadrightarrow Z$.

Proof: Left to the reader (see Exercise 7.2).

The definition of MVD requires that X and Y be disjoint in $X \twoheadrightarrow Y$. Suppose we remove this condition from the definition. Let relation $r(R)$ satisfy $X \twoheadrightarrow Y$ under the modified definition and let $Y' = Y - X$. Under either definition, r satisfies $X \twoheadrightarrow Y'$: Let $Z = R - (X\ Y) = R - (X\ Y')$. Let t_1 and t_2 be tuples in r with $t_1(X) = t_2(X)$. Since $X \twoheadrightarrow Y$, there must be a tuple t_3 in r with $t_3(X) = t_1(X)$, $t_3(Y) = t_1(Y)$, and $t_3(Z) = t_2(Z)$. If $t_3(Y) = t_1(Y)$, then $t_3(Y') = t_1(Y')$, since $Y' \subseteq Y$. So r satisfies $X \twoheadrightarrow Y'$.

Now suppose that X and Y are disjoint and relation $r(R)$ satisfies $X \twoheadrightarrow Y$. If $X' \subseteq X$, then $X \twoheadrightarrow Y X'$ under the modified definition of MVD: If tuples t_1 and t_2 are in r, and $t_1(X) = t_2(X)$, then there is a tuple t_3 in r with $t_3(X) = t_1(X)$, $t_3(Y) = t_1(Y)$, and $t_3(Z) = t_2(Z)$. It follows that $t_3(Y\ X') = t_1(Y X')$.

We adopt the modified definition in place of the original.

Example 7.2 The relation r shown below satisfies the MVD $A\ B \twoheadrightarrow B\ C$, hence it satisfies the MVD $A\ B \twoheadrightarrow C$.

$r(A$	B	C	$D)$
a	b	c	d
a	b	c'	d'
a	b	c	d'
a	b	c'	d
a	b'	c'	d
a'	b	c	d'

Let us investigate the meaning of the special cases $\emptyset \twoheadrightarrow Y$ and $X \twoheadrightarrow \emptyset$ for a relation $r(R)$. Recall our assumption that $t(\emptyset) = \lambda$ for any tuple t. Consider $\emptyset \twoheadrightarrow Y$. Let $Z = R - Y$. For any tuples t_1 and t_2 in r, $t_1(\emptyset) = t_2(\emptyset)$. If r satisfies $\emptyset \twoheadrightarrow Y$, there must be a tuple $t_3 \in r$ with $t_3(Y) = t_1(Y)$ and $t_3(Z) = t_2(Z)$. Therefore, r must be the cross product of the projections $\pi_Y(r)$ and $\pi_Z(r)$.

The MVD $X \twoheadrightarrow \emptyset$ is trivially satisfied by any relation on a scheme containing X.

7.2 PROPERTIES OF MULTIVALUED DEPENDENCIES

We have formalized the property that distinguishes the instances of the relation *service* in Tables 7.1 and 7.3. Let us see how MVDs are related to lossless decomposition.

Theorem 7.1 Let r be a relation on scheme R, and let X, Y, and Z be subsets of R such that $Z = R - (X\,Y)$. Relation r satisfies the MVD $X \twoheadrightarrow Y$ if the only if r decomposes losslessly onto the relation schemes $R_1 = X\,Y$ and $R_2 = X\,Z$.

Proof: Suppose the MVD holds. Let $r_1 = \pi_{R_1}(r)$ and $r_2 = \pi_{R_2}(r)$. Let t be a tuple in $r_1 \bowtie r_2$. There must be a tuple $t_1 \in r_1$ and a tuple $t_2 \in r_2$ such that $t(X) = t_1(X) = t_2(X)$, $t(Y) = t_1(Y)$, and $t(Z) = t_2(Z)$. Since r_1 and r_2 are projections of r, there must be tuples t_1' and t_2' in r with $t_1(X\,Y) = t_1'(X\,Y)$ and $t_2(X\,Z) = t_2'(X\,Z)$. The MVD $X \twoheadrightarrow Y$ implies that t must be in r, since r must contain a tuple t_3 with $t_3(X) = t_1'(X)$, $t_3(Y) = t_1'(Y)$, and $t_3(Z) = t_2'(Z)$, which is a description of t.

Suppose now that r decomposes losslessly onto R_1 and R_2. Let t_1 and t_2 be tuples in r such that $t_1(X) = t_2(X)$. Let r_1 and r_2 be defined as before. Relation r_1 contains a tuple $t_1' = t_1(X\,Y)$ and relation r_2 contains a tuple $t_2' = t_2(X\,Z)$. Since $r = r_1 \bowtie r_2$, r contains a tuple t such that $t(X\,Y) = t_1(X\,Y)$ and $t(X\,Z) = t_2(X\,Z)$. Tuple t is the result of joining t_1' and t_2'. Hence t_1 and t_2 cannot be used in a counterexample to $X \twoheadrightarrow Y$, hence r satisfies $X \twoheadrightarrow Y$.

Theorem 7.1 gives us a method to test if a relation $r(R)$ satisfies the MVD $X \twoheadrightarrow Y$. We project r onto $X\,Y$ and $X(R - XY)$, join the two projections, and test if the result is r. There is another method to test MVDs that does not require project and join, only some sorting and counting.

Let $Z = R - (X\,Y)$, $R_1 = X\,Y$, and $R_2 = X\,Z$. If

$$r_1 = \pi_{R_1}(r) \quad \text{and} \quad r_2 = \pi_{R_2}(r),$$

then $r_1 \bowtie r_2$ always contains r. For a given X-value x, suppose there are c_1 tuples in r_1 with X-value x and c_2 tuples in r_2 with X-value x. Let c be the number of tuples in r with X-value x. If $c = c_1 \cdot c_2$, for any X-value x, then $r = r_1 \bowtie r_2$ (see Exercise 7.4).

We define a function to assist us with our counting. The function $c_W[X = x]$ maps relations to non-negative integers as follows:

$$c_W[X = x](r) = |\pi_W(\sigma_{X=x}(r))|$$

Example 7.3 The value of $c_D[A\ B = a\ b](r)$ is 2 for the relation r in Example 7.2.

The function $c_W[X = x]$ counts the number of different W-values associated with a given X-value in a relation. The condition for the MVD $X \twoheadrightarrow Y$ we just discussed can be stated as

For any X-value x in r, $c_R[X = x](r) = c_{XY}[X = x](r) \cdot c_{XZ}[X = x](r)$.

Since $c_{WX}[X = x] = c_W[X = x]$, we can simplify this condition to

For any X-value x in r, $c_R[X = x](r) = c_Y[X = x](r) \cdot c_Z[X = x](r)$.

Example 7.4 For the relation r in Example 7.2, and the MVD $A\ B \twoheadrightarrow C$,

$$c_{ABCD}[A\ B = a\ b](r) = 4,$$
$$c_C[A\ B = a\ b](r) = 2, \text{ and}$$
$$c_D[A\ B = a\ b](r) = 2.$$

We see the condition is satisfied for the $(A\ B)$-value $a\ b$.

To test a relation $r(R)$ against the MVD $X \twoheadrightarrow Y$, first let $Z = R - (X\ Y)$. Next, sort the relation to bring equal X-values together. For each X-value, we count the number of tuples with the value, the number of different Y-values associated with the X-value, and the number of different Z-values associated with the X-value. Finally, we test if the first number is the product of the other two.

This test provides another definition of MVD (see Exercise 7.6).

Definition 7.2 Let r be a relation on scheme R, let X and Y be subsets of R, and let $Z = R - (X\ Y)$. Relation r satisfies the *multivalued dependency* $X \twoheadrightarrow Y$ if for every X-value x and Y-value y in r, such that xy appears in r,

$$c_Z[X = x](r) = c_Z[X\ Y = x\ y](r).$$

7.3 MULTIVALUED DEPENDENCIES AND FUNCTIONAL DEPENDENCIES

From Theorem 7.1 we can derive the following corollary.

Corollary Let r be a relation on scheme R and let X and Y be subsets of R. If r satisfies the FD $X \rightarrow Y$, then r satisfies the MVD $X \twoheadrightarrow Y$.

Proof From Exercise 6.4, we know that $X \rightarrow Y$ implies r decomposes losslessly onto $X\ Y$ and $X\ (R - (X\ Y))$. This result also follows directly from the counting definition of MVD.

Suppose we have a relation scheme R and a set of FDs F over R. We want to know which MVDs must hold in a relation $r(R)$ that satisfies F. From the last corollary, we know that if $X \rightarrow Y$ is in F^+, then r satisfies $X \twoheadrightarrow Y$, and, by Lemma 7.1, it follows that r satisfies $X \twoheadrightarrow R - (X\ Y)$. Are there any MVDs that will always hold on r that do not correspond directly to FDs? The answer is no.

Theorem 7.2 Let F be a set of FDs over R. Let X, Y, and Z be subsets of R, with $Z = R - (X\ Y)$. Let X^+ be the closure of X under F. If $Y \not\subseteq X^+$ and $Z \not\subseteq X^+$, then there is a relation $r(R)$ that satisfies F and does not satisfy the MVD $X \twoheadrightarrow Y$.

Proof The proof is similar to that of Theorem 4.1 on the completeness of the inference axioms for FDs. Assume $R = A_1\ A_2\ \cdots\ A_n$. We construct a relation $r(R)$ containing only two tuples, t_1 and t_2. Tuple t_1 is defined as

$$t_1(A_i) = a_i, \qquad 1 \leq i \leq n$$

and tuple t_2 is defined as

$$t_2\,(A_i) = \begin{cases} a_i & \text{if } A_i \in X^+ \\ b_i & \text{otherwise,} \end{cases} \qquad 1 \leq i \leq n.$$

By the proof of Theorem 4.1, r satisfies all the FDs in F. Since $Y \not\subseteq X^+$ and $Z \not\subseteq X^+$, Y must contain an attribute B_1 not in X^+, and Z must contain an attribute B_2 not in X^+. Thus, $t_2(B_1) = b_j$ and $t_2(B_2) = b_k$ for some j and k.

Since $X \subseteq X^+$, $t_1(X) = t_2(X)$. If r satisfies $X \twoheadrightarrow Y$, r must contain a tuple t_3 with $t_3(X) = t_1(X)$, $t_3(Y) = t_1(Y)$, and $t_3(Z) = t_2(Z)$. However, r has only two tuples, so $t_3 = t_1$ or $t_3 = t_2$. Suppose $t_3 = t_1$. Then $t_3(B_2) = t_1(B_2) \neq t_2(B_2)$, since $t_2(B_2)$ is b_k and t_1 is all a's, so $t_3(Z) \neq t_2(Z)$; a contradiction.

Similarly, we get a contradiction if we assume $t_3 = t_2$. Since $t_2\,(B_1) = b_j$ and t_1 is all a's, $t_3(B_1) = t_2(B_1) \neq t_1(B_1)$, so $t_3(Y) \neq t_1(Y)$. We must conclude that r does not satisfy the MVD $X \twoheadrightarrow Y$.

From Theorem 7.2 we see that the only MVDs implied by a set of FDs are those of the form $X \twoheadrightarrow Y$, where $Y \subseteq X^+$ or $R - (X\,Y) \subseteq X^+$.

Example 7.5 Let $R = A\,B\,C\,D\,E\,I$ and let $F = \{A \rightarrow B\,C,\ C \rightarrow D\}$. Then F implies $A \twoheadrightarrow B\,C\,D$ and $A \twoheadrightarrow C$, but F does not imply $A \twoheadrightarrow D\,E$.

7.4 INFERENCE AXIOMS FOR MULTIVALUED DEPENDENCIES

We have just seen exactly which MVDs are implied by a set of FDs. We now consider what MVDs are implied by a set of MVDs and what MVDs and FDs are implied by a set of MVDs and FDs.

7.4.1 Multivalued Dependencies Alone

The first six inference axioms below are analogs to the FD axioms with the same names, although only the first three have exactly the same statement. Axiom M7 has no FD counterpart.

Let r be a relation on scheme R and let W, X, Y, Z be subsets of R.

M1. Reflexivity
Relation r satisfies $X \twoheadrightarrow X$.

M2. Augmentation
If r satisfies $X \twoheadrightarrow Y$, then r satisfies $X\,Z \twoheadrightarrow Y$.

M3. Additivity
If r satisfies $X \twoheadrightarrow Y$ and $X \twoheadrightarrow Z$, then r satisfies $X \twoheadrightarrow Y\,Z$.

M4. Projectivity
If r satisfies $X \twoheadrightarrow Y$ and $X \twoheadrightarrow Z$, then r satisfies $X \twoheadrightarrow Y \cap Z$ and $X \twoheadrightarrow Y - Z$.

M5. Transitivity
If r satisfies $X \twoheadrightarrow Y$ and $Y \twoheadrightarrow Z$, then r satisfies $Y \twoheadrightarrow Z - Y$.

M6. Pseudotransitivity
If r satisfies $X \twoheadrightarrow Y$ and $Y\,W \twoheadrightarrow Z$, then r satisfies $X\,W \twoheadrightarrow Z - (Y\,W)$.

M7. Complementation
If r satisfies $X \twoheadrightarrow Y$ and $Z = R - (X\ Y)$, then r satisfies $X \twoheadrightarrow Z$.

Axioms M1 and M2 follow immediately from the first definition of MVD (see Exercise 7.8). Let us demonstrate the correctness of axiom M3. Let r contain tuples t_1 and t_2, with $t_1(X) = t_2(X)$. We must prove that r contains a tuple t such that

$$t(X) = t_1(X), \qquad t(Y\,Z) = t_1(Y\,Z), \quad \text{and} \quad t(U) = t_2(U),$$

where $U = R - (X\,Y\,Z)$. Since r satisfies $X \twoheadrightarrow Y$, it must contain a tuple t_3 such that

$$t_3(X) = t_1(X), \qquad t_3(Y) = t_1(Y), \quad \text{and} \quad t_3(V) = t_2(V),$$

where $V = R - (X\ Y)$. Since r satisfies $X \twoheadrightarrow Z$, it must contain a tuple t_4 such that

$$t_4(X) = t_1(X), \qquad t_4(Z) = t_1(Z), \quad \text{and} \quad t_4(W) = t_3(W),$$

where $W = R - (X\,Z)$.

We claim $t = t_4$. Clearly $t(X) = t_4(X)$.

Also

$$t_4(Z) = t_1(Z) = t(Z), \text{ and}$$
$$t_4(Y \cap W) = t_3(Y \cap W) = t_1(Y \cap W) = t(Y \cap W), \text{ so}$$
$$t_4(Y\,Z) = t(Y\,Z).$$

Since $U \subseteq W \cap V$,

$$t_4(U) = t_3(U) = t_2(U) = t(U).$$

We have shown $t_4 = t$, since $R = X\,Y\,Z\,U$.

We know axiom M7 is correct from Lemma 7.1. We can use axioms M3 and M7 to prove the correctness of axiom M4. If r satisfies $X \twoheadrightarrow Y$ and $X \twoheadrightarrow Z$, then, by axiom M3, r satisfies $X \twoheadrightarrow Y\,Z$. By axiom M7, r must also satisfy $X \twoheadrightarrow V$, where $V = R - (X\,Y\,Z)$. Using M3 again, we know r satisfies $X \twoheadrightarrow VZ$. A final application of M7 yields $X \twoheadrightarrow R - (X\ V\ Z)$. Substituting and simplifying gives us

$$R - (X\,V\,Z) =$$
$$R - (X\{R - (X\,Y\,Z)\}Z) =$$
$$R - (X\{R - Y\}Z) =$$
$$Y - (X\,Z) =$$
$$(Y - Z) - X.$$

Therefore, r satisfies $X \twoheadrightarrow (Y - Z) - X$, which implies $X \twoheadrightarrow Y - Z$ by the discussion in Section 7.1.

From $X \twoheadrightarrow Y$ we get $X \twoheadrightarrow W$ by axiom M7, where $W = R - (X\,Y)$. Combining this with $X \twoheadrightarrow Y - Z$ using axiom M3 yields $X \twoheadrightarrow W(Y - Z)$. One more application of axiom M7 gives us $X \twoheadrightarrow R - (X\,W(Y - Z))$. Substituting, we get

$$R - (W\,X(Y - Z)) =$$
$$R - (X\{R - (X\,Y)\}(Y - Z)) =$$
$$R - (X\{R - Y\}(Y - Z)) =$$
$$Y - (X(Y - Z)) =$$
$$(Y \cap Z) - X.$$

Thus r satisfies $X \twoheadrightarrow (Y \cap Z) - X$ and hence r satisfies $X \twoheadrightarrow Y \cap Z$.

To prove the correctness of axiom M5, we first show that $X \twoheadrightarrow Y$ and $Y \twoheadrightarrow Z$ imply $X \twoheadrightarrow Y\,Z$. Let $W = R - (X\,Y\,Z)$. We must show that if there are tuples t_1 and t_2 in r, with $t_1(X) = t_2(X)$, then r contains a tuple t such that

$$t(X) = t_1(X),$$
$$t(Y\,Z) = t_1(Y\,Z), \text{ and}$$
$$t(W) = t_2(W).$$

From $X \twoheadrightarrow Y$, we get a tuple t_3 such that

$$t_3(X) = t_1(X), \qquad t_3(Y) = t_1(Y), \quad \text{and} \quad t_3(V) = t_2(V),$$

where $V = R - (X\,Y)$. Using $Y \twoheadrightarrow Z$ we get a tuple t_4 such that

$$t_4(Y) = t_1(Y), \qquad t_4(Z) = t_1(Z), \quad \text{and} \quad t_4(U) = t_3(U),$$

where $U = R - (Y\,Z)$.

We know $t_4(X) = t_1(X)$, since there is only one possible value for each attribute $A \in X$. Clearly $t_4(Y\,Z) = t_1(Y\,Z)$. Since $W \subseteq U - X \subseteq V$, $t_4(W) =$

$t_2(W)$. Hence, t_4 is the tuple t we seek. We have shown r satisfies $X \twoheadrightarrow YZ$. Using axiom M4 and $X \twoheadrightarrow Y$, we finally get $X \twoheadrightarrow Z - Y$.

Axiom M6 follows from the other axioms and is left as an exercise (see Exercise 7.10).

Example 7.6 Let $R = A\ B\ C\ D\ E$ and let $F = \{A \twoheadrightarrow B\ C,\ D\ E \twoheadrightarrow C\}$. From $A \twoheadrightarrow B\ C$ we get $A \twoheadrightarrow D\ E$ by complementation. Transitivity then gives us $A \twoheadrightarrow C$. Using augmentation we get $A\ D \twoheadrightarrow C$. Finally, applying complementation again yields $A\ D \twoheadrightarrow B\ E$. Therefore $F \models A\ D \twoheadrightarrow B\ E$. Below is a relation $r(A\ B\ C\ D\ E)$ that satisfies all of these MVDs.

$r(A$	B	C	D	$E)$
a	b	c	d	e
a'	b'	c'	d	e
a'	b'	c	d	e
a	b	c'	d	e
a''	b'	c'	d'	e

7.4.2 Functional and Multivalued Dependencies

We now turn our attention to the implications we can make when we have FDs and MVDs together. There are only two axioms for FDs and MVDs combined.

Let r be a relation on R and let W, X, Y, Z be subsets of R.

C1. Replication
If r satisfies $X \rightarrow Y$, then r satisfies $X \twoheadrightarrow Y$.

C2. Coalescence
If r satisfies $X \twoheadrightarrow Y$ and $Z \rightarrow W$, where $W \subseteq Y$ and $Y \cap Z = \emptyset$, then r satisfies $X \rightarrow W$.

Axiom C1 is a consequence of the corollary to Theorem 7.1. We prove the correctness of axiom C2. Let t_1 and t_2 be tuples in r with $t_1(X) = t_2(X)$. Since r satisfies $X \twoheadrightarrow Y$, there must be a tuple t in r such that

$$t(X) = t_1(X), \qquad t(Y) = t_1(Y), \quad \text{and} \quad t(V) = t_2(V),$$

where $V = R - (X\ Y)$. Since $Y \cap Z = \emptyset$, $Z \subseteq X\ V$, hence $t(Z) = t_2(Z)$. The FD $Z \rightarrow W$ means that $t(W) = t_2(W)$. However, $W \subseteq Y$, so $t_1(W) = t(W) = t_2(W)$, hence r satisfies $X \rightarrow W$.

Example 7.7 Let $R = A\ B\ C\ D\ E$ and let $F = \{A \twoheadrightarrow BC, D \rightarrow C\}$. Axiom C2 implies $F \models A \rightarrow C$. Below is a relation $r(A\ B\ C\ D\ E)$ that satisfies these FDs and MVDs.

$r(A$	B	C	D	$E)$
a	b	c'	d	e
a	b'	c'	d'	e'
a	b'	c'	d	e
a	b	c'	d'	e'

7.4.3 Completeness of the Axioms and Computing Implications

We shall only state the completeness results for inference axioms involving MVDs; we shall not prove them here.

Theorem 7.3 Inference axioms M1–M7 are complete for sets of MVDs.

Theorem 7.4 Inference axioms F1–F6, M1–M7, and C1 and C2 are complete for sets of FDs and MVDs.

As a consequence of Theorem 7.4, we see that a set of MVDs alone implies no FDs other than trivial ones; that is, FDs of the form $X \rightarrow Y$, where X contains Y. This observation follows from the form of the inference axioms. F1–F6 can only derive trivial FDs from trivial FDs; M1–M7 and C1 cannot derive any FDs; axiom C2 does not apply when the FD involved is trivial.

Axioms C1 and C2 are necessary. Without axiom C1, MVDs could not be derived from a set of only FDs. It is left as an exercise to find an example where axiom C2 derives an FD that could not be derived from axioms F1–F6 alone from a given set of FDs and MVDs (see Exercise 7.12).

We shall not develop a membership algorithm for MVDs or FDs and MVDs, although polynomial-time algorithms exist in both cases. We shall, however, discuss some of the concepts used in these algorithms, since these concepts help give a better picture of the dependency structure implied by a set of MVDs.

Definition 7.3 Given a collection of sets $\mathbf{S} = \{S_1, S_2, \ldots, S_p\}$, where $\mathbf{U} = S_1 \cup S_2 \cup \cdots \cup S_p$, the *minimal disjoint set basis* of $\mathbf{S}$ ($mdsb(\mathbf{S})$) is the partition $T_1, T_2, \ldots, T_q$ of $\mathbf{U}$ such that:

1. Every S_i is a union of some of the T_j's.
2. No partition of $\mathbf{U}$ with fewer cells has the first property.

The reader should take a moment to convince himself or herself that the $mdsb(\mathbf{S})$ is unique as defined. The $mdsb(\mathbf{S})$ is formed by grouping together elements in $\mathbf{U}$ that are contained in exactly the same set of S_i's.

Example 7.8 Let $\mathbf{S} = \{A\ B\ C\ D,\ C\ D\ E,\ A\ E\}$. We have $\mathbf{U} = A\ B\ C\ D\ E$ and $mdsb(\mathbf{S}) = A,\ B,\ C\ D,\ E$.

Let F be a set of MVDs over R and let $X \subseteq R$. Define G as

$$G = \{Y | F \models X \twoheadrightarrow Y\}.$$

We claim $mdsb(G)$ is a subset of G. If there is a set Y_1 in G such that Y_1 contains attributes both in and out of some other set Y_2 in G, then, by axiom M4, there are sets $Y_3 = Y_1 - Y_2$ and $Y_4 = Y_1 \cap Y_2$ in G. $Mdsb(G)$ consists exactly of those nonempty sets of G that contain no other set of G as a subset. Note that if $X = A_1\ A_2\ \cdots\ A_n$, then $A_1,\ A_2,\ \ldots,\ A_n$ are all in $mdsb(G)$.

Definition 7.4 Let F, X, and G be as defined above. The *dependency basis of* X with respect to F is $mdsb(G)$ and is denoted $DEP(X)$. If $X = A_1\ A_2\ \cdots\ A_n$ and $DEP(X) = \{A_1, A_2, \ldots, A_n, Y_1, Y_2, \ldots, Y_m\}$, we write $X \twoheadrightarrow Y_1 | Y_2 | \cdots | Y_m$.

Example 7.9 Let $F = \{A \twoheadrightarrow BC,\ DE \twoheadrightarrow C\}$ be a set of MVDs over $ABCDE$. If $X = A$, then $G = \{A, BC, DE, C, BDE, B, BCDE, CDE\}$ and $DEP(A) = mdsb(G) = \{A,B,C,DE\}$.

We can recover all MVDs implied by F with X as the left side from $DEP(X)$. $F \models X \twoheadrightarrow Y$ if and only if Y is the union of some sets in $DEP(X)$. Y must be in G, so Y is the union of some sets in $DEP(X)$. In the other direction, by axiom M3, if $Y_1, Y_2, \ldots, Y_k$ are in $DEP(X)$, then $F \models X \twoheadrightarrow Y_1\ Y_2 \cdots Y_k$.

The membership algorithm for MVDs tests if a set of MVDs implies an MVD $X \twoheadrightarrow Y$ by first computing $DEP(X)$ with respect to F and then checking if Y can be formed from sets in $DEP(X)$. The procedure for computing the dependency basis of X has three stages.

1. Find the set G of all sets Y such that the MVD $X \twoheadrightarrow Y$ follows from F by augmentation of complementation. That is, for any MVD $X' \twoheadrightarrow Y'$ in F where $X' \subseteq X$, add Y' and $R - (X'\ Y')$ to G. Also add A to G for every $A \in X$.
2. Let $DEP(X) = mdsb(G)$.
3. Look for an MVD $W \twoheadrightarrow Z$ that can be used to refine $DEP(X)$ with

transitivity. That is, let $Y_1, Y_2, \ldots, Y_k$ be sets in $DEP(X)$ such that $W \subseteq Y_1 Y_2 \cdots Y_k$. Let $Y = Y_1 Y_2 \cdots Y_k$. By augmentation, since $W \subseteq Y$, $F \models Y \twoheadrightarrow Z$. By transitivity, $X \twoheadrightarrow Z - Y$. If $Z - Y$ is the union of some sets in $DEP(X)$, we cannot refine $DEP(X)$. If not, let $DEP(X) = mdsb(DEP(X) \cup \{Z - Y\})$. If no MVD in F can be used to change $DEP(X)$, stop.

Example 7.10 Let $F = \{A \twoheadrightarrow B\ C,\ D\ E \twoheadrightarrow C\}$ be a set of MVDs over $A\ B\ C\ D\ E$. To compute $DEP(A)$, we first find $G = \{BC,\ DE,\ A\}$. We then set $DEP(A) = \{B\ C,\ D\ E,\ A\}$. We then use transitivity on $D\ E \twoheadrightarrow C$ to get $A \twoheadrightarrow C$ and refine $DEP(A)$ to $mdsb(\{B\ C,\ D\ E,\ A\} \cup C) = \{B,\ C,\ D\ E,\ A\}$. We can make no further refinement to $DEP(X)$.

We shall not attempt to prove the correctness of the procedure for computing $DEP(X)$. Observe, however, that the time complexity of the procedure is bounded by a polynomial in the size of F. $DEP(X)$ can contain at most $|R|$ sets, thus $DEP(X)$ can be refined at most $|R - X| - 1$ times in step 3. (Any attribute in X is in $DEP(X)$ as a singleton set from the start.)

Computing directly which FDs and MVDs are implied by a set F of FDs and MVDs requires redefining X^+ and $DEP(X)$ to take account of the effects of axioms C1 and C2. For these redefinitions, there exists a polynomial-time algorithm to compute X^+ and $DEP(X)$, from which $F \models X \rightarrow Y$ or $F \models X \twoheadrightarrow Y$ can be decided. In Chapter 8 we shall develop another method to test if an FD or MVD follows from F.

7.5 FOURTH NORMAL FORM

We know that any relation $r(R)$ that satisfies the MVD $X \twoheadrightarrow Y$ decomposes losslessly onto the relation schemes $X\ Y$ and $X\ Z$, where $Z = R - (X\ Y)$. However, if $X \twoheadrightarrow Y$ is the only dependency on R, then R is in 3NF. Therefore, 3NF is not guaranteed to find all possible decompositions.

Definition 7.5 An MVD $X \twoheadrightarrow Y$ is *trivial* if for any relation scheme R with $X\ Y \subseteq R$, any relation $r(R)$ satisfies $X \twoheadrightarrow Y$.

It is left to the reader to show that the trivial MVDs on a relation $r(R)$ are exactly those of the form $X \twoheadrightarrow Y$ where $Y \subseteq X$ or $X\ Y = R$ (see Exercise 7.14). If $X \twoheadrightarrow Y$ is trivial, and we attempt to decompose a relation $r(R)$ using it, one of the projected relations will be all of r. There is no benefit in such a decomposition.

Definition 7.6 An MVD $X \twoheadrightarrow Y$ *applies* to a relation scheme R if $X\,Y \subseteq R$.

Definition 7.7 Let F be a set of FDs and MVDs over $\mathbf{U}$. A relation scheme $R \subseteq \mathbf{U}$ is in *fourth normal form* (4NF) with respect to F if for every MVD $X \twoheadrightarrow Y$ implied by F that applies to R either the MVD is trivial or X is a superkey for R. A database scheme $\mathbf{R}$ is in *fourth normal form* with respect to F if every relation scheme R in $\mathbf{R}$ is in fourth normal form with respect to F.

Example 7.11 Let relation scheme R = FLIGHT DAY-OF-WEEK PLANE-TYPE and let F = {FLIGHT $\twoheadrightarrow$ DAY-OF-WEEK}. R is not in 4NF with respect to F. The data-base scheme $\mathbf{R}$ = FLIGHT DAY-OF-WEEK, FLIGHT PLANE-TYPE is in 4NF with respect to F. Any relation $r(R)$ that satisfies F decomposes losslessly onto the relation schemes in $\mathbf{R}$.

Let us consider the case where we have the MVD $X \twoheadrightarrow Y$ holding on relation scheme R, but X is a key of R. For any relation $r(R)$ the projections

$$r_1 = \pi_{XY}(r) \text{ and } r_2 = \pi_{XZ}(r),$$

where $Z = R - (X\,Y)$, both have the same number of tuples as r. There are no duplicate X-values in r, so there are as many X-values as tuples. Any projection containing the attributes in X must contain all the different X-values.

There is never anything to be gained by such a decomposition. $X\,Y$-values and $X\,Z$-values are not duplicated in r, so no redundancy is removed by the decomposition. No space is saved either. Assuming that each entry in a relation takes one unit of storage space, the relation r takes $|\,r\,| \cdot |\,R\,|$ units (where $|\,r\,|$ is the number of tuples in r). The relations r_1 and r_2 together take $|r| \cdot (|R_1| + |R_2|)$.

Example 7.12 Let $F = \{A \rightarrow B\,C,\ C \twoheadrightarrow D\,E\}$ be a set of dependencies over the relation scheme $R = A\,B\,C\,D\,E$. R is not in 4NF with respect to F because of the MVD $C \twoheadrightarrow D\,E$. The database scheme $\mathbf{R}$ consisting of the two relation schemes

$$R_1 = A\,B\,C \quad \text{and} \quad R_2 = C\,D\,E$$

is in 4NF with respect to F, even though the MVD $A \twoheadrightarrow B$ is implied by F and applies to R_1. $A \twoheadrightarrow B$ is not trivial, but A is a key for R_1.

We can construct 4NF database schemes from a relation scheme R and a set F of FDs and MVDs by decomposition in much the same way we constructed 3NF database schemes. We start with relation R and look for a nontrivial MVD $X \twoheadrightarrow Y$ implied by F, where X is not a key for R. We split R into the two relation schemes

$$R_1 = X\,Y \quad \text{and} \quad R_2 = X\,Z,$$

where $Z = R - (X\,Y)$. The MVD $X \twoheadrightarrow Y$ is now trivial on R_1 and does not apply to R_2. If either of R_1 or R_2 is not in 4NF with respect to F, we repeat the decomposition process on the offending scheme. Since the MVDs we are using are not trivial, both newly formed relation schemes have fewer attributes than the original relation scheme. Therefore, the decomposition process eventually halts.

Let **R** be a 4NF database scheme obtained by decomposition from a relation scheme R and let F be a set of FDs and MVDs. Any relation $r(R)$ that satisfies F decomposes losslessly onto the relation schemes in **R** (see Exercise 7.15).

Example 7.13 Let $F = \{A \twoheadrightarrow B\,C\,D,\ B \rightarrow A\,C,\ C \rightarrow D\}$ be a set of dependencies over the relation scheme $R = A\,B\,C\,D\,E\,I$. Since $A \twoheadrightarrow B\,C\,D$ is a nontrivial MVD and A is not a key for R, we decompose R into the relation schemes

$$R_1 = A\,B\,C\,D \quad \text{and} \quad R_2 = A\,E\,I.$$

R_2 is in 4NF with respect to F. F implies the MVD $B \twoheadrightarrow A\,C$ on R, but this MVD is not a candidate for use in decomposition because B is a key for R_1, since $C \rightarrow D$. However, $C \rightarrow D$ implies the MVD $C \twoheadrightarrow D$, which we can use to decompose R_1. The result is the relation schemes

$$R_{11} = A\,B\,C \quad \text{and} \quad R_{12} = C\,D.$$

Both of these schemes are in 4NF with respect to F. The database scheme $\mathbf{R} = \{R_{11}, R_{12}, R_2\}$ is thus in 4NF with respect to F.

7.6 FOURTH NORMAL FORM AND ENFORCEABILITY OF DEPENDENCIES

We now ask if, for a set of FDs and MVDs F, we can always find a database scheme in 4NF with respect to F upon which F is enforceable. The first problem is that the question is not quite well-posed. The definition of enforceability we use for FDs does not make sense for MVDs.

A set of FDs F is enforceable on a database scheme $\mathbf{R}$ if there is a set of FDs G equivalent to F such that G applies to $\mathbf{R}$. This definition is a reasonable one for FDs for the following reason. Suppose $\mathbf{R}$ is a database scheme over $\mathbf{U}$ and d is a database on $\mathbf{R}$ that is the projection of a single relation $r(\mathbf{U})$. If we can find the actual functional relationship for each FD $X \rightarrow Y$ in G (that is, the corresponding Y-value for each X-value) from d, and $G \models V \rightarrow W$, then we can recover the actual functional relationship for $V \rightarrow W$ from d. The relationship can be reconstructed following the inference axioms as they are applied to derive $V \rightarrow W$ from G (see Exercise 7.16).

The same property is almost true for MVDs. The problem is the complementation axiom, M7. Consider the data base scheme $\mathbf{R} = \{R_1, R_2\}$, where $R_1 = A\ B$ and $R_2 = C$, and the set $F = \{A \rightarrow\!\!\!\rightarrow B\}$. Suppose d is a database on $\mathbf{R}$ obtained by projecting a relation $r(A\ B\ C)$. We can recover the multivalued relationship for $A \rightarrow\!\!\!\rightarrow B$ in r from d. However, $F \models A \rightarrow\!\!\!\rightarrow C$, but we cannot reconstruct the multivalued relationship for $A \rightarrow\!\!\!\rightarrow C$ from d. Any definition of enforceability for MVDs must deal with the problem of complementation.

Even if we can arrive at an appropriate definition of enforceability for MVDs, we still are not assured of having 4NF and enforceability, as the next result shows. (Recall that in Example 6.26 we saw a set of FDs that was not enforceable on any BCNF scheme.)

Lemma 7.2 If a relation scheme R is in 4NF with respect to a set F of FDs and MVDs, then R is in BCNF with respect to the set of FDs implied by F.

Proof Suppose R is not in BCNF. Then we must have subsets K, Y, and A of R such that K is a key for R, $A \not\subseteq K\ Y$ and $K \rightarrow Y$, $Y \not\rightarrow K$ and $Y \rightarrow A$ under F. The FD $Y \rightarrow A$ implies the MVD $Y \rightarrow\!\!\!\rightarrow A$. Y is not a key for R, since $Y \not\rightarrow K$. $Y \rightarrow\!\!\!\rightarrow A$ is not trivial, since A is not contained in Y and $YA \neq R$, because there must be some attribute B in K that is not in Y. Therefore, R is not in 4NF with respect to F.

There have been attempts at finding a synthetic approach to constructing 4NF database schemes from a set of MVDs and FDs. So far, these attempts have not met with as much success as the synthesis schemes for FDs alone.

7.7 JOIN DEPENDENCIES

MVDs are an attempt to detect lossless decompositions that will work for all relations on a given relation scheme. However, MVDs are not completely adequate in this regard. A relation can have a nontrivial lossless decomposition onto three schemes, but have no such decomposition onto any pair of schemes (see Exercise 6.7). By Theorem 7.1, such a relation satisfies only trivial MVDs (see Exercise 7.17).

Example 7.14 The relation $r(A\ B\ C)$ in Figure 7.1 decomposes losslessly

$r(A$	B	$C)$
a_1	b_1	c_1
a_1	b_2	c_2
a_3	b_3	c_3
a_4	b_3	c_4
a_5	b_5	c_5
a_6	b_6	c_5

Figure 7.1

onto the relation schemes $A\ B$, $A\ C$, and $B\ C$. The projections are shown in Figure 7.2. However, r satisfies no nontrivial MVDs, so it has no lossless

$\pi_{A B}(r) = A$	B
a_1	b_1
a_1	b_2
a_3	b_3
a_4	b_3
a_5	b_5
a_6	b_6

$\pi_{A C}(r) = A$	C
a_1	c_1
a_1	c_2
a_3	c_3
a_4	c_4
a_5	c_5
a_6	c_5

$\pi_{B C}(r) = B$	C
b_1	c_1
b_2	c_2
b_3	c_3
b_3	c_4
b_5	c_5
b_6	c_5

Figure 7.2

decomposition onto any pair of relation schemes R_1 and R_2 such that $R_1 \neq A\ B\ C$ and $R_2 \neq A\ B\ C$.

Definition 7.8 Let $\mathbf{R} = \{R_1, R_2, \ldots, R_p\}$ be a set of relation schemes over $\mathbf{U}$. A relation $r(\mathbf{U})$ satisfies the *join dependency* (JD) $*[R_1, R_2, \ldots, R_p]$ if r decomposes losslessly onto $R_1, R_2, \ldots, R_p$. That is,

$$r = \pi_{R_1}(r) \bowtie \pi_{R_2}(r) \bowtie \cdots \bowtie \pi_{R_p}(r).$$

We also write $*[R_1, R_2, \ldots, R_p]$ as $*[\mathbf{R}]$.

Example 7.15 Relation r in Figure 7.1 satisfies the JD $*[A\ B,\ A\ C,\ B\ C]$.

A necessary condition for a relation $r(\mathbf{U})$ to satisfy the JD $*[R_1, R_2, \ldots, R_p]$ is that $\mathbf{U} = R_1 R_2 \cdots R_p$. We also see from the definition that an MVD is a special case of a JD. A relation $r(R)$ satisfies the MVD $X \twoheadrightarrow Y$ if and only if r decomposes losslessly onto $X\ Y$ and $X\ Z$, where $Z = R - (X\ Y)$. This condition is just the JD $*[X\ Y,\ X\ Z]$. Looking from the other direction, the join dependency $*[R_1, R_2]$ is the same as the MVD $R_1 \cap R_2 \twoheadrightarrow R_1$.

We can also define JDs in a manner similar to the definition of MVDs. Let r satisfy $*[R_1, R_2, \ldots, R_p]$. If r contains tuples $t_1, t_2, \ldots, t_p$ such that

$$t_i(R_i \cap R_j) = t_j(R_i \cap R_j)$$

for all i and j, then r must contain a tuple t such that $t(R_i) = t_i(R_i)$, $1 \le i \le p$.

Example 7.16 Suppose relation $r(A\ B\ C\ D\ E)$ satisfies the JD $*[ABC,\ BD,\ CDE]$ and contains the three tuples shown below. Using our

	$r(A$	B	C	D	$E)$
t_1	a	b	c	d	e
t_2	a'	b	c'	d'	e''
t_3	a''	b'	c	d'	e'

alternative characterization of JDs, we see that r must also contain the tuple $t = \langle a\ b\ c\ d'\ e' \rangle$.

We shall not present inference axioms for JDs. In Chapter 8 we shall see a method for testing if a set of FDs and JDs (including MVDs) implies a given JD.

7.8 PROJECT-JOIN NORMAL FORM

The point of seeking lossless decomposition is to remove redundancy from relations. We have seen lossless decompositions that do not correspond to MVDs, hence 4NF is not the ultimate in terms of finding lossless decompositions. We shall first define project-join normal form with only decomposition in mind. We then modify the definition slightly to meet another criterion.

Definition 7.9 A JD $*[R_1, R_2, \ldots, R_p]$ over R is *trivial* if it is satisfied by every relation $r(R)$.

We leave it to the reader to show that the trivial JDs over R are JDs of the form $*[R_1, R_2, \ldots, R_p]$ where $R = R_i$ for some i (see Exercise 7.22).

Definition 7.10 A JD $*[R_1, R_2, \ldots, R_p]$ *applies* to a relation scheme R if $R = R_1 R_2 \cdots R_p$.

Definition 7.11 Let R be a relation scheme and let F be a set of FDs and JDs over R. R is in *project-join normal form* (PJNF) with respect to F if for every JD $*[R_1, R_2, \ldots, R_p]$ implied by F that applies to R, the JD is trivial or every R_i is a superkey for R. A database scheme **R** is in *project-join normal form* with respect to F if every relation scheme R in **R** is in project-join normal form with respect to F.

Example 7.17 Let $F = \{*[A\ B\ C\ D,\ C\ D\ E,\ B\ D\ I],\ *[A\ B,\ B\ C\ D,\ A\ D],\ A \rightarrow B\ C\ D\ E,\ B\ C \rightarrow A\ I\}$ be a set of dependencies over the relation scheme $R = A\ B\ C\ D\ E\ I$. R is not in PJNF with respect to F because of the JD $*[A\ B\ C\ D,\ C\ D\ E,\ B\ D\ I]$. The database scheme $\mathbf{R} = \{R_1, R_2, R_3\}$, where $R_1 = A\ B\ C\ D$, $R_2 = C\ D\ E$, and $R_3 = B\ D\ I$, is in PJNF with respect to F. The JD $*[A\ B,\ B\ C\ D,\ A\ D]$ is implied by F and applies to R_1, but each set of attributes is a superkey for R_1. The MVDs implied by the FDs are either trivial or have keys as left sides.

The reason for allowing a JD $*[R_1, R_2, \ldots, R_p]$ to apply to a relation scheme R and not violate PJNF when every R_i is a superkey is the same as for 4NF. If every R_i is a key, then all projections of a relation $r(R)$ onto the R_i's will have the same number of tuples as r and no redundancy will be removed.

The definition of PJNF above is a weaker condition than the original definition of PJNF as given by Fagin. Besides eliminating redundancy, the original definition ensures enforceability of dependencies by satisfying keys.

Definition 7.12 (revised) Let R be a relation scheme and let F be a set of FDs and JDs. R is in *projection-join normal form* (PJNF) with respect to F if for every JD $*\ [R_1, R_2, \ldots, R_p]$ implied by F that applies to R, $*[R_1, R_2, \ldots, R_p]$ is implied by the key FDs of R.

We leave it to the reader to show that the revised definition is stronger than the first one given (see Exercise 7.24). The following example shows it is strictly stronger.

Example 7.18 Let $R = A\ B\ C$ and let $F = \{A \rightarrow B\ C,\ C \rightarrow A\ B,\ *[A\ B,\ B\ C]\}$. Since $A\ B$ and $B\ C$ are superkeys of R, R satisfies the first definition of PJNF. However, R does not satisfy the revised definition (see Exercise 7.25a).

PJNF implies 4NF, so PJNF and enforceability of dependencies are not always compatible (see Exercise 7.23). PJNF schemes can be constructed by decomposition of a relation scheme using the JDs that cause PJNF violations as guides. We shall see in Chapter 8 how to test when a set of FDs implies a JD.

7.9 EMBEDDED JOIN DEPENDENCIES

Given a relation $r(R)$ and an FD $X \rightarrow Y$, if $X \rightarrow Y$ holds on $\pi_S(r)$, for $X\ Y \subseteq S \subseteq R$, then $X \rightarrow Y$ holds on all of r. The same is not true for JDs, as the next example shows.

Example 7.19 Consider the relation $r(A\ B\ C\ D)$ shown in Figure 7.3. The projection $\pi_{A\ B\ C}(r)$ satisfies the MVD $A \twoheadrightarrow B$, but r itself does not.

r(A	B	C	D)
a	b	c	d
a	b'	c	d
a	b	c'	d'
a	b'	c'	d
a'	b'	c'	d'

Figure 7.3

Definition 7.13 Relation $r(R)$ satisfies the *embedded join dependency* (EJD) $*[R_1, R_2, \ldots, R_p]$ if $\pi_S(r)$ satisfies $*[R_1, R_2, \ldots, R_p]$ as a regular JD, where $S = R_1 R_2 \cdots R_p$. We allow $R = S$. That is, every JD is an EJD. We also write the embedded multivalued dependency (EMVD) $*[X\ Y,\ X\ Z]$ as $X \twoheadrightarrow Y\ (Z)$ (read "X multivalued determines Y in the context of Z").

Example 7.20 The relation r in Figure 7.3 satisfies the EMVD $A \twoheadrightarrow B\ (C)$.

No complete axiomatizations are known for EJDs although complete proof procedures exist for classes of dependencies containing EJDs.

7.10 EXERCISES

7.1 Modify the relation r below to satisfy the MVDs $A \twoheadrightarrow B\ C$ and $C\ D \twoheadrightarrow B\ E$ by adding rows.

r(A	B	C	D	E)
a	b	c	d	e
a	b'	c	d'	e
a'	b	c	d	e'

7.2 Prove Lemma 7.1.

7.3 Prove that if the relation $r(R)$ satisfies the MVDs $X \twoheadrightarrow Y_1$, $X \twoheadrightarrow Y_2$, $\ldots$, $X \twoheadrightarrow Y_k$, where $R = X\ Y_1\ Y_2 \cdots Y_k$, then r decomposes losslessly onto the relation schemes $X\ Y_1$, $X\ Y_2$, $\ldots$, $X\ Y_k$.

7.4 Let $r(R)$ be a relation where $R_1 \subseteq R$, $R_2 \subseteq R$ and $R = R_1\ R_2$. Prove that $r = \pi_{R_1}(r) \bowtie \pi_{R_2}(r)$ if and only if $c_R[X{=}x](r) = c_{R_1}[X{=}x](r) \cdot c_{R_2}[X{=}x](r)$ for every X-value x in r.

7.5 Prove that if a relation $r(R)$ satisfies $X \twoheadrightarrow Y$ and $Z = R - (X\ Y)$, then

$$\pi_Z(\sigma_{X=x}(r)) = \pi_Z(\sigma_{XY=xy}(r))$$

for every $X\ Y$-value $x\ y$ in r.

7.6 Prove the equivalence of the two definitions of MVDs.

7.7 Characterize the set of MVDs implied by the single FD $X \rightarrow Y$.

7.8 Prove the correctness of inference axioms M1 and M2.

7.9 Let r be a relation on scheme R and let W, X, Y, Z be subsets of R. Show that if r satisfies $X \twoheadrightarrow Y$ and $Z \subseteq W$, then r satisfies $X\ W \twoheadrightarrow Y\ Z$.

7.10 Prove the correctness of inference axiom M6 using axioms M1-M5 and M7.

7.11 Let r be a relation on scheme R and let X, Y, Z be subsets of R. Show that if r satisfies $X \twoheadrightarrow Y$ and $X\ Y \rightarrow Z$, then r satisfies $X \rightarrow Z - Y$.

7.12 Give a set of FDs and MVDs from which an FD can be derived using axiom C2 that cannot be derived using axioms F1-F6.

7.13 Find $DEP(A\ C)$ under the set $F = \{A \twoheadrightarrow E\ I,\ C \twoheadrightarrow A\ B\}$ of MVDs over the relation scheme $R = A\ B\ C\ D\ E\ I$.

7.14 Show that an MVD $X \twoheadrightarrow Y$ over R is trivial if and only if $X \supseteq Y$ or $X\ Y = R$.

7.15 Let **R** be a 4NF database scheme obtained by decomposition from a relation scheme R and a set F of FDs and MVDs. Show that any relation $r(R)$ that satisfies F decomposes losslessly onto the relation schemes in **R**.

7.16 Let $\mathbf{R} = \{R_1, R_2, \ldots, R_p\}$ be a database scheme over **U** and let $d = \{r_1, r_2, \ldots, r_p\}$ be a database over **R** that is the projection of a single relation $r(\mathbf{U})$. That is, $r_i = \pi_{R_i}(r)$, $1 \leq i \leq p$. Show that if the FDs $X \rightarrow Y$ and $Y \rightarrow Z$ apply to **R**, then it is possible to recover the actual functional relationship for $X \rightarrow Z$ in r from d.

7.17 Show that a relation $r(R)$ has no lossless decompositions onto any pair of relation schemes R_1 and R_2, where $R_1 \neq R$ and $R_2 \neq R$, if and only if r satisfies only trivial MVDs.

7.18 Give an example of a relation $r(A\ B\ C\ D\ E)$ that satisfies the JD $*[A\ B\ C,\ B\ D\ E,\ A\ C\ E]$ but satisfies no nontrivial MVD.

7.19 What does it mean for a relation r to satisfy a JD $*[R_1, R_2, \ldots, R_p]$ where all the R_i's are disjoint?

7.20 Let relation r satisfy $*[R_1, R_2, \ldots, R_p]$. If $t_1, t_2, \ldots, t_p$ are tuples in r such that $t_i(R_i \cap R_j) = t_j(R_i \cap R_j)$ for all i and j, show that $t_1', t_2', \ldots, t_p'$ are joinable, where $t_i' = t_i(R_i)$.

7.21 Let $*[R_1, R_2, \ldots, R_p]$ and $*[S_1, S_2, \ldots, S_q]$ be JDs such that for each R_i, $1 \leq i \leq p$, there exists an S_j such that $R_i \supseteq S_j$. Show that $*[S_1, S_2, \ldots, S_q]$ implies $*[R_1, R_2, \ldots, R_p]$.

7.22 Show that a JD $*[R_1, R_2, \ldots, R_p]$ over R is trivial if and only if $R = R_i$ for some i.

7.23 Show that PJNF implies 4NF.

7.24 Show that the revised definition of PJNF implies the first definition given.

7.25 Refer to Example 7.18.
   (a) Give a relation over R with keys A and C that violates $*[A\ B,\ B\ C]$.
   (b) Show that decomposing a relation over R that satisfies F onto $\{A\ B,\ B\ C\}$ requires more space than the original relation.

7.26 Show that the JD $*[A\ B\ C,\ B\ D\ E,\ A\ E\ I]$ over $A\ B\ C\ D\ E\ I$ implies the EJD $*[A\ B,\ B\ E,\ A\ E]$, but not the EJD $*[B\ C,\ B\ D,\ A\ I]$.

7.11 BIBLIOGRAPHY AND COMMENTS

Multivalued dependencies were introduced by Fagin [1977c]. The same concept, under a different name, was independently put forth by Zaniolo [1976] and Delobel [1978]. Beeri, Fagin, and Howard [1977] introduced the first complete axiomatization for FDs and MVDs. Mendelzon [1979] discusses independence of these axioms. The construction of *DEP*(X) is from Beeri [1980]. Hagihara, Ito, *et al.* [1979], Galil [1979], and Sagiv [1980] give efficient algorithms for calculating *DEP*(X). Beeri [1979], Biskup [1978, 1980b], and Zaniolo [1979] also discuss inference rules for MVDs, particularly the applicability of complementation in the context of databases. Fischer, Jou, and Tsou [1981] discuss succinct representations for sets of MVDs. Katsuno [1981b] treats some semantic aspects of MVDs.

Fagin [1977a] introduced the fourth normal form. Beeri [1979] and Kambayashi [1979] give synthesis algorithms that incorporate MVDs. Beeri and Vardi [1981a] point out some problems in achieving 4NF. Other normal forms and decompositions strategies are treated by Armstrong and Delobel [1980], Fagin [1980b], Lien [1981], Namibar [1979], Tanaka, Kambayashi, and Yajima [1979a], and Zaniolo and Melkanoff [1981, 1982].

Join dependencies were first introduced in full generality by Rissanen [1977] and were extensively studied by Aho, Beeri, and Ullman [1979]. Sciore [1982] axiomatizes a class of dependencies slightly larger than the class of JDs. Beeri and Vardi [1981b] and Vardi [1980a, 1980b] give inference axioms for FDs and JDs together. Project-join normal form is from Fagin [1979].

Embedded cases of MVDs were recognized by both Fagin [1977c] and Delobel [1978]. Parker and Parsaye-Ghomi [1980], and Sagiv and Walecka [1979] showed there is no complete, finite axiomatization for EMVDs alone. Tanaka, Kambayashi, and Yajima [1979b] also discuss EMVDs. Sadri and Ullman [1980a] give a proof procedure for a more general class of dependencies (which we shall take up in Chapter 14). Beeri and Vardi [1980a, 1980b] and Chandra, Lewis, and Makowsky [1981] showed that implication for this class of dependencies is undecidable. There is no contradiction here, since the proof procedure is for finite and infinite relations. An implication statement can have an infinite counterexample but no finite counterexample.

Chapter 8

PROJECT-JOIN MAPPINGS, TABLEAUX, AND THE CHASE

We did not present a set of inference axioms for JDs in Chapter 7. Instead, in this chapter we present a method for deciding if a given FD or JD is implied by a set of FDs and JDs.

8.1 PROJECT-JOIN MAPPINGS

The criterion for a relation $r(R)$ decomposing losslessly onto a database scheme $\mathbf{R} = \{R_1, R_2, \ldots, R_p\}$ is that $r = \pi_{R_1}(r) \bowtie \pi_{R_2}(r) \bowtie \cdots \bowtie \pi_{R_p}(r)$. The right side of this equation is rather cumbersome, so we give a shorter notation for it.

Definition 8.1 Let $\mathbf{R} = \{R_1, R_2, \ldots, R_p\}$ be a set of relation schemes, where $R = R_1R_2 \cdots R_p$. The *project-join mapping* defined by $\mathbf{R}$, written $m_{\mathbf{R}}$, is a function on relations over R defined by

$$m_{\mathbf{R}}(r) = \pi_{R_1}(r) \bowtie \pi_{R_2}(r) \bowtie \cdots \bowtie \pi_{R_p}(r).$$

Example 8.1 Let $R = ABCDE$ and let $\mathbf{R} = \{ABD, BC, ADE\}$. Consider the relation $r(R)$ in Figure 8.1. The result of applying $m_{\mathbf{R}}$ to r is the relation $s(R)$ shown in Figure 8.2. Applying $m_{\mathbf{R}}$ to s gives back relation s.

r(A	B	C	D	E)
a	b	c	d	e
a	b'	c	d'	e
a	b'	c	d'	e'
a	b	c	d'	e'

Figure 8.1

s(A	B	C	D	E)
a	b	c	d	e
a	b′	c	d′	e
a	b′	c	d′	e′
a	b	c	d′	e′
a	b	c	d′	e

Figure 8.2

Saying that a relation $r(R)$ satisfies the JD $*[\mathbf{R}]$ is the same as saying $m_{\mathbf{R}}(r) = r$.

Definition 8.2 Let $\mathbf{R} = \{R_1, R_2, \ldots, R_p\}$, where $R = R_1R_2 \cdots R_p$. Relation $r(R)$ is a *fixed-point* of the mapping $m_{\mathbf{R}}$ if $m_{\mathbf{R}}(r) = r$. The set of all fixed-points of $m_{\mathbf{R}}$ is denoted *FIX*(**R**).

Example 8.2 If $\mathbf{R} = \{ABD, BC, ADE\}$, then the relation r in Figure 8.1 is not in *FIX*(**R**), while the relation s in Figure 8.2 is in *FIX*(**R**).

We present some other properties of project-join mappings.

Lemma 8.1 Let $\mathbf{R} = \{R_1, R_2, \ldots, R_p\}$ be a set of relation schemes where $R = R_1R_2 \cdots R_p$ and let r and s be relations over R. The project-join mapping $m_{\mathbf{R}}$ has the following properties:

1. $r \subseteq m_{\mathbf{R}}(r)$;
2. if $r \subseteq s$, then $m_{\mathbf{R}}(r) \subseteq m_{\mathbf{R}}(s)$ (monotonicity);
3. $m_{\mathbf{R}}(r) = m_{\mathbf{R}}(m_{\mathbf{R}}(r))$ (idempotence).

Proof The proof of part 1 is left to the reader (see Exercise 8.2). Part 2 follows from the observation that $r \subseteq s$ implies $\pi_{R_i}(r) \subseteq \pi_{R_i}(s)$, $1 \leq i \leq p$. Let $r' = m_{\mathbf{R}}(r)$; part 3 follows from the property that $\pi_{R_1}(r)$, $\pi_{R_2}(r)$, $\ldots$, $\pi_{R_p}(r)$ join completely (see Exercise 2.16), hence $\pi_{R_i}(r) = \pi_{R_i}(r')$, $1 \leq i \leq p$.

We would like to know when relations on a relation scheme R can be represented as databases on a database scheme **R** such that

1. there is no loss of information, and
2. redundancy is removed.

In practice, we are not interested in all possible relations on scheme R, only some subset. Call it **P**. The first point above corresponds to saying that for every relation r in **P**, $m_{\mathbf{R}}(r) = r$. That is, $\mathbf{P} \subseteq FIX(\mathbf{R})$. The second point seems to require that if we project a relation r in **P** into the schemes in **R**, some of the projections have fewer tuples than r.

The set **P** will usually be infinite, hence it cannot be described by enumeration. Rather, **P** will frequently be specified by a set of constraints (such as FDs or JDs) on relations on R.

Definition 8.3 Let **C** be a set of constraints on a relation scheme R. $SAT_R(\mathbf{C})$ is the set of all relations r on R that satisfy all the constraints in **C**. We write $SAT(\mathbf{C})$ for SAT_R (**C**) when R is understood, and we write $SAT_R(c)$ for $SAT_R(\{c\})$, where c is a single constraint.

We can now state precisely the notion of implication we have been using informally in our discussions of MVDs and JDs.

Definition 8.4 Let **C** be a set of constraints over relation scheme R. **C** *implies* c, written $\mathbf{C} \models c$, if $SAT_R(\mathbf{C}) \subseteq SAT_R(c)$.

If **P** = SAT(**C**) for some set of constraints **C**, then our condition requiring no loss of information for databases on database scheme **R** can be stated as

$$SAT(\mathbf{C}) \subseteq FIX(\mathbf{R}) \quad \text{or}$$
$$\mathbf{C} \models *[\mathbf{R}]$$

In subsequent sections we shall develop a test for this condition, when **C** is composed of JDs and FDs.

8.2 TABLEAUX

In this section we present a tabular means of representing project-join mappings; a *tableau*. A tableau is similar to a relation, except, in place of values, a tableau has variables chosen from a set V. V is the union of two sets, V_d and V_n. V_d is the set of *distinguished variables*, denoted by subscripted a's, and V_n is the set of *nondistinguished variables*, denoted by subscripted b's. (We shall use variable and symbol synonymously in this context.) A tableau, T, is shown in Figure 8.3. The set of attributes labeling columns in the tableau, in this case $A_1 A_2 A_3 A_4$, is the *scheme* of the tableau. What would be tuples in a relation are referred to as *rows* of the tableau.

$T(A_1$	A_2	A_3	$A_4)$
a_1	b_1	a_3	b_2
b_3	a_2	a_3	b_4
a_1	b_5	a_3	a_4

Figure 8.3

We restrict the variables in a tableau to appear in only one column. We make the further restriction that at most one distinguished variable may appear in any column. By convention, if the scheme of a tableau is $A_1 A_2 \cdots A_n$, then the distinguished variable appearing in the A_i-column will be a_i.

A tableau T with scheme R can be viewed as a pattern or template for a relation on scheme R. We get a relation from the tableau by substituting domain values for variables. Assume $R = A_1 A_2 \cdots A_n$ and let

$$\mathbf{D} = \cup_{i=1}^{n} dom(A_i).$$

A *valuation* for tableau T is a mapping ρ from V to $\mathbf{D}$ such that $\rho(v)$ is in $dom(A_i)$ when v is a variable appearing in the A_i-column. We extend the valuation from variables to rows and thence to the entire tableau. If $w = \langle v_1 v_2 \cdots v_n \rangle$ is a row in a tableau, we let $\rho(w) = \langle \rho(v_1)\ \rho(v_2) \cdots \rho(v_n) \rangle$. We then let

$$\rho(T) = \{\rho(w) \mid w \text{ is a row in } T\}.$$

Example 8.3 Let ρ be the valuation listed in Figure 8.4. The result of applying ρ to tableau T in Figure 8.3 is the relation r in Figure 8.5.

$\rho(a_1) = 1$	$\rho(b_1) = 4$
$\rho(a_2) = 3$	$\rho(b_2) = 8$
$\rho(a_3) = 5$	$\rho(b_3) = 2$
$\rho(a_4) = 7$	$\rho(b_4) = 7$
	$\rho(b_5) = 4$

Figure 8.4

$r(A_1$	A_2	A_3	$A_4)$
1	4	5	8
2	3	5	7
1	4	5	7

Figure 8.5

8.2.1 Tableaux as Mappings

We can interpret a tableau T with scheme R as a function on relations with scheme R. Let w_d be the row of all distinguished variables. That is, if $R = A_1 A_2 \cdots A_n$, $w_d = \langle a_1\ a_2\ \cdots\ a_n \rangle$. (Row w_d is not necessarily in T.) If r is a relation on scheme R, we let

$$T(r) = \{\rho(w_d) \mid \rho(T) \subseteq r\}.$$

This definition says that if we find a valuation ρ that takes every row in T to a tuple in r, then $\rho(w_d)$ is in $T(r)$.

Example 8.4 Let r be the relation shown in Figure 8.6 and let T be the tableau in Figure 8.3. The valuation ρ in Figure 8.4 shows us that the tuple $\langle 1\ 3\ 5\ 7 \rangle$ must be in $T(r)$. The valuation ρ' in Figure 8.7 puts $\langle 2\ 4\ 5\ 7 \rangle$ in $T(r)$. All of $T(r)$ is given as relation s in Figure 8.8.

$r(A_1$	A_2	A_3	$A_4)$
1	4	5	8
2	3	5	7
1	4	5	7
2	3	6	7

Figure 8.6

$\rho'(a_1) = 2$	$\rho'(b_1) = 3$
$\rho'(a_2) = 4$	$\rho'(b_2) = 7$
$\rho'(a_3) = 5$	$\rho'(b_3) = 1$
$\rho'(a_4) = 7$	$\rho'(b_4) = 8$
	$\rho'(b_5) = 3$

Figure 8.7

$T(r) = s(A_1$	A_2	A_3	$A_4)$
1	4	5	8
2	4	5	7
1	4	5	7
1	3	5	8
1	3	5	7
2	3	5	7
2	3	6	7

Figure 8.8

When evaluating $T(r)$, if the A_i-column in T has no distinguished variable in it, then there is no restriction on the value of $\rho(a_i)$. If $\rho(T) \subseteq r$, then $\rho'(T) \subseteq r$, for any ρ' that agrees with ρ on V except on a_i. Thus, if $dom(A_i)$ is infinite, $T(r)$ can have infinitely many tuples and hence will not be a relation. Whenever we want to consider a tableau T as a function from relations to relations, we require that T have a distinguished symbol in every column (see Exercise 8.5).

8.2.2 Representing Project-Join Mappings as Tableaux

It is always possible to find a tableau T that represents the same function as any project-join mapping $m_{\mathbf{R}}$. Let $\mathbf{R} = \{R_1, R_2, \ldots, R_p\}$ be a set of relation schemes, where $R = R_1 R_2 \cdots R_p$. The *tableau for* $\mathbf{R}$, $T_{\mathbf{R}}$, is defined as follows: The scheme for $T_{\mathbf{R}}$ is R. $T_{\mathbf{R}}$ has p rows, $w_1, w_2, \ldots, w_p$. Assume $R = A_1 A_2 \cdots A_n$. Row w_i has the distinguished variable a_j in the A_j-column exactly when $A_j \in R_i$. The rest of w_i is unique nondistinguished symbols—nondistinguished symbols that appear in no other rows of $T_{\mathbf{R}}$.

Example 8.5 Let $\mathbf{R} = \{A_1A_2, A_2A_3, A_3A_4\}$. The tableau $T_{\mathbf{R}}$ is shown in Figure 8.9.

$T_{\mathbf{R}}(A_1$	A_2	A_3	$A_4)$
a_1	a_2	b_1	b_2
b_3	a_2	a_3	b_4
b_5	b_6	a_3	a_4

Figure 8.9

Lemma 8.2 Let $\mathbf{R} = \{R_1, R_2, \ldots, R_p\}$ be a set of relation schemes, where $R = R_1 R_2 \cdots R_p$. The project-join mapping $m_{\mathbf{R}}$ and the tableau $T_{\mathbf{R}}$ define the same function between relations over R.

Proof Left to the reader (see Exercise 8.7).

Example 8.6 If $\mathbf{R} = \{A_1A_2, A_2A_3, A_3A_4\}$ and r is the relation shown in Figure 8.10, then $m_{\mathbf{R}}(r) = T_{\mathbf{R}}(r) = s$, where s is the relation in Figure 8.11.

$r(A_1$	A_2	A_3	$A_4)$
1	3	5	7
1	4	5	7
2	3	6	8

Figure 8.10

$s(A_1$	A_2	A_3	$A_4)$
1	3	5	7
1	3	6	8
1	4	5	7
2	3	5	7
2	3	6	8

Figure 8.11

8.3 TABLEAUX EQUIVALENCE AND SCHEME EQUIVALENCE

Definition 8.5 Let T_1 and T_2 be tableaux over scheme R. We write $T_1 \sqsupseteq T_2$ if $T_1(r) \supseteq T_2(r)$ for all relations $r(R)$. Tableaux T_1 and T_2 are *equivalent*, written $T_1 \equiv T_2$, if $T_1 \sqsupseteq T_2$ and $T_2 \sqsupseteq T_1$. That is, $T_1 \equiv T_2$ if $T_1(r) = T_2(r)$ for every relation $r(R)$.

Example 8.7 Let T_1 and T_2 be the tableaux in Figures 8.12 and 8.13, respectively. $T_1 \sqsupseteq T_2$. For example, if r is the relation in Figure 8.10, $T_1(r)$ is the relation s in Figure 8.11, while $T_2(r) = r$.

$T_1(A_1$	A_2	A_3	$A_4)$
a_1	a_2	b_1	b_2
b_3	a_2	a_3	b_4
b_5	b_6	a_3	a_4

Figure 8.12

$T_2(A_1$	A_2	A_3	$A_4)$
a_1	a_2	a_3	b_1
b_2	b_3	a_3	a_4

Figure 8.13

Definition 8.6 Let $\mathbf{R} = \{R_1, R_2, \ldots, R_p\}$ and $\mathbf{S} = \{S_1, S_2, \ldots, S_q\}$ be sets of relation schemes, where $R_1R_2 \cdots R_p = S_1S_2 \cdots S_q = R$. $\mathbf{R}$ *covers* $\mathbf{S}$, written $\mathbf{R} \geq \mathbf{S}$, if for every scheme S_j in $\mathbf{S}$, there exists an R_i in $\mathbf{R}$ such that $R_i \supseteq S_j$. We say $\mathbf{R}$ and $\mathbf{S}$ are *equivalent*, written $\mathbf{R} \simeq \mathbf{S}$, if $\mathbf{R} \geq \mathbf{S}$ and $\mathbf{S} \geq \mathbf{R}$.

Example 8.8 If $\mathbf{R} = \{A_1A_2, A_2A_3, A_3A_4\}$ and $\mathbf{S} = \{A_1A_2A_3, A_3A_4\}$, then $\mathbf{R} \leq \mathbf{S}$.

Theorem 8.1 Let $\mathbf{R} = \{R_1, R_2, \ldots, R_p\}$ and $\mathbf{S} = \{S_1, S_2, \ldots, S_q\}$ be sets of relation schemes, where $R_1 R_2 \cdots R_p = S_1 S_2 \cdots S_q = R$. The following are equivalent:

1. $m_{\mathbf{R}}(r) \supseteq m_{\mathbf{S}}(r)$ for all relations $r(R)$.
2. $\mathrm{T}_{\mathbf{R}} \sqsupseteq \mathrm{T}_{\mathbf{S}}$.
3. $FIX(\mathbf{R}) \subseteq FIX(\mathbf{S})$.
4. $\mathbf{R} \leq \mathbf{S}$.

Proof By Lemma 8.2, 1 and 2 are equivalent. We next show 1 and 3 are equivalent.

Suppose $m_{\mathbf{R}}(r) \supseteq m_{\mathbf{S}}(r)$ for all relations $r(R)$. Let s be in $FIX(\mathbf{R})$. Since $m_{\mathbf{R}}(s) = s$, $s \supseteq m_{\mathbf{S}}(s)$. But, by Lemma 8.1, $s \subseteq m_{\mathbf{S}}(s)$. Therefore $s = m_{\mathbf{S}}(s)$ and $s \in FIX(\mathbf{S})$. Thus we conclude $FIX(\mathbf{R}) \subseteq FIX(\mathbf{S})$.

Now suppose $FIX(\mathbf{R}) \subseteq FIX(\mathbf{S})$. By idempotence, for any relation $r(R)$,

$$m_{\mathbf{R}}(r) = m_{\mathbf{R}}(m_{\mathbf{R}}(r)).$$

Hence $m_{\mathbf{R}}(r)$ is in $FIX(\mathbf{R})$ and $FIX(\mathbf{S})$:

$$m_{\mathbf{S}}(m_{\mathbf{R}}(r)) = m_{\mathbf{R}}(r).$$

From Lemma 8.1 we know $m_{\mathbf{R}}(r) \supseteq r$, so by monotonicity

$$m_{\mathbf{S}}(m_{\mathbf{R}}(r)) \supseteq m_{\mathbf{S}}(r),$$

hence

$$m_{\mathbf{R}}(r) \supseteq m_{\mathbf{S}}(r).$$

Last, we show that 1 and 4 are equivalent.

Suppose $m_{\mathbf{R}}(r) \supseteq m_{\mathbf{S}}(r)$ for all relations $r(R)$. We assume for each attribute A in R, $dom(A)$ has at least two values, which we shall call 0 and 1. We construct a relation $s(R)$ as follows: Relation s has q tuples, $t_1, t_2, \ldots, t_q$. The tuple t_i is defined as

$$t_i(A) = \begin{cases} 0 & \text{if } A \in S_i \\ 1 & \text{otherwise,} \end{cases} \qquad 1 \leq i \leq q.$$

Let t_0 be the tuple of all 0's. It is not hard to see that t_0 must be in $m_{\mathbf{S}}(s)$. Therefore, t_0 is in $m_{\mathbf{R}}(s)$. By the nature of $m_{\mathbf{R}}$, for each relation scheme R_i in

R, there has to be a tuple t_j in s such that $t_j(R_i) = t_0(R_i)$. Thus, $R_i \subseteq S_j$ and $\mathbf{R} \leq \mathbf{S}$.

Now suppose $\mathbf{R} \leq \mathbf{S}$. Let $r(R)$ be an arbitrary relation and let t be any tuple in $m_{\mathbf{S}}(r)$. There must be tuples $t_1, t_2, \ldots, t_q$ in r such that $t_i(S_i) = t(S_i)$, $1 \leq i \leq p$. For any R_j such that $R_j \subseteq S_i$, $t_i(R_j) = t(R_j)$. Since $\mathbf{R} \leq \mathbf{S}$, for any R_j in **R** there is a tuple t_j' in r such that $t_j'(R_j) = t(R_j)$. We see that t is in $m_{\mathbf{R}}(r)$ and hence $m_{\mathbf{R}}(r) \supseteq m_{\mathbf{S}}(r)$.

Example 8.9 Let $\mathbf{R} = \{A_1A_2, A_2A_3, A_3A_4\}$ and $\mathbf{S} = \{A_1A_2A_3, A_3A_4\}$, as in Example 8.8. We see that tableau T_1 in Figure 8.12 is $T_{\mathbf{R}}$ and that Tableau T_2 in Figure 8.13 is $T_{\mathbf{S}}$. Since $\mathbf{R} \leq \mathbf{S}$, by Theorem 8.1, $T_{\mathbf{R}} \sqsupseteq T_{\mathbf{S}}$. For example, if r is the relation in Figure 8.14, then $T_{\mathbf{R}}(r)$ is given in Figure 8.15 and $T_{\mathbf{S}}(r)$ is given in Figure 8.16. Evidently, $T_{\mathbf{R}}(r) \supseteq T_{\mathbf{S}}(r)$.

$r(A_1$	A_2	A_3	$A_4)$
1	4	6	8
2	4	7	9
3	5	7	10

Figure 8.14

$T_{\mathbf{R}}(r)(A_1$	A_2	A_3	$A_4)$
1	4	6	8
1	4	7	9
1	4	7	10
2	4	6	8
2	4	7	9
2	4	7	10
3	5	7	9
3	5	7	10

Figure 8.15

$T_{\mathbf{S}}(r)(A_1$	A_2	A_3	$A_4)$
1	4	6	8
2	4	7	9
2	4	7	10
3	5	7	9
3	5	7	10

Figure 8.16

Corollary Let $\mathbf{R} = \{R_1, R_2, \ldots, R_p\}$ and $\mathbf{S} = \{S_1, S_2, \ldots, S_q\}$ be sets of relation schemes, where $R_1R_2 \cdots R_p = S_1S_2 \cdots S_q = R$. The following are equivalent.

1. $m_{\mathbf{R}} = m_{\mathbf{S}}$
2. $T_{\mathbf{R}} \equiv T_{\mathbf{S}}$
3. $FIX(\mathbf{R}) = FIX(\mathbf{S})$
4. $\mathbf{R} \simeq \mathbf{S}$

Condition 1 means $m_{\mathbf{R}}(r) = m_{\mathbf{S}}(r)$ for all relations $r(R)$. Note that conditions 2 and 4 use equivalence rather than equality. Equivalence can hold without equality.

Example 8.10 Let $\mathbf{R} = \{A_1A_2A_3, A_1A_4, A_1A_3A_4\}$ and $\mathbf{S} = \{A_1A_2A_3, A_3A_4, A_1A_3A_4\}$ be sets of relation schemes. $\mathbf{R} \geq \mathbf{S}$ and $\mathbf{S} \geq \mathbf{R}$, so $\mathbf{R} \simeq \mathbf{S}$. By the corollary to Theorem 8.1, $T_{\mathbf{R}} \equiv T_{\mathbf{S}}$. But as we see from Figures 8.17 and 8.18, $T_{\mathbf{R}} \neq T_{\mathbf{S}}$, even if we rename nondistinguished variables.

$T_{\mathbf{R}}(A_1$	A_2	A_3	$A_4)$
a_1	a_2	a_3	b_1
a_1	b_2	b_3	a_4
a_1	b_4	a_3	a_4

Figure 8.17

$T_{\mathbf{S}}(A_1$	A_2	A_3	$A_4)$
a_1	a_2	a_3	b_1
b_2	b_3	a_3	a_4
a_1	b_4	a_3	a_4

Figure 8.18

Although we can have $T_{\mathbf{R}} \equiv T_{\mathbf{S}}$ without $T_{\mathbf{R}} = T_{\mathbf{S}}$, if $T_{\mathbf{R}} \equiv T_{\mathbf{S}}$, then $T_{\mathbf{R}}$ and $T_{\mathbf{S}}$ will exhibit a certain similarity.

Definition 8.7 Let w_1 and w_2 be rows in a tableau T with scheme R. If for every attribute A in R, $w_2(A)$ is a distinguished variable implies $w_1(A)$ is a distinguished variable, then w_1 is said to *subsume* w_2.

Example 8.11 In Figure 8.17, the third row subsumes the second row. In Figure 8.18, the third row also subsumes the second row.

Definition 8.8 Let T be a tableau. T *reduced by subsumption*, denoted $SUB(T)$, is the tableau consisting of the set of rows in T that are not subsumed by any other row of T.

Example 8.12 $SUB(T_{\mathbf{R}})$ is given in Figure 8.19, for the tableau $T_{\mathbf{R}}$ in Figure 8.17.

$SUB(T_{\mathbf{R}})(A_1$	A_2	A_3	$A_4)$
a_1	a_2	a_3	b_1
a_1	b_4	a_3	a_4

Figure 8.19

Theorem 8.2 Let $\mathbf{R} = \{R_1, R_2, \ldots, R_p\}$ and $\mathbf{S} = \{S_1, S_2, \ldots, S_q\}$ be sets of relation schemes where $R_1R_2 \cdots R_p = S_1S_2 \cdots S_q = R$. $T_{\mathbf{R}} \equiv T_{\mathbf{S}}$ if and only if $SUB(T_{\mathbf{R}})$ is identical to $SUB(T_{\mathbf{S}})$, except for possibly a one-to-one renaming of the nondistinguished symbols.

Proof Left to the reader (see Exercise 8.13).

Example 8.13 Let $\mathbf{R} = \{A_1A_2A_3, A_1A_4, A_1A_3A_4\}$ and $\mathbf{S} = \{A_1A_2A_3, A_3A_4, A_1A_3A_4\}$ be sets of relation schemes, as in Example 8.10. $SUB(T_{\mathbf{R}})$, shown in Figure 8.19, is identical to $SUB(T_{\mathbf{S}})$.

Corollary $SUB(T_{\mathbf{R}}) \equiv T_{\mathbf{R}}$.

8.4 CONTAINMENT MAPPINGS

As we see from Theorem 8.2, there is a simple test for equivalence of tableaux that come from sets of schemes, namely, identity of subsumption-reduced versions. Any tableau where no nondistinguished variable occurs more than once comes from some set of schemes. Unfortunately, Theorem 8.2 does not hold for tableaux where some nondistinguished variables are duplicated.

Example 8.14 Consider the tableau T in Figure 8.20 and its subsumption-reduction $SUB(T)$ in Figure 8.21. Let r be the relation in Figure 8.22. Certainly $SUB(T)$ is identical to $SUB(SUB(T))$. However, $T(r) = r$, whereas $SUB(T)(r) = r'$, where r' is the relation given in Figure 8.23.

$T(A_1$	A_2	A_3	$A_4)$
a_1	a_2	b_1	b_2
b_3	a_2	a_3	a_4
b_4	a_2	a_3	b_2

Figure 8.20

$SUB(T)(A_1$	A_2	A_3	$A_4)$
a_1	a_2	b_1	b_2
b_3	a_2	a_3	a_4

Figure 8.21

$r(A_1$	A_2	A_3	$A_4)$
1	3	4	6
2	3	5	7

Figure 8.22

$r'(A_1$	A_2	A_3	$A_4)$
1	3	4	6
1	3	5	7
2	3	4	6
2	3	5	7

Figure 8.23

We want to formulate a condition for equivalence of arbitrary tableaux. To do so we introduce containment mappings of tableaux. A containment mapping is quite similar to a valuation, but instead of mapping tableau variables to domain values, it maps them to variables in a second tableau, in such a way that rows are mapped to rows.

Definition 8.9 Let T and T' be tableaux on scheme R, with variable sets V and V'. A mapping ψ: $V \rightarrow V'$ is a *containment mapping from* T *to* T$'$ if the following conditions hold:

1. If variable v is in the A-column of T then $\psi(v)$ is in the A-column of T'.
2. If variable v is distinguished, then $\psi(v)$ is distinguished. (By our naming convention, $\psi(v) = v$.)

3. $\psi(T) \subseteq T'$. That is, when ψ is extended to rows of T and thence to T itself, it maps every row of T to a row in T'.

Example 8.15 Let T and T' be the tableaux in Figures 8.24 and 8.25. There is a containment mapping from T to T', namely ψ, where

$$\begin{aligned} \psi(a_i) &= a_i, \qquad 1 \le i \le 4 \\ \psi(b_1) &= a_3 \\ \psi(b_2) &= b_1 \\ \psi(b_3) &= a_1 \\ \psi(b_4) &= b_2 \\ \psi(b_5) &= a_2. \end{aligned}$$

The first two rows of T are mapped to the first row of T' by ψ; ψ maps the third row of T to the second row of T'. There is no containment mapping from T' to T, since, for example, the first row of T' would have to map to a row with at least the distinguished variables a_1, a_2 and a_3.

$T(A_1$	A_2	A_3	$A_4)$
a_1	a_2	b_1	b_2
b_3	a_2	a_3	b_2
b_4	b_5	a_3	a_4

Figure 8.24

$T'(A_1$	A_2	A_3	$A_4)$
a_1	a_2	a_3	b_1
b_2	a_2	a_3	a_4

Figure 8.25

Theorem 8.3 Let T and T' be tableaux over scheme R. $T \sqsupseteq T'$ if and only if there is a containment mapping from T to T'.

Proof (if) Let ψ be a containment mapping from T to T'. Take any relation $r(R)$ and look at $T(r)$ and $T'(r)$. If ρ is a valuation for T' such that $\rho(T') \subseteq r$, then $\rho \circ \psi$ is a valuation for T such that $\rho \circ \psi(T) \subseteq r$. The inclusion follows from $\psi(T) \subseteq T'$ by applying ρ to both sides. If w_d is the row of all distinguished variables, since $\psi(w_d) = w_d$, $\rho \circ \psi(w_d) = \rho(w_d)$, so $T(r) \supseteq T'(r)$.

(only if) Suppose $T \sqsupseteq T'$. Consider T' also as a relation. We have $T(T') \supseteq T'(T')$. Consider the valuation ρ' that is the identity on the variables V' of T'. Clearly $\rho'(T') = T' \subseteq T'$, so $\rho'(w_d) = w_d \in T'(T')$. There must be a valuation ρ for T such that $\rho(T) \subseteq T'$ and $\rho(w_d) = w_d$. We see that ρ can also be construed as a containment mapping from T to T'.

Example 8.16 We see that $T \sqsupseteq T'$, where T and T' are the tableaux in Figures 8.24 and 8.25. For example, if r is the relation in Figure 8.26, then $T(r) = r'$, where r' is given in Figure 8.27, while $T'(r) = r$, so $T(r) \supseteq T'(r)$.

$r(A_1$	A_2	A_3	$A_4)$
1	4	6	8
2	4	7	8
3	5	7	9

Figure 8.26

$r'(A_1$	A_2	A_3	$A_4)$
1	4	6	8
1	4	7	8
1	4	7	9
2	4	7	8
2	4	7	9
3	5	7	8
3	5	7	9

Figure 8.27

Example 8.17 Let T'' be the tableau in Figure 8.28. There is a containment mapping from T'' to T (What is it?), so $T'' \sqsupseteq T$. For the relation r in Figure 8.26, $T''(r) = r''$, where r'' is given in Figure 8.29. We see $T''(r) \supseteq T(r)$.

$T''(A_1$	A_2	A_3	$A_4)$
a_1	a_2	b_1	b_2
b_3	a_2	a_3	b_4
b_5	b_6	a_3	a_4

Figure 8.28

$r''(A_1$	A_2	A_3	$A_4)$
1	4	6	8
1	4	7	8
1	4	7	9
2	4	6	8
2	4	7	8
2	4	7	9
3	5	7	8
3	5	7	9

Figure 8.29

Corollary Let T and T' be tableaux over scheme R. $T \equiv T'$ if and only if there is a containment mapping from T to T' and a containment mapping from T' to T.

Example 8.18 Let T be the tableau consisting of only the row w_d of all distinguished variables. Let T' be any tableau that contains w_d. $T \equiv T'$. The containment mapping from T to T' maps w_d to w_d. The containment mapping from T' to T maps every row to w_d.

8.5 EQUIVALENCE WITH CONSTRAINTS

We are trying to characterize when a relation can be faithfully represented by its projections. From the corollary to Theorem 8.1 and Theorem 8.2, we see that if $\mathbf{R} = \{R_1, R_2, \ldots, R_p\}$ is a database scheme over R, then $FIX(R)$ is the set of all relations over R only if $R_i = R$ for some i. If $R_i = R$, there is no need for the other relation schemes in $\mathbf{R}$, so $\mathbf{R}$ ends up being a single relation scheme. Thus, in general, the answer to the question, "When can relations over R be represented faithfully as database over a nontrivial database scheme $\mathbf{R}$?" is never.

We seldom deal in the most general case. We usually want to represent a set of relations over scheme R where some set of constraints is imposed. We can use those constraints to find nontrivial database schemes on which to represent the relations.

Definition 8.10 Let $\mathbf{P}$ be a set of relations over scheme R. If T_1 and T_2 are tableaux over R, then T_1 *contains* T_2 *on* $\mathbf{P}$, written $T_1 \sqsupseteq_{\mathbf{P}} T_2$, if $T_1(r) \supseteq T_2(r)$ for every relation r in P. T_1 *and* T_2 *are equivalent on* $\mathbf{P}$, written $T_1 \equiv_{\mathbf{P}} T_2$, if $T_1 \sqsupseteq_{\mathbf{P}} T_2$ and $T_2 \sqsupseteq_{\mathbf{P}} T_1$.

The set **P** will most often be expressed as $\mathbf{P} = SAT(\mathbf{C})$ for some set of constraints **C**. We abbreviate $\equiv_{\mathrm{SAT(C)}}$ as $\equiv_{\mathbf{C}}$. Recall that we are interested in when $SAT(\mathbf{C}) \subseteq FIX(\mathbf{R})$ for a database scheme **R**. That is, for a given database scheme **R**, can every relation in $SAT(\mathbf{C})$ be losslessly decomposed onto **R**? In terms of constraints, we are asking whether $\mathbf{C} \models *[\mathbf{R}]$. If T_I is a tableau for the identity mapping (T_I contains the row of all distinguished variables), then we want to know if $T_{\mathbf{R}}$ behaves as T_I on $SAT(\mathbf{C})$. That is, is $T_{\mathbf{R}} \equiv_{\mathbf{C}} T_I$? Theorem 8.3 gives a test for $\sqsupseteq$; we need a test for $\sqsupseteq_{\mathbf{C}}$.

For the next lemma, we need to view a tableau as a relation. We have already used this device in the proof of Theorem 8.3. We must be more precise now, since we want to know when tableau T, considered as a relation, is in set **P**. What we mean by this condition is that for any valuation ρ, $\rho(T) \in \mathbf{P}$. For an arbitrary set of relations **P**, this conditions is hard to test. However, when $\mathbf{P} = SAT(\mathbf{C})$, where **C** consists of FDs and JDs, if for some one-to-one valuation ρ, $\rho(T) \in \mathbf{P}$, then for any other valuation ρ', $\rho'(T) \in \mathbf{P}$ (see Exercise 8.20).

Lemma 8.3 Let T_1 and T_2 be tableaux over scheme R and let **P** be a set of relations over R. Let T_1' and T_2' be tableaux such that

1. $T_1 \equiv_{\mathbf{P}} T_1'$ and $T_2 \equiv_{\mathbf{P}} T_2'$, and
2. T_1' and T_2' considered as relations are both in **P**.

Then $T_1 \sqsubseteq_{\mathbf{P}} T_2$ if and only if $T_1' \sqsubseteq T_2'$.

Proof The if direction is immediate. Clearly $T_1' \sqsubseteq T_2'$ implies $T_1' \sqsubseteq_{\mathbf{P}} T_2'$, so $T_1' \sqsubseteq T_2'$, $T_1 \equiv_{\mathbf{P}} T_1'$, and $T_2 \equiv_{\mathbf{P}} T_2$ imply $T_1 \subseteq_{\mathbf{P}} T_2$. For the only if direction, $T_1 \sqsubseteq_{\mathbf{P}} T_2$, $T_1 \equiv_{\mathbf{P}} T_1'$ and $T_2 \equiv_{\mathbf{P}} T_2'$ imply $T_1' \sqsubseteq_{\mathbf{P}} T_2'$. We now show that $T_1' \sqsubseteq_{\mathbf{P}} T_2'$ implies $T_1' \sqsubseteq T_2'$.

Consider $T_1'(T_1')$. (We are treating T_1' simultaneously as a tableau and as a relation.) Since T_1', as a relation, is in **P**, $T_1'(T_1') \subseteq T_2'(T_1')$. Let w_d be the row of all distinguished variables and let ρ be the identity valuation for T_1'. Obviously, $\rho(T_1') \subseteq T_1'$, so $\rho(w_d) = w_d$ is in $T_1'(T_1')$ and hence in $T_2'(T_1')$. There must be a valuation η for T_2' such that $\eta(T_2') \subseteq T_1'$ and $\eta(w_d) = w_d$. The valuation η can be viewed as a containment mapping from T_2' to T_1'. Hence, by Theorem 8.3, $T_1' \sqsubseteq T_2'$.

Corollary For the hypotheses of Lemma 8.3, $T_1 \equiv_{\mathbf{P}} T_2$ if and only if $T_1' \equiv T_2'$.

Let us take stock. We are seeking a test for $T_1 \sqsubseteq_{\mathbf{C}} T_2$. We know how to test $T_1 \sqsubseteq T_2$. By Lemma 8.3, we could test $T_1 \sqsubseteq_{\mathbf{C}} T_2$ if we had a way to take an arbitrary tableau T and find a tableau T' such that $T \equiv_{\mathbf{C}} T'$ and T' as a relation is in $SAT(\mathbf{C})$. We shall introduce *transformation rules* for tableaux. A transformation rule for a set of constraints **C** is a means to modify a tableau T to a tableau T' so that $T \equiv_{\mathbf{C}} T'$.

We have seen a limited type of transformation rule in subsumption. For a tableau T with no duplicated nondistinguished variables, removing a subsumed row preserves equivalence. We shall look at transformation rules for a set of constraints **C** composed of FDs and JDs. The different transformation rules will actually correspond to individual FDs (F-rules) and JDs (J-rules). Repeated application of these transformation rules will yield a tableau that, as a relation, satisfies all the dependencies in **C**.

For the rest of this chapter, **C** will always be a set of FDs and JDs over a set of attributes **U**. **U** will be the scheme for all relations and tableaux.

8.5.1 F-rules

For every FD $X \rightarrow A$ in **C** there is an associated F-rule. The F-rule for $X \rightarrow A$ represents a class of transformations that can be applied to a tableau, depending on which rows are chosen.

Let tableau T have rows w_1 and w_2, where $w_1(X) = w_2(X)$. Let $w_1(A) = v_1$ and $w_2(A) = v_2$ and suppose $v_1 \neq v_2$. We apply the F-rule for $X \rightarrow A$ to T by identifying variables v_1 and v_2, to form a new tableau T'. Variables v_1 and v_2 are identified by renaming one of them to be the other. If one of v_1 and v_2 is distinguished, say v_1, then every occurrence of v_2 is replaced by v_1. If v_1 and v_2 are both non-distinguished, every occurrence of the one with the larger subscript is replaced by the one with the smaller subscript. Since a tableau is a set of rows, some rows may be identified by renaming.

Example 8.19 Let T be the tableau in Figure 8.30 and let $\mathbf{C} = \{A_1A_2 \rightarrow A_4, A_2A_4 \rightarrow A_3\}$. Applying the F-rule for $A_2A_4 \rightarrow A_3$ to the first and second rows of T identifies variables a_3 and b_3. Since a_3 is distinguished, it replaces b_3, to yield the tableau T' in Figure 8.31. The F-rule for $A_1A_2 \rightarrow A_4$ can be applied to the first and third rows of T' to identify variables b_1 and b_4. Since b_1 has the lower subscript, it replaces b_4. The first and third rows are now the same, so the result, T'' in Figure 8.32, has only two rows.

$T(A_1$	A_2	A_3	$A_4)$
a_1	a_2	a_3	b_1
b_2	a_2	b_3	b_1
a_1	a_2	b_3	b_4

Figure 8.30

$T'(A_1$	A_2	A_3	$A_4)$
a_1	a_2	a_3	b_1
b_2	a_2	a_3	b_1
a_1	a_2	a_3	b_4

Figure 8.31

$T''(A_1$	A_2	A_3	$A_4)$
a_1	a_2	a_3	b_1
b_2	a_2	a_3	b_1

Figure 8.32

Theorem 8.4 Let T' be the result of applying the F-rule for the FD $X \rightarrow A$ to tableau T. T and T' are equivalent on $SAT(X \rightarrow A)$.

Proof Left to the reader (see Exercise 8.23).

8.5.2 J-rules

Let $\mathbf{S} = \{S_1, S_2, \ldots, S_q\}$ be a set of relation schemes and let $*[\mathbf{S}]$ be a JD over $\mathbf{U}$. Let T be a tableau and let $w_1, w_2, \ldots, w_q$ be rows of T that are joinable on $\mathbf{S}$ with result w. Applying the J-rule for $*[\mathbf{S}]$ to T allows us to form the tableau $T' = T \cup \{w\}$.

Example 8.20 Let T be the tableau in Figure 8.33 and let $\mathbf{C} = \{*[A_1A_2A_4, A_1A_3A_4], *[A_1A_2, A_2A_3, A_3A_4]\}$. We can apply the J-rule for $*[A_1A_2, A_2A_3, A_3A_4]$ to the second row and the third row of T to generate the row $\langle a_1\, a_2\, b_3\, a_4\rangle$. The resulting tableau T' is given in Figure 8.34. The J-rule for $*[A_1A_2A_4, A_1A_3A_4]$ can be applied to the first and fourth rows of T' to generate the row $\langle a_1\, b_1\, b_3\, a_4\rangle$. Tableau T'' in Figure 8.35 is the result of this application.

$T(A_1$	A_2	A_3	$A_4)$
a_1	b_1	b_2	a_4
a_1	a_2	b_3	b_4
b_5	a_2	b_3	a_4

Figure 8.33

$T'(A_1$	A_2	A_3	$A_4)$
a_1	b_1	b_2	a_4
a_1	a_2	b_3	b_4
b_5	a_2	b_3	a_4
a_1	a_2	b_3	a_4

Figure 8.34

$T''(A_1$	A_2	A_3	$A_4)$
a_1	b_1	b_2	a_4
a_1	a_2	b_3	b_4
b_5	a_2	b_3	a_4
a_1	a_2	b_3	a_4
a_1	b_1	b_3	a_4

Figure 8.35

Theorem 8.5 Let $\mathbf{S} = \{S_1, S_2, \ldots, S_q\}$. Let T' be the result of applying the J-rule for $*[\mathbf{S}]$ to tableaux T. T and T' are equivalent on $SAT(*[\mathbf{S}])$.

Proof We must show that $T(r) = T'(r)$ for an arbitrary relation $r \in SAT(*[\mathbf{S}])$.

Let t' be any tuple in $T'(r)$. Let ρ be the valuation with $\rho(w_d) = t'$ (w_d is the all-distinguished row) and $\rho(T') \subseteq r$. We have $\rho(T) \subseteq \rho(T')$, since $T \subseteq T'$ (set containment), so $\rho(T) \subseteq r$, and $\rho(w_d) = t' \in T(r)$. Hence $T'(r) \subseteq T(r)$.

Now let t be any tuple in $T(r)$ and let ρ be the valuation with $\rho(w_d) = t$ and $\rho(T) \subseteq r$. The only tuple that could possibly be in $\rho(T')$ but not in $\rho(T)$ is $\rho(w)$, where w is the row generated by the J-rule for $*[\mathbf{S}]$ from rows $w_1, w_2, \ldots, w_q$ of T. It is left to the reader to show that if $w_1, w_2, \ldots, w_q$ are joinable on $\mathbf{S}$ with result w, then $\rho(w_1), \rho(w_2), \ldots, \rho(w_q)$ are joinable on $\mathbf{S}$ with result $\rho(w)$ (see Exercise 8.25). Since r is in $SAT(*[\mathbf{S}])$, and $\{\rho(w_1), \rho(w_2), \ldots, \rho(w_q)\} \subseteq \rho(T) \subseteq r$, $\rho(w)$ is in r. Therefore $\rho(T') \subseteq r$, and $\rho(w_d) = t \in T'(r)$. Hence $T(r) \subseteq T'(r)$ and $T(r) = T'(r)$.

8.6 THE CHASE

In this section we give a computation method, the *chase*, that finds, given a tableau T and set of dependencies $\mathbf{C}$, a new tableau T^* such that $T \equiv T^*$ and

T^* as a relation is in $SAT(\mathbf{C})$. Thus, using Lemma 8.3 and Exercise 8.18, we shall be able to test tableaux for equivalence under $\mathbf{C}$.

The chase computation is simply described. Given T and $\mathbf{C}$, apply the F- and J-rules associated with the FDs and JDs in $\mathbf{C}$, *as long as they make a change*. We shall prove that the order of application of the transformation rules is immaterial. By Theorems 8.4 and 8.5, if the computation terminates, it always yields a tableau $T^* \equiv_{\mathbf{C}} T$. What is harder to show is that the computation always halts and that the resulting tableau, T^*, is in $SAT(\mathbf{C})$.

Example 8.21 Let T be the tableau in Figure 8.36 and let $\mathbf{C} = \{*[ABC, BCD], B \to C, AD \to C\}$. (We use A, B, C, D for A_1, A_2, A_3, A_4 for readability.) Tableau $T = T_{\mathbf{R}}$ where $\mathbf{R} = \{AB, BD, ACD\}$. Applying the F-rule for $B \to C$ yields tableau T_1 in Figure 8.37. We then apply the J-rule for $*[ABC, BCD]$ to get T_2 in Figure 8.38 and apply the F-rule for $AD \to C$ to get T_3 in Figure 8.39. One more application of the J-rule for $*[ABC, BCD]$ yields tableau T^* in Figure 8.40. No more transformation rules that correspond to dependencies in $\mathbf{C}$ can be applied to change T^*. Also, T^*, as a relation, is in $SAT(\mathbf{C})$.

T(A	B	C	D)
a_1	a_2	b_1	b_2
b_3	a_2	b_4	a_4
a_1	b_6	a_3	a_4

Figure 8.36

T_1(A	B	C	D)
a_1	a_2	b_1	b_2
b_3	a_2	b_1	a_4
a_1	b_6	a_3	a_4

Figure 8.37

T_2(A	B	C	D)
a_1	a_2	b_1	b_2
b_3	a_2	b_1	a_4
a_1	b_6	a_3	a_4
a_1	a_2	b_1	a_4

Figure 8.38

$T_3(A$	B	C	$D)$
a_1	a_2	a_3	b_2
b_3	a_2	a_3	a_4
a_1	b_6	a_3	a_4
a_1	a_2	a_3	a_4

Figure 8.39

$T^*(A$	B	C	$D)$
a_1	a_2	a_3	b_2
b_3	a_2	a_3	a_4
a_1	b_6	a_3	a_4
a_1	a_2	a_3	a_4
b_3	a_2	a_3	b_2

Figure 8.40

Definition 8.11 A *generating sequence* for tableau T under constraints **C** is a sequence of tableaux $T_0, T_1, T_2, \ldots$ where $T = T_0$ and T_{i+1} is obtained from T_i by applying an F- or J-rule for a dependency in **C**, $0 \leq i$. We require $T_i \neq T_{i+1}$. If the generating sequence has a last element T_n such that no F- or J-rules for **C** can be applied to T_n to make a change, then T_n is called a *chase of* T *under* **C**. $Chase_{\mathbf{C}}(T)$ represents all such chases.

Example 8.22 Let T and **C** be as in Example 8.21. T, T_1, T_2, T_3, T^* is a generating sequence for T under **C**. Therefore, $T^* \in chase_{\mathbf{C}}(T)$.

We need to keep track of rows during the chase computation for some of our subsequent proofs. Let tableau T' be derived from tableau T by the application of a J-rule. If w is a row in T, the *row corresponding to* w in T' is w itself. Let T' be derived from T by an F-rule that changes variable v to variable v'. If w is a row in T, the *row corresponding to* w in T' is w', where w' is row w with v replaced by v'. (If w does not contain v, then $w = w'$.)

If $T_0, T_1, \ldots, T_i, \ldots, T_j, \ldots$ is a generating sequence, and w_i is a row in T_i, we can extend the "corresponds" relation transitively, and write of the row w_j in T_j corresponding to w_i. That is, there are rows $w_{i+1}, w_{i+2}, \ldots, w_{j-1}$ where $w_k \in T_k$, such that w_{i+1} corresponds to w_i, w_{i+2} corresponds to $w_{i+1}, \ldots, w_j$ corresponds to w_{j-1}.

Example 8.23 In the generating sequence T, T_1, T_2, T_3, T^* of Example 8.22, the first rows of tableaux T_1, T_2, T_3, T^* all correspond to the first row of T. Also, the fourth row of T_3 corresponds to the fourth row of T_2.

For any row w in a tableau in a generating sequence, there is always a row corresponding to w in any later tableau in the sequence. However, w does not necessarily correspond to some row in an earlier tableau in the sequence, since w could have been generated by a J-rule. Distinct rows in one tableau may correspond to the same row in a later tableau (see Exercise 8.27).

Theorem 8.6 Given a tableau T and constraints **C**, every generating sequence for T under **C** is finite. Thus, $chase_{\mathbf{C}}(T)$ is never empty.

Proof Since tableaux are sets of rows, and no F- or J-rule introduces new variables, there are only a finite number of tableaux that can appear in a generating sequence for T under **C**. If we can show that no tableau appears twice in a generating sequence, we are done.

Let T_i and T_j be tableaux in a generating sequence, where $i < j$. If at some point in the subsequence $T_i, T_{i+1}, \ldots, T_j$ an F-rule was used, then T_i has some variable that T_j lacks, so $T_i \neq T_j$. If only J-rules were used in the subsequence, then T_j has at least one more row than T_i, so $T_i \neq T_j$.

Theorem 8.7 For any tableau T^* in $chase_{\mathbf{C}}(T)$, T^*, as a relation, is in $SAT(\mathbf{C})$.

Proof If T^* violates an FD $X \rightarrow A$ in **C**, there must be two rows w_1 and w_2 in T^* with $w_1(X) = w_2(X)$, but $w_1(A) \neq w_2(A)$. The F-rule for $X \rightarrow A$ can be applied to rows w_1 and w_2 to change T^*, which means T^* cannot be the last tableau in a generating sequence under **C**. Hence T^* satisfies $X \rightarrow A$. Similarly, if T^* violates a JD in **C**, then the J-rule for that JD can be applied to T^* to make a change.

Example 8.24 The tableau T in Figure 8.41 is $T_{\mathbf{R}}$ for $\mathbf{R} = \{AE, ADE, BCD\}$. The tableau T^* in Figure 8.42 is in $chase_{\mathbf{C}}(T)$, where $\mathbf{C} = \{AE \rightarrow D, D \rightarrow C, *[AB, BCDE]\}$. The J-rule for the JD in **C** is never used. We see that T^* satisfies **C**.

$T(A$	B	C	D	$E)$
a_1	b_1	b_2	b_3	a_5
a_1	b_4	b_5	a_4	a_5
b_6	a_2	a_3	a_4	b_7

Figure 8.41

$T^*(A$	B	C	D	$E)$
a_1	b_1	a_3	a_4	a_5
a_1	b_4	a_3	a_4	a_5
b_6	a_2	a_3	a_4	b_7

Figure 8.42

Corollary $Chase_{\mathbf{C}}(T) = \{T\}$ if and only if T, as a relation, is in $SAT(\mathbf{C})$.

8.6.1 The Finite Church-Rosser Property

The chase computation is an example of a replacement system. A *replacement system* is a pair $(Q, \Rightarrow)$, where Q is a set of objects and $\Rightarrow$ is an antireflexive binary relation on Q, called the *transformation relation*.* In our case, the chase computation is a replacement system for every set of constraints $\mathbf{C}$. Q is the set of tableaux over $\mathbf{U}$, and $T \Rightarrow T'$ if T' is obtained from T by applying an F- or J-rule corresponding to a dependency in $\mathbf{C}$.

Definition 8.12 The relation $\overset{*}{\Rightarrow}$ is the reflexive, transitive closure of $\Rightarrow$. We read $T \overset{*}{\Rightarrow} T'$ as "T goes to T'" or "T' is reachable from T."

Definition 8.13 Given the replacement system $(Q, \Rightarrow)$, object $p \in Q$ is *irreducible* if $p \overset{*}{\Rightarrow} q$ implies $p = q$. That is, for no $q \neq p$ does $p \Rightarrow q$.

Definition 8.14 The replacement system $(Q, \Rightarrow)$ is *finite* if for every $p \in Q$ there is a constant c, depending on p, such that if $p \overset{*}{\Rightarrow} q$ in i steps, then $i \leq c$. That is, for any object p in Q, only a finite number of transformations can be applied to p before reaching an irreducible object.

Using Theorem 8.6, it follows that the replacement system for a given chase computation is finite. $Chase_{\mathbf{C}}(T)$ is all the irreducible tableaux reachable from T using F- and J-rules for $\mathbf{C}$.

Definition 8.15 A finite replacement system $(Q, \Rightarrow)$ is *finite Church-Rosser* (FCR) if for any object $p \in Q$, if $p \overset{*}{\Rightarrow} q_1$ and $p \overset{*}{\Rightarrow} q_2$ and q_1 and q_2 are both irreducible, then $q_1 = q_2$. That is, starting with any p, no matter how we apply transformations, we eventually end up at the same irreducible object.

*Replacement systems also sometimes include an equivalence relation over Q. Equivalence is then used in place of equality in the definition of Finite Church-Rosser and in Theorem 8.8.

Example 8.25 Let **B** be the set of all well-formed Boolean expressions using the symbols 0, 1, (,), ∨ or ∧. We assume the expressions are completely parenthesized. The pair $(B, \Rightarrow)$ is a replacement system, where $\Rightarrow$ is the relation summarized in Figure 8.43. We have $T \Rightarrow T'$ whenever T' is T with one of the strings in the left column replaced by the associated string in the right column.

string	replacement
(0)	0
(1)	1
0 ∧ 0	0
0 ∧ 1	0
1 ∧ 0	0
1 ∧ 1	1
0 ∨ 0	0
0 ∨ 1	1
1 ∨ 0	1
1 ∨ 1	1

Figure 8.43

We have, for example,

$$(((0 \vee 0) \vee 1) \wedge 0) \Rightarrow$$
$$(((0) \vee 1) \wedge 0) \Rightarrow ((0 \vee 1) \wedge 0) \Rightarrow$$
$$((1) \wedge 0) \Rightarrow$$
$$(1 \wedge 0) \Rightarrow$$
$$(0) \Rightarrow 0.$$

The strings 0 and 1 are the only irreducible expressions in **B**. Every expression in **B** goes to exactly one of 0 or 1 under $\overset{*}{\Rightarrow}$, and does so in a finite number of steps. Hence, $(\mathbf{B}, \Rightarrow)$ is FCR.

We shall show that the chase computation for a set of constraints **C** is FCR. That result implies that $chase_{\mathbf{C}}(T)$ always contains exactly one element. To show the chase computation is FCR, we cite the following theorem, which is a special case of a theorem due to Sethi.

Theorem 8.8 (Sethi) A replacement system $(Q, \Rightarrow)$ is FCR if and only if it is finite and, for any object $p \in Q$, if $p \Rightarrow q_1$ and $p \Rightarrow q_2$, then there is a q in Q such that $q_1 \overset{*}{\Rightarrow} q$ and $q_2 \overset{*}{\Rightarrow} q$. Diagramatically, we have

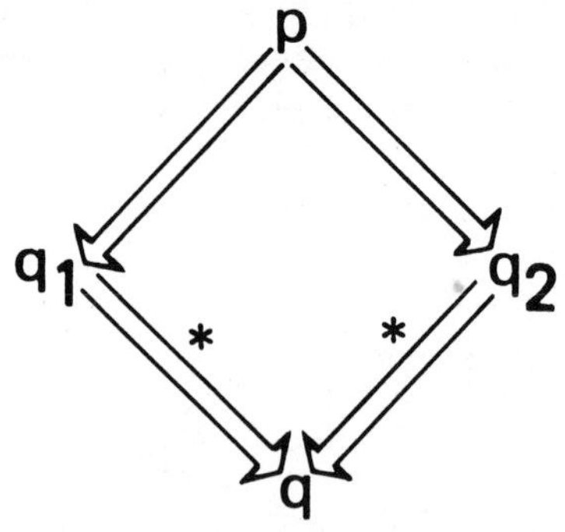

Example 8.26 For the replacement system (**B**, ⇒) of Example 8.26,

$$((0 \vee 0) \vee (1 \vee 1)) \Rightarrow ((0) \vee (1 \vee 1)) \text{ and}$$
$$((0 \vee 0) \vee (1 \vee 1)) \Rightarrow ((0 \vee 0) \vee (1)).$$

As required by the theorem

$$((0) \vee (1 \vee 1)) \overset{*}{\Rightarrow} (0 \vee 1) \text{ and}$$
$$((0 \vee 0) \vee (1)) \overset{*}{\Rightarrow} (0 \vee 1).$$

Theorem 8.9 The chase computation for a set of constraints is an FCR replacement system. Therefore, $chase_{\mathbf{C}}(T)$ is always a singleton set.

Proof We use Theorem 8.8. We have already observed that the chase is a finite replacement system. We must show that if we can obtain either tableau T_1 or tableau T_2 from tableau T by a single application of a transformation rule for **C**, then there is some tableau T^* that can be obtained from both T_1 and T_2 by 0 or more applications for the rules for **C**. We treat three cases:

Case 1:

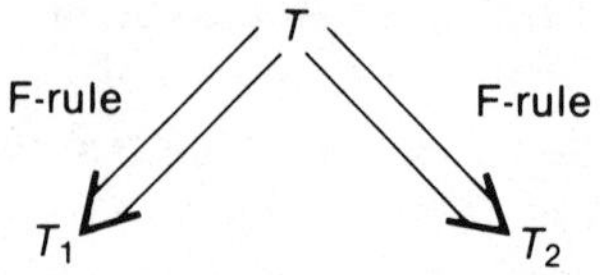

Case 2:

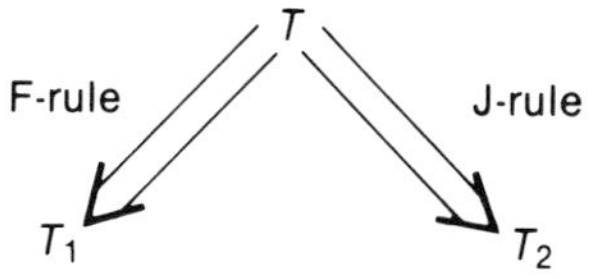

Case 3:

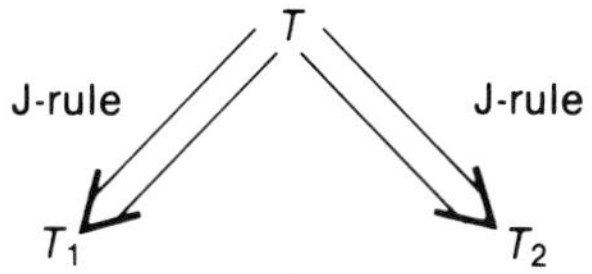

Observe that J-rules leave existing rows in a tableau unchanged, and that an F-rule cannot change one occurrence of a given variable without changing all other occurrences. Let w_1 and w_2 be rows in tableau T, and let u_1 and u_2 be the rows in tableau T' corresponding to w_1 and w_2, where T' can be obtained from T by application of F- and J-rules. By the observation, if $w_1(X) = w_2(X)$, then $u_1(X) = u_2(X)$. Thus, if some F-rule or J-rule is applicable to a set of rows in T, then the same rule applies to the corresponding set of rows in T'. We now treat the cases.

Case 1 Let T_1 be T with variables v_1 and v_2 identified using the F-rule for $X \rightarrow A$. Let T_2 be T with variables v_3 and v_4 identified using $Y \rightarrow B$.

If $A \neq B$, use the F-rule for $X \rightarrow A$ on T_2 to identify v_1 and v_2. The result is T^*, which is T with v_1 and v_2 identified, and v_3 and v_4 identified. T^* can also be obtained from T_1 by using $Y \rightarrow B$ to identify v_3 and v_4.

If $A = B$, the argument for $A \neq B$ holds when v_1, v_2, v_3, and v_4 are all distinct. If not, assume v_1 is a distinguished variable, or, if none of v_1, v_2, v_3 or v_4 is distinguished, v_1 is the nondistinguished variable with lowest subscript among the four variables. (We may have to reverse the roles of T_1 and T_2.) Also assume $v_3 = v_1$ or $v_3 = v_2$. We claim T^* is T with v_2, v_3, and v_4 replaced by v_1.

If $v_3 = v_1$, the argument above works again, or $T_1 = T_2 = T^*$, if $v_2 = v_4$. If $v_3 = v_2$, the argument is more involved. In T_1, v_2 $(= v_3)$ has been replaced by v_1. Since the F-rule for $Y \rightarrow B$ was applied to T to identify v_3 and v_4, the rule for $Y \rightarrow B$ also applies to T_1 to replace v_4 by v_1. This replacement yields T^*. In T_2, v_3 replaced v_4; or vice-versa. If v_3 replaced v_4, then the F-rule for

$X \to A$ can replace v_3 with v_1 in T_2. If v_4 replaced v_3, the F-rule for $X \to A$ will let v_1 replace v_4 in T_2. In either case, v_2, v_3, and v_4 are replaced by v_1, and the result is T^*.

Example 8.27 Let T be the tableau in Figure 8.44. Applying F-rules for $A \to B$ and $C \to B$, we get the tableaux T_1 and T_2, respectively, shown in Figures 8.45 and 8.46. Applying $C \to B$ to T_1 or $A \to B$ to T_2 gives tableau T^* in Figure 8.47.

$T(A$	B	$C)$
a_1	b_1	b_2
a_1	b_3	a_3
b_4	a_2	a_3

Figure 8.44

$T_1(A$	B	$C)$
a_1	b_1	b_2
a_1	b_1	a_3
b_4	a_2	a_3

Figure 8.45

$T_2(A$	B	$C)$
a_1	b_1	b_2
a_1	a_2	a_3
b_4	a_2	a_3

Figure 8.46

$T^*(A$	B	$C)$
a_1	a_2	b_2
a_1	a_2	a_3
b_4	a_2	a_3

Figure 8.47

Proof of Theorem 8.9 continued

Case 2 Assume the F-rule replaces variable v_1 by variable v_2 in T to form T_1. Assume the J-rule creates row w to add to T to form T_2. If w has no occurrence of v_1, then apply the J-rule to T_1 to generate w. The application is possible, because the portions of the rows that went into forming w are unchanged from T to T_1. Similarly, applying the F-rule to T_2 replaces v_1 by v_2, since addition of a row cannot bar application of a rule. The result of either rule application is tableau T^*, which is T with variable v_1 replaced by v_2 and row w added.

If row w contains v_1, T^* will be T with v_1 replaced by v_2 and row w' added, where w' is row w with v_1 replaced by v_2. Applying the F-rule used to transform T_1 to T_2 still changes v_1 to v_2, thereby changing row w to w'. The result is T^*. The J-rule used to generate w from T can be applied to the rows in T_1 that correspond to the rows in T to which the rule was originally applied. The resulting row from T_1 will be w' and so the result of the application is T^*. Note that some rows in T_1 may correspond to more than one row in T.

Example 8.28 Let T be the tableau in Figure 8.48. Applying the F-rule for $A \rightarrow B$ yields tableau T_1 in Figure 8.49; applying the J-rule for $*[AB, BC]$ yields tableau T_2 in Figure 8.50. Applying the J-rule to T_1 or the F-rule to T_2 will yield tableau T^*.

$T(A$	B	$C)$
a_1	b_1	b_2
b_3	b_1	a_3
a_1	a_2	a_3

Figure 8.48

$T_1(A$	B	$C)$
a_1	a_2	b_2
b_3	a_2	a_3
a_1	a_2	a_3

Figure 8.49

$T_2(A$	B	$C)$
a_1	b_1	b_2
b_3	b_1	a_3
a_1	a_2	a_3
a_1	b_1	a_3

Figure 8.50

Proof of Theorem 8.9 continued Case 3 is left to the reader (see Exercise 8.30). Since we are able to find an appropriate T^* in all three cases, the chase computation is FCR.

Since $chase_{\mathbf{C}}(T)$ is always a singleton set, we modify our notation to let $chase_{\mathbf{C}}(T)$ represent its only element.

Corollary If $SAT(\mathbf{C}) = SAT(\mathbf{C}')$, then $chase_{\mathbf{C}}(T) = chase_{\mathbf{C}'}(T)$ for any tableau T.

Proof We prove here the special case where $\mathbf{C}' = \mathbf{C} \cup \{c\}$ for any c such that $\mathbf{C} \models c$. Let $T^* = chase_{\mathbf{C}}(T)$. The same applications of rules will take us from T to T^* under $\mathbf{C}'$, since $\mathbf{C}' \supseteq \mathbf{C}$. Furthermore, Theorem 8.7 shows us that we cannot apply any rules for $\mathbf{C}'$ to T^*, because T^* as a relation is in $SAT(\mathbf{C})$ and hence in $SAT(\mathbf{C}')$. We see $chase_{\mathbf{C}'}(T) = T^*$.

The proof of the general version of the corollary is left to the reader (see Exercise 8.31). If $\mathbf{C}$ and $\mathbf{C}'$ are arbitrary equivalent sets of constraints, then $\mathbf{C} \models c'$ for any constraint $c' \in \mathbf{C}$. Likewise, for any c in $\mathbf{C}$, $\mathbf{C}' \models c$. If $\mathbf{C}'' = \mathbf{C} \cup \mathbf{C}'$, then $SAT(\mathbf{C}'') = SAT(\mathbf{C}) = SAT(\mathbf{C}')$. It can be shown, using the special case, that $chase_{\mathbf{C}}(T) = chase_{\mathbf{C}''}(T) = chase_{\mathbf{C}'}(T)$.

8.6.2 Equivalence of Tableaux under Constraints

We can now test equivalence of tableaux under constraints, which gives us a test for cases when a project-join mapping $m_{\mathbf{R}}$ is lossless on $SAT(\mathbf{C})$. By the remarks at the beginning of this section, we know $T \equiv_{\mathbf{C}} chase_{\mathbf{C}}(T)$. Theorem 8.7 tells us $chase_{\mathbf{C}}(T)$, as a relation, is in $SAT(\mathbf{C})$. Using Lemma 8.3, we have the following results.

Theorem 8.10 Let T_1 and T_2 be tableaux, and let $\mathbf{C}$ be a set of constraints. $T_1 \sqsubseteq_{\mathbf{C}} T_2$ if and only if $chase_{\mathbf{C}}(T_1) \sqsubseteq chase_{\mathbf{C}}(T_2)$.

Corollary $T_1 \equiv_{\mathbf{C}} T_2$ if and only if $chase_{\mathbf{C}}(T_1) \equiv chase_{\mathbf{C}}(T_2)$.

Example 8.29 Consider tableaux T_1 and T_2 in Figures 8.51 and 8.52. T_1 is the tableau for the set of schemes $\{AB, BC, AD\}$. T_2 is the tableau for the set $\{AB, BC, CD\}$. Let $\mathbf{C} = \{A \to D, *[AB, BCD]\}$. Figures 8.53 and 8.54 show $T_1^* = chase_{\mathbf{C}}(T_1)$ and $T_2^* = chase_{\mathbf{C}}(T_2)$.

$T_1(A$	B	C	$D)$
a_1	a_2	b_1	b_2
b_3	a_2	a_3	b_4
a_1	b_5	b_6	a_4

Figure 8.51

$T_2(A$	B	C	$D)$
a_1	a_2	b_1	b_2
b_3	a_2	a_3	b_4
b_5	b_6	a_3	a_4

Figure 8.52

$T_1^*(A$	B	C	$D)$
a_1	a_2	b_1	a_4
b_3	a_2	a_3	a_4
a_1	b_5	b_6	a_4
a_1	a_2	a_3	a_4
b_3	a_2	b_1	a_4

Figure 8.53

$T_2^*(A$	B	C	$D)$
a_1	a_2	b_1	b_2
b_3	a_2	a_3	b_2
b_5	b_6	a_3	a_4
a_1	a_2	a_3	b_2
b_3	a_2	b_1	b_2

Figure 8.54

Since T_1^* contains the row of all distinguished variables, it is not hard to find a containment mapping from T_2^* to T_1^*. Hence $T_2^* \sqsubseteq T_1^*$ and therefore $T_2 \sqsubseteq_{\mathbf{C}} T_1$.

8.6.3 Testing Implication of Join Dependencies

We desire a means to test when all the relations in $SAT(\mathbf{C})$ can be faithfully represented by their projections onto the relation schemes in some database scheme $\mathbf{R}$. This condition, equivalently stated as $\mathbf{C} \models *[\mathbf{R}]$ or $m_{\mathbf{R}}$, is the identity mapping on $SAT(\mathbf{C})$. In terms of tableau equivalence, $T_{\mathbf{R}} \equiv_{\mathbf{C}} T_I$ where

T_I is the tableau consisting only of w_d, the row of all distinguished variables. T_I is the identity mapping on all relations. By Theorem 8.10, we can test the equivalence above by checking if $chase_{\mathbf{C}}(T_{\mathbf{R}}) \equiv chase_{\mathbf{C}}(T_I)$. $Chase_{\mathbf{C}}(T_I) = T_I$ (why?), so we are checking whether $chase_{\mathbf{C}}(T_{\mathbf{R}}) \equiv T_I$. The test for that condition is simply whether or not $chase_{\mathbf{C}}(T_{\mathbf{R}})$ contains w_d (see Exercise 8.33).

Example 8.30 T_1 in Figure 8.51 is the tableau for the database scheme $\mathbf{R} = \{AB, BC, AD\}$. Let $\mathbf{C} = \{A \rightarrow D, *[AB, BCD]\}$. Since $chase_{\mathbf{C}}(T_1)$, given in Figure 8.53, contains w_d, any relation in $SAT(\mathbf{C})$ decomposes losslessly onto $\mathbf{R}$. T_2 in Figure 8.52 is the tableau for database scheme $\mathbf{S} = \{AB, BC, CD\}$. Since $chase_{\mathbf{C}}(T_2)$, given in Figure 8.54, does not contain w_d, there are some relations in $SAT(\mathbf{C})$ that have lossy decompositions onto $\mathbf{S}$.

Example 8.31 As promised in Section 6.5.4, we shall now show that if $\mathbf{R}$ is a database scheme over $\mathbf{U}$ that completely characterizes a set F of FDs and some scheme $R \in \mathbf{R}$ is a universal key for $\mathbf{U}$, then any relation in $SAT(F)$ decomposes losslessly onto $\mathbf{R}$.

Let G be the set of FDs expressed by the keys of the relation schemes in R. We know $G \models R \rightarrow \mathbf{U}$. Let $T_{\mathbf{R}}^* = chase_G(T_{\mathbf{R}})$. Let w be the row for R in $T_{\mathbf{R}}$ and let w^* be the corresponding row in $T_{\mathbf{R}}^*$. We claim w^* is the row of all distinguished variables.

Let H be a G-based DDAG for $R \rightarrow \mathbf{U}$. There is a computation for $chase_G(T_{\mathbf{R}})$ that mimics the construction of H. The correspondence will be that if Y is the set of node labels at some point in the construction of H, then the row corresponding to w in some tableau in the generating sequence for $T_{\mathbf{R}}^*$ has distinguished variables in all the Y-columns. More formally, let $H_0, H_1, \ldots, H_n = H$ be the successive DDAGs in the construction of H. We shall describe a generating sequence $T_{\mathbf{R}} = T_0, T_1, \ldots, T_n$ for $T_{\mathbf{R}}^*$.

Let w_i be the row in T_i corresponding to w in T_0. If Y_i is the set of node labels for DDAG H_i, we want w_i to have distinguished variables in all the Y_i-columns. Initially, the desired relationship holds. Y_0 is just R, and $w_0 = w$ is the row for R in T_R. Suppose the relationship holds for H_i and T_i. Suppose also that H_{i+1} is derived from H_i by adding a node labeled A, using the FD $K \rightarrow A$ from G. K must be a key for some relation scheme R_j in $\mathbf{R}$, where $A \in R_j$. There is a row u for R_j in T_0. Let u_i be the corresponding row in T_i. Row u_i has distinguished variables in the R_j-columns at least (see Lemma 8.4, to follow).

Since $K \rightarrow A$ was used to extend H_i, $K \subseteq Y_i$, hence w_i is distinguished in all the K-columns. Since $K \subseteq R_j$, u_i is distinguished in the K-columns. The F-rule for $K \rightarrow A$ is applicable to T_i on rows w_i and u_i, because $w_i(K) = u_i(K)$. Applying the F-rule sets $w_i(A) = u_i(A)$, which means that $w_i(A)$ is made distinguished, if it is not already. Hence in T_{i+1}, w_{i+1} is distinguished at least on $Y_iA = Y_{i+1}$.

As the result of our induction, we see that w_n in T_n is the row of all distinguished variables, since $H_n = H$ has all the attributes in **U** as node labels. One minor detail remains. There may be more rules for G that can be applied to T_n. Let the chase computation continue until it terminates: T_{n+1}, T_{n+2}, ..., $T^*_{\mathbf{R}}$. The row w^* in $T^*_{\mathbf{R}}$ corresponding to w_n in T_n is still all distinguished.

We see that $chase_G(T_{\mathbf{R}})$ contains the row of all distinguished variables, so $G \models *[R]$. Thus, any relation r in $SAT(G) = SAT(F)$ decomposes losslessly onto **R**.

8.6.4 Testing Implication of Functional Dependencies

We have a test for implication of JDs by a set **C** of FDs and JDs. We now turn to a test for implication of FDs by **C**. To test implication of JDs, we interpreted tableaux as mappings from relations to relations. For the FD test, we shall view tableaux as relations, or, more accurately, templates for relations. Before presenting the test, we need two lemmas.

Lemma 8.4 Let T be a tableau and let **C** be a set of constraints. Let ρ be a valuation for T such that $\rho(T) \subseteq r$, where r is chosen from $SAT(\mathbf{C})$. If $T = T_0, T_1, T_2, \ldots, T_n$ is a generating sequence for $chase_{\mathbf{C}}(T)$, then for $0 \leq i \leq n$,

1. $\rho(w_0) = \rho(w_i)$, where w_0 is any row in T_0 and w_i is the corresponding row in T_i. Also, w_i subsumes w_0.
2. $\rho(T_i) \subseteq r$.
3. $T_i \sqsupseteq T_{i+1}$ $i \neq n$.

Proof Parts 1 and 2. It suffices to say that if w_j is a row in T_j and w_{j+1} is the corresponding row of T_{j+1} then

$$\rho(w_j) = \rho(w_{j+1}) \text{ and}$$
$$w_{j+1} \text{ subsumes } w_j;$$

and if w is a row in T_{j+1} that corresponds to no row in T_j, then

$$\rho(w) \in r.$$

If T_{j+1} is obtained by an F-rule that changes no variable in w_j, or a J-rule, then $w_j = w_{j+1}$ and obviously $\rho(w_j) = \rho(w_{j+1})$ and w_{j+1} subsumes w_j. Otherwise, in going from T_j to T_{j+1}, for some attribute A, $w_j(A)$ changes from v_1 to v_2.

The change must be through the applications of an F-rule for an FD $X \rightarrow A$ to two rows u_1 and u_2 in T_j, where $u_1(X) = u_2(X)$, $u_1(A) = v_1$ and $u_2(A) = v_2$. By induction $\rho(u_1) = t_1$ and $\rho(u_2) = t_2$, where t_1 and t_2 are tuples in r. We must have $t_1(X) = t_2(X)$. Since r is in $SAT(\mathbf{C})$, $t_1(A) = t_2(A)$. Now $\rho(v_1) = \rho(u_1(A)) = t_1(A) = t_2(A) = \rho(u_2(A)) = \rho(v_2)$. Hence $\rho(w_j) = \rho(w_{j+1})$. Also, if one of v_1 or v_2 is distinguished, it must be v_2, so w_{j+1} subsumes w_j.

If w is a row in T_{j+1} that corresponds to no row in T_j, then w must be the result of joining rows $u_1, u_2, \ldots, u_q$ of T_j on $\mathbf{S}$, where $*[\mathbf{S}] \in \mathbf{C}$. By Exercise 8.25, $\rho(u_1), \rho(u_2), \ldots, \rho(u_q)$, which are all in r, are joinable on $\mathbf{S}$ with result $\rho(w)$. Since $r \in SAT(\mathbf{C})$, $\rho(w) \in r$.

The proof of part 3 is left to the reader (see Exercise 8.36).

Suppose we have a non-trivial FD $X \rightarrow A$, and we want to test whether $\mathbf{C} \models X \rightarrow A$. We construct a tableau T_X as follows. T_X has two rows, w_d and w_X. Row w_d is all distinguished symbols; w_X has distinguished symbols in the X-columns and distinct nondistinguished symbols elsewhere. That is, $T_X = T_{\mathbf{R}}$ for $\mathbf{R} = \{\mathbf{U}, X\}$.

Example 8.32 Figure 8.55 shows T_{BC} for $\mathbf{U} = ABCD$.

$T_{BC}(A$	B	C	$D)$
a_1	a_2	a_3	a_4
b_1	a_2	a_3	b_2

Figure 8.55

Theorem 8.11 $\mathbf{C} \models X \rightarrow A$ if and only if $chase_{\mathbf{C}}(T_X)$ has only distinguished variables in the A-column.

Proof Let $T^* = chase_{\mathbf{C}}(T_X)$. Suppose T^* has a nondistinguished symbol in the A-column. T^* considered as a relation is a counterexample to $\mathbf{C} \models X \rightarrow A$. By Theorem 8.7, T^* satisfies $\mathbf{C}$. However, every row of T^* has all distinguished symbols in the X-columns, since chase computation does not create new symbols. Row w_d remains unchanged throughout the chase, by Lemma 8.4. Thus T^* has two rows that agree on X but disagree on A: w_d and the row with a nondistinguished symbol in the A-column. Hence, T^* violates $X \rightarrow A$.

Suppose now that T^* has only a distinguished variable in the A-column, and let r be an arbitrary relation in $SAT(\mathbf{C})$. Let t_1 and t_2 be any pair of tuples in r with $t_1(X) = t_2(X)$. Consider the valuation ρ for T_X such that

$\rho(w_d) = t_1$ and $\rho(w_X) = t_2$. Such a valuation exists, because $w_d(X) = w_X(X)$. We just saw that w_d is the row in T^* corresponding to w_d in T_X. Let w_X^* be the row corresponding to w_X. By Lemma 8.4, $\rho(w_X^*) = \rho(w_X)$. Since T^* has only one variable in the A-column, $w_X^*(A) = w_d(A)$. Thus we see

$$t_1(A) = \rho(w_d(A)) = \rho(w_X^*(A)) = \rho(w_X(A)) = t_2(A).$$

Any two tuples in r that agree on X also agree on A. Since r was arbitrary, $SAT(\mathbf{C}) \subseteq SAT(X \rightarrow A)$ or $\mathbf{C} \vDash X \rightarrow A$.

Example 8.33 Suppose we wish to test $\mathbf{C} \vDash BC \rightarrow D$. If $\mathbf{C} = \{A \rightarrow D\}$, then $chase_{\mathbf{C}}(T_{BC}) = T_{BC}$. There is a b_2 in the D-column, so $BC \rightarrow D$ is not implied by $\mathbf{C}$. If $\mathbf{C}' = \{A \rightarrow D, *[ABC, CD]\}$, then $chase_{\mathbf{C}'}(T_{BC})$ is the tableau T^* in Figure 8.56. T^* has only a_4 in the D-column, so $\mathbf{C}' \vDash BC \rightarrow D$.

$T^*(A$	B	C	$D)$
a_1	a_2	a_3	a_4
b_1	a_2	a_3	a_4

Figure 8.56

We originally defined X^+ as the closure of a set of attributes X with respect to a set of FDs F. We can extend the definition consistently to include JDs as well as FDs.

Definition 8.16 Let $\mathbf{C}$ be a set of FDs and JDs and let X be a set of attributes. The *closure of* X with respect to $\mathbf{C}$, denoted X^+, is the largest set of attributes Y such that $\mathbf{C} \vDash X \rightarrow Y$. Note that if $\mathbf{C}$ is only FDs, the new definition reduces to the old definition.

Corollary For a given $\mathbf{C}$, X^+ is the set of all attributes A such that the A-columns of $chase_{\mathbf{C}}(T_X)$ has only distinguished variables.

Corollary If J is a set of JDs, then $J \vDash X \rightarrow Y$ implies $X \supseteq Y$. That is, a set of JDs implies only trivial FDs.

Proof $Chase_J(T_X)$ will have a nondistinguished variable in every column corresponding to an attribute in $\mathbf{U} - X$, since J-rules do not identify symbols.

8.6.5 Computing a Dependency Basis

Since MVDs are a special case of JDs, we can always test $\mathbf{C} \models X \twoheadrightarrow Y$ by testing $\mathbf{C} \models *[XY, XZ]$, where $Z = \mathbf{U} - XY$. However, the next theorem shows an alternate way to use the chase to find *all* sets Y such that $C \models X \twoheadrightarrow Y$, for a given X.

Theorem 8.12 Let $\mathbf{C}$ be a set of constraints, and let Y be a set of attributes disjoint from X^+ under $\mathbf{C}$. $\mathbf{C} \models X \twoheadrightarrow Y$ if and only if $chase_{\mathbf{C}}(T_X)$ contains a row u_Y with distinguished variables exactly in all the YX^+-columns.

Proof (if) Let T_X^* be $chase_{\mathbf{C}}(T_X)$. Let u_d and u_X be the rows in T_X^* corresponding to w_d and w_X. (We know $w_d = u_d$.) Let $\mathbf{R}$ be the database scheme $\{XY, XZ\}$ where $Z = \mathbf{U} - YX^+$. We shall show that $T_{\mathbf{R}}^* = chase_{\mathbf{C}}(T_{\mathbf{R}})$ must contain w_d, hence $\mathbf{C} \models *[XY, XZ]$, which is equivalent to $\mathbf{C} \models X \twoheadrightarrow Y$.

Let p_{XY} and p_{XZ} be the rows in $T_{\mathbf{R}}$ for relation schemes XY and XZ. Let q_{XY} and q_{XZ} be the corresponding rows in $T_{\mathbf{R}}^*$. Consider a mapping δ from variables in T_X to variables in $T_{\mathbf{R}}^*$ such that $\delta(w_d) = q_{XY}$ and $\delta(w_X) = q_{XZ}$. The mapping δ can be viewed as a valuation if $T_{\mathbf{R}}^*$ is considered as a relation; δ exists because $p_{XY}(X) = p_{XZ}(X)$, so $q_{XY}(X) = q_{XZ}(X)$. Since $T_{\mathbf{R}}^*$ as a relation is in $SAT(\mathbf{C})$, by Lemma 8.4, $\delta(T_X^*) \subseteq T_{\mathbf{R}}^*$, $\delta(w_d) = \delta(u_d)$, and $\delta(w_X) = \delta(u_X)$. Since $u_d(X^+) = u_X(X^+)$, $q_{XY}(X^+) = q_{XZ}(X^+)$. We see that δ maps distinguished variables in the X^+-columns of T_X^* to distinguished variables in the X^+ columns of $T_{\mathbf{R}}^*$.

We shall show that for row u_Y of T_X^*, with distinguished symbols in exactly the YX^+-columns, $\delta(u_Y)$ is the row w_d of all distinguished symbols in T_R^*. Since u_Y is distinguished in the X^+-columns, $\delta(u_Y)$ is distinguished in the X^+-columns by the argument in the previous paragraph. Since q_{XY} subsumes p_{XY}, q_{XY} is distinguished in all the Y-columns. We know $\delta(w_d) = q_{XY}$, so δ must map distinguished variables in the Y-columns of T_X^* to distinguished variables in the Y-columns of $T_{\mathbf{R}}^*$. Row u_Y is distinguished in all the Y-columns, so $\delta(u_Y)$ is distinguished in all the Y-columns. Since q_{XZ} subsumes p_{XZ}, q_{XZ} is distinguished in all the Z-columns. We know $\delta(w_X) = q_{XZ}$, so δ must map nondistinguished variables in the Z-columns of T_X^* to distinguished variables in the Z-columns of $T_{\mathbf{R}}^*$. Row u_Y is nondistinguished in all the Z-columns, so $\delta(u_Y)$ is distinguished in the Z-columns. $\mathbf{U} = YX^+Z$, so $\delta(u_Y)$ is distinguished everywhere. Therefore $T_{\mathbf{R}}^*$ contains w_d, so $\mathbf{C} \models X \twoheadrightarrow Y$.

(only if) Assume $\mathbf{C} \models X \twoheadrightarrow Y$. Let $\mathbf{C}' = \mathbf{C} \cup \{*[XY, XZ]\}$, where $Z = \mathbf{U} - YX^+$, as before. By the corollary to Theorem 8.9, $chase_{\mathbf{C}}(T_X) = chase_{\mathbf{C}'}(T_X)$ because $SAT(\mathbf{C}) = SAT(\mathbf{C}')$. Consider the computation for

$chase_{\mathbf{C}'}(T_X)$ where the first step is to apply the J-rule for $*[XY, XZ]$ to rows w_d and w_X. The result is a row w that is distinguished exactly in the XY-columns. During the remainder of the chase computation, any nondistinguished variables in the X^+-columns of w will be made distinguished. Thus the row in $chase_{\mathbf{C}'}(T_X)$ corresponding to w will have distinguished variables in exactly the YX^+-columns. (Why are there no distinguished variables elsewhere?) $Chase_{\mathbf{C}}(T_X) = chase_{\mathbf{C}'}(TX)$, so we are done.

Example 8.34 Let $\mathbf{C} = \{B \rightarrow C, *[ABC, CDE]\}$. Tableau T_B is given in Figure 8.57 and $T_B^* = chase_{\mathbf{C}}(T_B)$ is given in Figure 8.58. We see that $B^+ = BC$ and that $\mathbf{C}$ implies the MVDs $B \twoheadrightarrow ADE$, $B \twoheadrightarrow \emptyset$, $B \twoheadrightarrow A$ and $B \twoheadrightarrow DE$.

T_B(A	B	C	D	E)
a_1	a_2	a_3	a_4	a_5
b_1	a_2	b_2	b_3	b_4

Figure 8.57

T_B^*(A	B	C	D	E)
a_1	a_2	a_3	a_4	a_5
b_1	a_2	a_3	b_3	b_4
a_1	a_2	a_3	b_3	b_4
b_1	a_2	a_3	a_4	a_5

Figure 8.58

From $chase_{\mathbf{C}}(T_X)$, then, we can determine the set $Q = \{Y \mid \mathbf{C} \models X \twoheadrightarrow Y$ and $X^+ \cap Y = \emptyset\}$. Referring to Section 7.4.2, by replication, $\mathbf{C} \models X \twoheadrightarrow A$ for any $Z \in X^+$. Exercise 8.38 will show that $\mathbf{C} \models X \twoheadrightarrow Y$ if and only if Y can be written as $X'Y'$, where $X' \subseteq X^+$ and $Y' \in Q$. We can extend our definition of dependency basis to include JDs.

Definition 8.17 Let $\mathbf{C}$ be a set of constraints and let X be a set of attributes. The *dependency basis of* X with respect to $\mathbf{C}$, denoted $DEP(X)$, is $mdsb(\{Y \mid \mathbf{C} \models X \twoheadrightarrow Y\})$. (Recall that $mdsb$ is minimum disjoint set basis—see Section 7.4.3.)

As before, $\mathbf{C} \models X \twoheadrightarrow Y$ if and only if Y is the exact union of sets in $DEP(X)$. $DEP(X)$ can be calculated directly from Q and X^+ as $mdsb(Q) \cup \{\{A\} \mid A \in X^+\}$.

Example 8.35 Let $\mathbf{C} = \{B \to C, *[ABC, CDE]\}$, as in Example 8.34. We saw in that example that $B^+ = BC$ and $Q = \{ADE, \emptyset, A, DE\}$. We can calculate $DEP(B) = \{A, B, C, DE\}$.

8.7 TABLEAUX AS TEMPLATES

In this section we shall formalize the idea of a tableau as a template for relations.

Definition 8.18 Let **P** be a set of relations, and let r be any relation. A *completion of* r *under* **P** is a relation s in **P** such that $r \subseteq s$ and there is no relation s' in **P** such that $r \subseteq s' \subsetneq s$. $COMP_{\mathbf{P}}(r)$ is the set of all such completions; $COMP_{\mathbf{C}}(r)$ is shorthand for $COMP_{SAT(\mathbf{C})}(r)$.

Completions do not always exist.

Example 8.36 Let r be the relation in Figure 8.59. If $F = \{A \to C\}$, then $COMP_F(r)$ is empty. If $J = \{*[AB, BCD]\}$, then $COMP_J(r) = \{s\}$, where s is the relation in Figure 8.60.

r(A	B	C	D)
1	3	4	6
2	3	4	6
1	3	5	7

Figure 8.59

s(A	B	C	D)
1	3	4	6
2	3	4	6
1	3	5	7
2	3	5	7

Figure 8.60

Completions are not unique, given they exist.

Example 8.37 Let r be the relation of Figure 8.59. Let $\mathbf{P} = SAT(*[AB, BC])$. The dependency $*[AB,BC]$ is an embedded JD for the given relation scheme. $COMP_{\mathbf{P}}(r)$ contains relation s in Figure 8.60, and also the relation q in Figure 8.61. In fact, $COMP_{\mathbf{P}}(r)$ contains one relation for every value in the domain of attribute D.

q(A	B	C	D)
1	3	4	6
2	3	4	6
1	3	5	7
2	3	5	6

Figure 8.61

A set **P** of relations is closed under intersection if for every pair of relations r and s in **P**, $r \cap s$ is in **P**.

Lemma 8.5 **P** is closed under intersection if and only if completions under **P** are unique.

Proof Suppose **P** is closed under intersection. Let s and s' be completions of r under **P**. By closure, $s \cap s'$ is in **P**, and $s \cap s' \supseteq r$, so $s = s \cap s' = s'$. For the converse, suppose completions under **P** are unique. Let r and s be in **P**, and let $q = r \cap s$. There must be some subset r' of r (perhaps r itself) such that r' is a completion of q under **P**. Likewise, there is a subset s' of s that is a completion of q. By uniqueness of completion $r' = s'$, so $r' = q = s'$ and q is in **P**.

Corollary If **C** is a set of FDs and JDs, then completions under $SAT(\mathbf{C})$ are unique.

Proof Left to the reader (see Exercise 8.40).

Completions always exist for a set J of JDs only. Completions can be found in a manner similar to the chase computation. However, if **C** contains both FDs and JDs, completions do not always exist, even for relations that satisfy the FDs (see Exercise 8.41). For a set of FDs F, $COMP_F(r)$ exists exactly when $r \in SAT(F)$. In that case, $COMP_F(r) = r$. (We use $COMP_P(r)$ to stand for its only member when P is closed under intersection.)

We now give the set of relations a tableau represents.

Definition 8.19 Let T be a tableau and let **P** be a set of relations. The *representation set of* T *under* **P**, denoted $REP_{\mathbf{P}}(T)$, is

$$\{r \mid r \in COMP_{\mathbf{P}}(\rho(T)) \text{ for some valuation } \rho\}.$$

As usual, $REP_{\mathbf{C}}(T)$ stands for $REP_{SAT(\mathbf{C})}(T)$.

Lemma 8.6 Let **P** be a set of relations closed under intersection and let T_1 and T_2 be tableaux. If $T_1 \sqsubseteq_{\mathbf{P}} T_2$, then for every relation r in $REP_P(T_1)$, there is a relation s in $REP_{\mathbf{P}}(T_2)$ such that $s \subseteq r$.

Proof Let $r \in REP_{\mathbf{P}}(T_1)$, where r is $COMP_{\mathbf{P}}(\rho_1(T_1))$, and let w_d be the row of all distinguished variables. $T_1(r)$ contains $\rho_1(w_d)$, since $r \supseteq \rho_1(T_1)$. Since $T_1 \sqsubseteq_{\mathbf{P}} T_2$, $\rho_1(w_d) \in T_2(r)$. There must be a valuation ρ_2 such that $\rho_2(w_d) = \rho_1(w_d)$ and $\rho_2(T_2) \subseteq r$. Let $s = COMP_{\mathbf{P}}(\rho_2(T_2))$. Relation s exists because $\rho_2(T_2) \subseteq r \in \mathbf{P}$. It follows that $s \subseteq r$.

Example 8.38 Lemma 8.6 is quite weak when $\mathbf{P} = SAT(\mathbf{C})$, for **C** a set of FDs and JDs. No matter what **C** is, $SAT(\mathbf{C})$ contains all relations consisting of a single tuple. Suppose we have $T_1 \sqsubseteq_{\mathbf{C}} T_2$ and $r \in REP_{\mathbf{C}}(T_1)$. Let t be a tuple in r, let s be the relation consisting only of t, and let ρ be the valuation such that $\rho(T_2) = s$. Since $COMP_{\mathbf{C}}(s) = s$, $s \in REP_{\mathbf{C}}(T_2)$ and clearly $s \subseteq r$.

However, when $\mathbf{P} = SAT(\mathbf{C})$, we can prove a fairly strong result.

Theorem 8.13 Let **C** be a set of constraints and let T be a tableau. If $T^* = chase_{\mathbf{C}}(T)$, then $REP_{\mathbf{C}}(T) = REP_{\mathbf{C}}(T^*)$.

Proof Suppose $r \in REP_{\mathbf{C}}(T)$. Let ρ be the valuation such that $r = COMP_{\mathbf{C}}(\rho(T))$. Clearly, $\rho(T) \subseteq r$. Since $r \in SAT(\mathbf{C})$, from Lemma 8.4 we have

1. $\rho(T) \subseteq \rho(T^*)$ and
2. $\rho(T^*) \subseteq r$.

We see $COMP_{\mathbf{C}}(\rho(T^*)) = r$, so $REP_{\mathbf{C}}(T) \subseteq REP_{\mathbf{C}}(T^*)$.

Now suppose $r \in REP_{\mathbf{C}}(T^*)$. Let ρ be a valuation such that $r = COMP_{\mathbf{C}}(\rho(T^*))$. Since T^* as a relation is in $SAT(C)$, $\rho(T^*) \in SAT(\mathbf{C})$, so $r = \rho(T^*)$. T may have more variables than T^*, but ρ can be consistently extended to T in such a way that $\rho(T) \subseteq \rho(T^*)$. Let w be any row in T, and let w^* be the corresponding row in T^*. Set $\rho(w) = \rho(w^*)$. Let $T = T_0, T_1, T_2, \ldots, T_n = T^*$ be a generating sequence for T^*. By Lemma 8.4, we know that

$$\rho(T_1) \subseteq \rho(T_2) \subseteq \cdots \subseteq \rho(T_n).$$

Since $SAT(C)$ has the intersection property,

$$COMP_{\mathbf{C}}(\rho(T_1)) \subseteq COMP_{\mathbf{C}}(\rho(T_2)) \subseteq \cdots \subseteq COMP(\rho(T_n)).$$

(Here $COMP_C(s)$ stands for a relation.) Suppose one of the containments is proper:

$$COMP_C(\rho(T_i)) \subsetneq COMP_C((T_{i+1})).$$

There must be a tuple $\rho(w)$ in $\rho(T_{i+1})$ that is not in $COMP_C(\rho(T_i))$, otherwise $\rho(T_{i+1}) \subseteq COMP_C(\rho(T_i))$ and the two completions are equal. Therefore, $w \in T_{i+1}$, $w \notin T_i$. Row w must have been generated by a J-rule from rows in T_i, say rows $w_1, w_2, \ldots, w_q$ and the J-rule for *[**S**]. Now $\rho(w_1)$, $\rho(w_2), \ldots, \rho(w_q)$ are in $\rho(T_i)$, hence in $COMP_C(\rho(T_i))$. But $COMP_C(\rho(T_i)) \in SAT(\mathbf{C})$ and hence must satisfy *[**S**], so $\rho(w)$ is in $COMP_C(\rho(T_i))$, a contradiction. None of the containments are proper, so $COMP_C(\rho(T)) = COMP_C(\rho(T^*)) = r$.

We see that $REP_C(T) \subseteq REP_C(T^*)$, and so $REP_C(T) = REP_C(T^*)$.

Corollary For a set of constraints **C** and tableau T,

$$REP_C(T) = \{\rho(T^*) \mid T^* = chase_C(T) \text{ and } \rho \text{ is a valuation}\}.$$

Proof $REP_C(T) = REP_C(T^*) = \{COMP_C(\rho(T^*)) \mid \rho \text{ is a valuation}\}$. As we saw in the proof of the theorem, $COMP_C(\rho(T^*)) = \rho(T^*)$.

In light of the last theorem, we might expect some connection between the conditions $T_1 \equiv_C T_2$ and $REP_C(T_1) = REP_C(T_2)$. However, the first does not imply the second (Exercise 8.42), nor does the second imply the first, as the next example shows.

Example 8.39 Let T_1 and T_2 be the tableaux in Figures 8.62 and 8.63. Let $\mathbf{C} = \{A \rightarrow B\}$. Both the tableaux, as relations, are in $SAT(\mathbf{C})$, hence they are their own chases under **C**. There is no containment mapping from T_1 to T_2, so $T_1 \not\equiv_C T_2$. However, we see that for any valuation ρ_1 for T_1 there is a valuation ρ_2 for T_2 such that $\rho_1(T_1) = \rho_2(T_2)$, and vice-versa. By the corollary to Theorem 8.13, $REP_C(T_1) = REP_C(T_2)$.

$T_1(A$	B	$C)$
a_1	a_2	a_3
a_1	a_2	b_2
b_3	b_4	a_3

Figure 8.62

T_2(A	B	C)
a_1	b_1	a_3
a_1	b_1	b_2
b_3	a_2	a_3

Figure 8.63

8.8 COMPUTATIONAL PROPERTIES OF THE CHASE COMPUTATION

In general, the chase computation has exponential time complexity. If tableau T has k columns and m rows, $chase_{\mathbf{C}}(T)$ can have m^k rows (see Exercise 8.44). If we are using the chase computation to test for a lossless join, we need not always compute the entire chase. As soon as w_d, the all-distinguished row, is encountered, there is no need to continue. If w_d occurs in any tableau in a generating sequence, it will appear in the final tableau in the sequence. However, the problem of determining whether $w_d \in chase_{\mathbf{C}}(T)$ probably does not have a polynomial-time solution, because the problem of testing $\mathbf{C} \models *[\mathbf{S}]$ is known to be NP-hard. There are methods, other than the chase, that can be used to test $\mathbf{C} \models c$ in polynomial time, where c is an FD or MVD.

$Chase_F(T)$, for a set F of FDs, never has more rows that T, since F-rules do not create new rows. It is not suprising, then, that $chase_F(T)$ can be computed in polynomial time. We assume that the input to the problem is the tableau T and the set F. For simplicity, assume that one attribute or one tableau variable takes one unit of space to express. Let

$k = |\mathbf{U}| =$ the number of the columns in T.
$m =$ the number of rows in T, and
$p =$ the amount of space to express F.

The size of our input is

$$n = O(k \cdot m + p).$$

We now indicate how to compute $chase_{\mathbf{C}}(T)$ in $O(n^3)$ time. We shall make repeated passes through the set of FDs. For each FD $X \rightarrow A$, we do a bucket sort on the rows of the tableau to bring rows with equal X-components together. If $|X| = q$, the sort takes $O(q \cdot m)$ time. Once the rows are sorted, in $O(q \cdot m)$ time again, we can find rows with equal X-components and make them identical in their A-columns. Over all the FDs in F, the sum of the sizes of their left sides is no more than p. Thus, one pass through all the FDs takes $O(p \cdot m)$ time.

We continue to make passes through F until we make a pass where no changes occur. At that point, we are done. T can have at most $k \cdot m$ distinct variables to begin with. Every pass except the last decreases the number of variables by one, so we make $O(k \cdot m)$ passes at most. The total time spent on the chase is $O(k \cdot p \cdot m^2)$, which is no more than $O(n^3)$.

If the tableau corresponds to a database scheme, and only the relation schemes are given as input, the procedure above requires $O(n^4)$ time, where n is the size of the input (see Exercise 8.45). Other methods for computing the chase exist that can bring the time complexity down to $O(n^2/\log n)$.

Up to this point we have assumed all our FDs have single attributes on their right sides, in order to make the F-rule simple to state. The F-rule can be generalized to handle multiple attributes on the right side of an FD. If w_1 and w_2 are rows in a tableau such that $w_1(X) = w_2(X)$, and $X \to Y$ is an FD in the set of constraints, we can identify $w_1(A)$ and $w_2(A)$ for each attribute A in Y.

There is also an extension of the J-rule that allows us to generate more than one row at a time. If *[**S**] is a JD in the set of constraints, we may apply the project-join mapping $m_{\mathbf{S}}$ to a tableau and use the result as the next tableau in the generating sequence.

Example 8.40 Suppose T_1 in Figure 8.64 is a tableau in a generating sequence for $chase_{\mathbf{C}}(T)$, where **C** contains *[AB, BC, CD]. T_2 in Figure 8.65 can be the next tableau in the generating sequence.

T_1(A	B	C	D)
b_1	a_2	b_2	a_4
a_1	a_2	a_3	b_3
b_4	b_5	a_3	a_4

Figure 8.64

The astute reader may be wondering if the subscripts on nondistinguished variables can be dispensed with and these variables could be considered distinct until identified with a distinguished variable. The next example shows a tableau where nondistinguished variables must be equated to perform the chase.

$T_2(A$	B	C	$D)$
b_1	a_2	b_2	a_4
b_1	a_2	a_3	b_3
b_1	a_2	a_3	a_4
a_1	a_2	b_2	a_4
a_1	a_2	a_3	b_3
a_1	a_2	a_3	a_4
b_4	b_5	a_3	b_3
b_4	b_5	a_3	a_4

Figure 8.65

Example 8.41 Let T be the tableau in Figure 8.66 and let $\mathbf{C} = \{A \to C, B \to C, CD \to E\}$. In order to compute $chase_{\mathbf{C}}(T)$, we must be able to identify b_2, b_4 and b_8.

$T(A$	B	C	D	$E)$
a_1	b_1	b_2	a_4	b_3
a_1	a_2	b_4	b_5	b_6
b_7	a_2	b_8	a_4	a_5
b_9	b_{10}	a_3	b_{11}	a_4

Figure 8.66

The reader should check that the chase in Example 8.41 cannot proceed without equating nondistinguished variables, even if the closure of the FDs is used.

We shall briefly turn our attention to embedded join dependencies (EJDs). Let $\mathbf{S} = \{S_1, S_2, \ldots, S_q\}$ be a set of relation schemes where $S_1 S_2 \cdots S_q = S \subseteq \mathbf{U}$. To test $\mathbf{C} \models *[\mathbf{S}]$, form the tableau $T_{\mathbf{S}}$ over $\mathbf{U}$. Compute $T_{\mathbf{S}}^* = chase_{\mathbf{C}}(T_{\mathbf{S}})$. If $T_{\mathbf{S}}^*$ contains a row that is distinguished in all the S-columns, then $\mathbf{C} \models *[\mathbf{S}]$.

Example 8.42 Let $\mathbf{S} = \{AD, AB, BDE\}$, let $\mathbf{U} = A\,B\,C\,D\,E$, and let $\mathbf{C} = \{A \to C, B \to C, CD \to E, E \to B\}$. We form the tableau $T_{\mathbf{S}}$, as shown in Figure 8.67, and compute $T_{\mathbf{S}}^* = chase_{\mathbf{C}}(T_S)$, as shown in Figure 8.68. Since $T_{\mathbf{S}}^*$ contains a row distinguished in the $ABDE$-columns, the implication holds. Note that the C-column must be included. If $T_{\mathbf{S}}$ were formed over just $A\,B\,D\,E$, as shown in Figure 8.69, $chase_{\mathbf{C}}(T_{\mathbf{S}})$ would not contain the row of all distinguished variables.

T_S(A	B	C	D	E)
a_1	b_1	b_2	a_4	b_3
a_1	a_2	b_4	b_5	b_6
b_7	a_2	b_8	a_4	a_5

Figure 8.67

T_S^*(A	B	C	D	E)
a_1	a_2	b_2	a_4	a_5
a_1	a_2	b_2	b_5	b_6
b_7	a_2	b_2	a_4	a_4

Figure 8.68

T_S^*(A	B	D	E)
a_1	b_1	a_4	b_2
a_1	a_2	b_3	b_4
b_5	a_2	a_4	a_5

Figure 8.69

The chase computation does not generalize to include EJDs as part of **C**. The J-rule for an EJD would only generate a partial row. The partial row could be padded out with new nondistinguished variables, but then the proof of finiteness of the chase fails (Theorem 8.6).

8.9 EXERCISES

8.1 Let $\mathbf{R} = \{AB, BCD, AE\}$. Compute $m_{\mathbf{R}}(r)$ and $m_{\mathbf{R}}(s)$ for the relations r and s in Figures 8.1 and 8.2.

8.2 Prove part 1 of Lemma 8.1.

8.3 Let $\mathbf{R} = \{R_1, R_2, \ldots, R_p\}$ be a database scheme where $R = R_1R_2 \cdots R_p$. Show that for any relation $r(R)$

$$m_{\mathbf{R}}(r) \in FIX(\mathbf{R}).$$

8.4 Prove that for any tableau T with scheme R and any relation $r(R)$, $r \subseteq T(r)$.

8.5 Let T be a tableau with scheme R, and let $r(R)$ be a relation. Show that if T has a distinguished variable in every column, then $T(r)$ is a relation. That is, $T(r)$ is a *finite* set of tuples.

8.6 Apply the tableau

$T(A_1$	A_2	A_3	$A_4)$
a_1	a_2	a_3	b_1
b_2	a_2	a_3	a_4
a_1	b_3	b_4	a_4

to the relation

$r(A_1$	A_2	A_3	$A_4)$
1	3	5	7
1	3	5	8
2	4	6	8
1	4	6	7

8.7* Prove Lemma 8.2. Hint: Show that if tuples $t_1, t_2, \ldots, t_p$ are joinable on **R**, then there is a valuation ρ for $T_{\mathbf{R}}$ that maps w_i to t_i, $1 \leq i \leq p$, where w_i is the row with distinguished variables in the R_i-columns.

8.8 Show that if tableau T contains the row of all distinguished variables, then $T(r) = r$ for any relation r.

8.9 Let $\mathbf{R} = \{A_1A_2A_3A_4, A_2A_3A_4A_5\}$ and let $\mathbf{S} = \{A_1A_2A_3, A_2A_3A_4, A_4A_5\}$. How many sets of relation schemes **Q** are there such that $\mathbf{R} \geq \mathbf{Q} \geq \mathbf{S}$?

8.10 For the sets **R** and **S** of Exercise 8.9, show that the containment $FIX(\mathbf{R}) \supseteq FIX(\mathbf{S})$ is proper.

8.11* Prove a version of Theorem 8.1 where all the containments are proper.

8.12 What is the maximum number of rows a tableau T can have subject to the constraint $SUB(T) = T$?

8.13 Prove Theorem 8.2. Hint: Use the result that $T_{\mathbf{R}} \equiv T_{\mathbf{S}}$ if and only if $\mathbf{R} \simeq \mathbf{S}$.

8.14 Show that for an arbitrary tableau T, $SUB(T) \sqsubseteq T$.

8.15 Prove or disprove: $T_1 \sqsubseteq T_2$ implies $SUB(T_1) \sqsubseteq SUB(T_2)$.

8.16 For the tableaux

$T_1(A_1$	A_2	$A_3)$
a_1	a_2	b_1
b_2	a_2	a_3

and

$$\begin{array}{ccc} \multicolumn{3}{c}{T_2(A_1 \quad A_2 \quad A_3)} \\ \hline a_1 & a_2 & b_1 \\ b_2 & a_2 & a_3 \\ b_2 & b_3 & b_1 \end{array}$$

find a relation r such that the containment

$$T_1(r) \supseteq T_2(r)$$

is proper.

8.17 Given tableau T and rows w_1 and w_2 in T, say w_1 *supersedes* w_2 if w_1 subsumes w_2 and $w_1(A) \neq w_2(A)$ implies $w_2(A)$ is a nondistinguished variable appearing nowhere else in T. Let $SUP(T)$ be T with all superseded rows removed. Prove $SUP(T) \equiv T$.

8.18 Let T_1 and T_2 be tableaux. Prove that if $T_1 \supseteq T_2$ *as sets of rows*, then $T_1 \sqsubseteq T_2$ as mappings.

8.19 Given tableaux T_1 and T_2, give an algorithm to test if there is a containment mapping from T_1 to T_2. What is the time-complexity of your algorithm?

8.20 Let T be a tableau and $\mathbf{C}$ a set of FDs and JDs. Prove: If $\rho(T) \in SAT(\mathbf{C})$ for some 1-1 valuation ρ, then $\rho'(T) \in SAT(\mathbf{C})$ for any other valuation ρ'.

8.21 What equivalence preserving transformation rules exist for $\mathbf{C} = \emptyset$?

8.22 Apply the F-rules for the FDs $A_1 \to A_3$ and $A_3A_4 \to A_2$ to the tableau

$$\begin{array}{cccc} \multicolumn{4}{c}{T(A_1 \quad A_2 \quad A_3 \quad A_4)} \\ \hline a_1 & b_1 & a_3 & b_2 \\ b_3 & a_2 & a_3 & a_4 \\ a_1 & b_4 & b_5 & a_4 \end{array}$$

as many times as possible.

8.23 Prove Theorem 8.4. Hint: Show that if ρ is a valuation such that $\rho(T) \subseteq r$ for $r \in SAT(X \to A)$ and w_1 and w_2 are rows of T where $w_1(X) = w_2(X)$, then $\rho(w_1(A)) = \rho(w_2(A))$.

8.24 Continue applying the J-rules for $\mathbf{C}$ in Example 8.20 to tableau T'' until no more changes can be made.

8.25 Let $\mathbf{S} = \{S_1, S_2, \ldots, S_q\}$ be a set of relation schemes, let T be a tableau and let ρ be a valuation for T. Show that if $w_1, w_2, \ldots, w_q$ are rows of T joinable on $\mathbf{S}$ with result w, then $\rho(w_1), \rho(w_2), \ldots, \rho(w_q)$ are joinable on $\mathbf{S}$ with result $\rho(w)$.

8.26 Compute the chase of tableau

T(A	B	C	D	E)
a_1	b_1	a_3	b_2	a_5
a_1	b_3	b_4	a_4	a_5
b_5	a_2	a_3	a_4	b_6

under the set of constraints $\mathbf{C} = \{A \to B, E \to D, *[A\,B\,C\,D, D\,E]\}$.

8.27 Give an example of a generating sequence where two distinct rows in one tableau have the same corresponding row in a subsequent tableau.

8.28 Let $T_0, T_1, \ldots, T_n$ be a generating sequence for an arbitrary chase computation. Show that $T_0 \sqsupseteq T_1 \sqsupseteq \cdots \sqsupseteq T_n$.

8.29 Consider the replacement system of Example 8.25. Show that if the condition that parentheses explicitly express the precedence of $\wedge$ over $\vee$ is removed, then the system is not FCR.

8.30 Complete case 3 of the proof of Theorem 8.9.

8.31 Prove the general case of the corollary to Theorem 8.9.

8.32 Prove that the tableaux

T_1(A	B	C	D)
a_1	b_1	a_3	b_2
a_1	a_2	b_3	b_4
b_5	a_2	a_3	a_4

and

T_2(A	B	C	D)
a_1	a_2	b_1	b_2
b_3	a_2	b_4	a_4
b_5	b_6	a_3	a_4

are equivalent on $SAT(\mathbf{C})$, where $\mathbf{C} = \{A \to B, D \to C, *[AB, BC, CD]\}$.

8.33 Show that for a tableau T, if $T \equiv T_I$, where T_I is the tableau with just row w_d (of all distinguished variables), then T contains w_d.

8.34 For Example 8.30, find a relation in $SAT(\mathbf{C})$ that has a lossy decomposition onto database scheme **S**.

8.35 (a) Consider the database scheme $\mathbf{R} = \{ABC, ADEI, BDEI, CDEI\}$ and the set of constraints $\mathbf{C} = \{A \rightarrow D, B \rightarrow E, C \rightarrow I\}$. Show that $\mathbf{C} \models *[\mathbf{R}]$, but that for no proper subset **S** of **R** does $\mathbf{C} \models *[\mathbf{S}]$.

(b)* Generalize part (a) to show that for any $n \geq 3$ there is a set **R** of n relation schemes and a set **C** of functional dependencies such that $\mathbf{C} \models *[\mathbf{R}]$, but for no proper subset S of **R** does $\mathbf{C} \models *[\mathbf{S}]$.

(c) Show that if **R** consists of two relation schemes, X and Y, and **C** is only FDs,

$$\mathbf{C} \models *[X, Y] \text{ if and only if}$$
$$\mathbf{C} \models X \cap Y \rightarrow X \text{ or } \mathbf{C} \models X \cap Y \rightarrow Y.$$

8.36 Prove part 3 of Lemma 8.4.

8.37 What is $(AB)^+$ under the set of constraints

$$\mathbf{C} = \{*[ABC, BCD, DE], B \rightarrow D\}?$$

8.38 Let **C** be a set of constraints, X a set of attributes and $Q = \{Y \mid \mathbf{C} \models X \twoheadrightarrow Y \text{ and } X^+ \cap Y = \emptyset\}$. Show that $\mathbf{C} \models X \twoheadrightarrow Y$ if and only if Y can be written $X'\,Y'$, with $X' \subseteq X^+$ and $Y' \in Q$.

8.39 Find $DEP(BC)$ under the set of constraints $\{*[ABD, ACEI], *[ACDI, BCEI], B \rightarrow I\}$.

8.40 Show that if **C** is a set of FDs and JDs, then $SAT(\mathbf{C})$ is closed under intersection, but if **C** also has EJDs, it is not necessarily closed under intersection.

8.41 Show that if **C** contains only JDs, then $COMP_{\mathbf{C}}(r)$ always exists, but that if **C** also contains FDs, then $COMP_{\mathbf{C}}(r)$ does not necessarily exist, even if r satisfies all the FDs.

8.42 Given the set of constraints **C** and tableaux T_1 and T_2, show that $T_1 \equiv_{\mathbf{C}} T_2$ does not necessarily imply $REP_{\mathbf{C}}(T_1) = REP_{\mathbf{C}}(T_2)$. Note: In light of Theorem 8.13, you may assume T_1 and T_2, as relations, are in $SAT(\mathbf{C})$.

8.43 Construct an example along the lines of Example 8.39, where **C** consists only of JDs.

8.44 Give a general example of a tableau T with m rows and k columns, and a set **C** of constraints, such that $chase_{\mathbf{C}}(T)$ has m^k rows.

8.45 Show that the procedure for computing the chase given in Section 8.8 has time-complexity $O(n^4)$ if the input is given as a set of relation schemes and a set of FDs, rather than a complete tableau and FDs.

8.46* Suppose we generalize the J-rule to include EJDs, as described at the end of Section 8.8. Partial rows are padded with new nondistinguished variables. Give a set **C** of constraints, which will include EJDs, such that an infinite generating sequence T_0, T_1, T_2 ... exists under **C**. Moreover, the generating sequence must have the property that $T_i \not\equiv T_{i+1}$, $i \geq 0$.

8.10 BIBLIOGRAPHY AND COMMENTS

Most of the material from Sections 8.1–8.4 is due to Beeri, Mendelzon, et al. [1979] and Aho, Sagiv, and Ullman [1979a, 1979b]. Tableaux and the chase process with FDs alone are due to Aho, Beeri, and Ullman [1979], who used it to test when a set of FDs implies a JD. The extension of the chase to JDs, its use to solve other dependency problems, and the treatment of tableaux as templates are by Maier, Mendelzon, and Sagiv [1979].

Theorem 8.8 is from Sethi [1974]. Graham [1980] offers another proof that the chase is finite Church-Rosser. Liu and Demers [1978] and Downey, Sethi, and Tarjan [1980] have offered fast algorithms for the chase computation with FDs alone. With JDs, fast algorithms probably do not exist. It is NP-hard to test if a JD is implied by a JD and a set of FDs (Maier, Sagiv, and Yannakakis [1981]), a JD and a set of MVDs (Beeri and Vardi [1980b]), or a set of MVDs alone (Tsou [1980]). The first two problems have been shown to be in NP. Kanellakis [1980] has shown intractability when doing inferences from FDs where domain sizes are restricted.

The "if" part of Exercise 3.5c was first noted by Delobel and Casey [1973]. The "only if" part was noted by Rissanen [1977].

Chapter 9

REPRESENTATION THEORY

In this chapter we shall discuss several notions of when a relation is adequately represented by its decomposition onto a database scheme. We also introduce a new type of equivalence for database schemes, data equivalence. We first examine both topics for an arbitrary set of relations **P**, and then state further results for the case where $\mathbf{P} = SAT(\mathbf{C})$.

9.1 NOTIONS OF ADEQUATE REPRESENTATION

We state here some notations that will be used throughout the chapter. We want to represent members of a set **P** of relations. All relations in **P** are over the scheme **U**. **Q** denotes the set of all relations with scheme **U**. We shall refer to relations in **Q** as *instances*, to avoid confusion with relations that are components of databases. $\mathbf{R} = \{R_1, R_2, \ldots, R_p\}$ will be a database scheme such that $\mathbf{U} = R_1 R_2 \cdots R_p$. Let **M** be the set of all databases over **R**. We want to represent instances in **P** as databases in **M**, so we shall examine the restrictions on **R** necessary for an adequate representation.

In the chapters on normal forms, we were looking for database schemes that eliminated redundancy and gave lossless decompositions. In this chapter, we shall be concerned with enforcing constraints and unique representations. Lossless decomposition frequently will enter into the discussions of the second condition.

We have already seen the project-join mapping defined by **R**, $m_{\mathbf{R}}$. We shall find it useful to separate the projection and join functions.

Definition 9.1 The *project mapping for* **R**, $\pi_{\mathbf{R}}$, maps instances in **Q** to databases in **M**. For $r \in \mathbf{Q}$, we define

$$\pi_{\mathbf{R}}(r) = d$$

where $d = \{r_1, r_2, \ldots, r_p\}$ is the database in **M** such that

$$\pi_{R_i}(r) = r_i, \qquad 1 \leq i \leq p.$$

When it is understood we are projecting instances onto databases, we use π for $\pi_{\mathbf{R}}$.

Definition 9.2 The *join mapping for* **R**, $\bowtie$, maps databases in **M** to instances in **Q**. For database

$$\begin{aligned} d &= \{r_1, r_2, \ldots, r_p\} \text{ in } \mathbf{M}, \\ \bowtie(d) &= r_1 \bowtie r_2 \bowtie \cdots \bowtie r_p. \end{aligned}$$

Note that the description of **R** is implicit in the structure of d.

Example 9.1 Let $\mathbf{U} = ABC$ and $\mathbf{R} = \{AB, BC\}$. If r is the instance in Figure 9.1, then $\pi_{\mathbf{R}}(r)$ is the database $d = \{r_1, r_2\}$, where r_1 and r_2 are given in Figure 9.2. The result of $\bowtie(d)$ is the instance r' in Figure 9.3. Clearly $\pi_{\mathbf{R}}(r') = d$. If $d' = \{r_1, r_2'\}$, where r_2' is given in Figure 9.4, then $\bowtie(d')$ is the empty instance over **U**.

r(A	B	C)
1	3	5
1	4	6
2	4	5
2	4	6

Figure 9.1

r_1(A	B)
1	3
1	4
2	4

r_2(B	C)
3	5
4	5
4	6

Figure 9.2

r'(A	B	C)
1	3	5
1	4	5
1	4	6
2	4	5
2	4	6

Figure 9.3

$r_2'(B$	$C)$
7	5
8	6

Figure 9.4

Definition 9.3 For any subset **P** of **Q**, the *direct image of* **P** *under* **R**, written $\pi_{\mathbf{R}}\mathbf{P}$ (or $\pi\mathbf{P}$ when **R** is understood), is defined as

$$\pi_{\mathbf{R}}\mathbf{P} = \{d \in \mathbf{M} \mid d = \pi_{\mathbf{R}}(r) \quad \text{for some } r \in \mathbf{P}\}.$$

If R is a subset of **U**, the *image of* **P** *under* R, written $\pi_R\mathbf{P}$, is the set

$$\{s(R) \mid s = \pi_R(r) \quad \text{for some } r \in \mathbf{P}\}.$$

We see that $\pi\mathbf{P} \subseteq \pi\mathbf{Q} \subsetneq \mathbf{M}$. The last containment is proper because not every database d is $\pi_{\mathbf{R}}(r)$ for some instance $r \in \mathbf{Q}$.

Example 9.2 The database $d' = \{r_1, r_2'\}$, where r_1 is given in Figure 9.2 and r_2' is given in Figure 9.4, is not the projection of any instance on scheme ABC.

We shall only consider databases in $\pi\mathbf{Q}$ as candidates to represent instances in **P**, since we want π to be the mapping from **P** to **M**. The set $\pi\mathbf{Q}$ is exactly all those databases with scheme **R** that join completely (see Exercise 9.2). There is some controversy involved with this assumption, for three reasons.

1. It is an NP-complete problem to decide if a set of relations joins completely.
2. Databases where the relations do not join completely can still be meaningful.

It is sometimes desirable to store partial information.

Example 9.3 The database consisting of the relations *assigned* and *canfly* in Table 9.1 does not join completely, because Bentley is not assigned to any flight. We still might want to record the information that Bentley can fly a 727, even if he is not currently piloting any flight. However, we cannot represent that piece of information in an instance with scheme {PILOT, FLIGHT#, PLANE-TYPE} without using some special value in the FLIGHT# column.

3. The constraint that a database d is in $\pi\mathbf{Q}$ can only be checked by looking at the database as a whole. It is not sufficient to consider the relations in the database individually, or even in pairs.

Table 9.1 The relations *assigned* and *canfly*, constituting a database.

assigned (PILOT	FLIGHT#)
Bottom	62
Brown	113
Brown	114

canfly (PILOT	PLANE-TYPE)
Bentley	727
Bottom	727
Bottom	DC8
Brown	727
Brown	737

Example 9.4 The relations r_1, r_2 and r_3 in Figure 9.5 join completely when taken in pairs, but the three relations together do not join completely.

$r_1(A$	$B)$
a	b
a'	b'

$r_2(B$	$C)$
b	c
b'	c'

$r_3(A$	$C)$
a	c'
a'	c

Figure 9.5

We shall cover these three objections in further detail in Chapter 12.

Apart from the joinability condition, we want to enforce constraints on the databases in $\pi\mathbf{Q}$ by enforcing constraints on individual relations in the database. We do not want to construct the instance in $\mathbf{Q}$ we are representing every time we need to test a constraint.

Definition 9.4 For any subset $\mathbf{P}$ of $\mathbf{Q}$, the *component-wise image of* $\mathbf{P}$ *under* $\mathbf{R}$, written $CW_{\mathbf{R}}(\mathbf{P})$, is the set

$$\{d \in \mathbf{M} \mid d = \{r_1, r_2, \ldots, r_p\}, r_i \in \pi_{R_i}(\mathbf{P})\}.$$

That is, $CW_{\mathbf{R}}(\mathbf{P})$ consists of those databases over $\mathbf{R}$ where each relation is the projection of some instance in $\mathbf{P}$, but not necessarily the same instance.

Example 9.5 Clearly, $CW_{\mathbf{R}}(\mathbf{P}) \supseteq \pi\mathbf{P}$. The containment is generally proper. Suppose $\mathbf{U} = ABC$, $\mathbf{R} = \{AB, BC\}$ and $\mathbf{P} = SAT(A \rightarrow C)$. Then the database $d = \{r_1, r_2\}$, where r_1 and r_2 are given in Figure 9.6, is in $CW_{\mathbf{R}}(\mathbf{P})$ but not $\pi\mathbf{P}$.

$r_1(A$	$B)$
1	2
1	3

$r_2(B$	$C)$
2	4
3	5

Figure 9.6

To represent **P**, we are interested in using those databases that are projections of instances, and, component-wise, look like projections of instances in **P**. We call this set of interest **L**, which we define

$$\mathbf{L} = CW_{\mathbf{R}}(\mathbf{P}) \cap \pi\mathbf{Q}.$$

Since $\pi\mathbf{P} \subseteq \pi\mathbf{Q}$, $\pi\mathbf{P} \subseteq \mathbf{L}$. Figure 9.7 diagrams the relationship among sets introduced so far.

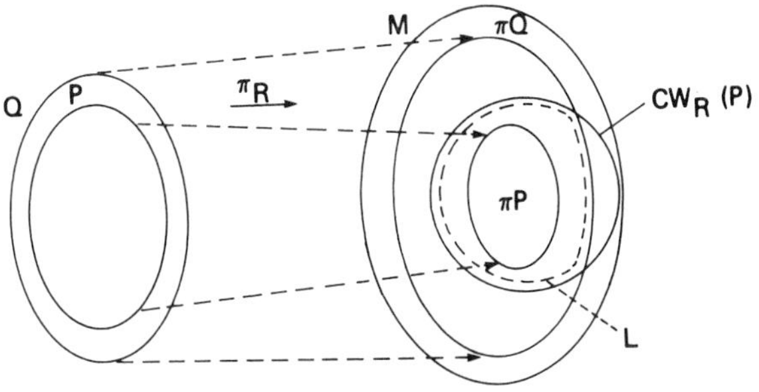

Figure 9.7

Definition 9.5 If **N** is a subset of **M**, we define $\bowtie\mathbf{N}$ to be the set of instances

$$\{\bowtie(d) \mid d \in \mathbf{N}\}.$$

We are ready to define our first notion of adequate representation, which is due to Rissanen.

Definition 9.6 Database scheme **R** *decomposes* **P** *into independent components* if the following two properties hold.

IC1. If $d \in \mathbf{L}$, then there is at most one instance $r \in \mathbf{P}$ with $\pi(r) = d$.
IC2. If $d \in \mathbf{L}$, then there is at least one instance $r \in \mathbf{P}$ with $\pi(r) = d$.

The first property is sometimes called *unique representation*. Properties IC1 and IC2 together are called the *independent component condition*.

The independent component condition requires π to be a one-to-one correspondence from **P** to **L**. For every database $d \in \mathbf{L}$, there is exactly one instance $r \in \mathbf{P}$ such that $\pi(r) = d$. Also, we can represent uniquely each instance in **P** by a database in **L**. We could write IC1 and IC2 as a single property, but we separate them because we use IC1 in our other notions of adequacy. Note that IC2 holds if and only if $\pi\mathbf{P} = \mathbf{L}$ (see Exercise 9.5).

The problem with the independent component condition is that it may be hard to compute the inverse of π if we ever want to go from databases to instances. IC1 and IC2 do not require $\bowtie$ to be the inverse of π. The situation shown in Figure 9.8 could hold.

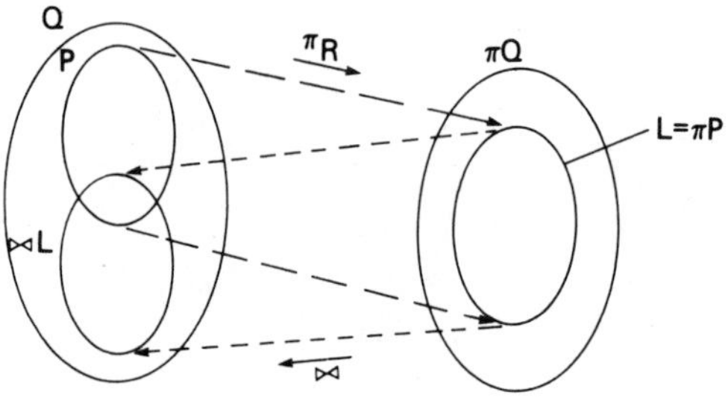

Figure 9.8

Example 9.6 This example is admittedly contrived. Let $\mathbf{U} = ABC$, $\mathbf{R} = \{AB, BC\}$ and $\mathbf{P}$ consists of all instances that satisfy the constraint:

For every pair of tuples t_1 and t_2 in r,
$t_1(A) \geq t_2(A)$ implies $t_1(C) \geq t_2(C)$.

We are assuming ordered domains for attributes A and C. $\mathbf{R}$ decomposes $\mathbf{P}$ into independent components (see Exercise 9.6), but the join mapping for $\mathbf{R}$ is not the inverse of the project mapping on $\mathbf{P}$. The instance r in Figure 9.9 decomposes over R into the database $d = \{r_1, r_2\}$ shown in Figure 9.10, but $\bowtie(d) \neq r$.

$r(A$	B	$C)$
1	3	4
2	3	5

Figure 9.9

$r_1(A$	$B)$
1	3
2	3

$r_2(B$	$C)$
3	4
3	5

Figure 9.10

The next notion of adequacy is due to Arora and Carlson.

Definition 9.7 Database scheme **R** describes an *information preserving decomposition of* **P** if the following two properties hold.

AC1. Same as IC1.
AC2. For any instance r in $\mathbf{Q}$, $\pi(r) \in \mathbf{L}$ implies $r \in \mathbf{P}$.

The second property is called *constraint containment*. AC1 and AC2 together are called the *information preservation condition*.

We now introduce a new set that will allow us to restate property AC2.

Definition 9.8 For any subset **N** of $\pi\mathbf{Q}$, the *preimage* of **N**, denoted $\mathbf{N}^{\leftarrow}$, is the set of instances

$$\{r \in \mathbf{Q} \mid \pi(r) \in \mathbf{N}\}.$$

The set we are interested in is $\mathbf{L}^{\leftarrow}$. The relationship of $\mathbf{L}^{\leftarrow}$ to other sets is shown in Figure 9.11.

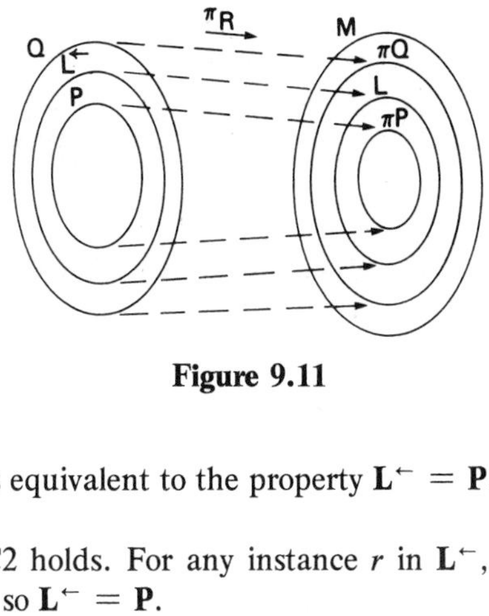

Figure 9.11

Lemma 9.1 AC2 is equivalent to the property $\mathbf{L}^{\leftarrow} = \mathbf{P}$.

Proof Suppose AC2 holds. For any instance r in $\mathbf{L}^{\leftarrow}$, $\pi(r) \in \mathbf{L}$, so $r \in \mathbf{P}$. Therefore $\mathbf{L}^{\leftarrow} \subseteq \mathbf{P}$, so $\mathbf{L}^{\leftarrow} = \mathbf{P}$.

Suppose now $\mathbf{L}^{\leftarrow} = \mathbf{P}$. For any instance $r \in \mathbf{Q}$ where $\pi(r) \in \mathbf{L}$, $r \in \mathbf{L}^{\leftarrow}$. Hence, $r \in \mathbf{P}$ and AC2 is satisfied.

Clearly, $\mathbf{L}^{\leftarrow} = \mathbf{P}$ implies $\mathbf{L} = \pi\mathbf{P}$, hence we have the following result relating the independent component condition and the information preservation condition.

Corollary AC2 implies IC2, hence AC1 and AC2 imply IC1 and IC2.

The implication does not go the other way (see Exercise 9.8). Properties AC1 and AC2 require not only that we can represent every instance r in **P** by a database d in **L**, but also that d could not possibly represent some other instance s in $\mathbf{Q} - \mathbf{P}$. It turns out that the information preservation condition actually specifies what the inverse of π must be.

Definition 9.9 The set of instances **P** satisfies the *lossless join property* for database scheme **R** if

LJ. $FIX(\mathbf{R}) \supseteq \mathbf{P}$.

That is, $\bowtie(\pi(r)) = r$ for all $r \in \mathbf{P}$. Note that $\bowtie(\pi(r))$ is the same as $m_{\mathbf{R}}(r)$, always.

Lemma 9.2 The LJ property implies the IC1 property.

Proof Suppose the LJ property holds. Let r and r' be instances in **P**. If $\pi(r) = \pi(r')$, then surely $\bowtie(\pi(r)) = \bowtie(\pi(r'))$. From the LJ property, $r = \bowtie(\pi(r))$, hence $r = r'$ and IC1 is satisfied.

Corollary LJ and AC2 imply AC1 and AC2.

Lemma 9.3 Properties AC1 and AC2 imply LJ.

Proof Assume the information preservation condition holds. Let r be an instance **P** and let $d = \pi(r)$. Now $\bowtie(d)$ is also an instance such that $\pi(\bowtie(d)) = d$. Since $d \in \mathbf{L}$, by AC2, $\bowtie d$ is in P. AC1 requires $\bowtie(d) = r$, since $\pi(r) = \pi(\bowtie(d))$. Hence we have $r = \bowtie(d) = \bowtie(\pi(r))$, which is property LJ.

To summarize the previous results:

Theorem 9.1 Given constraint containment (AC2), AC1 is equivalent to LJ.

It should now be clear that $\bowtie$ is the inverse of π on **P** under the information preservation condition.

Example 9.7 Let $\mathbf{U} = ABC$, $\mathbf{R} = \{AB, BC\}$ and $\mathbf{P} = SAT(B \rightarrow C)$. The FD $B \rightarrow C$ ensures that the LJ property holds. If instance r obeys $B \rightarrow C$, then $\pi_{BC}(r)$ obeys $B \rightarrow C$ and if $\pi_{BC}(r)$ obeys $B \rightarrow C$, r must obey $B \rightarrow C$ (see Exercise 9.10). Therefore, for any instance r such that $\pi(r) \in \mathbf{L}$, $r \in \mathbf{P}$. **P** satisfies AC2 and hence the information preservation condition.

We have noted that the independent component condition has the problem that the inverse mapping from databases to instances may not always be easily computable. Testing membership in **P** can be of arbitrary complexity, and sometimes the complexity carries over to testing which instance in **P** a given database represents. We have seen that AC1 and AC2 require join to be the inverse mapping, but they also require that for no instance r in $\mathbf{Q} - \mathbf{P}$ is $\pi(r)$ in **L**. That is, not only can we represent every instance r in **P** by a unique database d in **L**, but there is no possibility that d also represents some instance r' not in **P**. This property is overly restrictive. Surely if a database d in **L** could represent an instance r in **P** and an instance r' not in **P**, we can ignore r', since it is outside the realm of interest. We present a condition intermediate between independent component and information preservation.

Definition 9.10 Database scheme R satisfies the *join condition* for **P** if the following properties hold.

J1. Same as IC1.
J2. For every database $d \in \mathbf{L}$, $\bowtie(d) \in \mathbf{P}$.

It is not hard to see that J1 and J2 require $\bowtie$ to be the inverse of π on **P**. If r is an instance in **P**, then $\pi(r) \in \mathbf{L}$ and, by J2, $m_{\mathbf{R}}(r) \in \mathbf{P}$. But $\pi(m_{\mathbf{R}}(r)) = \pi(r)$, so, by J1, $m_{\mathbf{R}}(r) = r$. We have also shown that the LJ property holds on **P**. The join condition also says that we let any database $d \in \mathbf{L}$ represent the maximal instance r in **P** such that $\bowtie(r) = d$ (see Exercise 9.11). We now give an alternative characterization of property J2.

Lemma 9.4 Property J2 holds if and only if $FIX(\mathbf{R}) \cap \mathbf{L}^{\leftarrow} \subseteq \mathbf{P}$.

Proof (only if) Property J2 can be stated as $\bowtie\mathbf{L} \subseteq \mathbf{P}$. Let r be an instance in $FIX(\mathbf{R}) \cap \mathbf{L}^{\leftarrow}$. Since r is in $\mathbf{L}^{\leftarrow}$, $\pi(r) \in \mathbf{L}$. Since $r \in FIX(\mathbf{R})$, $r = \bowtie(\pi(r))$, so $r \in \bowtie\mathbf{L}$, hence $r \in \mathbf{P}$. We see $FIX(\mathbf{R}) \cap \mathbf{L}^{\leftarrow} \subseteq \mathbf{P}$.

(if) Suppose $FIX(\mathbf{R}) \cap \mathbf{L}^{\leftarrow} \subseteq \mathbf{P}$, and let r be an instance in $\bowtie\mathbf{L}$. Since $r \in \bowtie\mathbf{L}$, $r = \bowtie(d)$ for some database $d \in \mathbf{L}$. Clearly $\pi(r) = d$, so $m_{\mathbf{R}}(r) = r$ and hence $r \in FIX(\mathbf{R})$. Since $d \in \mathbf{L}$, $r \in \mathbf{R}^{\leftarrow}$. By our supposition, $r \in \mathbf{P}$. We have that $\bowtie\mathbf{L} \subseteq \mathbf{P}$, hence property J2 is satisfied.

We now compare the join condition with the independent component and information preservation conditions.

Lemma 9.5 Condition J2 implies condition IC2.

Proof Left to the reader (see Exercise 9.13).

Theorem 9.2 AC1 and AC2 imply J1 and J2, which in turn imply IC1 and IC2.

Proof Suppose AC1 and AC2 hold. J1 clearly holds. To see that J2 holds, pick any instance $r \in \mathbf{L}$, and let $r = \bowtie(d)$ for $d \in \mathbf{L}$. Since $\pi(r) = d \in \mathbf{L}$, AC2 requires r to be in $\mathbf{P}$. Hence $\bowtie\mathbf{L} \subseteq \mathbf{P}$ and J2 is satisfied. The other implication follows from Lemma 9.5.

To compare AC1 and AC2 to J1 and J2, we note that both require $\mathbf{P} \subseteq FIX(\mathbf{R})$ (LJ condition), but AC2 restricts $\mathbf{L}^{\leftarrow} = \mathbf{P}$, where J1 and J2 allow $\mathbf{P}$ to be properly contained in $\mathbf{L}^{\leftarrow}$. In Figure 9.12, the pair of instances s, s' could not exist under either pair of properties, but J1 and J2 allow the pair of instances r, r', while AC1 and AC2 do not.

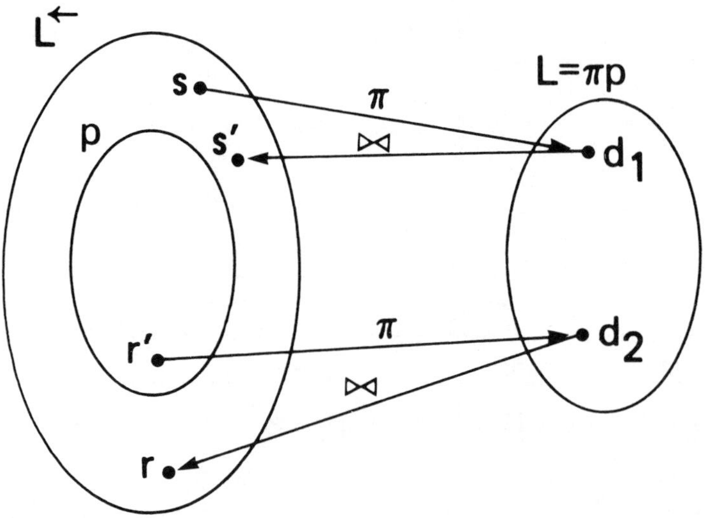

Figure 9.12

Example 9.6 shows that the independent components condition does not imply the join condition. The next example gives a database scheme and set of instances that satisfy the join condition, but not the information preservation condition.

Example 9.8 Let $\mathbf{U} = ABC$, let $\mathbf{R}$ be the database scheme $\{AB, BC\}$ and let $\mathbf{P} = SAT(B \twoheadrightarrow A)$. $\mathbf{L}$ consists of all pairs of completely joinable relations over AB and BC. $B \twoheadrightarrow A$ is another statement of $*[AB, BC]$, so $\mathbf{R}$ satisfies property LJ, hence property J1. The join of two relations over AB and BC

always satisfies $B \twoheadrightarrow A$, so property J2 holds. However, property A2 is violated, since for any instance $r \in \mathbf{Q}$, $\pi(r) \in \mathbf{L}$, and $\mathbf{P} \neq \mathbf{Q}$.

We now look at what property we can add to the independent components condition to get equivalence to the join condition, and also what property we can add to the join condition to get equivalence to the information preservation condition.

How can property IC2 hold while property J2 fails? This situation can only happen if there is some instance r in $\mathbf{P}$ such that $m_{\mathbf{R}}(r) \notin \mathbf{P}$. We formalize this property.

Definition 9.11 Database scheme $\mathbf{R}$ *preserves* $\mathbf{P}$ if the following property holds:

PR. For every instance r in $\mathbf{P}$, $m_{\mathbf{R}}(r) \in \mathbf{P}$. That is, $m_{\mathbf{R}}\mathbf{P} \subseteq \mathbf{P}$, where $m_{\mathbf{R}}\mathbf{P} = \bowtie \pi\mathbf{P}$.

Lemma 9.6 Property J2 implies property PR.

Proof Left to the reader (see Exercise 9.16).

Property PR does not imply property J2, however.

Example 9.9 Let $\mathbf{U} = ABC$, let database scheme $\mathbf{R} = \{AB, BC\}$, and let $\mathbf{P} = SAT(\{A \twoheadrightarrow B, B \twoheadrightarrow A\})$. Since $\mathbf{P} \subseteq SAT(B \twoheadrightarrow A)$, $m_{\mathbf{R}}\mathbf{P} = \mathbf{P}$, so PR is satisfied. Consider the database $d = \{r_1, r_2\}$, where relations r_1 and r_2 are given in Figure 9.13. Database d is in $\mathbf{L}$, since $r_1 = \pi_{AB}(s_1)$ and $r_2 = \pi_{BC}(s_2)$, where s_1 and s_2 are the instances from $\mathbf{P}$ shown in Figure 9.14. We see that $\bowtie(d)$, shown in Figure 9.15, is not in $\mathbf{P}$ (why?), so property J2 is violated.

r_1:

A	B
1	3
1	4
2	4

r_2:

B	C
3	5
3	6
4	5
4	6
4	7

Figure 9.13

s_1(A	B	C)
1	3	5
1	4	5
2	4	5

s_2(A	B	C)
1	3	5
1	3	6
2	4	5
2	4	6
2	4	7

Figure 9.14

$\bowtie(d)$(A	B	C)
1	3	5
1	3	6
1	4	5
1	4	6
1	4	7
2	4	5
2	4	6
2	4	7

Figure 9.15

Lemma 9.7 Properties PR and IC2 imply property J2.

Proof Let r be any instance in $\bowtie\mathbf{L}$ and let d be the database in $\mathbf{L}$ such that $r = \bowtie(d)$. By IC2, $\mathbf{P} = \mathbf{L}$, so $d \in \pi\mathbf{P}$. Let r' be an instance in $\mathbf{P}$ such that $\pi(r') = d$. By PR, $m_{\mathbf{R}}(r') \in \mathbf{P}$, but $m_{\mathbf{R}}(r') = r$, so, $r \in \mathbf{P}$. Hence $\bowtie\mathbf{L} \subseteq \mathbf{P}$ and J2 is satisfied.

Corollary Properties IC1, IC2, and PR hold if and only if J1 and J2 hold.

We can replace IC1 and PR in the corollary above by property LJ.

Lemma 9.8 Property LJ implies property PR.

Proof $FIX(\mathbf{R}) \supseteq \mathbf{P}$ implies $m_{\mathbf{R}}(\mathbf{P}) = \mathbf{P}$, which in turn implies $m_{\mathbf{R}}(\mathbf{P}) \subseteq \mathbf{P}$.

Theorem 9.3 Properties LJ and IC2 hold if and only if properties J1 and J2 hold.

Proof By Lemma 9.2, LJ implies IC1; by Lemma 9.8, LJ implies PR. Therefore, by the corollary to Lemma 9.7, LJ and IC2 imply the join condition. From Theorem 9.2, we know that J1 and J2 imply IC2. J1 and J2 also imply LJ (see Exercise 9.17), so they imply LJ and IC2.

We now look at what need be added to make the join condition equivalent to the information preservation condition.

Definition 9.12 Database scheme **R** satisfies *property S* if

S. $FIX(\mathbf{R}) \supseteq \mathbf{L}^{\leftarrow}$.

Theorem 9.4 Properties J1, J2, and S hold if and only if properties AC1 and AC2 hold.

Proof From Theorem 9.2, we know AC1 and AC2 imply J1 and J2. By Lemma 9.1, AC2 requires $\mathbf{L}^{\leftarrow} = \mathbf{P}$. By Lemma 9.3, AC1 and AC2 require property LJ, so $\mathbf{P} \subseteq FIX(\mathbf{R})$. Thus we have $\mathbf{L}^{\leftarrow} = \mathbf{P} \subseteq FIX(\mathbf{R})$, which implies property S.

We now show J2 and S imply AC2. Let r be an instance in $\mathbf{L}^{\leftarrow}$, where $\pi(r) = d$, for $d \in \mathbf{L}$. By J2, $\bowtie(d) \in \mathbf{P}$. But S says that $m_{\mathbf{R}}(r) = r$, so $r = \bowtie(d) \in \mathbf{P}$. Therefore, $\mathbf{L}^{\leftarrow} \subseteq \mathbf{P}$. Since we always have $\mathbf{L}^{\leftarrow} \supseteq \mathbf{P}$, $\mathbf{L}^{\leftarrow} = \mathbf{P}$ and AC2 is satisfied.

The difference between the join condition and the information preservation condition is whether we require only $FIX(\mathbf{R}) \supseteq \mathbf{P}$ or the stronger condition $FIX(\mathbf{R}) \supseteq \mathbf{L}^{\leftarrow}$ (see Exercise 9.18). We shall be most interested in cases where **P** is described by some set of constraints **C**. In that case, $FIX(\mathbf{R}) \supseteq \mathbf{P}$ is the same as $\mathbf{C} \models *[\mathbf{R}]$, which we have means to test if **C** is FDs and JDs. The condition $FIX(\mathbf{R}) \supseteq \mathbf{L}^{\leftarrow}$ is the same as $\pi\mathbf{C} \models *[\mathbf{R}]$. We use $\pi\mathbf{C}$ to denote the "projected constraints" of **C** on **R**: the constraints that necessarily hold in the various projections of an instance r onto the schemes in **R**, where r is in $SAT(\mathbf{C})$. That is, $\pi\mathbf{C}$ is the set of constraints such that $\mathbf{L}^{\leftarrow} = SAT(\pi\mathbf{C})$. $SAT(\pi\mathbf{C})$ is exactly those instances r such that $\pi(r) \in \mathbf{L}$. One problem, which we examine later, is that the constraints in $\pi\mathbf{C}$ are not necessarily of the same type as those in **C**, or even embedded versions thereof. There can be problems with testing $\pi\mathbf{C} \models *[\mathbf{R}]$, therefore. The other part of testing the join and information preservation conditions is determining whether $\bowtie\mathbf{L} \subseteq \mathbf{P}$ (see Exercise 9.18). In terms of projected constraints, we want to test $\pi\mathbf{C} \cup \{*[\mathbf{R}]\} \models \mathbf{C}$. For information preservation, the test reduces to $\pi\mathbf{C} \models \mathbf{C}$, by Theorem 9.4. We shall return to testing the various representation properties when **P** is defined by constraints in Section 9.3.

9.2 DATA-EQUIVALENCE OF DATABASE SCHEMES

In Chapter 8 we saw one notion of equivalence of database schemes **R** and **S** relative to a set **P** of instances, namely $T_\mathbf{R} \equiv_\mathbf{P} T_\mathbf{S}$. That is, **R** and **S** are equivalent on **P** if $T_\mathbf{R}(r) = T_\mathbf{S}(r)$ for all instances r in **P**. In Chapter 8 we were mainly concerned with testing whether $T_\mathbf{R} \equiv_\mathbf{P} T_I$, where T_I is a tableau for the identity mapping. This notion of equivalence says schemes **R** and **S** are equivalent on **P** if their respective project-join mappings behave identically on **P**. That is, for any instance $r \in \mathbf{P}$, decomposing r onto **R** involves the same loss of information as decomposing r onto **S**.

Suppose, however, we are only interested in those instances where no information is lost through decomposition. We may only care that **R** and **S** can faithfully represent the same set of instances in **P**, but not that **R** and **S** may mangle instances differently that are not represented faithfully by decomposition. We present this weaker notion of equivalence in this section.

Definition 9.13 Given database scheme **R** and a set of instances **P**, the *fixed points of* **P** *under* **R**, written $FIX_\mathbf{P}(\mathbf{R})$, is $FIX(\mathbf{R}) \cap \mathbf{P}$.

Definition 9.14 Database scheme **R** and **S** are *data-equivalent on* **P**, written $\mathbf{R} \approx_\mathbf{P} \mathbf{S}$, if $FIX_\mathbf{P}(\mathbf{R}) = FIX_\mathbf{P}(\mathbf{S})$. That is, **R** and **S** can faithfully represent the same subset of instances in **P**. When proving data-equivalence, we shall generally show two containments. Note that the containment $FIX_\mathbf{P}(\mathbf{R}) \subseteq FIX_\mathbf{P}(\mathbf{S})$ holds exactly when the containment $FIX_\mathbf{P}(\mathbf{R}) \subseteq FIX(\mathbf{S})$ holds.

Lemma 9.9 $T_\mathbf{R} \equiv_\mathbf{P} T_\mathbf{S}$ implies $\mathbf{R} \approx_\mathbf{P} \mathbf{S}$.

Proof Left to the reader (see Exercise 9.19).

The converse of Lemma 9.9 does not hold, as we expect.

Example 9.10 Let $\mathbf{U} = ABCD$, let **R** be the database scheme $\{ABC, CD\}$ and let **S** be the scheme $\{AB, BCD\}$. If **P** consists of just the two instances r and s in Figure 9.16, then **R** and **S** are data-equivalent on **P**. Instance r decomposes losslessly onto both **R** and **S**, while s has a lossy decomposition onto both schemes. However, $T_\mathbf{R}$ and $T_\mathbf{S}$ are not equivalent on **P**, because $s' = T_\mathbf{R}(s)$ is not the same as $s'' = T_\mathbf{S}(s)$, as shown in Figure 9.17.

Definition 9.15 Given database scheme **R**, the *preserved set of* **P** *under* **R**, denoted $PRES_\mathbf{P}(\mathbf{R})$, is $\{r \in \mathbf{P} \mid m_\mathbf{R}(r) \in \mathbf{P}\}$.

$r(A$	B	C	$D)$
1	3	5	7
1	3	6	8
2	4	6	8

$s(A$	B	C	$D)$
1	3	5	7
2	3	6	7
2	4	6	8

Figure 9.16

$s'(A$	B	C	$D)$
1	3	5	7
2	3	6	7
2	4	6	7
2	3	6	8
2	4	6	8

$s''(A$	B	C	$D)$
1	3	5	7
1	3	6	7
2	3	5	7
2	3	6	7
2	4	6	8

Figure 9.17

Using this definition, **R** preserves **P** can be written $PRES_{\mathbf{P}}(\mathbf{R}) = \mathbf{P}$. We also note $FIX_{\mathbf{P}}(\mathbf{R}) \subseteq PRES_{\mathbf{P}}(\mathbf{R})$ (see Exercise 9.21).

Theorem 9.5 Let **R** and **S** be database schemes and let **P** be a set of instances. Assume $\mathbf{P}'$ is any set of instances such that

$$FIX_{\mathbf{P}}(\mathbf{R}) \subseteq \mathbf{P}' \subseteq PRES_{\mathbf{P}}(\mathbf{R}).$$

Then $FIX_{\mathbf{P}}(\mathbf{R}) \subseteq FIX(\mathbf{S})$ if and only if $m_{\mathbf{S}}(r) \subseteq m_{\mathbf{R}}(r)$ for all r in $\mathbf{P}'$.

Proof (only if) Let r be an arbitrary instance in $\mathbf{P}'$. Since $r \in PRES_{\mathbf{P}}(\mathbf{R})$, instance $s = m_{\mathbf{R}}(r)$ is in **P**. Project-join mappings are idempotent, so s is in $FIX(\mathbf{R})$ and hence in $FIX_{\mathbf{P}}(\mathbf{R})$. By assumption, s is then in $FIX(\mathbf{S})$. Now $r \subseteq s$, so $m_{\mathbf{S}}(r) \subseteq m_{\mathbf{S}}(s)$. Since s is in $FIX(\mathbf{S})$, $m_{\mathbf{S}}(s) = s$. Combining equalities and containment we have $m_{\mathbf{S}}(r) \subseteq m_{\mathbf{R}}(r)$, as desired.

(if) Let r be an instance in $FIX_{\mathbf{P}}(\mathbf{R})$, which implies $r \in \mathbf{P}'$. By assumption, $m_{\mathbf{S}}(r) \subseteq m_{\mathbf{R}}(r)$. Now $m_{\mathbf{R}}(r) = r$ and $m_{\mathbf{S}}(r) \supseteq r$, so $m_{\mathbf{S}}(r) = r$ and $r \in FIX(\mathbf{S})$. Hence $FIX_{\mathbf{P}}(\mathbf{R}) \subseteq FIX(\mathbf{S})$.

Corollary The following are equivalent:

1. $FIX_{\mathbf{P}}(\mathbf{R}) \subseteq FIX(\mathbf{S})$.
2. $T_{\mathbf{S}} \sqsubseteq_K T_{\mathbf{R}}$ for $K = FIX_{\mathbf{P}}(\mathbf{R})$.
3. $T_{\mathbf{S}} \sqsubseteq_K T_{\mathbf{R}}$ for $K = PRES_{\mathbf{P}}(\mathbf{R})$.

Proof Left to the reader (see Exercise 9.22).

Corollary If $\mathbf{R}$ and $\mathbf{S}$ are database schemes where $\mathbf{R}$ preserves $\mathbf{P}$, then $FIX_{\mathbf{P}}(\mathbf{R}) \subseteq FIX(\mathbf{S})$ if and only if $T_{\mathbf{S}} \sqsubseteq_{\mathbf{P}} T_{\mathbf{R}}$.

Proof Immediate from the equivalence of 1 and 3 in the last corollary.

We have stumbled onto the result that data-equivalence and regular equivalence are the same when $\mathbf{P}$ is preserved.

Theorem 9.6 If $\mathbf{R}$ and $\mathbf{S}$ are database schemes that preserve $\mathbf{P}$, then $\mathbf{R} \approx_{\mathbf{P}} \mathbf{S}$ is equivalent to $T_{\mathbf{R}} \equiv_{\mathbf{P}} T_{\mathbf{S}}$.

We know that both the join and information preservation conditions require property PR. Thus, if we choose either condition as a notion of adequate representation, data-equivalence and regular equivalence are the same for adequate database schemes.

9.3 TESTING ADEQUATE REPRESENTATION AND EQUIVALENCE UNDER CONSTRAINTS

We have seen that when the mapping from databases in $\mathbf{L}$ to relations in $\mathbf{Q}$ is the join, then the independent component and join conditions are equivalent. The difference between the join and information preservation conditions is whether we require $\mathbf{P} \subseteq FIX(\mathbf{R})$ or the stronger condition $\mathbf{L}^{\leftarrow} \subseteq FIX(\mathbf{R})$. If $\mathbf{P}$ is defined as $SAT(\mathbf{C})$ for a set of constraints $\mathbf{C}$, the difference is whether $\mathbf{C} \models *[\mathbf{R}]$ or $\pi\mathbf{C} \models *[\mathbf{R}]$. Recall that $\pi\mathbf{C}$ is our informal notation for the *projected constraints of* $\mathbf{C}$ *on* $\mathbf{R}$: the constraints that define the set $\mathbf{L}^{\leftarrow}$. That is, $\pi\mathbf{C}$ is the set of restrictions that necessarily must apply to $\pi_R(r)$ for $r \in SAT(\mathbf{C})$ and for all relation schemes $R \in \mathbf{R}$.

We are defining $\pi\mathbf{C}$ in a backwards manner. We want $\pi\mathbf{C}$ to be a set of constraints such that $\mathbf{L}^{\leftarrow} = SAT(\pi\mathbf{C})$. One problem with providing a formal definition for $\pi\mathbf{C}$ is that $\pi\mathbf{C}$ cannot necessarily be expressed by the same types of dependencies as those in $\mathbf{C}$. There often are dependencies in $\pi\mathbf{C}$ of the same type as those in $\mathbf{C}$ (see Exercises 9.10 and 9.24), but there can be dependencies of other types.

Example 9.11 Let $\mathbf{U} = ABCDE$, let $R = ABDE$ and let $\mathbf{P} = SAT\{A \rightarrow E, B \rightarrow E, CE \rightarrow D\})$. For any relation $r \in \mathbf{P}$, the set of FDs $\pi_{\mathbf{R}}(r)$ must satisfy is $F = \{AC \rightarrow D, BC \rightarrow D\}$. Consider the relation s in Figure 9.18. Relation $s \in SAT(F)$, but s is not the projection of any instance in $\mathbf{P}$. (Add an E-column to s and try chasing under the FDs of **P**.) It turns out that any relation $\pi_{\mathbf{R}}(r)$ for $r \in \mathbf{P}$ must satisfy the curious dependency:

If t_1, t_2, and t_3 are tuples in $\pi_{\mathbf{R}}(r)$ such that

1. $t_1(A) = t_3(A)$
2. $t_1(C) = t_2(C)$
3. $t_2(B) = t_3(B)$

then

4. $t_1(D) = t_2(D)$.

This dependency is not equivalent to any set of FDs. Note that s does not satisfy the dependency.

s(A	B	C	D)
1	3	5	7
2	4	5	8
1	4	6	8

Figure 9.18

Example 9.12 Let $\mathbf{U} = ABCD$, let $R = ABC$ and let $\mathbf{P} = SAT(\{A \rightarrow\rightarrow BC, B \rightarrow\rightarrow AC, CD \rightarrow\rightarrow A\})$. Any relation $\pi_{\mathbf{R}}(r)$ for $r \in \mathbf{P}$ need only satisfy trivial MVDs. However, relation s in Figure 9.19 is not the projection of any instance in **P**. (Add a D-column and chase under the MVDs of **P**.)

s(A	B	C)
1	3	5
1	4	6
2	4	5

Figure 9.19

9.3.1 P Specified by Functional Dependencies Only

We see there are problems with specifying $\pi\mathbf{C}$, and hence with testing $FIX(\mathbf{R}) \supseteq \mathbf{L}^{\leftarrow}$. In Chapter 14 we shall examine classes of dependencies that can be used to characterize $\pi\mathbf{C}$ when **C** consists of FDs and JDs. However no decision procedure for implication exists for those more general dependency classes. When **C** is just FDs, even though we cannot express $\pi\mathbf{C}$ with just FDs, the set of FDs in $\pi\mathbf{C}$ suffices for our representation conditions.

Theorem 9.7 If $\mathbf{P} = SAT(F)$ for a set F of FDs, then the independent components, join and information preservation conditions are equivalent.

Proof By Theorem 9.2, it suffices to show that if AC1 or AC2 fails, then IC1 or IC2 fails. Clearly, if AC1 fails, then IC1 fails.

Suppose AC2 fails: $\mathbf{L}^{\leftarrow} \neq \mathbf{P}$. Let r be an instance in $\mathbf{L}^{\leftarrow} - \mathbf{P}$. We may assume r has only two tuples (see Exercise 9.27). Instance r must violate some FD implied by F, say $X \rightarrow A$. Since r has but two tuples, they must agree on X and disagree on A. Thus r has one value in each of the X-columns and two values in the A-column.

If IC2 fails, we are done. Suppose it holds. Let $d = \pi(r)$; d must be in $\mathbf{L}$. By IC2, there is an instance r' in $\mathbf{P}$ such that $\pi(r') = d$. Instance r' can only have a single value in each of its X-columns. (Why?) However, r' must have two values in its A-column, and therefore violates $X \rightarrow A$. Hence $r' \in \mathbf{P}$ and IC2 must fail.

We now consider testing the join condition (and hence the other two representation conditions) when $\mathbf{P} = SAT(F)$ for a set F of FDs. We shall test properties LJ and J2 (see Exercise 9.28). LJ translates to $F \models *[\mathbf{R}]$, which we know how to test using the chase. We consider testing J2, which is $\bowtie \mathbf{L} \subseteq \mathbf{P}$.

Definition 9.16 For a database scheme $\mathbf{R}$ and a set F of FDs, *F restricted to* $\mathbf{R}$, denoted $F_{\mathbf{R}}$, is the set of FDs in F^+ that apply to any relation scheme R in $\mathbf{R}$.

Example 9.13 Let $\mathbf{U} = ABCD$, $\mathbf{R} = \{ABC, CD\}$ and $F = \{AD \rightarrow C, CD \rightarrow A, B \rightarrow D\}$. The only nontrivial FDs in $F_{\mathbf{R}}$ are $BC \rightarrow A$, $BC \rightarrow AB$, $BC \rightarrow AC$, $BC \rightarrow ABC$, $AB \rightarrow C$, $AB \rightarrow AC$, $AB \rightarrow BC$ and $AB \rightarrow ABC$.

Recall that F is *enforceable* on $\mathbf{R}$ if $F_{\mathbf{R}} \equiv F$.

Lemma 9.10 Let $\mathbf{P} = SAT(F)$ for a set F of FDs. Property J2 holds if and only if F is enforceable on $\mathbf{R}$.

Proof We leave the if direction as Exercise 9.30 (only if). We shall show that if F is not enforceable on $\mathbf{R}$, then there is a database d in $\mathbf{L}$ such that $\bowtie d$ is not in $\mathbf{P}$. Let $X \rightarrow AY$ be an FD in F such that $X \rightarrow A$ is not in $G = F_{\mathbf{R}}^+$. Let Z be the closure of X under G. Clearly $A \notin Z$. We construct an instance r_X in $\mathbf{Q}$ as follows. Instance r_X has two tuples: t_0, which is 0 everywhere, t_Z, which is 0 on Z and 1 elsewhere.

Obviously, r_X is not in $\mathbf{P}$, since it violates F. Let $d = \pi(r_X)$. The instance $\bowtie(d)$ is not in $\mathbf{P}$ either, since $\bowtie(d) \supseteq r_X$ (see Exercise 9.26). We now show that each relation in d is the projection of some instance in $\mathbf{P}$. Let R be any relation scheme in $\mathbf{R}$. We define an instance r_R in $\mathbf{P}$ where $\pi_R(r_X) = \pi_R(r_R)$.

Let r_R contain two tuples: t_0 as in r_X, and t_1, which is all 1's except for 0's in $(Z \cap R)^+$ under F. Instance r_R cannot violate any FD in F, or else $(Z \cap R)^+$ would be incorrectly defined. To show that $\pi_R(r_X) = \pi_R(r_R)$, we must show $(Z \cap R)^+ \cap R = Z \cap R$. (Those sets are the columns where $\pi_R(r_R)$ and $\pi_R(r_X)$, respectively, contain two symbols.) Suppose B is an attribute that is in the first set but not the second. B is clearly in R. Since $B \in (Z \cap R)^+$, $F \models Z \cap R \rightarrow B$. But then $F \models Z \rightarrow B$, so $B \in Z$ and hence $B \in Z \cap R$, a contradiction. We have shown $d \in \mathbf{L}$. Since $\bowtie(d) \in \mathbf{P}$, property J2 is violated, as we predicted.

We saw in Chapter 8 that for a set of FDs F, $F \models *[\mathbf{R}]$ can be tested in time polynomial in the space required to write F and $\mathbf{R}$. We now present a polynomial-time test for F being enforceable on $\mathbf{R}$. This test will give us a polynomial-time test for the join condition when $\mathbf{P} = SAT(F)$.

The Algorithm 9.1 computes X^+ under $F_\mathbf{R}$. The closure taken in line 5 is the closure under F.

Algorithm 9.1 PCLOSURE

Input: A set of FDs F over $\mathbf{U}$, a database scheme $\mathbf{R}$ over $\mathbf{U}$ and a subset X of $\mathbf{U}$.

Output: The closure of X under $F_\mathbf{R}$.

PCLOSURE(F, $\mathbf{R}$, X)

```
1. begin
2. Y := X;
3. while there are changes to Y do
4.    for each R ∈ R do
5.       Y := ((Y ∩ R)+ ∩ R) ∪ Y;
6. return (Y);
7. end.
```

Example 9.14 Let $\mathbf{U} = ABCDE$, $R = \{AB, BC, CDE\}$ and $F = \{A \rightarrow D, D \rightarrow B, B \rightarrow CE\}$. PCLOSURE($F$, $\mathbf{R}$, A) is ABC. Note that A^+ under F is $ABCDE$.

Theorem 9.8 PCLOSURE(F, $\mathbf{R}$, X) returns X^+ under $F_\mathbf{R}$.

Proof Let Y be the set in the algorithm. Y is initially a subset of X^+, and remains so, since the FD being implicitly used in line 5 is $(Y \cap R) \rightarrow (Y \cap R)^+ \cap R$, which is in $F_\mathbf{R}$ (the closure $(Y \cap R)^+$ being taken under F). We want to show now that every attribute of X^+ is eventually added to Y.

Let H be an $F_\mathbf{R}$-based DDAG for $X \rightarrow X^+$. Assume that the successive sets of node labels during the construction of H are $Z_0, Z_1, Z_2, \ldots, Z_n$, where $X = Z_0$ and $X^+ = Z_n$. We claim $Z_i \subseteq Y$ at the end of the ith iteration of the **while**-loop. Clearly $Z_0 \subseteq Y$. Suppose to get from Z_i to Z_{i+1} the FD $V \rightarrow W$ is applied. Since $V \rightarrow W$ is in $F_{\mathbf{R}}$, there is some relation scheme $R \in \mathbf{R}$ such that $VW \subseteq R$. Moreover, $V \subseteq Z_i$, so $V \subseteq Y$ at the start of the $i + 1^{st}$ iteration. When R is reached in the **for**-loop, $V \subseteq Y \cap R$, so $W \subseteq (Y \cap R)^+ \cap R$, since $F \models F_{\mathbf{R}}$. Therefore, all of W is added to Y if it is not there already, and whatever attribute $A \in W$ was added to Z_i to get Z_{i+1} is also added to Y. Hence, when the algorithm terminates $Z_n \subseteq Y$, and so $Y = X^+$.

Lemma 9.11 PCLOSURE has time complexity $O(|\mathbf{U}| \cdot |\mathbf{R}| \cdot ||F||)$ where $||F||$ is the space required to write all the FDs in F.

Proof The **while**-loop in line 3 can execute no more than $|\mathbf{U}|-1$ times, since Y can grow no larger than $\mathbf{U}$. The **for**-loop at line 4 executes $|\mathbf{R}|$ times for each iteration of the **while**-loop. The dominating factor in the computation of line 5 is determining $(Y \cap R)^+$, which we can do in time linear in $||F||$. Hence we have a total time complexity of $O(|\mathbf{U}| \cdot |\mathbf{R}| \cdot ||F||)$.

Theorem 9.9 The join condition can be tested in time polynomial in $|\mathbf{U}|$, $|\mathbf{R}|$, and $||F||$ when $\mathbf{P} = SAT(F)$ and F is all FDs.

Proof By our previous discussion, property LJ is testable in polynomial time. From Lemma 9.10 we know property J2 holds if $F \equiv F_{\mathbf{R}}$. We need only test $F_{\mathbf{R}} \models F$, which we can do using PCLOSURE for each FD $X \rightarrow Y$ in F to see if X^+ under $F_{\mathbf{R}}$ contains Y. This test involves $|F|$ calls to PCLOSURE, which is certainly of polynomial time-complexity.

When $F \equiv F_{\mathbf{R}}$, we can find a cover G for $F_{\mathbf{R}}$ that applies to R in time polynomial in the input (see Exercise 9.32). However, when $F \not\equiv F_{\mathbf{R}}$, it is an NP-complete problem to determine for a set G of FDs that applies to R whether $F_{\mathbf{R}} \equiv G$, given $\mathbf{R}$, F and G.

The next two examples show that the properties LJ and J2 are indeed independent when $\mathbf{P}$ is described by FDs.

Example 9.15 Let $\mathbf{U} = ABC$, $\mathbf{R} = \{AC, AB\}$ and $\mathbf{P} = SAT(\{A \rightarrow C, B \rightarrow C\})$. LJ is satisfied, because the FD $A \rightarrow C$ holds. J2 fails, because $F_{\mathbf{R}} \not\models B \rightarrow C$, so F is not enforceable on $\mathbf{R}$.

Example 9.16 Let $\mathbf{U}$ and $\mathbf{P}$ be the same as in Example 9.15, but now let $\mathbf{R} = \{AC, BC\}$. F applies to $\mathbf{R}$, so it is enforceable, and J2 is satisfied. However, now LJ fails, since $\{A \rightarrow C, B \rightarrow C\} \not\models *[AC, BC]$.

9.3.2 P Specified by Functional and Multivalued Dependencies

In the last subsection we saw how to test the join condition when **P** is determined by a set of FDs. We now work on a test for that condition when $\mathbf{P} = SAT(\mathbf{C})$ for a set **C** of FDs and MVDs and **R** is a 4NF database scheme. We need to test the LJ and J2 properties. Testing LJ is done by determining whether $\mathbf{C} \models *[\mathbf{R}]$, using the chase. For J2, we want to determine whether $\bowtie\mathbf{L} \subseteq \mathbf{P}$, which is $\pi\mathbf{C} \cup \{*[\mathbf{R}]\} \models \mathbf{C}$ in terms of dependencies. We have seen there are problems in testing implications by $\pi\mathbf{C}$. We shall show that when **R** is in 4NF, it suffices to test $F_\mathbf{R} \cup \{*[R]\} \models \mathbf{C}$, where F is the set of FDs implied by **C**.

Lemma 9.12 Let **R** be a 4NF database scheme and let $\mathbf{P} = SAT(\mathbf{C})$ for **C** a set of FDs and MVDs. Let F be the set of FDs implied by **C**, and let $X \rightarrow A$ be an FD in F that is not implied by $F_\mathbf{R}$ and $*[\mathbf{R}]$. Then $X \rightarrow A$ is not implied by $\pi\mathbf{C}$ and $*[\mathbf{R}]$. (That is, some instance in $\bowtie\mathbf{L}$ violates $X \rightarrow A$.)

Proof In this proof, for any set of attributes $V \subseteq \mathbf{U}$, r_V is the instance with one tuple of all 0's and a second tuple that is all 0's on V and 1's elsewhere.

We may assume that $X = X^+$ under $F_\mathbf{R}$ and $*[\mathbf{R}]$, since $F_\mathbf{R}$ and $*[\mathbf{R}]$ do not imply $X^+ \rightarrow A$ and if instance r in $\bowtie$L violates $X^+ \rightarrow A$, it also violates $X \rightarrow A$. Let r_X be defined as above, and let d be the database $\pi(r_X)$. Since $d \supseteq r_X$ and r_X violates $X \rightarrow A$, so does d. We need to show that $\bowtie(d)$ is in $\bowtie\mathbf{L}$, so we show that d is in **L**. To do so, we show that every relation in d is the projection of an instance in **P**.

Let R be any relation scheme in **R**. Let $Y = R \cap X$ and let $r^* = chase_\mathbf{C}(r_Y)$. (Treat the 0's as distinguished variables and the 1's as nondistinguished variables.) The set of columns in r^* that are all 0's will be Y^+ under **C**. Now $Y^+ \cap R = X \cap R$, for if B is an attribute of B in Y^+ then $Y \rightarrow B$ is in F and hence in $F_\mathbf{R}$, so $B \in X$.

Suppose $\pi_R(r_X) \neq \pi_R(r^*)$. There must be tuple t in R^* that is 0 exactly on W, where $W \cap R \neq X \cap R = Y$. By Theorem 8.12, $\mathbf{C} \models Y \twoheadrightarrow W$, so $Y \twoheadrightarrow R \cap W$ holds on R (see Exercise 9.23). Now $\mathbf{C} \not\models Y \rightarrow W \cap R$, or else $W \cap R \subseteq X$. Therefore $\mathbf{C} \not\models Y \rightarrow R$. We see that R is not in 4NF, a contradiction. The projections above must be equal, and hence $d \in \bowtie\mathbf{L}$.

Lemma 9.13 Let **R** be a 4NF database scheme, let $\mathbf{P} = SAT(\mathbf{C})$ for **C** a set of FDs and MVDs, and assume property LJ holds. Let F be the set of FDs implied by **C**, and let $X \twoheadrightarrow Y$ be an MVD implied by **C** that is not implied by $F_\mathbf{R}$ and $*[\mathbf{R}]$. Then $X \twoheadrightarrow Y$ is not implied by $\pi\mathbf{C}$ and $*[\mathbf{R}]$.

Proof We shall assume Y is minimal with respect to the hypotheses given. That is, for no proper subset Y' of Y does $\mathbf{C} \models X \rightarrow\rightarrow Y'$ and $F_{\mathbf{R}} \cup \{*[\mathbf{R}]\} \not\models X \rightarrow\rightarrow Y'$. We also assume that X is maximal with respect to the hypotheses. First, $X = X^+$ under $F_{\mathbf{R}}$ and $*[\mathbf{R}]$, as in the proof of Lemma 9.12. Second, for no $Z \subsetneq \mathbf{U} - XY$ does $\mathbf{C} \models XZ \rightarrow\rightarrow Y$ while $F_{\mathbf{R}} \cup \{*[\mathbf{R}]\} \not\models XZ \rightarrow\rightarrow Y$.

Let r_X be as defined in the proof of Lemma 9.12. Instance r_X clearly satisfies F_R; we claim it also satisfies $*[\mathbf{R}]$. Suppose not. Chasing r_X under $F_{\mathbf{R}}$ and $*[\mathbf{R}]$ must yield new tuples. Let t be one of these new tuples; say that XW is the set of attributes where t is 0 and X is disjoint from W. By Theorem 8.12, $*[\mathbf{R}] \models X \rightarrow\rightarrow W$. By property LJ, $\mathbf{C} \models *[\mathbf{R}]$, so $\mathbf{C} \models X \rightarrow\rightarrow W$. Surely $Y \neq W$. If $Y \subseteq W$, then $\mathbf{C} \models XZ \rightarrow\rightarrow Y$, where $Z = \mathbf{U} - WXY$. Z is nonempty because $XW \neq \mathbf{U}$. $F_{\mathbf{R}}$ and $*[\mathbf{R}]$ cannot imply $XZ \rightarrow\rightarrow Y$, since $XZ \rightarrow\rightarrow Y$ and $X \rightarrow\rightarrow W$ imply $X \rightarrow\rightarrow Y$. (This implication may easily be tested using the chase.) So $Y \subseteq W$ leads to a contradiction to the maximality of X. If W and Y are disjoint, then $W' = \mathbf{U} - WX$ contains Y and $*[\mathbf{R}] \models X \rightarrow\rightarrow W'$, leading to the same contradiction.

The only possibility left is that W partially intersects Y. Let $Y' = Y - W$ and $Y'' = Y \cap W$. By projectivity, $\mathbf{C} \models \{X \rightarrow\rightarrow Y', X \rightarrow\rightarrow Y''\}$. $F_{\mathbf{R}}$ and $*[\mathbf{R}]$ cannot imply both $X \rightarrow\rightarrow Y'$ and $X \rightarrow\rightarrow Y''$, since these two MVDs imply $X \rightarrow\rightarrow Y$ by additivity. This situation contradicts the minimality of Y. We see that chasing r_X under $*[\mathbf{R}]$ adds no new tuples, hence r_X satisfies $F_{\mathbf{R}}$ and $*[\mathbf{R}]$.

We now only need to show that the database $d = \pi(r_X)$ is in $\mathbf{L}$, since then $\bowtie(d) = r_X$ will be in $\bowtie\mathbf{L}$. Since $X = X^+$ under $F_{\mathbf{R}}$ and $*[\mathbf{R}]$, the proof of Lemma 9.12 suffices to show d is in $\mathbf{L}$.

We now have the tools for testing the join condition for a 4NF database scheme R and a set of instances $\mathbf{P}$ defined by a set $\mathbf{C}$ of FDs and MVDs. First we test property LJ, $\mathbf{C} \models *[\mathbf{R}]$, using the chase. Then we must find the set F of FDs implied by $\mathbf{C}$, or some cover for F. Unfortunately, no methods are known for finding F other than straightforward enumeration and testing. We next need to find $F_{\mathbf{R}}$. By Lemmas 9.12 and 9.13, we can then check property J2 by testing $F_{\mathbf{R}} \cup \{*[\mathbf{R}]\} \models \mathbf{C}$ using the chase. This process is nowhere near as efficient as the test in the case that $\mathbf{C}$ is only FDs. However, no test at all is known for the join condition when $\mathbf{C}$ is FDs and JDs and $\mathbf{R}$ is arbitrary.

Example 9.17 Let $\mathbf{U} = ABCDE$, $\mathbf{R} = \{ABC, BCD, DE\}$ and let $\mathbf{C} = \{D \rightarrow E, BC \rightarrow\rightarrow A, AD \rightarrow\rightarrow E\}$. If F is the set of FDs implied by $\mathbf{C}$, then $\{D \rightarrow E\}$ is a cover for $F_{\mathbf{R}}$. We see that $\mathrm{C} \models *[\mathbf{R}]$ and that $F_{\mathbf{R}}$ and $*[\mathbf{R}]$ imply $\mathbf{C}$, so the join condition is satisfied in this case.

Example 9.18 Let $\mathbf{U} = ABCDE$, $\mathbf{R} = \{ABC, BCD, DE\}$ and let $\mathbf{C} = \{D \to E, BC \twoheadrightarrow A, A \twoheadrightarrow E\}$. Again, $\{D \to E\}$ is a cover for $F_{\mathbf{R}}$, but $F_{\mathbf{R}}$ and $*[\mathbf{R}]$ do not imply $A \twoheadrightarrow E$, so the join condition does not hold here.

9.3.3 Testing Data-Equivalence

When $\mathbf{P} = SAT(\mathbf{C})$, and $\mathbf{R}$ and $\mathbf{S}$ are database schemes, in order to test $\mathbf{R} \approx_{\mathbf{P}} \mathbf{S}$, we must determine whether $FIX_{\mathbf{C}}(\mathbf{R}) = FIX_{\mathbf{C}}(\mathbf{S})$. The equality holds, of course, when there is containment in both directions. As previously noted, $FIX_{\mathbf{C}}(\mathbf{R}) \subseteq FIX_{\mathbf{C}}(\mathbf{S})$ exactly when $FIX_{\mathbf{C}}(\mathbf{R}) \subseteq FIX(\mathbf{S})$. That containment holds if and only if $\mathbf{C} \cup \{*[\mathbf{R}]\} \models *[\mathbf{S}]$, which we can test with the chase when $\mathbf{C}$ is FDs and JDs.

When $\mathbf{R}$ preserves $SAT(\mathbf{C})$, a corollary to Theorem 9.5 tells us that $FIX_{\mathbf{C}}(\mathbf{R}) \subseteq FIX(\mathbf{S})$ is equivalent to $T_{\mathbf{S}} \sqsubseteq_{\mathbf{C}} T_{\mathbf{R}}$. The following lemma can be useful for testing that containment.

Lemma 9.14 Let $\mathbf{R}$ and $\mathbf{S}$ be database schemes, let $\mathbf{C}$ be a set of FDs and JDs and let $T_{\mathbf{R}}^* = chase_{\mathbf{C}}(T_{\mathbf{R}})$. Then $T_{\mathbf{R}} \sqsubseteq_{\mathbf{C}} T_{\mathbf{S}}$ if and only if $T_{\mathbf{R}}^* \sqsubseteq T_{\mathbf{S}}$.

Proof Left to the reader (see Exercise 9.34).

Lemma 9.14 is useful because $T_{\mathbf{R}}^* \sqsubseteq T_{\mathbf{S}}$ is quite easy to test. We need to find a containment mapping from $T_{\mathbf{S}}$ to $T_{\mathbf{R}}^*$ in order for the containment to hold. Since $T_{\mathbf{S}}$ has no duplicated nondistinguished variables, we need only check that for each row w in $T_{\mathbf{S}}$ there is a row w' in $T_{\mathbf{R}}^*$ that subsumes w.

Example 9.19 Let $\mathbf{U} = ABCDE$, let $\mathbf{R} = \{ABC, BCD, DE\}$, let $\mathbf{S} = \{ACE, BCD\}$, and let $\mathbf{P} = SAT(\mathbf{C})$ where $\mathbf{C} = \{B \to E, D \twoheadrightarrow B\}$. $T_{\mathbf{R}}^* = chase_{\mathbf{C}}(T_{\mathbf{R}})$ and $T_{\mathbf{S}}^* = chase_{\mathbf{C}}(T_{\mathbf{S}})$ are shown in Figures 9.20 and 9.21. There is a containment mapping from $T_{\mathbf{S}}$ to $T_{\mathbf{R}}^*$, so $T_{\mathbf{R}} \sqsubseteq_{\mathbf{C}} T_{\mathbf{S}}$. However, there is not a containment mapping from $T_{\mathbf{R}}$ to $T_{\mathbf{S}}^*$, so $\mathbf{R} \not\approx_{\mathbf{C}} \mathbf{S}$. Actually, the simplified test of Theorem 9.5 for $\mathbf{R} \approx_{\mathbf{C}} \mathbf{S}$ does not apply here, since neither $\mathbf{R}$ nor $\mathbf{S}$ preserves $SAT(\mathbf{C})$. However, the negative result carries through (see Exercise 9.35).

$T_{\mathbf{R}}^*(A$	B	C	D	$E)$
a_1	a_2	a_3	b_1	a_5
b_3	a_2	a_3	a_4	a_5
b_5	b_6	b_7	a_4	a_5
b_3	b_6	a_3	a_4	a_5
b_5	a_2	b_7	a_4	a_5

Figure 9.20

$T_S^*(A$	B	C	D	$E)$
a_1	b_1	a_3	b_2	a_5
b_3	a_2	a_3	a_4	b_4

Figure 9.21

In the case that **R** and **S** preserve $SAT(\mathbf{C})$, we know $\mathbf{R} \approx_{\mathbf{C}} \mathbf{S}$ is equivalent to $T_{\mathbf{R}} \equiv_{\mathbf{C}} T_{\mathbf{S}}$. If **C** is a set of FDs only, then we can calculate the chases of $T_{\mathbf{R}}$ and $T_{\mathbf{S}}$ in time polynomial in the space required to represent $T_{\mathbf{R}}$, $T_{\mathbf{S}}$, and **C**. Let $T_{\mathbf{R}}^*$ and $T_{\mathbf{S}}^*$ be those two chases. We can test $T_{\mathbf{R}}^* \sqsubseteq T_{\mathbf{S}}$ and $T_{\mathbf{R}} \sqsupseteq T_{\mathbf{S}}^*$, and hence $T_{\mathbf{R}} \equiv_{\mathbf{C}} T_{\mathbf{S}}$, in polynomial time, because containment mappings are easy to find in these cases, as we stated before. The next result gives us a polynomial time test for whether a database scheme **R** preserves a set of FDs F.

Definition 9.17 Let T be a tableau. *T embeds an FD* $X \rightarrow Y$ if some row w in T is distinguished on at least its XY-columns. *T embeds a set of FDs* F if T embeds every FD in F.

Evidently, a set of FDs F is enforceable on database scheme R if and only if $T_{\mathbf{R}}$ embeds some cover G of F.

Example 9.20 The tableau T in Figure 9.22 embeds the set of FDs $F = \{C \twoheadrightarrow AB, E \rightarrow B\}$.

$T(A$	B	C	D	$E)$
a_1	a_2	a_3	b_1	b_2
b_3	a_2	b_4	a_4	b_5
a_1	a_2	a_3	b_6	a_5

Figure 9.22

Theorem 9.10 Let **R** be a database scheme and let F be a nonredundant set of FDs. **R** preserves $SAT(F)$ if and only if $T_{\mathbf{R}}^* = chase_F(T_{\mathbf{R}})$ embeds F.

Proof Suppose **R** preserves $SAT(F)$. We show a property of $T_{\mathbf{R}}^*$. If w is a row of $T_{\mathbf{R}}^*$ and X is the set of columns where w has a distinguished variable, then $X = X^+$ under F. Suppose $X \neq X^+$. Let A be an attribute in $X^+ - X$. We know $F \models X \rightarrow A$. Also, $T_{\mathbf{R}}^*$ as an instance is in $SAT(F)$ so $m_{\mathbf{R}}(T_{\mathbf{R}}^*)$ is in $SAT(F)$, since **R** preserves $SAT(F)$. But $m_{\mathbf{R}}(T_{\mathbf{R}}^*)$ contains both w and w_d, the row of all distinguished variables. (Why?) Now $w(X) = w_d(X)$, but

$w(A) \neq w_d(A)$, which is a violation of $X \rightarrow A$. We conclude from this contradiction that $X^+ = X$. Furthermore, it can be shown that $T^*_{\mathbf{R}}$ contains no duplicated nondistinguished variables (see Exercise 9.36).

Let $X \rightarrow Y$ be an arbitrary FD in F. We want to show that $X \rightarrow Y$ is embedded in $T^*_{\mathbf{R}}$. Let w_X be a row with distinguished variables in exactly the X-columns, and nondistinguished variables that do not appear elsewhere in $T^*_{\mathbf{R}}$. Let T be the tableau $T^*_{\mathbf{R}}$ with row w_X added. Let $T^* = chase_F(T)$ and let w^*_X be the row in T^* that corresponds to w_X in T. Let w^*_X be distinguished in exactly the Z-columns. We claim $Z = X^+$. By the argument in the previous paragraph, $Z = Z^+$, so $Z \supseteq X^+$. By Exercise 9.37, if $A \in Z$, then $F \models X \rightarrow A$. So $Z \subseteq X^+$ and hence $Z = X^+$.

Furthermore, we claim that T^* is just T with w_X changed to w^*_X. That is, none of $T^*_{\mathbf{R}}$ in T changes in the computation of $chase_F(T)$. Consider the first F-rule applied in computing $chase_F(T)$. Say it is the F-rule for $W \rightarrow B$ in F. Row w_X must be involved in the application, since $T^*_{\mathbf{R}}$ satisfies $W \rightarrow B$. For $W \rightarrow B$ to be applicable to T, $W \subseteq X$ and there must be a row w in $T^*_{\mathbf{R}}$ with $w(W) = w_X(W)$. We conclude that w is distinguished on all the W-columns, Since the set of distinguished columns of w is closed under F, w is distinguished on B as well. Thus the application of the F-rule for $W \rightarrow B$ to T changes $w_X(B)$ to a distinguished variable. The rows of $T^*_{\mathbf{R}}$ in T are unchanged. The same argument then applies to the second application of an F-rule, the third application, and so forth. Therefore, none of the rows of $T^*_{\mathbf{R}}$ change during the computation of $chase_F(T)$.

We know that w_X ends up as w^*_X in T^*, where w^*_X is distinguished in exactly the X^+ columns. F is nonredundant, so there is a nonempty subset Y' of Y such that $X \rightarrow Y'$ is not implied by $F - \{X \rightarrow Y\}$. At some point in computing $chase_F(T)$, then, we have to use an F-rule for $X \rightarrow A$, for some $A \in Y'$, in order to distinguish w_X on Y'. By the results of the previous paragraph, there is some row w in $T^*_{\mathbf{R}}$ that is distinguished on its X-columns. Since the set of columns where w has distinguished variables is closed under F, w is distinguished on its Y-columns as well. Hence $T^*_{\mathbf{R}}$ embeds $X \rightarrow Y$.

Now suppose $T^*_{\mathbf{R}}$ embeds F. Let $X \rightarrow Y$ be an FD in F. Let r be an instance in $SAT(F)$. Since r satisfies $X \rightarrow Y$, so does $T^*_{\mathbf{R}}(r)$ (see Exercise 9.39). Further, $T^*_{\mathbf{R}}(r) = T_{\mathbf{R}}(r) = m_{\mathbf{R}}(r)$, so $m_{\mathbf{R}}(r)$ satisfies $X \rightarrow Y$. We conclude that $\mathbf{R}$ preserves $SAT(F)$.

Example 9.21 Let $\mathbf{R}$ be the database scheme $\{ABC, CD, DEI\}$ and let $F = \{AB \rightarrow C, C \rightarrow D, D \rightarrow A, ADE \rightarrow I\}$. F is nonredundant. $T^*_{\mathbf{R}} = chase_F(T_{\mathbf{R}})$ is shown in Figure 9.23. $T^*_{\mathbf{R}}$ embeds F, so $\mathbf{R}$ perserves $SAT(F)$. Note, however, that F is not enforceable on $\mathbf{R}$ ($D \rightarrow \mathbf{A}$ is the problem) nor does $F \models *[\mathbf{R}]$.

$T^*_{\mathbf{R}}$(A	B	C	D	E	I)
a_1	a_2	a_3	a_4	b_2	b_3
a_1	b_5	a_3	a_4	b_6	b_7
a_1	b_9	b_{10}	a_4	a_5	a_6

Figure 9.23

The final result of this chapter relates preservation of a set of FDs to the fix-points of a database scheme that naturally arises from the set.

Definition 9.18 Let F be a set of FDs, and let G be a nonredundant cover for F. The *intended database scheme of* F, which we denote as $\boldsymbol{R}_F$, is

$$\{X^+ \mid X \rightarrow Y \in G\}.$$

The definition does not depend on the choice of G (see Exercise 9.40).

Example 9.22 Let $F = \{AB \rightarrow C,\ C \rightarrow E,\ D \rightarrow A,\ ADE \rightarrow I\}$ as in Example 9.21. We have $(AB)^+ = ABC$, $C^+ = ACD$, $D^+ = AD$, and $(ADE)^+ = ADEI$, so $\mathbf{R}_F = \{ABC, ACD, AD, ADEI\}$.

In the case that $*[\mathbf{R}_F]$ is a full JD (mentions all the attributes of $\mathbf{U}$), we have the following result.

Theorem 9.11 Let $\mathbf{R}$ be a database scheme, and let F be a set of FDs. Suppose $*[\mathbf{R}_F]$ is a full JD. Then $FIX_F(\mathbf{R}_F) \subseteq FIX(\mathbf{R})$ if and only if $\mathbf{R}$ preserves $SAT(F)$.

Proof (if) By Exercise 9.36, $chase_F(T_{\mathbf{R}}) = T_{\mathbf{S}}$ for some database scheme $\mathbf{S}$. Furthermore, from the proof of Theorem 9.10, for any relation scheme $S \in \mathbf{S}$, $S = S^+$. Let G be a nonredundant cover for F. $T_{\mathbf{S}}$ embeds G by Theorem 9.10. For any FD $X \rightarrow Y$ in G, there is a relation scheme S in $\mathbf{S}$ such that $XY \subseteq S$. Since $S = S^+$, $X^+ \subseteq S^+$. We conclude $\mathbf{S} \geq \mathbf{R}_F$. Therefore, $FIX(\mathbf{S}) \supseteq FIX(\mathbf{R}_F)$, and so $FIX_F(\mathbf{S}) \supseteq FIX_F(\mathbf{R}_F)$. By the definition of $\mathbf{S}$, $FIX_F(\mathbf{R}) = FIX_F(\mathbf{S})$. We see that $FIX_F(\mathbf{R}_F) \subseteq FIX(\mathbf{R})$.

(only if) Obviously, R_F preserves $SAT(F)$. By the second corollary to Theorem 9.5, $T_{\mathbf{R}} \sqsubseteq_F T_{\mathbf{R}_F}$. We know $m_{\mathbf{R}_F}(r)$ is in $SAT(F)$ for any instance r in $SAT(F)$. Also, $m_{\mathbf{R}}(r) \subseteq m_{\mathbf{R}_F}(r)$, so by Exercise 9.26, $m_{\mathbf{R}}(r)$ is in $SAT(F)$. Hence R preserves $SAT(F)$.

Example 9.23 Let $\mathbf{R} = \{ABC, CD, DEI\}$ and let $F = \{AB \rightarrow C, C \rightarrow D, D \rightarrow A, ADE \rightarrow I\}$, as in Examples 9.21 and 9.22. We saw in Example 9.22 that $\mathbf{R}_F = \{ABC, ACD, AD, ADEI\}$. Tableau T in Figure 9.24 is the chase of $T_\mathbf{R}$ under F and $*[\mathbf{R}_F]$. T contains the row of all distinguished variables, so F and $*[\mathbf{R}_F]$ imply $*[\mathbf{R}]$. Hence $FIX_F(\mathbf{R}_F) \subseteq FIX(\mathbf{R})$ and $\mathbf{R}$ preserves F, as we previously determined in Example 9.21.

T(A	B	C	D	E	I)
a_1	a_2	a_3	a_4	b_2	b_3
a_1	b_5	a_3	a_4	b_6	b_7
a_1	b_9	b_{10}	a_4	a_5	a_6
a_1	a_2	a_3	a_4	a_5	a_6
a_1	b_5	a_3	a_4	a_5	a_6
a_1	a_2	a_3	a_4	b_6	b_7
a_1	b_5	a_3	a_4	b_2	b_3
a_1	b_9	b_{10}	a_4	b_6	b_7
a_1	b_9	b_{10}	a_4	b_2	b_3

Figure 9.24

9.4 EXERCISES

9.1 Suppose all domains for attributes in $\mathbf{U}$ are finite. Compare the cardinalities of $\mathbf{Q}$, $\mathbf{P}$, $\mathbf{M}$, $\pi\mathbf{Q}$, $\pi\mathbf{P}$, $\mathbf{L}$ and $\bowtie\mathbf{L}$.

9.2 Prove that $\pi\mathbf{Q}$ is the set of all databases over scheme $\mathbf{R}$ where the relations join completely.

9.3 Show that for arbitrary $n \geq 3$ there is always a set of n relations such that any $n - 1$ join completely, but all n do not.

9.4 Show that the containment $\mathbf{L} \supseteq \pi\mathbf{P}$ is proper.

9.5 Prove that condition IC2 is equivalent to $\pi\mathbf{P} = \mathbf{L}$.

9.6 Show that database scheme $\mathbf{R}$ decomposes $\mathbf{P}$ into independent components, where $\mathbf{R}$ and $\mathbf{P}$ are given in Example 9.6. Describe the inverse mapping to $\pi_\mathbf{R}$.

9.7 Give an example of a database scheme $\mathbf{R}$ and an infinite set of instances $\mathbf{P}$ such that $\mathbf{R}$ satisfies AC1 but not AC2.

9.8 Show that the condition $\mathbf{L} = \pi\mathbf{P}$ does not necessitate AC2.

9.9 Show that AC1 and LJ can be inequivalent when AC2 does not hold.

9.10 Let X, Y, and Z be subsets of $\mathbf{U}$. Show that for an instance $r \in \mathbf{Q}$, r satisfies $X \rightarrow Y$ if and only if $\pi_{XYZ}(r)$ satisfies $X \rightarrow Y$. Show that the statement is false if $X \rightarrow Y$ is replaced by $X \twoheadrightarrow Y$.

9.11 Show that for any instance $r \in \mathbf{Q}$ where $\pi(r) = d$, $\bowtie d \supseteq r$.
9.12 Show that the join condition requires $\bowtie$ to be the inverse of π on $\mathbf{P}$.
9.13 Prove Lemma 9.5.
9.14 Prove that given condition J1, $FIX(\mathbf{R}) \cap \mathbf{L}^{\leftarrow} \subseteq \mathbf{P}$ implies $FIX(\mathbf{R}) \cap \mathbf{L}^{\leftarrow} = \mathbf{P}$.
9.15 Show that IC1 and IC2 do not require condition LJ.
9.16 Prove Lemma 9.6.
9.17 Show that conditions LJ and J2 hold if and only if conditions J1 and J2 hold.
9.18 (a) Show that information preservation is equivalent to property J2 and $FIX(\mathbf{R}) \supseteq \mathbf{L}^{\leftarrow}$.
(b) Show that the join condition is equivalent to property J2 and $FIX(\mathbf{R}) \supseteq \mathbf{P}$.
9.19 Prove Lemma 9.9.
9.20 Prove that $\mathbf{R} \approx_{\mathbf{P}} I$ is equivalent to $T_{\mathbf{R}} \equiv_{\mathbf{P}} T_I$, where I is a database scheme containing $\mathbf{U}$ as the only relation scheme.
9.21 Show that $FIX_{\mathbf{P}}(\mathbf{R})$ is contained by $PRES_{\mathbf{P}}(\mathbf{R})$, and that the containment can be proper.
9.22 Prove the first corollary to Theorem 9.5.
9.23 Show that if instance $r \in \mathbf{P}$ satisfies the MVD $X \twoheadrightarrow Y$, then $\pi_{\mathbf{R}}(r)$ satisfies the MVD $X \twoheadrightarrow Y \cap R$ if $X \subseteq R$.
9.24* Characterize the join dependencies that must hold in $\pi_R(r)$ when instance r satisfies some join dependency $*[\mathbf{S}]$.
9.25 In Example 9.12, find a data dependency that $\pi_R(r)$ must satisfy if r is in $\mathbf{P}$, but which s violates.
9.26 Show that if r is an instance violating a set of FDs F, then any instance containing r violates F. Show that if r satisfies F, then every relation contained in r satisfies F.
9.27 Let $\mathbf{P} = SAT(F)$ for a set of FDs F. Show that $\mathbf{L}^{\leftarrow} - \mathbf{P}$ contains an instance with two tuples.
9.28 Show properties LJ and J2 are equivalent to the join condition.
9.29* Characterize when $SAT(F_{\mathbf{R}}) = SAT(\pi F)$ for a set F of FDs over $\mathbf{U}$.
9.30 Complete the proof of Lemma 9.10.
9.31 Compute $(AC)^+$ under $F_{\mathbf{R}}$ where $\mathbf{U} = ABCDEI$, $\mathbf{R} = \{ABC, CDE, AEI\}$, and $F = \{AB \rightarrow D, D \rightarrow I, E \rightarrow I, BC \rightarrow A, I \rightarrow B\}$.
9.32* Find a polynomial-time algorithm that given $\mathbf{R}$ and F produces a cover G for $F_{\mathbf{R}}$ such that every FD in G applies to some relation scheme $R \in \mathbf{R}$, *provided* $F \equiv F_{\mathbf{R}}$. Show that your algorithm fails to produce a cover for $F_{\mathbf{R}}$ when $F \not\equiv F_{\mathbf{R}}$. (How did I know that would happen?)
9.33 For Example 9.18, exhibit an instance in $\bowtie \mathbf{L}$ that is not in $SAT(\mathbf{C})$.
9.34 Prove Lemma 9.14.

9.35 For database schemes **R** and **S**, and a set **C** of dependencies, show that $T_{\mathbf{R}} \not\equiv_{\mathbf{C}} T_{\mathbf{S}}$ implies $\mathbf{R} \not\approx_{\mathbf{C}} \mathbf{S}$.

9.36 Let **R** be a database scheme that preserves $SAT(F)$ for a set F of FDs. Show that $chase_F(T_{\mathbf{R}})$ is $T_{\mathbf{S}}$ for some database scheme **S**. Describe **S** in terms of **R** and F.

9.37 Let **R** be a database scheme and let F be a set of FDs. Prove the following. Let w be a row of $T_{\mathbf{R}}$ and let w^* be the corresponding row of $chase_F(T_{\mathbf{R}})$. If w is distinguished on exactly X and w^* is distinguished on Y, then $F \models X \rightarrow Y$.

9.38 Let **R** be a database scheme, let F be a set of FDs and let $X \subseteq \mathbf{U}$. Show that if **R** preserves $SAT(F)$, then $R \cup \{X\}$ preserves $SAT(F)$.

9.39 Let T be a tableau that embeds the FD $X \rightarrow Y$. Show that for any instance r in $SAT(X \rightarrow Y)$, $T(r) \in SAT(X \rightarrow Y)$.

9.40 Prove that different choices for G in definition of $\mathbf{R}_F$ do not yield different sets of attributes.

9.5 BIBLIOGRAPHY AND COMMENTS

The material from Section 9.1 is largely from Maier, Mendelzon, *et al.* [1980]. Sections 9.2 and 9.3 follow from Beeri, Mendelzon, *et al.* [1979]. Rissanen [1977] proposed the IC conditions; the AC conditions are from Arora and Carlson [1978]. The algorithm for determining enforceability of a set F of FDs is due to Beeri and Honeyman [1981], who also show it is NP-complete to test if a set G is a cover for the subset of F^+ enforceable on a scheme. Beeri and Rissanen [1980] and Graham [1981a, 1981b] have also dealt with equivalence database schemes under constraints and preserving dependencies.

Ginsburg and Hull [1980] and Ginsburg and Zaiddan [1981] have studied the structure of $SAT(F)$ for a set F of FDs. In particular, Ginsburg and Zaiddan noted that $\pi_R(SAT(F))$ is not necessarily $SAT(F')$ for any set of FDs F' over **R**. Sadri [1980a] noted the similar situation for JDs.

Chapter 10

QUERY SYSTEMS

To this point, we have seen two systems for manipulating relational databases. In Chapter 1 we saw update commands for adding, deleting, and modifying tuples in relations. In Chapters 2 and 3 we introduced the relational algebra to express selections, restrictions, and combinations of relations in a database. We call a formal system that can express updates to relations an *update system*. A *query* is a computation upon relations that yields other relations. A *query system*, such as the relational algebra, is a formal system for expressing queries. Query systems form the underlying structure of *query languages*: the special purpose programming languages used in database systems to formulate commands. We examine several query languages for relational database systems in Chapter 15.

In this chapter we cover three other query systems. The *tuple relational calculus* is essentially a formalization of the set-former notation we used to define the operators in relational algebra. *Domain relational calculus* is similar, except the variables range over single domain values rather than entire tuples. We shall see that both tuple calculus and domain calculus are equivalent in expressive power to relational algebra. We also introduce a modification of tableaux as a means to express queries. While tableaux cannot express all of the queries representable in relational algebra, the subclass they can represent seems to include many of the queries that might naturally arise in a real application. Furthermore, they lend themselves well to testing of equivalence and transformations, as we shall see in the next chapter.

Although a few query languages are based on relational algebra, most are based on either calculus or tableaux. The main reason is that the algebra is a procedural system, while the other three are non-procedural. That is, an expression in relational algebra gives a set of operations on relations and an order in which to perform them (up to certain associativities). We shall see that the calculi and tableaux simply express *what* the result of the computation should be, but *not how* to carry out the computation. Thus, query languages based on non-procedural systems tend to be higher-level, relieving the user of such languages from having to determine how to derive a desired answer. The burden for this determination naturally falls to the query language processor of the given database system. In this chapter we shall show that expressions in either calculus can be translated effectively into algebraic expressions. However, the algebraic expressions we end up with can by no means be expected to be efficient means to evaluate the calculus expressions. In the next chapter we explore ways of modifying algebraic expressions to make them easier to evaluate.

We shall also, briefly, introduce conjunctive queries, which are a subclass of domain calculus expressions. Conjunctive queries are similar to tableaux queries, and also lend themselves well to equivalence testing and transformation.

10.1 EQUIVALENCE AND COMPLETENESS

The expressions in the various query systems we shall study can be viewed as mappings from databases to relations. That is, for an expression E, and a database d, we can evaluate E on d and get a particular relation r. We call r the *value* of expression E on d, and denote it $E(d)$.* We would like to say two expressions E_1 and E_2 are *equivalent*, written $E_1 \equiv E_2$, when $E_1(d) = E_2(d)$ for every database state d. The problem is that we must know the scheme of the database to decide equivalence. For example,

$$\pi_{AB}(r \bowtie s) \quad \text{and} \quad \pi_{AB}(r) \bowtie \pi_{AB}(s)$$

would be equivalent if we consider the schemes of r and s to be ABC and ABD, but not if the schemes were $ABCD$ and $ABCE$. We therefore consider equivalence to be relative to a particular database scheme. Sometimes the particular database scheme is immaterial, since the two expressions are equivalent for every database scheme where they are both properly formed. For example,

$$\sigma_{A=a}(r \bowtie s) \quad \text{and} \quad \sigma_{A=a}(r) \bowtie s$$

are equivalent for any database scheme where the relation scheme for r contains A.

The last example suggests a stronger notion of equivalence: $E_1 \equiv E_2$ if $E_1(d) = E_2(d)$ for every database d over every database scheme that is consistent with both E_1 and E_2. Unfortunately, this definition of equivalence is not transitive.

---

*In Chapter 3, before the introduction of databases, we were denoting $E(d)$ as $E(s_1, s_2, \ldots, s_k)$ where d is the database $\{s_1, s_2, \ldots, s_k\}$.

Example 10.1 Consider the following algebraic expressions:

$$E_1 = \pi_{AB}(r \cap s),$$
$$E_2 = \pi_{AB}(r) \cap s, \text{ and}$$
$$E_3 = \pi_{AB}(r) \cap \pi_{AB}(s).$$

E_1 and E_2 are equivalent under the alternative definition above. In any database consistent with E_1 and E_2, the schemes of r and s must both be AB. E_1 requires the two schemes be the same, where E_2 requires the scheme of s be AB. Similarly, E_2 and E_3 can be shown equivalent under the alternative definition. However, E_1 and E_3 are not equivalent, since there are databases consistent with both where the schemes of r and s are both ABC.

The situation can be worse than that given in Example 10.1. Under the alternative definition, there are expressions E_1, E_2, and E_3, with $E_I \equiv E_2$ and $E_2 \equiv E_3$, where E_1 and E_3 do not even define relations over the same scheme for some mutually consistent databases (see Exercise 10.1). Hence, we shall always assume equivalence is relative to a fixed database scheme.

Once we define the other query systems, we shall discuss equivalence of expressions in different systems. One comparison we shall make between systems is *expressive power*. Query system QS_1 is *as expressive* as query systems QS_2 if for every expression E_2 of QS_2, and every database scheme compatible with E_2, there is an expression E_1 of QS_1 such that $E_1 \equiv E_2$. Note that E_1 may depend upon the particular database scheme. QS_1 and QS_2 are *equally expressive* if each is as expressive as the other. A query system is *complete* if it is as expressive as relational algebra. We shall see that tuple calculus and domain calculus are both complete, while tableau queries and conjunctive queries are not.*

In Chapter 3 we defined the relational algebra $\mathcal{R}$ for a universe of attributes $\mathbf{U}$, with corresponding domains, a set of relations $\{r_1, r_2, \ldots, r_p\}$, and a set of binary comparators Θ, using constant relations and the operators union, intersection, difference, select, project, natural join, renaming, divide, theta-join, and active complement. The relational algebra with complement also allowed complement. However, we also saw, in Theorem 3.1, that for any relational algebra expression E, there is an equivalent expression E' using only single-attribute, single-tuple constant relations, renaming, select with a single comparison, projection, natural join, union, difference, and possibly complement (if the original expression used complement). The subalgebra of relational algebra using only the constants and operators above

---

*Traditionally, completeness has been defined as being as expressive as tuple calculus.

is equally expressive with the full relational algebra, and hence complete. Thus when we want to show that some query system QS is as expressive as relational algebra, we need only consider expressions using the subalgebra above. On the other hand, if we want to show relational algebra is as expressive as QS, we may use any of the relational operators, to simplify our task.

Although relational algebra is our benchmark for completeness, we shall see in Chapter 14 that there are some natural computations on relations that cannot be expressed by any algebraic expression (see Exercise 10.2).

10.2 TUPLE RELATIONAL CALCULUS

The tuple relational calculus should appear a natural notation to the reader, since it is quite similar to the set-former expressions used in Chapters 2 and 3 to define some of the operators in relational algebra. Where the relational algebra has relations as its basic units for manipulation, tuple relational calculus (tuple calculus, for short) builds its expressions from tuples.

Recall the definition of divide from Section 3.1. If $r(R)$ and $s(S)$ are relations, with $S \subseteq R$, and $R' = R - S$, then $r \div s$ is the relation

$$r'(R') = \{t \mid \text{for every tuple } t_s \in s \text{ there is a tuple } t_r \in r \text{ with } t_r(R') = t \text{ and } t_r(S) = t_s\}.$$

Tuple calculus expressions will have the form

$$\{x(R) \mid f(x)\},$$

where f is some Boolean predicate on tuple variable x. The expression denotes the relation $r(R)$ that consists of all tuples $t(R)$ where $f(t)$ is true. We shall shortly give a formal definition of the set of legal formulas, but first we give some informal examples.

Consider the database consisting of the three relations in Table 10.1. The database describes replacement parts for aircraft. Relation *pinfo* gives part numbers, other parts of which the part is an immediate subpart (not a subpart of a subpart) and the name of the part. Relation *usedon* gives the quantity of each part that is used on each type of aircraft. Relation *instock* gives the quantity of each part on hand at various repair locations. Some of the relations are incomplete. The value 0 for SUBPARTOF means the part is not a subpart.

Table 10.1 The relations *pinfo*, *usedon*, and *instock*.

pinfo

PART#	SUBPARTOF	PARTNAME
211	0	coach seat
2114	211	seat cover
2116	211	seat belt
21163	2116	seat belt buckle
21164	2116	seat belt anchor
318	21164	funny little bolt
206	0	overhead console
2061	206	paging switch
2066	206	light switch
2068	206	air nozzle

usedon

PART#	PTYPE	NUSED
211	707	86
211	727	134
2114	707	86
2114	727	134
2116	707	244
2116	727	296
21164	707	488
21164	727	592

instock

PART#	LOCATION	QUANTITY
211	JFK	106
211	Boston	28
211	O'Hare	77
2114	JFK	6
2114	O'Hare	28
2116	Boston	341
2116	O'Hare	29
21164	Atlanta	36,391

Example 10.2 For the question "What are the subparts of part number 211," we might express the answer as

$$\{x(\text{PART\# PARTNAME}) \mid x \in pinfo \text{ and } x(\text{SUBPARTOF}) = 211\}$$

The value of this expression is given in Table 10.2. The expression may not interpret the question correctly, if subparts of subparts, subparts of subparts of subparts, and so forth, were also meant to be included.

Table 10.2 Subparts of part 211.

(PART#	PARTNAME)
2114	seat cover
2116	seat belt

Example 10.3 The answer to the question "How many coach seats are used on a 727?" can be expressed as

$\{x(\text{NUSED}) \mid x \in \textit{usedon}$ and $x(\text{PTYPE}) = 727$ and there is a $y \in \textit{pinfo}$ where $x(\text{PART\#}) = y(\text{PART\#})$ and $y(\text{PARTNAME}) =$ "coach seat"$\}$

The value of this expression on the database in Table 10.1 is given in Table 10.3.

Table 10.3 Number of coach seats used on a 727.

(NUSED)
134

10.2.1 Tuple Calculus Formulas

The set of legal tuple calculus formulas will be defined relative to

1. A universal set of attributes **U**, with a domain, $dom(A)$, for each attribute A in **U**;
2. A set Θ of binary comparators on domains; and
3. A set d of relation names $\{r_1, r_2, \ldots, r_p\}$ on schemes $R_1, R_2, \ldots, R_p$, all subsets of **U**.

We first give the rules for building formulas, and then distinguish a subset of legal formulas according to a set of restrictions. We give the intuitive meaning of each formula as we go, but postpone the precise definition of the interpretation of a formula until after the set of legal formulas has been defined.

Tuple variables will generally be lower case letters from the very end of the alphabet, while we reserve t, u and v to stand for individual tuples.

The basic building blocks of formulas are *atoms*, of which there are three kinds:

a1. For any relation name r in d, and for any tuple variable x, $r(x)$ is an atom; $r(x)$ stands for $x \in r$.

a2. For any tuple variables x and y (not necessarily distinct), any comparator $\theta \in \Theta$, and any attributes A and B in **U** that are θ-comparable, $x(A)\ \theta\ y(B)$ is an atom.

a3. For any tuple variable x, any comparator $\theta \in \Theta$ and any attributes A and B in U that are θ-comparable, if c is a constant in $dom(A)$, then $c\ \theta\ x(B)$ is an atom; if c is a constant in $dom(B)$, then $x(A)\ \theta\ c$ is an atom.

Example 10.4 For the database of Table 10.1, some atoms are $pinfo(x)$, $x(\text{PART\#}) = y(\text{PART\#})$, and $x(\text{QUANTITY}) \leq 20$.

We use the connectives $\neg$(not), $\wedge$(and), $\vee$(or), $\exists$(there exists) and $\forall$(for all) to recursively build *formulas* from atoms, according to the following six rules. The formulas are similar to those of first-order predicate calculus using $r_1, r_2, \ldots, r_p$ as unary relation symbols.

f1. Any atom is a formula.

f2. If f is a formula, then $\neg f$ is a formula; $\neg f$ is true exactly when f is false.

f3. If f and g are formulas, then $f \wedge g$ and $f \vee g$ are formulas; $f \wedge g$ is true exactly when both f and g are true, $f \vee g$ is true when either f or g is true.

f4. If x is a tuple variable, f is a formula involving x, and R is a subset of **U**, then $\exists x(R)f$ is a formula. That formula is true if there is some tuple t over R that makes f true when substituted for x in R.

f5. If x is a tuple variable, f is a formula involving x, and R is a subset of **U**, then $\forall x(R)f$ is a formula. That formula is true if for every tuple t over R, f is true when t is substituted for x.

f6. If f is a formula, then (f) is a formula.

Parentheses are used to override the precedence of the connectives. We assume $\exists$ and $\forall$ are of highest and equal precedence, followed by $\neg$, $\wedge$, and $\vee$ in decreasing precedence.

Example 10.5 The atoms in Example 10.4 are all formulas by f1. By f2,

$$\neg x(\text{QUANTITY}) \leq 20$$

is a formula. By f3 and f6,

$$(x(\text{PART\#}) = y(\text{PART\#}) \vee \neg x(\text{QUANTITY}) \leq 20)$$

is a formula. By f3 again,

$$\mathit{instock}(x) \wedge (x(\text{PART\#}) = y(\text{PART\#}) \vee \neg x(\text{QUANTITY}) \leq 20)$$

is a formula. Finally, by f6 and f4,

$$\exists x(\text{PART\# LOCATION QUANTITY})$$
$$(\mathit{instock}(x) \wedge (x(\text{PART\#}) = y(\text{PART\#}) \vee \neg x(\text{QUANTITY}) \leq 20))$$

is a formula. The parentheses added by f6 are necessary, for the unparenthesized formula

$$\exists x(\text{PART\# LOCATION QUANTITY})$$
$$\mathit{instock}(x) \wedge x(\text{PART\#}) = y(\text{PART\#}) \vee \neg x(\text{QUANTITY}) \leq 20$$

is equivalent to

$$((\exists x(\text{PART\# LOCATION QUANTITY})\, \mathit{instock}\,(x)) \wedge$$
$$x(\text{PART\#}) = y(\text{PART\#})) \vee x(\text{QUANTITY}) \leq 20$$

by the precedence of the connectives given.

10.2.2 Types, and Free and Bound Occurrences

Before we formally define the interpretation of a formula, we must be precise about what "f is a formula involving x" and "when t is substituted for x" mean. We also want to exclude certain nonsensical formulas, such as

$$\mathit{usedon}(x) \wedge x(\text{LOCATION}) = \text{"JFK"}$$

There is a typing problem with x, for $\mathit{usedon}(x)$ implies x is a tuple variable on PART# PTYPE NUSED, but x(LOCATION) implies a different scheme.

We shall define the *type* of a tuple variable x, that is, the scheme for x. We also define the *mention set* of x, which is the set of attributes x occurs with in a formula. We shall always want the mention set of x to be contained in the type of x. We also define when an occurrence of x is *free* or *bound* in a formula.

The idea of free and bound occurrences of tuple variables is analogous to global and local program variables in a language with nested procedure declaration.

Example 10.6 Consider the program sketched in Figure 10.1. Any mention of X, Y or Z in the body of MAIN refers to the variable declared in declaration 1. Any mention of Y or Z in the body of SUB1 also refers to declaration 1, while any mention of X or W refers to declaration 2. Y and Z are global to SUB1; they reference the same storage location at some procedure outside of SUB1. X and W are local to SUB1; they reference storage locations that are unseen by procedures outside of SUB1, although they can be seen by procedures inside SUB1. In the body of SUB12, X, Y and W are global, but Z is local. Note that in procedure SUB12, every occurrence of Z in declaration 3 and the body can be changed to another variable without changing the meaning of the program, as long as the new variable is not one that is global to SUB12. However, changing every occurrence of W in SUB12 could substantially alter the meaning of the program, since those occurrences of W are global to SUB12. Also note that *occurrences* of variable are global or local. An occurrence of Z in the body of SUB12 is local, while an occurrence in SUB1 is global.

```
        proc MAIN;
(1)       decl X, Y, Z;
          [body of MAIN]
               :
          proc SUB1;
(2)         decl X, W;
            [body of SUB1]
                 :
            proc SUB12;
(3)           decl Z;
              [body of SUB12]
              end SUB12;
            end SUB1;
          end MAIN.
```

Figure 10.1

In a formula, free and bound variable occurrences correspond to global and local occurrences of variables in a program. The connectives $\exists$ and $\forall$, called *quantifiers*, correspond to declarations; they bind occurrences of variables in their scope. Quantifiers will also serve to type variables in our formulas, just as declarations can do in programs. We shall define free and bound occurrences recursively, along with $type(x, f)$, the type of variable x in formula f, and $men(x, f)$, the mention set of x in f. Both $type(x, f)$ and $men(x, f)$ are defined only when x has a free occurrence in f (x "occurs free" in f). We also use freedom, boundness, *type*, and *men* to define the class of *legal formulas*, through restrictions on when different connectives can be used.

First, consider the cases where f is an atomic formula.

a1. If f is $r(x)$, then x is free in f, and $type(x, f) = men(x, f) = R$, where R is the relation scheme for r.

a2. If f is $x(A)\ \theta\ y(B)$, then x and y are both free in f, $type(x, f)$ and $type(y, f)$ are both undefined, $men(x, f) = A$, and $men(y, f) = B$.

a3. If f is $x(A)\ \theta\ c$ or $c\ \theta\ x(A)$, then x is free in f, $type(x, f)$ is undefined, and $men(x, f) = A$.

Atomic formulas, as long as they obey the requirement on comparators and domains, are all legal. Next, consider the cases where f is built from smaller formulas. Assume g and h are both legal formulas.

f2. If $f = \neg g$, then f is legal, and all occurrences of variables in f are free or bound as they are in g. For every variable x that occurs free in f, $type(x, f) = type(x, g)$ and $men(x, f) = men(x, g)$.

f3. If $f = g \wedge h$ or $f = g \vee h$, then all occurrences of variables in f are free or bound as their corresponding occurrences are in g and h. For every variable x that occurs free in f, if $type(x, g)$ and $type(x, h)$ are both defined, they must be equal for f to be legal. If the type of x is defined for only one subformula, say $type(x, g)$, and x occurs free in h, then $type(x, g) \supseteq men(x, h)$ must hold for f to be legal. In either case, $type(x, f) = type(x, g)$. If the type of x is undefined for both subformulas, then $type(x, f)$ is undefined. In all cases, $men(x, f) = men(x, g) \cup men(x, h)$.

f4. If $f = \exists x(R)g$, then x must occur free in g for f to be legal. Furthermore, $type(x,g)$ must be R, if it is defined, and R must contain $men(x,g)$. All occurrences of x in f are bound; $type(x,f)$ and $men(x,f)$ are not defined, since x does not occur free in f. Any occurrence of a variable $y \neq x$ is free or bound in f as it was in g; $type(y,f) = type(y,g)$ and $men(y,f) = men(y,g)$.

f5. If $f = \forall x(R)g$, then all restrictions and definitions are the same as in f4.

f6. If $f = (g)$, then f is legal, and freedom, boundness, *type* and *men* are the same as for g.

In a formula such as $\exists x(R)g$ or $\forall x(R)g$, it is useful to distinguish which occurrences of x in g are actually bound by the quantifier. An occurrence of x in $\exists x(R)g$ is bound to $\exists x(R)$ if that occurrence of x is free in g. The same holds for $\exists$ replaced by $\forall$. If the occurrence of x in g is bound, then it must be bound to some quantifier contained in g.

The next five examples refer to the database given in Table 10.1. For these examples let

$$R_1 = \text{PART\# SUBPARTOF PARTNAME},$$
$$R_2 = \text{PART\# PTYPE NUSED, and}$$
$$R_3 = \text{PART\# LOCATION QUANTITY}.$$

Example 10.7 Let f be the formula

$$\forall x(R_3)\,(\neg\, instock(x) \vee x(\text{QUANTITY}) \leq 100).$$

All occurrences of x are bound; they are in the scope of $x(R_3)$. This formula is true if for every tuple t in *instock*, $t(\text{QUANTITY}) \leq 100$.

As shorthand notation, we shall use

$$\forall x(R) \in r\, f \quad \text{for} \quad \forall x(R)\,(\neg\, r(x) \vee f).$$

Similarly, we shall use

$$\exists x(R) \in r\, f \quad \text{for} \quad \exists x(R)\,(r(x) \wedge f).$$

Example 10.8 Let f be the formula

$$\forall x(R_3) \in instock(\exists y(R_3) \in instock$$
$$(x(\text{LOCATION}) = y(\text{LOCATION}) \wedge x(\text{PART\#}) = z(\text{PART\#}))).$$

All occurrences of x and y are bound. Each x is bound to $\forall x(R_3)$; each y is bound to $\forall y(R_3)$. The lone occurrence of z is free; $type(z,f)$ is undefined; $men(z,f) = \text{PART\#}$.

Example 10.9 Let f be the formula

$$\begin{aligned}&\exists x(R_3) \in instock(x(\text{LOCATION}) = \text{“JFK”} \wedge \\ &\quad \forall y(R_2) \in usedon((x(\text{PART\#}) \neq y(\text{PART\#}) \vee y(\text{PTYPE}) \neq \text{“747”}) \vee \\ &\quad\quad \exists x(R_3) \in instock(x(\text{PART\#}) = y(\text{PART\#}) \wedge x(\text{LOCATION}) \\ &\qquad\qquad = z(\text{LOCATION}))))\end{aligned}$$

(We use double quotes around domain values that come from non-numeric domains, so that values are not confused with variables. For consistency, we use the quotes even when the specific value is numeric.) Let $x_1, x_2, \ldots, x_6$ be the six occurrences of x in the order they occur in f. All occurrences of x are bound, however, x_1, x_2, and x_3 are bound to the first $\exists x(R_3)$, while x_4, x_5, and x_6 are bound to the second $\exists x(R_3)$. All occurrences of y are bound, but the lone occurrence of z is free. Note that the subformula

$$\begin{aligned}&\exists x(R_3) \in instock(x(\text{PART\#}) = y(\text{PART\#}) \wedge x(\text{LOCATION}) \\ &\qquad = z(\text{LOCATION}))\end{aligned}$$

could be changed to

$$\begin{aligned}&\exists w(R_3) \in instock(w(\text{PART\#}) = y(\text{PART\#}) \wedge w(\text{LOCATION}) \\ &\qquad = z(\text{LOCATION}))\end{aligned}$$

to make f easier to read.

Example 10.10 Let f be the formula

$$\exists x(R_2)\,(usedon(x) \wedge x(\text{LOCATION}) = y(\text{LOCATION})).$$

We see that for the subformulas

$$\begin{aligned}g &= usedon(x) \text{ and}\\ h &= (x(\text{LOCATION}) = y(\text{LOCATION})),\end{aligned}$$

$type(x,g) = R_2$, while $men(x,h) =$ LOCATION. Hence the subformula $g \wedge h$ is not legal, so f is not legal.

Example 10.11 Let f be the formula

$$\exists x(R_2)\,(instock(x) \wedge x(\text{LOCATION}) = y(\text{LOCATION})).$$

for the subformula

$$g = (instock(x) \wedge x(\text{LOCATION}) = y(\text{LOCATION})).$$

$type(x,g) = R_3$, hence formula f is not legal.

Another shorthand notation, which did not arise in the examples, is

$$x(S) = y(S)$$

where S is a set of attributes $A_1 A_2 \cdots A_k$. It stands for the formula

$$(x(A_1) = y(A_1) \wedge x(A_2) = y(A_2) \wedge \cdots \wedge x(A_k) = y(A_k)).$$

When discussing formulas, we shall write $f(x_1, x_2, \ldots, x_n)$ to indicate that there are free occurrences of variables $x_1, x_2, \ldots, x_n$ in f. However, $f(x_1, x_2, \ldots, x_n)$ does not necessarily mean that $x_1, x_2, \ldots, x_n$ are the only variables that occur free in f.

10.2.3 Tuple Calculus Expressions

We denote a tuple calculus $\mathfrak{TC}$ as a sextuple

$$(\mathbf{U}, \mathfrak{D}, dom, \mathbf{R}, d, \Theta),$$

where $\mathbf{U}$ is the universe of attributes, $\mathfrak{D}$ is the set of domains, dom is a mapping from $\mathbf{U}$ to $\mathfrak{D}$, $\mathbf{R}$ is a set of relation schemes over $\mathbf{U}$, d is a database on the schemes in $\mathbf{R}$, and Θ is a set of comparators that includes at least equality and inequality for every domain in $\mathfrak{D}$. A *tuple calculus expression* over $\mathfrak{TC}$ has the form

$$\{x(R) | f(x)\},$$

where

1. f is a legal formula relative to $\mathbf{U}$, $\mathfrak{D}$, dom, $\mathbf{R}$, d and Θ.
2. x is the only tuple variable that occurs free in f.
3. R is a subset of $\mathbf{U}$.
4. If $type(x,f)$ is defined, it is equal to R, otherwise, $R \supseteq men(x,f)$.

By a slight manipulation of notation, we let $dom(R)$ stand for the set of all tuples with scheme R. To define the value for a tuple calculus expression, we need to substitute tuples for tuple variables.

Definition 10.1 Let $f(x)$ be a legal formula. Let R be $type(x,f)$, if $type(x,f)$ is defined, otherwise let R be any subset of **U** containing $men(x,f)$. Then f *with* t *substituted for* x, denoted $f(t/x)$, is the formula obtained by modifying each atom in f containing a free occurrence of x, as follows.

a1. If the x in $r(x)$ is free, replace $r(x)$ by *true* if $t \in r$, otherwise, replace $r(x)$ by *false*.

a2. If the x in $x(A)\ \theta\ y(B)$ is free, replace $x(A)$ by the constant $c \in dom(A)$ where $t(A) = c$, provided $x \neq y$. The same holds for $y(B)\ \theta\ x(A)$. If $x = y$, that is, the atom is actually $x(A)\ \theta\ x(B)$, replace the entire atom by *true* if $c_1\ \theta\ c_2$, where $c_1 = t(A)$ and $c_2 = t(B)$, otherwise, replace the atom by *false*.

a3. If the x in $x(A)\ \theta\ c$ is free, replace the entire atom by *true* if $c_1\ \theta\ c$, where $c_1 = t(A)$. Otherwise, replace the atom by *false*. Handle $c\ \theta\ x(A)$ in a similar manner.

Note we are slightly extending the definition of formula here to include the Boolean constants *true* and *false* as atoms. Under this extension, if $f(x)$ is a legal formula, so is $f(t/x)$ (see Exercise 10.4).

Example 10.12 Let $f(x)$ be the formula

$$\forall y(R_3)\,(\neg\,instock(y) \vee \neg y(\text{PART\#}) = x(\text{PART\#})$$
$$\vee y(\text{QUANTITY}) \leq x(\text{QUANTITY}) \vee x(\text{LOCATION}) = \text{“JFK”})$$

If t is the tuple ⟨2114 O'Hare 28⟩ over scheme R_3 = PART# LOCATION QUANTITY, then $f(t/x)$ is

$$\forall y(R_3)\,(\neg\,instock(y) \vee \neg y(\text{PART\#}) = 2114$$
$$\vee y(\text{QUANTITY}) \leq 28 \vee false).$$

Example 10.13 Let $f(y)$ be the formula

$$\neg\,instock(y) \vee \neg y(\text{PART\#}) = 2114$$
$$y(\text{QUANTITY}) \leq 28 \vee false.$$

If t is the tuple ⟨2116 Boston 341⟩ over scheme R_3, then $f(t/y)$ is

$$\neg\,\text{true} \vee \neg false \vee false \vee false.$$

If t = ⟨2114 JFK 6⟩, then $f(t/y)$ is

$$\neg\,true \vee \neg\,true \vee true \vee false.$$

Definition 10.2 Let f be a legal formula with no free tuple variables, but where *true* and *false* may appear as atoms. The *interpretation* of f, denoted $I(f)$, is defined recursively as follows.

f1. If f is *true*, then $I(f) = true$.
If f is *false*, then $I(f) = false$.
f2. If f is $\neg g$, then g must have no free variables. Let $I(f) = false$ if $I(g) = true$, otherwise let $I(f) = true$.
f3. If f is $g \wedge h$ or $g \vee h$, then neither g or h have free variables. If f is $g \wedge h$, let $I(f) = true$ exactly when $I(g) = I(h) = true$, otherwise, $I(f) = false$. If f is $g \vee h$, let $I(f) = false$ exactly when $I(g) = I(h) = false$, otherwise, $I(f) = true$.
f4. If f is $\exists x(R)g$, then x is the only variable that occurs free in g, (see Exercise 10.5). $I(f) = true$ if there is at least one tuple t in $dom(R)$ such that $I(g(t/x)) = true$, otherwise, $I(f) = false$.
f5. If f is $\forall x(R)g$, then x is the only variable that occurs free in g. $I(f) = true$ if for every tuple t in $dom(R)$, $I(g(t/x)) = true$, otherwise $I(f) = false$.
f6. If f is (g), then $I(f) = I(g)$.

Example 10.14 Let f be the formula

$$\begin{aligned}&\exists x(R_3)\,(instock(x) \wedge x(\text{LOCATION}) = \text{"JFK"} \wedge\\ &\quad\forall y(R_3)\,(\neg\, instock(y) \vee \neg\, y(\text{PART\#}) = x(\text{PART\#}) \vee\\ &\qquad y(\text{QUANTITY}) \leq x(\text{QUANTITY}))),\end{aligned}$$

where R_3 = PART# LOCATION QUANTITY, as before. Intuitively, $I(f)$ is true if there is some part such that more of that part is stored at JFK than anywhere else. Let us compute $I(f)$ for the database of Table 10.1. Formula f has the form $\exists x(R_3)\, g(x)$, so we need to know if $I(g(t/x)) = true$ for some $t \in dom(R_3)$. Rather than trying all such tuples, we also note that $g(x)$ has the form $instock(x) \wedge g'(x)$, so we only need check tuples from $dom(R_3)$ that are in *instock*. (Using shorthand notation, f could be written $\exists x(R_3) \in instock\ g'(x)$.)

A little more inspection tells us that we only need try tuples in *instock* where the LOCATION-value is JFK. Let us first try the tuple $t = \langle 2114 \text{ JFK } 6\rangle$. We have

$$\begin{aligned}&g(t/x) = (true \wedge true \wedge\\ &\quad\forall y(R_3)\,(\neg\, instock(y) \vee \neg\, y(\text{PART\#}) = 2114 \vee\\ &\qquad y(\text{QUANTITY}) \leq 6)),\end{aligned}$$

which simplifies to

$$\forall y(R_3)\,(\neg\, instock(y) \lor \neg\, y(\text{PART\#}) = 2114 \lor y(\text{QUANTITY}) \leq 6).$$

This formula has the form $\forall y(R_3)\; h(y)$, so we need to test whether $I(h(u/y)) = true$ for every tuple $u \in dom(R_3)$. Again, we can limit the search: since $h(y)$ has the form $\neg\, instock(y) \lor h'(y)$, we need only consider tuples in *instock*. Getting straight to the point, choosing $u = \langle 2114 \text{ O'Hare } 28\rangle$, we have

$$h(u/y) = (\neg\, true \lor \neg\, true \lor false).$$

Clearly $I(h(u/y)) = false$, so $I(g(t/x)) = false$.

We back up and try $t = \langle 211 \text{ JFK } 106\rangle$. Now

$$g(t/x) = (true \land true \land \forall y(R_3)\,(\neg\, instock(y) \lor \neg\, y(\text{PART\#}) = 211 \lor y(\text{QUANTITY}) \leq 106)),$$

which simplifies to

$$\forall y(R_3)\,(\neg\, instock(y) \lor \neg\, y(\text{PART\#}) = 211 \lor y(\text{QUANTITY}) \leq 106).$$

Again, we have a formula of the form $\forall y(R_3)\; h(y)$, so we have to check that $I(h(u/y)) = true$ for every tuple $u \in dom(R_3)$. As before, we need only test tuples in *instock*. Every choice for u makes $I(h(u/y)) = true$. For example, if $u = \langle 2116 \text{ O'Hare } 29\rangle$, we have

$$h(u/y) = (\neg\, true \lor \neg\, false \lor true),$$

so $I(h(u/y)) = true$. If $u = \langle 211 \text{ Boston } 28\rangle$, then

$$h(u/y) = (\neg\, true \lor \neg\, true \lor true),$$

so $I(h(u/y)) = true$. Hence $I(g(t/x)) = true$ and it follows $I(f) = true$. Note that $I(f) = false$ if $y(\text{QUANTITY}) \leq x(\text{QUANTITY})$ is changed to $y(\text{QUANTITY}) < x(\text{QUANTITY})$ (see Exercise 10.7).

We can now say what relation a tuple calculus expression defines.

Definition 10.3 Let $E = \{x(R) | f(x)\}$ be a tuple calculus expression over the tuple calculus $\mathfrak{TC}$ =

$$(\mathbf{U}, \mathfrak{D}, dom, \mathbf{R}, d, \Theta).$$

The *value* of expression E on the current state of database d, denoted $E(d)$, is the relation r on scheme R containing every tuple $t \in dom(R)$ such that

$$I(f(t/x)) = true.$$

Example 10.15 The expression E =

$$\{x(\text{PART\# PARTNAME}) | \exists y(R_1) \in pinfo\ (y(\text{SUBPARTOF}) = 211 \\ \wedge x(\text{PART\# PARTNAME}) = y(\text{PART\# PARTNAME}))\}$$

is a formalization of the expression in Example 10.2, where R_1 = PART# PARTNAME SUBPARTOF. Let $f(x)$ denote the formula in this expression. To evaluate $E(d)$ for d, the database in Table 10.1, we need to find every tuple $t \in dom$(PART# PARTNAME) such that $I(f(t/x)) = true$. Inspection shows that we need only consider tuples in $\pi_{\text{PART\# PARTNAME}}(pinfo)$. Choosing $t = \langle 211 \text{ coach seat}\rangle$,

$$f(t/x) = \exists y(R_1) \in pinfo\ (y(\text{SUBPARTOF}) = 211 \\ \wedge 211 = y(\text{PART\#}) \wedge \text{“coach seat”} = y(\text{PARTNAME})).$$

$I(f(t/x))$ will be true only if there is a tuple $\langle 211 \text{ coach seat}\rangle$ in *pinfo*, which there is not. Thus, $\langle 211 \text{ coach seat}\rangle$ is not in $E(d)$.

Choosing $t = \langle 2114 \text{ seat cover}\rangle$,

$$f(t/x) = \exists y(R_1) \in pinfo\ (y(\text{SUBPARTOF}) = 211 \\ \wedge 2114 = y(\text{PART\#}) \wedge \text{“seat cover”} = y(\text{PARTNAME})).$$

$I(f(t/x)) = true$ in this case, so 2114 seatcover is in $E(d)$. The only other choice of t that makes $I(f(t/x)) = true$ is $t = \langle 2116 \text{ seat belt}\rangle$, so $E(d)$ is as given in Table 10.2.

Example 10.16 The expression in Example 10.3 can be formalized to

$$E = \{x(\text{NUSED}) \mid \exists z(R_2) \in \textit{usedon}\ (x(\text{NUSED}) = z(\text{NUSED})$$
$$\wedge\ z(\text{PTYPE}) = \text{“727”} \wedge \exists y(R_1) \in \textit{pinfo}\ (z(\text{PART\#}) = y(\text{PART\#})$$
$$\wedge\ y(\text{PARTNAME}) = \text{“coach seat”}))\},$$

where R_2 = PART# PTYPE NUSED and R_1 is as in the last example. $E(d)$, for the database given in Table 10.1, is given in Table 10.3. Note that in both this example and the last, an extra tuple variable was necessary going from the informal to the formal version of each expression. The extra variables handle the implicit projection in the informal versions.

Example 10.17 Consider the expression

$$E = \{x(R_2) \mid \neg\, \textit{usedon}(x) \vee x(\text{PTYPE}) \neq \text{“707”}\}.$$

where R_2 is as in the last example. If any of the domains for PART#, PTYPE and NUSED is infinite, then $E(d)$ will be an infinite relation, since there will be infinitely many tuples not in *usedon*. The *complement* of $E(d)$, for d the database in Table 10.1, is given in Table 10.4. In this case, but not always, the complement is finite (see Exercise 10.13).

Table 10.4 Complement of $E(d)$.

(PART#	PTYPE	NUSED)
211	727	134
2114	727	134
2116	727	296
21164	727	592

Example 10.18 Again refering to the database d in Table 10.1, consider the expression

$$E = \{x(\text{PARTNAME PTYPE}) \mid \exists y(R_1) \in \textit{pinfo}$$
$$\exists z(R_2) \in \textit{usedon}\ (y(\text{PART\#}) = z(\text{PART\#})$$
$$\wedge\ x(\text{PARTNAME}) = y(\text{PARTNAME}) \wedge z(\text{NUSED}) > 200$$
$$\wedge\ x(\text{PTYPE}) = z(\text{PTYPE}))\},$$

where R_1 and R_2 are as given in previous examples. $E(d)$ gives all part names and plane types where more than 200 of the part are used on a plane of that type. $E(d)$ is shown in Table 10.5.

Table 10.5 Relation Between Part Name and Plane Type.

(PARTNAME	PTYPE)
seat belt	707
seat belt	727
seat belt anchor	707
seat belt anchor	727

10.3 REDUCING RELATIONAL ALGEBRA WITH COMPLEMENT TO TUPLE RELATIONAL CALCULUS

In this section we show that tuple calculus is as expressive as relational algebra with complement. We shall eventually show that they are equally expressive. In Section 10.4 we shall give an alternative interpretation for tuple calculus formulas. Under the alternative interpretation, tuple calculus and relational algebra without complement are equally expressive.

Theorem 10.1 Let $\mathcal{R} = (\mathbf{U}, \mathfrak{D}, dom, \mathbf{R}, d, \Theta, O)$ be a relational algebra with complement and let $\mathfrak{TC} = (\mathbf{U}, \mathfrak{D}, dom, \mathbf{R}, d, \Theta)$ be a tuple calculus. For any algebraic expression E over $\mathcal{R}$, there is an equivalent tuple calculus expression F over $\mathfrak{TC}$. That is, for any state of d, $E(d) = F(d)$.

Proof As we noted in Section 10, it is sufficient to assume E comes from the subalgebra $\mathcal{R}'$ where O is replaced by the set of operations renaming, select with a single comparison, projection, natural join, union, difference, and complement, and where only single-attribute, single-tuple constant relations are allowed. The proof proceeds by induction on the number of operators in E.

Basis No operators. Then E is either a constant relation or a single relation from d. If $E = \langle a{:}A \rangle$, then $F = \{x(A) | x(A) = a\}$. If $E = r$, where r is a relation on R, then $F = \{x(R) | r(x)\}$.

Induction Assume the theorem holds for any relational algebra expression with fewer than k operators. Let E have k operators.

Case 1 (renaming): $E = \delta_{A_1, A_2, \ldots, A_m \leftarrow B_1, B_2, \ldots, B_m}(E_1)$. E_1 has less than k operators. Let $\{x(R) | f(x)\}$ be a tuple calculus expression equivalent to E_1. Then F is

$$\{y(S) \mid \exists x(R)\,(f(x) \wedge g(x,y))\},$$

where $S = (R - A_1A_2 \cdots A_m)B_1B_2 \cdots B_m$ and $g(x, y)$ is the formula that is the "and" of the atoms $y(C) = x(C)$ for each C in $R - A_1A_2 \cdots A_m$ and $y(B_i) = x(A_i)$ for $1 \le i \le m$.

Case 2 (select): $E = \sigma_{A\theta c}(E_1)$ or $\sigma_{A\theta B}(E_1)$. Let $\{x(R) \mid f(x)\}$ be a tuple calculus expression equivalent to E_1. Then F is

$$\{x(R) \mid f(x) \wedge x(A)\,\theta\, c\}$$

or

$$\{x(R) \mid f(x) \wedge x(A)\,\theta\, x(B)\}.$$

Case 3 (projection): $E = \pi_X(E_1)$. This case is left to the reader (see Exercise 10.10).

Case 4 (join): $E = E_1 \bowtie E_2$. Let $\{x(QR) \mid f(x)\}$ be a tuple calculus expression for E_1 and let $\{y(RS) \mid g(y)\}$ be a tuple calculus expression for E_2, where $QR \cap RS = R$. Then F is

$$\{z(QRS) \mid \exists x(QR)\, \exists y(RS)\,(f(x) \wedge g(y) \wedge z(QR) = x(QR) \wedge z(RS) = y(RS)\}.$$

Case 5 (union): $E = E_1 \cup E_2$. This case is left to the reader (see Exercise 10.10).

Case 6 (difference): $E = E_1 - E_2$. This case is left to the reader (see Exercise 10.10).

Case 7 (complement): $E = \bar{E}_1$. Let $\{x(R) \mid f(x)\}$ be a tuple calculus expression for E_1. Then

$$F = \{x(R) \mid \neg f(x)\}.$$

Example 10.19 Consider the algebraic expression

$$E = \pi_{\text{SUBPARTOF NUSED}}(pinfo \bowtie \sigma_{\text{PTYPE} = 747}(usedon)).$$

for the database in Table 10.1. Equivalent tuple calculus expressions for *pinfo* and *usedon* are

$$\{x(R_1) | pinfo(x)\} \text{ and } \{y(R_2) | usedon(y)\},$$

where R_1 = PART# SUBPARTOF PARTNAME and R_2 = PART# PTYPE NUSED. For $\sigma_{\text{PTYPE} = 747}(usedon)$ we have

$$\{y(R_2) | usedon(y) \wedge y(\text{PTYPE}) = \text{"747"}\}.$$

Letting R = PART# SUBPARTOF PARTNAME PTYPE NUSED, an equivalent expression for $pinfo \bowtie \sigma_{\text{PTYPE} = 747}(usedon)$ is

$$\{z(R) | \exists x(R_1)\ \exists y(R_2)\ (pinfo(x) \wedge usedon(y) \\ \wedge y(\text{PTYPE}) = \text{"747"} \wedge z(R_1) = x(R_1) \wedge z(R_2) = y(R_2)\}.$$

Finally, an equivalent tuple calculus expression for E is

$$\{w(\text{SUBPART NUSED}) | \exists z(R)\ (\exists x(R_1)\ \exists y(R_2) \\ (pinfo(x) \wedge usedon(y) \wedge y(\text{PTYPE}) = \text{"747"} \wedge \\ z(R_1) = x(R_1) \wedge z(R_2) = y(R_2)) \wedge w(\text{SUBPART}) = \\ z(\text{SUBPART}) \wedge w(\text{NUSED}) = z(\text{NUSED}))\}.$$

10.4 LIMITED INTERPRETATION OF TUPLE CALCULUS FORMULAS

The interpretation given for tuple calculus formulas presents some practical problems when tuple calculus is considered as the basis for a query system. First, tuple calculus expressions can define infinite relations. Second, it is not clear that arbitrary formulas of the forms

$$\exists x(R) f(x) \quad \text{and} \quad \forall x(R) f(x)$$

can be effectively interpreted. The interpretation given would seem to require searching through all of $dom(R)$, which could be infinite. Even if all the attributes in R have finite domains, $dom(R)$ could be unmanageably large. We shall present an alternative interpretation for formulas where tuples are restricted to being composed of domain values that appear in a formula or in relations mentioned in a formula. The original interpretation shall be called *unlimited*, while the alternative interpretation shall be called *limited*. We shall also introduce a class of tuple calculus expressions for which both interpretations always yield the same value.

For the following development, we assume, as in Chapter 3, that domains of different attributes are either equal or disjoint. This restriction is for simplification only. We could allow arbitrary intersection of domains, so long as there is a means to specify all the values of a given domain that appear anywhere in a relation.

Definition 10.4 Let f be a tuple calculus formula and let A be an attribute. The *extended active domain* of A relative to f, denoted $edom(A,f)$, is the set of all values from $dom(A)$ that appear in relations mentioned in f or as constants in f.

If no attribute with a domain the same as $dom(A)$ is mentioned in f, it is possible for $edom(A,f) = \emptyset$. For a set of attributes R, we let $edom(R,f)$ consist of all tuples t such that $t(A) \in edom(A,f)$ for every $A \in R$.

Example 10.20 Assume that the attributes PART# and SUBPARTOF, in the database of Table 10.1, have the same domain. Let f be the formula

$$\begin{aligned} &\forall y(R_1) \in pinfo(217 \neq y(\text{SUBPARTOF}) \vee \\ &\quad \exists z(R_3) \in instock\ (z(\text{PART\#}) = y(\text{PART\#}) \wedge \\ &\qquad z(\text{LOCATION}) = x(\text{LOCATION}) \wedge z(\text{QUANTITY}) > 0))), \end{aligned}$$

where R_1 and R_3 are as in previous examples. This formula describes all the locations that stock all the subparts of part 217. Using the states of *pinfo* and *instock* in Table 10.1,

$$\begin{aligned} &edom(\text{PART\#}, f) = edom(\text{SUBPARTOF}, f) = \\ &\quad \{0, 206, 211, 217, 318, 2061, 2066, 2068, 2114, 2116, 21163, 21164\}. \end{aligned}$$

There is an algebraic expression for $edom(\text{PART\#},f)$ that accounts for the current state of *pinfo* and *instock*. It is

$$\begin{aligned} &\pi_{\text{PART\#}}(pinfo) \cup \pi_{\text{PART\#}}(instock) \cup <217{:}\text{PART\#}> \\ &\cup\ \delta_{\text{SUBPARTOF} \leftarrow \text{PART\#}}(\pi_{\text{SUBPARTOF}}(pinfo)). \end{aligned}$$

By Theorem 10.1, there is also a tuple calculus expression for $edom(\text{PART\#},f)$. Note that if g is a subformula of a tuple calculus formula f, then $edom(A,g) \subseteq edom(A,f)$ for every attribute A.

We now give the *limited interpretation* of a tuple calculus formula f with no free variables. The limited interpretation of f is denoted $i(f)$, and the definition is the same as for $I(f)$, except for the cases f4 and f5 on $\exists$ and $\forall$. These cases are replaced by

f4′. If f is $\exists x(R)g$, then $i(f) = true$ if there is at least one tuple t in $edom(R,g)$ such that $i(g(t/x)) = true$. Otherwise, $i(f) = false$.
f5′. If f is $\forall x(R)g$, then $i(f) = true$ if for every tuple t in $edom(R,g)$ $i(g(t/x)) = true$. Otherwise, $i(f) = false$.

The *limited evaluation* of a tuple calculus expression $E = \{x(R) | f(x)\}$ is the relation on R consisting of every tuple $t \in edom(R,f)$ such that $i(f(t/x)) = true$.

The previous interpretation and evaluation shall be called *unlimited*. For Examples 10.15, 10.16 and 10.18, the unlimited and limited evaluations yield the same value. However, the value for the expression in Example 10.17 is a finite relation under limited evaluation. Limited evaluation always yields a finite relation, since, given finite relations to start with, $edom(R,f)$ is finite for any formula f. Also, the limited interpretation of formulas such as $\exists x(R)g$ and $\forall x(R)g$ is effective, since $i(g(t/x))$ need only be computed for tuples in $edom(R,g)$.

Example 10.21 The following expression over the database in Table 10.1 always yields the empty relation under limited evaluation:

$$\{x(\text{PART\#}) | \forall y(R_3) \in \textit{instock}\ x(\text{PART\#}) \neq y(\text{PART\#})\}.$$

Tuple variable x ranges only over parts that appear in *instock*.

Example 10.22 Assuming that $dom(\text{PART\#}) = dom(\text{SUBPARTOF})$ in the database of Table 10.1, the expression

$$E = \{x(\text{SUBPARTOF}) | \forall y(R_1) \in \textit{pinfo}\ x(\text{SUBPARTOF}) \neq y(\text{SUBPARTOF})\}$$

does not necessarily yield an empty relation under limited interpretation. Tuple variable x ranges over all parts that appear in either the PART# or SUBPARTOF columns of *pinfo*. If d, the current state of the database, is as given in Table 10.1, then $E(d)$ under limited evaluation is given in Table 10.6.

Table 10.6 $E(d)$ Under Limited Evaluation.

(PART#)
21163
2061
2066
2068

10.4.1 Reducing Relational Algebra to Tuple Calculus with Limited Evaluation

As we have noted, tuple calculus expressions denote only finite relations under limited evaluation. Algebraic expressions without complement denote only finite relations. This similarity is no coincidence.

Theorem 10.2 Let $\mathcal{R} = (\mathbf{U}, \mathfrak{D}, dom, \mathbf{R}, d, \Theta, O)$ be a relational algebra (without complement), and $\mathfrak{T}\mathcal{C} = (\mathbf{U}, \mathfrak{D}, dom, \mathbf{R}, d, \Theta)$ be a tuple calculus. For any algebraic expression E over $\mathcal{R}$ there is a tuple calculus expression F over $\mathfrak{T}\mathcal{C}$ such that E is equivalent to F under limited evaluation.

Proof The proof follows that of Theorem 10.1 with case 7 of the induction omitted. Every tuple calculus expression used in the rest of the proof has the same value under unlimited and limited interpretation. The details are left to the reader (see Exercise 10.18).

10.4.2 Safe Tuple Calculus Expressions

Tuple calculus under the limited evaluation, although as expressive as relational algebra, leaves something to be desired as the basis for a query language. The value of an expression can depend on columns in relations corresponding to attributes not even mentioned in the expression. Another approach to the problem of keeping values of expressions finite and having effective interpretation of formulas with quantifiers is to use only expressions where the unlimited and limited evaluations are guaranteed to be the same.

Definition 10.5 A tuple calculus expression $\{x(R) | f(x)\}$ is *safe* if the following three conditions hold.

s1. $I(f(t/x)) = true$ implies that $t \in edom(R,f)$.

s2. For every subformula of f of the form $\exists y(S)\ g(y, z_1, z_2, \ldots, z_k)$, $I(g(t/y, u_1/z_1, u_2/z_2, \ldots, u_k/z_k)) = true$ implies $t \in edom(S,g)$, where $y, z_1, z_2, \ldots, z_k$ are all the free tuple variables in g.

s3. For every subformula of f of the form $\forall y(S)\ g(y, z_1, z_2, \ldots, z_k)$, $t \notin edom(S,g)$ implies $I(g,(t/y, u_1/z_1, u_2/z_2, \ldots, u_k/z_k)) = true$ where $y, z_1, z_2, \ldots, z_k$ are all the free tuple variables in g.

Condition s1 guarantees that the value of the expression will be a finite relation under the unlimited evaluation. Conditions s2 and s3 guarantee that the unlimited interpretation of formulas can be made effective, since only a finite number of tuples need be considered to interpret $\exists y(S)g$ or $\forall y(S)g$. If every place a quantifier is used in formula f, it is involved in the shorthand $\exists y(S) \in s\ g(y)$ or $\forall y(S) \in s\ g(y)$, then conditions s2 and s3 will be satisfied. The notation $\exists y(S) \in s\ g(y)$ stands for $\exists y(S)\ h(y)$, where $h(y)$ is $s(y) \wedge g(y)$. Any tuple $t \in s$ is clearly in $edom(S,h)$, and the $s(y)$ atom in $h(y)$ means that $h(t/y)$ cannot interpret to *true* no matter what the other free variables in h are. Similarly, $\forall y(S) \in s\ g(y)$ stands for $\forall y(S)\ h(y)$, where $h(y)$ in this case is $\neg s(y) \vee g(y)$. Any tuple t not in $edom(S,h)$ is surely not in s, so $g(t/y)$ interprets to *true* for any such tuple.

If the formula $f(x)$ actually has the form $r(x) \wedge f'(x)$, for some relation r, then condition s1 is satisfied.

Example 10.23 By what we observed above, the expression

$$\{x(R_2) | usedon(x) \wedge \exists y(R_3) \in instock \\ (x(\text{PART\#}) = y(\text{PART\#}) \wedge y(\text{QUANTITY}) \geq 100)\}$$

on the database of Table 10.1 is safe. R_2 and R_3 are the relation schemes of *usedon* and *instock*, as before.

Example 10.24 The expression

$$\{x(R_2) | usedon(x) \vee \exists y(R_3) \in instock \\ (x(\text{PART\#}) = y(\text{PART\#}) \wedge y(\text{QUANTITY}) \geq 100)\}$$

is not safe. The unlimited evaluation of this expression for the database in Table 10.1 contains the tuple $\langle 2116\ 707\ 83\rangle$, for example, which is not in the extended active domain of R_2 for the formula in the expression.

Example 10.25 The expression

$$\{x(\text{PARTNAME PTYPE}) \mid \exists y(R_1) \in \textit{pinfo}\ \exists z(R_2) \in \textit{usedon}$$
$$(y(\text{PART\#}) = z(\text{PART\#}) \wedge x(\text{PARTNAME}) = y(\text{PARTNAME})$$
$$\wedge\ x(\text{PTYPE}) = y(\text{PTYPE}))\}$$

is safe, even though there is no $r(x)$ term. Any tuple t in the value of the expression must have a PARTNAME-value that appears in *pinfo* and a PTYPE-value that appears in *usedon*. A class of safe expressions, of which this expression is a member, is described in Exercise 10.20.

Lemma 10.1 For any safe tuple calculus expression E, the unlimited and limited evaluations of E are the same.

Proof Left to the reader (see Exercise 10.21).

Theorem 10.3 Given any tuple calculus expression E, there is a safe tuple calculus expression F that is equivalent to E under limited evaluation for E.

Proof Exercise 10.22 shows that for any tuple calculus formula g there is another formula h such that the value of $\{y(X) \mid h(y)\}$ under unlimited evaluation is $edom(X,g)$ for a given set of attributes S. Furthermore, $edom(S,g) = edom(S,h)$, so $edom(S,g) = edom(S,g \wedge h) = edom(S,g \vee \neg h)$.

Given an expression $E = \{x(R) \mid f(x)\}$, we first want to find a formula f' such that $i(f(t/x)) = I(f'(t/x))$ for all $t \in dom(R)$. The only place i and I diverge is on subformulas involving quantifiers. We produce f' by modifying such subformulas. For a subformula $\exists y(S)\ g(y)$, let $h(y)$ be as outlined above. Replace this subformula by $\exists y(S)\ (g(y) \wedge h(y))$. We have $i(g(t/y)) = I(g(t/y) \wedge h(t/y))$ for any $t \in edom(S,g)$ and $I(g(t/y) \wedge h(t/y)) = \textit{false}$ for any $t \notin edom(S,g)$, provided $i(g(t/y)) = I(g(t/y))$. Hence the modified subformula has an unlimited interpretation equal to the limited interpretation of the original subformula.

For a subformula $\forall y(S)\ g(y)$, let $h(y)$ be as above and substitute $\forall y(S)\ (g(y) \vee \neg h(y))$. Assuming $i(g(t/y)) = I(g(t/y))$, $i(g(t/y)) = I(g(t/y) \wedge \neg h(t/y))$ for any $t \in edom(S,g)$ and $I(g(t/y) \vee \neg h(t/y)) = \textit{true}$ for any $t \notin edom(S,g)$. Hence the modified subformula has an unlimited interpretation equal to the limited interpretation of the original subformula.

If we make these modifications to all such subformulas of f working from the inside out, the end result is a formula f' where $i(f(t/x)) = I(f'(t/x))$. Note that we do not modify subformulas in the h's, so the process does terminate. To complete the proof, let h' be a formula such that the unlimited evaluation of $\{x(R) \mid h'(x)\}$ is $edom(R,f)$. The desired expression F is then

$$\{x(R) \mid f'(x) \wedge h'(x)\}.$$

10.5 DOMAIN RELATIONAL CALCULUS

Domain relational calculus is quite similar to tuple relational calculus, except variables represent single domain values rather than entire tuples. Also, relation symbols can now be multiplace rather than simply unary. To keep the notation reasonable, it is necessary to assume a fixed order on the attributes in a relation. Since tuple calculus and domain calculus are so similar, the treatment of domain calculus will be much briefer. We first give some informal examples, again using the database of Table 10.1.

Example 10.26 The expression

$$\{x\,y \mid pinfo(x\,z\,y) \wedge z = 206\}$$

represents all part number-part name pairs that are subparts of part 206. The expression

$$\{x\,y \mid pinfo(x\;206\,y)\}$$

represents the same pairs. The value of both these expressions is shown in Table 10.7.

Table 10.7 Partname-Partnumber Pairs.

(PART#	PARTNAME)
2061	paging switch
2066	light switch
2068	air nozzle

Example 10.27 The expression

$$\{x\,y \mid \exists z\;\exists w\;(usedon(z\,x\,y) \wedge pinfo(z\;w\;\text{“coach seat”})\}$$

represents the number of coach seats used on each plane type. The value of this expression is shown in Table 10.8.

Table 10.8 Number of Coach Seats Used.

(PTYPE	NUSED)
707	86
727	134

A domain calculus $\mathfrak{DC}$ is denoted the same way as a tuple calculus, namely as a sextuple (**U**, $\mathfrak{D}$, *dom*, **R**, *d*, Θ). *Domain calculus formulas* are built from domain variables using relations, comparators, and the connectives $\neg$, $\wedge$, $\vee$, $\exists$ and $\forall$. The basic building blocks are *atoms*:

a1. If r is a relation in d with scheme $A_1 A_2 \cdots A_n$, then $r(a_1 a_2 \cdots a_n)$ is an atom, where each a_i is either a domain variable or a constant from $dom(A_i)$.
a2. If x and y are domain variables, θ is a comparator and c is an appropriate constant, then $x \theta y$, $x \theta c$ and $c \theta x$ are all atoms.
a3. The Boolean constants *true* and *false* are atoms.

The atoms are combined recursively into formulas:

f1. Any atom is a formula.
f2. If f is a formula, then $\neg f$ is a formula.
f3. If f and g are formulas, so are $f \wedge g$ and $f \vee g$.
f4. If f is a formula, so is $\exists x(A)f$, where A is an attribute in **U** and x is a domain variable.
f5. If f is a formula, so is $\forall x(A)f$, where A is an attribute in **U** and x is a domain variable.
f6. If f is a formula, so is (f).

The precedence of connectives is the same as for tuple calculus formulas.

Example 10.28 The following domain calculus formula is similar to the tuple calculus formula of Example 10.5:

$$\exists x_1(\text{PART\#})\ \exists x_2(\text{LOCATION})\ \exists x_3(\text{QUANTITY})$$
$$(instock(x_1\, x_2\, x_3) \wedge (x_1 = y \wedge \neg x_3 \leq 20)).$$

The rules for free and bound occurrences of variables are analogous to those for tuple calculus formulas. To discuss legal domain calculus formulas, we need to type domain variables. The type of a variable x in formula f, denoted $type(x,f)$, is either a domain in $\mathfrak{D}$ or undefined. We again assume for simplicity that the domains of two attributes are either equal or disjoint. We shall not formally define the type of a variable or legal formulas. As with tuple calculus, legality simply requires that there is consistency as to the type of a variable and that a quantified variable occur free in the quantified formula.

Example 10.29 Let $r(A\ B\ C)$ and $s(C\ D)$ be relations. For the formula

$$f = \exists x(E)\, \forall y(A)\, (r(y\,z\,x) \wedge s(x\,x) \wedge y \leq z)$$

to be legal, we must have $dom(C) = dom(D) = dom(E)$ and attributes A and B must be $\leq$-comparable. In that case, $type(z,f) = dom(B)$. If g is the subformula

$$(r(y\,z\,x) \wedge s(x\,x) \wedge y \leq z),$$

then $type(x,g) = dom(C)$ and $type(y,g) = dom(A)$.

When quantifying variables, we could use domains rather than attributes to type them. However, it will be useful to have attributes when reducing domain calculus to relational algebra.

The *substitution* of a domain constant c for a domain variable x that occurs free in a formula f, denoted $f(c/x)$, is analogous to substitution for tuple calculus formulas. We assume $c \in type(x,f)$. Every free occurrence of x in f is replaced by c, and then atoms composed entirely of constants are replaced by *true* and *false* as appropriate.

Example 10.30 Consider the formula

$$\begin{aligned} f = {} & usedon(x \text{ “707” } y) \wedge \forall w(\text{QUANTITY}) \\ & (\neg\, instock(x \text{ “JFK” } w) \vee w \geq y \vee x = 2116). \end{aligned}$$

Variable x is free in f; $f(211/x)$ is the formula

$$\begin{aligned} g = {} & usedon(211 \text{ “707” } y) \wedge \forall w(\text{QUANTITY}) \\ & (\neg\, instock(211 \text{ “JFK” } 2) \vee w \geq y \vee false). \end{aligned}$$

Variable y is free in g; $g(86/y)$ is

$$\begin{aligned} & true \wedge \forall w(\text{QUANTITY}) \\ & (\neg\, instock(211 \text{ “JKF” } 2) \vee w \geq 86 \vee false), \end{aligned}$$

which simplifies to

$$\forall w(\text{QUANTITY})\, (\neg\, instock(211 \text{ “JFK” } 2) \vee w \geq 86).$$

The *unlimited interpretation* of a domain calculus formula f with no free occurrences of variables is denoted $I(f)$. The definition is essentially that for tuple calculus formulas. For a formula $f = \exists x(A)\, g(x)$, $I(f) = true$ if and only if there is a $c \in dom(A)$ such that $I(g(c/x)) = true$. For a formula $f = \forall x(A)\, g(x)$, $I(f) = true$ if and only if for every $c \in dom(A)$, $I(g(c/x)) = true$.

Example 10.31 Let h be the formula

$$\forall w(\text{QUANTITY})\, (\neg\, instock(211\ \text{“JFK”}\ w) \vee w \geq 86)$$

from the end of Example 10.30. To calculate $I(h)$, we need to know $I(h'(c/x))$ for every $c \in dom(\text{QUANTITY})$ where $h'(w)$ is the formula

$$\neg\, instock(211\ \text{“JFK”}\ w) \vee w \geq 86.$$

The first disjunct in $h'(w)$ interprets to *true* for all choices of w except 106, and the second disjunct interprets to *true* for every $c \in dom(\text{QUANTITY})$. Hence $I(h) = true$.

A *domain calculus expression* over $\mathfrak{DC}$ has the form

$$\{x_1(A_1)\, x_2(A_2) \cdots x_n(A_n) | f(x_1, x_2, \ldots, x_n)\}$$

where

1. f is a legal domain calculus formula with exactly the free variables $x_1, x_2, \ldots, x_n$,
2. $A_1, A_2, \ldots, A_n$ are distinct attributes in $\mathbf{U}$, and
3. $type(x_i, f) = dom(A_i)$ for $1 \leq i \leq n$.

The *value* of this expression under *unlimited evaluation* is the relation over scheme $A_1\ A_2 \cdots A_n$ containing every tuple $\langle c_1\ c_2 \cdots c_n \rangle$ such that $c_i \in dom(A_i)$, for $1 \leq i \leq n$, and $I(f(c_1/x_1, c_2/x_2, \ldots, c_n/x_n) = true$. As before, the value of expression E for database d is denoted $E(d)$.

Example 10.32 Using the formula from Example 10.30, we have the domain calculus expression

$$E = \{x(\text{PART\#})\, y(\text{NUSED}) | usedon(x\ \text{“707”}\ y) \wedge \\ \forall w(\text{QUANTITY})\, (\neg\, instock(x\ \text{“JFK”}\ w) \vee w \geq y \vee x = 2116)\}.$$

E denotes the part number and number used for each part used on a 707 such that the quantity of that part *instock* at JFK is at least the number used or the part number is 2116. $E(d)$, under unlimited evaluation, for the state of the database d given in Table 10.1 is shown in Table 10.9.

Table 10.9 Part Number and Number Used.

(PART#	NUSED)
211	86
2116	244

As with tuple calculus, we can give a limited interpretation for formulas and limited evaluation for expressions. The *extended active domain* of an attribute A in a domain calculus formula f, denoted $edom(A,f)$, is the set of all elements of $dom(A)$ that occur as constants in f or in relations mentioned in f. The *limited interpretation* of a domain calculus formula f with no free variables, denoted $i(f)$, differs from the unlimited interpretation only for quantified formulas. If f is $\exists x(A)\, g(x)$, then $i(f) = true$ if and only if there is a constant $c \in edom(A,g)$ such that $I(g(c/x)) = true$. Similarly, if f is $\forall x(A)$ $g(x)$, then $i(f) = true$ if for every constant $c \in edom(A,f)\; I(g(c/x)) = true$. To get the limited evaluation of an expression

$$\{x_1(A_1)\, x_2(A_2) \cdots x_n(A_n) | f(x_1, x_2, \ldots, x_n)\},$$

x_i ranges over $edom(A_i,f)$, for $1 \leq i \leq n$, and limited interpretation is used for f.

Example 10.33 Consider the expression

$$\{x(\text{PART\#}) | \forall y(\text{PART\#})\, \forall z(\text{PARTNAME})$$
$$\neg\, pinfo(y\ x\ z) \wedge x \neq 318\}$$

for the database of Table 10.1, where we assume dom(PART#) = dom(SUBPARTOF) = non-negative integers. The unlimited evaluation of this expression yields an infinite relation. The value under limited interpretation is given in Table 10.10.

We can also define the class of *safe* domain calculus expressions. An expression

$$\{x_1(A_1)\, x_2(A_2) \cdots x_n(A_n) | f(x_1, x_2, \ldots, x_n)\}$$

is safe if the following three conditions hold.

s1. If for constants $c_1, c_2, \ldots, c_n$ $I(f(c_1/x_1, c_2/x_2, \ldots, c_n/x_n)) = true$, then $c_i \in edom(A_i, f)$ for $1 \leq i \leq n$.

s2. For each subformula of f of the form $\exists y(A)\, g(y)$, $I(g(c/y)) = true$ implies $c \in dom(A,g)$.

s3. For each subformula of f of the form $\forall y(A)\, g(y)$, $c \notin edom(A,g)$ implies $I(g(c/y)) = true$.

These three conditions serve the same purpose as the corresponding conditions for safe type calculus expressions.

Table 10.10 Value under Limited Interpretation.

(PART#)
21163
2061
2066
2068

Example 10.34 The expression in Example 10.32 is safe. Both x and y must appear in *usedon*, and $\neg$ *instock*(x "JFK" 2) $\vee$ $w \geq y \vee x = 2116$ interprets to *true* if w does not appear in *instock*. The expression in Example 10.33 is not safe. There are values for x that do not appear in *pinfo* that make the formula true.

The following two results are analogs of Lemma 10.1 and Theorem 10.3, and are stated without proof.

Lemma 10.2 For any safe domain calculus expression E, the unlimited and limited evaluations of E are the same.

Theorem 10.4 Given any domain calculus expression E, there is a safe domain calculus expression F that is equivalent to E under limited evaluation for E.

10.6 REDUCTION OF TUPLE CALCULUS TO DOMAIN CALCULUS

As we saw in Example 10.9, any tuple calculus formula can be modified to an equivalent formula where the same tuple variable is not bound in two places. For this section, we assume that in a tuple calculus expression

$$\{x(R) \mid f(x)\},$$

x does not occur bound in f, nor is any other tuple variable bound in more than one place.

The translation of a tuple calculus expression E to an equivalent domain calculus expression is straightforward. Let $E = \{x(R) | f(x)\}$. Any tuple variable y appearing in f is associated with a unique relation scheme S. Either y appears in $\exists y(S)$ or $\forall y(S)$, or $y = x$ and $S = R$. Let $S = A_1 A_2 \cdots A_k$. Tuple variable y is replaced by k domain variables $y_1, y_2, \ldots y_k$. Any atom $r(y)$ becomes $r(y_1 y_2 \cdots y_k)$. Any atom $y(A_i)\ \theta\ a$ or $a\ \theta\ y(A_i)$, for a a constant or another tuple variable component, becomes $y_i\ \theta\ a$ or $a\ \theta\ y_i$, respectively. A quantified subformula $\exists y(S)\ g$ becomes

$$\exists y_1(A_1)\ \exists y_2(A_2) \cdots \exists y_k(A_k)\, g,$$

while $\forall y(S)\ g$ becomes

$$\forall y_1(A_1)\ \forall y_2(A_2) \cdots \forall y_k(A_k)\, g.$$

If $y = x$ and $S = R$, then $x(R)$ at the beginning of the expression is replaced by

$$y_1(A_1)\, y_2(A_2) \cdots y_k(A_k).$$

Example 10.35 The tuple calculus expression

$$\begin{aligned} E = \{&x(\text{NUSED}) | \exists z(R_2)\ (usedon(z) \wedge x(\text{NUSED}) = z(\text{NUSED}) \wedge \\ &z(\text{PTYPE}) = \text{“727”} \wedge y(R_1)\ (pinfo(y) \wedge \\ &z(\text{PART\#}) = y(\text{PART\#}) \wedge y(\text{PARTNAME}) = \text{“coach seat”}))\} \end{aligned}$$

is that of Example 10.16 with the shorthand notation written out. We replace x by x_1, z by z_1, z_2, z_3, and y by y_1, y_2, y_3 to get the domain calculus expression

$$\begin{aligned} F = \{&x_1(\text{NUSED}) | \exists z_1(\text{PART\#})\ \exists z_2(\text{PTYPE})\ \exists z_3(\text{NUSED}) \\ &(usedon(z_1\, z_2\, z_3) \wedge x_1 = z_3 \wedge z_2 = \text{“727”} \wedge \\ &\exists y_1(\text{PART\#})\ \exists y_2(\text{SUBPARTOF})\ \exists y_3(\text{PARTNAME}) \\ &(pinfo(y_1\, y_2\, y_3) \wedge z_1 = y_1 \wedge y_3 = \text{“coach seat”}))\}. \end{aligned}$$

F can be simplified to

$$\begin{aligned} \{&x_1(\text{NUSED}) | \exists z_1(\text{PART\#})\ (usedon(z_1\ \text{“727”}\ x_1) \\ &\wedge \exists y_2(\text{SUBPARTOF})\ (pinfo(z_1\, y_2\ \text{“coach seat”})))\}. \end{aligned}$$

Theorem 10.5 Let E be a tuple calculus expression and let F be the domain calculus expression obtained from F by the translation given above. Then

1. $E \equiv F$ under unlimited evaluation,
2. $E \equiv F$ under limited evaluation, and
3. If E is safe, then F is safe.

Proof 1. Left to the reader (see Exercise 10.27).

2. The equivalence follows from part 1 and the observation that for any attribute A, if g is a subformula of E and g' is the corresponding subformula of F, $edom(A,g) = edom(A,g')$. The equality follows since g and g' mention exactly the same relations and constants.
3. Any place the formation $\exists y_i(A_i)$ occurs in F, it is actually part of a subformula

$$\exists y_1(A_1)\, \exists y_2(A_2) \cdots \exists y_k(A_k)\, g'(y_1, y_2, \ldots, y_k)$$

that was the translation of a subformula $\exists y(S)\, g(y)$ in E, where $S = A_1\, A_2 \cdots A_k$. Let $c_i \in dom(A_i)$ for $1 \le i \le k$, and suppose $I(g'(c_1/y_1, c_2/y_2, \ldots, c_k/y_k)) = true$. By the correspondence of g and g', $I(g(t/y)) = true$ for t the tuple $c_1\, c_2 \cdots c_k$. If E is safe, then $t \in edom(R,g)$. It follows that $c_i \in edom(A_i,g')$. Hence condition s2 of the definition of a safe domain calculus expression is satisified for F. Conditions s1 and s3 can similarly be shown to be satisfied if E is safe.

10.7 REDUCTION OF DOMAIN CALCULUS TO RELATIONAL ALGEBRA

In this section we show that relational algebra with complement is as expressive as domain calculus with unlimited evaluation, and also that relational algebra (without complement) is as expressive as domain calculus with limited evaluation. These results, combined with those of Sections 10.3, 10.4.1 and 10.6, show that relational algebra with complement and tuple and domain calculus under unlimited evaluation are equally expressive. Relational algebra and tuple and domain calculus under limited evaluation are also equally expressive, hence the tuple and domain calculi under limited evaluation are complete.

Theorem 10.6 Let E be an expression over a domain calculus $\mathfrak{DC} = (\mathbf{U}, \mathfrak{D}, dom, \mathbf{R}, d, \Theta)$. Let $\mathfrak{R} = (\mathbf{U}, \mathfrak{D}, dom, \mathbf{R}, d, \Theta, O)$ be a relational algebra with complement. There is an algebraic expression F over $\mathcal{R}$ that is equivalent to E under unlimited evaluation, provided there are sufficient attributes in **U** for each domain in $\mathcal{D}$.

Proof Let $E = \{x_1(A_1)\, x_2(A_2) \cdots x_n(A_n) | f(x_1,x_2, \ldots, x_n)\}$.
For each subexpression g of f we shall find an algebraic expression F_g for

$$\{y_1(B_1)\, y_2(B_2) \cdots y_m(B_m) | g(y_1,y_2, \ldots, y_m)\}$$

where $y_1, y_2, \ldots, y_m$ are all the free domain variables in g and the B_i's are chosen to have appropriate domains.

First, replace domain variables in f so that no variable is bound in two places or occurs both free and bound in f. Next, note that every variable is associated with an attribute, either by a quantifier ($\exists x(A)$ or $\forall x(A)$), or by appearing to the left of the bar in the expression E ($x(A)$). For each domain variable x, if A is the attribute associated with x, let $att(x)$ be an attribute B such that $dom(A) = dom(B)$. Furthermore, let $att(x)$ be chosen such that for any domain variable $y \neq x$, $att(y) \neq att(x)$. It is at this step that the requirement for a sufficient number of attributes for each domain arises.

For any attribute A, there is an algebraic expression for $dom(A)$. One such expression is

$$\langle c{:}A \rangle \cup \overline{\langle c{:}A \rangle},$$

where c is an arbitrary element of $dom(A)$. In what follows, $[A]$ will stand for an algebraic expression for $dom(A)$.

We now recursively define the algebraic expression F_g for each subformula g of f. F_g will be equivalent to the domain calculus expression

$$\{y_1(att(y_1))\, y_2(att(y_2)) \cdots y_m(att(y_m)) | g(y_1, y_2, \ldots, y_m)\}.$$

Case 1 Subformula g is an atom of the form $x \,\theta\, y$, $x \,\theta\, x$, $x \,\theta\, c$, or $c \,\theta\, x$, for x and y domain variables and c a domain constant. Let $A = att(x)$ and $B = att(y)$. The algebraic expressions for these atoms are

$$\sigma_{A\theta B}([A] \bowtie [B]),$$
$$\sigma_{A\theta A}([A]),$$
$$\sigma_{A\theta c}([A]), \text{ and}$$
$$\sigma_{c\theta A}([A]), \text{ respectively.}$$

Note the join in the first instance is necessarily a Cartesian product.

Case 2 Subformula g is an atom of the form $r(a_1 \, a_2 \, \cdots \, a_k)$ where a_i is either a constant or a domain variable. Let $D_1 \, D_2 \, \cdots \, D_k$ be the relation scheme for r. Let $B_i = att(a_i)$ if a_i is a variable; let $B_i = D_i$ otherwise. The algebraic expression F_g is

$$\pi_X(\delta_N(\sigma_C(r)))$$

where

C is the selection condition made up of the "and" of comparisons $D_i = a_i$ for each a_i that is a constant,
N is the renaming $D_1, D_2, \ldots, D_k \leftarrow B_1, B_2, \ldots, B_k$, and
X is the set of attributes $\{B_i | a_i$ is a variable$\}$.

Case 3 Subformula g is $\neg h$. Let F_h be the algebraic expression for h. Then $F_g = \bar{F}_h$.

Case 4 Subformula g is $h \wedge h'$. Let h have free variables $z_1, z_2, \ldots, z_k, v_1, v_2, \ldots, v_p$ and let h' have free variables $z_1, z_2, \ldots, z_k, w_1, w_2, \ldots, w_q$, where $v_1, v_2, \ldots, v_p$ and $w_1, w_2, \ldots, w_q$ are distinct. F_h and F_h' are the algebraic expressions for h and h'. Let $att(v_i) = B_i$, $1 \leq i \leq p$, and $att(w_i) = C_i$, $1 \leq i \leq q$. Let

$$F_1 = F_h \bowtie [C_1] \bowtie [C_2] \bowtie \cdots \bowtie [C_q]$$

and let

$$F_2 = F_h' \bowtie [B_1] \bowtie [B_2] \bowtie \cdots \bowtie [B_p].$$

F_1 is F_h with columns added for all the attributes in $sch(F_h') - sch(F_h) = C_1 C_2 \cdots C_q$. F_2 is F_h' with columns added for all the attributes in $sch(F_h) - sch(F_h') = B_1 B_2 \ldots B_p$. Note that $sch(F_1) = sch(F_2) = \{att(y) | y$ is free in $g\}$. The algebraic expression F_g is $F_1 \cap F_2$.

Case 5 Subformula g is $h \vee h'$. This case is left to the reader (see Exercise 10.28).

Case 6 Subformula g has the form $\exists x(A) \, h$. F_h is the algebraic expression for h. Let $att(x) = B$. Note that $dom(A) = dom(B)$. The algebraic expression F_g for g is simply $\pi_{X-B}(F_h)$ where $X = sch(F_h)$.

Case 7 Subformula g is $\forall x(A)\ h$. F_h is the algebraic expression for h. Let $att(x) = B$. The algebraic expression F_g for g is $F_h \div [B]$. (This one case is the only reason we ever bothered with division.)

Recursively, using these seven cases, we can build up an expression F_f that is equivalent to

$$\{x_1(att(x_1))\, x_2(att(x_2)) \cdots x_n(att(x_n)) \mid f(x_1, x_2, \ldots, x_n)\}.$$

We are not assured that $att(x_i)$ is necessarily A_i, so we need one final renaming operation to actually obtain the algebraic expression F equivalent to E.

Example 10.36 $E =$

$$\{x(\text{PART\#})\ y(\text{NUSED}) \mid usedon(x \text{ “707” } y)$$
$$\forall w(\text{QUANTITY})\,(\neg\, instock(x \text{ “JFK” } w) \vee w \geq y \vee x = 2116)\}$$

is the domain calculus expression from Example 10.32. Let $att(x) =$ PART#, $att(y) =$ NUSED, and $att(w) =$ QUANTITY. To keep things tidy, let F_P = [PART#], F_N = [NUSED], and F_Q = [QUANTITY]. The algebraic expression for $instock(x$ "JFK" $w)$ is

$$F_1 = \pi_{\text{PART\# QUANTITY}}(\sigma_{\text{LOCATION} = \text{JFK}}(instock)).$$

(Renaming is unnecessary in this instance.) The algebraic expression for $\neg\, instock(x$ "JFK" $w)$ is $\overline{F_1}$. The algebraic expressions for $w \geq y$ and $x =$ 2116 are

$$F_2 = \sigma_{\text{QUANTITY} \geq \text{NUSED}}(F_Q \bowtie F_N) \text{ and}$$
$$F_3 = \sigma_{\text{PART\#} = 2116}(F_P).$$

An algebraic expression for

$$\neg\, instock(x \text{ “JFK” } w) \vee w \geq y \vee x = 2116$$

is

$$F_4 = (\overline{F_1} \bowtie F_N) \cup (F_2 \bowtie F_P) \cup (F_3 \bowtie F_Q \bowtie F_N).$$

Adding the quantifier $\forall w$(QUANTITY), we get the algebraic expression

$$F_5 = F_4 \div F_Q.$$

The algebraic expression for *usedon*(*x* "707" *y*) is

$$F_6 = \pi_{\text{PART\# NUSED}}(\sigma_{\text{PTYPE} = 707}(usedon)).$$

The equivalent algebraic expression for E is $F = F_6 \cap F_5$. No final renaming is necessary.

Just for fun, we can write F out:

$$\begin{aligned}&\pi_{\text{PART\# NUSED}}(\sigma_{\text{PTYPE} = 707}(usedon)) \cap\\ &\quad(((\pi_{\text{PART\# QUANTITY}}(\sigma_{\text{LOCATION} = \text{JFK}}(instock)) \bowtie F_N) \cup\\ &\quad\ (\sigma_{\text{QUANTITY} \geq \text{NUSED}}(F_Q \bowtie F_N) \bowtie F_P) \cup\\ &\quad\ (\sigma_{\text{PART\#} = 2116}(F_P) \bowtie F_Q \bowtie F_N)) \div F_Q).\end{aligned}$$

If we look back at the meaning of E given in Example 10.32, we see that a simpler algebraic expression equivalent to E exists, namely

$$\pi_{\text{PART\# NUSED}}(\sigma_{\text{QUANTITY} \geq \text{NUSED} \vee \text{PART\#} = 2116}(usedon \bowtie instock)).$$

Corollary For $\mathfrak{DC}$, $\mathfrak{R}$ and E as given in Theorem 10.6, there is an algebraic expression F over $\mathfrak{R}$ without complement that is equivalent to E under limited evaluation.

Proof The details are left mainly to the reader (see Exercise 10.30).

The proof here is similar to that of Theorem 10.6, with some modifications. The first problem is the correct expression for $[A]$. Expression E can be further modified so that where $\exists x(A)$ or $\forall x(A)$ appear, $att(x) = \text{A}$. Also, in $x_1(A_1)\, x_2(A_2) \cdots x_n(A_n)$, we can choose $att(x_i) = A_i$, $1 \leq i \leq n$, since $A_i \neq A_j$ for $i \neq j$. With this modification of E, any attribute symbol A appears at most once in E. If A appears in $\exists x(A)g$ or $\forall x(A)g$, then $[A]$ should be an algebraic expression for $edom(A,f)$.

The second problem is removing the use of complement from case 3.

The third problem is that the algebraic expression F_g for each subformula g of f will not be equivalent to

$$E_g = \{y_1(att(y_1))\, y_2(att(y_2)) \cdots y_m(att(y_m)) | g(y_1,y_2, \ldots, y_m)\}$$

under limited interpretation, as one might think. Rather, F_g will represent E_g where quantified formulas are given the limited interpretation, but y_i ranges over $[att(y_i)]$, $1 \leq i \leq m$, which may properly contain $edom(att(y_i),g)$.

10.8 TABLEAU QUERIES

This section covers a query system based on tableaux, namely *tableau queries*. Tableau queries are not as expressive as relational algebra, but they can represent any algebraic expression involving only select with an equality comparison, project, and join. With certain extensions, algebraic expressions involving union and difference can be handled. Tableau queries are of particular interest because they can be optimized to minimize the number of joins in the corresponding algebraic expression, although the optimization process can be somewhat expensive computationally. There is a subclass of the tableau queries that can be so optimized efficiently. It is also possible to modify tableau queries to take advantage of FDs and other data dependencies in a database, in a manner similar to the chase computation.

Tableau queries come in two flavors, "untagged" and "tagged." The first flavor is for queries against a single relation. Queries against a multirelation database can also be handled, if the relations are the projection of a common instance. The second flavor is used for queries against multirelation databases where the relations do not necessarily come from a common instance.

We present a class of algebraic expressions we can represent with tableau queries.

Definition 10.6 A *restricted algebraic expression E* is an algebraic expression built up from relations and single-tuple constant relations using

1. select in the form $\sigma_{A=c}$
2. project, and
3. natural join.

Intersection could also be allowed, as it can be expressed by join, and select is not strictly necessary, since it can be expressed by join with a constant relation. While restricted algebraic expressions exclude many interesting queries, there are many queries they can express.

Example 10.37 The query "What are the parts used on a 747?" against the database in Table 10.1 can be expressed by the restricted algebraic expression

$$\pi_{\text{PARTNAME}}(\sigma_{\text{PTYPE}\,=\,747}(pinfo \bowtie usedon)).$$

10.8.1 Single Relation Tableau Queries

This section develops tableau queries for a single relation database. While such queries are not in themselves very interesting, they will serve to demonstrate techniques and proofs that carry over to the multirelation case. Also, single relation tableau queries will serve to represent queries for a multirelation database where all the relations in the database are the projection of a common instance. Since the parts database is getting a little old, we introduce a new database for future examples. The database shown in Table 10.11 describes meals for our little airline. The attributes FL, ME, DT, OP, NM stand for flight, meal, date, option and number. The relation *serves* tells what meals are normally served on each flight. Relation *choice* tells what the different options are for each meal for a given date. Relation *ordered* tells how many of each option have been ordered for a given flight on a given date. Only the portion of the figure to the dashed line is *ordered*. Note that the three relations given join completely. We let *meals* be the relation that is the join of the three relations in the database, which is just *ordered* with the column to the right of the dashed line added.

A *tableau query* is a modified version of a tableau as introduced in Chapter 8. As before, there are distinguished and non-distinguished variables. In addition, there are constants and blanks. Distinguished variables, non-distinguished variables, and constants are collectively called *symbols*. A tableau query also has a *summary*, which is a special row of the tableau. We shall write the summary between two lines above the rows in the tableau query. A tableau query for a relation $r(A_1\ A_2\ \cdots\ A_k)$ must satisfy the following restrictions:

q1. The columns are labeled $A_1, A_2, \ldots, A_k$.
q2. Any variable may appear in only one column.
q3. If a distinguished variable appears in a column, it must also appear in the summary for that column.
q4. Only symbols (no blanks) may appear in the rows.
q5. Only distinguished variables, constants, and blanks may appear in the summary.
q6. If constant c appears in the A-column, then $c \in dom(A_i)$.

Generally, we denote the summary as w_0, and the rows as $w_1, w_2, \ldots, w_n$.

Example 10.38 Table 10.12 gives a tableau query for the relation *meals* that is the join of the relations in Table 10.11.

To evaluate a tableau query Q for a relation $r(R)$, we must extend the definition of a valuation. A *valuation* ρ *of a tableau query* Q is a function from the symbols of Q to domain values such that if α is a symbol in the A-column of Q, $\rho(\alpha) \in dom(A)$ and if c is a constant, then $\rho(c) = c$. Valuation ρ can naturally be extended to map rows of Q to tuples in $dom(R)$, and to map the summary of Q to $dom(S)$, where S is the set of columns of Q where the summary does not contain a blank. We then extend ρ to map Q to

Table 10.11 The Relations *serves, choice*, and *ordered*.

serves(FL	ME)
56	B
56	L
57	D
106	L
106	D
107	D

choice(ME	DT	OP)
B	15 Aug	eggs
B	15 Aug	waffles
B	16 Aug	eggs
L	15 Aug	sandwich
L	16 Aug	lasagne
L	16 Aug	salad
D	15 Aug	pot roast
D	15 Aug	seafood crepe
D	16 Aug	pot roast
D	16 Aug	flounder
D	16 Aug	chicken

ordered(FL	DT	OP	NM)	(ME)
56	15 Aug	eggs	27	B
56	15 Aug	waffles	23	B
56	16 Aug	eggs	50	B
56	15 Aug	sandwich	50	L
56	15 Aug	salad	50	L
57	15 Aug	pot roast	55	D
57	16 Aug	pot roast	60	D
106	16 Aug	sandwich	80	L
106	16 Aug	lasagne	45	L
106	16 Aug	salad	35	L
106	15 Aug	pot roast	40	D
106	15 Aug	seafood crepe	40	D
106	16 Aug	flounder	40	D
106	16 Aug	chicken	40	D
107	15 Aug	pot roast	60	D
107	16 Aug	chicken	60	D

Table 10.12 Tableau Query for the Relation *meals*.

	Q(FL	DT	OP	NM	ME)
w_0		a_2	a_3	a_4	
w_1	b_1	b_2	a_3	a_4	b_5
w_2	106	a_2	a_3	a_4	b_5
w_3	107	b_6	b_7	b_8	b_4

a relation, namely $\rho(Q)=\{\rho(w_i)|w_i$ is a row in $Q\}$. Note that $\rho(w_0)$ is not included in $\rho(Q)$.

Example 10.39 If Q is the tableau query in Table 10.12 and ρ is the valuation shown in Table 10.13, then $\rho(w_0) = \langle$15 Aug pot roast 40$\rangle$ and $\rho(Q)$ is shown in Table 10.14.

Table 10.13 Valuation Table for ρ.

$\rho(a_2) =$ 15 Aug	$\rho(b_1) =$ 57
$\rho(a_3) =$ pot roast	$\rho(b_2) =$ 15 Aug
$\rho(a_4) =$ 40	$\rho(b_3) =$ 60
$\rho(106) =$ 106	$\rho(b_4) =$ D
$\rho(107) =$ 107	$\rho(b_5) =$ D
	$\rho(b_6) =$ 15 Aug
	$\rho(b_7) =$ pot roast
	$\rho(b_8) =$ 60

Table 10.14 Valuation Table for $\rho(Q)$.

$\rho(Q)$(FL	DT	OP	NM	ME)
57	16 Aug	pot roast	60	D
106	15 Aug	pot roast	40	D
107	15 Aug	pot roast	60	D

The *value* of tableau query Q on relation r, denoted $Q(r)$, is the relation

$$\{\rho(w_0)|\rho \text{ is a valuation for } Q \text{ and } \rho(Q) \subseteq r\}.$$

Example 10.40 Let Q be the tableau query in Table 10.12 $Q(meals)$, for *meals* the join of the relations in Table 10.11, contains the tuple $\langle$15 Aug pot roast 40$\rangle$; $\rho(w_0) = \langle$15 Aug pot roast 40$\rangle$ and $\rho(Q) \subseteq$ *meals*, for ρ the valuation of Table 10.13. $Q(meals)$ is the answer to the question "For any meal that flight 107 serves, and for any option available for that meal, how many of that option does flight 106 have ordered for that meal on each day?" $Q(meals)$ is shown in Table 10.15.

Table 10.15 $Q(meals)$.

$Q(meals)$(DT	OP	NM)
15 Aug	pot roast	40
15 Aug	seafood crepe	40
16 Aug	flounder	40
16 Aug	chicken	40

It happens that Q is equivalent to the algebraic expression

$$\pi_{\text{DT OP NM}}(\pi_{\text{OP ME}}(\textit{meals}) \bowtie \pi_{\text{DT OP NM}}(\sigma_{\text{FL}=106}(\textit{meals}) \bowtie \pi_{\text{ME}}(\sigma_{\text{FL}=107}(\text{meals})))).$$

This algebraic expression is equivalent to

$$\pi_{\text{DT OP NM}}(\pi_{\text{OP ME}}(\textit{choice}) \bowtie \pi_{\text{DT OP NM}}(\sigma_{\text{FL}=106}(\textit{ordered})) \bowtie \pi_{\text{ME}}(\sigma_{\text{FL}=107}(\textit{serves})))$$

if *serves*, *choice* and *ordered* are projections of meals.

We can immediately derive a tuple calculus expression equivalent to a given tableau query. Let Q be a tableau query for relation $r(R)$ with summary w_0 and rows $w_1, w_2, \ldots, w_n$. Let S be the set of attributes where w_0 is non-blank. The equivalent tuple calculus expression is

$$E = \{x(S) \mid \exists y_1(R) \in r\, \exists y_2(R) \in r \cdots \exists y_n(R) \in r\; f(x, y_1, y_2, \ldots, y_n)\}$$

where f is the conjunction of the atoms

1. $x(A) = y_i(A)$ where w_0 and w_i have the distinguished variable for the A-column,
2. $y_i(A) = y_j(A)$ where $w_i(A) = w_j(A)$ and $w_i(A)$ is not a constant,
3. $x(A) = c$ where $w_0(A) = c$, c a constant, and
4. $y_i(A) = c$ where $w_i(A) = c$, c a constant.

Expression E is safe, and moreover, is equivalent to an algebraic expression involving at most $n-1$ joins (see Exercise 10.35). Note that the choices for $y_1, y_2, \ldots, y_n$ in r correspond to $\rho(w_1), \rho(w_2), \ldots, \rho(w_n)$ for some valuation ρ such that $\rho(Q) \subseteq r$.

Example 10.41 Let R_m = FL DT OP NM ME. An equivalent tuple calculus expression to tableau query in Figure 10.13 is

$$\{x(\text{DT OP NM}) \mid \exists y_1(R_m)\, \exists y_2(R_m)\, \exists y_3(R_m)\; (x(\text{DT}) = y_2(\text{DT}) \wedge x(\text{OP}) = y_1(\text{OP}) \wedge x(\text{OP}) = y_2(\text{OP}) \wedge x(\text{NM}) = y_2(\text{NM}) \wedge y_1(\text{ME}) = y_3(\text{ME}) \wedge y_2(\text{FL}) = 106 \wedge y_3(\text{FL}) = 107)\}.$$

Note that the atom $y_1(\text{OP}) = y_2(\text{OP})$ could have been included, but would be redundant.

Definition 10.7 Let Q be a tableau query with scheme R and let w be a row of Q. If A is an attribute in R, then w is *matched in the* A-*column* if $w(A) = c$ for some constant c, $w(A) = w_0(A)$ for the summary w_0, or $w(A) = w'(A)$ for another row w' in Q. We call $w(A)$ a *matched symbol*. Let $match(w) = \{A | w$ is matched in the A-column$\}$.

Definition 10.8 Let Q be a tableau query on scheme R. Let d be a database over R with scheme $\mathbf{R} = \{R_1, R_2, \ldots, R_p\}$. Q *applies* to database d if for each row w in Q there is a relation scheme $R_i \in \mathbf{R}$ with $match(w) \in R_i$.

Example 10.42 For the tableau query Q in Table 10.12,

$$\begin{aligned} match(w_1) &= \text{DT OP ME} \\ match(w_2) &= \text{FL DT OP NM} \\ match(w_3) &= \text{FL ME}. \end{aligned}$$

Q applies to the database of Table 10.11. Q would not apply to a database d with database scheme {DT OP, OP ME, FL DT OP NM, FL ME}.

Let Q be a tableau query with summary w_0 and rows $w_1, w_2, \ldots, w_n$ that applies to database d. If the relations of d are all projections of a common instance r, then Q can be evaluated against d as follows. For each row w_i in Q, let $r_i(R_i)$ be a relation in d such that $match(w_i) \subseteq R_i$. For a valuation ρ on Q, we let $\rho(Q) \subseteq d$ mean that $\rho(w_i(R_i)) \subseteq r_i$. That is, ρ maps a portion of w_i containing $match(w_i)$ to a tuple in r_i. We can then let

$$Q(d) = \{\rho(w_0) | \rho \text{ is a valuation for } Q \text{ where } \rho(Q) \subseteq d\}.$$

It should be clear that $Q(d) = Q(r)$. For a valuation ρ such that $\rho(Q) \subseteq r$ it also happens that $\rho(Q) \subseteq d$. For any valuation ρ such that $\rho(Q) \subseteq d$, there is a valuation ρ' such that $\rho(w_0) = \rho'(w_0)$ and $\rho'(Q) \subseteq r$. Valuation ρ' always exists, since if $\rho(w_i(R_i)) = t_i \in r_i$, there is a tuple $t \in r$ such that $t(R_i) = t_i$. We can consistently choose ρ' such that $\rho'(w_i) = t$.

The condition that the relations in d be the projections of a common instance r must hold for $Q(d)$ to be well-defined. The choice of relation r_i for row w_i can affect $Q(d)$ if the condition does not hold.

Example 10.43 Let d be the database shown in Figure 10.2. If Q is the tableau query

$$\begin{array}{c|ccc} A(& A & B & C) \\ \hline & a_1 & & \\ \hline w_1 & a_1 & b_1 & b_2, \end{array}$$

then $Q(d)$ can be either $\langle 1{:}A \rangle$ or $\langle 2{:}A \rangle$, depending on whether r_1 or r_2 is chosen for w_1.

$r_1(A$	$B)$
1	3

$r_2(A$	$C)$
2	4

Figure 10.2

10.8.2 Tableau Queries for Restricted Algebraic Expressions

In this section we shall see how to translate a restricted algebraic expression over a relation r into an equivalent tableau query. By the nature of the operators in a restricted algebraic expression, if any subexpression is identically the empty relation, then the entire expression is identically the empty relation. We shall use $Q_\emptyset$ to denote a special tableau query that always evaluates to the empty relation.

For a given restricted algebraic expression E for relation r, we define an equivalent tableau query Q recursively. Let the relation scheme for r be $A_1 A_2 \cdots A_m$.

Case 1 E is r. Then Q is

$$\begin{array}{c|cccc} & A_1 & A_2 & \cdots & A_m \\ \hline w_0 & a_1 & a_2 & \cdots & a_m \\ \hline w_1 & a_1 & a_2 & \cdots & a_m \,. \end{array}$$

Case 2 E is $\langle c_1{:}B_1\ c_2{:}B_2\ \cdots\ c_k{:}B_k \rangle$, where $B_1 B_2 \cdots B_k \subseteq A_1 A_2 \cdots A_m$ and c_i is a constant in $dom(B_i)$. Q is the tableau query consisting only of a summary w_0, where w_0 has c_i in the B_i-column, $1 \le i \le k$, and is blank elsewhere (see Exercise 10.34).

Case 3 E is $\sigma_{A_i=c}(E')$. Let Q' be the tableau query for E'. There are three possibilities for Q.

a. If $Q'=Q_\emptyset$, then $Q = Q_\emptyset$.
b. If w_0' is the summary for Q', and $w_0'(A_i) = c'$, then if $c = c'$, $Q = Q'$. Otherwise, when $c \neq c'$, Q is $Q_\emptyset$.

c. If w_0' is the summary for Q', and $w_0'(A_i) = a_i$, then Q is Q' with every occurrence of a_i replaced by c.

Case 4 E is $\pi_X(E')$. Let Q' be the tableau query for E'. If $Q' = Q_\emptyset$, then $Q = Q_\emptyset$. Otherwise, let w_0' be the summary of Q'. The summary w_0 for Q has $w_0(A_i) = w_0'(A_i)$ for $A_i \in X$ and is blank elsewhere. The rows of Q are the rows of Q', except if a_i is the distinguished variable for the A_i column, and $A_i \notin X$, then a_i is replaced by a new nondistinguished variable.

Case 5 E is $E' \bowtie E''$. Let Q' and Q'' be tableau queries for E' and E''. Assume that no nondistinguished variable appears both in E' and E''. There are three possibilities for Q.

a. If Q' or Q'' is $Q_\emptyset$, then $Q = Q_\emptyset$.
b. If w_0' and w_0'' are the summaries of Q' and Q'', and $w_0'(A_i) = c'$ and $w_0''(A_i) = c''$ for some A_i, and constants c' and c'' are unequal, then Q is $Q_\emptyset$.
c. Otherwise, the summary w_0 has
   i. $w_0(A_i) = c$ if either $w_0'(A_i) = c$ or $w_0''(A_i) = c$ (if a_i is changed to c in the summary, it is changed everywhere).
   ii. $w_0(A_i) = a_i$ if i. does not apply and either $w_0'(A_i) = a_i$ or $w_0''(A_i) = a_i$, and
   iii. $w_0(A_i) =$ blank elsewhere

   and the rows of Q are the rows of Q' and Q''.

Example 10.44 Let E be the restricted algebraic expression

$$\pi_{\mathrm{FL\,DT}}(\pi_{\mathrm{DT\,ME}}(\pi_{\mathrm{FL\,OP\,ME}}(\sigma_{\mathrm{FL}=56}(\mathit{meal})) \bowtie \pi_{\mathrm{DT\,OP}}(\mathit{meal})) \bowtie \mathit{meal})$$

for the relation *meal* that is the join of the relations in Table 10.11. We shall translate E to a tableau query, combining steps as we go. A query tableau for $\sigma_{\mathrm{FL}=56}(\mathit{meal})$ is shown in Figure 10.3. A tableau for $\pi_{\mathrm{FL\,OP\,ME}}(\sigma_{\mathrm{FL}=56}(\mathit{meal}))$ is shown in Figure 10.4. Figure 10.5 gives the tableau for $\pi_{\mathrm{FL\,OP\,ME}}(\sigma_{\mathrm{FL}=56}(\mathit{meal})) \bowtie \pi_{\mathrm{DT\,OP}}(\mathit{meal})$. Figure 10.6 gives the tableau for $\pi_{\mathrm{DT\,ME}}(\sigma_{\mathrm{FL\,OP\,ME}}(\sigma_{\mathrm{FL}=56}(\mathit{meal})) \bowtie \pi_{\mathrm{DT\,OP}}(\mathit{meal})) \bowtie \mathit{meal}$, and Figure 10.7 gives a tableau query for all of E.

Theorem 10.7 If E is a restricted algebraic expression for relation r, and Q is the tableau query obtained by the method given above, then E is equivalent to Q.

(FL	DT	OP	NM	ME)
56	a_2	a_3	a_4	a_5
56	a_2	a_3	a_4	a_5

Figure 10.3

(FL	DT	OP	NM	ME)
56		a_3		a_5
56	b_1	a_3	b_2	a_5

Figure 10.4

(FL	DT	OP	NM	ME)
56	a_2	a_3		a_5
56	b_1	a_3	b_2	a_5
b_3	a_2	a_3	b_4	b_5

Figure 10.5

(FL	DT	OP	NM	ME)
a_1	a_2	a_3	a_4	a_5
56	b_1	b_6	b_2	a_5
b_3	a_2	b_6	b_4	b_5
a_1	a_2	a_3	a_4	a_5

Figure 10.6

(FL	DT	OP	NM	ME)
a_1	a_2			
56	b_1	b_6	b_2	b_7
b_3	a_2	b_6	b_4	b_5
a_1	a_2	b_8	b_9	b_7

Figure 10.7

Proof We proceed by cases.

Case 1 E is r. The reader should recognize the corresponding tableau query Q as the identity mapping, hence $Q(r) = r$.

Case 2 E is $\langle c_1{:}B_1\ c_2{:}B_2\ \cdots\ c_k{:}B_k \rangle$. If w_0 is the summary of Q and ρ is a valuation of Q, then $\rho(w_0(B_i)) = c_i$, $1 \le i \le k$, so $Q(r) = \langle c_1{:}B_1\ c_2{:}B_2\ \cdots\ c_k{:}B_k \rangle$.

Case 3 E is $\sigma_{A_i=c}(E')$. It should be obvious that Q is equivalent to E for possibilities a and b. For possibility c, suppose t is a tuple in $E(r)$. Then $t(A_i) = c$ and t is a tuple in $E'(r)$. It follows that there is a valuation ρ of Q' where $\rho'(Q') \subseteq r$ such that $\rho(w_0') = t$ and hence $\rho(a_i) = c$. Extending ρ, if necessary, so that $\rho(c) = c$, we see that $\rho(Q) \subseteq r$ and $\rho(w_0) = t$, hence $t \in Q(r)$. Similarly, it follows that if t is a tuple in $Q(r)$, $t \in E(r)$. We conclude E and Q are equivalent.

Case 4 E is $\pi_X(E')$. If $Q' = Q_\emptyset$, then E' is identically the empty relation on $sch(E')$, hence E will be identically the empty relation on X, so Q is correctly chosen. Otherwise, let t be a tuple in $E(r)$. There must be a tuple t' in $E'(r)$ with $t'(X) = t$. Let ρ be a valuation such that $\rho(Q') \subseteq r$ and $\rho(w_0') = t'$. If for any attribute A_i that is projected away by π_X we let $\rho(b_j) = \rho(a_i)$, where b_j is the nondistinguished variable that replaced a_i in Q', then $\rho(Q) \subseteq r$ and $\rho(w_0) = t$, so $t \in Q(r)$. A similar argument shows that any t in $Q(r)$ is also in $E(r)$, so E and Q are equivalent.

Case 5 is left to the reader (see Exercise 10.38).

Although every restricted algebraic expression has an equivalent tableau query, not every tableau query comes from a restricted algebraic expression.

Example 10.45 Consider the tableau query Q in Figure 10.8. Q is not the translation of any restricted algebraic expression using the method previously given. Suppose that Q came from expression E. E must be of the form $E' \bowtie E''$. Let Q' and Q'' be the tableau queries for E' and E''. Which rows of Q came from Q' and which came from Q''? Assume without loss of

$Q(A$	$B)$
a_1	a_2
a_1	b_2
b_1	b_2
b_1	a_2

Figure 10.8

generality that row w_1 came from Q'. Row w_2 must also come from Q', since it agrees with w_1 on a non-distinguished symbol. Likewise, w_3 comes from Q'. No rows come from Q'', so E'' must be a constant relation, which is a contradiction, since Q contains no constants. Hence Q does not come from any restricted algebraic expression (see Exercise 10.39).

The method given for translating restricted algebraic expressions over a single relation also works for expressions over a database d if all the relations in d are projections of a common instance r. If E is a restricted algebraic expression over d, replace each occurrence of r_i by $\pi_{R_i}(r)$, where R_i is the scheme of r_i, and proceed as before. The resulting tableau query Q is guaranteed to apply to database d. Any row w in Q can be traced to a subexpression $\pi_{R_i}(r)$, which means $match(w) \subseteq R_i$. Suppose, for example, that r is a relation on $ABCD$ and $R_i = AC$. The tableau query for $\pi_{R_i}(r)$ is

Q'	A	B	C	D
	a_1		a_2	
w'	a_1	b_1	a_2	b_2

Row w' eventually becomes w in Q. The nondistinguished symbols in w' can never become matched, either through selection or joining. Hence $match(w)$ in Q will be contained in $R_i = AC$.

Example 10.46 Let E be the expression

$$\pi_{\text{OP ME}}(\sigma_{\text{FL}=106,\ \text{DT}=15\ \text{Aug}}(serves \bowtie choice))$$

for the database in Table 10.11. Figure 10.9 shows a tableau query equivalent to E.

FL	DT	OP	NM	ME
		a_3		a_5
106	b_1	b_2	b_3	a_5
b_4	15 Aug	a_3	b_5	a_5

Figure 10.9

10.8.3 Tableau Queries that Come from Algebraic Expressions

Although we shall not characterize all tableau queries that come from restricted algebraic expressions, the following theorem does characterize some of those tableau queries.

Theorem 10.8 Let Q be a tableau query for relation $r(R)$. If Q has at most one matched symbol in every column, then Q can be derived from some restricted algebraic expression by the translation method given.

Proof It suffices to consider only tableau queries with no constants in the summary. If Q has constants $c_1, c_2, \ldots, c_k$ in columns $B_1, B_2, \ldots, B_k$ of the summary, then Q is the tableau query for the expression

$$\langle c_1{:}B_1\, c_2{:}B_2 \cdots c_k{:}B_k \rangle \bowtie E',$$

where E' is the tableau query for Q with all its constants in the summary changed to blanks.

Let $w_1, w_2, \ldots, w_n$ be the rows of Q. For each w_i we form an algebraic expression E_i. Let X_i be the set of columns where w_i has a constant. Let $Y_i = match(w_i) - X_i$. Start with the expression r. For every attribute $A \in X_i$, apply the selection $\sigma_{A=w_i(A)}$ to the expression. Finally, apply the projection π_{Y_i} to get E_i. Let $E = \pi_Y(E_1 \bowtie E_2 \bowtie \cdots \bowtie E_n)$, where Y is the set of columns where the summary of Q is not blank. It is left to the reader to show that E translates into Q by the correct choice of nondistinguished variables at each stage (see Exercise 10.41).

Note that the proof only depends on there not being both a distinguished variable (necessarily matched) and a matched nondistinguished variable in each column. Any number of constants can appear in a column, in addition to another matched symbol.

Example 10.47 Let r be a relation on scheme $ABCD$ and let Q be the tableau query for r shown in Figure 10.10. Q can be derived from the restricted algebraic expression

$$\pi_{AB}(\pi_{ACD}(r) \bowtie \pi_C(\sigma_{B=2}(\sigma_{D=3}(r)) \bowtie \pi_{BD}(r)).$$

The tableau queries Q_1, Q_2 and Q_3 to be used for subexpressions $\pi_{ACD}(r)$, $\pi_C(\sigma_{B=2}(\sigma_{D=3}(r))$, and $\pi_{BD}(r)$ are shown in Figure 11.11.

$A(A$	B	C	$D)$
a_1	a_2		
a_1	b_1	b_2	b_3
b_4	2	b_2	3
b_5	a_2	b_6	b_3

Figure 10.10

Q_1	A	B	C	D
	a_1		a_3	a_4
	a_1	b_1	a_3	a_4

Q_2	A	B	C	D
			a_3	
	b_4	2	a_3	3

Q_3	A	B	C	D
		a_2		a_4
	b_5	a_2	b_6	a_4

Figure 10.11

10.8.4 Tableau Queries for Multirelation Databases

We now modify tableau queries so they can represent restricted algebraic expressions on databases where the relations are not necessarily the projection of some common instance. We associate a particular relation with each row in the query. Actually, we assume that all the relations in the database have distinct schemes, so we simply associate relation schemes with rows.

Let d be a database with scheme $\mathbf{R}$ over R. *A tagged tableau query* Q for d is similar to a regular tableau query with scheme R, except the rows of Q may contain blanks and every row has a *tag*. The tag of row w, denoted $tag(w)$, is some relation scheme $S \in \mathbf{R}$. Row w is blank in exactly the columns in $R - S$. We view a valuation ρ for Q as mapping row w to a tuple over $tag(w)$. The notation $\rho(Q) \subseteq d$ then means that for each row w in Q, $\rho(w) \in s$, where s is the relation in d with scheme $tag(w)$. If w_0 is the summary of Q, we let

$$Q(d) = \{\rho(w_0) \mid \rho \text{ is a valuation of } Q \text{ such that } \rho(Q) \subseteq d\}.$$

Example 10.48 Harking back to the database d in Table 10.1, we can construct the tagged tableau query Q shown in Figure 10.12. P#, SP, PN, PT, NU, LC, and QY are abbreviations for PART#, SUBPARTOF, PARTNAME, PTYPE, NUSED, LOCATION, and QUANTITY. Tags are shown in parentheses to the right of each row. $Q(d)$ is shown in Figure 10.13.

Q(P#	SP	PN	PT	NU	LC	QY)	
				a_5	a_6	a_7	
b_1	211	b_2					(P# SP PN)
b_1			707	a_5			(P# PT NU)
b_1					a_6	a_7	(P# LC QY)
b_1			727	b_3			(P# PT NU)

Figure 10.12

$Q(d)$(NU	LC	QY)
86	JFK	6
86	O'Hare	28
244	Boston	341
244	O'Hare	29

Figure 10.13

The tags are written in Figure 10.12 only for emphasis. They can be inferred from the non-blank portion of each row.

The translation from restricted algebraic expressions to tagged tableau queries is essentially the same as for the single-relation case. The only difference is the tableau query for a single relation s with scheme $A_1 A_2 \cdots A_k$. The tableau for s has a summary with distinguished symbols in the columns corresponding to $A_1 A_2 \cdots A_k$ and blanks elsewhere. It also has a single row that is identical to the summary.

Example 10.49 The tableau query Q in Figure 10.12 is the translation of the algebraic expression

$$\pi_{\text{NU LC QY}}(\sigma_{\text{SP}=211}(\mathit{pinfo}) \bowtie \sigma_{\text{PT}=707}(\mathit{usedon}) \bowtie \mathit{instock} \bowtie \\ \pi_{\text{P\#}}(\sigma_{\text{PT}=727}(\mathit{usedon}))).$$

For a database where all the relations are the projection of a common instance, the tagged tableau query derived from an algebraic expression is equivalent to the untagged version. The two tableaux will be essentially identical, except some unmatched symbols in the untagged version will be blanks in the tagged version.

10.8.5 Tableau Set Queries

The range of algebraic expressions that can be modeled by tableaux can be extended if we allow sets of tableaux to denote a query. In this section we return to regular tableau queries, although the extension described works for tagged tableau queries as well.

Definition 10.9 A *monotonic algebraic expression* E is an algebraic expression built up from relations and single-tuple constant relations using

1. select in the form $\sigma_{A=c}$,
2. project,
3. natural join, and
4. union.

Note that with *union* and *intersection*, selection conditions with $\wedge$ and $\vee$ are possible. Also, *union* can be used to construct multiple-tuple constant relations.

Definition 10.10 Tableau queries Q_1 and Q_2 are *compatible* if they have the same scheme and their summaries are blank in the same columns. A set of tableau queries is compatible if each pair of queries in the set is compatible.

Definition 10.11 A *tableau set query* over scheme R is a set $\mathbf{Q} = \{Q_1, Q_2, \ldots, Q_m\}$ of compatible tableau queries, all with scheme R. For a relation $r(R)$, the *value* of $\mathbf{Q}$ on r, denoted $\mathbf{Q}(r)$ is

$$Q_1(r) \cup Q_2(r) \cup \cdots \cup Q_m(r).$$

Example 10.50 Let *meals* be the join of the relations in Table 10.11. Let $\mathbf{Q}$ be the tableau set query $\{Q_1, Q_2\}$, where Q_1 and Q_2 are shown in Figure 10.14. $\mathbf{Q}(meals)$ is given in Figure 10.15.

Theorem 10.9 Let E be a monotonic algebraic expression. There is a tableau set query Q that is equivalent to E.

Proof By Theorem 10.7, it is sufficient to show that any monotonic algebraic expression E is equivalent to a monotonic algebraic expression

$$E_1 \cup E_2 \cup \cdots \cup E_m$$

where each E_i is a restricted algebraic expression. The equivalence follows because *select*, *project*, and *join* all distribute over *union*.

Q_1(FL	DT	OP	NM	ME)
a_1		a_3	a_4	
56	15 Aug	a_3	b_2	b_3
a_1	15 Aug	a_3	a_4	b_3

Q_2(FL	DT	OP	NM	ME)
a_1		a_3	a_4	
56	16 Aug	a_3	b_2	b_3
a_1	16 Aug	a_3	a_4	b_3

Figure 10.14

Q(*meals*)(FL	OP	NM)
56	eggs	27
56	waffles	23
56	eggs	50
56	sandwich	50
56	salad	50
106	sandwich	80

Figure 10.15

From Section 2.2 we know that

$$\sigma_{A=c}(E_1 \cup E_2) = \sigma_{A=c}(E_1) \cup \sigma_{A=c}(E_2)$$

for expressions E_1 and E_2. Exercise 2.8 a) gives us

$$\pi_X(E_1 \cup E_2) = \pi_X(E_1) \cup \pi_X(E_2).$$

It is not hard to show that

$$E_1 \bowtie (E_2 \cup E_3) = (E_1 \bowtie E_2) \cup (E_1 \bowtie E_3)$$

as well. Repeated application of these identities will transform a monotonic algebraic expression into the union of restricted algebraic expressions. Note that if E contains k unions, m can be a large as 2^k.

Example 10.51 The tableau set of query **Q** of Example 10.50 can be derived from the expression

$$\pi_{\mathrm{FL\ OP\ NM}}(\pi_{\mathrm{DT\ OP\ ME}}(\sigma_{\mathrm{FL}=56}(\sigma_{\mathrm{DT}=15\ \mathrm{Aug}}(meals) \cup \sigma_{\mathrm{DT}=16\ \mathrm{Aug}}(meals))) \bowtie meals).$$

10.9 CONJUNCTIVE QUERIES

Conjunctive queries are a subset of domain calculus expressions. Although they are not as expressive as domain calculus, they can express many useful queries, and do occur as subexpressions in domain calculus expressions. Their main interest, as with tableau queries, is that they can be optimized effectively.

A *conjunctive query* for database d is a domain calculus expression of the form

$$\{x_1(A_1)\, x_2(A_2) \cdots x_n(A_n) \mid \exists y_1(B_1)\ \exists y_2(B_2) \cdots \exists y_m(B_m)\ f(x_1, x_2, \ldots, x_n, y_1, y_2, \ldots, y_m)\}$$

such that f is the conjunction of atoms of the form $r(a_1\, a_2 \cdots a_p)$, where $r \in d$ and each a_i is either a constant, x_j for some j, or y_k for some k.

Example 10.52 The tagged tableau query Q in Figure 10.12 is equivalent to the conjunctive query

$$\{x_1(\mathrm{NU})\, x_2(\mathrm{LC})\, x_3(\mathrm{QY}) \mid \exists y_1(\mathrm{P\#})\ \exists y_2(\mathrm{PN})\ \exists y_3(\mathrm{NU})\ pinfo(y_1\ 211\ y_2) \wedge usedon(y_1\ \text{“707”}\ x_1) \wedge instock(y_1\ x_2\ x_3) \wedge usedon(y_1\ \text{“727”}\ y_3)\}.$$

Every conjunctive query is a safe domain calculus expression. They are as expressive as tagged tableau queries that do not contain constants in the summary (see Exercise 10.45). Conjunctive queries are basically tagged tableau queries where a symbol may appear in multiple columns. Conjunctive queries are easily translated into equivalent algebraic expressions (see Exercise 10.46).

10.10 EXERCISES

10.1 Using the alternative definition of equivalence where expressions must have the same value on all mutually consistent databases, exhibit algebraic expressions E_1, E_2, and E_3, where $E_1 \equiv E_2$ and $E_2 \equiv E_3$, and where there exists a database d that is mutually consistent with E_1 and E_3, but $E_1(d)$ and $E_3(d)$ are relations over different schemes.

10.2* Consider databases with the same scheme as the one in Table 10.1. Prove that there is no expression in relational algebra that denotes the relation r(PART SUBPART′) that contains a tuple $p\ s$ if and only if s is a subpart of p, or a subpart of a subpart, or a subpart of a subpart of a subpart, and so on. That is, s is used somewhere in p.

Many of the following exercises refer to the database pictured in Table 10.16. The *usage* relation gives, for each aircraft type, the number in service, the combined miles of flight (in ten thousands), and the combined hours of flight (in hundreds). The *accidents* relation gives, for each aircraft type and type of accident, the number of accidents and the number of people injured.

Table 10.16 Relations *accidents* and *usage*.

usage(PTYPE	INSERV	TMILES	THOURS)
707	14	7,358	1,839
727	12	6,621	1,642
747	8	3,784	841
A100	3	1,213	397
DC8	21	11,016	2,803

accidents(PTYPE	TACC	NACC	INJURED)
707	takeoff	2	6
727	takeoff	1	3
727	landing	4	17
A100	landing	1	12
A100	inflight	1	6
DC8	inflight	1	26

The domain of INSERV, TMILES, THOURS, NACC, and INJURED is the non-negative integers; *dom*(PTYPE) = {707, 727, 747, A100, DC8, DC10}; and *dom*(TACC) = {takeoff, landing, inflight, taxiing}. The comparators for the non-negative integers are $=, \neq, <, \leq, \geq, >$. The comparators for the other two domains are just $=$ and $\neq$. Let R_1 be the scheme of *usage* and R_2 be the scheme of *accidents*.

10.3 For each of the formulas, state which are legal. For the legal formulas, state for each tuple variable occurrence whether it is free or bound; if it is bound, indicate to which quantifier it is bound. Also for the legal formulas, for each tuple variable that occurs free in the formula, give *type* and *men*. Recall R_1 is the scheme of *usage* and R_2 is the scheme of *accidents*.

(a) $x(\text{PTYPE}) = y(\text{PTYPE}) \wedge y(\text{THOURS}) \geq 1{,}000$.

(b) $x(\text{TACC}) \wedge x(\text{INSERV})$.

(c) $x(\text{TACC}) \wedge usage(x)$.

(d) $\exists x(R_1)\ (usage(x) \wedge \exists x(R_2)$
$(accidents(x) \wedge x(\text{PTYPE}) = x(\text{PTYPE}) \wedge x(\text{NACC}) =$
$y(\text{NACC}))))$.

(e) $\forall x(R_1) \in accidents\ (x(\text{PTYPE}) = y(\text{PTYPE}) \wedge$
$\exists z(R_1R_2)\ (z(\text{INSERV}) \geq y(\text{INSERV}) \wedge$
$z(\text{PTYPE}) \geq x(\text{PTYPE})))$.

(f) $\forall x(R_1)\ \exists x(R_2)\ (x(\text{NACC}) \leq 6)$.

(g) $\forall x(R_2) \in accidents(\neg x(\text{PTYPE TACC}) =$
$y(\text{PTYPE TACC}) \vee (x(\text{NACC}) \geq y(\text{NACC}) \wedge$
$x(\text{INJURED}) \geq y(\text{INJURED})))$.

10.4 Assuming the atoms *true* and *false* are both legal formulas, show that $f(t/x)$ is legal if $f(x)$ is legal.

10.5 Show that if legal formula $f = \exists x(R)g$ has no free variables, then x is the only variable that occurs free in g.

10.6 Using the database of Table 10.16, give the (unlimited) interpretation of each of the following formulas, where R_1 and R_2 are the schemes of *usage* and *accidents*.

(a) $\forall x(R_1)\ (x(\text{INSERV}) < 60)$.

(b) $\forall x(R_1)\ (\neg usage(x) \vee x(\text{INSERV}) < 60)$.

(c) $\forall x(R_2) \in accidents\ (x(\text{PTYPE}) \neq \text{"727"} \wedge$
$(x(\text{TACC}) = \text{"landing"} \vee x(\text{TACC}) = \text{"takeoff"})$.

(d) $\exists x(R_1) \in usage\ \exists y(R_2) \in accidents$
$(x(\text{PTYPE}) = y(\text{PTYPE}) \wedge y(\text{TACC}) = \text{"inflight"} \wedge$
$x(\text{TMILES}) \geq 5{,}000 \wedge y(\text{NACC}) \leq 1)$.

(e) $\exists x(R_1) \in usage\ \exists y(R_1) \in usage\ \forall z(R_2) \in accidents$
$\forall w(R_2) \in accidents\ (\neg(x(\text{PTYPE}) = z(\text{PTYPE}) \wedge$
$y(\text{PTYPE}) = w(\text{PTYPE})) \vee z(\text{TACC}) \neq w(\text{TACC}) \vee$
$z(\text{NACC}) \leq w(\text{NACC}))$.

Hint: There is a join going on here.

10.7 Let f be the formula

$$\exists x(R_3)\ (instock(x) \wedge x(\text{LOCATION} = \text{"JFK"} \vee$$
$$\forall y(R_3)\ (\neg instock(y) \vee \neg y(\text{PART\#}) = x(\text{PART\#}) \vee$$
$$y(\text{QUANTITY}) < x(\text{QUANTITY}))$$

for the database in Table 10.1, where R_3 = PART# LOCATION QUANTITY. Show that $I(f) = false$ for any state of the relation *instock*.

10.8 Using the database in Table 10.16, give the value of $\{x(R_1) \lfloor f(x)\}$ for each of the following choices for f (under the unlimited evaluations). (You can write an infinite relation on a single sheet of paper as follows. Write the first tuple on half the sheet. Write the next two tuples on half of what remains. Write the next four tuples on half of what now remains. Continue in this manner until you have written all the tuples. *Warning*: This method does not work for uncountably infinite relations.)

(a) $f(x) = usage(x) \wedge x(\text{THOURS}) \geq 1{,}000$.

(b) $f(x) = usage(x) \wedge \forall y(R_2) \in accidents$
$(x(\text{PTYPE}) \neq y(\text{PTYPE}))$.

(c) $f(x) = \exists y(R_1) \in usage$
$(x(\text{PTYPE INSERV TMILES}) = y(\text{PTYPE INSERV TMILES}))$

(d) $f(x) = usage(x) \wedge \forall y(R_2) \in accident$
$(x(\text{PTYPE}) \neq y(\text{PTYPE}) \vee \forall z(R_2) \in accident$
$(y(\text{PTYPE}) = z(\text{PTYPE}) \vee y(\text{TACC}) \neq z(\text{TACC})$
$\vee\, y(\text{NACC}) > z(\text{NACC})))$.

(e) $f(x) = \exists y(R_1) \in usage\ (x(\text{PTYPE}) = y(\text{PTYPE}) \wedge$
$\exists z(R_i) \in usage(x(\text{INSERV TMILES THOURS}) =$
$z(\text{INSERV TMILES THOURS}) \wedge$
$z(\text{INSERV}) \leq 5))$.

(f) $f(x) = \exists y(R_2) \in accidents(x(\text{PTYPE}) = y(\text{PTYPE}) \wedge$
$\exists z(R_1) \in usage(x(\text{INSERV TMILES THOURS}) =$
$z(\text{INSERV TMILES THOURS}) \wedge$
$z(\text{INSERV}) \leq 5))$.

10.9 For the database in Table 10.16, give tuple calculus expressions that will provide the answers to the following questions:

(a) Which plane types have no inflight accidents listed?

(b) Which plane type has logged the most miles and how many miles is that?

(c) Which plane types have more hours but less inflight accidents than other plane types? (Assume that there is an attribute PTYPE′ with the same domain as PTYPE and that no entry for a plane type and accident type in accidents means no accidents of that type.)

10.10 Complete cases 3, 5, and 6 of Theorem 10.1.

10.11 Give equivalent tuple calculus expressions for the following algebraic expressions over the database in Table 10.16.

(a) $\pi_{\mathrm{PTYPE}}(usage \bowtie accidents)$.

(b) $\sigma_{\mathrm{PTYPE}=707 \vee \mathrm{INSERV} \leq 10}(usage)$.

(c) $\overline{accidents}$.

(d) $\langle 707{:}\mathrm{PTYPE}\ 12{:}\mathrm{INSERV}\ 1{,}213{:}\mathrm{TMILES}\rangle$

10.12 Let E be the algebraic expression $E_1 \div E_2$, where $sch(E_1) = RS$ and $sch(E_2) = S$. Give a tuple calculus expression equivalent to E in terms of formulas in the expressions $\{x(RS) | f(x)\}$ and $\{y(S) | g(y)\}$ for E_1 and E_2.

10.13 Give a tuple calculus expression E for the database d in Table 10.16 such that $E(d)$ and its complement are both infinite under the unlimited interpretation.

10.14 For the following formulas, let r be a relation on $ABCD$ and S a relation on CDE where $dom(A) = dom(C) = dom(E) =$ positive integers. For each formula f, give an algebraic or tuple calculus expression for $edom(A,f)$.

(a) $r(x) \wedge x(c) \leq 10$.

(b) $\exists z(ABCD)\ \exists y(CDE)\ (z(B) = x(B) \wedge z(D) = y(D) \wedge x(CD) = y(CD))$.

(c) $\exists x(ABCD)\ (x(C) \leq z(C) \vee (z(E) \leq 15 \wedge z(E) \geq 5))$

10.15 Repeat Exercise 10.6 using the limited interpretation of formulas.

10.16 Repeat Exercise 10.8 using the limited evaluation of expressions.

10.17 Give a tuple calculus expression E for the database d in Table 10.16 such that $E(d)$ is finite under both the unlimited and limited interpretations, but such that the value is different under the two interpretations.

10.18 Show that every tuple calculus expression used in the proof of Theorem 10.1, except for case 7, has the same value under unlimited and limited evaluation (provided you did Exercise 10.10 properly).

10.19 Which expressions in Exercise 10.8 are safe?

10.20 Let $r_1, r_2, \ldots, r_p$ be relations on schemes $R_1, R_2, \ldots, R_p$. Let E be any expression of the form

$$\{x(S) | \exists y_1(R_1) \in r_1\ \exists y_2(R_2) \in r_2 \cdots \exists y_p(R_p) \in r_p\ (f(x, y_1, y_2, \ldots, y_p) \wedge g(x, z_1, z_2, \ldots, z_q))\}$$

where

1. f is an arbitrary legal tuple calculus formula with no quantifiers,
2. $\{z_1, z_2, \ldots, z_q\}$ is a subset of $\{y_1, y_2, \ldots, y_p\}$, and

3. g is the conjunction of atoms, where for every attribute $A \in S$ there is an atom $x(A) = z_i(A)$ or $x(A) = c$ in g.

Show that E is safe. Is E safe if some of the $\exists$'s are changed to $\forall$'s? If f may contain quantifiers?

10.21 Prove Lemma 10.1. You may wish to define safe tuple calculus formulas as those satisfying conditions s2 and s3 of the definition of safe expression.

10.22 Let R be a set of attributes. Show that for a legal tuple calculus formula g there is another formula h such that the value of $\{y(R) | g(y)\}$ under unlimited evaluation is $edom(R, g)$, and such that $edom(R,g) = edom(R, h)$.

10.23 Give the unlimited and limited evaluations of the following domain calculus expressions for the database in Table 10.16

(a) $\{x(\text{PTYPE})\ y(\text{INSERV}) | (\exists z(\text{TMILES})\ \exists w(\text{THOURS})$
$(usage(x\ y\ z\ w) \wedge (z \geq 4{,}000 \vee w \geq 1{,}000))\}$.

(b) $\{x(\text{TACC}) | \forall y(\text{PTYPE})\ \forall z(\text{NACC})\ \forall w(\text{INJURED})$
$\neg\, accidents(y\ x\ z\ w)\}$.

(c) $\{x(\text{PTYPE})\, y(\text{INSERV}) | y \geq 10 \wedge \forall z_1(\text{TMILES})\ \forall z_2(\text{THOURS})$
$(\neg\, usage(x\ y\ z_1\ z_2)\ \exists w(\text{INJURED})$
$accidents(x \text{ “inflight” } 1\ w))\}$.

10.24 Which expressions in Exercise 10.23 are safe?

10.25 Give domain calculus expressions to answer the questions in Exercise 10.9.

10.26 Convert the tuple calculus expressions in Exercise 10.8 to equivalent domain calculus expressions, and simplify where possible.

10.27 Prove part 1 of Theorem 10.5.

10.28 Complete case 5 of the proof of Theorem 10.6.

10.29 For each domain calculus expression E in Exercise 10.23 give an equivalent algebraic expression, assuming unlimited evaluation of E.

10.30* Complete the proof of the corollary to Theorem 10.6.

10.31 Which of the tuple calculus expressions in Exercise 10.23 have equivalent restricted algebraic expressions?

10.32 Compute $Q(meals)$ for the following tableau queries, where *meals* is the join of the relations in Table 10.12.

(a) Q(

FL	DT	OP	NM	ME)
a_1	a_2			
a_1	a_2	eggs	b_1	b_2

(b) Q

FL	DT	OP	NM	ME
a_1	a_2		a_4	
a_1	15 Aug	b_1	b_2	b_3
a_1	a_2	b_1	a_4	b_4

(c) Q

FL	DT	OP	NM	ME
57	a_2			
57	15 Aug	b_1	b_2	b_3
57	a_2	b_1	a_4	b_4

(d) Q

FL	DT	OP	NM	ME
a_1		a_3		a_4
a_1	b_1	b_2	b_3	a_4
b_4	b_5	a_3	b_6	a_4

10.33 Give algebraic expressions equivalent to the tableau queries in Exercise 10.32.

10.34 What is the difference between tableau queries Q and Q' below?

$Q(A)$
5
b_1

$Q'(A)$
5

10.35 Let R be a relation scheme and let $A_1 A_2 \cdots A_m \subseteq R$. Consider a tuple calculus expression

$$E = \{x(A_1A_2 \cdots A_m) \mid \exists y_1(R) \in r\ \exists y_2(R) \in r \cdots \exists y_n(R) \in r\ x(A_1) = b_1 \wedge x(A_2) = b_2 \wedge \cdots \wedge x(A_m) = b_m \wedge g(y_1, y_2, \ldots, y_n)\}$$

where b_i is either a constant in $dom(A_i)$ or $y_j(A_i)$ for some $1 \leq j \leq n$ and, g is the conjunction of atoms of the forms $y_i(A_k) = y_j(A_k)$ and $y_i(A_k) = c$, c a constant, in $dom(A_k)$.

(a) Show that E is safe.

(b) Show that E is equivalent to an algebraic expression with at most n-1 natural joins and no theta-joins.

(c) Show that E is equivalent to a tableau query.

(d) Show that if g is an arbitrary formula without quantifiers that may contain atoms of the form $y_i(A_k)\ \theta\ y_j(A_l)$ and $y_i(A_k) = c$, then (a) and (b) can be shown, but not (c).

10.36 Let Q be a tableau query that applies to database d. Assuming the relations of d are projections of a single relation r, show how to derive a tuple calculus expression on database d that is equivalent to Q.

10.37 Give equivalent tableau queries for the following restricted algebraic expressions on the database of Table 10.12, assuming the relations are all projections of a common instance.

(a) $\pi_{\text{OP ME}}(\sigma_{\text{FL}=106}(\textit{serves}) \bowtie \sigma_{\text{DT}=15\ \text{Aug}}(\textit{choice}))$.

(b) $\pi_{\text{OP ME}}(\sigma_{\text{FL}=106}(\textit{serves}) \bowtie \sigma_{\text{DT}=15\ \text{Aug}}(\textit{ordered}) \bowtie \textit{choice})$.

(c) $\langle \text{B:ME eggs:OPTION} \rangle \bowtie \textit{ordered}$.

(d) $\pi_{\text{FL}}(\sigma_{\text{DT}=15\ \text{AUG OP}=\text{salad}}(\textit{serves} \bowtie \textit{choice}))$.

10.38 Prove case 5 of Theorem 10.7.

10.39* Show that the tableau query Q in Figure 10.8 is not equivalent to any tableau query Q' that comes from a restricted algebraic expression.

10.40 Give a tableau query that comes from a restricted algebraic expression, but that is not characterized by Theorem 10.8.

10.41 Complete the proof of Theorem 10.8.

10.42 Repeat Exercise 10.37 without the assumption that the relations are projected from a common instance.

10.43 Let r be a relation on scheme $ABCD$. Give tableau set queries for the following algebraic expressions.

(a) $\sigma_{A=6 \vee (B=7 \wedge C=2)}(r)$

(b) $(\sigma_{A=6}(r) \cup \sigma_{A=7}(r)) \bowtie \pi_{CD}(\sigma_{A=B}(r))$.

10.44 Let E be an algebraic expression involving relation r, single-tuple constant relations, select in the form $\sigma_{A=c}$, project, join, union, and difference. Are there necessarily tableau set queries $\mathbf{Q}_1$ and $\mathbf{Q}_2$ such that

$$E(r) = \mathbf{Q}_1(r) - \mathbf{Q}_2(r)?$$

10.45 Show that there is a conjunctive query equivalent to any tagged tableau query that does not have constants in its summary.

10.46 Show that a conjunctive query

$$\{x_1(A_1)\,x_2(A_2) \cdots x_n(A_n) \mid \exists y_1(B_1)\,\exists y_2(B_2) \cdots \exists y_m(B_m)\ f(x_1, x_2, \ldots, x_n, y_1, y_2, \ldots, y_m)\},$$

where f is the conjunction of k atoms, has an equivalent algebraic expression using renaming, $k-1$ equijoins, and a single projection.

10.11 BIBLIOGRAPHY AND COMMENTS

Codd [1971a, 1972b] proposed relational calculus as the benchmark for query language completeness and showed its equivalence to relational algebra. The concept of safe expressions, as well as the general structure of the equivalence proofs, are from Ullman [1980]. However, Codd's and Ullman's proofs are for the case where relations have ordered columns and no attribute names.

Conjunctive queries are due to Chandra and Merlin [1976], and are the basis for tableau queries introduced by Aho, Sagiv, and Ullman [1979a, 1979b]. Tableau set queries are due to Sagiv and Yannakakis [1978], who also handle the difference operator in a limited form. Klug [1980b, 1980c] has extended tableau queries to handle inequality comparisons.

As the structure of tuple and domain calculus indicates, there is a close connection between predicate logic and databases. Gallaire and Minker [1979] have edited a collection of papers on that connection. Jacobs [1979, 1980a, 1980b] has dealt extensively with the use of logic in database theory.

In Chapter 14 we shall see that there are natural operations on relations that cannot be expressed in relational algebra, thus questioning the aptness of the definition of a complete query system.

Chapter 11

QUERY MODIFICATION

The query processor is a central component in any database system. The job of the query processor is to take a query expressed in the system's query language, analyze it, and perform the file accesses and computations necessary to evaluate the query. Alternatively, it may generate code to perform those accesses and computations, rather than evaluating the query itself. There is generally a package of file management routines available to the query processor for performing the actual file accesses. As part of its analysis, the query processor might modify the query, usually for reasons of computational efficiency.

If the query language is based on tuple or domain calculus, the first modification that generally takes place is the translation of the query into relational algebra (although the algebraic expression may be present only implicitly in some internal representation of the query). The tuple and domain calculi are basically non-procedural query systems: they express *what* the value of a query should be, but do not express *how* to compute the value. We do have methods to evaluate safe tuple and domain calculus expressions directly, but if the formulas involved contain quantifiers, those methods are computationally prohibitive. Algebraic expressions, on the other hand, can be evaluated directly if procedures exist for each of the operators involved. Thus, translation of a query to an algebraic expression is a means to specify how the value of the query should be computed. Note that the translations used in the theorems of Chapter 10 are not the ones used in query processors. Query languages based on tuple or domain calculus usually represent only some restricted subset of the possible tuple or domain calculus expressions. The restricted form of the expressions usually allows more direct translation schemes that produce fairly succinct algebraic expressions.

The next modification the query processor is likely to make is substitution for virtual relations. Relational systems often support two types of relations: *base relations*, which are physically stored, and *virtual relations*, which are defined in terms of the base relations. Virtual relations, singly or collectively, are sometimes called *views*. The virtual relations are not stored, but the users of the system may use them to formulate queries, along with the base relations. During query processing, occurrences of virtual relations within expressions must be replaced by expressions for those relations in terms of the base relations. The result is an equivalent expression involving only base relations.

Example 11.1 In our little airline, pilots are periodically tested by examiners and rated. The information on these tests is kept in three relations,

rp(P# PN BD)
re(E# EN)
rt(P# E# DT RG),

where P#, PN, BD, E#, EN, DT, and RG stand for pilot number, pilot name, based, examiner number, examiner name, date, and rating. We might have a virtual relation *low*, which gives information on pilots with low ratings, defined as

$$low = rp \bowtie \pi_{\text{P\# DT RG}}(\sigma_{\text{RG} \leq 6.5}(rt)).$$

An expression such as

$$\sigma_{\text{PN = Jacobs}}(low)$$

would be modified to

$$\sigma_{\text{PN = Jacobs}}(rp \bowtie \pi_{\text{P\# DT RG}}(\sigma_{\text{RG} \leq 6.5}(rt))$$

before evaluation.

Some relational systems, such as INGRES, enforce integrity constraints and security through query modification.

Example 11.2 For the database of Example 11.1, suppose we wanted to grant only limited access to the rp relation to someone. Say we only allowed him to access tuples for pilots based at JFK or Atlanta. In INGRES, it is possible to stipulate that each time this person uses rp, the selection

$$\sigma_{\text{BD=JFK} \vee \text{BD=Atlanta}}$$

is applied to it.

Modifications are also made because not every algebraic operator may be supported, or some may be supported only in limited form. Some systems support only joins involving a single attribute in each relation. Joins involving multiple attributes in each relation must be converted to a single-attribute join followed by a series of selections. Some systems support only selections involving the conjunction and negation of comparisons. Selections with disjunctions are converted to the union of selections of the restricted type for evaluation.

A large class of modifications are lumped together under the heading of *query optimization*. The purpose of such modifications is to find an expression that is equivalent to a given expression, but whose evaluation will be more time- or space-efficient. "Improvement" might be a better term than "optimization," for it is seldom possible to efficiently find an equivalent expression that minimizes the time or space required for evaluation.

Some optimizations are merely simplifications to remove redundant operations, or to combine two operations into one.

Example 11.3 Using the relations in Example 11.1, if we start with the expression

$$\pi_{\mathrm{PN}}(rp \bowtie low),$$

substitution gives us

$$\pi_{\mathrm{PN}}(rp \bowtie rp \bowtie \pi_{\mathrm{P\#\ DT\ RG}}(\sigma_{\mathrm{RG} \leq 6.5}(rt))),$$

which simplifies to

$$\pi_{\mathrm{PN}}(rp \bowtie \pi_{\mathrm{P\#\ DT\ RG}}(\sigma_{\mathrm{RG} \leq 6.5}(rt))),$$

since $rp \bowtie rp = rp$.

The expression

$$\pi_{\mathrm{P\#}}(\pi_{\mathrm{P\#\ DT\ DG}}(rt))$$

can have its projections combined to get

$$\pi_{\mathrm{P\#}}(rt).$$

Other optimizations are made to take advantage of the form of the operations that are supported by the query processor.

Example 11.4 Suppose there is a "restrict" operation available that performs a selection followed by a projection. The expression

$$\sigma_{\text{DT}=7\text{ Jun}}(\pi_{\text{P\# E\# DT}}(rt)),$$

for relation rt of Example 11.1, requires two invocations of restrict, since the selection follows the projection. However, the equivalent expression

$$\pi_{\text{P\# E\# DT}}(\sigma_{\text{DT}=7\text{ Jun}}(rt))$$

requires only one invocation, since the projection follows the selection.

The goal of all optimization is efficiency of execution. Even if the original query is seemingly written to execute efficiently, translation to another query system, virtual relation substitution and other modifications can yield a result that is not so efficient. Joins are a critical operation for efficiency, since the time required for a join is often proportional to the product of the sizes of the operands. Query modifications that reduce the size of join operands will improve time-efficiency.

Example 11.5 Consider the expression

$$\sigma_{\text{PN}=\text{Jacobs}}(rp \bowtie \pi_{\text{P\# DT RG}}(\sigma_{\text{RG}\leq 6.5}(rt))$$

from Example 11.1, which was obtained by virtual relation substitution. Presumably, $\sigma_{\text{PN}=\text{Jacobs}}(rp)$ has only a single tuple, hence is much smaller than rp. To reduce the time needed for the join, the equivalent expression,

$$\sigma_{\text{PN}=\text{Jacobs}}(rp) \bowtie \pi_{\text{P\# DT RG}}(\sigma_{\text{RG}\leq 6.5}(rt))$$

should be used.

Sometimes constraints on a database can be helpful in optimizing queries.

Example 11.6 Suppose that for the relations rp and rt in Example 11.1 every pilot number that appears in rp must also appear in rt. The expression

$$\pi_{\text{PN}}(rp \bowtie rt)$$

can be replaced by simply $\pi_{\text{PN}}(rp)$. Without the constraint, the two expressions are not equivalent.

Picking the order of evaluation for an expression also falls under the heading of optimization. The query processor must decide which intermediate results to compute first and how to associate and commute operations. If an expression has a repeated subexpression, it may save time to save the value of that subexpression rather than computing it twice. The order that joins are taken in a string of joins is also important.

Example 11.7 Consider the expression

$$\pi_{\text{P\#}}(\sigma_{\text{DT}=7\text{ Jun}}(rt \bowtie \sigma_{\text{EN}=\text{Lewin}}(re))) - \pi_{\text{P\#}}(\sigma_{\text{DT}=8\text{ Jun}}(rt \bowtie \sigma_{\text{EN}=\text{Lewin}}(re)))$$

for the relations of Example 11.1. It may prove profitable to first compute

$$r = rt \bowtie \sigma_{\text{EN}=\text{Lewin}}(re)$$

and then compute

$$\pi_{\text{P\#}}(\sigma_{\text{DT}=7\text{ Jun}}(r)) - \pi_{\text{P\#}}(\sigma_{\text{DT}=8\text{ Jun}}(r)).$$

Example 11.8 Consider the join

$$rp \bowtie re \bowtie rt$$

for the relations of Example 11.1. If this join is evaluated as

$$(rp \bowtie re) \bowtie rt,$$

an intermediate result larger than the final result may be obtained, since $rp \bowtie re$ is a Cartesian product. A better way to evaluate it is

$$rp \bowtie (re \bowtie rt),$$

so that no joins are Cartesian products.

Finally, query optimization includes choosing the method of evaluation. The query processor may have several options as to how to perform a given operation. The option selected may depend on how a relation is stored, and what auxiliary structures exist. A selection can be computed by scanning the entire relation a tuple at a time. However, if an index exists for the attribute on which the selection is performed, the selection can be computed through index look-up. Projection may be implemented with and without duplicate removal. If one projection is nested within another, duplicate removal need only be done at the outermost, if that choice is more efficient. Pointers from tuples in one relation to tuples in another are sometimes maintained to help compute joins.

Although the order of tuples in a relation is immaterial in the formal model, in query evaluation, order is important. Almost every query language allows the user to specify that a result be sorted by one or more attributes. Ordering an intermediate result can make a subsequent operation easier. Union, intersection, and difference can be computed on a single pass through each operand if both operands are sorted in the same order. The ordering of operands also makes a difference as to the best method to compute a join.

Example 11.9 Suppose we want to compute the join $r \bowtie s$ where the scheme of r is AB and the scheme of s is BC. Assume that each relation is stored on disk, with 20 tuples per disk block, and that input from the disk comes only in entire blocks. Assume that r requires 30 disk blocks and that s requires 40 blocks, and that there is room in memory for 5 disk blocks at a time. We shall count complexity by the number of disk accesses made.

If neither r nor s is sorted on B, we cannot do much better than the following method. Read the blocks of s into memory, 4 at a time. For each four blocks of s, we read in the blocks of r, one at a time. joining all possible tuples from the block of r with those in the four blocks of s. Each block of s is accessed once, and each block r is accessed 10 times, for a total of 340 accesses. This method of computing the join can be viewed as one loop nested within another. The outside loop steps through blocks of r, and the inside loop steps through blocks of s.

If r and s are both sorted on B, a more efficient method is available. Assume tuples with a given B-value do not span more than two blocks of r or s. We compute $r \bowtie s$ by considering each B-value in turn, and joining all the tuples from r and s with that B-value. At most, two blocks of r and two blocks of s need be in memory at a time. If we consider B-values in sort order, each block of r and s is accessed once, for a total of 70 accesses. This method of computing the join can be viewed as merging r and s by simultaneously making a single pass through each.

The query modifications we shall cover will not depend a lot on implementation details, for to do so we would have to delve into file management techniques and trade-offs between secondary storage access and computation time. We shall try to use general principles that are valid in most implementations, such as reducing the number of joins or the size of intermediate results improves efficiency. However, the reader should be familiar with file structures and indexing techniques used for secondary storage, to have an intuition for the general principles.

11.1 LEVELS OF INFORMATION IN QUERY MODIFICATION

This section is a short aside to indicate how the range of modifications available depends on the amount of information available on a particular database and the system that supports it. Even if a lot of information is available, it may not be worthwhile to take the time to consult it for every query. For a query that must be evaluated only once, it is counter-productive to spend more time to obtain an optimized version than it takes to evaluate the original query. For a query that is expected to be evaluated many times, a large amount of time spent on optimization can be made up over the life of the query.

At the lowest level of information, nothing is known about the relations in a database but their names.

Example 11.10 The expressions

$r \cap r$,
$\pi_X(r \cup s)$, and
$\sigma_{A=B \wedge B=C \wedge A=C}(r)$

can be modified to the equivalent expressions

r,
$\pi_X(r) \cup \pi_X(s)$, and
$\sigma_{A=B \wedge B=C}(r)$

knowing nothing about the schemes of r and s except what is implicit in the expressions. Note, however, if we are given

$$\pi_X(r) \cup \pi_X(s)$$

originally, we cannot be sure that

$$\pi_X(r \cup s)$$

is a well-formed expression, so we do not allow that modification.

With information about schemes of relations, a wider class of modifications is available.

Example 11.11 Given relations $r(A\ B)$ and $s(B\ C)$, the expression

$$\sigma_{A=a}(r \bowtie s)$$

is equivalent to

$$\sigma_{A=a}(r) \bowtie s.$$

The equivalence does not hold if the schemes of the two relations are reversed.

Constraints on relations allow more modifications.

Example 11.12 If relation r satisfies the FD $B \rightarrow C$, then

$$\pi_{AB}(r) \bowtie \pi_{BC}(r)$$

can be replaced with

$$\pi_{ABC}(r).$$

The usefulness or necessity of certain modifications depends upon the operations supported by a specific database system and what retrieval methods are available for secondary storage. Multiple-relation joins might be implemented as a single operation. If selection is supported only where the condition is the conjunction of comparisons, selections with conditions involving disjunction then must be converted to a union of selections. It is possible in some systems to apply a selection and projection during the retrieval of a relation from secondary storage.

Some modifications depend upon the particular implementation of a database on a given system. The presence or absence of an index can dictate how to evaluate a selection or join. At the highest level of information, the state of the database comes into play. In the join $q \bowtie r \bowtie s$, the relative sizes of q, r, and s can dictate which pair of relations to join first. Even if $q \bowtie r$ is a Cartesian product, it is probably best to evaluate it first if $|q| \cdot |r| < |s|$. The method used to evaluate an expression might depend on which intermediate results are likely to fit in main memory. The decision whether to store the value of a common subexpression or recompute it can also hinge on the size of the relations involved.

11.2 SIMPLIFICATIONS AND COMMON SUBEXPRESSIONS IN ALGEBRAIC EXPRESSIONS

The following equivalences can be used to eliminate useless operations from an expression:

$$\begin{aligned} r \cup r &\equiv r \\ r \cap r &\equiv r \\ r \bowtie r &\equiv r \\ r - r &\equiv \emptyset \end{aligned}$$

where $\emptyset$ is the empty relation with the appropriate scheme. Once the empty relation can appear in expressions, other simplifications present themselves:

$$\begin{aligned} r \cup \emptyset &\equiv r & \pi_X(\emptyset) &\equiv \emptyset \\ r \cap \emptyset &\equiv \emptyset & \sigma_C(\emptyset) &\equiv \emptyset \\ r \bowtie \emptyset &\equiv \emptyset & r[C]\emptyset &\equiv \emptyset \\ r - \emptyset &\equiv r & \emptyset[C]r &\equiv \emptyset \\ \emptyset - r &\equiv \emptyset & \delta_N(\emptyset) &\equiv \emptyset \end{aligned}$$

where C is an arbitrary condition for selection or theta-join, and N is an arbitrary renaming.

Example 11.13 The expression

$$(r - r) \bowtie (r \cup r)$$

simplifies to

$$\emptyset \bowtie r$$

and thence to $\emptyset$.

The equivalences above also apply for an arbitrary expression E in place of r, such as $(r \bowtie s) \cup (r \bowtie s) \equiv r \bowtie s$. In order to apply such simplifications, we must locate common subexpressions within an expression. Ideally, we would like to locate equivalent subexpressions, such as $r \bowtie s$ and $s \bowtie r$. We shall describe a method that detects common subexpressions as well as some equivalent subexpressions that come from associativity and commutativity. As we have noted, detecting such subexpressions is useful for deciding how to evaluate an expression, as well as for applying simplifications.

We shall represent algebraic expressions by *expression trees*. An expression tree is a directed tree with interior nodes labeled by operators and leaves labeled by relations and constants. The outgoing edges from an interior node point to the operands for its operator.

Example 11.14 An expression tree for

$$\pi_X(s \bowtie r) - \pi_X(q \bowtie r \bowtie s)$$

is shown in Figure 11.1.

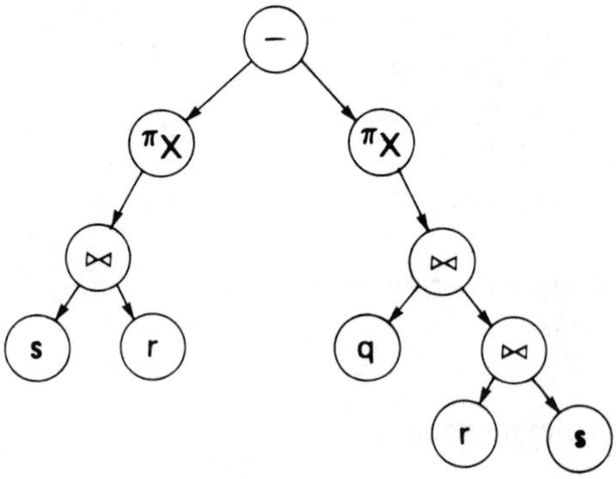

Figure 11.1

The idea is to convert an expression tree into a DAG by first merging identical leaves, and then merging interior nodes labeled with the same operator and having the same operands. For interior nodes with two operands, the order of the operands only matters for difference and theta-join.

Example 11.15 Starting with the expression tree in Figure 11.1, we can merge leaves to obtain the DAG in Figure 11.2. Two join nodes can then be merged to get the DAG in Figure 11.3.

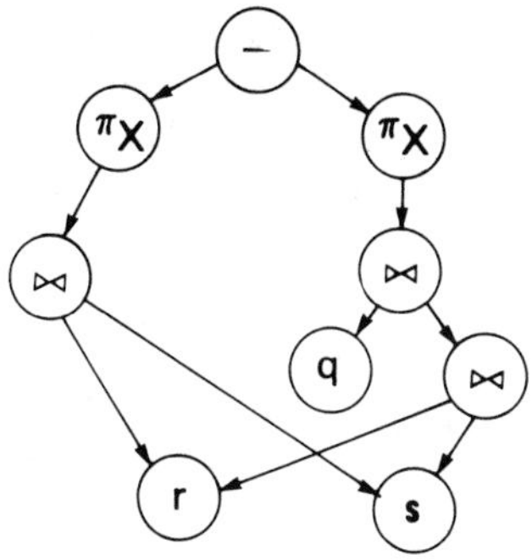

Figure 11.2

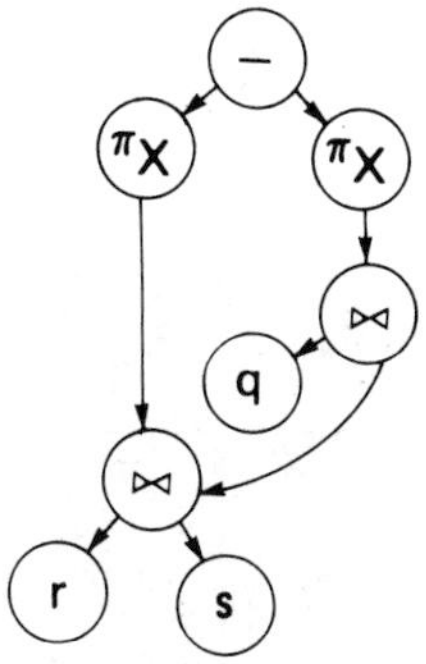

Figure 11.3

If associative operations in an expression are not completely parenthesized, there is a choice as to how to form the expression tree. The choice might preclude finding equivalent subexpressions.

Example 11.16 The subtree for $q \bowtie r \bowtie s$ in the expression tree of Figure 11.1 might have been formed as shown in Figure 11.4. In that case, no common subexpression would be detected.

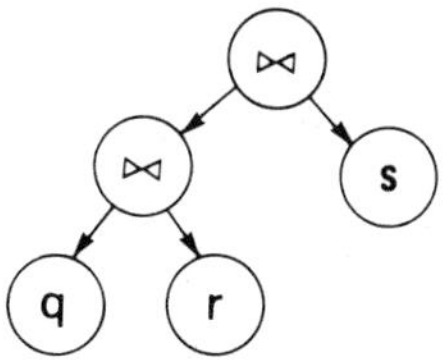

Figure 11.4

To avoid missing subexpressions because of the wrong choice of expression tree, we allow any number of out edges from an interior node representing an associative and commutative operation. If two interior nodes with the same label have sets of operands that overlap by two or more, the overlap can be brought out as a subexpression.

Example 11.17 The expression tree for

$$(r_1 \bowtie r_2 \bowtie r_3) \cup (r_2 \bowtie r_3 \bowtie r_4)$$

is shown in Figure 11.5. A merged version is shown in Figure 11.6.

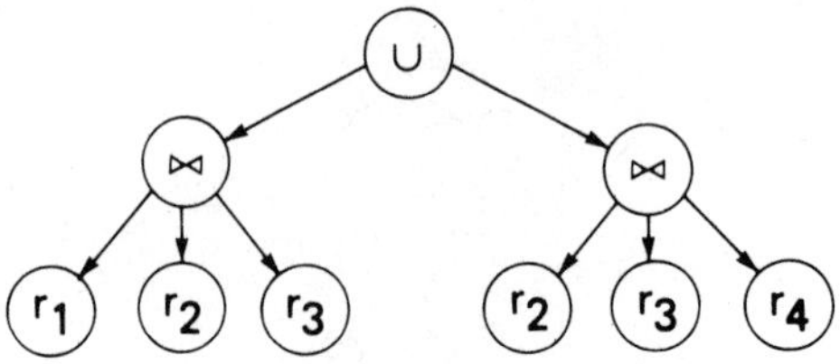

Figure 11.5

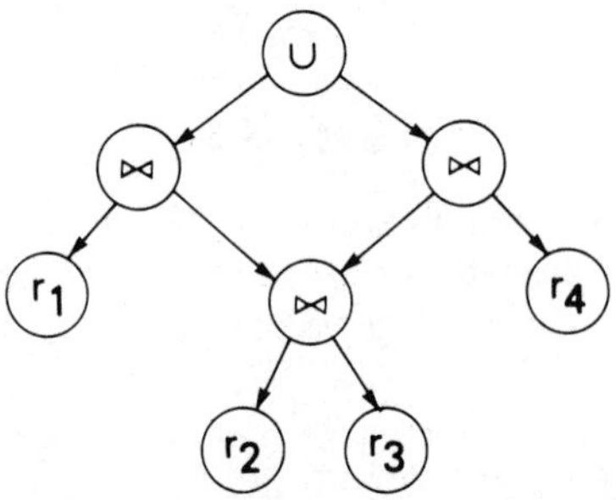

Figure 11.6

Even allowing more than two operands for interior nodes does not guarantee that every common subexpression will be found. Certain choices for merging will preclude others. If the expression of Example 11.17 is actually part of a larger expression that also includes $r_1 \bowtie r_2$, the merging done in Figure 11.6 means $r_1 \bowtie r_2$ will not be identified as a common subexpression. For small expressions, it might be possible to try all mergings in order to detect all subexpressions.

As common subexpressions are detected, we can check to see if any simplifications can be made.

Example 11.18 The expression tree for

$$q \bowtie \pi_X(r \bowtie s) \bowtie \pi_X(r \bowtie s)$$

can have its nodes merged to obtain the DAG in Figure 11.7, which can then be simplified to the DAG in Figure 11.8.

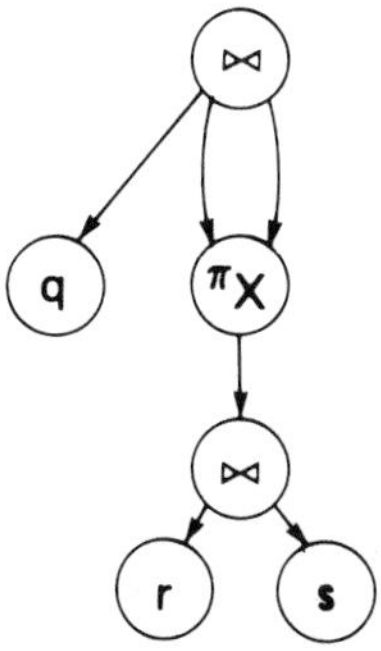

Figure 11.7

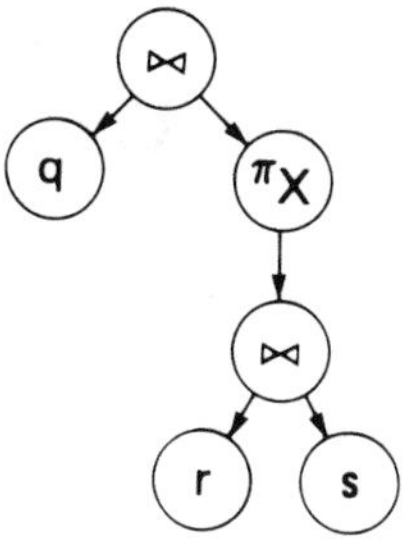

Figure 11.8

There are also simplifications based upon containment, some of which are covered in Exercise 11.1. While containment of relations might be unusual in a database, containment can readily arise at the expression level.

Example 11.19 A DAG obtained from the expression

$$((r - (r \cup s)) \bowtie q) \cup \sigma_{A=a}(s)$$

is given in Figure 11.9. If we can recognize that $r \subseteq r \cup s$, then we can make the sequence of simplifications shown in Figure 11.10.

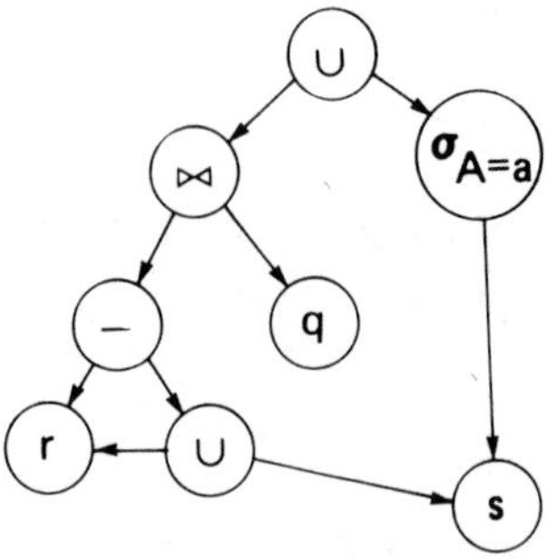

Figure 11.9

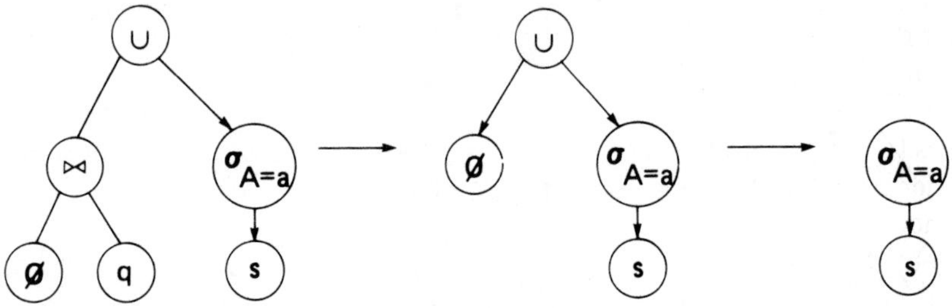

Figure 11.10

Unary operators can be combined to simplify expressions, using the following equivalences:

$$\sigma_{C_1}(\sigma_{C_2}(r)) \equiv \sigma_{C_1 \wedge C_2}(r)$$
$$\pi_X(\pi_Y(r)) \equiv \pi_X(r)$$
$$\delta_{N_1}(\delta_{N_2}(r)) \equiv \delta_{N_3}(r),$$

for the appropriate choice of N_3. Of course, such simplifications may mask common subexpressions. It is possible to apply these equivalences to split an operator and then get a common subexpression.

Example 11.20 In the expression

$$(r \bowtie \sigma_{A=a}(q \bowtie s)) - (r \bowtie \sigma_{A=a \wedge B=b}(q \bowtie s)),$$

it might prove fruitful to split $\sigma_{A=a} \wedge \sigma_{B=b}(q \bowtie s)$ into $\sigma_{B=b}(\sigma_{A=a}(q \bowtie s))$ to exploit the subexpression $\sigma_{A=a}(q \bowtie s)$.

11.3 OPTIMIZING ALGEBRAIC EXPRESSIONS

For the optimizations presented in this chapter, the general principle is that the time and space required to perform a binary operation grows with the number of tuples in each operand and the size of the scheme of each operand. The strategy we employ here is to push selections and projections down the expression tree. Pushing selections down reduces the number of tuples in the operands of binary operations. Pushing projections down also reduces the number of tuples and it decreases the size of schemes. Also, as a general principle, we want to perform selections before projections, because selection requires at most a single pass through a relation, while projection can require sorting to remove duplicates.

Our goal is to start with an expression tree, push selections and projections as far down the tree as possible, and combine projections and selections such that in any path down the tree, between any two nodes for binary operations there is at most one projection and one selection node. The intuition here comes from the way an expression tree (or DAG) might be evaluated. For any interior node whose operands are all relations, we evaluate the operation at the node, store the result in a temporary relation, and replace the interior node by a leaf labeled with that relation. The process is repeated until only a single leaf is left in the tree.

Example 11.21 Consider the expression tree in Figure 11.11. We compute $s_1 = r_1 \bowtie r_2$ and modify the tree as shown in Figure 11.12. We next compute $s_2 = \pi_X(s_1)$ and modify the tree as shown in Figure 11.13. The evaluation is completed by computing $s_3 = s_2 \bowtie r_3$.

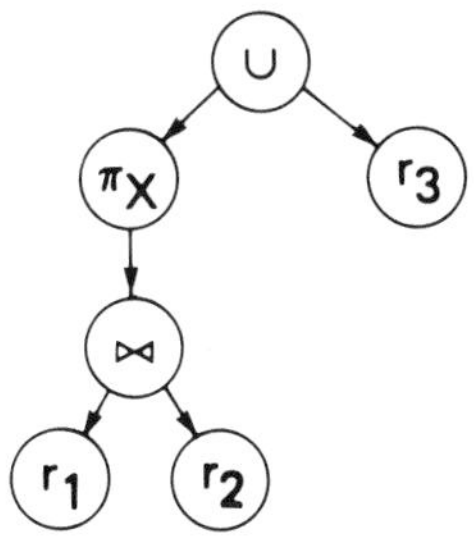

Figure 11.11

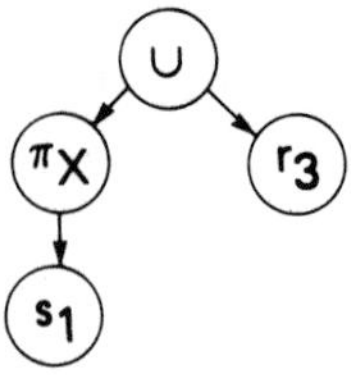

Figure 11.12

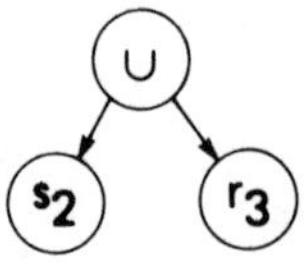

Figure 11.13

The reason for wanting a single projection and selection between nodes for binary operations is that the unary operations can easily be performed at the same time as the preceding or following binary operation. When retrieving tuples from a relation for binary operations, it is a simple matter to drop attributes or screen out tuples to perform projection or selection. The same can be done when storing tuples that are the result of the binary operation. In addition, the file manager might be able to remove duplicates during storage.

Example 11.22 In Example 11.21, the projection can be combined with the subsequent join, and the temporary relation s_2 need not be stored.

Below we give the equivalences that can be used to push selection down an expression tree. We assume that theta-join $r[C]s$ is transformed to $\sigma_C(r \bowtie s)$, where the natural join is necessarily a Cartesian product. The equivalences are

$$\sigma_C(\pi_X(r)) \equiv \pi_X(\sigma_C(r))$$
$$\sigma_C(\delta_N(r)) \equiv \delta_N(\sigma_{C'}(r))$$
$$\sigma_C(r \cup s) \equiv \sigma_C(r) \cup \sigma_C(s)$$
$$\sigma_C(r \cap s) \equiv \sigma_C(r) \cap \sigma_C(s)$$
$$\sigma_C(r - s) \equiv \sigma_C(r) - \sigma_C(s),$$

where condition C' is condition C with appropriate renamings. Joins present a problem, since C might contain comparisons that involve attributes in both relations. Given relations $r(R)$ and $s(S)$, suppose C can be written as $C_1 \wedge C_2 \wedge C_3$, where C_2 applies only to attributes in R and C_3 applies only to attributes in S. We then have the equivalence

$$\sigma_{C_1 \wedge C_2 \wedge C_3}(r \bowtie s) \equiv \sigma_{C_1}(\sigma_{C_2}(r) \bowtie \sigma_{C_3}(s)).$$

Example 11.23 Let q, r, and s be relations with schemes AB, BC, and CD. Then the expression

$$\sigma_{B \leq C \wedge C=4 \wedge D<A}(q \bowtie r \bowtie s)$$

can be modified to

$$\sigma_{D<A}(q \bowtie \sigma_{B \leq C \wedge C=4}(r) \bowtie \sigma_{C=4}(s)).$$

Note that

$$\sigma_{D<A}(q \bowtie \sigma_{B \leq C}(r) \bowtie \sigma_{C=4}(s))$$

is also an equivalent expression, but we always choose to push selection down as many branches of the expression tree as possible.

All of the equivalences above for selection, of course, work when relations r and s are replaced by arbitrary algebraic expressions E_1 and E_2. The following equivalences are used to push projection down the expression tree:

$$\pi_X(\delta_N(r)) \equiv \delta_N(\pi_{X'}(r))$$
$$\pi_X(\sigma_C(r)) \equiv \pi_X(\sigma_C(\pi_{XY}(r))$$
$$\pi_X(r \cup s) \equiv \pi_X(r) \cup \pi_X(s),$$

where X' is the appropriate renaming of X, and Y is the smallest set of attributes such that XY contains all the attributes mentioned in C. Note that projection cannot be pushed past an intersection or difference. Join, once again, is a little tricky. Let R and S be the relation schemes of r and s. Let $R' = R \cap XS$ and $S' = S \cap XR$. We can then use the equivalence

$$\pi_X(r \bowtie s) \equiv \pi_X(\pi_{R'}(r) \bowtie \pi_{S'}(s)).$$

We must retain all the attributes in X plus all the attributes in $R \cap S$. As before, the equivalences hold with expressions substituted for relations.

Algebraic optimization proceeds by using the equivalences above to push selections and projections down the expression tree as far as possible. Where there is a conflict between pushing a selection or pushing a projection, the selection goes lower than the projection, for reasons already discussed. A project-select-project sequence is simplified to a project-select sequence. Any projections onto the entire scheme of an operand are removed.

Example 11.24 Consider the following expression using the relations of Example 11.1, which gives all the pilots that have been given a low rating by Randolph and who are based in the same place as some other pilot who has been given a low rating since 1 June.

$$\pi_{\mathrm{PN}}(\sigma_{\mathrm{PN} \neq \mathrm{PN}'}(\sigma_{\mathrm{EN}=\mathrm{Randolph} \wedge \mathrm{RG} \leq 6.5}(rp \bowtie re \bowtie rt)$$
$$\bowtie \pi_{\mathrm{PN}'\ \mathrm{BD}}(\delta_{\mathrm{PN} \leftarrow \mathrm{PN}'}(\sigma_{\mathrm{DT} \geq 1\ \mathrm{June} \wedge \mathrm{RG} \leq 6.5}(rp \bowtie rt))))).$$

The expression tree for this expression is shown in Figure 11.14. The topmost selection cannot be pushed through the join, but the other two selections can be pushed downward through joins, as shown in Figure 11.15. Figure 11.16 shows the topmost projection pushed down through a selection and join. Figure 11.17 shows projections pushed further down the tree, and the next-to-topmost projection removed. If we do not worry about removing duplicates in the two projections that lie below all binary operations, and perform the three-way join as two binary joins, then the tree in Figure 11.17 can be evaluated in four stages. If duplicates are eliminated for those projections, then the tree can be evaluated in six stages:

$$r_1 \leftarrow \pi_{\mathrm{P\#\ E\#\ RG}}(\sigma_{\mathrm{RG} \geq 6.5}(rt))$$
$$r_2 \leftarrow \sigma_{\mathrm{EN}=\mathrm{Randolph}}(re) \bowtie r_1$$
$$r_3 \leftarrow \pi_{\mathrm{PN\ BD}}(rp \bowtie r_2)$$
$$r_4 \leftarrow \sigma_{\mathrm{P\#}}(\sigma_{\mathrm{DT} \geq 1\ \mathrm{June} \wedge RG \leq 6.5}(rt))$$
$$r_5 \leftarrow \delta_{\mathrm{PN} \leftarrow \mathrm{PN}'}(\pi_{\mathrm{PN\ BD}}(rp \bowtie r_4))$$
$$r_6 \leftarrow \pi_{\mathrm{PN}}(\sigma_{\mathrm{PN} \neq \mathrm{PN}'}(r_3 \bowtie r_5)).$$

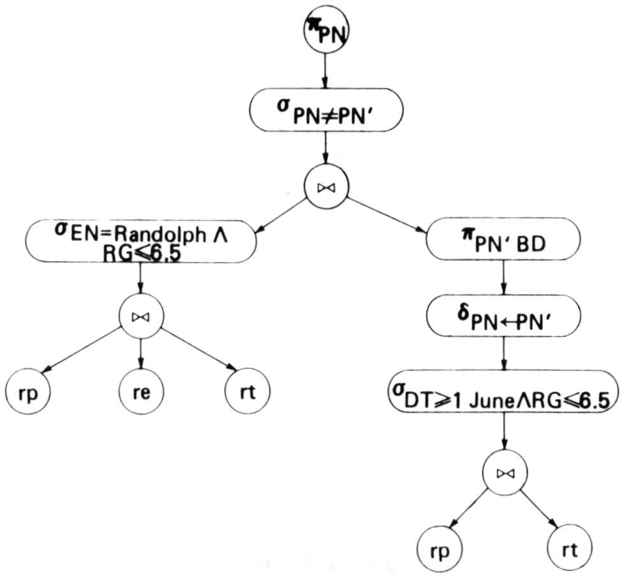

Figure 11.14

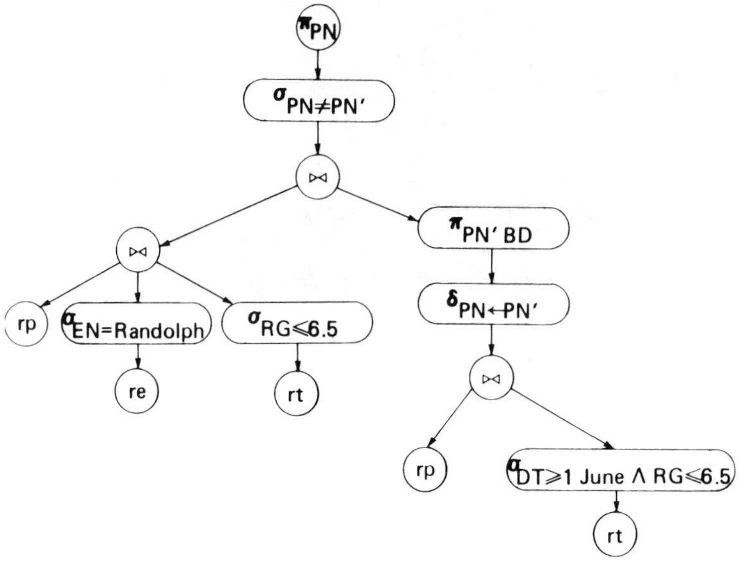

Figure 11.15

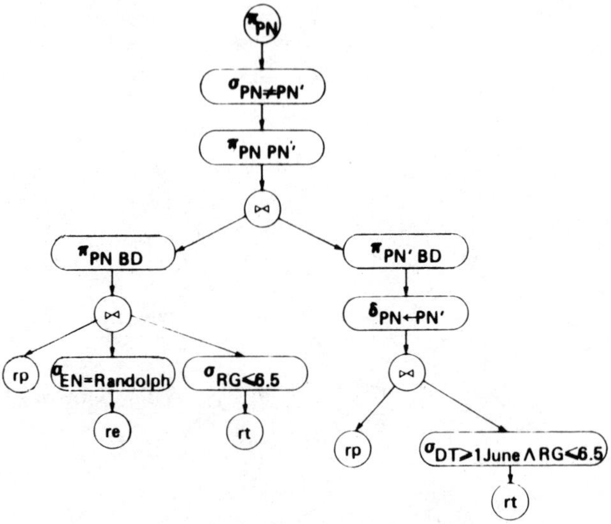

Figure 11.16

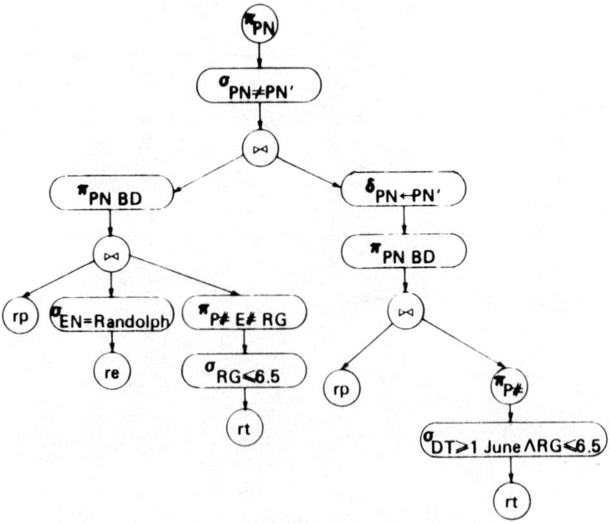

Figure 11.17

The interaction between finding common subexpressions and algebraic optimization is complex. Certainly, performing algebraic optimizations can mask common subexpressions. In Example 11.24, the common subexpression $rp \bowtie rt$ is present in the original tree but not in the optimized tree. However, it is not obvious that computing $rp \bowtie rt$ and using the result in two subtrees saves any time over the optimized version. There is also a problem in pushing selections and projections down a DAG, since one node can represent the operand of multiple operations. It would seem best to optimize first and then look for common subexpressions. The optimized expression may even contain common subexpressions that were not present in the original expression.

Example 11.25 Let q, r and s be relations on schemes AB, BC, and CD. The expression

$$(q \bowtie r) - \pi_{ABC}(q \bowtie \sigma_{D=d}(r \bowtie s))$$

has no common subexpressions. The optimized version of the expression,

$$(q \bowtie r) - \pi_{ABC}(q \bowtie r \bowtie \pi_C(\sigma_{D=d}(s)))$$

has the common subexpression $q \bowtie r$.

We state again that "optimization" is somewhat of a misnomer for what we are doing. Pushing selections and projections down a tree is a heuristic; there is no guarantee that the modified expression will actually save any time or space for a particular state of the database.

11.4 QUERY DECOMPOSITION

This section deals with a method for evaluating queries that is used by the QUEL query processor in the INGRES relational database system. The goal is to reduce each query to a program involving only assignment, selection, projection, and **for**-loops. The INGRES algorithm also uses recursive calls, but we shall use assignments in their place for simplicity.

The decomposition method works on a class of queries described by tuple calculus expressions of the form

$$\{x(A_1 A_2 \cdots A_n) | \exists y_1(R_1) \in r_1 \ \exists y_2(R_2) \in r_2 \cdots \exists y_m(R_m) \in r_m \\ (f(x, y_1, y_2, \ldots, y_m) \wedge g(y_1, y_2, \ldots, y_m))\}.$$

The formula f is a conjunction of atoms. For each i, $1 \leq i \leq n$, it contains the atoms $x(A_i) = y_j(B)$ for some y_j and some attribute B. The formula g contains no quantifiers, nor atoms of the form $r(z)$. Such a tuple calculus expression can be easily translated to an equivalent algebraic expression. Let s_i stand for $\delta_{N_i}(r_i)$, where N_i renames each attribute B in R_i to "$y_i.B$". The equivalent algebraic expression has the form

$$\delta_N(\pi_X(\sigma_C(s_1 \bowtie s_2 \bowtie \cdots \bowtie s_m))).$$

For each atom $x(A_i) = y_j(B)$ in f, N includes $A_i \leftarrow y_j.B$ and X contains B. C is the selection condition obtained from g by converting each atom $y_i(A)\ \theta\ y_j(B)$ to the comparison $y_1.A\ \theta\ y_j.B$. Note that by the way attributes are named in the s_i's, all the joins are Cartesian products.

Example 11.26 Consider the expression

$$\{x(\text{PN RG}) \mid \exists y_1(\text{P\# PN BD}) \in rp\ \exists y_2(\text{P\# E\# DT RG}) \in rt$$
$$((x(\text{PN}) = y_1(\text{PN}) \wedge x(\text{RG}) = y_2(\text{RG})) \wedge$$
$$(y_1(\text{BD}) = \text{“JFK”} \wedge y_1(\text{P\#}) = y_2(\text{P\#}) \wedge y_2(\text{RG}) > 9))\},$$

using the relations rp and rt from Example 11.1. An equivalent algebraic expression is

$$\delta_{\text{PN}\leftarrow y_1.\text{PN},\text{RG}\leftarrow y_2.\text{RG}}(\pi_{y_1.\text{PN}\ y_2.\text{RG}}$$
$$(\sigma_{y_1.\text{BD}=\text{“JFK”}\wedge y_1.\text{P\#}=y_2.\text{P\#}\wedge y_2.\text{RG}>9}(rp' \bowtie rt'))).$$

where rp' and rt' are rp and rt with appropriate renamings.

We shall present a graphical representation of algebraic expressions of the form

$$\sigma_C(s_1 \bowtie s_2 \bowtie \cdots \bowtie s_m),$$

but first we need to massage C into a certain form.

Definition 11.1 A selection condition C is in *conjunctive normal form* (CNF) if it has the form $C_1 \wedge C_2 \wedge \cdots \wedge C_k$ where no C_i contains $\wedge$ and negation applies only to individual comparisons.

An arbitrary selection condition C can easily be put in CNF. First, apply the following two identities (De Morgan's Laws) to move negations inward until they apply to individual comparisons:

1. $\neg(C_1 \wedge C_2) = \neg C_1 \vee \neg C_2$
2. $\neg(C_1 \vee C_2) = \neg C_1 \wedge \neg C_2$.

Next, apply the following equalities to distribute $\vee$ over $\wedge$:

3. $(C_1 \wedge C_2) \vee C_3 = (C_1 \vee C_3) \wedge (C_2 \vee C_3)$
4. $(C_1 \vee (C_2 \wedge C_3) = (C_1 \vee C_2) \wedge (C_1 \vee C_3)$.

Example 11.27 Starting with the selection condition

$$\neg((A_1 = A_2 \vee A_2 < a) \vee \neg(A_1 = A_3 \vee A_3 = a)),$$

we move the first negation inward to get

$$\neg(A_1 = A_2 \vee A_2 < a) \wedge (A_1 = A_3 \vee A_3 = a).$$

Moving negation inward once more, we get

$$(\neg A_1 = A_2 \wedge \neg A_2 < a) \wedge (A_1 = A_3 \vee A_3 = a)),$$

which has negation applying only to individual comparisons. We can then distribute to get

$$(\neg A_1 = A_2 \vee (A_1 = A_3 \vee A_3 = a))$$
$$\wedge (\neg A_2 < a \vee (A_1 = A_3 \vee A_3 = a)),$$

which is in CNF.

Let E be the algebraic expression

$$\sigma_C(s_1 \bowtie s_2 \bowtie \cdots \bowtie s_m),$$

where $C = C_1 \wedge C_2 \wedge \cdots \wedge C_k$ is in CNF and the joins are all Cartesian products. We represent E by a labeled hypergraph H_E, called the *connection graph* for E. In a hypergraph, edges may contain one or more nodes, rather than just two as in regular graphs. H_E has a node for each of $s_1, s_2, \ldots, s_m$. H_E contains an edge e_i for each conjunct C_i. Edge e_i contains node s_j if $y_j.B$ appears in C_i for some attribute B. Edge e_i is labeled by C_i.

Example 11.28 Let E be the algebraic expression

$$\sigma_C(s_1 \bowtie s_2 \bowtie s_3 \bowtie s_4 \bowtie s_5)$$

where C is the selection condition

$$y_1.A = y_2.A \wedge y_1.B = y_2.B \wedge y_3.D = d \wedge$$
$$(y_2.G = y_3.G \vee y_2.F < y_4.F) \wedge y_4.A < y_5.A.$$

The connection graph H_E for E is shown in Figure 11.18. Edges are depicted with dashed lines. Note that two edges can have the same nodes, but the edges will have different labels.

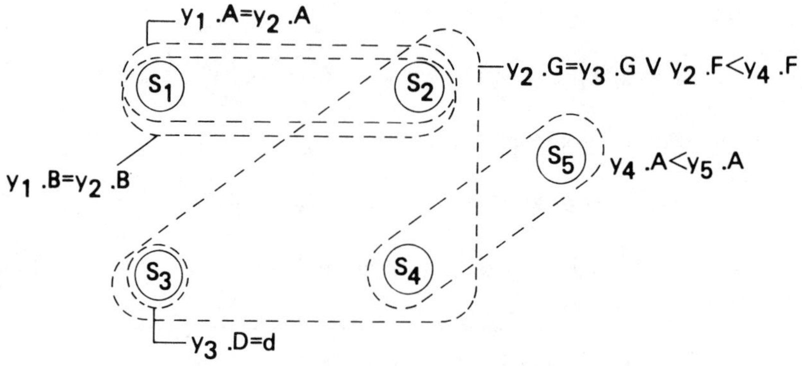

Figure 11.18

In all subsequent examples, edges will have at most two nodes, for simplicity. We shall draw the connection graphs as regular graphs. An edge containing only one node is represented as a loop from the node to itself.

Query decomposition starts with a one-statement program of the form

$$r \leftarrow \pi_X \sigma_C(s_1 \bowtie s_2 \bowtie \cdots \bowtie s_m),$$

where the schemes of the s_i's are disjoint. The end result is a multiple-statement program that contains assignment, selection, projection, and **for**-loops, but no joins. The joins are performed via **for**-loops instead. Two transformations on programs, called *instantiation* and *iteration*, are used to achieve that goal. The transformations correspond to edge removal and node removal in connection graphs, and the goal is to transform the connection graph for

$\sigma_C(s_1 \bowtie s_2 \bowtie \cdots \bowtie s_m)$ to a graph with no edges. We examine each transformation in detail.

11.4.1 Instantiation

Instantiation is analogous to pushing selections down an expression tree. We start with the statement

$$r \leftarrow \pi_X\, \sigma_C(s_1 \bowtie s_2 \bowtie \cdots \bowtie s_m),$$

where $C = C_1 \wedge C_2 \wedge \cdots \wedge C_k$ is a CNF selection condition. Let E denote the expression.

$$\sigma_C(s_1 \bowtie s_2 \bowtie \cdots \bowtie s_m).$$

Instantiation starts with the choice of some subset of the relations $\{s_1, s_2, \ldots, s_m\}$ to instantiate. Suppose we choose $\{s_1, s_2, \ldots, s_p\}$. Let $e_1, e_2, \ldots, e_q$ be the edges in H_E that consist only of nodes in $\{s_1, s_2, \ldots, s_p\}$. Recall that edge e_i is labeled with conjunct C_i. The transformed program for this instantiation has two statements:

$$r' \leftarrow \pi_Y(\sigma_{C_1 \wedge C_2 \wedge \cdots \wedge C_q}(s_1 \bowtie s_2 \bowtie \cdots \bowtie s_p));$$
$$r \leftarrow \pi_X(\sigma_{C_{q+1} \wedge C_{q+2} \wedge \cdots \wedge C_k}(r' \bowtie s_{p+1} \bowtie s_{p+2} \bowtie \cdots \bowtie s_m)).$$

Y is the set of attributes in relations $s_1, s_2, \ldots, s_p$ that are mentioned in $C_{q+1}, C_{q+2}, \ldots, C_k$ or contained in X. Relation r' is a temporary relation to hold the intermediate result.

The corresponding change in the connection graph substitutes r' for $s_1, s_2, \ldots, s_k$ in the edges $e_{q+1}, e_{q+2}, \ldots, e_k$. The result is a graph with two components, one with nodes $s_1, s_2, \ldots, s_p$ and edges $e_1, e_2, \ldots, e_q$, and the other with nodes $r', s_{p+1}, s_{p+2}, \ldots, s_m$ and modified edges $e_{q+1}, e_{q+2}, \ldots, e_k$.

Example 11.29 Consider the statement

$$r \leftarrow \pi_{y_1.A\; y_3.B\; y_4.G}(\sigma_C(s_1 \bowtie s_2 \bowtie s_3 \bowtie s_4))$$

where

$$C \text{ is } y_1.A = y_2.A \wedge y_2.A = y_3.A \wedge y_2.B \leq y_3.B$$
$$\wedge\, y_3.D \leq y_4.D \wedge y_4.F = 6.$$

The connection graph for the selection is shown in Figure 11.19. Instantiating on $\{s_2, s_3\}$ gives the statements

$$r' \leftarrow \pi_{y_2.A\, y_3.B\, y_3.D}(\sigma_{C'}(s_2 \bowtie s_3));$$
$$r \leftarrow \pi_{y_1.A\, y_3.B\, y_4.G}(\sigma_{C''}(r' \bowtie s_1 \bowtie s_4)),$$

where

C' is $y_2.A = y_3.A \wedge y_2.B \leq y_3.B$ and
C'' is $y_1.A = y_2.A \wedge y_3.D \leq y_4.D \wedge y_4.F = 6$.

The modified connection graph is shown in Figure 11.20.

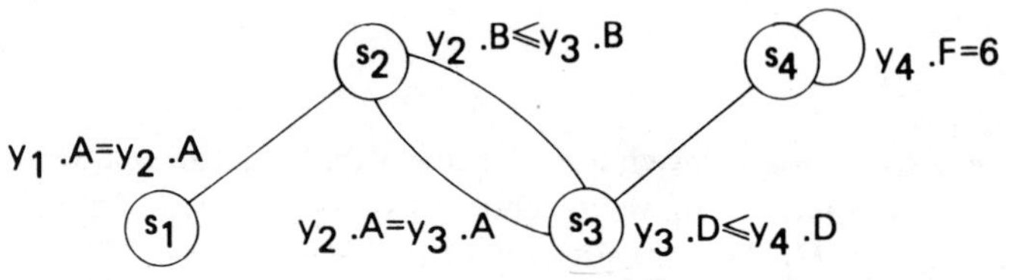

Figure 11.19

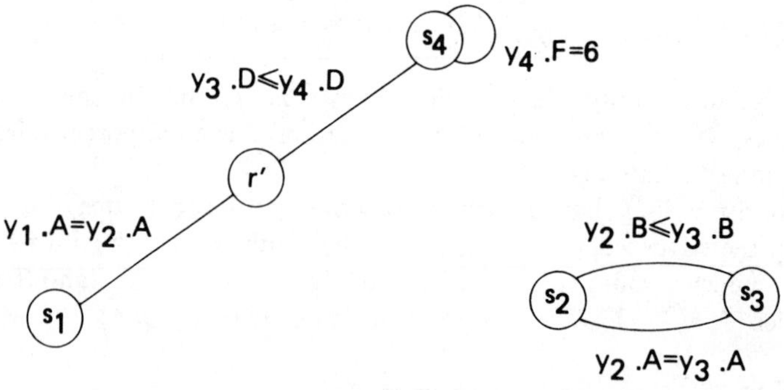

Figure 11.20

A useful special case is where a single relation, say s_1, is chosen for instantiation. In that case the two statements in the transformed program are

$$r' \leftarrow \pi_Y(\sigma_{C_1 \wedge C_2 \wedge \cdots \wedge C_q}(s_1));$$
$$r \leftarrow \pi_X(\sigma_{C_{q+1} \wedge C_{q+2} \wedge \cdots \wedge C_k}(r' \bowtie s_2 \bowtie s_3 \bowtie \cdots \bowtie s_m)).$$

Example 11.30 Suppose we start with the program in Example 11.29 and instantiate $\{s_4\}$ instead. The resulting program is

$$r' \leftarrow \pi_{y_4.D\, y_4.G}(\sigma_{y_4.F=6}(s_4));$$
$$r \leftarrow \pi_{y_1.A\, y_3.B\, y_4.G}(\sigma_{C'}(r' \bowtie s_1 \bowtie s_2 \bowtie s_3)),$$

where C' is C without the comparison $y_4.F = 6$. The modified connection graph is in Figure 11.21.

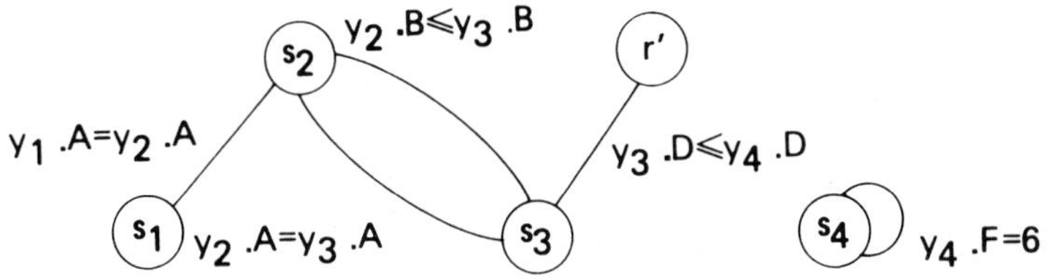

Figure 11.21

11.4.2 Iteration

This transformation is also called tuple substitution. It starts with a single statement

$$r \leftarrow \pi_X \sigma_C(s_1 \bowtie s_2 \bowtie \cdots \bowtie s_m)$$

as before. One of the relations, say s_1, is then chosen for iteration. The transformed program is

$r \leftarrow \emptyset$
for each tuple t in s_1 **do**
  begin
  $r' \leftarrow \pi_Y \sigma_{C(t)}(s_2 \bowtie s_3 \bowtie \cdots \bowtie s_m);$
  add r' to r with appropriate padding
  end.

Here $C(t)$ means C with every occurrence of an attribute $y_1.A$ replaced by the value $t(y_1.A)$. Y contains those attributes in X that are not in the scheme of s_1. The appropriate padding for r' is $t(X-Y)$. That is, r' is extended by the portion of t that is included in X.

The corresponding change in the connection graph is to remove the node s_1. Any edges that were incident upon s_1 become loops.

Example 11.31 Consider the statement

$$r \leftarrow \pi_{y_1.A\, y_2.B\, y_3.G}(\sigma_C(s_1 \bowtie s_2 \bowtie s_3)),$$
$$C \text{ is } y_1.A = y_2.A \wedge y_2.D \leq y_3.D \wedge y_3.F = 6.$$

This statement is the same as one of the statements in Example 11.29 with some renaming. The connection graph for this statement is shown in Figure 11.22. Iterating on s_2 gives the transformed program

$r \leftarrow \emptyset$
for each tuple t in s_2 **do**
  begin
  $r' \leftarrow \pi_{y_1.A\, y_3.G}(\sigma_{C(t)}(s_1 \bowtie s_3));$
  add $r' \bowtie \langle t(y_2.B)\rangle$ to r
  end.

$$C(t) \text{ is } y_1.A = t(y_2.A) \wedge t(y_2.D) \leq y_3.D \wedge y_3.F = 6.$$

The modified connection graph is shown in Figure 11.23.

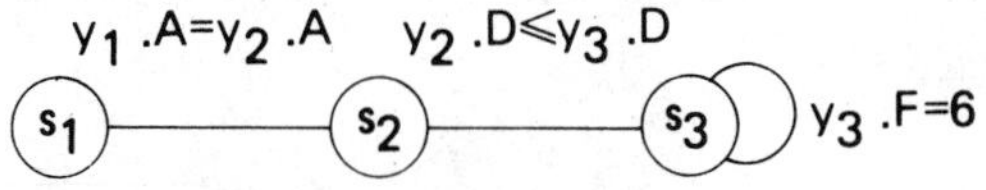

Figure 11.22

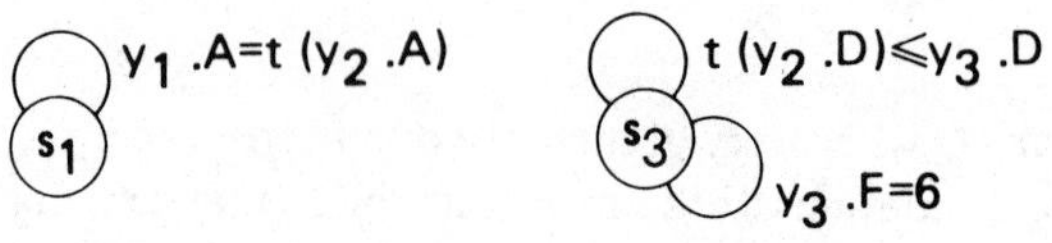

Figure 11.23

11.4.3 The Query Decomposition Algorithm

The query decomposition algorithm is simply stated as: start with a single-statement program, and repeatedly apply the instantiation and iteration transformations until all assignment statements have the form

$$r \leftarrow \pi_X \sigma_C(s),$$
$$r \leftarrow \pi_X(s_1 \bowtie s_2 \bowtie \cdots \bowtie s_k) \text{ or}$$
$$r \leftarrow \emptyset.$$

The second form can be transformed further by more applications of iteration. However, since no selection in involved, we use that form as shorthand for the k-1 **for**-loops necessary to compute the Cartesian product. Also, depending on the attributes in the projection, a **for**-loop might not be necessary for every join (see Exercise 11.6). In terms of the connection graph, the goal of the algorithm is essentially to isolate every node. That is, no edge connects two different nodes. Actually, once all the nodes are isolated, some applications of instantiation might still be necessary.

Example 11.32 In the connection graph (Figure 11.23) for the transformed program of Example 11.31, all nodes are isolated. The second assignment statement has a selection applied to a join. However, since the selection condition has no comparisons between attributes of s_1 and s_3, iteration is not necessary, only instantiation. A fully transformed version of the program is

$r \leftarrow \emptyset$
for each tuple t in s_2 **do**
  begin
  $r_1' \leftarrow \pi_{y_1.A}(\sigma_{C_1(t)}(s_1))$;
  $r_3' \leftarrow \pi_{y_3.G}(\sigma_{C_2(t)}(S_3))$;
  $r' \leftarrow r_1' \bowtie r_3'$;
  add $r' \bowtie \langle t(y_2.B)\rangle$ to r
  end.

$C_1(t)$ is $y_1.A = t(y_2.A)$ and $C_2(t)$ is $t(y_2.D) \leq y_3.D \wedge y_3.F = 6$.

Example 11.33 For this example we shall use relations s_w, s_x, s_y, and s_z, and assume attributes from s_w are prefaced with "w.", attributes from s_x with "x.", and so forth. Assume that we start with the single statement

$$r \leftarrow \pi_{w.A\ z.G}(\sigma_{C_1 \wedge C_2 \wedge C_3 \wedge C_4 \wedge C_5 \wedge C_6}(s_w \bowtie s_x \bowtie s_y \bowtie s_z))$$

where

C_1 is $w.B \leq 7$	C_4 is $x.D = y.D$
C_2 is $w.A = x.A$	C_5 is $y.F = z.F$
C_3 is $w.A \leq y.A$	C_6 is $x.F \leq z.F$.

The connection graph for this statement is shown in Figure 11.24.

We start by iterating s_z to get

1. $r \leftarrow \emptyset$
   for each tuple t in s_z **do**
   begin
2. $r_1 \leftarrow \pi_{w.A}(\sigma_{C_1 \wedge C_2 \wedge C_3 \wedge C_4 \wedge C_5(t) \wedge C_6(t)}(s_w \bowtie s_x \bowtie s_y))$
   add $r_1 \bowtie \langle t(z.G) \rangle$ to r
   end.

where

$C_5(t)$ is $y.F = t(z.F)$ and $C_6(t)$ is $x.F \leq t(z.F)$.

The connection graph for this program is shown in Figure 11.25.

We now instantiate s_w, s_x, and s_y, in turn, in statement 2 to get

2.1. $r_2 \leftarrow \pi_{w.A}(\sigma_{C_1}(s_w))$;
2.2. $r_3 \leftarrow \pi_{x.A\ x.D}(\sigma_{C_6(t)}(s_x))$;
2.3. $r_4 \leftarrow \pi_{y.A\ y.D}(\sigma_{C_5(t)}(s_y))$;
2.4. $r_1 \leftarrow \pi_{w.A}(\sigma_{C_2 \wedge C_3 \wedge C_4}(r_2 \bowtie r_3 \bowtie r_4))$.

The connection graph is now as shown in Figure 11.26.

We next iterate r_3 in statement 2.4 to get

2.4.1. $r_1 \leftarrow \emptyset$;
   for each tuple u in r_3 **do**
   begin
2.4.2. $r_5 \leftarrow \pi_{w.A}(\sigma_{C_2(u) \wedge C_3 \wedge C_4(u)}(r_2 \bowtie r_4))$;
   add r_5 to r_1
   end.

where

$$C_2(u) \text{ is } w.A = u(x.A) \text{ and } C_4(u) \text{ is } u(x.D) = y.D.$$

The connection graph is now as shown in Figure 11.27. Finally, we instantiate r_4, then iterate the resulting relation, r_6, in statement 2.4.2 to get

2.4.2.1. $r_6 \leftarrow \pi_{y.A}(\sigma_{C_4(r)}(r_4))$;
2.4.2.2. $r_5 \leftarrow \emptyset$;
for each tuple v in r_6 **do**
begin
2.4.2.3. $r_7 \leftarrow \pi_{w.A}(\sigma_{C_2(u) \wedge C_3(v)}(r_2))$;
add r_7 to r_5
end.

where

$$C_3(v) \text{ is } w.A \leq v(y.A).$$

The final connection graph is shown in Figure 11.28.

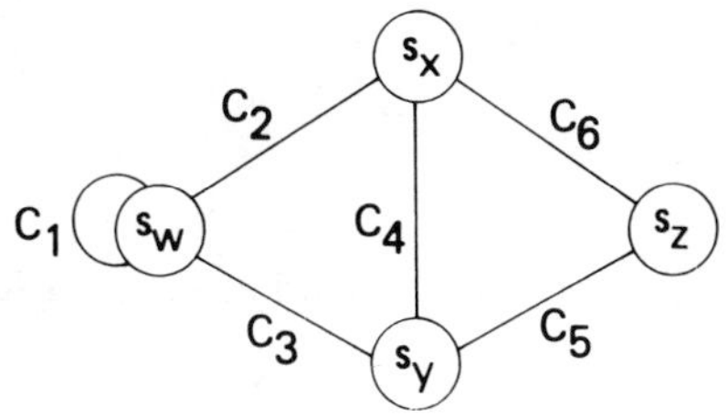

Figure 11.24

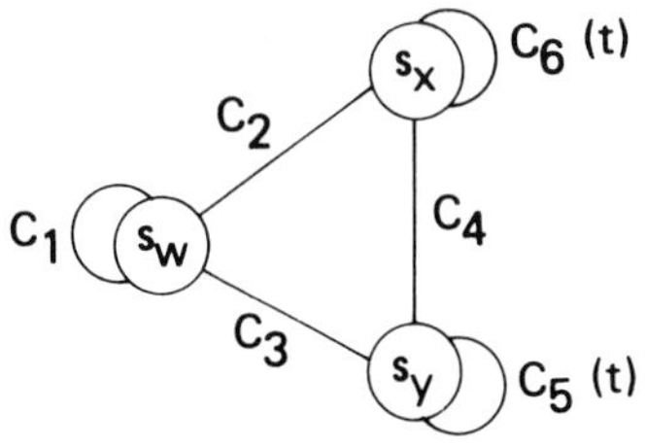

Figure 11.25

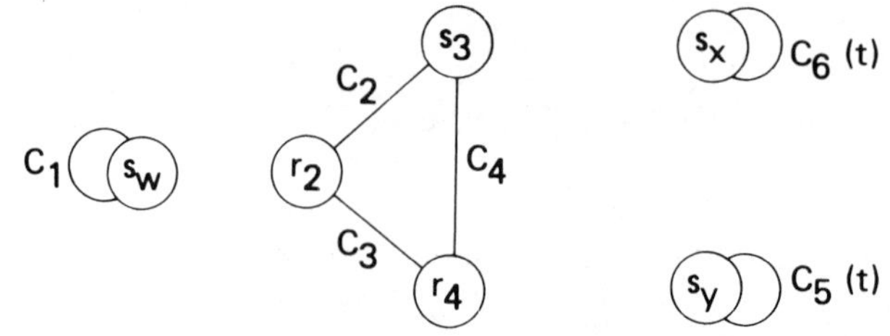

Figure 11.26

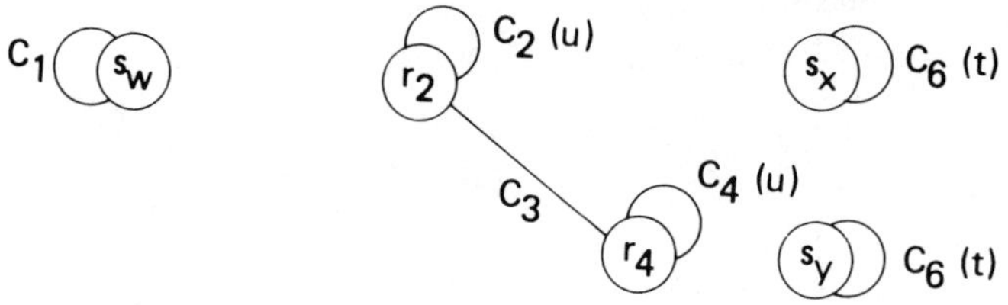

Figure 11.27

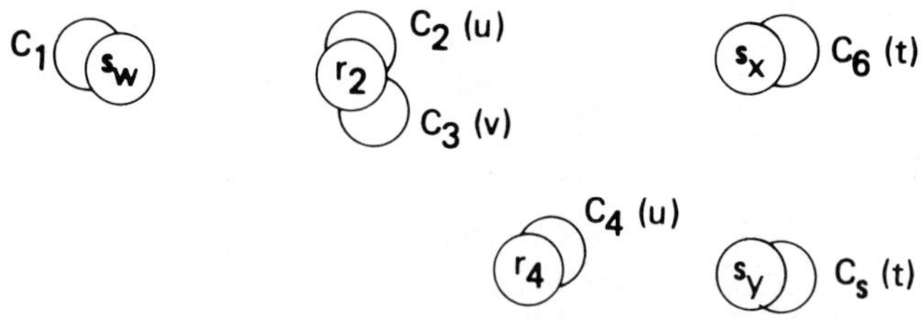

Figure 11.28

The query decomposition algorithm as described leaves a lot of leeway, since it does not say which instantiations or iterations to perform, nor in what order to perform them. Some final programs will be better than others. We present a heuristic method for applying the transformations in the decomposition algorithm to minimize the time complexity of the resulting program. We note here that the QUEL query processor does not use multiple-relation instantiation (see Exercise 11.8). While multiple-relation instantiation is not necessary to get a program in the desired form, it is useful for applying heuristics during decomposition.

The first principle is to minimize the number of repetitions for each **for**-loop. Hence, we want to instantiate a relation before iterating it whenever possible, to reduce the number of tuples that must be considered in the **for**-loop. The second principle is to minimize the number of times the iteration transformation must be applied. In general, the number of iterations required will be one fewer than the number of relations involved. Sometimes, however, not all the iterations need be performed for a statement of the form $r \leftarrow \pi_X(s_1 \bowtie s_2 \bowtie \cdots \bowtie s_k)$ (see Exercise 11.8). The third principle is to minimize the depth of the nesting of **for**-loops, since nesting has a multiplicative effect upon time complexity (see Exercise 11.10).

The second and third principles are served by always trying to choose a relation to iterate whose node, if removed, disconnects some portions of the connection graph.

Example 11.34 If we are working on a statement with the connection graph shown in Figure 11.29, picking s_1 to iterate means at least one more application of iteration. If s_2 is iterated first, no more applications of iteration are necessary.

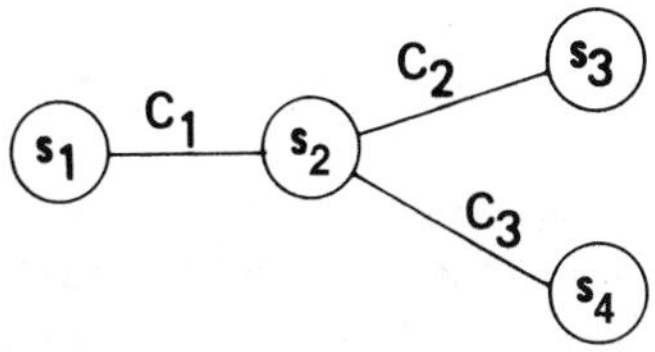

Figure 11.29

In the following method, we make crude estimates on the sizes of relations. A *simple* edge in the connection graph is a one- or two-node edge whose selection condition is the disjunction of equality comparisons. Let r be a new relation generated by instantiating a single relation s:

$$r \leftarrow \pi_X(\sigma_C(s)).$$

If any of the selection conditions in C comes from a simple edge, we label r "small," since presumably the equalities hold for only a few tuples in s.

The heuristic is described in terms of the connection graph by the following options. During the query decomposition algorithm, always choose the lowest numbered option possible.

1. Instantiate a relation that is contained in some one-node edge. If a simple edge is involved in the instantiation, label the newly generated relation "small."
2. Iterate a "small" relation. Prefer one in simple edges.
3. Iterate a relation whose removal disconnects some portion of the graph. Prefer one in simple edges.

4. Instantiate a set of relations whose removal disconnects some portion of the graph. Give preference to sets
   a. with few relations,
   b. that are connected in the graph, and
   c. that are in simple edges.
5. Iterate a relation. Prefer one in simple edges.

The idea behind option 4 is that the new relation generated by the instantiation is a candidate for option 3 during the next transformation.

Example 11.35 We repeat the query decomposition algorithm on the initial statement of Example 11.33, this time using the heuristic. In the connection graphs, we denote "small" relations by heavy circles. The graph for the initial statement is shown in Figure 11.24. Note that the edges for C_2, C_4, and C_5 are simple. Option 1 applies to relation s_w, so we instantiate s_w to get

1. $r_1 \leftarrow \pi_{w.A}(\sigma_{C_1}(s_w));$
2. $r \leftarrow \pi_{w.A\ z.G}(\sigma_{C_2 \wedge C_3 \wedge C_4 \wedge C_5 \wedge C_6}(r_1 \bowtie s_x \bowtie s_y \bowtie s_z)).$

The edge labeled C_1 is not simple, so r_1 is not "small." The modified connection graph is shown in Figure 11.30. None of options 1-3 now apply, so we apply option 4. We instantiate $\{s_x, s_y\}$ in statement 2 to get

2.1. $r_2 \leftarrow \pi_{x.A\ x.F\ y.A\ y.F}(\sigma_{C_4}(s_x \bowtie s_y));$
2.2. $r \leftarrow \pi_{x.A\ z.G}(\sigma_{C_2 \wedge C_3 \wedge C_5 \wedge C_6}(r_1 \bowtie r_2 \bowtie s_z)).$

The new connection graph is shown in Figure 11.31.

We now use option 3 and iterate r_2 in statement 2.2 to get

2.2.1. $r \leftarrow \emptyset;$
  for each tuple t in r_2 **do**
    begin
2.2.2. $r_3 \leftarrow \pi_{w.A\ z.G}(\sigma_{C_2(t) \wedge C_3(t) \wedge C_5(t) \wedge C_6(t)}(r_1 \bowtie s_z));$
    add r_3 to r
    end.

where

$C_2(t)$ is $w.A = t(x.A)$ $\quad C_5(t)$ is $t(y.F) = z.F$
$C_3(t)$ is $w.A \leq t(y.A)$ $\quad C_6(t)$ is $t(x.F) \leq z.F$.

The new connection graph is shown in Figure 11.32.

Using option 1, we can instantiate r_1 and s_z in statement 2.2.2 to get

2.2.2.1. $r_4 \leftarrow \pi_{w.A}(\sigma_{C_2(t) \wedge C_3(t)}(r_1));$
2.2.2.2. $r_5 \leftarrow \pi_{z.G}(\sigma_{C_5(t) \wedge C_6(t)}(s_z);$
2.2.2.3. $r_3 \leftarrow r_4 \bowtie r_5.$

The new connection graph is given in Figure 11.33. Since the edges for $C_2(t)$ and $C_5(t)$ are simple, r_4 and r_5 are "small" relations. However, that fact does not affect the rest of the decomposition. Finally, we iterate s_x in statement 2.1 to get

2.1.1. $r_2 \leftarrow \emptyset$;
for each tuple u in s_x **do**
begin
2.1.2. $r_6 \leftarrow \pi_{y.A\ y.F}(\sigma_{C_4(u)}(s_y))$;
add $r_6 \bowtie \langle u(x.A)\ u(x.F)\rangle$ to r_2
end.

where $C_4(u)$ is $u(x.D) = y.D$. The final connection graph is shown in Figure 11.34.

Note that the order of instantiation and iteration would be completely different under the heuristic if C_1 were $w.B = 7$. After instantiating s_w, r_1 would be "small," and hence would be iterated at the next step (see Exercise 11.7 d).

Comparing the decomposition obtained in this example to the decomposition in Example 11.33, we see that there we had 3 explicit iterations, all nested, while here we have two explicit iterations, not nested.

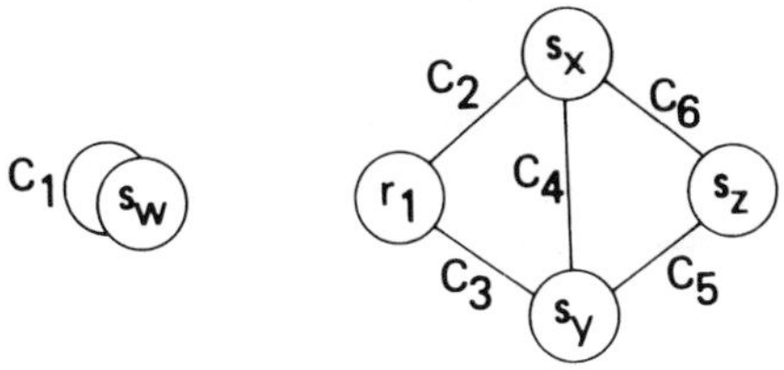

Figure 11.30

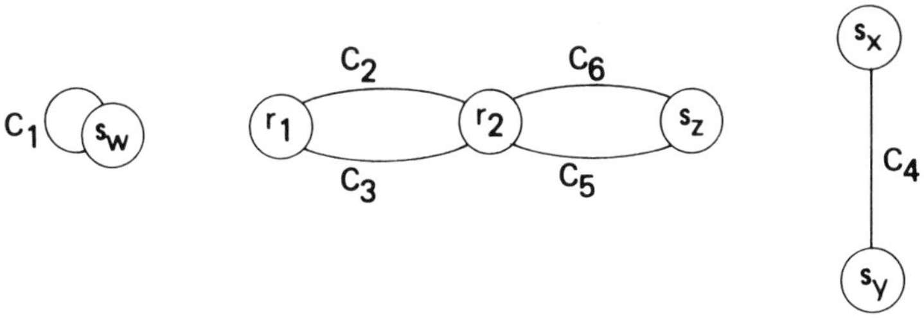

Figure 11.31

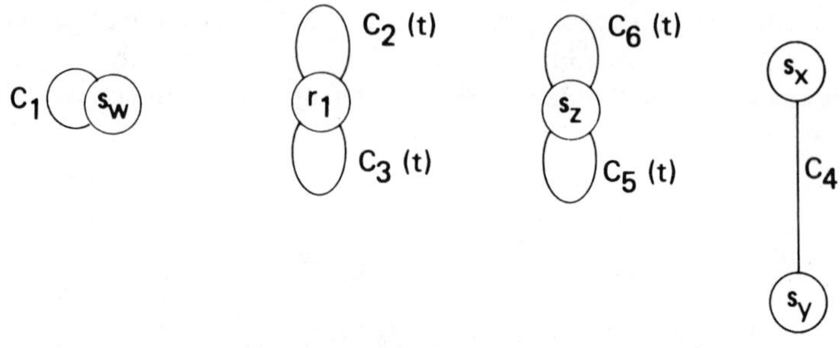

Figure 11.32

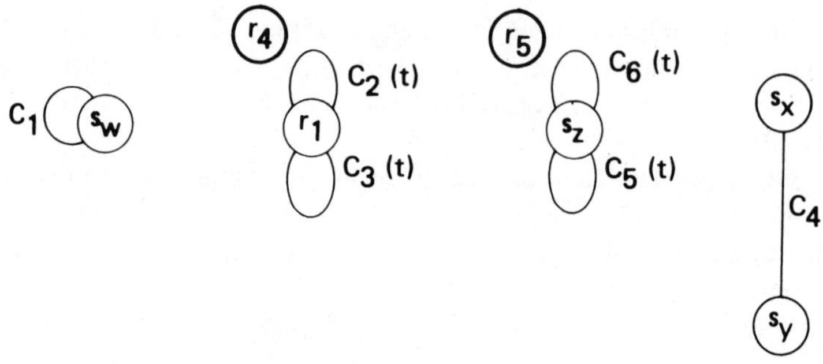

Figure 11.33

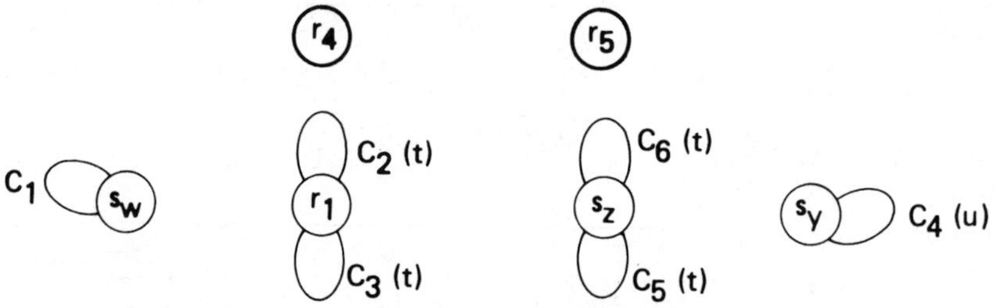

Figure 11.34

Our heuristic could be improved by several methods. One is to have different degrees of "small," depending upon the selection conditions involved. Another is to take into account the current sizes of relations in the database when making choices for instantiation and iteration. If the relative sizes of the relations change significantly, however, the decomposition may have to be redone.

11.5 TABLEAU QUERY OPTIMIZATION

The number of rows in a tableau query is a measure of the number of joins required in an equivalent algebraic expression. Given a tableau query, our goal will be to find an equivalent tableau query with the minimum number of rows. While in general such a search is NP-complete, the search is efficient for a subset of tableau queries: the *simple* tableau queries.

We shall also explore how to use data dependencies to reduce the number of rows in a tableau query. The method is a variant of the chase computation.

Many results in this section are similar to results in Chapter 8. We shall not spend much time on proofs that are similar to ones there. Our development will focus on untagged tableau queries. We shall discuss the modifications for tagged queries at the end of the section.

11.5.1 Tableau Query Equivalence

Definition 11.2 Let Q_1 and Q_2 be compatible tableau queries with scheme R. Q_1 *contains* Q_2, written $Q_1 \sqsupseteq Q_2$, if for every relation $r(R)$, $Q_1(r) \sqsupseteq Q_2(r)$. Q_1 and Q_2 are *equivalent*, written $Q_1 \equiv Q_2$, if for every relation $r(R)$, $Q_1(r) = Q_2(r)$. Evidently, $Q_1 \equiv Q_2$ if and only if $Q_1 \sqsupseteq Q_2$ and $Q_2 \sqsupseteq Q_1$.

In the following definition, a mapping of tableau symbols to tableau symbols extends to a mapping of rows to rows in the obvious way.

Definition 11.3 Let Q_1 be a tableau query on scheme $A_1 A_2 \cdots A_n$ with summary w_0 and rows $w_1, w_2, \ldots, w_p$. Let Q_2 be a tableau query with summary v_0. Let a_i be the distinguished variable for the A_i-column in both tableaux. A mapping ψ from the symbols of Q_1 to the symbols of Q_2 is a *containment mapping* from Q_1 to Q_2 if

1. $\psi(c) = c$ for every constant c in Q_1,
2. $\psi(w_0) = v_0$, and
3. $\psi(w_i)$ is a row of Q_2 for $1 \leq i \leq p$.

Conditions 2 and 3 require that Q_1 and Q_2 are compatible. Condition 2 also requires that $\psi(a_i)$ be a_i or the constant in the A_i-column of v_0. We let $\psi(Q_1) = \{\psi(w_i) | 1 \leq i \leq p\}$.

Theorem 11.1 Let Q_1 and Q_2 be compatible tableau queries with scheme R. Let w_0 be the summary of Q_1 and v_0 the summary of Q_2. $Q_1 \sqsupseteq Q_2$ if and only if there is a containment mapping ψ from Q_1 to Q_2.

Proof (if) Let r be a relation with scheme R. If ρ is a valuation of Q_2 such that $\rho(Q_2) \subseteq r$, then $\rho \circ \psi$ is a valuation of Q_1 where $\rho \circ \psi(Q_1) \subseteq r$ and $\rho \circ \psi(w_0) = \rho(v_0)$. Hence every tuple of $Q_2(r)$ is in $Q_1(r)$.

(only if) We treat Q_2 as both a relation and as a tableau query. When treating it as a relation, we ignore the summary. Since $Q_1 \sqsupseteq Q_2$, $Q_1(Q_2) \supseteq Q_2(Q_2)$. Let ρ_I be the identity valuation for Q_2. Clearly $\rho_I(Q_2) \subseteq Q_2$, so $\rho_I(v_0) = v_0 \in Q_2(Q_2)$. Therefore, v_0 must be in $Q_1(Q_2)$. Let ψ be the valuation of Q_1 such that $\psi(Q_1) \subseteq Q_2$ and $\psi(w_0) = v_0$. Clearly, ψ is a containment mapping from Q_1 to Q_2.

Corollary Compatible tableau queries Q_1 and Q_2 are equivalent if and only if there is a containment mapping from Q_1 to Q_2 and another from Q_2 to Q_1.

Note that if Q_1 and Q_2 are equivalent, they necessarily have identical summaries, so the containment mappings in the corollary always map distinguished variables to distinguished variables.

Q_1

A_1	A_2	A_3	A_4
a_1		a_3	
a_1	b_1	b_2	b_3
b_4	b_1	a_3	4

Q_2

A_1	A_2	A_3	A_4
a_1		a_3	
a_1	b_1	b_2	b_3
b_4	b_1	a_3	4
a_1	b_1	b_5	b_6
b_7	b_1	b_8	4

Q_3

A_1	A_2	A_3	A_4
a_1		a_3	
a_1	b_1	b_2	b_3
6	b_1	a_3	4

Figure 11.35

Example 11.36 Consider tableau queries Q_1, Q_2, and Q_3 in Figure 11.35. Using the identity containment mapping from Q_1 to Q_2, we see $Q_1 \sqsupseteq Q_2$. The containment mapping ψ_1 from Q_2 to Q_1 in Figure 11.36 shows that $Q_2 \sqsupseteq Q_1$, hence $Q_1 \equiv Q_2$. The containment mapping ψ_2 from Q_1 to Q_3 in Figure 11.37 shows $Q_1 \sqsupseteq Q_3$. However $Q_3 \not\sqsupseteq Q_1$, since there is no containment mapping from Q_3 to Q_1. The second row of Q_3 contains a 6, and hence cannot be mapped to any row of Q_1.

$\psi_1(a_1) = a_1$	$\psi_1(b_1) = b_1$
$\psi_1(a_3) = a_3$	$\psi_1(b_2) = b_2$
$\psi_1(4) = 4$	$\psi_1(b_3) = b_3$
	$\psi_1(b_4) = b_4$
	$\psi_1(b_5) = b_2$
	$\psi_1(b_6) = b_3$
	$\psi_1(b_7) = b_4$
	$\psi_1(b_8) = a_3$

Figure 11.36

$\psi_2(a_1) = a_1$	$\psi_2(b_1) = b_1$
$\psi_2(a_3) = a_3$	$\psi_2(b_2) = b_2$
$\psi_2(4) = 4$	$\psi_2(b_3) = b_3$
	$\psi_2(b_4) = 6$

Figure 11.37

Corollary If tableau queries Q_1 and Q_2 are identical up to a one-to-one renaming of nondistinguished variables, then $Q_1 \equiv Q_2$.

The converse of this corollary is not true, as we can see from tableau queries Q_1 and Q_2 of Example 11.36.

The following definitions extend the definitions for subsumes (Section 8.3) and supersedes (Exercise 8.17).

Definition 11.4 Let w_1 and w_2 be rows over scheme R. Row w_1 *subsumes* row w_2 if for every attribute $A \in R$ such that $w_2(A)$ is a distinguished variable or constant, $w_1(A) = w_2(A)$.

Definition 11.5 Let T_1 and T_2 be sets of rows on scheme R. T_1 *covers* T_2 if for every row v in T_2 there exists a row w of T_1 that subsumes v. Tableau query Q_1 *covers* tableau query Q_2 if the rows of Q_1 cover the rows of Q_2. We write $Q_1 \simeq Q_2$ if Q_1 covers Q_2 and Q_2 covers Q_1.

Definition 11.6 Let Q be a tableau query with scheme R and let w_1 and w_2 be rows of Q. Row w_1 *supersedes* row w_2 if $w_1(A) = w_2(A)$ for every attribute A in $match(w_2)$.

Example 11.37 Let Q be the tableau query of Figure 11.38. Row w_2 subsumes row w_4, but does not supersede it. Row w_3 supersedes row w_4. Q covers tableau query Q_3 in Figure 11.35.

$Q($	A_1	A_2	A_3	$A_4)$
w_0	a_1	a_2	a_3	
w_1	a_1	a_2	b_1	b_2
w_2	6	a_2	a_3	4
w_3	b_3	a_2	a_3	b_2
w_4	b_5	a_2	b_6	b_2

Figure 11.38

Lemma 11.1 Let Q_1 be a tableau query. Let Q_2 be Q_1 with one or more superseded rows removed. $Q_1 \equiv Q_2$.

Proof Left to the reader (see Exercise 11.13).

Example 11.38 In tableau query Q_2 of Figure 11.35, the first row supersedes the third and the second supersedes the fourth. Q_1 is Q_2 with the third and fourth rows removed. We saw in Example 11.35 that $Q_1 \equiv Q_2$.

Definition 11.7 A tableau query Q is *minimum* if no tableau query equivalent to Q has fewer rows than Q.

Note that a minimum equivalent tableau query for a tableau query Q is the same as an equivalent minimum tableau query for Q.

Definition 11.8 Let Q_1 and Q_2 be compatible tableau queries. Q_2 is a *subtableau* of Q_1 if Q_2 is Q_1 with 0 or more rows removed.

Theorem 11.2 For any tableau query Q_1, there is a subtableau Q_2 of Q_1 that is a minimum equivalent tableau for Q_1.

Proof Let Q_3 be a minimum equivalent tableau for Q_1. Let ψ_{13} be a containment mapping from Q_1 to Q_3 and let ψ_{31} be a containment mapping from Q_3 to Q_1. Let Q_2 be the subtableau of Q_1 containing the rows in $\psi_{31}(\psi_{13}(Q_1))$. The composition $\psi_{31} \circ \psi_{13}$ is a containment mapping from Q_1 to Q_2; $\psi_{13} \circ \psi_{31}$ is a containment mapping from Q_2 to Q_1. Hence $Q_1 \equiv Q_2$. Since $\psi_{13}(Q_1)$ is a subset of the rows of Q_3, $\psi_{31}(\psi_{13}(Q_1))$ has no more rows than Q_3, hence Q_2 is also minimum.

The next result is a partial converse to the second corollary of Theorem 11.1.

Theorem 11.3 Let Q_1 and Q_2 be compatible minimum tableau queries. $Q_1 \equiv Q_2$ if and only if there is a one-to-one containment mapping from Q_1 to Q_2 whose inverse is a containment mapping from Q_2 to Q_1. That is, Q_1 and Q_2 are identical up to a one-to-one renaming of nondistinguished variables.

Proof Left to the reader (see Exercise 11.14).

In general, testing equivalence of tableau queries is hard. It is an NP-complete problem given tableau queries Q_1 and Q_2 to decide whether $Q_1 \equiv Q_2$. The problem is NP-complete even if Q_1 and Q_2 come from restricted algebraic expressions and Q_2 is a subtableau of Q_1.

11.5.2 Simple Tableau Queries

In this section we introduce the simple tableau queries and show that they can be minimized efficiently. We shall also show that equivalence of minimum simple queries can be decided efficiently, which means equivalence can be decided efficiently for arbitrary simple queries.

Definition 11.9 A tableau query Q is *simple* if in any column where a nondistinguished variable is matched, no other symbol is repeated.

Example 11.39 Consider tableau queries Q_1 and Q_2 in Figure 11.39. Q_1 is not simple, because b_4 is matched in the A_2-column and a_2 repeats, and b_3 is matched in the A_4-column and 4 repeats. Q_2 is the same as Q_1 except for the last row, but Q_2 is simple.

$Q_1(A_1$	A_2	A_3	$A_4)$
a_1	a_2	a_3	
a_1	a_2	b_1	4
b_2	a_2	a_3	b_3
a_1	b_4	a_3	b_3
a_1	b_4	b_5	4

$Q_2(A_1$	A_2	A_3	$A_4)$
a_1	a_2	a_3	
a_1	a_2	b_1	4
b_2	a_2	a_3	b_3
a_1	b_4	a_3	b_3
a_1	a_2	b_5	b_3

Figure 11.39

Our task is to show that simple tableau queries can be minimized efficiently and equivalence of minimum simple queries is easy to test, thus deriving an efficient algorithm for equivalence of simple queries.

Let Q_1 be a simple tableau query that is not minimum. By Theorem 11.2 there is an equivalent subtableau Q_2 of Q_1 that is equivalent to Q_1. Let w be a row of Q_1 that does not appear in Q_2. There is a containment mapping ψ from Q_1 to Q_2 and a row v in Q_2 such that $\psi(w) = \psi(v) = v$ (see Lemma 11.2 below).

Given a simple tableau query Q_1, in order to minimize it, we try to find rows w, v, and a containment mapping ψ from Q_1 to Q_1 such that $\psi(w) = \psi(v) = v$. To aid in the search, we compute the *companion set of* w *relative to* v, $COMP_v(w)$, that contains all the rows ψ must map to v if ψ maps w to v. If $\{v\}$ covers $COMP_v(w)$, then ψ can be chosen to map every row in $COMP_v(w)$ to v and every other row to itself. The subtableau Q_2 of Q_1 containing the rows in $\psi(Q_1)$ is equivalent to Q_1 but has fewer rows. If Q_2 is not minimum, we can repeat the process with a new w, v and ψ.

We now fill in the details and prove the correctness of the method above.

Lemma 11.2 Let Q_1 be a tableau query, and let Q_2 be a proper subtableau of Q_1. If ψ is a containment mapping from Q_1 to Q_2 and w is a row in Q_1 not in Q_2, then there is a containment mapping ψ_0 from Q_1 to Q_2 and a row v of Q_2 such that $\psi_0(w) = \psi_0(v) = v$.

Proof We first note that composition of containment mappings is a containment mapping. Let ψ^i be the containment mapping obtained by composing ψ with itself i times. Consider the sequence of rows $\psi^1(w)$, $\psi^2(w)$, $\psi^3(w)$, ... Since each row is contained in Q_1, the sequence must contain a duplicate. Select i and j such that $i \leq j$ and $\psi^i(w) = \psi^j(w)$. Let $\psi_0 = \psi^{i(j-i)}$ and let $v = \psi_0(w)$. We show that $\psi_0(v) = v$.
First,

$$\psi_0(v) = \psi^{i(j-i)}(v) = \psi^{2i(j-i)}(w).$$

We can rewrite $\psi^{2i(j-i)}(w)$ as

$$\psi^{i(j-i-1)}(\psi^{i(j-i)}(\psi^i(w))),$$

which simplifies to

$$\psi^{(j-i-1)}(\psi^i(w)),$$

since

$$\psi^{(j-i)}(\psi^i(w)) = \psi^j(w) = \psi^i(w).$$

Finally,

$$\psi^{i(j-i-1)}(\psi^i(w)) = \psi^{i(j-i)}(w) = \psi_0(w) = v.$$

Definition 11.10 Let Q be a simple tableau query with scheme R, and let w and v be rows of Q. The *companion set of* w *relative to* v, denoted $COMP_v(w)$, is the smallest set T containing v subject to the following closure condition:

> If w_1 is a row in T, w_2 is a row of Q, and A is an attribute in R such that $w_1(A)$ is a nondistinguished variable and $w_1(A) = w_2(A) \neq v(A)$, then w_2 is in T.

Example 11.40 Let Q be the tableau in Figure 11.40. Let us compute $COMP_{w_3}(w_4)$. We start with row w_4. For row w_5 we have $w_5(A_4) = w_4(A_4) = b_{11} \neq w_3(A_4)$, so w_5 is included. Also, $w_5(A_5) = w_6(A_5) = b_{16} \neq w_3(A_5)$, so w_6 is included. Hence, $COMP_{w_3}(w_4) = \{w_4, w_5, w_6\}$. Row w_2 is not included, even though $w_2(A_2) = w_6(A_2) = b_1$, since $w_3(A_2) = b_1$.

	$Q(A_1$	A_2	A_3	A_4	$A_5)$
w_0	a_1		a_3		
w_1	a_1	b_1	b_2	4	b_3
w_2	a_1	b_1	b_4	b_5	b_6
w_3	b_7	b_1	a_3	b_8	7
w_4	b_9	b_{10}	a_3	b_{11}	b_{12}
w_5	b_{13}	b_{14}	b_{15}	b_{11}	b_{16}
w_6	b_{17}	b_1	b_{18}	b_{19}	b_{16}

Figure 11.40

Lemma 11.3 Let Q be a simple tableau query and let w and v be rows of Q. If ψ is a containment mapping from Q to Q such that $\psi(w) = v$, then $\psi(u) = v$ for every row u in $COMP_v(w)$.

Proof Left to the reader (see Exercise 11.23).

Theorem 11.4 Let Q be a simple tableau query with scheme R and let w and v be distinct rows of Q. There is a containment mapping ψ from Q to Q such that $\psi(u) = v$ for all u in $COMP_v(w)$ if and only if $\{v\}$ covers $COMP_v(w)$.

Proof (if) Let ψ be the identity on all symbols except nondistinguished variables appearing in the rows of $COMP_v(w)$. For each attribute $A \in R$ and each row u in $COMP_v(w)$, let $\psi(u(A)) = \psi(v(A))$. (Since v and w are distinct, $COMP_v(w)$ does not contain v. Why?)

We claim ψ is well-defined. Let b be a nondistinguished variable in the A-column. If b appears both in a row u_1 in $COMP_v(w)$ and a row u_2 not in $COMP_v(w)$, then $u_1(A) = u_2(A) = v(A)$ or else u_2 would be in $COMP_v(w)$. Hence $\psi(b) = b$, which implies ψ is the identity on rows not in $COMP_v(w)$. Also, if some row u in $COMP_v(w)$ has a distinguished variable or a constant in the A-column, so does v, since v subsumes u. Hence ψ is the identity on distinguished symbols and constants.

It is not hard to verify that $\psi(u) = u$ if $u \notin COMP_v(w)$ and $\psi(u) = v$ if $u \in COMP_v(w)$. Hence ψ is the desired containment mapping.

(only if) Since ψ is a containment mapping, it maps constants to themselves. It must also be the identity on distinguished variables, since if Q contains a distinguished variable in the A-column, there is no constant in the

A-column of the summary. For any row $u \in COMP_v(w)$, since $\psi(u) = v$, every place u has a distinguished variable or constant, v has the same symbol. Thus v subsumes u and so $\{v\}$ covers $COMP_v(w)$.

Example 11.41 As we saw in Example 11.40, for the tableau query Q in Figure 11.40, $COMP_{w3}(w_4) = \{w_4, w_5, w_6\}$. We see that $\{w_3\}$ covers $\{w_4, w_5, w_6\}$. Hence, there is a containment mapping ψ from Q to Q such that $\psi(w_1) = w_1$, $\psi(w_2) = w_2$, and $\psi(w_3) = \psi(w_4) = \psi(w_5) = \psi(w_6) = w_3$.

$COMP_{w6}(w_3) = \{w_3, w_4, w_5\}$. However $\{w_6\}$ does not cover $\{w_3, w_4, w_5\}$. No containment mapping maps w_3 to w_6, since $w_3(A_5) = 7$ and $w_6(A_5) = b_{16}$.

We combine our results into the algorithm MINEQ in Figure 11.41. Given a simple tableau query Q, we search for distinct rows w and v such that $\{v\}$ covers $COMP_v(w)$. By Lemmas 11.2, 11.3, and Theorem 11.4, if Q is not minimum, v and w will exist. The rows of $COMP_v(w)$ can be removed from Q to get a smaller equivalent tableau. If no such w and v exist, Q must be minimum.

```
Input:  A simple tableau query Q.
Output: A minimum equivalent subtableau of Q.
MINEQ(Q)
  begin
  let T be the rows of Q;
  while changes to T occur do
    for each row v in T do
      for each row w ≠ v in T do
        if v covers COMP_v(w) in T
        then T := T − COMP_v(w);
  let Q′ be T with the summary of Q;
  return (Q′)
  end.
```

Figure 11.41

Example 11.42 Let Q_1 be the tableau query in Figure 11.42. $COMP_{w1}(w_2) = \{w_2\}$, and $\{w_1\}$ covers $\{w_2\}$, so we remove row w_2. $COMP_{w1}(w_3) = \{w_3\}$, and $\{w_1\}$ covers $\{w_3\}$, so we also remove w_3. We are left with rows w_1, w_4, w_5, w_6, w_7. $COMP_{w5}(w_6) = \{w_6, w_7\}$ and is covered by $\{w_5\}$, so we remove w_6 and w_7. No more rows can be removed. The minimum equivalent subtableau Q_1' is shown in Figure 11.43.

	$Q_1(A_1$	A_2	A_3	A_4	$A_5)$
w_0	a_1			7	a_5
w_1	a_1	b_1	5	b_2	b_3
w_2	a_1	b_1	b_4	b_5	b_6
w_3	a_1	b_7	b_8	b_9	b_{10}
w_4	b_{11}	b_1	b_{12}	7	b_{14}
w_5	b_{15}	b_{16}	b_{17}	7	a_5
w_6	b_{18}	b_{19}	b_{20}	7	b_{21}
w_7	b_{22}	b_{23}	b_{20}	b_{24}	a_5

Figure 11.42

	$Q_1'(A_1$	A_2	A_3	A_4	$A_5)$
w_0	a_1			7	a_5
w_1	a_1	b_1	5	b_2	b_3
w_4	b_{11}	b_1	b_{12}	7	b_{14}
w_5	b_{15}	b_{16}	b_{17}	7	a_5

Figure 11.43

Let us determine the time complexity of MINEQ. Assume Q has k rows and n columns. $COMP_v(w)$ can be found in $O(k^2n)$ time (see Exercise 11.24). Testing whether v covers $COMP_v(w)$ can be done in $O(kn)$ time. Each **for**-loop iterates at most k times, so the body of the **while**-loop takes $O(k^4n)$ time. Each time a change occurs to T, at least one row is removed, so the **while**-loop iterates for at most k times. Hence the total time-complexity of *MINEQ* is $O(k^5n)$.

Actually, the time-complexity is no more than $O(k^4n)$. The **while**-loop need only execute once, for if a row is not removed on the first iteration, it will not be removed on any subsequent iteration, as the following lemma shows.

Definition 11.11 Let Q be a simple tableau query with scheme R and let v and w be rows of Q. Let $K = w_1, w_2, \ldots, w_m$ be a sequence of distinct rows for Q. K is a *construction sequence* for $COMP_v(w)$ if

1. $COMP_v(w) = \{w_1, w_2, \ldots, w_m\}$, and
2. For each j, $1 < j \leq m$, there is an $i < j$ and an attribute A in R such that $w_i(A)$ and $w_j(A)$ are the same nondistinguished variable and $w_j(A) \neq v(A)$.

Clearly, every companion set has a construction sequence. The first row in the sequence may be any row of the companion set.

Lemma 11.4 Let Q be a simple tableau query with scheme R. Assume Q contains distinct rows v_0 and w_0 such that $COMP_{v_0}(w_0)$ is covered by $\{v_0\}$. Let Q' be the subtableau obtained from Q by removing the rows in $COMP_{v_0}(w_o)$. (That is, Q' is Q after one step of MINEQ.) Let v and w be rows of Q' and let $COMP_v(w)$ and $COMP_v'(w)$ be the companion sets of w relative to v in Q and Q', respectively. If $\{v\}$ covers $COMP_v'(w)$, then $\{v\}$ covers $COMP_v(w)$.

Proof We focus on the identities of v_0 and w_0. Note that if w' is a row in $COMP_v(w)$, then $COMP_v(w) = COMP_v(w')$ (see Exercise 11.26).

$COMP_{v_0}(w_0)$ must contain some row u in $COMP_v(w)$, or else $COMP_v(w) = COMP_v'(w)$ and we are finished. If $v = v_0$, then $COMP_{v_0}(w_0) = COMP_{v_0}(u) = COMP_v(u) = COMP_v(w)$, so w would not be a row of Q'. Thus, the rows removed going from Q to Q' are $COMP_{v_0}(u)$ where $v_0 \neq v$.

We claim v_0 is in $COMP_v(w)$. Why? First, note that $COMP_{v_0}(u) \not\supseteq COMP_v(w)$, or else w would not be a row of Q'. Let $u_1, u_2, \ldots, u_m$ be a construction sequence for $COMP_v(w)$ such that $u_1 = u$. Let j be the smallest integer such that u_j is not in $COMP_{v_0}(u)$. There must be an $i < j$ and an attribute A in R such that $u_i(A)$ and $u_j(A)$ are the same nondistinguished variable and $u_i(A) \neq v(A)$. We must have $u_i(A) = u_j(A) = v_0(A)$, or else u_j would be in $COMP_{v_0}(u)$. We know $u_i(A)$ and $v_0(A)$ are the same nondistinguished symbol. Since $u_i(A)$ is in $COMP_v(w)$ and $v_0(A) = u_i(A) \neq v(A)$, v_0 is also in $COMP_v(w)$, as we claimed.

We next show that v_0 is in $COMP_v'(w)$. Let $w_1, w_2, \ldots, w_p$ be a prefix of a generating sequence for $COMP_v(w)$ such that $w = w_1$ and $v_0 = w_p$. If all of $w_1, w_2, \ldots, w_p$ are in Q', we have proved that v_0 is in $COMP_v'(w)$, so let j, $z < j \leq p$, be the least integer such that w_j is not a row of Q'. There must be an $i < j$ and an attribute B in R such that $w_i(B)$ and $w_j(B)$ are the same nondistinguished symbol, which is not $v(B)$. We know w_i was not in $COMP_{v_0}(u)$ but that w_j was. We conclude $w_i(B) = w_j(B) = v_0(B)$. All of $w_1, w_2, \ldots, w_i$ are in $COMP_v'(w)$ and $v_0(B) = w_i(B) \neq v(B)$, so v_0 is also in $COMP_v'(w)$, as desired.

To conclude, any row u_0 in $COMP_v'(w)$ must be in $COMP_{v_0}(u)$. Since v_0 is in $COMP_v'(w)$ and $\{v\}$ covers $COMP_v'(w)$, v subsumes u_0 and so $\{v\}$ covers $COMP_v(w)$.

We can use MINEQ to construct an efficient test for equivalence. Let Q_1 and Q_2 be simple tableau queries with scheme R that we wish to test for equivalence. We first compute $Q_1' = \text{MINEQ}(Q_1)$ and $Q_2' = \text{MINEQ}(Q_2)$, and then test Q_1' and Q_2' for equivalence. Q_1' and Q_2' are both minimum. If Q_1' and Q_2' are equivalent, by Theorem 11.3 there is a one-to-one containment mapping ψ from Q_1' to Q_2' that is the identity on distinguished variables and whose inverse is a containment mapping from Q_1' to Q_2'. If Q_1' has a repeated nondistinguished variable b_1 in the A-column, for some attribute A in R, then $\psi(b_1) = b_2$ must be a repeated nondistinguished variable in the A-column of Q_2'. If we formed Q_1'' and Q_2'' by replacing b_1 and b_2 by a new constant c in Q_1' and Q_2', then Q_1'' and Q_2'' will also be equivalent.

To test Q_1' and Q_2' for equivalence, we proceed as follows. For each attribute A such that Q_1' has a repeated nondistinguished variable b_1 in the A-column, we check if Q_2' has a repeated nondistinguished variable, say b_2, in its A-column. If so, we replace b_1 and b_2 by some new constant c. If not, Q_1' and Q_2' are not equivalent. We attempt such a substitution for every repeated nondistinguished variable in Q_1'. Call the resulting tableau queries Q_1'' and Q_2''.

Q_1' and Q_2' are equivalent if and only if Q_1'' and Q_2'' are. If Q_2'' has any repeated, nondistinguished variables, then it is not equivalent to Q_1''. Otherwise, we can test $Q_1'' \equiv Q_2''$ by checking that the summaries are the same and that $Q_1'' \simeq Q_2''$. (Recall that $Q_1'' \simeq Q_2''$ means each tableau query covers the other.)

Example 11.43 Let Q_1 be the tableau query in Figure 11.42 and let Q_2 be the tableau query in Figure 11.44. $Q_1' = \text{MINEQ}(Q_1)$ is shown in Figure 11.43. $Q_2' = \text{MINEQ}(Q_2)$ is shown in Figure 11.45. Q_1' has repeated nondistinguished variable b_1 in the A_2-column, and Q_2' has b_2 repeated in the same column. We replace b_1 and b_2 by the constant 1 to get tableau queries Q_1'' and Q_2'' in Figure 11.46. Q_1'' and Q_2'' are equivalent, for we can map rows w_1, w_4, and w_5 to rows v_5, v_1, and v_4 by renaming only nondistinguished variables. Hence $Q_1 \equiv Q_2$.

For tableau query Q_3 in Figure 11.46, $Q_3 = \text{MINEQ}(Q_3)$. $Q_1 \not\equiv Q_3$, since Q_3 has a repeated nondistinguished variable in the A_4-column, where Q_1' has none.

Q_2	A_1	A_2	A_3	A_4	A_5
v_0	a_1			7	a_5
v_1	b_1	b_2	b_3	7	b_4
v_2	b_5	b_2	b_6	7	b_7
v_3	b_8	b_9	b_6	7	b_{10}
v_4	b_{11}	b_{12}	b_{13}	7	a_5
v_5	a_1	b_2	5	b_{14}	b_{15}

Figure 11.44

Q_2'	A_1	A_2	A_3	A_4	A_5
v_0	a_1			7	a_5
v_1	b_1	b_2	b_3	7	b_4
v_4	b_{11}	b_{12}	b_{13}	7	a_5
v_5	a_1	b_2	5	b_{14}	b_{15}

Figure 11.45

Q_1''	A_1	A_2	A_3	A_4	A_5
w_0	a_1			7	a_5
w_1	a_1	1	5	b_2	b_3
w_4	b_{11}	1	b_{12}	7	b_{14}
w_5	b_{15}	b_{16}	b_{17}	7	a_5

Q_2''	A_1	A_2	A_3	A_4	A_5
v_0	a_1			7	a_5
v_1	b_1	1	b_3	7	b_4
v_4	b_{11}	b_{12}	b_{13}	7	a_5
v_5	a_1	1	5	b_{14}	b_{15}

Figure 11.46

Q_3: A_1	A_2	A_3	A_4	A_5
a_1			7	a_5
b_1	b_2	b_3	b_4	b_5
b_6	b_7	b_8	b_4	a_5
a_1	b_2	5	b_9	b_{10}

Figure 11.47

11.5.3 Equivalence with Constraints

As we might expect, in the presence of FDs and JDs otherwise inequivalent tableau queries can be equivalent.

Example 11.44 Tableau query Q_1 in Figure 11.48 comes from Example 10.38 in the last chapter. Q_2 in Figure 11.49 is another tableau query on the same scheme. $Q_1 \sqsupseteq Q_2$, since there is a containment mapping that takes the first two rows of Q_1 to the first row of Q_2 and the last row of Q_1 to the last row of Q_2. However, $Q_2 \not\sqsupseteq Q_1$. Both Q_1 and Q_2 are simple, and both are left unchanged by MINEQ hence both are minimum. Since Q_1 has more rows than Q_2, $Q_1 \not\equiv Q_2$.

Suppose we are only interested in relations that satisfy the FD OP → ME. No option is available for more than one meal. (No more pizza for breakfast.) Let r be a relation in SAT(OP → ME). Any valuation ρ for Q_1 such that $\rho(Q_1) \subseteq r$ must have $\rho(b_4) = \rho(b_5)$. Hence $\rho(Q_2) \subseteq r$ and so $Q_1(r) \subseteq Q_2(r)$. Q_1 and Q_2 define the same mapping on SAT(OP → ME).

Q_1(FL	DT	OP	NM	ME)
	a_2	a_3	a_4	
b_1	b_2	a_3	b_3	b_4
106	a_2	a_3	a_4	b_5
107	b_6	b_7	b_8	b_4

Figure 11.48

Q_2(FL	DT	OP	NM	ME)
	a_2	a_3	a_4	
106	a_2	a_3	a_4	b_4
107	b_6	b_7	b_8	b_4

Figure 11.49

If Q_1 and Q_2 are compatible tableau queries on scheme R and **C** is a set of FDs and JDs, $Q_1 \sqsupseteq_{\mathbf{C}} Q_2$ means $Q_1(r) \supseteq Q_2(r)$ for every relation $r(R)$ in $SAT(\mathbf{C})$. Similarly, $Q_1 \equiv_{\mathbf{C}} Q_2$ means $Q_1(r) = Q_2(r)$ for every relation in $SAT(\mathbf{C})$.

We can extend the chase computation to a tableau query Q with two slight modifications. First, the F-rule gives priority to constants in renaming. Suppose we have an FD $X \rightarrow A$ and two rows w_1 and w_2 where $w_1(X) = w_2(X)$. If $w_1(A)$ and $w_2(A)$ are unequal constants, we replace the entire tableau query by the tableau query $\emptyset$ that maps every relation to the empty relation. Clearly, for any relation $r \in SAT(X \rightarrow A)$, there can be no valuation ρ such that $\rho(Q) \subseteq r$. If $w_1(A)$ is a constant and $w_2(A)$ is not, we set $w_2(A)$ to be that constant. The second modification is that if ever a distinguished variable is changed to a constant, the change carries through to the summary.

We let $chase_{\mathbf{C}}(Q)$ be the result of applying F- and J-rules for **C** to Q until no more changes can be made. The proofs of Chapter 8 work with minor changes to show that $chase_{\mathbf{C}}(Q)$ is thereby well-defined. We also state the following two theorems without proof.

Theorem 11.5 Let Q be a tableau query and let **C** be a set of FDs and JDs. $Q \equiv_{\mathbf{C}} chase_{\mathbf{C}}(Q)$.

Theorem 11.6 Let Q_1 and Q_2 be tableau queries and let **C** be a set of FDs and JDs. $Q_1 \sqsupseteq_{\mathbf{C}} Q_2$ if and only if $chase_{\mathbf{C}}(Q_1) \sqsupseteq chase_{\mathbf{C}}(Q_2)$.

Corollary $Q_1 \equiv_{\mathbf{C}} Q_2$ if and only if $chase_{\mathbf{C}}(Q_1) \equiv chase_{\mathbf{C}}(Q_2)$.

Example 11.45 Returning to the last example, if $\mathbf{C} = \{\mathrm{OP} \rightarrow \mathrm{ME}\}$, then $Q_1^* = chase_{\mathbf{C}}(Q_1)$ is shown in Figure 11.50. $Q_2 = chase_{\mathbf{C}}(Q_2)$. Also, MINEQ $(Q_1^*) = Q_2$, so $Q_1 \equiv_{\mathbf{C}} Q_2$.

Q_1^*(FL	DT	OP	NM	ME)
	a_2	a_3	a_4	
b_1	b_2	a_3	b_3	b_4
106	a_2	a_3	a_4	b_4
107	b_6	b_7	b_8	b_4

Figure 11.50

Example 11.46 Tableau queries Q_1 and Q_2 in Figure 11.51 clearly are not equivalent, since their summaries are different. If $\mathbf{C} = \{A_1 \rightarrow A_2, A_4 \twoheadrightarrow A_1\}$, then $Q_1^* = chase_{\mathbf{C}}(Q_2)$ are shown in Figure 11.52. The third row of Q_1^* supersedes all the rest, so $Q_1^* \equiv Q_3$, where Q_3 is shown in Figure 11.53. Similarly, the first row of Q_2^* supersedes the last, so $Q_2^* \equiv Q_3 \equiv Q_1^*$. Hence $Q_1 \equiv_{\mathbf{C}} Q_2$.

Definition 11.12 Let **C** be a set of FDs and JDs. A tableau query Q_1 is **C**-*minimum* if there is no tableau query Q_2 with fewer rows than Q_1 such that $Q_1 \equiv_{\mathbf{C}} Q_2$.

Certainly, finding a **C**-minimum equivalent tableau query given a tableau query Q and a set **C** of FDs and JDs is no easier than finding a minimum

Q_1	A_1	A_2	A_3	A_4
	a_1	a_2	a_3	
	a_1	a_2	b_1	b_2
	b_3	7	a_3	b_2

Q_2	A_1	A_2	A_3	A_4
	a_1	7	a_3	
	a_1	b_1	a_3	b_2
	a_1	7	b_3	b_4

Figure 11.51

Q_1^*	A_1	A_2	A_3	A_4
	a_1	7	a_3	
	a_1	7	b_1	b_2
	b_3	7	a_3	b_2
	a_1	7	a_3	b_2
	b_3	7	b_1	b_2

Q_2^*	A_1	A_2	A_3	A_4
	a_1	7	a_3	
	a_1	7	a_3	b_2
	a_1	7	b_3	b_4

Figure 11.52

Q_3	A_1	A_2	A_3	A_4
	a_1	7	a_3	
	a_1	7	a_3	b_2

Figure 11.53

equivalent tableau query. We might hope to combine MINEQ and the chase computation to get an algorithm for **C**-minimum equivalence of simple tableau queries. If Q is a simple tableau query, we cannot necessarily apply MINEQ to $chase_{\mathbf{C}}(Q)$. Note that in Example 11.46, Q_1 was simple, but $chase_{\mathbf{C}}(Q_1)$ was not. The problem can arise even with FDs alone, and removing superseded rows does not always restore simplicity (see Exercise 11.29). Applying the chase to MINEQ(Q) does not necessarily yield the desired result either (see Exercise 11.30).

11.5.4 Extensions for Multiple-Relation Databases

We first consider a database d on database scheme **R** over **U** where every relation is the projection of a common instance r(**U**). Our results on equivalence carry over easily, since if a tableau query Q applies to d, then so does any minimum equivalent query for Q.

Example 11.47 Let d be the database $\{q(AB), r(BC), s(AC)\}$ that is the projection of some common instance over ABC. Figure 11.54 shows a tableau query Q_1 for the algebraic expression

$$\pi_{BC}(\sigma_{B=c}(q) \bowtie r \bowtie s).$$

Q_1 is simple, so we may apply MINEQ to get tableau query Q_1' in Figure 11.55. The algebraic expression above is equivalent to $\sigma_{B=c}(r)$. However, the tableau query Q_2 in Figure 11.56 for the algebraic expression

$$\pi_{BC}(\sigma_{A=c}(q) \bowtie r \bowtie s)$$

is minimum.

Q_1(A	B	C)
	c	a_3
b_1	c	a_3
b_2	c	b_4
b_2	b_5	a_3

Figure 11.54

Q_1'(A	B	C)
	c	
b_1	c	a_3

Figure 11.55

$Q_2(A$	B	$C)$
	a_2	a_3
b_1	a_2	a_3
c	a_2	b_2
c	b_3	a_3

Figure 11.56

When we introduce dependencies, problems arise, for $chase_{\mathbf{C}}(Q)$ might not apply to d, even if Q did. We might interpret our result $Q \equiv_{\mathbf{C}} chase_{\mathbf{C}}(Q)$ as a statement about equivalence of queries over different databases that are projections of the same instance.

Example 11.48 Let $\{q(AB), r(BC), s(CD)\}$ and $d' = \{q'(ABC), r'(BCD)\}$ both be databases that are the projections of the same instance over $A\ B\ C\ D$. Let $\mathbf{C} = \{C \rightarrow D\}$. Q in Figure 11.57 is the tableau query for the algebraic expression

$$\pi_{AD}(q \bowtie r \bowtie s)$$

on database d. $Q' = chase_{\mathbf{C}}(Q)$ is shown in Figure 11.58 and $Q'' =$ MINEQ (Q') is shown in Figure 11.59. Neither Q' nor Q'' applies to d. However, both apply to d'. We can interpret $Q \equiv Q'$ as saying the algebraic expression

$$\pi_{AD}(\pi_{AB}(q') \bowtie r')$$

for database d' is equivalent to the expression above for database d whenever instance r is in $SAT(\mathbf{C})$.

$Q(A$	B	C	$D)$
a_1			a_4
a_1	b_1	b_2	b_3
b_4	b_1	b_5	b_6
b_7	b_8	b_5	a_4

Figure 11.57

Q′(A	B	C	D)
a_1			a_4
a_1	b_1	b_2	b_3
b_4	b_1	b_5	a_4
b_7	b_8	b_5	a_4

Figure 11.58

Q″(A	B	C	D)
a_1			a_4
a_1	b_1	b_2	b_3
b_4	b_1	b_5	a_4

Figure 11.59

When **C** consists of only FDs, there is another way to interpret $chase_{\mathbf{C}}(Q)$. The rows that do not correspond to any relation for database d can be regarded as corresponding to joins of relations, provided that F-rules were applied in a certain restricted manner. The joins are ones that can be computed efficiently, so any minimization that takes place in computing $chase_{\mathbf{C}}(Q)$ can be viewed as replacing arbitrary joins by efficient joins. We now take up this type of join.

Let d be a database over database scheme R that is the projection of a common instance $r(U)$. Let F be a set of FDs that r satisfies. If $r_1(XY)$ and $r_2(YZW)$ are two relations in d such that $XY \cap YZW = Y$, and $Y \rightarrow Z$ is an FD in F^+, then the *r_2-extension of r_1 by $Y \rightarrow Z$* is $r_1 \bowtie \pi_{YZ}(r_2)$. The r_2-extension of r_1 by $Y \rightarrow Z$ has the same number of tuples as r_1 and can be computed by a single pass through r_1 and r_2 if both relations are sorted on Y. Note that $r_1 \bowtie \pi_{YZ}(r_2) = \pi_{XYZ}(r)$. Such a join, where the common attributes of the two relations functionally determine all the attributes of one of the relations, is called an *extension join*.

A subset R of **U** is an $\mathbf{R}_F$-extension if $\pi_R(r)$ can be computed from database d only using extension joins and projection. That is, R is a subscheme of some relation in d or there is a program P of the form

$$
\begin{aligned}
&q_1 \leftarrow s_1 \bowtie \pi_{Y_1Z_1}(s_1');\\
&q_2 \leftarrow s_2 \bowtie \pi_{Y_2Z_2}(s_2');\\
&\vdots\\
&q_k \leftarrow s_k \bowtie \pi_{Y_kZ_k}(s_k')
\end{aligned}
$$

where

1. s_i is either a relation in d or q_j for $j < i$; the same for s_i',
2. q_i is the s_i'-extension of s_i by $Y_i \rightarrow Z_i$ for some FD $Y_i \rightarrow Z_i$ in F^+, and
3. the scheme of q_k is $R' \supseteq R$.

(See Exercise 11.34.)

Example 11.49 Let $d = \{r_1(AB), r_2(BC), r_3(CD), r_4(BDEI)\}$ be a database over database scheme $\mathbf{R} = \{AB, BC, CD, BDEI\}$. Assume d is the projection of an instance $r(A\ B\ C\ D\ E\ I)$ in $SAT(F)$, where $F = \{C \rightarrow D, BD \rightarrow E\}$. CE is an $\mathbf{R}_F$-extension, for consider the program

$$q_1 \leftarrow r_2 \bowtie r_3;$$
$$q_2 \leftarrow q_1 \bowtie \pi_{BDE}(r_4).$$

Both joins are extension joins and the scheme of q_2 is $BCDE$, which contains CE. AE is not an $\mathbf{R}_F$-extension. A only appears in relation r_1, which can never participate in an extension join because none of A, B, and AB appear as the left side of a nontrivial FD in F^+.

Given a set of FDs F and a database scheme $\mathbf{R}$ over $\mathbf{U}$, we can modify the chase computation to decide whether some set $R \subseteq \mathbf{U}$ is an $\mathbf{R}_F$-extension. The modification is that an F-rule cannot be applied to equate two nondistinguished variables. However, any FD in F^+ may be used as the basis for an F-rule. We call this computation the *extension chase with respect to* F, denoted $echase_F$.

Theorem 11.7 Let F be a set of FDs and let $\mathbf{R}$ be a database scheme over attributes $\mathbf{U}$. Let $T_{\mathbf{R}}$ be the tableau for $\mathbf{R}$. Let $R \subseteq \mathbf{U}$. If $echase_F(T_{\mathbf{R}})$ has a row that is distinguished on all the attributes in R (and possibly more), then R is an $\mathbf{R}_F$-extension.

Proof Initially, if some row in $T_{\mathbf{R}}$ is distinguished on the attributes in R, there must be some relation scheme R' in $\mathbf{R}$ with $R' \supseteq R$, so R is in an $\mathbf{R}_F$-extension.

The inductive hypothesis is that at any point of the computation of $echase_F(T_{\mathbf{R}})$, if some row w is distinguished on the attributes in S, then S is an $\mathbf{R}_F$-extension. Assume at some point in the computation we have rows w_1 and w_2 that are distinguished on S_1 and S_2, and that we apply the F-rule for $X \rightarrow A$ to make $w_1(A)$ distinguished (hence $w_2(A)$ already is). Since no nondistinguished variable is ever repeated, and $w_1(X) = w_2(X)$, we must have $X \subseteq S_1$ and $X \subseteq S_2$.

We need to show that S_1A is an $\mathbf{R}_F$-extension. Assume d is a database on $\mathbf{R}$ that is the projection of an instance $r(\mathbf{U})$. Since S_1 and S_2 are $\mathbf{R}_F$-extensions, we can construct relations $q_1(S_1) = \pi_{S_1}(r)$ and $q_2(S_2) = \pi_{S_2}(r)$ using only extension joins and projection. We can then construct $q_3(S_1A)$ as the q_2-extension of q_1 by $X \to A$. Hence S_1A is an $\mathbf{R}_F$-extension. Note that the only way $w_1(A)$ can become distinguished is through the direct application of an F-rule to w_1.

Example 11.50 Figure 11.60 shows $T_{\mathbf{R}}$ for the database scheme $\mathbf{R} = \{AB, BC, CD, BDEI\}$ of Example 11.49. Figure 11.61 shows $echase_F(T_{\mathbf{R}})$ for $F = \{C \to D, BD \to E\}$. We see that R is an $\mathbf{R}_F$-extension if $R \subseteq AB$, $R \subseteq BCDE$ or $R \subseteq BDEI$.

$T_{\mathbf{R}}$(A	B	C	D	E	I)
a_1	a_2	b_1	b_2	b_3	b_1
b_5	a_2	a_3	b_6	b_7	b_8
b_9	b_{10}	a_3	a_4	b_{11}	b_{12}
b_{13}	a_2	b_{14}	a_4	a_5	a_6

Figure 11.60

$echase_F(T_{\mathbf{R}})$(A	B	C	D	E	I)
a_1	a_2	b_1	b_2	b_3	b_4
b_5	a_2	a_3	a_4	a_5	b_8
b_9	b_{10}	a_3	a_4	b_{11}	b_{12}
b_{13}	a_2	b_{14}	a_4	a_5	a_6

Figure 11.61

It is not sufficient for R to be an $\mathbf{R}_F$-extension that $chase_F(T_{\mathbf{R}})$ be distinguished on R. In fact, the converse of Theorem 11.7 holds (see Exercise 11.37).

Example 11.51 Figure 11.62 shows the tableau $T_{\mathbf{R}}$ for database scheme $\mathbf{R} = \{AD, AB, BDE, CE\}$, which we last saw in Example 8.41. Let $F = \{A \to C, B \to C, CD \to E\}$. We see that $echase_F(T_{\mathbf{R}}) = T_{\mathbf{R}}$. However, $chase_F(T_{\mathbf{R}}) \neq T_{\mathbf{R}}$, as we see in Figure 11.63. There is a row of $chase_F(T_{\mathbf{R}})$ distinguished on CDE, but ADE is not an $\mathbf{R}_F$-extension (see Exercise 11.39).

$T_{\mathbf{R}}$(A	B	C	D	E)
a_1	b_1	b_2	a_4	b_3
a_1	a_2	b_3	b_4	b_5
b_6	a_2	b_7	a_4	a_5
b_8	b_9	a_3	b_{10}	a_5

Figure 11.62

$chase_F(T_{\mathbf{R}})$(A	B	C	D	E)
a_1	b_2	b_2	a_4	a_5
a_1	a_2	b_2	b_4	b_5
b_6	a_2	b_2	a_4	a_5
b_8	b_9	a_3	b_{10}	a_5

Figure 11.63

Returning to tableau queries, let d be a database on database scheme $\mathbf{R}$ that is the projection of an instance $r(\mathbf{U})$. Let Q be a tableau query that applies to d. For a set of FDs F, we can apply $echase_F$ to Q. However, rather than requiring that a symbol may only be replaced by a distinguished variable, we require that a symbol may only be replaced by a matched symbol. The matched symbols in Q correspond to distinguished variables in $T_{\mathbf{R}}$. Since Q applies to d, for any row w in Q, there is always a relation scheme S in $\mathbf{R}$ such that $match(W) \subseteq S$.

Consider $Q' = echase_F(Q)$. There may be a row w' in Q' such that $S' = match(w')$ is not contained in any scheme in $\mathbf{R}$. However, S' will always be an $\mathbf{R}_F$-extension. Thus, Q' applies to some database $d' = \{r_1(R_1), r_2(R_2), \ldots, r_p(R_p)\}$ where R_i is an $\mathbf{R}_F$-extension for $1 \leq i \leq p$. Every relation in d' can be computed from relations in d through extension joins and projections. If Q is the tableau query for some restricted algebraic expression for d, Q' will be a tableau query for some restricted algebraic expression for d' (see Exercise 11.40).

Example 11.52 Referring back to Example 11.47, Figure 11.57 shows the tableau query for the algebraic expression

$$\pi_{AD}(q \bowtie r \bowtie s)$$

for the database $d = \{q(AB), r(BC), s(CD)\}$. It turns out that $Q' = chase_F(Q) = echase_F(Q)$ for $F = \{C \rightarrow D\}$, so $Q \equiv_F Q'$ for the tableau query Q' in Figure 11.58. Q'' does not apply to d, because the matched set of the second row is BD. However, BD is an R_F-extension for database scheme $\mathbf{R} = \{AB, BC, CD\}$. Thus, the algebraic expression above is equivalent under F to

$$\pi_{AD}(q \bowtie r'),$$

where r' can be computed by extension joins and projections from r and s.

We actually have slightly more leeway in computing $echase_F(Q)$. Suppose w is a row in Q and $match(w) = S$, and suppose there is a relation $s(S')$ in d such that $S' \supseteq S$. We can treat $w(A)$ as a matched symbol for any $A \in S'$, even if $A \notin S$. Consider: If we add a row w' to Q, where $w'(S') = q(S')$ and w' is new nondistinguished variables elsewhere, then we have not changed the mapping Q defines, since w supersedes w'. Furthermore, Q still applies to d and $match(w) = S'$.

Finally, in this section, we turn to tagged tableau queries and extensions of our equivalence results to databases that are not projections of a common instance. The fundamental change to validate the results is that a containment mapping between tagged tableau queries must preserve tags. That is, we require that a containment mapping always maps blanks to blanks, and never maps a symbol to a blank.

Example 11.53 Let d be a database $\{q(AD), r(BC), s(AC)\}$ that is not necessarily the projection of any common instance. Figure 11.64 shows the tagged tableau query Q_1 for the algebraic expression

$$\pi_{BC}(\sigma_{B=c}(q) \bowtie r \bowtie s).$$

Figure 11.65 shows the tagged tableau query Q_2 for the algebraic expression

$$\pi_{BC}(r \bowtie s).$$

The mapping ψ defined by

$$\psi(a_2) = c$$
$$\psi(a_3) = a_3$$
$$\psi(b_1) = b_1$$

is a containment mapping from Q_2 to Q_1, so $Q_2 \sqsupseteq Q_1$. We conclude

$$\pi_{BC}(\sigma_{B=c}(q) \bowtie r \bowtie s) \subseteq \pi_{BC}(r \bowtie s)$$

for any choices of q, r, and s.

Recall that in Example 11.46 we saw that

$$\pi_{BC}(\sigma_{B=c}(q) \bowtie r \bowtie s) = \sigma_{B=c}(r)$$

if q, r, and s are all projections of a common instance. Q_3 in Figure 11.66 is the tagged tableau query for $\sigma_{B=c}(r)$. Note that $Q_1 \not\equiv Q_3$, because no containment mapping is possible from Q_1 to Q_3.

Q_1(A	B	C)	
	c	a_3	
b_1	c		(AB)
	c	a_3	(BC)
b_1		a_3	(AC)

Figure 11.64

Q_2(A	B	C)	
	a_2	a_3	
	a_2	a_3	(BC)
b_1		a_3	(AC)

Figure 11.65

Q_3(A	B	C)	
	c	a_3	
	c	a_3	(BC)

Figure 11.66

The results for data dependencies in the single relation case do not carry over entirely to tagged tableau queries. In general, in computing the chase of a tagged tableau query, only F-rules may be applied, and then only to rows with the same tag.

Example 11.54 Figure 11.67 shows two tagged tableau queries, Q_1 and Q_2, for the database $d = \{r(A\ B\ C), s(B\ C\ D)\}$. Given that r and s both satisfy $F = \{B \rightarrow C\}$, we might conclude that Q_1 and Q_2 are equivalent under F. However, as the reader may verify, $Q_1(d) \not\equiv Q_2(d)$ for the states of r and s given in Figure 11.68.

Q_1

A	B	C	D	
a_1			a_4	
a_1	b_1	b_2		(ABC)
	b_1	b_3	a_4	

Q_2

A	B	C	D	
a_1			a_4	
a_1	b_1	b_2		(ABC)
	b_1	b_2	a_4	(BCD)

Figure 11.67

r

A	B	C
1	3	5
2	4	5

s

B	C	D
3	5	7
4	6	8

Figure 11.68

The problem in Example 11.54 is that while r and s both satisfy $B \rightarrow C$, the function from B to C defined by r is not consistent with the function from B to C defined by s. F-rules can only be applied to rows with different tags if consistency of FDs is required. Note that if a database d has a minimal BCNF database scheme with respect to the FDs in F, then the issue is moot. No FD in F^+ applies to two rows in a tagged tableau query for d if the rows have different tags.

11.5.5 Tableau Set Query Equivalence

Here we return to untagged tableau queries. Recall that a tableau set query $\mathbf{Q}$ with scheme R is a set of compatible tableau queries $\{Q_1, Q_2, \ldots, Q_p\}$, all with scheme R (necessarily). Recall also that $\mathbf{Q}(r)$ is

$$Q_1(r) \cup Q_2(r) \cup \cdots \cup Q_p(r).$$

The notions of containment and equivalence extend directly to tableau set queries.

Definition 11.13 Let $\mathbf{Q}_1$ and $\mathbf{Q}_2$ be tableau set queries with scheme R. Then $\mathbf{Q}_1 \sqsubseteq \mathbf{Q}_2$ if $\mathbf{Q}_1(r) \subseteq \mathbf{Q}_2(r)$ for every relation $r(R)$. $\mathbf{Q}_1 \equiv \mathbf{Q}_2$ if $\mathbf{Q}_1(r) = \mathbf{Q}_2(r)$ for every relation $r(R)$.

The following theorem characterizes containment of tableau set queries.

Theorem 11.8 Let $\mathbf{Q}_1$ and $\mathbf{Q}_2$ be compatible tableau set queries with scheme R. $\mathbf{Q}_1 \sqsupseteq \mathbf{Q}_2$ if and only if for each tableau query Q_2 in Q_2 there is a tableau query Q_1 in Q_1 such that $Q_1 \sqsupseteq Q_2$.

Proof The if direction follows directly from the definition of $\mathbf{Q}_1(r)$ and $\mathbf{Q}_2(r)$. For the only if direction, we again use the technique of regarding the rows of a tableau query as a relation. Let Q_2 be any tableau query in $\mathbf{Q}_2$ and consider $\mathbf{Q}_2(Q_2)$. If w_0 is the summary of Q_2, then $w_0 \in \mathbf{Q}_2(Q_2)$, since $w_0 \in Q_2(Q_2)$ (by the identity valuation). Since $\mathbf{Q}_1 \sqsupseteq \mathbf{Q}_2$, $w_0 \in \mathbf{Q}_1(Q_2)$. There must be a tableau query Q_1 in S_1 such that $w_0 \in Q_1(Q_2)$. Let v_0 be the summary of Q_1. The valuation ρ such that $\rho(Q_1) \subseteq Q_2$ and $\rho(v_0) = w_0$ is a containment mapping from Q_1 to Q_2. Hence $Q_1 \sqsupseteq Q_2$.

Example 11.55 Using the tableau queries $Q_1 = Q_4$ in Figure 11.69,\we define tableau set queries $\mathbf{Q}_1 = \{Q_1, Q_2, Q_3\}$ and $\mathbf{Q}_2 = \{Q_3, Q_4\}$. $\mathbf{Q}_2 \sqsupseteq \mathbf{Q}_1$, since $Q_4 \sqsupseteq Q_1$, $Q_4 \sqsupseteq Q_2$, and $Q_3 \sqsupseteq Q_3$. $\mathbf{Q}_1 \not\sqsupseteq \mathbf{Q}_2$, since none of Q_1, Q_2, or Q_3 contain Q_4.

Definition 11.14 A tableau set query $\mathbf{Q}$ is *nonredundant* if it does not contain distinct tableau queries Q_1 and Q_2 such that $Q_1 \sqsupseteq Q_2$.

Theorem 11.9 Let $\mathbf{Q}_1$ and $\mathbf{Q}_2$ be nonredundant tableau set queries. If $\mathbf{Q}_1 \equiv \mathbf{Q}_2$, then for every tableau query $Q_1 \in \mathbf{Q}_1$, there is one and only one tableau query $Q_2 \in \mathbf{Q}_2$ such that $Q_1 \equiv Q_2$.

Q_1

A	B	C
a_1		4
a_1	b_1	b_2
3	b_1	4

Q_2

A	B	C
a_1		4
a_1	b_1	b_2
b_3	b_1	4

Q_3

A	B	C
3		a_3
3	b_1	a_3
3	5	b_2

Q_4

A	B	C
a_1		a_3
a_1	b_1	b_2
b_3	b_1	a_3

Figure 11.69

Proof Let Q_1 be a tableau query in $\mathbf{Q}_1$. Since $\mathbf{Q}_1 \sqsubseteq \mathbf{Q}_2$, there is a tableau query $Q_2 \in \mathbf{Q}_2$ such that $Q_1 \sqsubseteq Q_2$. Similarly, since $\mathbf{Q}_1 \sqsupseteq \mathbf{Q}_2$, there is a tableau query Q_3 in $\mathbf{Q}_1$ such that $Q_3 \supseteq Q_2$. We see $Q_1 \sqsubseteq Q_3$, which means $Q_1 = Q_3$, or else $\mathbf{Q}_1$ is not nonredundant. We conclude $Q_1 \equiv Q_2$. If there is another tableau query Q_4 in $\mathbf{Q}_2$ such that $Q_1 \equiv Q_4$, then $Q_2 \equiv Q_4$ and $\mathbf{Q}_2$ is not nonredundant. Hence Q_2 is the only tableau query in $\mathbf{Q}_2$ equivalent to Q_1.

Corollary If $\mathbf{Q}$ is a nonredundant tableau set query, there is no tableau set query equivalent to $\mathbf{Q}$ with fewer tableau queries.

Proof Left to the reader (see Exercise 11.43).

Example 11.56 Consider the tableau set query $\mathbf{Q}_1 = \{Q_1, Q_2, Q_3\}$ in Example 11.55. $\mathbf{Q}_1$ is not nonredundant, since $Q_2 \sqsupseteq Q_1$. If we let $\mathbf{Q}_3 = \{Q_2, Q_3\}$, then $\mathbf{Q}_1 \equiv \mathbf{Q}_3$. $\mathbf{Q}_3$ is nonredundant, since $Q_2 \not\sqsupseteq Q_3$ and $Q_3 \not\sqsupseteq Q_2$.

11.6 OPTIMIZING CONJUNCTIVE QUERIES

Recall that a conjunctive query over a database d is a domain calculus expression E of the form

$$\{x_1(A_1)\, x_2(A_2) \cdots x_n(A_n) | \exists y_1(B_1)\, \exists y_2(B_2) \cdots \exists y_m(B_m)$$
$$f(x_1, x_2, \ldots, x_n, y_1, y_2, \ldots, y_m).\}$$

such that f is the conjunction of atoms of the form

$$r(a_1\, a_2 \cdots a_k)$$

where $r \in d$ and each a_i is one of the x's, one of the y's, or a constant. Each atom in f represents a relation to be joined in evaluating E. We would like to find a conjunctive query equivalent to E that minimizes the number of atoms. The approach to minimizing conjunctive queries is almost exactly that of minimizing tableau queries.

One obvious requirement for equivalence of conjunctive queries is that they define relations over the same scheme. Any conjunctive query E' that is equivalent to E above must have the form

$$\{w_1(A_1)\, w_2(A_2) \cdots w_n(A_n) | \exists z_1(C_1)\, \exists z_2(C_2) \cdots \exists z_p(C_p)$$
$$g(w_1, w_2, \ldots, w_n, z_1, z_2, \ldots, z_p)\}.$$

A *folding* ψ from E to E' is a mapping of the domain variables and constants of E to the domain variables and constants of E' such that

c1. $\psi(x_i) = w_i$, $1 \leq i \leq n$;
c2. $\psi(c) = c$ for any constant c; and
c3. If $r(a_1\, a_2 \cdots a_k)$ is any atom in f, then $r(\psi(a_i)\, \psi(a_2) \cdots \psi(a_k))$ is an atom in g.

Foldings are quite similar to containment mappings of tagged tableau queries.

Example 11.57 Let d be the database $\{q(ABC), r(BCD), s(AD)\}$. Assume $dom(C) = dom(D)$. Let E be the conjunctive query

$$\{x_1(A)\, x_2(D) \mid \exists y_1(B)\, \exists y_2(C)\, \exists y_3(D)\, \exists y_4(D)$$
$$q(x_1\, y_1\, y_2) \wedge r(y_1\, y_2\, x_2) \wedge r(y_1\, x_2\, y_3) \wedge s(x_1\, y_4)\}$$

and let E' be the conjunctive query

$$\{w_1(A)\, w_2(D) \mid \exists z_1(B)\, q(w_1\, z_1\, w_2) \wedge r(z_1\, w_2\, w_2) \wedge s(w_1\, 6)\}.$$

The mapping ψ in Figure 11.70 is a folding from E to E'. There is no folding from E' to E, since the atom $s(w_1\ 6)$ in E' cannot map to any atom of E.

$\psi(x_1) = w_1$	$\psi(y_1) = z_1$
$\psi(x_2) = w_2$	$\psi(y_2) = w_2$
	$\psi(y_3) = w_2$
	$\psi(y_4) = 6$

Figure 11.70

For conjunctive queries E_1 and E_2, let $E_1 \sqsupseteq E_2$ mean the obvious thing. The proof of the following theorem is similar to that of Theorem 11.1, and is left as Exercise 11.44.

Theorem 11.10 Let E_1 and E_2 be conjunctive queries that define relations over the same scheme. $E_1 \sqsupseteq E_2$ if and only if there is a folding from E_1 to E_2.

Definition 11.15 A conjunctive query E is *minimum* if there is no conjunctive query E' equivalent to E with fewer atoms in its formula.

From Theorem 11.10 we can show that any minimum equivalent conjunctive query for a given conjunctive query E is unique up to a one-to-one renaming of domain variables. That is, if E_1 and E_2 are minimum equivalent conjunctive queries for E, then there is a folding ψ from E_1 to E_2 whose inverse is a folding from E_2 and E_1.

Let E_1 be

$$\{x_1(A_1)\, x_2(A_2) \cdots x_n(A_n) \mid \exists y_1(B_1)\, \exists y_2(B_2) \cdots \exists y_m(B_m)$$
$$f(x_1, x_2, \ldots, x_n, y_1, y_2, \ldots, y_m)\}$$

and let E_2 be

$$\{w_1(A_1)\, w_2(A_2) \cdots w_n(A_n) \mid \exists z_1(C_1)\, \exists z_2(C_2) \cdots \exists z_p(C_p)$$
$$g(w_1, w_2, \ldots, w_n, z_1, z_2, \ldots, z_p)\}.$$

By Theorem 11.10, there is a folding ψ_{12} from E_1 to E_2 and a folding ψ_{21} from E_2 to E_1. If ψ_{12} maps two atoms of f to the same atom of g, then $\psi_{21} \circ \psi_{12}$ is a folding from the atoms of E_1 to a proper subset of those atoms. The identity mapping is a folding from this subset to all the atoms. We conclude that we can remove some atoms (and possibly some of the y's) from E_1 to get an equivalent conjunctive query, a contradiction. Thus ψ_{12} must be one-to-one on the atoms of f. By a similar argument, we can show ψ_{12} is one-to-one as a mapping of variables and constants. (If not, there must be some y_i that is not mentioned in f.) Thus, the inverse of ψ_{12} is indeed a function. The inverse of ψ_{12} must also be defined on all variables and constants in E_2, or else there is some atom of g not mapped to by ψ_{12}, which implies E_2 is not minimum.

To show that ψ_{12}^{-1} is indeed a folding, we must show that conditions c1-c3 in the definition of folding hold. We have $\psi_{12}^{-1}(w_i) = x_i$, since $\psi_{12}(x_i) = w_i$. If $r(b_1\ b_2\ \cdots\ b_k)$ is an atom in g, it must be mapped to by some atom $r(a_1\ a_2\ \cdots\ a_k)$ in f, or else E_2 would not be minimum. Therefore, $r(\psi_{12}^{-1}(b_1)\ \psi_{12}^{-1}(b_2)\ \cdots\ \psi_{12}^{-1}(b_k)) = r(a_1\ a_2\ \cdots\ a_k)$ is in f. The only condition left to check is c2: $\psi_{12}^{-1}(c) = c$ for any constant c. The only way a problem can arise is if $\psi_{12}(y_i) = c$ for some $1 \le i \le m$.

For an atom $r(a_1\ a_2\ \cdots\ a_k)$ in f and a folding ψ, let $\psi(r(a_1\ a_2\ \cdots\ a_k))$ be $r(\psi(a_1\ \psi(a_2)\ \cdots\ \psi(a_k))$. Consider the folding $\psi_{11} = \psi_{21} \circ \psi_{12}$ from E_1 to itself. Everything we have shown so far about ψ_{12} applies to ψ_{21} by symmetry. The folding ψ_{11} must be a one-to-one mapping on atoms of E_1, since it is the composition of two such mappings. Let α_1 be an atom of E_1 that contains y_i in the jth position. Consider the sequence $\alpha_1, \alpha_2, \alpha_3, \ldots$ of atoms from E_1 such that $\psi_{11}(\alpha_l) = a_{l+1}$, $l \ge 1$. The sequence must eventually repeat an atom. Suppose $\alpha_q = \alpha_{q'}$ for $q < q'$. If $q > 1$ then $\psi_{11}(\alpha_{q-1}) = \alpha_q = \psi_{11}(\alpha_{q'-1})$ and ψ_{11} is not one-to-one on atoms. Hence $q = 1$. But since $\psi_{12}(y_i) = c$ and $\psi_{21}(c) = c$, $\psi_{11}(y_i) = c$. Also, $\psi_{11}(c) = c$, so each of $\alpha_2, \alpha_3, \alpha_4, \ldots$ must have c in the jth position, which contradicts $\alpha_1 = \alpha_{q'}$. The premise that $\psi_{12}(y_i) = c$ must be incorrect.

We summarize our argument in the following theorem.

Theorem 11.11 Let E_1 and E_2 be two minimum conjunctive queries. $E_1 \equiv E_2$ if and only if there is a folding ψ from E_1 to E_2 such that ψ^{-1} is a folding from E_2 to E_1.

As a consequence of Theorem 11.11, it is not hard to show that for any conjunctive query E there is a minimum equivalent conjunctive query E' that is E with some atoms and quantified variables removed. Minimizing a conjunctive query E reduces to finding a folding from E to E' that maps the atoms of E to a proper subset of themselves.

Example 11.58 Let d be the same database as used in Example 11.57. Consider the conjunctive query

$$E = \{x_1(A)\, x_2(D) \mid \exists y_1(C)\ \exists y_2(B)\ \exists y_3(C)\ \exists y_4(C)\ \exists y_5(D)\ q(x_1\ 3\ y_1) \wedge q(x_1\ y_2\ y_3) \wedge r(3\ y_1\ x_2) \wedge r(y_2\ y_4\ x_2) \wedge s(x_1\ 5) \wedge s(x_1\ y_5)\}$$

over database d. The folding ψ_1 for E that maps y_2 to 3, y_3 and y_4 to y_1, and everything else to itself shows that the conjunctive query

$$E' = \{x_1(A)\, x_2(A) \mid \exists y_1(C)\ \exists y_5(D)\ q(x_1\ 3\ y_1) \wedge r(3\ y_1\ x_2) \wedge s(x_1\ 5) \wedge s(x_1\ y_5)\}$$

is equivalent to E. The folding ψ_2 for E' that maps y_5 to 5 and everything else to itself shows that

$$E'' = \{x_1(A)\, x_2(A) \mid \exists y_1(C)\ q(x_1\ 3\ y_1) \wedge r(3\ y_1\ x_2) \wedge s(x_1\ 5)\}$$

is equivalent to E' and hence to E. E'' is clearly minimum (why?), so E'' is a minimum equivalent conjunctive query for E.

Determining whether a given conjunctive query E is minimum is an NP-complete problem. No known method for testing minimality is significantly better than examining all foldings from E to itself to see if one maps the atoms of E to a proper subset of themselves. Nevertheless, if E contains only a few atoms, such a search will not be prohibitive, especially if E is to be evaluated many times.

11.7 QUERY MODIFICATION FOR DISTRIBUTED DATABASES

Some database systems support relational databases whose parts are physically separated. Different relations might reside at different sites, multiple copies of a single relation might be distributed among several sites, or one relation might be broken into pieces and the pieces distributed. In order to evaluate a query posed at one site, it may be necessary to transfer data between various sites. The dominant element in the time required to process such a query will often be the time spent transferring data between sites, rather than the time spent on retrieval from secondary storage or computation. Efficient query evaluation depends on minimizing communication between sites.

Example 11.59 Suppose that the expression $r \bowtie \sigma_{A=a}(s)$ must be evaluated at site 1 of a distributed database system, where r is stored at site 1, but s is at site 2. Site 1 could ask site 2 to transmit all of relation s, and then compute the selection itself. A more reasonable approach, if s is large, if for site 1 to transmit the selection condition $A = a$ to site 2. Site 2 then performs the selection and transmits the result, which is presumably much smaller than s, to site 1.

In this section we shall look at semijoin, which is a useful operation for computing joins in a distributed system, and fragmented relations, which are relations that have been horizontally decomposed and stored at multiple sites.

11.7.1 Semijoins

Before defining semijoin, we demonstrate its utility with an example.

Example 11.60 Let relations $r(A\ B)$ and $s(B\ C\ D)$, as shown in Figure 11.71, be stored at site 1 and site 2, respectively, of a distributed database. Suppose we wish to compute $r \bowtie s$ at site 1. We could transmit all of s from site 2 to site 1 and compute the join at site 1. There would be 21 values sent in that transmission. Alternatively, we can compute $r' = \pi_B(r)$ at site 1, send r' to site 2, compute $s' = r' \bowtie s$, and send s' to site 1. We can then compute $r \bowtie s$ as $r \bowtie s'$. Relations r' and s' are shown in Figure 11.72. For this method, only 15 values must be transmitted: 6 for r' and 9 for s'.

r(A	B)
1	4
1	5
1	6
2	4
2	6
3	7
3	8
3	9

s(B	C	D)
4	13	16
4	14	16
7	13	17
10	14	16
10	15	17
11	15	16
11	15	16
12	15	16

Figure 11.71

$r'(A)$
4
5
6
7
8
9

$s'(B$	C	$D)$
4	13	16
4	14	16
7	13	17

Figure 11.72

Definition 11.16 Let $r(R)$ and $s(S)$ be two relations. The *semijoin of* r *with* s, denoted $r \ltimes s$, is the relation $\pi_R(r \bowtie s)$. That is, $r \ltimes s$ is the portion of r that joins with s.

Recalling some of the transformations from Section 11.3, we have

$$\pi_R(r \bowtie s) = \pi_R(r) \bowtie \pi_{R \cap S}(s) = r \bowtie \pi_{R \cap S}(s).$$

Thus, $r \ltimes s$ can be computed knowning only $\pi_{R \cap S}(s)$; all of s is not necessary. (In Example 11.60, $r' = \pi_B(r)$ and $s' = s \ltimes r$.) The property of semijoin that interests us is that $(r \ltimes s) \bowtie s = r \bowtie s$ (see Exercise 11.46). If r and s are at different sites, computing $r \bowtie s$ as $(r \ltimes s) \bowtie s$ saves transmitting data whenever r is larger than $\pi_{R \cap S}(r)$ and $r \ltimes s$ put together. If r and s join completely, there is no savings, of course. However, even in a database where all relations are projections of a common instance, queries can involve joins between relations that do not join completely, as a result of selections. In such cases, semijoins may be effective. Sometimes semijoins can replace joins completely.

Example 11.61 Let $q(A\ B)$, $r(B\ C)$, and $s(C\ D)$ be the three relations shown in Figure 11.73. Suppose q, r, and s are dispersed at sites 1, 2, and 3, respectively, and that we wish to evaluate the algebraic expression

$$E = \pi_D(\sigma_{A=1}(q \bowtie r \bowtie s))$$

at site 3. First we note that E is equivalent to

$$E' = \pi_D(\sigma_{A=1}(q) \bowtie r \bowtie s).$$

To evaluate E', we first compute $q' = \sigma_{A=1}(q)$ at site 1. We next send $\pi_B(q')$ to site 2 and compute $r' = r \ltimes q'$ there. We then send $\pi_C(r')$ to site

3 and compute $s' = s \ltimes r'$ at site 3. The desired result is $\pi_D(s')$, which we also compute at site 3. Relations q', r', and s' are shown in Figure 11.74. Note that no relation was transmitted in its entirety.

$q(A$	$B)$	$r(B$	$C)$	$s(C$	$D)$
1	4	4	7	7	11
1	5	5	7	8	11
2	4	5	8	9	12
2	6	6	9	10	11
3	6	6	10		

Figure 11.73

$q'(A$	$B)$	$r'(B$	$C)$	$s'(C$	$D)$
1	4	4	7	7	11
1	5	5	7	8	11
		5	8		

Figure 11.74

Frequently during the evaluation of a query in a distributed database, there is a point at which intermediate result relations $r_1, r_2, \ldots, r_p$ exist at different sites, and the next step is to compute $r_1 \bowtie r_2 \bowtie \cdots \bowtie r_p$ at a single site. It is helpful if we can easily compute the portion of each relation that takes part in the join.

Definition 11.17 Given database d and a relation $r(R)$ in d, the *full reduction of* r *relative to* d, denoted $FR(r, d)$, is $\pi_R(\bowtie(d))$. That is, $FR(r, d)$ is the portion of r that takes part in the join with all the other relations in d.

Example 11.62 Let d be the database $\{q(A\ B), r(B\ C), s(A\ C)\}$ for the relations q, r, and s in Figure 11.75. $FR(q, d) = q'$, $FR(r, d) = r'$, and $FR(s, d) = s'$ are shown in Figure 11.76.

$q(A$	$B)$	$r(B$	$C)$	$s(A$	$C)$
1	4	4	7	1	8
1	5	5	7	2	7
2	4	5	8	2	8
2	6	6	8	3	7
3	6				

Figure 11.75

$q'(A$	$B)$	$r'(B$	$C)$	$s'(A$	$C)$
1	5	4	7	1	8
2	4	5	8	2	7
2	6	6	8	2	8

Figure 11.76

Definition 11.18 Let $d = \{r_1, r_2, \ldots, r_p\}$ be a database. A *semijoin program SP* for d is a sequence of assignment statements of the form

$$r_i \leftarrow r_i \ltimes r_j$$

We let $SP(r_i, d)$ denote the final value of r_i after executing SP on d.

Definition 11.19 A semijoin program SP for database $d = \{r_1, r_2, \ldots, r_p\}$ is a *full-reducer* if for any state of d,

$$FR(r_i, d) = SP(r_i, d),\ 1 \le i \le p.$$

Note that $FR(r_i, d) \subseteq SP(r_i, d)$ whether or not SP is a full reducer for d (see Exercise 11.48).

Example 11.63 Let d be the database $\{r_1(A_1\ A_2), r_2(A_2\ A_3\ A_4\ A_5), r_3(A_3\ A_4\ A_6), r_4(A_4\ A_5\ A_7)\}$. Figure 11.77 shows a semijoin program SP_1 for d. SP_1 is not a full-reducer for d. Consider the state of d shown in Figure 11.78. $SP_1(r_2, d)$ is shown in Figure 11.79. It contains the tuple ⟨4 5 7 10⟩, which is not in $FR(r_2, d)$, since it joins with no tuple in r_i.

The semijoin program SP_1 in Figure 11.78 is a full-reducer for d. For example, using the state of d in Figure 11.75, $SP_2(r_2, d)$ is the relation in Figure 11.79, which is $FR(r_2, d)$. Proving that SP_2 is indeed a full reducer is not a trivial task, nor is SP_2 the shortest full-reducer for d (see Exercise 11.49). We indicate here why, for example, $SP_2(r_2, d)$ is necessarily $FR(r_2, d)$.

By Exercise 11.48, $SP_2(r_2, d) \supseteq FR(r_2, d)$. We need to show that every tuple in $SP_2(r_2, d)$ will actually join with tuples from the other three relations. Note that of the other three relations, only r_3 and r_4 have intersecting schemes, and the intersection is contained in the scheme of r_2. If a tuple t_2 from r_2 joins individually with tuples t_1, t_3, and t_4 from r_1, r_3, and r_4, it will join with them collectively. Since r_2 is semijoined with r_1, r_3, and r_4 in steps 3, 4, and 5 of SP_2, such tuples t_1, t_3, and t_4 must be present for any tuple t_2 in r_2.

SP_1:

1. $r_2 \leftarrow r_2 \ltimes r_3$;
2. $r_2 \leftarrow r_2 \ltimes r_4$;
3. $r_1 \leftarrow r_1 \ltimes r_1$.

Figure 11.77

r_1

A_1	A_2
1	3
2	3

r_2

A_2	A_3	A_4	A_5
3	5	7	9
3	6	7	9
4	5	7	10

r_3

A_3	A_4	A_6
5	7	11
6	8	12

r_4

A_4	A_5	A_7
7	9	13
7	10	13

Figure 11.78

$SP_1(r_2,d)$

A_2	A_3	A_4	A_5
3	5	7	9
4	5	7	10

Figure 11.79

SP_2:

1. $r_3 \leftarrow r_3 \ltimes r_4$;
2. $r_4 \leftarrow r_4 \ltimes r_3$;
3. $r_2 \leftarrow r_2 \ltimes r_3$;
4. $r_2 \leftarrow r_2 \ltimes r_4$;
5. $r_2 \leftarrow r_2 \ltimes r_1$;
6. $r_1 \leftarrow r_1 \ltimes r_2$;
7. $r_3 \leftarrow r_3 \ltimes r_2$;
8. $r_4 \leftarrow r_4 \ltimes r_2$.

Figure 11.80

$SP_2(r_2,d)$

A_2	A_3	A_4	A_5
3	5	7	9

Figure 11.81

Example 11.64 The database d in Example 11.62 has no full-reducer. The state of d shown in Figure 11.75 remains unchanged no matter what semijoins are performed, yet none of the relations in d is fully reduced.

In Chapter 13 we shall return to semijoin programs and characterize those databases for which full-reducers exist.

11.7.2 Fragments of Relations

In a distributed database, a given relation is not necessarily stored in its entirety at any single site. Its tuples may be dispersed among several sites for performance considerations. For example, a database of airline reservations might be broken up to put all tuples for each flight at the site where the flight originates. Sometimes, the same tuple is stored at several sites. We shall call the pieces of a relation that reside at each site *fragments* of the relation. Processing a query at one site may involve retrieving fragments from other sites. If the assignment of tuples to fragments follows some rule, then that rule can be used to reduce the number of fragments accessed in processing a query.

We shall define fragments using selection conditions. A fragment of a relation r will be $\sigma_C(r)$ for some selection condition C.

For the following discussion, let $s_1, s_2, \ldots, s_p$ be the fragments of relation r, where s_i, $1 \leq i \leq p$, is defined as $\sigma_{C_i}(r)$ for some selection condition C_i. We call $\{C_1, C_2, \ldots, C_p\}$ the *fragmentation scheme* for f. One condition we wish always to hold is

$$r = s_1 \cup s_2 \cup \cdots \cup s_p.$$

That is, we can recover r from its fragments. We assume there is also a condition C_0 that r is guaranteed to satisfy: $r = \sigma_{C_0}(r)$. To be certain that r can always be represented as the union of its fragments, the fragmentation scheme must have the property

$$C_0 \rightarrow C_1 \vee C_2 \vee \cdots \vee C_p.$$

That is, any tuple that satisfies C_0 must necessarily satisfy one of the conditions in the fragmentation scheme. We call any fragmentation scheme that has the property above *valid*.

Example 11.65 Let r be a relation on scheme $A\ B\ D$, where the domain of each attribute is the positive integers. Assume r always satisfies the condition C_0 where

$$C_0 \text{ is } (A \leq B \vee B \leq D) \wedge A \neq D.$$

The fragmentation scheme $\{C_1, C_2, C_3\}$ for r where

$$C_1 \text{ is } A = B$$
$$C_2 \text{ is } B = D, \text{ and}$$
$$C_3 \text{ is } A \leq D$$

is valid for f (why?).

Knowing the fragmentation scheme for r can help in processing queries. Suppose, perhaps as part of a larger query, we want to evaluate $\sigma_C(r)$ at a given site. We could send out a request for $\sigma_C(s_i)$ for each fragment s_i that is not at the site. However, we are guaranteed to get nothing back whenever $C \wedge C_i \equiv$ *false*. Thus, we need only ask for $\sigma_C(s_i)$ whenever $C \wedge C_i \not\equiv$ *false*.

We can actually do better at eliminating fragments from consideration. Suppose that for condition C_1 there is a condition C_j such that

$$C \wedge C_1 \Rightarrow C \wedge C_j.$$

Any tuple t in r that appears in fragment s_1 and satisfies C will also appear in fragment s_j. Thus, fragment s_1 need not be consulted to evaluate $\sigma_C(r)$. In general, if

$$C \wedge C_1 \Rightarrow [(C \wedge C_2) \vee (C \wedge C_3) \vee \cdots \vee (C \wedge C_p)]$$

then fragment s_1 can be removed from consideration. We call this implication the *elimination requirement*.

Example 11.66 Let r be a relation on scheme $A\ B\ D$, where the domain of each attribute is the positive integers. Assume r satisfies the condition C_0 where

$$C_0 \text{ is } A \leq B \wedge B \leq D.$$

Let s_1, s_2, s_3, and s_4 be fragments for r corresponding to the fragmentation scheme $\{C_1, C_2, C_3, C_4\}$ where

C_1 is $A < B$,
C_2 is $B \leq 3 \wedge B < D$,
C_3 is $B > 3$, and
C_4 is $A = D$.

The reader should check that this fragmentation scheme is valid.

Suppose we want to evaluate $\sigma_C(r)$ where

$$C \text{ is } A < B \wedge B < D.$$

Which fragments must we consult? Fragment s_4 is out, since $C \wedge C_4 \equiv false$. Also, since

$$C \wedge C_1 \Rightarrow [(C \wedge C_2) \vee (C \wedge C_3)],$$

s_1 could be eliminated. Alternatively, since

$$C \wedge C_2 \Rightarrow C \wedge C_1 \text{ and}$$
$$C \wedge C_3 \Rightarrow C \wedge C_1,$$

s_2 and s_3 could be eliminated, and only s_1 retained.

In general, when determining which fragment can be eliminated in evaluating $\sigma_C(r)$, $C' = C \wedge C_0$ can be used in place of C. If $C \not\Rightarrow C_0$, this replacement could allow more fragments to be eliminated.

We have not touched on algorithms to test validity or the elimination requirement. The complexity of such algorithms depends heavily on the particular domains for attributes and the permissible forms of selection conditions. As we saw in the last example, there can be more than one possibility for a minimal set of fragments to consult to evaluate $\sigma_C(r)$. The smallest set among the minimal sets might not be the optimal choice for evaluating the query. There are other considerations, such as communications costs (it could cost more to talk to one site than another), whether one of the fragments is already at the site where the query is being evaluated, and the amount of duplication among tuples in the minimal sets.

11.8 EXERCISES

11.1 Let r and s be the relations from Example 11.9. Give the number of disk accesses necessary to compute $r \bowtie s$ by the following methods.

(a) Read the blocks of r into memory 4 at a time, and for each group of 4, read in the blocks of s one at a time.

(b) Read the blocks of s into memory 2 at a time, and for each group of 2, read in the blocks of r three at a time.

11.2 For the relations r and s of Example 11.9, suppose only r is sorted on B. Can you find a more efficient way to compute $r \bowtie s$ than the one where neither r nor s is sorted on B. Suppose each disk block only contains 5 tuples?

11.3 Assume r and s are relations such that $r \subseteq s$. Simplify the following expressions.

(a) $r \bowtie s$

(b) $\sigma_{A=a}(r) - s$

(c) $\pi_X(r) \cap \pi_X(s)$

11.4 Give the expression tree for each of the following expressions, then merge nodes and simplify where possible.

(a) $(r_1 \bowtie r_2 \bowtie r_3) \cup (r_2 \bowtie r_3 \bowtie r_4) \cup (r_1 \bowtie r_3 \bowtie r_4) \cup (r_1 \bowtie r_2 \bowtie r_4)$

(b) $(r \bowtie q) \cap (\sigma_{A=a}(s) - s)$

(c) $\pi_{\mathrm{P\#\,PN\,BD\,DT\,RG}}(rp \bowtie low)$, for rp and low as given in Example 11.1.

11.5 Give the expression tree for each of the following expressions, then apply algebraic optimization to each. The schemes of q, r, and s are ABD, BDF, and FG.

(a) $\sigma_{D=d}(\pi_{BDF}(q \bowtie r) - \pi_{BDF}(r \bowtie s))$

(b) $\pi_{AD}(q \bowtie r \bowtie \sigma_{G=g}(s))$

(c) $\pi_B(\sigma_{A=a}(\sigma_{D=d}(q) \bowtie (r - \pi_{BDF}(r \bowtie s))))$

11.6 Consider the statement

$$r \leftarrow \pi_X(s_1 \bowtie s_2 \bowtie \cdots \bowtie s_k)$$

where the schemes of $s_1, s_2, \ldots, s_k$ are all disjoint. Suppose X only contains attributes from $s_1, s_2, \ldots, s_p$ for some $p < k$. Show a way to transform the statement to a program containing only $p-1$ **for**-loops, given that you may easily test if a relation is empty.

11.7 Apply the query decomposition algorithm to the initial statement of Example 11.33 using the following alternatives for comparisons C_1-C_6.

(a) C_1, C_2, C_3, C_5, and C_6 are the same, C_4 is $z.\mathrm{G} \leq 3$

(b) C_1, C_2, C_3, and C_6 are the same, C_4 is $z.\mathrm{G} \leq 3$, C_5 is $y.F = 4$

(c) C_1, C_3, C_4, and C_5 are the same, C_2 is $x.A = 5$, C_6 is $x.F \leq 9$
(d) C_2-C_6 are the same, C_1 is $w.B = 7$

11.8 For the statement

$$r \leftarrow \pi_X(\sigma_C(s_1 \bowtie s_2 \bowtie \cdots \bowtie s_k))$$

let P_1 be the program that results from query decomposition where $\{s_1, s_2, \ldots, s_p\}$, $p < k$ is instantiated, then $s_1, s_2, \ldots, s_p$ are all iterated. Compare the structure of P_1 to the program P_2 that results where $s_1, s_2, \ldots, s_p$ are iterated without the instantiation first.

11.9 Consider the tuple calculus expression and the corresponding algebraic expression at the beginning of Section 11.4. Let h be the formula

$$\exists y_1(R_1) \in r_1 \ \exists y_2(R_2) \in r_2 \cdots \exists y_m(R_m) \in r_m \ g(y_1, y_2, \ldots, y_m).$$

Let E be the corresponding part of the algebraic expression, namely

$$\sigma_C(s_1 \bowtie s_2 \bowtie \cdots \bowtie s_m).$$

Can you find modifications to h that correspond to applying instantiation and iteration to the statement $r \leftarrow E$? Hint: For instantiation, it is necessary to introduce a new tuple variable into h.

11.10 Consider relations $r_1(A_1\ A_2)$, $r_2(A_2\ A_3)$, $r_3(A_3\ A_4)$, and $r_4(A_4\ A_5)$. Below are two methods to compute $r_1 \bowtie r_2 \bowtie r_3 \bowtie r_4$. Assuming each relation has n tuples, under what conditions will the second method require less time. Assume time is measured by the number of executions of assignment statements. Single tuples are treated as one tuple relations in the assignment statements.

Method 1:
$r \leftarrow \emptyset$;
for each tuple t_1 in r_1 **do**
  for each tuple t_2 in r_2 **do**
    for each tuple t_3 in r_3 **do**
      for each tuple t_4 in r_4 **do**
        $r \leftarrow r \cup (t_1 \bowtie t_2 \bowtie t_3 \bowtie t_4)$

Method 2:

```
s1 ← ∅;
for each tuple t1 in r1 do
    for each tuple t2 in r2 do
        s1 ← s1 ∪ (t1 ⋈ t2);
s2 ← ∅;
for each tuple t3 in r3 do
    for each tuple t4 in r4 do
        s2 ← s2 ∪ (t3 ⋈ t4);
r ← ∅;
for each tuple u1 in s1 do
    for each tuple u2 in s2 do
        r ← r ∪ (u1 ⋈ u2)
```

11.11 Give an example where option 5 of the query decomposition heuristic would be used. That is, give a connection graph where options 1-4 do not apply.

11.12 Find two tableau queries Q_1 and Q_2 such that Q_1 covers Q_2 but $Q_2 \not\sqsupseteq Q_1$.

11.13 Prove Lemma 11.1.

11.14 Find two tableau queries Q_1 and Q_2 such that $Q_1 \equiv Q_2$, Q_2 is Q_1 with a single row removed, but the row is not superseded in Q_1.

11.15 Show that removing all superseded rows from a tableau query does not necessarily guarantee a minimum tableau query.

11.16 Prove Theorem 11.3. Note that the containment mapping can do nothing more than rename nondistinguished variables.

11.17 Give an algorithm to decide if two tableau queries are identical up to a one-to-one renaming of nondistinguished variables.

Definition 11.20 An *expression tableau query* is a tableau query that can be derived from a restricted algebraic expression by the method of Chapter 10.

11.18 Prove the following:

(a) If Q_1 is an expression tableau query, and Q_2 is a subtableau of Q_1 that is minimum and equivalent to Q_1, then Q_2 is an expression tableau query.

(b) Tableau query Q is equivalent to an expression tableau query if and only if every and any minimum equivalent tableau query for Q is an expression query.

(c) There is a tableau query that is equivalent to an expression tableau query but is not itself an expression tableau query.

11.19 Find an efficient method to determine if a simple tableau query is an expression tableau query.

11.20 Let Q be an expression tableau query that is not simple. What is the fewest rows Q can have?

11.21 Show that a minimum equivalent tableau query for a simple tableau query Q is also simple.

11.22 For the tableau query Q in Figure 11.40, compute $COMP_{w_i}(w_j)$ where

(a) $i = 1$ and $j = 2$, (c) $i = 3$ and $j = 6$,
(b) $i = 2$ and $j = 1$, (d) $i = 4$ and $j = 3$.

11.23 Prove Lemma 11.3. The proof depends on the simplicity of Q.

11.24 Find an algorithm to compute $COMP_v(w)$ in $O(k^2 n)$ for a tableau query Q with k rows and n columns.

11.25 Find MINEQ(Q) for tableau query Q in Figure 11.40.

11.26 Let Q be a simple tableau query and let v and w be rows of Q. Show that if w' is a row in $COMP_v(w)$, then $COMP_v(w) = COMP_v(w')$.

11.27 Are any of the following tableau queries equivalent?

Q_1(A_1	A_2	A_3	A_4)
a_1	a_2		
a_1	b_1	b_2	4
b_3	a_2	b_2	b_3

Q_2(A_1	A_2	A_3	A_4)
a_1	a_2		
b_1	a_2	b_2	b_3
b_4	a_2	b_5	b_6
b_7	b_8	b_2	b_6
a_1	b_9	b_2	4

Q_3(A_1	A_2	A_3	A_4)
a_1	a_2		
a_1	b_1	b_2	4
a_1	b_3	b_4	b_5
b_6	a_2	b_2	b_5

$Q_4(A_1$	A_2	A_3	$A_4)$
a_1	a_2		
a_1	a_2	b_2	4
b_3	a_2	b_2	b_3
b_5	a_2	b_2	4

11.28 Which tableau queries in Exercise 11.27 are equivalent on $SAT(A_3 \rightarrow A_4)$?

11.29 Exhibit a tableau query Q and a set **C** of FDs such that Q is simple but $chase_{\mathbf{C}}(Q)$ is not, nor can $chase_{\mathbf{C}}(Q)$ be made simple be removing superseded rows.

11.30 Given a simple tableau query Q and a set **C** of FDs and JDs, show that $chase_{\mathbf{C}}(\text{MINEQ}(Q))$ is not necessarily a **C**-minimum equivalent tableau query for Q.

11.31 If Q is an expression tableau query, and C is a set of FDs and JDs, is $chase_{\mathbf{C}}(Q)$ necessarily an expression tableau query?

11.32 Let $d = \{q(AB), r(BC), s(AC)\}$ be a database that is the projection of a common instance over $A\ B\ C$. Use tableau query optimization to find algebraic expressions equivalent to the following with fewer joins, if such exist.

(a) $\pi_B(q \bowtie r \bowtie s)$
(b) $\pi_{AC}(q \bowtie r)$
(c) $\pi_{AC}(q \bowtie r \bowtie s)$
(d) $\pi_{AC}(\sigma_{A=c_1}(q) \bowtie \sigma_{C=c_2}(r) \bowtie s)$.

11.33 Let d be a database over database scheme **R**. Assume d is the projection of an instance $r(\mathbf{U})$ in $SAT(F)$ for some set F of FDs. Let $q_1, q_2, \ldots, q_m$ be a sequence of relations such that w_i, $1 \leq i \leq m$ is either

i. a relation in d, or
ii. the q_j-extension of q_k by $Y \rightarrow Z$ for $j < i$, $k < i$ and $Y \rightarrow Z \in F$.

Let S be the scheme of q_m. Show that $q_m = \pi_S(r)$.

11.34 Let F be a set of FDs. Let $\mathbf{R} = \{R_1, R_2, \ldots, R_p\}$ be SYNTHESIZE(F) for the SYNTHESIZE algorithm of Chapter 6. Let $\mathbf{U} = R_1 R_2 \cdots R_p$. Under what condition is **U** an $\mathbf{R}_F$-extension?

11.35 Let F be a set of FDs and let $\mathbf{R} = \{R_1, R_2, \ldots, R_p\}$ be a database scheme, where $\mathbf{U} = R_1 R_2 \cdots R_p$. Suppose $F \models *[\mathbf{R}]$. Is **U** necessarily an $\mathbf{R}_F$-extension?

11.36 Let F be a set of FDs and let **R** be a database scheme over **U**. Show that if $R \subseteq \mathbf{U}$ is an $\mathbf{R}_F$-extension, then $echase_F(T_{\mathbf{R}})$ contains a row distinguished at least on the attributes in R.

11.37 Let F be a set of FDs and let $\mathbf{R}$ be a database scheme. Prove that if F is enforceable on $\mathbf{R}$, then $echase_F(T_{\mathbf{R}}) = chase_F(T_{\mathbf{R}})$. Recall that F is enforceable on $\mathbf{R}$ if some cover G of F applies to R.

11.38 Show the ADE is not an $\mathbf{R}_F$-extension for $F = \{A \rightarrow C, B \rightarrow C, CD \rightarrow E\}$ and $\mathbf{R} = \{AD, AB, BDE, CE\}$.

11.39 Show that if F is a set of FDs and Q is an expression tableau query, then $echase_F(Q)$ is an expression tableau query.

11.40 Find the containment relationships between the tableau set queries

$$\begin{aligned}
\mathbf{Q}_1 &= \{Q_1, Q_3\}\\
\mathbf{Q}_2 &= \{Q_2, Q_3\}\\
\mathbf{Q}_3 &= \{Q_1, Q_2, Q_4\}\\
\mathbf{Q}_4 &= \{Q_3, Q_4\}
\end{aligned}$$

where tableau queries Q_1, Q_2, Q_3, and Q_4 are given below. Which of $\mathbf{Q}_1$-$\mathbf{Q}_4$ are nonredundant?

$$\mathbf{Q}_1(\begin{array}{cccc} A & B & C & D \\ \hline a_1 & & a_3 & \\ \hline a_1 & b_1 & b_2 & b_3 \\ b_4 & b_1 & a_3 & b_5 \\ b_4 & b_6 & b_7 & b_3 \end{array})$$

$$\mathbf{Q}_2(\begin{array}{cccc} A & B & C & D \\ \hline a_1 & & a_3 & \\ \hline a_1 & b_1 & b_2 & b_3 \\ b_4 & b_1 & a_3 & b_5 \end{array})$$

$$\mathbf{Q}_3(\begin{array}{cccc} A & B & C & D \\ \hline a_1 & & a_3 & \\ \hline a_1 & b_1 & b_2 & b_3 \\ b_4 & b_1 & a_3 & b_3 \end{array})$$

$Q_4(A$	B	C	$D)$
a_1		a_3	
a_1	5	b_1	b_2
b_3	5	a_3	b_4

11.41 Prove the corollary to Theorem 11.9.

11.42 Prove Theorem 11.10.

11.43 Let d be the database $\{q(A\,B\,C), r(B\,C\,D), s(A\,D)\}$ where $dom(B) = dom(C)$. Find minimum equivalent conjunctive queries for the following conjunctive queries. Give a folding to justify each answer.

(a) $\{x_1(A)\, s_2(B)\, x_3(C) | \exists y_1(D)\, \exists y_2(C)$
$q(x_1\, x_2\, x_3) \wedge r(x_2\, x_2\, y_1) \wedge r(x\, y_2\, y_1) \wedge r(x_2\, x_3\, 6)\}$

(b) $\{x_1(B)\, x_2(D) | \exists y_1(A)\, \exists y_2(C)\, \exists y_3(A)$
$\exists y_4(B)\, \exists y_5(C)\, \exists y_6(A)\, \exists y_7(B)\, \exists y_8(D)$
$q(y_1\, x_1\, y_2) \wedge q(y_3\, y_4\, y_5) \wedge q(y_6\, y_7\, y_5)$
$\wedge\, s(y_1\, y_8) \wedge s(y_3\, y_8) \wedge s(y_6\, x_2)\}$

(c) $\{x_1(A)\, x_2(D) | \exists y_1(D)\, \exists y_2(A)$
$s(x_1\, y_1) \wedge s(y_2\, y_1) \wedge s(y_2\, x_2)\}$

11.44 For relations r and s, prove $r \bowtie s = (r \ltimes s) \bowtie s$.

11.45 For relations r and s, show that

$$r' = r \ltimes s \text{ and}$$
$$s' = s \ltimes r'$$

always join completely, and that $r \bowtie s = r' \bowtie s'$.

11.46 If SP is a semijoin program for database d, and r is a relation in d, show that $SP(r,d) \supseteq FR(r,d)$.

11.47 (a) Show that the semijoin program SP_2 in Example 11.63 is a full-reducer for d.

(b) For database d in Example 11.63, give a full-reducer with fewer statements than SP_2.

(c)*Prove: If database $d = \{r_1, r_2, \ldots, r_p\}$ has a full-reducer, it has one with $2p$-2 statements.

11.48 Let r be a relation on scheme $A\,B\,D\,E$, where the domain of each attribute is the positive integers. Assume r always satisfies the condition C_0 where

$$C_0 \text{ is } A \leq B \wedge B \leq D \wedge D \leq E.$$

Let

C_1 be $A < B \wedge B < D$
C_2 be $A = D$
C_3 be $A < D$
C_4 be $A \neq B \vee B \neq D$
C_5 be $B < E$

Which of the following fragmentation schemes are valid for r?
(a) $\{C_1, C_2\}$
(b) $\{C_2, C_3\}$
(c) $\{C_1, C_4, C_5\}$
(d) $\{C_2, C_4, C_5\}$.

11.49 Let r be as in Exercise 11.48. Let s_1, s_2, s_3, s_4 be fragments for r corresponding to the fragmentation scheme $\{C_1, C_2, C_3, C_4\}$ for the conditions C_1-C_4 given in Exercise 11.48. Give minimal sets of fragments that can be used to evaluate $\sigma_C(r)$ for the following choices of C.
(a) $A \neq B \wedge B = D$
(b) $B < D \wedge D < E$
(c) $A < 5 \wedge E < 6$

11.9 BIBLIOGRAPHY AND COMMENTS

Query modification in the INGRES database system is discussed by Stonebraker and Wong [1974], Stonebraker [1975], and Stonebraker and Rubenstein [1976].

Numerous researchers have investigated algorithms and complexity of operators in relational algebra. Gotlieb [1975] and Pecherer [1975] both showed a lower bound on the join of two relations proportional to $n \log n$, where n is the number of tuples in each relation. Blasgen and Eswaren [1977] compare various algorithms for computing a join. Stockmeyer and Wong [1979] showed that computing the intersection of two relations of k columns takes at least $(m+n)\log m + (m+n-1)k$ comparisons in the worst case, where the relations have m and n tuples, $m \leq n$. Kim [1980, 1981b] considers the best way of utilizing main memory in computing joins.

Section 11.2 on simplifications and common subexpressions follows largely from Hall [1976]. The utility of pushing selections down an expression tree was recognized by several researchers; Palermo [1974] seems to have been first. Section 11.3 on optimizing algebraic expressions follows the treatment given in Ullman [1980]. Smith and Chang [1975] discuss several strategies for efficient relational query evaluation, such as exploiting sort orders of intermediate results and directory information. Yao [1977] gives methods for estimating the cost of different strategies in select-project-join expressions. Selinger, Astrahan, *et al.* [1979] and Chamberlin, Astrahan, *et al.* [1981] describe the queries processing strategies used by IBM's System/R relational data base system. System/R makes extensive use of database statistics to select among different retrieval methods, orders for intermediate results, and types and arrangements of joins. Kim [1981a, 1981b] covers types of nesting and optimizing sets of queries in the System/R environment.

The QUEL decomposition algorithm is due to Wong and Youssefi [1976]. The graphical representation is due to Ullman [1980].

The results on tableau query equivalence and simple query minimization are from Aho, Sagiv, and Ullman [1979a, 1979b], who also show testing tableau query equivalence is NP-complete, even in several very restricted cases. Extension joins are from Honeyman [1980a], who refined the ideas of Osborn [1979b]. Others have looked at the problem of computing a lossless join to cover a specified set of attributes: Kambayashi [1979], Lozinskii [1980], Schenk and Pinkert [1977], Tanaka and Tsuda [1977]. The material on tableau set queries is from Sagiv and Yannakakis [1979]. Chandra and Merlin [1976] presented foldings as a means to minimize conjunctive queries, although they show the problem is NP-complete.

Semijoins were introduced in Bernstein and Chiu [1981], where the answer to exercise 11.47c may also be found. We shall treat semijoins further in Chapter 13. The material on fragments is from Maier and Ullman [1981b]. Fragments are used extensively in the SDD-1 distributed database system, described by Goodman, Bernstein, *et al.* [1979] and Rothnie, Bernstein, *et al.* [1981]. Epstein, Stonebraker, and Wong [1978], Ceri and Pelagatti [1980], Paredaens [1980], and Paredaens and DeBra [1981] have examined various aspects of "horizontal" decompositions in relation databases.

Exercises 11.18a and 11.19 are from Aho, Sagiv, Szymanski, and Ullman [1979]. Exercise 11.18b is from Connors and Vianu [1981].

Minker [1975a, 1975b, 1978] studied relational query processing in the framework of inductive inference. Shopiro [1979] has designed a programming language for relational manipulation. Lozinskii [1978] and Schkolnick and Sorenson [1981] examine the trade-offs between storage redundancy and speed of query evaluation. Klug [1980a], Klug and Price [1980], and Tanaka and Kambayashi [1980] show how to calculate constraints on the value of an algebraic expression given the constraints that hold on the component relations.

Chapter 12

NULL VALUES, PARTIAL INFORMATION AND DATABASE SEMANTICS

The reader is warned that the topics in this chapter are matters of personal taste. Whether the definitions and approaches offered seem right depends on individual intuition. This chapter presents some of the problems that arise from the assumption that all information fits into the relational model. The problems are not completely solved, but some partial solutions are offered as guidance for future work. The following line, overheard at a discussion of data semantics, gives the proper frame of mind: "It all makes sense if you squint a little and don't think too hard."

Underlying the relational database model is a blithe assumption that the information to be represented fits nicely into little boxes arranged in rectangular tables. The assumption can fail for two reasons:

1. The structure of the information does not fit the mold.
2. The information fits the mold, but part of the information is missing.

As an example of the first, recall the problem in the *pinfo*(PART# SUBPART PARTNAME) relation of Section 10.2. We needed an artificial value for SUBPARTOF whenever a part was not a subpart. We chose 0 as the artificial value. There is some danger in that approach. The domain calculus expression

$$\{x(\text{PART\#})\ y(\text{PART\#2}) \mid \exists z_1\ \exists z_2\ \exists z_3\ (pinfo(x\ z_1\ z_2) \wedge pinfo(y\ z_1\ z_3))\}$$

might at first seem the correct query to find all pairs of parts that are subparts of the same part. However, it also associates all pairs of parts that are not subparts of any part. The problem is that we need a way to represent *partial information*—we would like to have tuples that range over only a part of the relation scheme.

As an aside, we note that there are some cases where "no value" could properly be considered a value. Consider a relation *books*(TITLE FIRSTNAME MIDDLENAME LASTNAME) for recording titles and authors of books. If some author has no middle name, a special domain value could properly be used to represent the middle name. If two full names agree in the first name and the last name, and have no middle name, they are the same name. In this example, it is appropriate to augment the domain for MIDDLENAME with a "none" or "does not exist" element that is treated identically to any other domain value. Note the difference from the SUBPARTOF example. Contrast the statements "Two authors with no middle names can be considered to have the same middle name" and "Two parts that are not subparts can be considered to be subparts of a common part."

Turning to the second reason given above, recall the relation *usedon*(PART# PTYPE NUSED), also from Section 10.2. Suppose we know that part 318 is used on a 1011, but we do not know the number used. We would like to store a tuple with the information that we do have; a tuple t with t(PART#) = 318 and t(PTYPE) = 1011. What value should we store for t(NUSED)? Unlike the SUBPARTOF example, we know there is some domain value that could correctly fill the slot. However, using any particular domain value would give incorrect answers for queries, unless we happened to guess the correct value. We need a means to represent *unknown values*.

We shall first look at the problem of unknown values. We introduce *nulls* to represent the unknown values. We then show that functional dependencies and *marked nulls* may be used to fill in unknown values at times. We consider *existence constraints* as a means to control the use of nulls. Finally, we introduce *possibility functions* as a tool for comparing extensions of relational algebra to handle nulls. We then turn to the partial information problem. This problem is related to the problem of treating a database as a single semantic entity. We introduce *window functions* as a tool for viewing a database as a unit.

12.1 NULLS

The term *null* has been applied widely in database literature to special domain values that arise for a variety of reasons. Here we use it narrowly to mean "value exists but unknown." We use the symbol $\perp$ to denote a null. Although we may use the null symbol several places in a relation, each occurrence represents a potentially different unknown value.

Example 12.1 Suppose the personnel department at our airline is rather snoopy, and maintains a relation *history*(EMPLOYEE SALARY PREVEMP

PREVJOB PREVSAL). The relation records the previous employer, job title, and salary of an employee, as well as the current salary. However, personnel may not be able to wheedle all this information from every employee, so the relation may be incomplete, as shown in Table 12.1.

Table 12.1 Relation Table Comprising Employee *history*.

history(EMPLOYEE		SALARY	PREVEMP	PREVJOB	PREVSAL)
t_1	Lambert	39,500	SWA	pilot	36,000
t_2	Larson	24,100	$\perp$	$\perp$	$\perp$
t_3	Lathen	17,300	WIA	clerk	$\perp$
t_4	Liu	18,260	WIA	$\perp$	17,800

Since the problems of unknown values and partial information are so slippery, and have not been completely solved, our treatment will tend toward examples more than proofs. However, what we lack in rigor we shall make up in notation.

Notation A tuple containing 0 or more nulls is *partial*. A tuple with no nulls is *total*. Thus, every total tuple is a partial tuple (similarly to partial and total functions). A tuple t whose scheme includes attribute A is *definite* on A, written $t(A)\downarrow$, if $t(A)$ is not null. This notation extends to sets of attributes: $t(X)\downarrow$ means $t(A)\downarrow$ for every attribute $A \in X$. We use $t\downarrow$ to mean that t is total. If t is a tuple over scheme R, we let $DEF(t) = \{A \in R \mid t(A)\downarrow\}$. For tuples t and u on the same scheme, t *subsumes* u, written $t \geq u$, if $u(A)\downarrow$ implies $u(A) = t(A)$ for every attribute A in X. If $t \geq u$ and $t\downarrow$, we call t an *extension* of u, written $t \downarrow\geq u$.

Example 12.2 In Table 12.1, all the tuples are partial, while t_1 is also total. For t_2, t_2(EMPLOYEE)$\downarrow$, t_2(SALARY)$\downarrow$ and $DEF(t_2)$ = EMPLOYEE SALARY. The tuple $t = \langle$Larson 24,100 $\perp$ manager $\perp\rangle$ subsumes tuple t_2. For the tuple $u = \langle$Larson 24,100 WIA manager 22,050$\rangle$, $u \downarrow\geq t$.

More Notation A relation r is *total*, written $r\downarrow$, if all its tuples are total. Relations containing 0 or more nulls are *partial*. For relation scheme R, we let $Rel\uparrow(R)$ be the set of all partial relations over R and let $Rel(R)$ be the set of all total relations over R. Through Section 12.4, relation will mean partial relation. For relations r and s over R, r *subsumes* s, written $r \geq s$, if for every tuple $t_s \in s$ there is a tuple $t_r \in r$ such that $t_r \geq t_s$. If $r \geq s$ and $s \geq r$, we write $r \simeq s$. If r is total, then r is an *extension* of s, written $r \downarrow\geq s$.

If r can be obtained from s by changing some nulls in s to values, then r *augments* s, written $r \underline{\geq} s$. Clearly, $r \underline{\geq} s$ implies $r \geq s$. If r is total, then r

completes s, or r is a *completion* of s, written $r \downarrow \succeq s$. If $r \succeq s$ and $s \succeq r$, then $r = s$ (see Exercise 12.4). Evidently, r augments s if there is a mapping α of the tuples of s *onto* the tuples of r such that $\alpha(t) \geq t$ for every tuple $t \in s$. Note that the term *completion* is given a different meaning in this chapter than in Section 8.7.

Example 12.3 The relation *history'* in Table 12.2 is an extension of the relation *history* in Table 12.1, but not a completion, because of the tuples ⟨Lathen 17,300 WIA clerk 16,400⟩ and ⟨Lathen 17,300 WIA clerk 16,850⟩. The relation *history''* in Table 12.3 is a completion of *history*. Note that in general, neither $r \geq s$ nor $r \succeq s$ imply $|r| \geq |s|$.

Table 12.2 Extension of Relation *history*.

history'(EMPLOYEE	SALARY	PREVEMP	PREVJOB	PREVSAL)
Lambert	39,500	SWA	pilot	36,000
Larson	24,000	WIA	manager	22,050
Lathen	17,300	WIA	clerk	16,400
Lathen	17,300	WIA	clerk	16,850
Liu	18,260	WIA	agent	17,800

Table 12.3 Completion of Relation *history*.

history''(EMPLOYEE	SALARY	PREVEMP	PREVJOB	PREVSAL)
Lambert	39,500	SWA	pilot	36,000
Larson	24,000	WIA	manager	22,050
Lathen	17,300	WIA	clerk	16,400
Liu	18,260	WIA	agent	17,800

We can view a partial relation as a set of axioms about the total relation that the partial relation represents.

Example 12.4 We can view the relation *history* in Table 12.1 as a set of axioms (in domain calculus notation) about a total relation *history*:

1. *history*(Lambert 39,500 SWA pilot 36,000)
2. $\exists x_1 \exists x_2 \exists x_3$ *history*(Larson 24,100 x_1 x_2 x_3)
3. $\exists x_4$ *history*(Lathen 17,300 WIA clerk x_4)
4. $\exists x_5$ *history*(Liu 18,260 WIA x_5 17,800).

If r is a partial relation, then any extension of r can be interpreted as a finite model satisfying the axioms denoted by r. Also, if $r \geq s$, then, as sets of axioms about a total relation, r logically implies s.

For the moment, we shall be interested in those extensions that are completions. That is, every tuple in a partial relation is seen as representing a single tuple of a total relation. However, two tuples in the partial relation may represent the same tuple in the total relation. The principle is that we do not assume any more information than we need to in order to satisfy the axioms denoted by the partial relation. There are some subtle problems here. If relation r' is obtained from relation r by removing a tuple t from r, where t is subsumed by another tuple in r, then $r' \geq r$ and so $r' \simeq r$. Thus r' and r have the same set of extensions. While $r' \underline{\geq} r$ (why?), it is *not* necessarily true that $r \underline{\geq} r'$. In fact, it is never true that $r \underline{\geq} r'$, since that would imply $r = r'$, by Exercise 12.4. Thus there are completions of r that are not completions of r'.

The relationship $\underline{\geq}$ does not correspond to logical implication of sets of axioms, because we use the form of the axioms to limit the possible models. Logicians may be troubled by a system where models are restricted by the syntax of the axioms; where seemingly equivalent sets of axioms have different models. Linguists will be less troubled, for they know "It's not what you say, it's how you say it." Researchers in artificial intelligence won't see what all the fuss is about. We shall see in Chapter 14 that even the assumption that our models are finite has interesting effects upon the implication of dependencies. One way around the problem of subsumed tuples is to consider only relations with no such tuples, although we do not adopt that assumption here.

Given that we allow partial relations in a database, the problem of evaluating queries immediately arises. We briefly describe the *null substitution principle* for interpreting calculus formulas over partial relations. We examine only the single-relation case: multiple-relation formulas can be treated similarly. We define an interpretation function $\hat{I}$ that maps calculus formulas to the set $\{true, unknown, false\}$. Let f be a tuple calculus formula that mentions only a single relation, $r(R)$. Assume further that f has no free variables. Let $I_s(f)$ stand for the usual interpretation of formula f, using total relation $s(R)$ in place of r. We define

$\hat{I}(f) = true$ if $I_s(f) = true$ for every completion s of r,
$\hat{I}(f) = false$ if $I_s(f) = false$ for every completion s of r, and
$\hat{I}(f) = unknown$ otherwise.

That is, $\hat{I}(f)$ is *true* exactly when every possible substitution of values for nulls in r makes f a true formula in the usual sense.

Example 12.5 Let *history* be the relation in Table 12.1, and let R denote its scheme. Consider the formula f_1 defined as

$$\exists x(\mathrm{R}) \in \mathit{history}\ (x(\mathrm{PREVEMP}) = \text{“WIA”} \wedge x(\mathrm{PREVJOB}) = \text{“clerk”}).$$

$\hat{I}(f_1) = \mathit{true}$, since no matter how the null in tuple t_3 of *history* is filled in, $t_3(\mathrm{PREVEMP}) = \text{“WIA”} \wedge t_3(\mathrm{PREVJOB}) = \text{“clerk”}$ will be true. Next, consider the formula f_2 defined as

$$\exists x(R) \in \mathit{history}\ (x(\mathrm{EMPLOYEE}) = \text{“Liu”} \wedge \forall y(R) \in \mathit{history}\\ (x(\mathrm{PREVSAL}) \geq y(\mathrm{PREVSAL}))).$$

$\hat{I}(f_2) = \mathit{false}$, because no matter how nulls are filled in, t_4 is the only tuple that could make $x(\mathrm{EMPLOYEE}) = \text{“Liu”}$ true and choosing t_1 for y makes the formula as a whole false. Finally, consider the formula f_3 defined as

$$\exists x(R) \in \mathit{history}\ (x(\mathrm{EMPLOYEE}) = \text{“Lambert”} \wedge \forall y(R) \in \mathit{history}\\ (x(\mathrm{PREVSAL}) \geq y(\mathrm{PREVSAL}))).$$

$\hat{I}(f_3) = \mathit{unknown}$, since f_3 can become either true or false depending on how $t_2(\mathrm{PREVSAL})$ and $t_3(\mathrm{PREVSAL})$ are filled in.

A problem with the null substitution principle is that it does not admit a recursive definition of $\hat{I}$. That is, we cannot define $\hat{I}(f)$ in terms of $\hat{I}$'s value on the immediate subformulas of f. The next example shows that if $f = g \vee h$, then $\hat{I}(f)$ cannot be defined as $\hat{I}(g) \vee \hat{I}(h)$.

Example 12.6 Let *history* be the relation in Table 12.1 and let R represent its scheme. Let f be

$$\exists x(R) \in \mathit{history}\ (x(\mathrm{PREVEMP}) = \text{“WIA”} \wedge x(\mathrm{PREVSAL}) \leq 16{,}000) \vee\\ \exists y(R) \in \mathit{history}\ (y(\mathrm{PREVJOB}) = \text{“clerk”} \wedge y(\mathrm{PREVSAL}) > 16{,}000).$$

$\hat{I}(f) = \mathit{true}$, but $\hat{I}(g) = \hat{I}(h) = \mathit{unknown}$, where g and h are the two disjuncts of f.

While there is no recursive definition of $\hat{I}$, it is not necessary to try all possible substitutions of domain values for nulls in a formula f to compute $\hat{I}(f)$.

We need only look at enough domain values to allow any atom to become either true or false (if possible). For the formula f in Example 12.6, 16,000 and 15,999 are the only values that need be considered for nulls in the PREVSAL column of *history*. Nevertheless, evaluating $\hat{I}(f)$ is computationally hard, since it is basically the problem of testing for a tautology.

12.2 FUNCTIONAL DEPENDENCIES AND NULLS

We may have some restrictions on the total relation that a partial relation can represent. In particular, it may be that the total relation must satisfy some FDs.

Example 12.7 Consider the version of *history* shown in Table 12.4. We assume that the total relation that *history* represents has EMPLOYEE as a key. Hence, we would allow the completion *history*′ shown in Table 12.5, but not the completion *history*″ shown in Table 12.6.

Table 12.4 Relation *history* with EMPLOYEE as a Key.

history(EMPLOYEE	SALARY	PREVEMP	PREVJOB	PREVSAL)
Lathen	17,300	WIA	clerk	$\perp$
$\perp$	18,260	WIA	$\perp$	17,800

Table 12.5 Completion of Relation *history* (allowed).

history′(EMPLOYEE	SALARY	PREVEMP	PREVJOB	PREVSAL)
Lathen	17,300	WIA	clerk	16,400
Liu	18,260	WIA	agent	17,800

Table 12.6 Completion of Relation *history* (not allowed).

history″(EMPLOYEE	SALARY	PREVEMP	PREVJOB	PREVSAL)
Lathen	17,300	WIA	clerk	16,400
Lathen	18,260	WIA	agent	17,800

One thing we would like to test given a relation $r \in Rel\uparrow(R)$ and a set of FDs F is whether any completion of r satisfies F.

Definition 12.1 Let $r \in Rel\uparrow(R)$ and let F be a set of FDs over R. Relation r is *permissible* with respect to F if some completion s of r satisfies F. A completion that satisfies F is a *permissible completion* under F.

Example 12.8 Let F be {EMPLOYEE → SALARY PREVEMP PREVJOB PREVSAL}. The version of *history* shown in Table 12.4 is permissible with respect to F, while the version of Table 12.7 is not.

Table 12.7 Relation *history* (not permissible with respect to F).

history(EMPLOYEE	SALARY	PREVEMP	PREVJOB	PREVSAL)
Lathen	17,300	WIA	clerk	⊥
Lathen	⊥	SWA	⊥	17,800

We seek a test for permissibility of partial relations. As it turns out, FDs are not just constraints on possible completions. They can also be used to fill in nulls. For a particular null, there may be only a single way to fill in that null in order to satisfy a set of FDs.

Example 12.9 Consider the relation *vacation*(EMPLOYEE YEARS ANNUALDAYS ACCDAYS) in Table 12.8 that gives the number of years employees have been with the airline, how many days of vacation they accumulate annually, and the total days accumulated. We assume the set of FDs F = {EMPLOYEE → YEARS ANNUALDAYS ACCDAYS, YEARS → ANNUALDAYS} applies. In any completion of vacation that satisfies F, t_1(ACCDAYS) = 17, t_2(YEARS) = 3, t_2(ANNUALDAYS) = 21 and t_3(ANNUALDAYS) = 21. Thus we can fill in these nulls to get a more complete relation, *vacation*′, as shown in Table 12.9. It may seem that all the problems go away if *vacation* is decomposed using the FD YEARS → ANNUALDAYS, but there are similar examples where all the FDs involved have keys on the left. In later sections we shall see cases where we want to combine several relations in order to fill in nulls.

Table 12.8 The Relation *vacation*.

vacation	(EMPLOYEE	YEARS	ANNUALDAYS	ACCDAYS)
t_1	Udall	3	21	⊥
t_2	Udall	⊥	⊥	17
t_3	Unthank	3	⊥	⊥

Table 12.9 Partial completion of the Relation *vacation*.

vacation′	(EMPLOYEE	YEARS	ANNUALDAYS	ACCDAYS)
$t_1 = t_2$	Udall	3	21	17
t_3	Unthank	3	21	⊥

Our strategy for testing permissibility will be to fill in as many nulls as possible using information given by the FDs. How may we fill in nulls in a relation r given a set of FDs F? The last example gives one obvious rule as to how a null may be filled in. Let $X \rightarrow A$ be an FD in F. Let t_1 and t_2 be two tuples in r such that $t_1(X)\downarrow$, $t_2(X)\downarrow$, and $t_1(X) = t_2(X)$. Suppose that $t_1(A) = \perp$, but that $t_2(A) = a$. We can change $t_1(A)$ to a, since in any permissible completion of r, $t_1(A)$ must be a to satisfy $X \rightarrow A$.

The rule just given is correct, but it does not go far enough.

Example 12.10 Consider the relation $r(A\ B\ C\ D)$ in Figure 12.1, and the set of FDs $F = \{A \rightarrow C, C \rightarrow D\}$. A moment's inspection will show that $t_1(D) = d$ in any permissible completion of r, although the rule just given cannot be used to fill in any nulls in r.

r	A	B	C	D
t_1	a	b	$\perp$	$\perp$
t_2	a	$\perp$	$\perp$	d

Figure 12.1

In the last example, $t_1(D)$ can be filled in using the FDs in F^+, namely $A \rightarrow D$. There are examples where even F^+ does not suffice (see Exercise 12.10). The problem is that we need to indicate that two nulls represent the same value, even though that value is unknown. In the last example, we need to indicate $t_1(C) = t_2(C)$ in any permissible completion of r. To that end, we introduce *marked nulls*. We subscript the null symbol to get an infinite collection of different nulls: $\{\perp_1, \perp_2, \perp_3, \ldots\}$. Marked nulls will be assumed distinct unless they have the same subscript. Let t_1 and t_2 be two tuples over scheme R involving marked nulls. If A is an attribute in R, t_1 and t_2 *agree on* A if either

1. $t_1(A)\downarrow$ and $t_2(A)\downarrow$ and $t_1(A) = t_2(A)$, or
2. $t_1(A) = \perp_i$, $t_2(A) = \perp_j$ and $i = j$.

The tuples agree on a set of attributes X in R if they agree on every attribute in X. For the rest of this section, all nulls in partial relations are assumed to be marked. Any relation with unmarked nulls may be converted to one with marked nulls by appending distinct subscripts to unmarked nulls. We consider two relations in $Rel\uparrow(R)$ to be the same if they are identical except for a one-to-one renaming of marked nulls.

Example 12.11 The relation r in Figure 12.1 could appear as shown in Figure 12.2 with marked nulls.

$r(A$	B	C	$D)$
t_1 a	b	$\perp_1$	$\perp_2$
t_2 a	$\perp_3$	$\perp_4$	d

Figure 12.2

We need two definitions before giving the rule for filling in marked nulls.

Definition 12.2 Let $r \in Rel\!\uparrow\!(R)$, let $X \rightarrow A$ be an FD over R and let t_1 and t_2 be tuples in r that agree on X. If t_1 and t_2 are both definite on A, but $t_1(A) \neq t_2(A)$, r has a *hard violation* of $X \rightarrow A$. If t_1 and t_2 disagree on A, and at least one is null, then r has a *soft violation* of $X \rightarrow A$. Hard violations cannot be removed by filling in nulls, while soft violations can.

The *fill-in rule for marked nulls* mimics the F-rule of the chase computation. The rule fills in or equates marked nulls whenever they participate in a soft violation. Let $r \in Rel\!\uparrow\!(R)$ and let F be a set of FDs over R. Let t_1 and t_2 be tuples in r that participate in a soft violation of the FD $X \rightarrow A$ in F.

1. If $t_1(A)\!\downarrow$ and $t_2(A) = \perp_i$, change every occurrence of $\perp_i$ in r to $t_1(A)$.
2. If $t_2(A)\!\downarrow$ and $t_1(A) = \perp_i$, change every occurrence of $\perp_i$ in r to $t_2(A)$.
3. If $t_1(A) = \perp_i$, $t_2(A) = \perp_j$, and $i < j$, change every occurrence of $\perp_j$ to $\perp_i$; if $i > j$, change every occurrence of $\perp_i$ to $\perp_j$.

These changes remove the soft violation, although they may introduce new violations.

Example 12.12 Starting with relation r in Figure 12.2 and the FDs $F = \{A \rightarrow C, C \rightarrow D\}$, we apply the fill-in rule using $A \rightarrow C$ to change $\perp_4$ to $\perp_1$. We may then use the fill-in rule with $C \rightarrow D$ to change $\perp_2$ to d. The result is shown in Figure 12.3.

$r(A$	B	C	$D)$
t_1 a	b	$\perp_1$	d
t_2 a	$\perp_3$	$\perp_1$	d

Figure 12.3

The repeated application of the fill-in rule for a set of FDs F is similar to the chase computation on a tableau. Values correspond to distinguished variables and marked nulls correspond to nondistinguished variables. However, where a tableau has only one distinguished symbol per column, a relation can have many values in a column. The result of repeated application of the fill-in rule need not be unique.

Example 12.13 Let $r(A\ B\ C)$ be the relation in Figure 12.4. Let $F = \{A \rightarrow B, C \rightarrow B\}$. We see there are two ways to fill in $\perp_2$, one using $A \rightarrow B$ and the other using $C \rightarrow B$.

r(A	B	C)
1	2	$\perp_1$
1	$\perp_2$	3
$\perp_3$	4	3

Figure 12.4

While the relation in the example above could be filled in two ways using the given set of FDs, either way gives a hard violation. We shall show, and it should be apparent, that any relation with a hard violation has no permissible completions. To assure a unique result when applying the fill-in rule to a relation, we assume when a relation has a hard violation, the fill-in rule changes it to some special value, which we call HV. We let $nchase_F(r)$ stand for the result of applying the fill-in rule with FDs from f to relation r until no changes can be made. $Nchase_F(r)$ will either be a relation or the special value HV.

We want to show that r is permissible with respect to F exactly when $nchase_F(r)$ is not HV. $Nchase_F(r)$ can have multiple copies of a marked null. We update the definitions of *augment* and *completion* to handle the multiple copies. We still view a relation with marked nulls as a set of axioms (actually a single axiom) about a total relation that the partial relation represents. The difference is that tuples no longer generate separately quantified axioms.

Example 12.14 The relation $r(A\ B\ C)$ in Figure 12.5 represents the axiom (in domain calculus form):

$$\exists x_1\ \exists x_2\ (r(1\ 2\ x_1) \wedge r(x_2\ 2\ 3) \wedge r(x_2\ 4\ x_1)).$$

Note this formula is not equivalent to

$$\exists x_1\ (r(1\ 2\ x_1)) \wedge \exists x_2\ (r(x_2\ 2\ 3)) \wedge \exists x_1\ \exists x_2\ (r(x_2\ 4\ x_1)).$$

r(A	B	C)
1	2	$\perp_1$
$\perp_2$	2	3
$\perp_2$	4	$\perp_1$

Figure 12.5

We leave an updated definition of subsumes to Exercise 12.12. For r and s in $Rel\uparrow(R)$, r *augments* s, written $r \succeq s$, if r is obtained from s by filling in some nulls in s with values or other nulls. The restriction is that whenever a null $\perp_i$ is changed, every copy of $\perp_i$ must be changed in the same way. Also, we do not allow a marked null to appear in more than one column of a relation. If, in addition, $r\downarrow$, we say r is a *completion* of s, written $r \downarrow\!> s$. These definitions reduce to the ones for the unmarked null case when neither r nor s contains a repeated marked null.

We now show two results. Assume HV has no permissible completions under any set of FDs. First, $nchase_F(r)$ and r always have the same permissible completions under F. Second, if $nchase_F(r) \neq HV$, then r has at least one permissible completion.

We actually show that if r' is obtained from r by a single application of the fill-in rule using an FD form F, then r and r' have the same permissible completions under F. If r' is actually HV, then r had a hard violation. The tuples in r constituting the hard violation will still exhibit the hard violation when filled in. Therefore, r has no permissible completions. If r' is a relation, then r' came from r by replacing a marked null with another marked null or with a value. In either case, $r' \succeq r$, so any permissible completion of r' is a permissible completion of r.

Consider how r' was obtained from r. There must be an FD $X \rightarrow A$ in F and tuples t_1 and t_2 in r such that t_1 and t_2 agree on X. Further, either $t_1(A) = \perp_i$ and $t_2(A) = a$, or $t_1(A) = a$ and $t_2(A) = \perp_i$, or $t_1(A) = \perp_i$ and $t_2(A) = \perp_j$, where $i \neq j$. In any completion s of r, $t_1(X) = t_2(X)$. For s to satisfy F, t_1 and t_2 must agree on A. In the first two cases, both must be a on A, as is the case in r'. If s is a permissible completion of r, then s is a permissible completion of r'. Similarly, in the third case, $\perp_i$ and $\perp_j$ must be replaced by the same value if s is to satisfy F. Hence, again, if s is permissible for r, it is a completion for r', and so a permissible completion for r'. We conclude r and r' have the same permissible completions under F.

From this argument it follows that r and $nchase_F(r)$ have the same permissible completions under F.

Consider the case where $r^* = nchase_F(r)$ is not HV. Form a completion s of r^* by replacing every marked null in r^* with a value distinct from any value in r^* and distinct from the value used to replace any other null. We claim s satisfies F (see Exercise 12.14).

Example 12.15 Let $r(A\ B\ C\ D\ E)$ be the relation in Figure 12.6. Let $F = \{A \rightarrow B, B\,D \rightarrow C\}$. $Nchase_F(r)$ is the relation r^* shown in Figure 12.7. Filling in nulls with distinct values gives the completion s shown in Figure 12.8, which indeed satisfies F.

r(A	B	C	D	E)
1	$\perp_1$	$\perp_2$	2	3
1	$\perp_3$	4	5	$\perp_4$
6	7	8	5	9
1	$\perp_5$	$\perp_6$	2	9

Figure 12.6

r*(A	B	C	D	E)
1	$\perp_1$	$\perp_2$	2	3
1	$\perp_1$	4	5	$\perp_4$
6	7	8	5	9
1	$\perp_1$	$\perp_2$	2	9

Figure 12.7

s(A	B	C	D	E)
1	10	11	2	3
1	10	4	5	12
6	7	8	5	9
1	10	11	2	9

Figure 12.8

To see why s must satisfy F, choose an arbitrary FD $X \rightarrow A$ from F. Let t_1 and t_2 be tuples in s that agree on X. In r^*, t_1 and t_2 must agree on X, otherwise filling in nulls would have made them disagree. Since r^* cannot have a soft or hard violation, $t_1(A) = t_2(A)$ in r^*. Hence $t_1(A) = t_2(A)$ in s. Thus s satisfies $X \rightarrow A$. Since $X \rightarrow A$ was arbitrary, s satisfies F and is therefore a permissible completion of r^* and r.

Nchase gives a method for testing whether a relation r is permissible with respect to a set of FDs F, as well as filling in all nulls possible, assuming infinite domains (see Exercise 12.15). There is still some information about the permissible completions of r that $nchase_F(r)$ does not capture: certain nulls may not take on certain values. If some domains are finite, rather than infinite as we have assumed, it may be possible to determine values for more nulls using FDS.

Example 12.16 Consider the relation *restrooms* in Table 12.10. Assume it obeys the FD FLOOR SEX → ROOM# (only one restroom of each type per floor). We can conclude that t_3(SEX) $\neq$ *women*. If the domain of sex is {*men*, *women*}, then we can change t_3(SEX) to *men*, since it must be so in any permissible completion of restrooms.

Table 12.10. The Relation *restrooms.*

restrooms	FLOOR	ROOM#	SEX
t_1	1	8B	women
t_2	2	8B	women
t_3	2	8D	$\perp_1$

There does not seem to be any labeling scheme to capture information about which values a null may not assume and which nulls must be filled in with different values in a permissible completion. There are other problems to be examined in connection with nulls. Can marked nulls be used to fill in values across relations in a database? Can other dependencies be used to fill in values in partial relations? Should relations such as

r	A	B
	1	$\perp_1$
	1	$\perp_2$

be allowed? Note that r has more completions than

s	A	B
	1	$\perp_1$.

In Section 12.4 we shall examine some ways other than completions to denote what a partial relation represents.

12.3 CONSTRAINTS ON NULLS

In practice, there will usually be restrictions on where nulls should appear in a relation. Typically, nulls are forbidden in any components of the primary key of a relation. We give a means to express such restrictions. For this section it does not matter if nulls are marked or not.

Definition 12.3 Let R be a relation scheme. An *existence constraint* (EC) over R is a statement of the form $X \urcorner Y$ (read "X requires Y") for X and Y subsets of R. A relation $r \in Rel\uparrow(R)$ satisfies $X \urcorner Y$ if for every tuple t in r, $t(X)\downarrow$ implies $t(Y)\downarrow$.

Example 12.17 Let $r(A\ B\ C\ D)$ be the relation shown in Figure 12.9. Relation r satisfies the ECs $D \urcorner A$, $C\ D \urcorner A$ and $\emptyset \urcorner B$. The last EC requires that all tuples be definite on B. The EC A $\urcorner D$ is not satisfied (because of t_2), nor is $B\ A \urcorner C$.

r	$(A$	B	C	$D)$
t_1	1	2	$\perp$	3
t_2	1	4	$\perp$	$\perp$
t_3	$\perp$	2	5	$\perp$
t_4	6	2	7	8

Figure 12.9

A relation satisfies an EC if each of its tuples individually satisfies the EC. This situation is unlike FDs, where pairs of tuples must be considered. Suprisingly, inference axioms for ECs take the exact form of inference axioms for FDs. For example, if $X \urcorner Y$, then $X\ A \urcorner Y$ for any attribute A. Also, if $X \urcorner Y$ and $Y \urcorner Z$, we may conclude $X \urcorner Z$ (see Exercise 12.16). If we have only ECs to check as constraints, it is a simple matter to test whether a given update will cause a relation to violate the ECs. Any deletion is acceptable. Insertion and modification depend only on the tuple involved. When FDs also are being enforced, and are used to fill in nulls, other tuples may be affected by an insertion or modification. The tuple to be inserted may initially satisfy the ECs, but some nulls may be filled in using FDs and cause an EC violation. It is also possible that a tuple already in the relation will be made to violate the ECs.

Example 12.18 The relation $r(A\ B\ C\ D)$ in Figure 12.10 satisfies the EC A $\urcorner B\ C$, and is permissible with respect to the FD $B \rightarrow A$. Adding the tuple $t_3 = \langle 5\ 1\ 4\ \perp \rangle$ will cause t_1 to violate $A \urcorner B\ C$ when $t_1(A)$ is filled in as 5 using $B \rightarrow A$.

There remains much work to be done on which sets of FDs and ECs behave nicely together (see Exercise 12.17).

r	A	B	C	D
t_1	$\perp$	1	$\perp$	6
t_2	2	3	4	$\perp$

Figure 12.10

12.4 RELATIONAL ALGEBRA AND PARTIAL RELATIONS

We now turn to extending relational algebra to relations with nulls. For this section, we let $Rel\uparrow$ and Rel denote the sets of all partial and total relations whose schemes are taken from some fixed universe **U** of attributes. Also, we return to the use of unmarked nulls. We shall view a relation r in $Rel\uparrow(R)$ as denoting a set of total relations from $Rel(R)$. This set of possibilities we call $POSS(r)$. In previous sections we have used $POSS(r) = \{s | s \text{ is a completion of } r\}$. Here we shall consider other definitions for $POSS$. Relative to $POSS$, we consider ways to extend relational operators from Rel to $Rel\uparrow$. Suppose we want to extend the join operator to partial relations. Ideally we would like an extended operator $\bowtie'$ such that

$$POSS(r \bowtie' s) = POSS(r) \bowtie POSS(s)$$

for r and s in $Rel\uparrow$. By $P_1 \bowtie P_2$, for sets of relations P_1 and P_2, we mean

$$\{q_1 \bowtie q_2 | q_1 \in P_1 \quad \text{and} \quad q_2 \in P_2\}.$$

We shall first discuss what properties $POSS$ should possess, and what constitutes a reasonable extension of a relational operator relative to a given possibility function. We then look at proposals for an extended join operator and discuss their shortcomings. Finally, we consider for which definitions of $POSS$ there exist reasonable extensions of the relational operators.

12.4.1 Possibility Functions

Definition 12.4 A *possibility function* is a function $POSS$: $Rel\uparrow \rightarrow 2^{Rel}$. That is, $POSS$ assigns every partial relation a set of total relations. We require that if $r \in Rel\uparrow(R)$, then $POSS(r) \subseteq Rel(R)$.

As the definition stands, there is nothing to indicate that a possibility function is supposed to represent possible total relations for a partial relation. The definition allows a possibility function that maps every partial relation to the empty relation over the same scheme. While such a stonewalling possibility function might have use in political circles, we choose to impose additional restrictions on possibility functions.

Definition 12.5 Let q and r be relations over scheme R such that $q \downarrow\geq r$. If for every tuple $t_q \in q$ there is a tuple $t_r \in r$ such that $t_q \geq t_r$, we say q is a *close extension* of r. If no proper subrelation of q is an extension of r, but q is an extension of r, then q is a *minimal extension* of r. Any minimal extension is also a close extension (see Exercise 12.18).

Example 12.19 Consider the relation $r(A\ B\ C)$ in Figure 12.11. Relation q in Figure 12.12 is a close extension of r, but not a minimal extension, because tuples t_2 and t_3 could be eliminated. Relation q' in Figure 12.13 is a minimal extension of r.

r(A	B	C)
1	2	⊥
⊥	2	3
1	⊥	3

Figure 12.11

q	(A	B	C)
t_1	1	2	3
t_2	4	2	3
t_3	1	5	3

Figure 12.12

q'(A	B	C)
1	2	6
7	2	3
1	8	3

Figure 12.13

Any possibility function *POSS* gives rise to a partial ordering on $Rel\uparrow(R)$ for any R. If $r, s \in Rel\uparrow(R)$, r is *stronger than* s, relative to *POSS*, written $r \sqsupseteq_{POSS} s$, if $POSS(r) \subseteq POSS(s)$. If $r \sqsupseteq_{POSS} s$ and $s \sqsupseteq_{POSS} r$, we say r and s are *equally strong*, written $r \equiv_{POSS} s$. We write $\sqsupseteq$ and $\equiv$ for $\sqsupseteq_{POSS}$ and $\equiv_{POSS}$ when *POSS* is understood.

We can now describe further restrictions on possibility functions.

Definition 12.6 A possibility function *POSS* is *reasonable* if

1. every element of $POSS(r)$ is an extension of r,
2. $POSS(r)$ contains every minimal extension of r, and
3. for every r and s over the same scheme, $s \in POSS(r)$ if and only if $s \sqsupseteq r$ and $s\downarrow$.

Definition 12.7 *POSS* is *closed* if $POSS(r)$ contains only close extensions of r.

Condition 1 arises from viewing r as axioms about a total relation. The condition says that every relation in $POSS(r)$ satisfies the axioms that r denotes. Condition 2 says there are no "hidden axioms." Any total relation that satisfies the axioms r denotes, and has no superfluous tuples in that regard, is in $POSS(r)$. Condition 3 captures the idea that a total relation interpreted as a set of axioms agrees with the relation as a model for a set of axioms. If *POSS* is closed, $s\downarrow$ implies $POSS(s) = \{s\}$, so condition 3 is trivially satisfied.

A closed possibility function corresponds to a "closed world assumption" in heuristic inference systems. The closed world assumption states that what is not provably true is assumed to be false. In our situation, where some of our information is incomplete, it is not clear which statements should be construed as true. This uncertainty allows several variations on the closed world assumption.

Example 12.20 We have already seen one possibility function, $POSS_C(r) = \{s | s \downarrow \succeq r\}$. The subscript C stands for "completion." We leave it to the reader to show that $POSS_C$ is reasonable and closed. The possibility function $POSS_O(r) = \{s | s \downarrow \geq r\}$ is also reasonable, but it is not closed. (The O is for "open.") It is the only possibility function we shall consider that is not closed. Notice $r \sqsupseteq_{POSS_O} s$ holds exactly when $r \geq s$ (see Exercise 12.25). The possibility function $POSS_E(r) = \{s | s \downarrow \geq r$ and s has an even number of tuples$\}$ is not reasonable, since it violates conditions 2 and 3.

Henceforth, we consider only reasonable possibility functions.

If $r \in Rel(R)$, $s \in Rel\!\uparrow\!(R)$ and $r \sqsupseteq s$ for some possibility function *POSS*, then $r \in POSS(s)$ and $r \geq s$, by conditions 3 and 1 of the definition of reasonable possibility function. These results also hold when $r \in Rel\!\uparrow\!(R)$.

Lemma 12.1 Let *POSS* be a possibility function, $\sqsupseteq$ its associated strength ordering, and r and s partial relations on scheme R. Then $r \sqsupseteq s$ implies $r \geq s$.

Proof Suppose $r \not\geq s$. Let t_s be a tuple in s that is not subsumed by any tuple in r. It is possible to construct an extension q of r such that for any tuple $t_q \in q$, $t_q \not\geq t_s$. Furthermore, we can assume q is minimal. (Otherwise, remove tuples from q.) Since q is a minimal extension of r, $q \in POSS(r)$, but $q \notin POSS(s)$, since $q \not\geq s$. Therefore, $POSS(r) \not\subseteq$ POSS(s) and so $r \not\sqsupseteq s$. We have shown the contrapositive of the lemma.

Corollary If $r \equiv s$, then $r \simeq s$.

We shall see cases where the converse of Lemma 12.1 fails: $r \geq s$ does not imply $r \sqsupseteq s$. Let $r \lessgtr s$ mean $r \not\geq s$ and $s \not\geq r_m$ (r and s are incomparable under subsumption). We may conclude from the lemma that $r \lessgtr s$ implies $r \not\equiv s$.

12.4.2 Generalizing the Relational Operators

We shall use possibility functions to characterize when the generalization of an algebraic operator from *Rel* to *Rel*↑ is reasonable. There is one criterion, however, that is independent of the choice of possibility function. We want the generalized operator to agree with the regular operator on *Rel*.

Definition 12.8 Let γ be an operator on *Rel* and let γ' be an operator on *Rel*↑; γ' is *faithful* to γ if

1. when γ and γ' are unary operators, $\gamma(r) = \gamma'(r)$ for every $r \in Rel$ for which $\gamma(r)$ is defined, or
2. when γ and γ' are binary operators, $r\ \gamma\ s = r\ \gamma'\ s$ for every $r, s \in Rel$ for which $r\ \gamma\ s$ is defined.

The next definition gives the ideal behavior of a generalized operator.

Definition 12.9 Let γ be an operator on *Rel* and let γ' be an operator on *Rel*↑. Operator γ' is a *precise* generalization of γ relative to possibility function *POSS* if

1. when γ and γ' are unary operators, $POSS(\gamma'(r)) = \gamma(POSS(r))$ for every $r \in Rel$↑; or
2. when γ and γ' are binary operators, $POSS(r\ \gamma'\ s) = POSS(r)\ \gamma\ POSS(s)$ for every $r, s \in$ Rel↑.

Here, for sets P_1 and P_2 of total relations,

$$\gamma(P_1) = \{\gamma(q) | q \in P_1\} \text{ and}$$
$$P_1 \, \gamma \, P_2 = \{q_1 \, \gamma \, q_2 | q_1 \in P_1, q_2 \in P_2\}.$$

Unfortunately, for some possibility functions, $\gamma(POSS(r))$ or $POSS(r) \, \gamma \, POSS(s)$ may not be regular enough to describe as $POSS(q)$ for any q. In such cases we settle for a generalization of γ that captures everything in $\gamma(POSS(r))$ or $POSS(r) \, \gamma \, POSS(s)$ and as little extra as possible.

Definition 12.10 Let γ be an operator on *Rel* and let γ' be an operator on $Rel\uparrow$. Let *POSS* be a possibility function. Operator γ' is *adequate* for γ relative to *POSS* if

1. when γ and γ' are unary operators, $POSS(\gamma'(r)) \supseteq \gamma(POSS(r))$ for every $r \in Rel\uparrow$, or
2. when γ and γ' are binary operators, $POSS(r \, \gamma' \, s) \supseteq POSS(r) \, \gamma \, POSS(s)$ for every $r, s \in Rel\uparrow$.

Operator γ' is *restricted* for γ relative to *POSS* if

1. when γ and γ' are unary operators, for every $r \in Rel\uparrow$, there is no q in $Rel\uparrow$ such that
$$POSS(\gamma'(r)) \supsetneq POSS(q) \supseteq \gamma(POSS(r)), \text{ or}$$
2. When γ and γ' are binary operators, for every $r, s \in Rel\uparrow$, there is no q in $Rel\uparrow$ such that
$$POSS(r \, \gamma' \, s) \supsetneq POSS(q) \supseteq POSS(r) \, \gamma \, POSS(s).$$

Clearly, if γ' is precise for γ, then γ' is adequate and restricted for γ. We shall content ourselves with an adequate and restricted generalization when no precise generalization is available. We would also like the generalized operators to have properties that the regular operator possesses, such as commutativity or associativity. For example, if γ is an associative binary operator, we want a generalization γ' to satisfy

$$(q \, \gamma' \, r) \, \gamma' \, s \equiv q \, \gamma' \, (r \, \gamma' \, s)$$

for $q, r, s \in Rel\uparrow$. We now consider some generalizations of equijoin and natural join that have been proposed previously.

Example 12.21 Codd defined a "maybe" equijoin for use with relations containing nulls. We examine a simple form of it. Let $r(R)$ and $s(S)$ be relations in $Rel\uparrow$, with $A \in R$, $C \in S$, and $R \cap S = \emptyset$. We extend the equijoin $[A = C]$ as $[A = C]'$ where

$$r[A = C]'\, s = \{t(RS) | t(R) \in r, t(S) \in s \text{ and } t(A) = t(C), \text{ or at least one of } t(A) \text{ and } t(C) \text{ is null}\}.$$

(This definition is actually a combination of Codd's "definite" and "maybe" equijoins.) If we let $r(A\ B)$ and $s(C\ D)$ be as shown in Figure 12.14, then $r[A = C]'\, s$ is given in Figure 12.15. Note that this generalization of equijoin cannot be used to derive a generalization of natural join because the A and C values of a tuple do not necessarily agree.

r(A	B)
1	2
4	⊥

s(C	D)
2	3
⊥	5

Figure 12.14

r[A = C]′s(A	B	C	D)
1	2	2	3
4	⊥	2	3
1	2	⊥	5
4	⊥	⊥	5

Figure 12.15

If we take the three relations

q(A	B)
1	2

r(C	D)
⊥	3

s(E	F)
4	5

and compute $(q\ [A = C]'\ r)\ [C = E]'\ s$, we get

q′(A	B	C	D	E	F)
1	2	⊥	3	4	5

Note that for no (reasonable) possibility function *POSS* is the empty relation in $POSS(q')$. However, if $[A = C]'$ and $[C = E]'$ are adequate for $[A = C]$ and $[C = E]$ under *POSS*, then

$$POSS(q') \supseteq POSS(q[A = C]'\ r)\ [C = E]\ POSS(s) \supseteq (POSS(q)\ [A = C]\ POSS(r))\ [C = E]\ POSS(s),$$

which contains the empty relation. Take any close extensions $\hat{q}$, $\hat{r}$, and $\hat{s}$ for q, r, and s;

$$(\hat{q}\ [A = C]\ \hat{r})\ [C = E]\ \hat{s}$$

is the empty relation. We see that this generalization of equijoin is not adequate for any choice of *POSS*. The problem is that the null in relation r is assumed to equal 1 in one case and 4 in another. We shall see in the next section a modification of Codd's notions that does work out.

Example 12.22 LaCroix and Pirotte propose a generalized natural join operator, denoted $\overset{+}{\bowtie}$, that guarantees every tuple enters a join. Tuples that do not join with other tuples are padded with nulls and added to the result. For the relations $r(A\ B)$ and $s(B\ C)$ in Figure 12.16, $r \overset{+}{\bowtie} s$ is shown in Figure 12.17. LaCroix and Pirotte give several choices as to how to proceed when a null appears in a join column. No matter what choice is taken, $\overset{+}{\bowtie}$ is not associative. Consider the relations

q(A	B)
1	2

r(B	C)
2	3

s(A	C)
1	4

Computing $(q \overset{+}{\bowtie} r) \overset{+}{\bowtie} s$ we get

q′(A	B	C)
1	2	3
1	⊥	4

while $q \overset{+}{\bowtie} (r \overset{+}{\bowtie} s)$ gives

q″(A	B	C)
1	2	4
⊥	2	3

Now $q' \not\asymp q''$, so for any reasonable possibility function $q' \not\equiv q''$, by Lemma 12.1.

r(A	B)
1	2
1	4

s(B	C)
2	3
5	6

Figure 12.16

$r \overset{+}{\bowtie} s$(A	B	C)
1	2	3
1	4	⊥
⊥	5	6

Figure 12.17

Example 12.23 Zaniolo proposed a generalization of join, which we shall denote $\bowtie^Z$, where tuples join if on each common attribute either they agree or exactly one is null. If one tuple is null on an attribute, the joined tuple takes its value from the other tuple. If a tuple does not join with any tuples, it is padded with nulls and added to the result. For the relations $r(A\ B)$ and $s(B\ C)$ in Figure 12.18, $r \bowtie^Z s$ is shown in Figure 12.19.

r(A	B)
1	2
4	5

s(B	C)
2	3
⊥	6
7	8

Figure 12.18

$r \bowtie^Z s$(A	B	C)
1	2	3
1	2	6
4	5	6
⊥	7	8

Figure 12.19

There is no reasonable possibility function for which $\bowtie^Z$ is associative. Consider

q(A	B)
1	2
⊥	5

r(A	B)
⊥	3
⊥	6

s(A	B)
⊥	4
7	8

Computing $(q \bowtie^Z r) \bowtie^Z s$ gives

q'(A	B	C	D)
1	2	3	4
1	2	6	4
7	5	⊥	8

while $q \bowtie^Z (r \bowtie^Z s)$ gives

$q''(A$	B	C	$D)$
7	5	3	8
7	5	6	8
1	2	$\perp$	4

Since $q' \not\approx q''$, we conclude from Lemma 12.1 that $q' \not\equiv q''$ for any reasonable possibility function.

12.4.3 Specific Possibility Functions

In this section we examine several possibility functions to see if adequate and restricted generalized operators exist for them. We shall limit our attention to four operators: (natural) join, union, project, and select on equality.

We first consider $POSS_O$, the "open" possibility function. Recall

$$POSS_O(r) = \{s \mid s\downarrow \geq r\},$$

and that for $POSS_O$, $r \sqsupseteq s$ exactly when $r \geq s$.

Consider a join operator for $POSS_O$; call it $\bowtie^O$. It cannot be precise. For partial relations $r(R)$ and $s(S)$, $POSS_O(r) \bowtie POSS_O(s)$ is a subset of $SAT(*[R\ S])$. For any relation $q \in Rel\uparrow(R\ S)$, $POSS_O(q)$ is not a subset of $SAT(*[R\ S])$ (see Exercise 12.26). We can give an adequate and restricted definition for $\bowtie^O$. Let $r(R)$ and $s(S)$ be in $Rel\uparrow$, with $R \cap S = X$. Let

$$r \bowtie^O s = \{t(R\ S) \mid \text{there are } t_r \in r \text{ and } t_s \in s \text{ with } t_r(X)\downarrow,\ t_s(X)\downarrow,\ t(R) = t_r, \text{ and } t(S) = t_s\}.$$

We join tuples from r and s if they are definite on and agree on X.

Example 12.24 The generalized join of relations $r(A\ B\ C)$ and $s(B\ C\ D)$ in Figure 12.20 is shown in Figure 12.21.

$r(A$	B	$C)$
1	2	$\perp$
$\perp$	3	4
1	3	5

$s(B$	C	$D)$
2	7	3
$\perp$	4	8
3	4	9
3	4	10
3	5	$\perp$

Figure 12.20

$r \bowtie^O s(A$	B	C	$D)$
$\perp$	3	4	9
$\perp$	3	4	10
1	3	5	$\perp$

Figure 12.21

As defined, $\bowtie^O$ is adequate. Let $q = r \bowtie^O s$ and let $\hat{q}$ be any relation in $POSS_O(r) \bowtie POSS_O(s)$. We must show $\hat{q} \geq q$, from which it immediately follows that $\hat{q} \downarrow\geq q$, hence $\hat{q} \in POSS_O(q)$, hence $POSS_O(q) \supseteq POSS_O(r) \bowtie POSS_O(s)$. Let $\hat{q} = \hat{r} \bowtie \hat{s}$ for $\hat{r} \in POSS_O(r)$ and $\hat{s} \in POSS_O(s)$. Let t_q be any tuple in q. There must exist tuples $t_r \in r$ and $t_s \in s$ such that $t_r(X)\downarrow$, $t_s(X)\downarrow$, $t_q(R) = t_r$ and $t_q(S) = t_s$. We conclude $t_r(X) = t_s(X)$. Since $\hat{r} \geq r$, there must be a tuple $t_{\hat{r}} \in \hat{r}$ such that $t_{\hat{r}} \geq t_r$ and so $t_{\hat{r}}(X) = t_r(X)$. Likewise, there is a tuple $t_{\hat{s}} \in \hat{s}$ such that $t_{\hat{s}} \geq t_s$ and so $t_{\hat{s}}(X) = t_s(X)$. Relation $\hat{q}$ must contain a tuple $t_{\hat{q}}$ such that $t_{\hat{q}}(R) = t_{\hat{r}}$ and $t_{\hat{q}}(S) = t_{\hat{s}}$. It follows $t_{\hat{q}} \geq t_q$. Since the choice of t_q was arbitrary, $\hat{q} \geq q$, as desired. We leave the proof that $\bowtie^O$ is restricted as Exercise 12.27.

Union has a precise generalization for $POSS_O$. Let r and s be in $Rel\uparrow(R)$, and let

$$r \cup^O s = \{t \mid t \in r \text{ or } t \in s\}.$$

Suppose $q = r \cup^O s$. We first show $POSS_O(q) \supseteq POSS_O(r) \cup POSS_O(s)$. (Union here is an element-wise union.) Let $\hat{q} \in POSS_O(r) \cup POSS_O(s)$. There must be $\hat{r} \in POSS_O(r)$ and $\hat{s} \in POSS_O(s)$ such that $\hat{q} = \hat{r} \cup \hat{s}$. Let t_q be a tuple in q. Either $t_q \in r$ or $t_q \in s$. If $t_{\hat{q}} \in \hat{r}$, there is a tuple $t_{\hat{q}} \in \hat{r}$, and hence in $\hat{q}$, such that $t_{\hat{q}} \geq t_q$. If $t_q \in s$, there is similarly a tuple $t_{\hat{q}}$ in $\hat{q}$ with $t_{\hat{q}} \geq t_q$. We conclude $\hat{q} \geq q$, hence $\hat{q} \downarrow\geq q$ and so $\hat{q} \in POSS_O(q)$.

Suppose now that $\hat{q} \in POSS_O(q)$. Since $q \geq r$ (Why?), $\hat{q} \downarrow\geq r$ and so $\hat{q} \in POSS_O(r)$. Similarly, $\hat{q} \in POSS_O(s)$. Therefore $\hat{q} \in POSS_O(r) \cup POSS_O(s)$ and so $POSS_O(q) \subseteq POSS_O(r) \cup^O POSS_O(s)$. We conclude $\cup^O$ is precise for $POSS_O$.

Project also has a precise generalization for $POSS_O$. We leave the definition to the reader (see Exercise 12.28).

We turn to select with equality comparisons between two attributes or an attribute and a value. Let $r \in Rel\uparrow(R)$ and let $A \in R$. We define

$$\sigma^O_{A=a}(r) = \{t(R) \mid t \in r \text{ and } t(A) = a\}.$$

Example 12.25 Let $r(A\ B\ C)$ be the relation in Figure 12.22; $\sigma^O_{A=1}(r)$ is shown in Figure 12.23

$r(A$	B	$C)$
1	1	2
1	$\perp$	3
$\perp$	4	5
4	4	6

Figure 12.22

$\sigma^O_{A=1}(r)(A$	B	$C)$
1	1	2
1	$\perp$	3

Figure 12.23

For comparing two attributes $A, B \in R$ we have

$$\sigma^O_{A=B}(r) = \{t(R) | t \in r,\ t(A)\downarrow,\ t(B)\downarrow \text{ and } t(A) = t(B)\}.$$

Example 12.26 The relation r in Figure 12.22, $\sigma^O_{A=B}(r)$ is shown in Figure 12.24.

$\sigma^O_{A=B}(r)(A$	B	$C)$
1	1	2
4	4	6

Figure 12.24

These two definitions are not precise, but precise definitions are not possible. For $\sigma^O_{A=a}$, note that for any relation $s \in \sigma_{A=a}(POSS_O(r))$, every tuple $t \in s$ has $t(A) = a$. For any relation q, $POSS_O(q)$ contains relations whose tuples are not all a on A. The two definitions are adequate and restricted (see Exercise 12.29).

We now examine closed possibility functions. There does not seem to be any closed possibility function that has adequate and restricted generalizations for all of join, union, project, and select. While we do not exhaust all reasonable closed possibility functions, we do treat the three most natural ones.

The most liberal definition for a closed possibility function is

$$POSS_{CE}(r) = \{s | s \text{ is a close extension of } r\}.$$

For $POSS_{CE}$, $r \geq s$ does *not* imply $r \sqsupseteq s$. Consider relations

$r(A \quad B)$ and $s(A \quad B)$

A	B
1	2
⊥	2

A	B
1	2

We have $r \geq s$, but

$\hat{r}(A \quad B)$

A	B
1	2
3	2

is a close extension of r but not of s. Hence, $POSS_{CE}(r) \not\subseteq POSS_{CE}(s)$ and so $r \not\sqsupseteq s$. $POSS_{CE}$ has adequate and restricted generalizations of union and project (see Exercise 12.31a). No adequate generalization exists for select. Consider $\sigma_{A=1}(POSS_{CE}(r))$ for

$\hat{r}(A \quad B)$

A	B
⊥	2 .

There is no relation q in $Rel\uparrow(A\ B)$ such that $POSS_{CE}(q) \supseteq \sigma_{A=1}(POSS_{CE}(r))$. $POSS_{CE}(q)$ can contain either non-empty relations, or just the empty relation, while $\sigma_{A=1}(POSS_{CE}(r))$ contains the empty relation and the relation

$\hat{r}(A \quad B)$

A	B
1	2 .

A similar argument shows there is no adequate generalization of join for $POSS_{CE}$ (see Exercise 12.31b).

Another closed possibility function is

$$POSS_C(r) = \{s \mid s \downarrow\geq r\}.$$

There is no adequate generalization of project for $POSS_C$. Consider

$r(A \quad B)$

A	B
⊥	1
⊥	2 .

The set π_A $(POSS_C(r))$ is all one- and two-tuple total relations on scheme A. There is no relation $q \in Rel\uparrow(A)$ such that $POSS_C(q)$ contains all such relations. The same problem arises for the possibility function $POSS_{ME}$ where

$$POSS_{ME}(r) = \{s \mid s \text{ is a minimal extension of } r\}.$$

$POSS_{ME}$ is the most conservative closed possibility function.

The chances seem bleak for a closed possibility function with adequate and restricted definitions for join, union, select, and project. Biskup has a possibility function using a modification of partial relations for which such generalizations exist. His approach divides a relation into *sure* tuples and *maybe* tuples. We shall call this variety of partial relation a *partitioned relation*. A partitioned relation can be viewed as an ordered pair of partial relations. If r is a partitioned relation, we let $SURE(r)$ be the set of sure tuples for f and let $MAYBE(r)$ be the set of maybe tuples for r. If r is a partitioned relation with scheme R, and s is a partial relation on the same scheme, s *approximates* r, written $s \rhd r$, if $SURE(r) \cup MAYBE(r) \supseteq s \supseteq SURE(r)$. The possibility function we shall use for partitioned relations is

$$POSS_B(r) = \{q \mid q \text{ is a close extension of some } s \text{ such that } s \rhd r\}.$$

In writing partitioned relations, we include a dashed line to separate the sure tuples above from the maybe tuples below.

Example 12.27 Figure 12.25 shows a partitioned relation $r(A\ B\ C)$. The partial relations s_1 and s_2 in Figure 12.26 both approximate r, hence the close extensions q_1 of s_1 and q_2 of s_2 in Figure 12.27 are both in $POSS_B(r)$.

$r(A$	B	$C)$
1	⊥	2
⊥	3	2
- - -	- - -	- - -
1	3	⊥
⊥	⊥	4

Figure 12.25

$s_1(A$	B	$C)$
1	⊥	2
⊥	3	2
⊥	⊥	4

$s_2(A$	B	$C)$
1	⊥	2
⊥	3	2

Figure 12.26

q_1(A	B	C)		q_2(A	B	C)
1	3	2		1	3	2
1	5	2				
1	3	4				
1	5	4				

Figure 12.27

If r contains only maybe tuples, $POSS_B(r)$ will contain the empty relation along with non-empty relations. Such a situation is not possible for partial relations with any closed possibility function.

We now syntactically characterize strength under $POSS_B$.

Lemma 12.2 For partitioned relations r and s over scheme R and the possibility function $POSS_B$, $r \sqsupseteq s$ if and only if

1. every sure tuple in s is subsumed by a sure tuple of r, and
2. every tuple in r subsumes some tuple in s.

Proof (if) We must show that if the two conditions hold, then $POSS_B(r) \subseteq POSS_B(s)$. Let $\hat{r}$ be a relation in $POSS_B(r)$. In order to show $\hat{r} \in POSS_B(s)$, we must show that every sure tuple in s is subsumed by some tuple in $\hat{r}$ and that every tuple in $\hat{r}$ subsumes some tuple in s. Let t_s be any sure tuple in s. By condition 1, there is a sure tuple $t_r \in r$ such that $t_r \geq t_s$. By the choice of $\hat{r}$, $\hat{r}$ contains a tuple $t_{\hat{r}}$ such that $t_{\hat{r}} \geq t_r$. Therefore, $t_{\hat{r}} \geq t_s$. Now take an arbitrary tuple $u_{\hat{r}}$ in $\hat{r}$. There must be a tuple u_r in r such that $u_{\hat{r}} \geq u_r$. By condition 2, s contains a tuple u_s such that $u_r \geq u_s$, so $u_{\hat{r}} \geq u_s$. Since the choice of $\hat{r}$ was arbitrary, $POSS_B(r) \subseteq POSS_B(s)$ and so $r \sqsupseteq s$.

(only if) Assume $r \sqsupseteq s$. Let $q = SURE(r)$. Form a completion $\hat{q}$ of q by filling in nulls in q with values that appear nowhere in s. By this construction of $\hat{q}$, $\hat{q} \in POSS_B(r)$. Since $r \sqsupseteq s$, $\hat{q}$ is in $POSS_B(s)$, so for any sure tuple $t_s \in s$, q contains a tuple $t_{\hat{q}}$ such that $t_{\hat{q}} \geq t_s$. Tuple $t_{\hat{q}}$ came from a sure tuple t_r in r by using values that do not appear in t_s. Hence, t_r must subsume t_s, and condition 1 is met.

Suppose now $q = SURE(r) \cup MAYBE(r)$. Form a completion $\hat{q}$ of q by filling in nulls using values that do not appear in s. As before, $\hat{q} \in POSS_B(r)$, hence $\hat{q}$ is in $POSS_B(s)$. Take any tuple $t_r \in r$ and let t_q be the tuple in $\hat{q}$ obtained by filling t_r (which appears in q). Since $\hat{q} \in POSS_B(s)$, s contains a tuple t_s such that $t_{\hat{q}} \geq t_s$. Since the filled-in values of $t_{\hat{q}}$ could not match t_s, we must have $t_r \geq t_s$, which fulfills condition 2.

Example 12.28 Let r be the partitioned relation in Figure 12.25 and let s be the partitioned relation shown in Figure 12.28. From Lemma 12.2 we see that $s \sqsupseteq r$, but $r \not\sqsupseteq s$. Indeed, the total relation q_2 in Figure 12.27 is in $POSS_B(r)$ but not in $POSS_B(s)$.

s(*A*	*B*	*C*)
1	⊥	2
⊥	3	2
1	3	4
----	----	----
1	⊥	4
7	⊥	4

Figure 12.28

Lemma 12.2 lets us characterize redundant tuples: those whose removal does not change the strength of a relation.

Corollary Let r be a partitioned relation over scheme R and let t be a tuple in r. Let r' be the partitioned relation formed by removing t from r. Then $r \equiv r'$ if and only if

1. $t \in SURE(r)$, t is subsumed by a sure tuple of r, and t subsumes a sure or maybe tuple of r; or
2. $t \in MAYBE(r)$ and t subsumes a sure or maybe tuple of r.

Proof Left to the reader (see Exercise 12.37).

The second case of the corollary implies that any $t \in SURE(r) \cap MAYBE(r)$ can be removed from $MAYBE(r)$. If r' is formed from r by removing a maybe tuple, then $r' \sqsupseteq r$. If r' is formed by removing a sure tuple, we could have r' and r incomparable in strength.

Example 12.29 Consider the partitioned relations $r(A\ B\ C)$ and $r'(A\ B\ C)$ in Figure 12.29. Neither r nor r' has any maybe tuples; r' is r with a sure tuple removed. Total relation $\hat{r}$ in Figure 12.30 is in $POSS_B(r)$ but not in $POSS_B(r')$; $\hat{r}'$ is in $POSS_B(r')$ but not in $POSS_B(r)$.

r(*A*	*B*	*C*)
1	⊥	2
⊥	3	4
----	----	----

r'(*A*	*B*	*C*)
1	⊥	2
----	----	----

Figure 12.29

$\hat{r}(A$	B	$C)$
1	5	2
6	3	4

$\hat{r}'(A$	B	$C)$
1	5	2

Figure 12.30

For discussing restricted generalizations, we need to characterize when one partitioned relation is strictly stronger than another. Assume r and s are partitioned relations such that $r \sqsupseteq\!\!\!\!/\; s$. There must be a total relation $\hat{s}$ in $POSS_B(s)$ that is not in $POSS_B(r)$. How could s fail to be in $POSS_B(r)$? The first possibility is that r contains a sure tuple t_r that is not subsumed by any tuple in $\hat{s}$. It follows that there is no tuple in s that subsumes t_r. The second possibility is that $\hat{s}$ has a tuple $t_{\hat{s}}$ that does not subsume any tuple in r. It follows that the tuple $t_s \in s$ from which $t_{\hat{s}}$ came does not subsume any tuple in r. To summarize:

Lemma 12.3 Let r and s be partitioned relations such that $r \sqsupseteq s$. If $r \sqsupseteq\!\!\!\!/\; s$, then

1. r contains a sure tuple that is not subsumed by any tuple in s, or
2. s contains a tuple that does not subsume any tuple in r.

The converse of Lemma 12.3 is left as Exercise 12.38.

We are ready to consider generalizations of relational operators under $POSS_B$. Projection has a natural generalization. If r is a partitioned relation with scheme R and $X \subseteq R$, we define

$$\pi_X^B(r) = s(X)$$

where

$$SURE(s) = \{t(X) | t \text{ in } SURE(r)\} \text{ and}$$
$$MAYBE(s) = \{t(X) | t \text{ in } MAYBE(r)\}.$$

Example 12.30 Let $r(A\ B\ C)$ be the partitioned relation in Figure 12.31. Figure 12.32 shows $s = \pi_{BC}^B(r)$. The maybe tuple $\langle \perp\ 4\rangle$ can be removed from s by the corollary to Lemma 12.2.

The proof that π^B is adequate and precise is left as Exercise 12.39. We next generalize select with an equality to constant comparison. Let r be a partitioned relation on scheme R and let $A \in R$. Define

$$\sigma_{A=a}^B(r) = s(R)$$

where

$$\begin{aligned} SURE(s) &= \{t \mid t \in SURE(r) \text{ and } t(A) = a\} \\ MAYBE(s) &= \{t \mid t \in MAYBE(r) \text{ and } t(A) = a\} \cup \\ &\quad \{t' \mid \text{there is a } t \in r \text{ such that } t(R - A) = \\ &\quad t'(R - A),\ t(A) = \bot \text{ and } t'(A) = a\}. \end{aligned}$$

Example 12.31 Let r be the partitioned relation in Figure 12.31. Figure 12.33 shows $s = \sigma^B_{A=1}(r)$.

r(A	B	C)
1	⊥	4
⊥	5	6
- - -	- - -	- - -
2	⊥	4
1	3	6

Figure 12.31

s(B	C)
⊥	4
5	6
- - -	- - -
⊥	4
3	6

Figure 12.32

s(A	B	C)
1	⊥	4
- - -	- - -	- - -
1	5	6
1	3	6

Figure 12.33

Lemma 12.4 The operator $\sigma^B_{A=a}$ is a precise generalization of $\sigma_{A=a}$ for $POSS_B$.

Proof Let $s = \sigma^B_{A=a}(r)$ for an arbitrary partitioned relation $r(R)$ with $A \in R$. First, we show $POSS_B(s) \supseteq \sigma_{A=a}(POSS_B(r))$. Let q be in $\sigma_{A=a}(POSS_B(r))$.

Let $\hat{r}$ be a relation in $POSS_B(r)$ such that $q = \sigma_{A=a}(\hat{r})$. We must show $q \in POSS_B(s)$. Let t be in $SURE(s)$. We must exhibit a tuple t_q of q such that $t_q \geq t_s$. Since $t_s \in SURE(s)$, $t_s(A) = a$ and $t_s \in SURE(r)$. Hence, $\hat{r}$ has a tuple $t_r \geq t_s$. We see that $t_{\hat{r}}(A)=a$, so $t_{\hat{r}} \in q$ and is the desired tuple t_q above. We next must show that for any tuple $t_q \in q$ there is a tuple $t_s \in s$ such that $t_q \geq t_s$. We know $t_q \in \hat{r}$, so there is a tuple $t_r \in r$ such that $t_q \geq t_r$. Either $t_r(A) = a$ or $t_r(A) = \perp$. In the former case, $t_r \in s$. In the latter case, $t_r' \in s$, where $t_r'(A) = a$ and $t_r'(R - A) = t_r(R - A)$. Since $t_q \geq t_r$, and $t_q(A) = a$, $t_q \geq t_r'$. We conclude $q \in POSS_B(s)$, as desired.

Second, we show $POSS_B(s) \subseteq \sigma_{A=a}(POSS_B(r))$. Let $q \in POSS_B(s)$. We must find $\hat{r}$ in $POSS_B(r)$ such that $q = \sigma_{A=a}(\hat{r})$. Note that $q = \sigma_{A=a}(q)$. If $q \notin POSS_B(r)$, it can only be because r contains a sure tuple t_r that is not subsumed by any tuple in q. Let $\hat{r}$ include q and a total tuple t_r' for every sure tuple t_r in r not covered by q. Choose t_r' so that $t_r'(A) \neq a$. We have $\hat{r} \in POSS_B(r)$, $q = \sigma_{A=a}(r)$, hence $q \in \sigma_{A=a}(POSS_B(r))$. We have shown $POSS_B(s) = \sigma_{A=a}(POSS_B(r))$, so $\sigma^B_{A=a}$ is precise.

We leave it to the reader to generalize $\sigma_{A=B}$ for $POSS_B$.

Let r and s both be partitioned relations on scheme r. The generalized union given by

$$r \cup^B s = q(R)$$

where

$$SURE(q) = SURE(r) \cup SURE(s) \text{ and}$$
$$MAYBE(q) = MAYBE(r) \cup MAYBE(s)$$

is precise (see Exercise 12.42).

Finally, we generalize join for $POSS_B$. Let $r(R)$ and $s(S)$ be partitioned relations where $R \cap S = X$. Say that $t_r \in r$ and $t_s \in s$ are *compatible on* X if for every $A \in X$, $t_r(A) = t_s(A)$ or at least one of $t_r(A)$ and $t_s(A)$ is null. Define

$$r \bowtie^B s = q(R\,S)$$

where

$$SURE(q) = \{t(RS) \mid \text{there are } t_r \in SURE(r),\ t_s \in (SURE(s) \text{ such that } t_r(X)\downarrow,\ t_s(X)\downarrow,\ t(R) = t_r \text{ and } t(S) = t_s\} \text{ and}$$

$$\begin{aligned} MAYBE(q) = \{t(RS) \mid & \text{there are compatible tuples } t_r \in r \\ & \text{and } t_s \in s \text{ such that } t(R-X) = t_r(R-X), \\ & t(S-X) = t_s(R-X), \text{ and for each } A \in X, \\ & \text{if } t_r(A)\downarrow, \text{ then } t(A) = t_r(A), \text{ else } t(A) = t_s(A)\}. \end{aligned}$$

The "*MAYBE*" part of the definitions says we join compatible tuples by following the more definite tuple on each attribute in X. This definition makes $SURE(q)$ a subset of $MAYBE(q)$, but we may drop the duplicate tuples from $MAYBE(q)$.

Example 12.32 Let $r(A\ B)$ and $s(B\ C)$ be the partitioned relations in Figure 12.34. Figure 12.35 shows $q = r \bowtie^B s$.

$r(A$	$B)$
⊥	1
3	⊥
- - -	- - -
4	1

$s(B$	$C)$
1	2
- - -	- - -
5	2
⊥	6

Figure 12.34

$q(A$	B	$C)$
1	1	2
- - -	- - -	- - -
⊥	1	6
3	1	2
3	5	6
3	⊥	6
4	1	2
4	1	6

Figure 12.35

This generalization of join is not precise. Referring to the last example, any relation in $POSS_B(r) \bowtie POSS_B(s)$ satisfies the JD $*[AB,\ BC]$. There are total relations in $POSS_B(q)$ that do not satisfy this JD.

Lemma 12.5 The operator $\bowtie^B$ is an adequate and restricted generalization of $\bowtie$ for $POSS_B$.

Proof For the proof, let $r(R)$ and $s(S)$ be partitioned relations, let $X = R \cap S$ and let $q = r \bowtie^B s$.

($\bowtie^B$ adequate) Let $\hat{r} \in POSS_B(r)$ and $\hat{s} \in POSS_B(s)$. Let $\hat{q} = \hat{r} \bowtie \hat{s}$. We must show $\hat{q} \in POSS_B(q)$. Let t_q be any tuple in $SURE(q)$. There must be tuples $t_r \in r$ and $t_s \in s$ that join to form t_q, and, furthermore, $t_r(X)\downarrow$, $t_s(X)\downarrow$ and $t_r(X) = t_s(X)$. By the choice of $\hat{r}$, it contains a tuple $t_{\hat{r}}$ such that $t_{\hat{r}} \geq t_r$. Likewise, s contains a tuple $t_{\hat{s}}$ with $t_{\hat{s}} \geq t_s$. Let $t_{\hat{q}} = t_{\hat{r}} \bowtie t_{\hat{s}}$. We have $t_{\hat{q}} \geq t_q$. Suppose now that u_q is an arbitrary tuple from $\hat{q}$. This tuple must be $u_{\hat{r}} \bowtie u_{\hat{s}}$ for some $u_{\hat{r}} \in \hat{r}$ and $u_{\hat{s}} \in \hat{s}$. In turn, r must contain a u_r such that $u_{\hat{r}} \geq u_r$, and $s \in u_s$ such that $u_{\hat{s}} \geq u_s$. Tuples u_r and u_s must becompatible and q therefore contains a maybe tuple u_q constructed from u_r and u_s. It follows fairly directly that $u_q \geq u_{\hat{q}}$. Thus, q is in $POSS_B(q)$ and so $POSS_B(q) \supseteq POSS_B(r) \bowtie POSS_B(s)$, as desired.

($\bowtie^B$ restricted) Suppose q' is a partitioned relation such that $q' \sqsupseteq\!\!\!\!/\; q$ and $POSS_B(q) \supseteq POSS_B(r) \bowtie POSS_B(s)$. Lemma 12.3 provides two cases to consider.

Case 1 $SURE(q')$ contains a tuple t_q' that is not subsumed by any tuple in q. We make the following claim.

Claim Any completion $\hat{q}$ of $SURE(q)$ is in $POSS_B(r) \bowtie POSS_B(s)$.

The proof of the claim is left as Exercise 12.42. Form a completion $\hat{q}$ of $SURE(q)$ using values not in q' to fill in nulls in $SURE(q)$. By its construction, no tuple in $\hat{q}$ subsumes tuple t_q' in q', so $\hat{q} \notin POSS_B(q')$. By the claim, we have a contradiction to $POSS_B(q') \supseteq POSS_B(r)$.

Case 2 Relation q contains a tuple t_q that does not subsume any tuple in q'. Consider the tuple $t_q \downarrow\geq t_q$ that is obtained by filling in t_q with values not in q'. No tuple in q' is subsumed by $t_{\hat{q}}$. By the construction of $\hat{t}_q$, r must contain a tuple t_r such that $\hat{t}_q(R) \downarrow\geq t_r$, and s must contain t_s where $\hat{t}_q(S) \downarrow\geq t_s$. Choose $\hat{r} \in POSS_B(r)$ that contains $\hat{t}_q(R)$ and choose $\hat{s} \in POSS_B(s)$ that contains $\hat{t}_q(S)$. We see $\hat{r} \bowtie \hat{s}$ contains $\hat{t}_q$, so $\hat{r} \bowtie \hat{s} \notin POSS_B(q')$, a contradiction. We conclude q' as described cannot exist, so $\bowtie^B$ is restricted.

In this section we have considered generalizing relational operators relative to various possibility functions. Only by introducing partitioned relations were we able to obtain a closed possibility function with adequate and restricted generalizations of union, select, project, and join. There may yet exist a closed possibility function for partial relations that admits such generalizations. It is also plausible that incorporating marked nulls would allow precise generalizations where only adequate and restricted ones are achievable now.

12.5 PARTIAL INFORMATION AND DATABASE SEMANTICS

We now turn to handling "subtuples" over a relation scheme. At times it would be useful to view a relation as a set of inhomogeneous tuples. Different tuples could have different schemes.

Example 12.33 Consider the attributes ADVISOR, DEPT, and STUDENT. We might want to store a tuple $\langle a\ d \rangle$ over ADVISOR DEPT, meaning a does advising for department d. We might also want a tuple $\langle d\ s \rangle$ over DEPT STUDENT, representing that d is the major department for s. We also might want a tuple $\langle a\ d\ s \rangle$ over all three attributes, meaning a is the advisor of s for department d. Possibly, we may want tuples over STUDENT alone, simply to record all the students.

The problems in handling a relation with inhomogeneous tuples are similar to those in treating a database as a single semantic entity. We might view a database as a single relation with inhomogeneous tuples. In Chapter 9, we were interested in databases that represented instances over a universal scheme, although we saw there that a database can have states that represent no universal instance. There is no efficient algorithm known to test if a given database state is the projection of a common instance. (In Chapter 13 we explore a class of database schemes for which such a test can be done efficiently.) It may be too restrictive to insist a database represent a single relation. If we do not adopt that view, though, how can we treat a database as a unit and how do we discuss enforcing constraints on the database as a whole?

12.5.1 Universal Relation Assumptions

The requirement that the relations in a database all be projections of some common instance is called the *universal instance assumption* (UIA). A database is seen as representing a single relation over a universal scheme—usually the join of all the relations in the database. The UIA is often a reasonable assumption for design purposes, even if actual states of the database will not always conform to it. It is particularly apt when the design starts with a single scheme. We can draw a broad analogy between the UIA and the assumption that a programming language can be described by a context-free grammar. While the basic syntax of the language may be described by a set of productions, the semantic actions associated with those productions may actually make certain constructs context-sensitive. Nevertheless, the context-free grammar is a useful tool for organizing a compiler for the language.

Why prefer a database over a single relation? First, we may eliminate redundancy going from the single relation to the database. Second, we may find it useful to store states of the database that do not correspond to any single relation.

Example 12.34 We could represent the history relation of Table 12.1 as a database of two relations: *info*(EMPLOYEE SALARY) and *pastinfo*(EMPLOYEE PREVEMP PREVJOB PREVSAL). We could then store a tuple ⟨Lombardi 13,200⟩ in *info* without storing a tuple for Lombardi in *pastinfo*, in the case that Lombardi had no previous job. The tuple ⟨Lombardi 13,200⟩ in *info* would *not* have the same meaning as the tuple ⟨Lombardi 13,200 ⊥ ⊥ ⊥⟩ in *history*, since the latter asserts Lombardi had a previous job, but we do not know the details.

There are situations where the UIA does not make sense, even at the design level. The design process does not necessarily start from a single relation scheme. The database can include facts on a wide range of subjects, where it is not meaningful or natural to discuss a tuple that ranges over the entire set of attributes. The design process can start with a set of relation schemes, and proceed by combining and decomposing those schemes. We do not want the UIA, but we do want some consistency assumption about the meaning of attributes in different schemes. If in one scheme DATE means the birthdate of an employee, and somewhere else it means the date of appointment, we have semantic problems with combining relations using natural join. If we assume that two occurrences of the same attribute in different schemes always have different meanings we can miss important connections.

The *universal relation scheme assumption* (URSA) on a database scheme requires an attribute mean the same everywhere it appears, that it represents a single role of a class of entities. DATE, as used above, represented different roles for the class of dates. URSA is always satisfied when a database scheme is obtained from a single relation scheme by decomposition. A consequence of URSA is that tuples over a given set of attributes have a single meaning. Hence, an URSA database should never contain two relations over the same scheme, for both relations would contain the same set of tuples. In an URSA database, the scheme is sufficient to identify a relation. A set of attributes determines a unique semantic connection among them, if any connection at all exists. To contrast the UIA and URSA, the UIA requires a "universal extension," while URSA only requires "universal intension."

To satisfy URSA, it may be necessary to rename attributes.

Example 12.35 Suppose we start with a relation *advises*(FACULTY STUDENT) to record advisors of students and a relation *teaches*(FACULTY COURSE STUDENT) to record students' instructors and courses. URSA is violated because of the two connections between FACULTY and STUDENT. To satisfy URSA, we can rename the two occurrences of FACULTY to ADVISOR and INSTRUCTOR, to reflect the different roles involved. Some information is lost here—that ADVISOR and INSTRUCTOR are different roles for the same class of entities. This connection may be discernable from the domains involved. It can be recaptured explicitly in a generalization hierarchy, which relates the different roles of a class of entities.

12.5.2 Placeholders and Subscheme Relations

We return to the problem of inhomogeneous tuples in a single relation. In Example 12.34 we saw that decomposing a relation into database let us represent facts over a subscheme of the original relation. Decomposition is not always the answer.

Example 12.36 Referring back to Example 12.33, we wanted to represent tuples over the schemes ADVISOR DEPT, DEPT STUDENT and ADVISOR DEPT STUDENT. Using a database with two relations, r_1(ADVISOR DEPT) and r_2(DEPT STUDENT), is not sufficient. We have no way to represent tuples over ADVISOR DEPT STUDENT. We cannot use the join of r_1 and r_2, since an advisor advising for a department and a student majoring in the same department do not necessarily imply that advisor advises that student.

One approach is to introduce a new special symbol, called a *placeholder*, to pad out a tuple over a subscheme to the entire relation scheme. We use a dash as the placeholder symbol. We treat a padded tuple as a tuple over the subscheme of attributes where the placeholder does not appear.

Example 12.37 Table 12.11 shows a relation r(ADVISOR DEPT STUDENT) with subtuples represented using placeholders. The tuple t_2 =

⟨Thorton Math -⟩ is interpreted as a regular tuple over the scheme ADVISOR DEPT. Tuple t_2 states only that Thorton does advising for the Math department. There is no assertion that Thorton actually advises some students, which the tuple ⟨Thorton Math-⟩ makes.

Table 12.11 Relation r.

	r(ADVISOR	DEPT	STUDENT)
t_1	Thomas	Math	Walker
t_2	Thorton	Math	-
t_3	-	Econ	Wilson
t_4	-	-	Wu

While nulls and placeholders can both appear in a relation, we restrict ourselves to just placeholders for the moment. As with nulls, we may want to control the use of placeholders in a relation. We may allow subtuples only over certain schemes. In the last example, we might disallow subtuples over just ADVISOR and STUDENT. We could use a formalism similar to existence constraints to restrict the legal schemes for subtuples, but it seems more natural here to simply list the allowable schemes for subtuples. We call an allowable scheme for a subtuple an *object*. Objects are basically those sets of attributes over which tuples "make sense." We constrain a relation $r(R)$ by giving a set of objects $\mathbf{O} = \{W_1, W_2, \ldots, W_n\}$, where $W_i \subseteq R$, $1 \leq i \leq n$. Relation r *satisfies* $\mathbf{O}$ if for any tuple t in r, the set of attributes where placeholders appear for t is $R - W_i$ for some object $W_i \in \mathbf{O}$.

Example 12.38 Relation r in Table 12.11 satisfies the set of objects $\mathbf{O} = \{$ADVISOR DEPT STUDENT, ADVISOR DEPT, DEPT STUDENT, DEPT, STUDENT$\}$.

While placeholders are adequate for representing subtuples in a single relation, we use another method when working with databases. Given a set of objects $\mathbf{O}$, we represent subtuples in a database that has one relation for each object $W \in \mathbf{O}$. Naturally, the relation on W contains all the subtuples with scheme W. That is, we use $\mathbf{O}$ as a database scheme. We are departing from our usual practice. Up to now, we never had two relations $r(R)$ and $s(S)$ in a database if $R \subseteq S$. Under the UIA, there is no point in such an arrangement, since $r = \pi_R(s)$. With just URSA, however, the arrangement makes sense.

The use of separate relations for subtuples also avoids a consistency problem. If placeholders are used, a given subtuple could properly appear in multiple relations. A tuple $\langle b\ c \rangle$ over $B\ C$ could be padded to appear in a relation $r(A\ B\ C)$ or a relation $s(B\ C\ D)$. To obey URSA, it seems that if a BC-tuple appears in r, it should also appear in s. When inserting a subtuple into a relation, we must test to see if that subtuple could properly be included in another relation. Using a separate relation for each type of subtuple removes the need for such cross-checking.

Example 12.39 Consider the set of objects $\mathbf{O}$ = {ADVISOR DEPT, DEPT STUDENT, ADVISOR DEPT STUDENT, DEPT STUDENT MATRIC}. MATRIC is the date when a student reaches upper-division standing in a department. We could store tuples over these objects in two relations, r_1(ADVISOR DEPT STUDENT) and r_2(DEPT STUDENT MATRIC), using placeholders. It is necessary to check that a DEPT STUDENT-tuple inserted into one relation is also inserted into the other. With one relation per object, no checking is necessary.

12.5.3 Database Semantics and Window Functions

In this and subsequent sections we consider treating a database as a semantic unit. We allow that a database contain relations on schemes that are subschemes of other relations. To be consistent with URSA, there are restrictions on such relations. Let $r(R)$ and $s(S)$ be relations in the same database, where $R \subseteq S$. By URSA, a set of attributes uniquely determines a semantic connection among themselves. Since R is a subset of S, whatever the connection among the attributes of R, it must be an aspect of the connection among the attributes in S. Thus, if t is a tuple of s, $t(R)$ should be a tuple in r. Equivalently, r should contain $\pi_R(s)$. This constraint is the *containment condition on objects*. While the containment condition seems to require storing much redundant information, it is easy to think of implementations that remove the redundancy.

Example 12.40 We consider a database where the containment condition is not met, and see how URSA is violated. Consider a database of just two relations, r(DEPT STUDENT) and s(ADVISOR DEPT STUDENT.) Suppose a tuple $\langle d\ s \rangle \in r$ means student s is taking a course from department d, and a tuple $\langle a\ d\ s \rangle \in s$ means a advises s for department d. The containment condition will be violated if we allow that a student can receive advising from a department before taking any courses offered by the department. The connection between DEPT and STUDENT given by r does not agree with the connection implied by s. At least one of DEPT or STUDENT must represent different roles in r and s, so URSA is violated.

We make a brief detour to consider the containment condition in light of updates. For a database, it is usual to restrict the set of users who can update a particular relation. Suppose a database contains relations $r(R)$ and $s(S)$ where $R \subseteq S$. At first it may seem permission to update s should imply permission to update r. Actually, it is quite reasonable to give update permission for s without permission for r. Having update permission for r means one can constrain updates to s, since a tuple t cannot be added to s unless $t(R) \in r$.

Example 12.41 Consider a database d on the set of objects {DEPT, DEPT COURSE#, DEPT COURSE SEMESTER YEAR, STUDENT, DEPT COURSE# SEMESTER YEAR STUDENT}. By the containment condition, a tuple ⟨Econ 101 Spring 1980⟩ over DEPT COURSE# SEMESTER YEAR could only be added to the database if there is already a tuple ⟨Econ 101⟩ over DEPT COURSE#. That is, a course cannot be scheduled for a given semester unless the course actually exists. Typically, the president of the university has authority to authorize an insertion of a DEPT-tuple (creating a new department). An academic vice-president or dean can authorize insertions over DEPT COURSE# (creating new courses). The admissions office authorizes STUDENT-tuples (admitting new students). A department chairman can add tuples over DEPT COURSE# SEMESTER YEAR (deciding course offerings). A student authorizes tuples over DEPT COURSE# SEMESTER YEAR STUDENT (enrolling in a course).

We return to the ramifications of URSA in a database. There are connections among attributes that are not captured directly by any relation in a database. Rather, the connections are realized by combining two or more relations. Such derived connections should be consistent with the connection embodied explicitly in relations.

Example 12.42 Consider a database d with relations r_1(FACULTY CLASS), giving the classes a faculty member teaches, and r_2(CLASS ROOM), giving the room where a class meets. It seems reasonable to connect FACULTY, CLASS, and ROOM by joining r_1 and r_2. Suppose, however, there is also a relation r_3(FACULTY ROOM) giving offices for faculty members. There is a disagreement between the explicit connection of FACULTY and ROOM in r_3 and the derived connection given by $r_1 \bowtie r_2$. Considered individually, it is not immediately apparent that r_1, r_2, and r_3 violate URSA. It is the derived connection from $r_1 \bowtie r_2$ that causes problems.

Whatever implicit connections among attributes we derive from a database should be consistent with each other and the explicit connections given in relations. We extend the meaning of *object* to include the schemes of derived relations on a database. The meanings associated with objects must be consistent, whether the objects correspond to stored or derived relations in a database.

To afford a uniform view of objects, stored and derived, we use a *window function*, so called because it gives a consistent set of views of the database, one for each object. A window function maps an object and a database to the relation, stored or derived, that the database assigns to that object. We denote the value of a window function on object W and database d by $[W, d]$, or simply $[W]$ where d is understood. Thus, $[W, d]$ is always a relation with scheme W, whose value depends on the state of d.

A window function allows no room for multiple meanings for objects, since it returns a unique relation for any object. Unique meanings for objects is certainly dictated by URSA, but meanings for different objects must be consistent. Hence, we make a *containment condition for windows*: If W and Z are objects for a database d, and $W \subseteq Z$, then $[W, d] \supseteq \pi_W([Z, d])$.

A window function can easily be extended to map every set of attributes to a relation over those attributes. Let X be a set of attributes and let **O** be a set of objects for a database d. We let

$$[X, d] = \bigcup_{\substack{W \in \mathbf{O} \\ W \supseteq X}} \pi_X([W, d]).$$

The meaning for a set of attributes that is not an object comes from the meaning of objects containing that set. If the original window function satisfies the containment condition, then the extended window function satisfies the containment condition, and agrees with the original function on any object (see Exercise 12.45). If a set of attributes X is not contained in any object in **O**, $[X, d]$ will always be the empty relation. The database assigns no meaning to the attributes in X taken as a group.

Some of the window functions we consider are defined directly for arbitrary sets of attributes. They do not make use of objects besides those corresponding to stored relations. Such a definition gives rise implicitly to a set of objects, however. From the containment condition, for any set of attributes X,

$$[X] \supseteq \bigcup_{Y \supsetneq X} \pi_X([Y]).$$

For some sets X, the containment will always be equality. For other X, there will be states of the database for which the containment is strict. Such an X is an *implicit object* of the window.

We consider one simple window function, and a problem with it, which will motivate another condition on window functions. Let $\mathbf{U}$ be the set of all attributes appearing in the schemes of a database d. We define a window function with $\mathbf{U}$ as the only object. Let $[\mathbf{U}, d]_1 = \bowtie d$. (The subscript will distinguish this particular window function from others.) This window function treats the database as representing a single relation over scheme $\mathbf{U}$. Extending this function to arbitrary sets of attributes we get

$$[X]_1 = \pi_X[\mathbf{U}]_1.$$

The problem with $[\cdot]_1$ is that for a relation $r(R)$ in d, $[R]_1$ does not necessarily equal r, although it is always contained in r. The meaning the window function gives r is not the one given in the database. While the interpretation of a database given by $[\cdot]_1$ satisfies URSA, and the database itself may satisfy URSA, considered together they violate URSA.

In an URSA database, no two stored relations may have the same scheme, so we may use schemes alone to distinguish relations. If R is a relation scheme, we use $\bar{r}(R)$ to denote the database relation with scheme R, whatever its actual name. We impose a *faithfulness condition* on window functions: for any relation scheme R of a database d, $[R, d] = \bar{r}(R)$. The window function $[\cdot]_1$ violates the faithfulness condition. Unless constraints are imposed on the database state, the faithfulness condition means relation schemes are always implicit objects of window functions.

In subsequent sections we examine several window functions. The first is defined using joins of relations, but not all the relations in the database at once. The others are defined as projections from a single relation, albeit one with nulls.

12.5.4 A Window Function Based on Joins

We assume a set of objects $\mathbf{O}$, of which a subset, $\mathbf{R}$, constitute the database scheme for a database d. As before, we let $\bar{r}(R)$ denote the relation on R for any $R \in \mathbf{R}$. We allow that one relation scheme be a subscheme of another, but require that the relations involved satisfy the containment condition. Because of the nature of the window function we shall define, we also require that every object W in $\mathbf{O}$ be the union of objects (schemes) in $\mathbf{R}$. We define a window function

$$[W, d]_{\mathbf{R},\mathbf{O}} = \mathop{\bowtie}_{\substack{R \in \mathbf{R} \\ R \subseteq W}} \bar{r}(R), \text{ for } W \in \mathbf{O}.$$

The relation for an object is the join of all stored relations whose schemes are contained in the object.

Example 12.43 Consider the set of objects $\mathbf{O}$ = {DEPT, DEPT COURSE#, DEPT COURSE# INSTRUCTOR, DEPT COURSE# CREDITS, DEPT COURSE# STUDENT, DEPT COURSE# STUDENT CREDITS, DEPT COURSE# STUDENT INSTRUCTOR} and a database d over the subset $\mathbf{R}$ = {DEPT, DEPT COURSE#, DEPT COURSE# INSTRUCTOR, DEPT COURSE# CREDITS, DEPT COURSE# STUDENT}. The sets $\mathbf{R}$ and $\mathbf{O}$ are pictured in Figure 12.36. Solid lines indicate schemes in R; dashed lines indicate objects in $\mathbf{O} - \mathbf{R}$. Table 12.12 gives a state of d. Table 12.13 gives the values of [DEPT COURSE# INSTRUCTOR STUDENT]$_{\mathbf{R},\mathbf{O}}$ and [DEPT COURSE# CREDITS STUDENT]$_{\mathbf{R},\mathbf{O}}$.

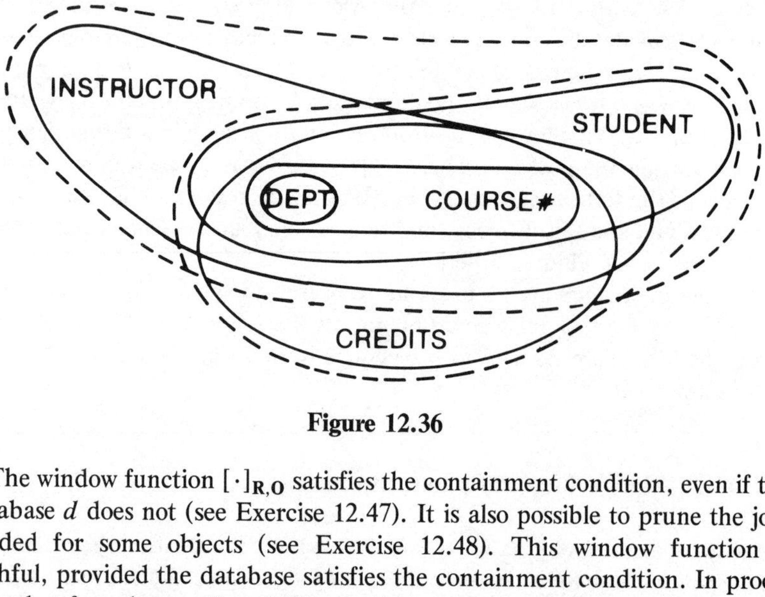

Figure 12.36

The window function $[\cdot]_{\mathbf{R},\mathbf{O}}$ satisfies the containment condition, even if the database d does not (see Exercise 12.47). It is also possible to prune the join needed for some objects (see Exercise 12.48). This window function is faithful, provided the database satisfies the containment condition. In proof, note that for schemes R and S in $\mathbf{R}$, if $R \subseteq S$, then $\bar{r}(R) \bowtie \bar{r}(S) = \bar{r}(S)$. Thus, for any $S \in \mathbf{R}$

$$\mathop{\bowtie}_{\substack{R \in \mathbf{R} \\ R \subseteq S}} \bar{r}(R) = \bar{r}(S).$$

Table 12.12 State of d.

$\bar{r}$(DEPT)
Econ
Math
History
English

$\bar{r}$(DEPT	COURSE#)
Econ	101
Econ	102
Math	120
History	306
History	308

$\bar{r}$(DEPT	COURSE#	INSTRUCTOR)
Econ	101	Galler
Econ	102	Garvey
Math	120	George
History	306	Gunther

$\bar{r}$(DEPT	COURSE#	CREDITS)
Econ	101	4
Econ	102	3
Math	120	4
History	306	4
History	308	3

$\bar{r}$(DEPT	COURSE#	STUDENT)
Econ	101	Adams
Econ	101	Allen
Econ	102	Andrews
History	308	Adams
History	308	Andrews

We extend $[\cdot]_{\mathbf{R},\mathbf{O}}$ to arbitrary sets of attributes as indicated in the last section.

Example 12.44 Continuing Example 12.43, $[\text{STUDENT CREDITS}]_{\mathbf{R},\mathbf{O}}$ and $[\text{STUDENT INSTRUCTOR}]_{\mathbf{R},\mathbf{O}}$ are shown in Table 12.14. The value of $[\text{INSTRUCTOR CREDITS}]_{\mathbf{R},\mathbf{O}}$ will always be empty because no object in **O** contains both INSTRUCTOR and CREDITS.

We shall return to this join-based window function when we examine the PIQUE query language in Chapter 15.

Table 12.13 Values of Windows.

DEPT	COURSE#	INSTRUCTOR	STUDENT
Econ	101	Galler	Adams
Econ	101	Galler	Allen
Econ	102	Garvey	Andrews

$[\text{DEPT COURSE\# INSTRUCTOR STUDENT}]_{\mathbf{R},\mathbf{O}}$

DEPT	COURSE#	CREDITS	STUDENT
Econ	101	4	Adams
Econ	101	4	Allen
Econ	102	3	Andrews
History	308	3	Adams
History	308	3	Andrews

$[\text{DEPT COURSE\# CREDITS STUDENT}]_{\mathbf{R},\mathbf{O}}$

Table 12.14 Values of Windows (continued)

STUDENT	CREDITS
Adams	4
Adams	3
Allen	4
Andrews	3
Andrews	3

$[\text{STUDENT CREDITS}]_{\mathbf{R},\mathbf{O}}$

STUDENT	INSTRUCTOR
Adams	Galler
Allen	Galler
Andrews	Garvey

$[\text{STUDENT INSTRUCTOR}]_{\mathbf{R},\mathbf{O}}$

12.5.5 Weak Instances

The underlying concept for the next definitions of window functions arose from the problems of enforcing data dependencies globally on a database.

Example 12.45 Consider the database in Table 12.15, with relations on the schemes DEPT COURSE# CREDITS SEMESTER and DEPT COURSES# CREDITS STUDENT. Both relations satisfy the FD DEPT COURSE# → CREDITS, but they represent different functions from DEPT COURSE# to CREDITS.

While a database state need not be the projection of a common instance, every database state is in a sense contained in a universal instance.

Definition 12.11 Let d be a database over the scheme $\mathbf{R} = \{R_1, R_2, \ldots, R_p\}$, where $\mathbf{U} = R_1 R_2 \cdots R_p$. A relation s over scheme $\mathbf{U}$ is a *weak instance* for d if

$$\pi_{R_i}(s) \supseteq \bar{r}(R_i)$$

for every scheme $R_i \in \mathbf{R}$.

Table 12.15 Inconsistent Database.

$\bar{r}$(DEPT	COURSE#	CREDITS	SEMESTER)
Econ	106	4	Spring
Econ	108	4	Fall
Math	211	3	Fall
Math	211	3	Spring
Math	286	3	Fall

$\bar{r}$(DEPT	COURSE#	CREDITS	STUDENTS)
Econ	106	4	Balfour
Econ	106	4	Berents
Econ	108	3	Balfour
Math	286	4	Berents
Math	286	4	Brown

The view here is that a database stands for its set of weak instances. Using weak instances to discuss a database does assume that a tuple over the universal scheme **U** makes sense, if not a universal instance over that scheme. We can use weak instances to discuss applying data dependencies globally to a database.

Definition 12.12 Let d be a database over the database scheme $\mathbf{R} = \{R_1, R_2, \ldots, R_p\}$, where $\mathbf{U} = R_1 R_2 \cdots R_p$. Let $\mathbf{C}$ be a set of dependencies over $\mathbf{U}$. Database d *globally satisfies* $\mathbf{C}$, if d has a weak instance that satisfies $\mathbf{C}$ in the usual sense.

Example 12.46 If d is the database of Example 12.45, and $F = \{$DEPT COURSE# $\rightarrow$ CREDITS$\}$, then d does not globally satisfy F. If we changed $\bar{r}$(DEPT COURSE# CREDITS STUDENT) to be as shown in Table 12.16, then d will globally satisfy F. A weak instance s of d satisfying F is shown in Table 12.17.

Table 12.16 Modified Relation.

$\bar{r}$(DEPT	COURSE#	CREDITS	STUDENT)
Econ	106	4	Balfour
Econ	106	4	Berents
Econ	108	4	Balfour
Math	286	3	Berents
Math	286	3	Brown

Table 12.17 Weak Instance s.

s(DEPT	COURSE#	CREDITS	SEMESTER	STUDENT)
Econ	106	4	Spring	Balfour
Econ	106	4	Spring	Berents
Econ	108	4	Fall	Balfour
Math	211	3	Fall	Butcher
Math	211	3	Spring	Butcher
Math	286	3	Fall	Berents
Math	286	3	Fall	Brown

For a database d over $\mathbf{U}$ and a set $\mathbf{C}$ of dependencies on $\mathbf{U}$, a relation $s(\mathbf{U})$ is a **C**-*weak instance*, (**C**-WI) for d if s is a weak instance for d satisfying $\mathbf{C}$. Evidently, d has a **C**-WI if and only if d globally satisfies $\mathbf{C}$.

We can define window functions using representative instances. We look for the common parts of all representative instances for a database. Let d be a database over $\mathbf{U}$, let $\mathbf{C}$ be a set of dependencies over $\mathbf{U}$, and let X be an arbitrary subset of $\mathbf{U}$. We define

$$[X,d]_{\mathbf{C}} = \bigcap_{\substack{s \text{ a } \mathbf{C}\text{-WI} \\ \text{for } d}} \pi_X(s).$$

That is, $[X,d]_{\mathbf{C}}$ consists of the X-values that appear in some tuple of every **C**-WI for d. This definition satisfies the containment condition. For sets X and Y where $X \subseteq Y$, if t is a tuple that is in $\pi_Y(s)$ for every **C**-WI s for d, then $t(X)$ is surely in $\pi_X(s)$ for every such s. The definition of $[\cdot]_{\mathbf{C}}$ does not immediately give rise to an effective procedure for its evaluation. A database d could have an infinite number of **C**-WIs. Fortunately, when $\mathbf{C}$ is FDs and JDs, *nchase* can be used to compute $[\cdot]_{\mathbf{C}}$.

Definition 12.13 Let r be a relation in $Rel\uparrow(R)$ and let $X \subseteq R$. The *X-total projection of* r, denoted $\pi{\downarrow}_X(r)$, is $\{t(X) | t \in r \text{ and } t(X){\downarrow}\}$. The X-total projection of r is the X portion of all tuples in r that are definite on X.

If r is a relation on scheme R and **U** is a set of attributes containing R, $PAD(r,\mathbf{U})$ is the relation s in $Rel\uparrow(\mathbf{U})$ obtained by padding out each tuple in r to have scheme **U**. The padding is done with distinct marked nulls. (The relations we shall be padding have no nulls of their own.) For a database d over **U**, $PAD(d)$ is $\bigcup_{r \in d} PAD(r,\mathbf{U})$. We pad out all the relations in d to a common scheme.

Example 12.47 Let d be the database in Figure 12.37. $PAD(d)$ is the relation s shown in Figure 12.38.

$\bar{r}$(A	B)
1	4
1	5
2	4
2	6

$\bar{r}$(B	C)
4	7
5	7
6	8

$\bar{r}$(A	C)
1	7
2	8
3	8
3	9

Figure 12.37

s(A	B	C)
1	4	$\perp_1$
1	5	$\perp_2$
2	4	$\perp_3$
2	6	$\perp_4$
$\perp_5$	4	7
$\perp_6$	5	7
$\perp_7$	6	8
1	$\perp_8$	7
2	$\perp_9$	8
3	$\perp_{10}$	8
3	$\perp_{11}$	9

Figure 12.38

Nchase from Section 12.2 can be extended to include an analogue of the J-rule in regular chase computation. There is no hard violation of JDs, however, as there was for FDs. The extension is straightforward.

Theorem 12.1 Let d be a database over **U** and let **C** be a set of FDs and JDs over **U**. For any subset X of **U**,

$$[X]_{\mathbf{C}} = \pi{\downarrow}_X(nchase_{\mathbf{C}}(PAD(d))).$$

Proof Left to the reader (see Exercise 12.56).

Different choices for **C** give different flavors of window functions. One possibility is to simply let $\mathbf{C} = \{*[R_1, R_2, \ldots, R_p]\}$ where $\mathbf{R} = \{R_1, R_2, \ldots, R_p\}$ is the database scheme. For this choice of **C**, we use $[\cdot]_{*\mathbf{R}}$ to denote the window function, rather than $[\cdot]_{\mathbf{C}}$.

Example 12.48 Let d be the database of Figure 12.37, for which $\mathbf{R} = \{AB, BC, AC\}$. $Nchase_J(s)$ is shown in Figure 12.39, where $J = \{*[\mathbf{R}]\}$ and $s = PAD(d)$. Figure 12.40 shows $[A\ B\ C]_{*\mathbf{R}}$.

$nchase_J(s)$ (A	B	C)
1	4	$\perp_1$
1	5	$\perp_2$
2	4	$\perp_3$
2	6	$\perp_4$
$\perp_5$	4	7
$\perp_6$	5	7
$\perp_7$	6	8
1	$\perp_8$	7
2	$\perp_9$	8
3	$\perp_{10}$	8
3	$\perp_{11}$	9
1	4	7
2	6	8

Figure 12.39

[A	B	C]$_{*\mathbf{R}}$
1	4	7
2	6	8

Figure 12.40

The window function $[\cdot]_{*\mathbf{R}}$ is faithful as long as the database d satisfies the containment condition (see Exercise 12.57). For an arbitrary database scheme **R**, $[\cdot]_{*\mathbf{R}}$ is probably hard to compute, since given a set of attributes X

and a tuple t over X, determining if $t \in [X]_{*\mathbf{R}}$ is NP-complete. In Chapter 13 we shall see a class of database schemes for which $[\cdot]_{*\mathbf{R}}$ can be readily evaluated.

There is a problem in using $[\cdot]_{\mathbf{C}}$ if $\mathbf{C}$ includes a set F of FDs. The database d may not globally satisfy F, hence there are no $\mathbf{C}$-WIs. If we plan to use F to define a window function, we want to constrain d to globally satisfy F. Enforcing F on the relations individually is not sufficient, as Examples 12.45 and 12.46 show. Computing $nchase_F(PAD(d))$ for every update to the database is prohibitive. If the FDs of F are embodied in keys of the database scheme, there is a more efficient way to ensure d has an F-WI.

Definition 12.14 Let d be a database over the scheme $\mathbf{R} = \{R_1, R_2, \ldots, R_p\}$. Let $\mathbf{K}_i$ be a set of keys for R_i, $1 \le i \le p$. Let F be a set of FDs that is completely characterized by the keys of $\mathbf{R}$. Database d satisfies the *modified foreign key constraint** (MFKC) relative to F if for every $R_i \in \mathbf{R}$, if $t \in \bar{r}(R_i)$, there is a tuple t' over R_i^+ such that for any $R_j \subseteq R_i^+$, $t'(R_j) \in \bar{r}(R_j)$, and, in particular $t'(R_i) = t$.

Example 12.49 Consider the database d over scheme $\mathbf{R} = \{\underline{A}\, B, \underline{B}\, D, \underline{A}\, C, \underline{C}\, D\}$ shown in Figure 12.41. The single key for each scheme is underlined. The keys completely characterize the set of FDs $F = \{A \rightarrow B, B \rightarrow D, A \rightarrow C, C \rightarrow D\}$. Database d does not satisfy the MFKC for F. Consider $\bar{r}(A\, B)$ and the tuple $t = \langle 7\ 8 \rangle$. We see $(A\, B)^+ = A\, B\, C\, D$, but there is no tuple t' over $A\, B\, C\, D$ such that $t'(A\, B) = t$ and $t'(R) \in \bar{r}(R)$ for every other scheme $R \subseteq A\, B\, C\, D$. If we add $\langle 7\ 5 \rangle$ to $\bar{r}(A\, C)$, such a tuple exists, namely $t' = \langle 7\ 8\ 5\ 6 \rangle$. With the addition of $\langle 7\ 5 \rangle$, d does satisfy the MFKC relative to F.

$\bar{r}(A$	$B)$
1	2
7	8

$\bar{r}(B$	$C)$
2	3
5	3
8	6

$\bar{r}(A$	$C)$
1	4

$\bar{r}(C$	$D)$
4	3
5	6
5	6

Figure 12.41

If every relation in a database d satisfies its keys, and d satisfies the MFKC relative to a completely characterized set of dependencies F, then d globally satisfies F. The reason is the structure $nchase_F(PAD(d))$ will have. Let t be a tuple in $PAD(d)$ such that $DEF(t) = R_i$. That is, t came from relation $\bar{r}(R_i)$

*The *foreign key constraint* requires that if R_i contains a key K_j for R_j and $t_i \in \bar{r}(R_i)$, there is a tuple t_j in R_j such that $t_i(K_j) = t_j(K_j)$.

in d. If t^* is the corresponding tuple for t in $nchase_F(PAD(d))$, $DEF(t^*) \supseteq R_i^+$, by the MFKC. In fact, $t^*(R_i^+)$ will be exactly the tuple t' for t required by the MFKC. It follows $t^*(R_j) \in \bar{r}(R_j)$ for any relation scheme $R_j \subseteq R_i^+$. $DEF(t^*)$ can be no larger than R_i^+, because we are chasing with the key dependencies of d (or an equivalent set of FDs).

Suppose t^* enters into a violation of F along with another tuple u^* in $nchase_F(PAD(d))$. Assume u^* came from a tuple u in $PAD(d)$ where $DEF(u) = R_k$. Since the keys of d completely characterize F, t^* and u^* must violate $K_j \to R_j$ for some relation scheme R_j and key $K_j \in \mathbf{K}_j$. Both R_i^+ and R_k^+ contain R_j, since they are both definite on K_j. By the remarks in the last paragraph, $t^*(R_j) \in \bar{r}(R_j)$ and $u^*(R_j)$. If t^* and u^* violate $K_j \to R_j$, so does $\bar{r}(R_j)$. We have argued for the following result.

Theorem 12.2. Let d be a database scheme, and let F be a set of FDs completely characterized by the keys of d. If d satisfies the MFKC relative to F, and each relation in d satisfies its keys, then d globally satisfies F.

Example 12.50 Figure 12.42 shows $s = PAD(d)$ for the database d of Figure 12.41, with the addition of $\langle 7\ 5 \rangle$ to $\bar{r}(A\ C)$. Figure 12.43 shows $s = nchase_F(PAD(d))$, where F is the set of FDs from Example 12.48. The nulls in s can be filled in to get an F-WI for d.

$PAD(d)$(	A	B	C	D)
	1	2	$\perp_1$	$\perp_2$
	7	8	$\perp_3$	$\perp_4$
	$\perp_5$	2	$\perp_6$	3
	$\perp_7$	5	$\perp_8$	3
	$\perp_9$	8	$\perp_{10}$	6
	1	$\perp_{11}$	4	$\perp_{12}$
	7	$\perp_{13}$	5	$\perp_{14}$
	$\perp_{15}$	$\perp_{16}$	4	3
	$\perp_{17}$	$\perp_{18}$	5	6

Figure 12.42

12.5.6 Independence

Enforcing the MFKC still involves checking multiple relations when making updates to a single relation. We would like a way to guarantee global satisfaction that only requires checking the relation being updated.

s(A	B	C	D)
$\perp_5$	2	$\perp_6$	3
1	2	4	3
7	8	5	6
$\perp_7$	5	$\perp_8$	3
$\perp_9$	8	$\perp_{10}$	6
$\perp_{15}$	$\perp_{16}$	4	3
$\perp_{17}$	$\perp_{18}$	5	6

Figure 12.43

Definition 12.15 Let **R** be a database scheme and let F be a set of FDs that applies to **R**. **R** is *independent for* F if every database d over **R** that obeys F (each relation satisfies the applicable FDs) globally satisfies F.

Independence can be paraphrased as "local satisfaction guarantees global satisfaction." In the case where F is embodied by the keys of **R**, there is a necessary and sufficient condition for independence. For the remainder of this section we assume that we have a relation scheme $\mathbf{R} = \{R_1, R_2, \ldots, R_p\}$, where each R_i has a set of keys $\mathbf{K}_i$. Let $F_i = \{K \rightarrow R_i | K \in \mathbf{K}_i\}$, $1 \leq i \leq p$. Let

$$F = \bigcup_{i=1}^{p} F_i \text{ and } F_{-j} = \bigcup_{\substack{i=1 \\ i \neq j}}^{p} F_i.$$

X^+ will denote the closure of a set of attributes relative to F, while X^+_{-j} denotes the closure relative to F_{-j}.

Definition 12.16 Let **R** and F be as given above. Relation scheme $R_i \in \mathbf{R}$ satisfies the *uniqueness condition* relative to F if there is no $R_j \in \mathbf{R}$, $i \neq j$, such that for some key $K \in \mathbf{K}_j$ and some attribute $B \in R_j - K$,

$$K\,B \in (R_i)^+_{-j}.$$

R satisfies the *uniqueness condition* relative to F if every $R_i \in \mathbf{R}$ satisfies it.

The uniqueness condition captures the idea that for any set of attributes X, there is exactly one way to compute X^+. That is, for any two F-based DDAGs H_1 and H_2 for $X \rightarrow X^+$, if attribute B was added to H_1 using an FD in F_i, then some FD in F_i was used to add B to H_2 (see Exercise 12.57). If **R** satisfies the uniqueness condition relative to F, then $\mathbf{R}$ is in BCNF under F (see Exercise 12.58). In particular, no dependency $K \rightarrow A$ in F may apply to more than one scheme in $\mathbf{R}$.

Example 12.51 Let $\mathbf{R} = \{R_1, R_2, R_3, R_4\}$ for $R_1 = \underline{A}\, B$, $R_2 = \underline{B}\, D$, $R_3 = \underline{A}\, C$ and $R_4 = \underline{C}\, D$, where each scheme has the single key underlined. These keys embody the set of dependencies $F = \{A \rightarrow B, B \rightarrow D, A \rightarrow C, C \rightarrow D\}$, with extraneous attributes removed. $\mathbf{R}$ does not satisfy the uniqueness condition relative to F. Consider R_1 and R_4. $F_{-4} = \{A \rightarrow B, B \rightarrow D, A \rightarrow C\}$. Thus $(R_i)^+_{-4} = A\,B\,C\,D$. C is a key of R_4, and $D \in R_4 - B$. $B\,D \subseteq (R_1)^+_{-4}$, so R_1 violates the uniqueness assumption.

Example 12.52 Let $\mathbf{R} = \{R_1, R_2, R_3\}$ for $R_1 = \underline{A\,B}\,C$, $R_2 = \underline{B\,C}\,D$ and $R_3 = \underline{A\,D}\,E$, where each scheme has the single key underlined. $F = \{A\,B \rightarrow C, B\,C \rightarrow D, A\,D \rightarrow E\}$. $\mathbf{R}$ satisfies the uniqueness assumption relative to F. For example, $(R_1)^+_{-2} = R_1$, which contains $B\,C$ but not D from R_2. Also, $(R_1)^+_{-3} = A\,B\,C\,D$, which contains $A\,D$ but not E from R_3.

Before presenting the main theorem of this section, we make two observations.

Observation 1 Let d be a database over $\mathbf{U}$ and let F be a set of FDs over $\mathbf{U}$. Suppose we form d' by adding tuples to some or all of the relations in d. If d' has any F-WI s, then s is an F-WI for d.

Definition 12.17 Let $s \in Rel\uparrow(R)$. Let t and u be tuples in s. We say t *supersedes* u in s if $t_1(A) = t_2(A)$ whenever $t_2(A)$ is a value, or a marked null that appears elsewhere in s.

Observation 2 Let $s \in Rel\uparrow(R)$ and let F be a set of FDs over R. Let t be a tuple in s that supersedes another tuple u in s. If t^* and u^* are the tuples in $s^* = nchase_F(s)$ corresponding to t and u in s, then t^* supersedes u^* in s^*.

From Observation 2 we conclude that if we are computing $nchase_F$ $(PAD(d))$ to determine if d has an F-WI, we can delete a superseded tuple at any time, without changing the determination.

Theorem 12.3 Let $\mathbf{R} = \{R_1, R_2, \ldots, R_p\}$ be a database scheme over $\mathbf{U}$ and let $\mathbf{K}_i$, $1 \leq i \leq p$, F_i, $1 \leq i \leq p$, and F be as defined previously. $\mathbf{R}$ is independent for F if and only if $\mathbf{R}$ satisfies the uniqueness condition relative to F.

Proof (if) We assume **R** satisfies the uniqueness condition relative to F. We show that any database d over R that satisfies the keys of **R** has an F-WI. We exhibit a database d' that has an F-WI and is an extension of d. By Observation 1, we conclude d has an F-WI. We shall compute $nchase_F(PAD(d'))$ and show that we never encounter a hard violation. We actually start off computing $nchase_F(PAD(d))$. Along the way we add tuples to d and hence to $PAD(d)$. Adding tuples in the middle of the *nchase* computation will not cause problems, for we can pretend the tuples were present from the beginning and we simply did not touch them before a certain point.

We shall organize the computation of the *nchase* in such a way that if t^* is a tuple in $PAD(d)$ at some intermediate step, $DEF(t^*)$ will be the union of schemes from **R**. Further, t^* will never have any nulls that appear elsewhere in $PAD(d)$.

Let $s^* \in Rel\uparrow(\mathbf{U})$ be the state of $PAD(d)$ at some point in the *nchase* computation. Suppose we are about to apply an FD $K \rightarrow A$ to tuples t^* and u^* in s^* that agree on K. Assume, inductively, that $t^*(K)\downarrow$. By the nature of F, K is a key for some scheme R_i, and $A \in R_i - K$. First, instead of just equating t^* and u^* on A, we equate them on all of $R_i - K$ at once (a slight extension of the fill-in rule). Second, we want to avoid equating marked nulls between t^* and u^*. If there is a tuple $v \in \overline{r}(R_i)$ such that $v(K) = t^*(K) = u^*(K)$, we have no problem. There must be a tuple v^* in s^* such that $v^*(K) = t^*(K) = u^*(K)$ and $v^*(R_i)\downarrow$. Instead of equating nulls between t^* and u^*, we change $t^*(R_i - K)$ and $u^*(R_i - K)$ to match $v^*(R_i - K)$. (Equating t^*, u^* and v^* on $R_i - K$ actually takes two steps in the *nchase* computation.)

Unfortunately, we have no guarantee that $\overline{r}(R_i)$ contains a tuple v with $v(K) = t^*(K) = u^*(K)$. At this point we must add such a tuple v to $\overline{r}(R_i)$. If we let $v(R_i - K)$ be values not already appearing in $\overline{r}(R_i)$, no keys for R_i will be violated. (Why?) We then pad v using new marked nulls to be a partial tuple over **U**, call it v^*. We add v^* to s^* and proceed to change $t^*(R_i - K)$ and $u^*(R_i - K)$ to match $v^*(R_i - K)$. Watch carefully, please. After the changes to t^*, $t^*(R_i) = v^*(R_i)$, and v^* is unmatched marked nulls on $\mathbf{U} - \mathbf{R_i}$. By Observation 2, we may remove v^* from s^*, since t^* supersedes it. We remove v^* to ensure the *nchase* computation eventually halts.

The effect of this maneuvering is tantamount to promoting $t^*(B)$ to a value whenever $t^*(B)$ and $u^*(B)$ are marked nulls, for $B \in R_i - K$. We assume for the rest of the proof that if s^* is some state in the computation of $nchase_F(PAD(d))$, and t^* is a tuple in s^*, then $DEF(t^*)$ is the union of schemes in **R**. Furthermore, we assume t^* contains no matched nulls.

As a consequence of these assumptions about computing $nchase_F(PAD(d))$, we can guarantee certain other conditions. Let t be a tuple in $PAD(d)$ such that $DEF(t) = R_i$. Let t^* be the corresponding tuple in some state s^* of the computation of $nchase_F(PAD(d))$. For $R_j \in \mathbf{R}$, if $R_j \not\subseteq DEF(t^*)$, then $(R_i)^{+}_{-j} \supseteq DEF(t^*)$. No dependency arising from keys in R_j has been used to fill-in t^*, or else $DEF(t^*) \supseteq R_j$. It follows that if $DEF(t^*)$ contains a key K of R_j and an attribute $A \in R_j - K$, then $DEF(t^*)$ contains all of R_j. Otherwise, $(R_i)^{+}_{-j}$ contains KA, and the uniqueness condition is violated.

After all these machinations, we must still show that we never encounter a hard violation when computing $nchase_F(PAD(d))$. Initially, there is no hard violation in $PAD(d)$, since all the relations in d obey their keys and no two relation schemes can embody a common dependency. Tuples added to $PAD(d)$ along the way are chosen so as not to violate keys. Suppose at some state in the computation of $nchase_F(PAD(d))$ we first encounter a hard violation. Let s^* be the state, and let t^* and u^* violate the FD $K \rightarrow A$. Recall that t^* and u^* must both be definite on KA. Let $t^*(A) = a$ and $u^*(A) = a'$. Since the hard violation first appeared at state s^*, one of t^* or u^* must have just been changed. Assume t^* was changed, and roll the computation back one step, to before t^* was changed. We consider three cases, which depend upon which parts of t^* are about to be filled in.

Case 1 An FD $Y \rightarrow A$ was used to fill in $t^*(A)$ as a using a tuple v^*. $K \neq Y$, otherwise, there is already a hard violation of $K \rightarrow A$ between u^* and v^*. K and Y are not in the same $\mathbf{K}_j$. If they were, then $R_j \supseteq KYA$. $DEF(t^*)$ contains K and Y, but not A, hence not R_j. We noted that such a situation does not occur, from the way we are computing the *nchase*. Let t be the tuple in $PAD(d)$ from which t^* came. Let $DEF(t) = R_i$. Assume $Y \rightarrow A$ comes from R_j. Before $t^*(A)$ is filled in, $DEF(t^*) \not\supseteq R_j$, so $(R_i)^{+}_{-j} \supseteq KY$. $K \rightarrow A$ does not come from R_j, so $(R_i)^{+}_{-j} \supseteq KYA$, which means R_i violates the uniqueness condition with respect to R_j.

Case 2 An FD $Y \rightarrow K'$ was used to fill in $t^*(K')$ from a tuple v^*, where $K = K'W$ for some set W (possibly empty). K and Y are not from the same $\mathbf{K}_j$, since t^* is definite on Y and W, but not K', hence not on R_j. (If $W = \emptyset$, $A \notin Y$, or else u^* and v^* violate $K \rightarrow A$. If $A \notin Y$, we have $DEF(t^*)$ containing YA but not $K' = K$, hence not R_j.) Assume t^* came from t in $PAD(d)$ where $DEF(t) = R_i$. Assume $K \rightarrow A$ comes from R_j. Before t^* is filled in on K', $DEF(t^*) \not\supseteq R_j$, so $(R_i)^{+}_{-j} \supseteq YWA$. Since $Y \rightarrow K'$ is not from R_j, $(R_i)^{+}_{-j} \supseteq YK'WA = YKA$. Thus, R_i violates the uniqueness condition relative to R_j.

Case 3 $Y \rightarrow K'A$ was used to fill in $t^*(K'A)$ from v^*, where $K = K'W$ for some W. $W \neq \emptyset$, or else u^* and v^* violate $K \rightarrow A$. K and Y are not from the same R_j, since $DEF(t^*)$ contains YW but not K', hence not R_j. Let t^* come from t in $PAD(d)$ where $DEF(t) = R_i$. Assume $K \rightarrow A$ is from R_j. Before t^* is filled in on $K'A$, $DEF(t^*) \not\supseteq R_j$, so $(R_i)^+_{-j} \supseteq YW$. $Y \rightarrow K'A$ is not from R_j, so $(R_i)^+_{-j} \supseteq YK'WA = YKA$. Hence, R_i violates the uniqueness condition relative to R_j.

In every case, we get a contradiction to the uniqueness assumption. We conclude the computation of $nchase_F(PAD(d'))$ never encounters a hard violation of F, where d' is d with some tuples added. Database d', and hence database d, has an F-WI. **R** is independent relative to F.

(only if) This part of the proof is simpler and is left to the reader (see Exercise 12.59).

Returning to window functions, consider $[\cdot]_F$ where F is the set of FDs embodied by the keys of the database scheme, **R**. Assume **R** satisfies the uniqueness condition. There will be no problems computing $[X,d]_F$ if d locally satisfies the keys of R, since an F-WI is guaranteed to exist. In that case, $[X,d]_F$ can be computed efficiently with joins (see Exercise 12.60). Also, $[\cdot]_F$ is faithful, if every relation has a non-trivial key (see Exercise 12.61).

12.5.7 A Further Condition on Window Functions

In this final section, we consider a further condition on window functions, which some will, and some will not, construe as a consequence of URSA. The faithfulness condition was imposed to insure agreement between stored relations and the window function. Still, the faithfulness condition does not totally guarantee the integrity of the semantics of stored relations. A window function can be faithful, yet induce connections on subsets of a relation scheme that are not part of the meaning of the scheme.

Example 12.53 Consider the database scheme **R** = {PLANE# CITY HANGAR#, CITY HANGAR# MECHANIC, PLANE# MECHANIC LASTSERV}, where the only keys are those underlined. **R** is the same scheme as in Example 12.52, up to renaming. Let F be the embodied FDs for **R**. The intended meaning of a tuple $\langle p\ c\ h \rangle$ over PLANE# CITY HANGAR# is that plane p goes to hangar h for servicing when in city c. A tuple $\langle c\ h\ m \rangle$ over CITY HANGAR# MECHANIC means that m is in charge of service for hangar h in city c. A tuple $\langle p\ m\ l \rangle$ over PLANE# MECHANIC LASTSERV means mechanic m last serviced plane p on date l. The window function $[\cdot]_F$ is the same as the window function $[\cdot]_{\mathbf{R},\mathbf{O}}$, where $\mathbf{O} = \mathbf{R} \cup$ {PLANE# CITY HANGAR# MECHANIC, PLANE# CITY HANGAR# MECHANIC LASTSERV}. **R** and **O** are diagrammed in Figure 12.52.

Consider a tuple $\langle p\ m \rangle$ from $[\text{PLANE\# MECHANIC}]_F$. If we just consider the meaning of PLANE# MECHANIC LASTSERV, we would conclude that $\langle p\ m \rangle$ means there is some date l such that m serviced p on l. However, it could result from tuples $\langle p\ c\ h \rangle$ and $\langle c\ h\ m \rangle$ in $\bar{r}$(PLANE# CITY HANGAR#) and $\bar{r}$(CITY HANGAR# MECHANIC). That is, if p were serviced in city c, it would be by m. This second meaning does not follow from PLANE# MECHANIC LASTSERV, which implies m already worked on p. The difference is potentiality versus actuality. Somehow, $[\cdot]_F$ does not preserve the integrity of PLANE# MECHANIC LASTSERV.

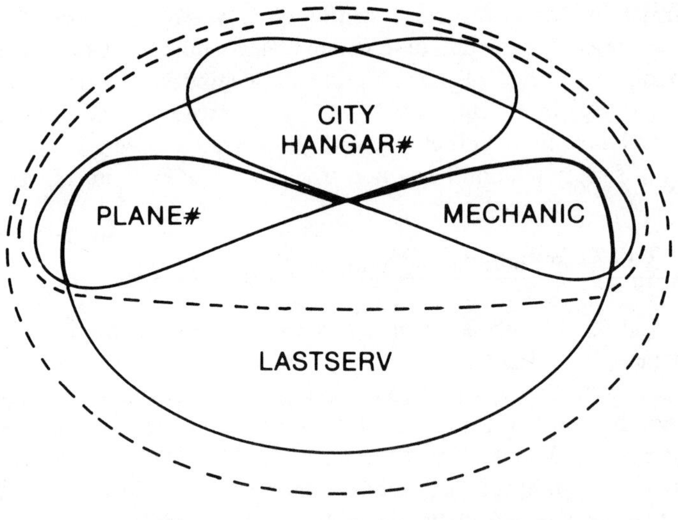

Figure 12.44

Definition 12.18 Let **R** be a database scheme and let $[\cdot]$ be a window function for databases over **R**. The *strong faithfulness condition* on $[\cdot]$ requires that for any scheme $R \in \mathbf{R}$, any $X \subseteq R$, and any database d over **R**, $[X, d]$ depends only on the states of relations whose schemes are contained in R, that is

$$\{\bar{r}(S) \mid S \in \mathbf{R}, S \subseteq R\}.$$

Strong faithfulness is violated in Example 12.53, since $[\text{PLANE\# MECHANIC}]_F$ does not depend solely on $\bar{r}$(PLANE# MECHANIC LASTSERV). Recall from Example 12.52 that **R** does satisfy the uniqueness condition, so the uniqueness condition does not assure a window function is strongly faithful (see Exercise 12.70). For window functions of the type $[\cdot]_{\mathbf{R},\mathbf{O}}$, we can give a sufficient condition for strong faithfulness.

Theorem 12.4 Let $\mathbf{R}$ be a database scheme over $\mathbf{U}$ and let $\mathbf{O}$ be a set of objects containing R. Assume every object in $\mathbf{O}$ is the union of schemes in $\mathbf{R}$. The window function $[\cdot]_{\mathbf{R},\mathbf{O}}$ is strongly faithful if $\mathbf{O}$ is closed under nonempty intersection. (That is, for $W, Z \in \mathbf{O}$, if $W \cap Z \neq \emptyset$ then $W \cap Z \in \mathbf{O}$.)

Proof We first show that for any subset X of $\mathbf{U}$ and database d, $[X,d]_{\mathbf{R},\mathbf{O}}$ can be computed from $[Y,d]_{\mathbf{R},\mathbf{O}}$ for a single $Y \in \mathbf{O}$, provided $\mathbf{O}$ is closed under intersection. Recall

$$[X]_{\mathbf{R},\mathbf{O}} = \bigcup_{\substack{Y \in \mathbf{O} \\ Y \supseteq X}} \pi_X([Y]_{\mathbf{R},\mathbf{O}}).$$

Let Y_1 and Y_2 both be in $\mathbf{O}$ and both contain X. $Y_1 \cap Y_2 = Y_3$ is nonempty, hence in $\mathbf{O}$. By the containment condition on the window function, $\pi_X([Y_3]_{\mathbf{R},\mathbf{O}})$ contains both $\pi_X([Y_1]_{\mathbf{R},\mathbf{O}})$ and $\pi_X([Y_2]_{\mathbf{R},\mathbf{O}}$. Hence Y_1 and Y_2 can be dropped from the union for computing $[X]_{\mathbf{R},\mathbf{O}}$ without changing the result. Proceeding in this manner, we may remove all but one object from the union, call it Y. We then have

$$[X]_{\mathbf{R},\mathbf{O}} = \pi_X([Y]_{\mathbf{R},\mathbf{O}}).$$

What we have demonstrated is that if X is contained in some object of $\mathbf{O}$, there is a unique minimum object Y that contains X. That is, for any W in $\mathbf{O}$ that contains X, $W \supseteq Y$. Further, $[X]_{\mathbf{R},\mathbf{O}}$ takes its value from $[Y]_{\mathbf{R},\mathbf{O}}$. Thus, if R is a scheme in $\mathbf{R}$ and $X \subseteq R$, there is a unique minimum Y in $\mathbf{O}$ with $X \subseteq Y \subseteq R$ (since $R \in \mathbf{O}$). The window function on X depends on the window function on Y, which in turn depends on

$$\{\bar{r}(S) \mid S \in \mathbf{R},\ S \subseteq Y\},$$

a subset of

$$\{\bar{r}(S) \mid S \in \mathbf{R},\ S \subseteq R\}.$$

Closure under intersection is not necessary for strong faithfulness.

Example 12.54 If $\mathbf{R} = \{B, C, AB, BD, AC, CD\}$ and $\mathbf{O} = \mathbf{R} \cup \{ABC, BCD\}$, then $[\cdot]_{\mathbf{R},\mathbf{O}}$ is strongly faithful but $\mathbf{O}$ is not closed under intersection. $ABC \cap BCD = BC$, which is not in $\mathbf{O}$.

There is a condition on window functions of the type $[\cdot]_{\mathbf{R},\mathbf{O}}$ that is equivalent to $\mathbf{O}$ being closed under intersection. The definition does not apply to window functions that are not defined directly from objects.

Definition 12.19 Let $\mathbf{R}$ be a database scheme and let $\mathbf{O}$ be a set of objects containing $\mathbf{R}$. The window function $[\cdot]_{\mathbf{R},\mathbf{O}}$ is *faithful for objects* if for any object $W \in \mathbf{O}$ and any $X \subseteq W$, $[X]_{\mathbf{R},\mathbf{O}}$ depends only on $\{\overline{r}(R) | R \in \mathbf{R}, R \subseteq W\}$.

Object-faithfulness prevents a little knowledge from being a dangerous thing. If $[\cdot]_{\mathbf{R},\mathbf{O}}$ is faithful for objects, knowing the meaning of $\overline{r}(R)$ for every scheme R contained in an object W provides the meaning for $[X]_{\mathbf{R},\mathbf{O}}$ for any $X \subseteq W$. Such is not the case when $[\cdot]_{\mathbf{R},\mathbf{O}}$ is not faithful for objects, as we saw in the last example. (Object-faithfulness implies strong faithfulness.)

Theorem 12.5 Let $\mathbf{R}$ be a database scheme over $\mathbf{U}$ and let $\mathbf{O}$ be a set of objects containing $\mathbf{R}$. Assume every object in $\mathbf{O}$ is the union of schemes in $\mathbf{R}$. The window function $[\cdot]_{\mathbf{R},\mathbf{O}}$ is faithful for objects if and only if $\mathbf{O}$ is closed under nonempty intersection.

Proof The "if" part follows from Theorem 12.4. The "only if" portion is left as Exercise 12.65. The basic idea is that if X is the intersection of objects Z and W, but not itself an object, then $[X]_{\mathbf{R},\mathbf{O}}$ depends on both relations from W and relations from Z.

There are generally several ways to modify a database scheme and a set of objects to make objects closed under intersection.

Example 12.55 Figures 12.45 and 12.46 show two ways to modify $\mathbf{R}$ and $\mathbf{O}$ from Example 12.53 to get closure of $\mathbf{O}$ under intersection. Under the first modification, PLANE#-MECHANIC pairs can exist independently. Under the second modification, PLANE#-MECHANIC pairs mean only that the mechanic could potentially work on the plane. A mechanic cannot have serviced a plane unless he or she could potentially have worked on it.

There are reasons for preferring closure of objects under intersection other than object faithfulness. There is a computational advantage, as shown in the proof of Theorem 12.4. A semantic argument can also be made for closure under intersection. Let W and Z be objects, with $X = W \cap Z \neq \emptyset$.

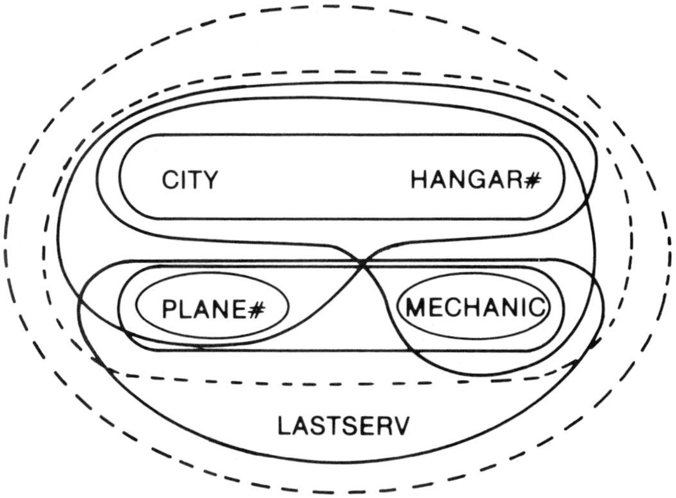

Figure 12.45

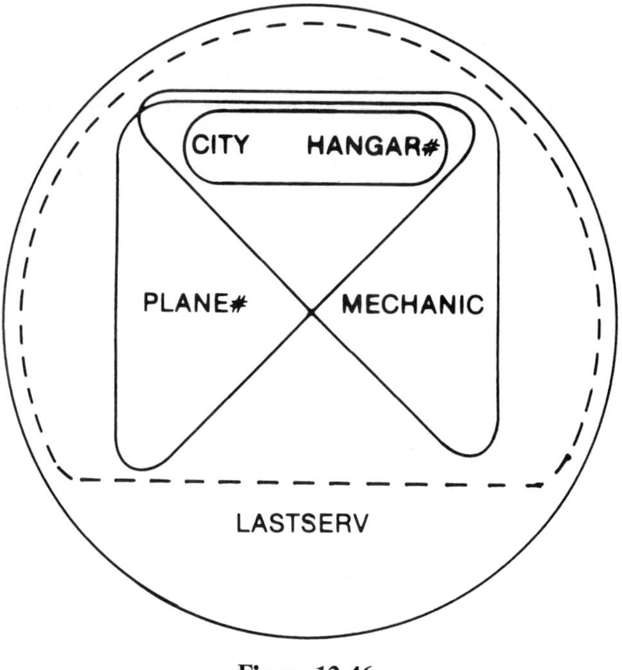

Figure 12.46

We know X-values make sense without $(W - X)$-values (in Z) and X-values make sense without $(Z - X)$-values (in W). It seems X-values should make sense with neither $(W - X)$-values nor $(Z - X)$-values: X should be an object in its own right.

Example 12.56 Referring to Example 12.53, consider CITY and HANGAR#. We can connect a CITY-HANGAR# pair without a PLANE# in $\bar{r}$(CITY HANGAR# MECHANIC). We can connect a CITY-HANGAR# pair without a MECHANIC in $\bar{r}$(PLANE# CITY HANGAR#). It would seem that a CITY-HANGAR# pair could exist without PLANE# or MECHANIC, but there is no place to store a pair. There is no place to assert that city c has a hangar h. Both the modified schemes of Example 12.55 have CITY HANGAR# as a relation scheme, and hence can store such pairs.

12.6 EXERCISES

12.1 True or False?

(a) For relations r and s, if $r \geq s$ and r and s have the same number of tuples, then $r > s$.

(b) For relations r and s, if $r \geq s$ and for every tuple $t_r \in r$ there is a tuple $t_s \in s$ such that $t_r \geq t_s$, then $r > s$.

12.2 Find a completion of the relation r below with a minimum number of tuples

r(A	B	C	D)
1	⊥	⊥	6
1	3	⊥	⊥
⊥	3	⊥	7
⊥	⊥	5	7
⊥	4	5	⊥
2	4	⊥	⊥

12.3* For a relation r with n columns and k tuples, what is the fewest tuples that any completion of r may have?

12.4 Show that $r > s$ and $s > r$ imply $r = s$.

12.5 Give relations r and s such that $r > s$ and there is a completion of s that is not a completion of r.

12.6 Let r and s be relations over scheme R. Show that if every completion of r is a completion of s, then $r > s$.

12.7 Let f be a tuple calculus formula with a single free variable, x, and that mentions a single relation, r. Give a method for evaluating the expression $\{x(R) | f(x)\}$ when r is partial. Does your method allow the value of the expression itself to be a partial relation? You might want the value to include a "sure" and a "maybe" component.

12.8 Give a tuple calculus formula involving a partial relation r such that $I_s(f)$ is *false* for every completion s of r, but $I_q(f) =$ *true* for some extension q of r.

12.9 Show that in the definition of permissible in Section 12.2, if "extension" is used instead of "completion," an equivalent definition results.

12.10 Give a set of FDs F and a relation r such that a particular null must take the same value in any permissible completion of r, but this value cannot be inferred using the fill-in rule for unmarked nulls. Hint: Think about nondistinguished variables in a tableau.

12.11 Characterize when two partial relations with marked nulls have the same set of completions.

12.12 Give a definition of *subsumes* for relations with marked nulls. We want a syntactic condition that characterizes when one relation, treated as a set of axioms, logically implies another.

12.13 Show that if in the definition of *augments* for relations with marked nulls, only values may replace nulls, an equivalent definition of *completion* results.

12.14 Let $r \in Rel\uparrow(R)$ and let F be a set of FDs over R. Show that arbitrary completions of $nchase_F(r)$ need not be permissible.

12.15 Let $r \in Rel\uparrow(R)$ and let F be a set of FDs over R. Let $r^* = nchase_F(r)$. Assume $r^* \neq HV$ and suppose t is a tuple in r^* with $t(A) = \perp_i$, $A \in R$. Show that r^* has permissible completions under F that do not agree on $t(A)$.

12.16 Give a correct and complete set of inference axioms for existence constraints.

12.17 Let E be a set of ECs over relation scheme R. For a subset X of R, let X^* denote the maximal set of attributes Y such that $X \urcorner Y$ is implied by E. (X^* is analogous to X^+ for FDs.) Let F be a set of FDs over R. When adding a tuple t to a relation $r \in Rel\uparrow(R)$, it may be that t initially satisfies E, but filling in nulls using F after the addition causes t to violate E. Alternatively, t may violate E initially, but filling in nulls after the addition makes t satisfy E. Using X^+, X^* and $DEF(t)$, characterize when

(a) t is guaranteed to satisfy E after insertion into r,

(b) t will possibly satisfy E after insertion, and

(c) t will surely violate E after insertion.

12.18 Show that if q is a minimal extension of r, then q is a close extension of r.

12.19 Is a minimal extension of a relation r necessarily a completion of r? Is a completion necessarily a minimal extension?

12.20 Which of the following possibility functions are reasonable?
(a) $POSS_1(r) = \{s \mid s \downarrow\geq r \text{ and } |s| = |r|\}$.
(b) $POSS_2(r) = \{s \mid s \downarrow\geq r \text{ and } |s| \leq |r|\}$.
(c) $POSS_3(r) =$
$\{s \mid s \downarrow\geq r$ and no proper subrelation of s completes $r\}$.
(d) $POSS_4(r) =$
$\{s \mid s \downarrow\geq r$ and no relation with fewer tuples than s extends $r\}$.

12.21 Show that for any closed possibility function $POSS$, the collection of sets $\{POSS(r) \mid r \in Rel\uparrow(R)\}$ is not closed under intersection.

12.22 Show that the collection of sets $\{POSS_O(r)\ r \in Rel\uparrow(R)\}$ is closed under intersection.

12.23 Prove that no precise generalization for join exists for any closed possibility function.

12.24 Show that if γ' is an adequate and restricted generalization of γ for a closed possibility function, then γ' is faithful to γ.

12.25 Show that for $POSS_O$, $r \sqsupseteq s$ if and only if $r \geq s$, and that $r \not\sqsupseteq s$ if and only if $r \not\geq s$.

12.26 Prove that for any relation $r \in Rel\uparrow(R)$ and any nontrivial JD $*[\mathbf{R}]$ over R, there is an extension of r that does not satisfy $*[\mathbf{R}]$.

12.27 Show that $\bowtie^O$ is restricted for $POSS_O$. Hint: If $q = r \bowtie^O s$ and there is a q' such that $POSS_O(q) \sqsupseteq POSS_O(q') \sqsupseteq POSS_O(r) \bowtie POSS_O(s)$, then $q' \sqsupseteq q$ and hence $q' \geq q$. Consider a tuple t in q' that is not subsumed by any tuple in q.

12.28 Give a precise generalization of project for $POSS_O$.

12.29 Show that $\sigma^O_{A=a}$ and $\sigma^O_{A=B}$ are adequate and restricted for $POSS_O$.

12.30 Prove that $POSS_{CE}$ and $POSS_{ME}$ are reasonable possibility functions.

12.31 (a) Give adequate and restricted generalizations of union and project for $POSS_{CE}$.
(b) Show that there is no adequate and restricted generalization of join for $POSS_{CE}$.

12.32 Do adequate and restricted generalizations for union, join, and select exist for $POSS_C$ and $POSS_{ME}$?

12.33* Give syntactic characterizations for $r \sqsupseteq s$ for the possibility functions $POSS_{CE}$, $POSS_C$ and $POSS_{ME}$.

12.34 Are there adequate and restricted generalizations for intersection, complement, and select with inequality comparisons for any of $POSS_O$, $POSS_{CE}$, $POSS_C$, and $POSS_{ME}$?

12.35 Show that if an operator γ has an adequate and restricted generalization γ' for possibility function, and γ' is not precise, then no precise generalization of γ exists.

12.36 Give rules for redundant tuple removal for $POSS_{CE}$, $POSS_C$ and $POSS_{ME}$.

12.37 Prove the corollary to Lemma 12.2.

12.38 Prove the converse of Lemma 12.3.

12.39 Show that the definition of π_X^B is adequate and restricted for $POSS_B$. Is it precise?

12.40 Give an adequate and restricted generalization $\sigma_{A=B}^B$ of $\sigma_{A=B}$ for $POSS_B$. What can be deduced about $\sigma_{A=B}^B(\sigma_{A=a}^B(r))$ versus $\sigma_{A=a}^B(\sigma_{A=B}^B(r))$?

12.41 Show that $\cup^B$ is precise for $POSS_B$.

12.42 Prove the claim in the proof of Lemma 12.5.

12.43 Which of the generalized operators defined for $POSS_O$ and $POSS_B$ are faithful? Which of the generalized binary operators are associative and commutative?

12.44* Let **O** be a set of objects over a set of attributes **U** and suppose **U** is one of the objects in **O**. Show that there exists a set E of ECs such that

$$\{DEF(t) | t \text{ satisfies } E\} = \mathbf{O}$$

12.45 Show that the extension of a window function from objects to all sets of attributes given in Section 12.5 preserves the containment condition and gives the same value as the original function on objects.

Definition 12.20 Given a set of objects **O** and a set of attributes X, $W \in \mathbf{O}$ is a *minimal object for* X if $W \supseteq X$ and there is no object Z in **O** such that $W \supseteq Z \supseteq X$.

12.46 Prove that the value of an extended window function on a set of attributes X can be computed from the value of the original window function on the minimal objects for X.

12.47 Show that the window function defined in Section 12.5.4 satisfies the containment condition, even if the underlying database does not.

Definition 12.21 Given a database scheme **R** and a set of attributes X, $R \in \mathbf{R}$ is a *maximal scheme for* X if $X \supseteq R$ and there is no scheme S in **R** such that $X \supseteq S \supsetneq R$.

12.48 Using the window function from Section 12.5.4, and assuming the underlying database satisfies the containment condition, show that $[X,d]_{\mathbf{R},\mathbf{O}}$ is the join of every relation $\bar{r}(R)$ where R is a maximal scheme for object $X \in \mathbf{O}$.

12.49 Does a database d necessarily have a representative instance s such that for at least one relation $r(R)$ in d, $\pi_R(s) = r$?

12.50 Prove Theorem 12.1. You will need to make some assumptions to handle the case where $nchase_{\mathbf{C}}(PAD(d)) = HV$.

12.51 Show that the window function $[\cdot]_{*\mathbf{R}}$ is faithful on any database satisfying the containment condition.

12.52* What are the implicit objects for $[\cdot]_{*\mathbf{R}}$ for $\mathbf{R} = \{R_1, R_2, \ldots, R_p\}$? Define $[W]_{*\mathbf{R}}$ for implicit object W in terms of joins.

12.53 Let d be a database with scheme $\mathbf{R}$ over $\mathbf{U}$ and let F be a set of FDs over $\mathbf{U}$. Let t be a tuple in $PAD(d)$. Let t^* be the corresponding tuple in $nchase_F(PAD(d))$. Prove $DEF(t)^+ \supseteq DEF(t)$.

12.54 Show that the foreign key constraint is not sufficient to guarantee that a locally satisfying database globally satisfies a set of FDs.

12.55 Show that $[\cdot]_F$ is faithful for a database d that satisfies the MFKC relative to F.

12.56* Consider $[\cdot]_F$ on databases over scheme $\mathbf{R} = \{R_1, R_2, \ldots, R_p\}$ that satisfy the MFKC relative to F. Give the implicit objects for $[\cdot]_F$, and for each object W, give a definition of $[W]_F$ using joins.

12.57 Let $\mathbf{R} = \{R_1, R_2, \ldots, R_p\}$, $F_1, F_2, \ldots, F_p$, and F be defined as in Section 12.5.6. Let $\mathbf{U} = R_1R_2 \cdots R_p$ and let $X \subseteq \mathbf{U}$. Assuming $\mathbf{R}$ satisfies the uniqueness condition, show that the construction of any F-based DDAG for $X \rightarrow X^+$ is unique relative to $F_1, F_2, \ldots, F_p$. For any attribute $A \in X^+ - X$, there is a unique j, depending on A and X, such that a node for A can only be added to the DDAG by using an FD from F_j.

12.58 Prove that the uniqueness condition implies BCNF.

12.59 Prove the "only if" portion of Theorem 12.3. If $\mathbf{R}$ violates the uniqueness condition relative to F, exhibit a database d that locally satisfies F but does not globally satisfy F. Hint: Such a database exists where every relation has but a single tuple.

12.60* Let $\mathbf{R}$ be a database scheme and let F be the set of FDs embodied in the keys of $\mathbf{R}$. For a database d on $\mathbf{R}$ and a set of attributes X, show that $[X,d]_F$ can be computed using union, projection, and extension joins.

12.61* The uniqueness condition does not allow database schemes where one relation scheme is the subscheme of another, unless the subscheme has a single, trivial key. Suppose we modify the definition of the uniqueness condition so that $(R_i)^{\pm}_j$ may contain a key and another attribute from R_j if $R_i \supseteq R_j$. Alter the definition of independence to be that local satisfaction *and* the containment condition imply global satisfaction. Show that Theorem 12.3 holds under the altered definitions.

12.62 Let **R** be a database scheme whose keys embody the set of FDs F. Show that $[\cdot]_F$ is faithful if **R** satisfies the uniqueness condition. Show that $[\cdot]_F$ can be faithful even if **R** violates the uniqueness condition and every relation has a non-trivial key.

12.63 Show that for any database scheme **R**, the window function $[\cdot]_{*\mathbf{R}}$ is strongly faithful.

12.64 Let **R** be a database scheme whose keys embody a set F of FDs. Find a necessary condition for $[\cdot]_F$ to be strongly faithful.

12.65 Complete the proof of Theorem 12.4. Let X be a non-object that is the intersection of objects W and Z. Show that $[X]_{\mathbf{R},\mathbf{O}}$ can be modified by changing relations whose schemes are in Z but not in W.

12.7 BIBLIOGRAPHY AND COMMENTS

Missing and partial information are problems in any database model. The ANSI/X3/SPARC report [1975] lists over a dozen types of nulls, although some are artifacts of the workings of the database system. Codd [1975] suggested the null substitution principle for evaluating expressions with partial relations. Grant [1977] pointed out that no recursive interpretation function can be defined for null substitution. Vassiliou [1979] considers algorithms for evaluating expressions under null substitution.

Walker [1979, 1980b] first suggested using dependencies to fill in nulls, although his method deals only with unmarked nulls. Marked nulls are from Maier [1980a], Vassiliou [1980a] and Honeyman [1980b, 1980c]. Lien [1979] considers the interaction of nulls and MVDs. Grant [1979] and Lipski [1979b, 1981] treat nulls that represent intervals or sets of values, rather than all possible values. Existence constraints are from Maier [1980a]. Goldstein [1981a] generalizes ECs to constraints on all types of values. Rozenshtein [1981] looks at efficient implementations of partial relations. Possibility functions follow from Biskup [1980a, 1981], who also introduces $POSS_B$ and generalized operators for $POSS_B$. Codd [1975], Lacroix and Pirotte [1976], and Zaniolo [1977] present generalized join operators. Reiter [1978] discussed the closed world assumption as it applies to databases.

Honeyman, Ladner, and Yannakakis [1980] show that testing the UIA is NP-complete in general. Other criticism of the UIA and URSA is given by Kent [1979b], Bernstein and Goodman [1980b], and Atzeni and Parker

[1981]. Objects are briefly mentioned by Zaniolo [1977] and are treated in detail by Sciore [1980b]. Carlson and Kaplan [1976] and Osborn [1979b] discuss automatically connecting relations in a database. Window functions are from Maier [1980a]. The window function $[\cdot]_{\mathbf{R,O}}$ was developed in a series of papers by Korth and Ullman [1980], Maier and Ullman [1980], Korth [1981], and Maier and Warren [1981b]. Representative instances were developed by Honeyman [1980b, 1980c], Graham [1981a], and Mendelzon [1981]. The window function $[\cdot]_{*\mathbf{R}}$ is from Yannakakis [1981]. The MFKC was proposed by Sagiv [1981a]. Stein [1981] considers efficiently enforcing the MFKC. The uniqueness condition and its equivalence to independence are due to Sagiv [1981b]. The proof of Theorem 12.8 used here was arrived at with the help of Ed Sciore.

Numerous semantic extensions to the relation model have been proposed, such as those by Schmid and Swenson [1975], Codd [1979], Kent [1979a], and Housel, Waddle, and Yao [1979]. Clifford and Warren [1981] consider the semantics of time in relational databases. The usefulness of summary information in databases is studied by LeViet, Kambayashi, *et al.* [1979], Walker [1980a], and Bernstein, Blaustein, and Clarke [1980].

URSA requires renaming related attributes. Bachman and Daya [1977], Smith and Smith [1977a, 1977b], Gewirtz [1979], and Sciore [1979, 1980a] all deal with renaming attributes or capturing information about related attributes, particularly where one attribute represents a specialized role of another attribute.

For more material on semantics of databases, the reader is referred to Sundgren [1975], Chen [1976], Sowa [1976], the collections edited by Nijssen [1976, 1977], Brodie [1978], and Hammer and McLeod [1978, 1980].

Exercise 12.44 is from Goldstein [1980, 1981b]. Exercise 12.53 is motivated by Yannakakis [1981]. Sagiv [1981a, 1981b] gives answers to parts of Exercises 12.56 and 12.60.

Chapter 13

ACYCLIC DATABASE SCHEMES

In this chapter we introduce a class of database schemes, the *acyclic* database schemes, that possess several desirable properties. We first enumerate the properties, then give three syntactic characterizations of acyclic schemes, give algorithms for two of the characterizations, and prove equivalence of the properties and characterizations.

13.1 PROPERTIES OF DATABASE SCHEMES

In this section we introduce five properties that a database scheme may possess. The properties are mainly "extensional"—they refer to a condition that must hold for all databases on the database scheme. The next section deals with "intensional" properties—ones that involve conditions on the database scheme alone.

13.1.1 Existence of a Full Reducer

We return to the semijoin operator introduced in Chapter 11. Consider a relational expression

$$E = \pi_X(\sigma_C(r_1 \bowtie r_2 \bowtie \cdots \bowtie r_p))$$

where C is some Boolean combination of comparison conditions. Such project-select-join expressions occur frequently as subexpressions when converting calculus-based queries to relational algebra. Suppose we are evaluating the expression on a distributed database system where the relations are spread over multiple sites. It is not unusual in such a system for communication costs between sites to greatly exceed processing costs at a single site. We consider evaluating E while trying to minimize data transmitted between sites, paying no attention to local processing costs.

A naive approach to evaluating E is to ship all the relations to a single site and evaluate the expression at that site. The problem with this approach is that only a small portion of each relation may be needed in the evaluation of E. Tuples and parts of tuples may be excluded from the evaluation by the projection, the selection condition, and the joins. The naive approach can be improved by using the algebraic optimization techniques of Chapter 11 to push parts of the projection and selection down the tree to individual relations. The result is an expression

$$E' = \pi_X(\sigma_{C'}(\pi_{Y_1}(\sigma_{C_1}(r_1)) \bowtie \pi_{Y_2}(\sigma_{C_2}(r_2)) \bowtie \cdots \bowtie \pi_{Y_p}(\sigma_{C_p}(r_p)))).$$

We can compute

$$s_i = \pi_{Y_i}(\sigma_{C_i}(r_i)),$$

for $1 \leq i \leq p$, at individual sites, to be left with the expression

$$E'' = \pi_X(\sigma_{C'}(s_1 \bowtie s_2 \bowtie \cdots \bowtie s_p)$$

to evaluate, where presumably some of the s_i's are smaller then the corresponding r_i's.

Example 13.1 Consider the database $d = \{r_1, r_2, r_3\}$ on the database scheme $\mathbf{R}_a = \{ABC, BCD, CDE\}$ shown in Figure 13.1. ($\mathbf{R}_a$ will be used as a running example throughout this chapter.) Suppose we want to evaluate the expression

$$E = \pi_{AD}(\sigma_{(E<4) \wedge (A \neq D) \wedge (B \neq 8)}(r_1 \bowtie r_2 \bowtie r_3)).$$

We transform E to

$$E' = \pi_{AD}(\sigma_{A \neq D}(\sigma_{B \neq 8}(r_1) \bowtie \sigma_{B \neq 8}(r_2) \bowtie \pi_{CD}(\sigma_{E<4}(r_3)))).$$

We can evaluate

$$s_1 = \sigma_{B \neq 8}(r_1)$$
$$s_2 = \sigma_{B \neq 8}(r_2)$$
$$s_3 = \pi_{CD}(\sigma_{E<4}(r_3))$$

locally to get the database $d' = \{s_1, s_2, s_3\}$ shown in Figure 13.2. The task is now to evaluate

$$E'' = \pi_{AD}(\sigma_{A \neq D}(s_1 \bowtie s_2 \bowtie s_3)).$$

r_1(A	B	C)
7	4	6
8	4	6
7	5	6
8	8	6
9	8	2
9	4	11
8	5	11

r_2(B	C	D)
4	6	7
5	6	7
8	6	9
8	11	9
4	11	9
5	11	9
4	12	9

r_3(C	D	E)
6	7	1
6	7	2
6	7	5
6	9	3
8	7	5
8	9	3
11	9	3
12	7	4

Figure 13.1

s_1(A	B	C)
7	4	6
8	4	6
7	5	6
9	4	11
8	5	11

s_2(B	C	D)
4	6	7
5	6	7
4	11	9
5	11	9
4	12	9

s_3(C	D)
6	7
6	9
8	9
11	9

Figure 13.2

Once the relations have been reduced as far as possible using projection and selections, it may be possible to reduce them further still through semijoins. We are interested in removing all the tuples of the database $d = \{s_1, s_2, \ldots, s_p\}$ that do not participate in the join $s_1 \bowtie s_2 \bowtie \cdots \bowtie s_p$. Recall: The *full reduction* of s_i relative to d, $FR(s_i,d)$, is the set of all tuples of s_i that participate in $\bowtie d$. A *semijoin program SP* is a series of assignments of the form $s_i \leftarrow s_i \ltimes s_j$. SP is a *full reducer* relative to the database scheme **R** if $SP(s_i,d) = FR(s_i,d)$ for every database $d(\mathbf{R})$ and relation $s_i \in d$.

If **R** has a full reducer, we can use semijoins to fully reduce $s_1, s_2, \ldots, s_p$ before transmitting them to a common site for joining. Whether or not it pays to apply a particular semijoin program in a distributed system depends on the states of individual relations. In computing $r(R) \bowtie s(S)$ in a distributed system, it could be cheaper to send all of r to s than to send $\pi_{R \cap S}(s)$ to r and then send $r \ltimes s$ back to s. For a given database d, it can happen that one full reducer is beneficial to apply while another is not (see Exercise 13.1).

Example 13.2 The database scheme $\mathbf{R} = \{ABC, BCD, CD\}$ has a full reducer. One full reducer is

$s_2 \leftarrow s_2 \ltimes s_1$;
$s_3 \leftarrow s_3 \ltimes s_2$;
$s_2 \leftarrow s_2 \ltimes s_3$;
$s_1 \leftarrow s_1 \ltimes s_2$.

The result of applying this semijoin program to the relations in Figure 13.2 is shown in Figure 13.3.

s_1:

A	B	C
7	4	6
8	4	6
7	5	6
9	4	11
8	5	11

s_2:

B	C	D
4	6	7
5	6	7
4	11	9
5	11	9

s_3:

C	D
6	7
11	9

Figure 13.3

Example 13.3 Consider the database scheme $\mathbf{R}_c = \{ABC, BCD, CE, DE\}$. ($\mathbf{R}_c$ will also be used for many examples in this chapter.) $\mathbf{R}_c$ has no full-reducers. The database on $\mathbf{R}_c$ shown in Figure 13.4 is not fully reduced, yet no semijoin reduces it further.

r_1:

A	B	C
1	2	3
7	8	9

r_2:

B	C	D
2	3	4
8	9	10

r_3:

C	E
3	5
9	11

r_4:

D	E
4	11
10	5

Figure 13.4

13.1.2 Equivalence of a Join Dependency to Multivalued Dependencies

Every database scheme **R** corresponds to a unique JD, namely *[**R**]. Every JD implies a set of MVDs. The general implication of one JD by another is given in the next lemma.

Lemma 13.1 If **R** and **S** are database schemes over the same set of attributes, then *[**R**] $\models$ *[**S**] if and only if **S** $\leq$ **R**.*

*Recall that **S** $\geq$ **R** means every relation scheme in **R** is contained in some relation scheme in **S**.

Proof Immediate consequence of Theorem 8.1. $FIX(\mathbf{R}) = SAT(*[\mathbf{R}])$ and $FIX(\mathbf{S}) = SAT(*[\mathbf{S}])$, so $\mathbf{S} \geq \mathbf{R}$ if and only if $FIX(\mathbf{R}) \subseteq FIX(\mathbf{S})$ if and only if $*[\mathbf{R}] \models *[\mathbf{S}]$.

We are interested in the MVDs implied by a JD $*[\mathbf{R}]$. We want to know all pairs of schemes S_1, S_2 such that $*[\mathbf{R}] \models *[S_1, S_2]$. It is sufficient to consider JDs $*[S_1, S_2]$ where S_1 and S_2 are exact unions of schemes in $\mathbf{R}$. In particular we assume there is a function

$$f:\{1, 2, \ldots, p\} \rightarrow \{1,2\}$$

such that

$$S_i = \bigcup_{f(j)=i} R_j, \; i = 1, 2.$$

Let $MVD(\mathbf{R})$ be all the nontrivial MVDs (two-scheme JDs) that can be so defined.

Example 13.4 For $\mathbf{R}_a = \{ABC, BCD, CDE\}$, $MVD(\mathbf{R}_a) = \{*[ABC, BCDE], *[ABCD, CDE]\}$. For $\mathbf{R}_c = \{ABC, BCD, CE, DE\}$, $MVD(R) = \{*[ABC, BCDE], *[ABCD, CDE], *[ABCE5, BCDE]\}$.

Exercise 13.4 shows that any MVD implied by $*[\mathbf{R}]$ is the direct consequence of some MVD in $MVD(\mathbf{R})$. We are interested when $MVD(\mathbf{R}) \models *[\mathbf{R}]$, for a database $\mathbf{R}$. $MVD(\mathbf{R}_a) \models *[\mathbf{R}_a]$, while $MVD(\mathbf{R}_c) \not\models *[\mathbf{R}_c]$ (see Exercise 13.6). Basically, $MVD(\mathbf{R}) \models *[\mathbf{R}]$ means that the lossless decomposition of a relation r onto $\mathbf{R}$ can be captured as a set of two-way decompositions. Also, if $MVD(\mathbf{R}) \models *[\mathbf{R}]$, an efficient test for satisfaction of $*[\mathbf{R}]$ can be devised.

13.1.3 Unique 4NF Decomposition

In this section we formalize the condition that a unique 4NF decomposition follows from a set of MVDs M over a scheme $\mathbf{U}$.

Definition 13.1 Let M be a set of MVDs over a scheme $\mathbf{U}$. A pair of relation schemes (R,S) is a *decomposition* for $\mathbf{U}$ under M if $M \models *[R,S]$. A decomposition (R,S) of $\mathbf{U}$ is *tight* if there is no other decomposition (R',S') with $R' \cap S'$ properly contained in $R \cap S$. That is, (R,S) is tight if the overlap of R and S is minimal.

We are actually interested in decomposing $\mathbf{U}$ until it is in 4NF. We can view M as applying to a subscheme $\mathbf{U}'$ of $\mathbf{U}$ by considering the MVDs that necessarily apply in $\pi_{\mathbf{U}'}(SAT(M))$. Thus "decomposition under M" and "tight decomposition under M" make sense for subschemes of $\mathbf{U}$.

Definition 13.2 Let $\mathbf{R}$ be a scheme over $\mathbf{U}$ and let M be a set of MVDs over $\mathbf{U}$. $\mathbf{R}$ is in *tight fourth normal form* (tight 4NF) for M if $\mathbf{R}$ is in 4NF relative to M and $\mathbf{R}$ can be obtained by a series of tight decompositions. *M uniquely decomposes* $\mathbf{U}$ if there is only one database scheme $\mathbf{R}$ over $\mathbf{U}$ that is in tight 4NF for M.

Definition 13.3 A database scheme $\mathbf{R}$ over $\mathbf{U}$ is a *unique decomposition* if some set M of MVDs uniquely decomposes $\mathbf{U}$ into $\mathbf{R}$.

Example 13.5 Consider database scheme $\mathbf{R}_a = \{ABC, BCD, CDE\}$ from previous examples. $\mathbf{R}_a$ is a unique decomposition of $A\ B\ C\ D\ E$. Let $M = \{BC \twoheadrightarrow A, CD \twoheadrightarrow E\}$ (which is $MVD(\mathbf{R}_a)$). We can either start by decomposing $ABCDE$ into $\{ABC, BCDE\}$ or $\{ABCD, CDE\}$, but at the next step we always reach $\{ABC, BCDE, CDE\}$, which is in 4NF relative to M. $\mathbf{R}_c = \{ABC, BCD, CE, DE\}$ is not a unique decomposition (see Exercise 13.11).

13.1.4 Pairwise Consistency Implies Total Consistency

Let $\mathbf{R} = \{R_1, R_2, \ldots, R_p\}$ be a database scheme and let $d = \{r_1, r_2, \ldots, r_p\}$ be a database over $\mathbf{R}$. We have noted in previous chapters that it is computationally hard to test if $r_1, r_2, \ldots, r_p$ join completely. We say that d is *totally consistent* (TC) if $r_1, r_2, \ldots, r_p$ join completely. Database d is *pairwise consistent* (PC) if every pair of relations r_i and r_j join completely. Testing PC is a polynomial computation in the size of a database. TC necessitates PC (Exercise 13.12), but PC is not always sufficient for TC. We are interested in database schemes where every PC database is also TC.

Example 13.6 PC does imply TC for databases on our old friend $\mathbf{R}_a = \{ABC, BCD, CDE\}$. Consider a database $d(\mathbf{R}_a) = \{r_1(ABC), r_2(BCD), r_3(CDE)\}$ that is PC. We show that every tuple in r_2 enters into the join $r_1 \bowtie r_2 \bowtie r_3$. Let t_2 be a tuple in r_2. Since r_1 joins completely with r_2, it contains a tuple t_1 that joins with t_2. Likewise, r_3 contains a tuple t_3 that joins with t_2. The three tuples all join together since $t_1(C) = t_2(C) = t_3(C)$, and C is the only attribute where t_1 and t_3 overlap.

PC is not sufficient for TC for databases on $\mathbf{R}_c = \{ABC, BCD, CE, DE\}$. Figure 13.4 shows a PC database on $\mathbf{R}_c$ that is not TC.

13.1.5 Small Intermediate Joins

Consider the problem of computing $\bowtie d$ for a database $d = \{r_1(R_1), r_2(R_2), \ldots, r_p(R_p)\}$ over scheme R by a series of binary joins. Even if all the relations in d are fully reduced, a poor choice of joins can lead to intermediate results larger than the final result.

Example 13.7 Consider computing $r_1 \bowtie r_2 \bowtie r_3$ for the database on $\mathbf{R}_a = \{ABC, BCD, CDE\}$ shown in Figure 13.5. If we begin by computing $r_1 \bowtie r_3$, we get an intermediate result with 10 tuples, where the complete join has only 6 tuples. If we start with $r_1 \bowtie r_2$, the intermediate result has only 6 tuples.

$r_1(A$	B	$C)$
1	3	5
1	4	5
2	3	5
2	4	6

$r_2(B$	C	$D)$
3	5	7
4	5	8
3	5	9
4	6	8

$r_3(C$	D	$E)$
5	7	10
5	8	10
5	9	11
6	8	11

Figure 13.5

Example 13.8 Consider computing $r_1 \bowtie r_2 \bowtie r_3 \bowtie r_4$ for the database on $\mathbf{R}_c = \{ABC, BCD, CE, DE\}$ given in Figure 13.6. Any sequence of pairwise joins gives at least one intermediate result with more tuples than the final result (see Exercise 13.14). Note that this database is fully reduced.

$r_1(A$	B	$C)$
1	2	3
1	2	4
1	2	5
1	2	6
1	2	7

$r_2(B$	C	$D)$
2	3	8
2	4	8
2	5	11
2	5	12
2	6	16
2	7	17

$r_3(C$	$E)$
3	9
4	10
5	14
6	15
7	15

$r_4(D$	$E)$
8	9
8	10
11	13
12	14
16	15
17	15

Figure 13.6

We are interested in database schemes where every fully reduced database can be joined through a sequence of pairwise joins where no intermediate result has more tuples than the final result. Moreover, we desire a sequence of joins that works for any database on the scheme and where intermediate results are always "growing." We actually look at a stronger condition, that when a join is taken, the relations involved join completely.

Definition 13.4 Let $\mathbf{R} = \{R_1, R_2, \ldots, R_p\}$ be a database scheme. A *join plan* for **R** is a rooted binary tree P with leaves labeled by relation schemes in R and every scheme in R labeling at least one leaf of P. Let $d = \{r_1, r_2, \ldots, r_p\}$ be a database on **R**. The *instantiation of* P *by* d, denoted $P(d)$, is obtained by associating r_i, $1 \leq i \leq p$, with the leaves labeled R_i. After relations are associated with the leaves, associate, recursively, the join of relations at the children with each interior node. The relation $r_1 \bowtie r_2 \bowtie \cdots \bowtie r_p$ is, of course, associated with the root of P.

Example 13.9 Figure 13.7 gives a join plan P for database scheme $\mathbf{R}_a = \{ABC, BCD, CDE\}$. If d is the database in Figure 13.5, Figure 13.8 shows the relations r_a, r_b, and r_c associated with interior nodes, a, b, and c in $P(d)$.

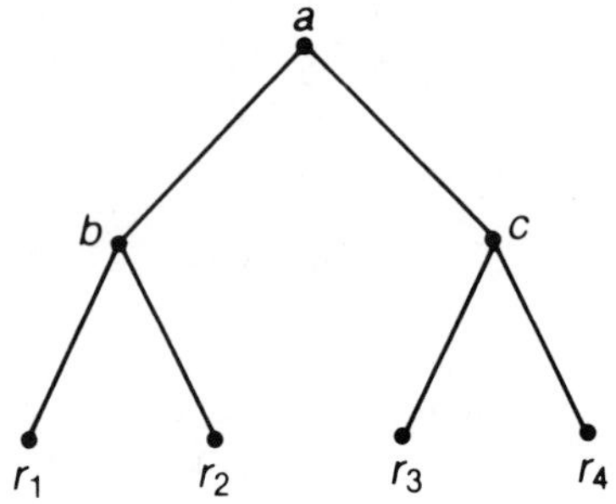

Figure 13.7

r_a(A	B	C	D	E)
1	3	5	7	10
1	3	5	9	11
1	4	5	8	10
2	3	5	7	10
2	3	5	9	11
2	4	6	8	11

r_b(A	B	C	D)
1	3	5	7
1	3	5	9
1	4	5	8
2	3	5	7
2	3	5	9
2	4	6	8

r_c(B	C	D	E)
3	5	7	10
4	5	8	10
3	5	9	11
4	6	8	11

Figure 13.8

Every join plan corresponds to a completely-parenthesized join expression. The join plan in Figure 13.7 corresponds to $(r_1 \bowtie r_2) \bowtie (r_3 \bowtie r_2)$.

Definition 13.5 If P is a join plan for **R** and d is a database on **R**, then $P(d)$ is *monotone* if for every interior node b of P, the relation associated with b is the complete join of the relations associated with its children. P is *monotone* if $P(d)$ is *monotone* for every PC database d on R.

Example 13.10 Referring back to Example 13.9, $P(d)$ is monotone, and, in fact, P is monotone.

Example 13.11 The join plan P for $\mathbf{R}_c = \{ABC, BCD, CE, DE\}$ given in Figure 13.9 is not monotone. In particular, $P(d)$ is not monotone, where d is the database of Figure 13.6.

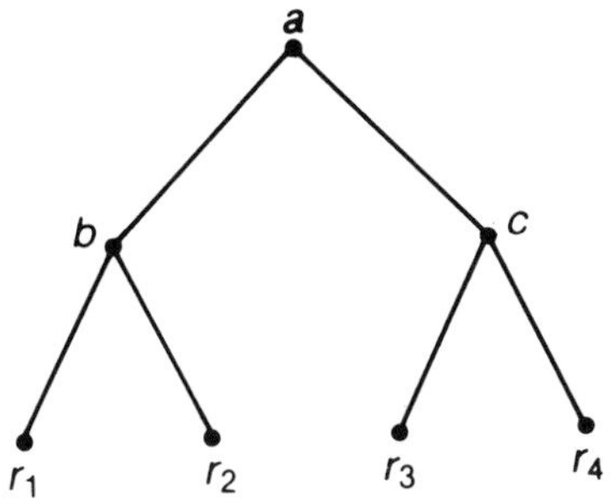

Figure 13.9

Definition 13.6 A database scheme $\mathbf{R}$ has the *increasing join property* if it has a monotone join plan.

13.2 SYNTACTIC CONDITIONS ON DATABASE SCHEMES

This section introduces three syntactic conditions on database schemes: acyclicity, existence of a join tree, and the running intersection property. In the next section we introduce algorithms for testing two of these conditions. We also demonstrate there the equivalence of the syntactic conditions of this section and the more extensional properties of the last section.

13.2.1 Acyclic Hypergraphs

A hypergraph is similar to an ordinary undirected graph, except that edges are arbitrary nonempty sets of nodes, rather than just doubletons.

Definition 13.7 A *hypergraph* H is a pair $(\mathfrak{N},\mathcal{E})$ where $\mathfrak{N}$ is a set of items, called *nodes*, and $\mathcal{E}$ consists of nonempty subsets of $\mathfrak{N}$, called *hyperedges*. If it is clear we are dealing with hypergraphs, we may use "edges" for "hyperedges." H is *reduced* if no edge in $\mathcal{E}$ properly contains another edge and every node is in some edge. The *reduction* of H, written $RED(H)$, is H with any contained edges and non-edge nodes removed.

A database scheme is naturally viewed as a hypergraph. If **R** is a database scheme over **U**, then **R** may be viewed as the hypergraph (**U**,**R**). That is, the attributes in **R** are the nodes in the hypergraph and the relation schemes of **R** are the hyperedges. We shall simply use **R** in place of (**U**,**R**) when dealing with the hypergraph that **R** represents. Saying that **R** is reduced is saying that **R** is reduced as a hypergraph: no relation scheme in **R** properly contains another.

Example 13.12 In drawing hypergraphs, nodes are represented by their labels and hyperedges are represented by closed curves around the nodes. The hypergraph for $\mathbf{R}_a = \{ABC, BCD, CDE\}$ is given in Figure 13.10. The hypergraph for $\mathbf{R}_c = \{ABC, BCD, CE, DE\}$ is given in Figure 13.11.

Definition 13.8 Let $H = (\mathfrak{N},\mathcal{E})$ be a hypergraph, with A and B nodes in $\mathfrak{N}$. A *path* from A to B in H is a sequence of edges $E_1, E_2, \ldots, E_k$, $k \leq 1$, such that $A \in E_1$, $B \in E_k$ and $E_i \cap E_{i+1} \neq \emptyset$ for $1 \leq i < k$. We also say that $E_1, E_2, \ldots, E_k$ is a path from E_1 to E_k.

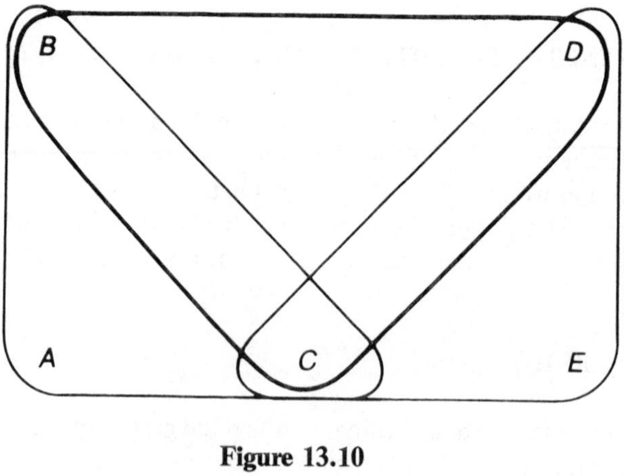

Figure 13.10

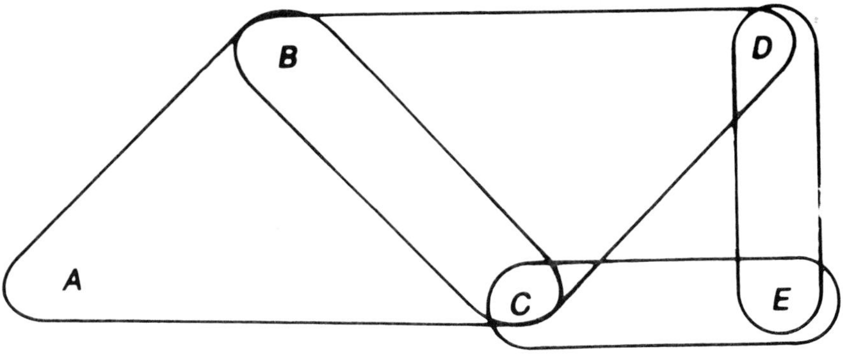

Figure 13.11

Definition 13.9 In a hypergraph $H = (\mathfrak{N}, \mathcal{E})$, two nodes or edges are *connected* if there is a path between them. A set of edges is *connected* if every pair of edges is connected. A *connected component* of H is a maximal connected set of edges.

Example 13.13 Let H be the hypergraph shown in Figure 13.12. ABC, BCD, DE is a path from A to E and from ABC to DE, so A and E are connected, as are ABC and DE. The connected components of H are $\{ABC, BCD, DE\}$ and $\{IJ, JKL, IKL\}$.

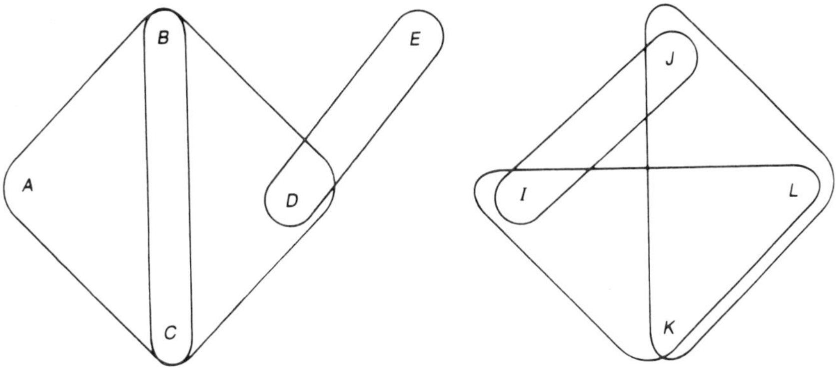

Figure 13.12

We shall be concerned mainly with hypergraphs that consist of a single connected component. Most of what we do generalizes to hypergraphs with multiple components.

Definition 13.10 Let $H = (\mathcal{N},\mathcal{E})$ and $H' = (\mathcal{N}',\mathcal{E}')$ be hypergraphs. H' is a *subhypergraph* of H if $\mathcal{N}' \subseteq \mathcal{N}$ and $\mathcal{E}' \subseteq \mathcal{E}$.

Definition 13.11 Let $H = (\mathcal{N},\mathcal{E})$ be a hypergraph and let $\mathcal{M} \subseteq \mathcal{N}$. The *$\mathcal{M}$-induced hypergraph for* H, denoted $H_{\mathcal{M}}$, is the hypergraph $RED((\mathcal{M},\mathcal{E}_{\mathcal{M}}))$ where

$$\mathcal{E}_{\mathcal{M}} = \{E \cap \mathcal{M} | E \in \mathcal{E}\}.$$

$H_{\mathcal{M}}$ is not necessarily a subhypergraph of H, since $\mathcal{E}_{\mathcal{M}}$ may contain edges not in $\mathcal{E}$.

Example 13.14 Let H be the hypergraph ($ABCDEIJK$, {ABC, BD, CDE, DEI, IJK}) shown in Figure 13.13. $H' = $ ($ABCDE$, {ABC, BD, CDE}) is a subhypergraph of H, as well as being the $ABCDE$-induced hypergraph for H. $H_{ABCD} = $ ($ABCD$, {ABC, BD, CD}), as shown in Figure 13.14. H_{ABCD} is not a subhypergraph of H, since CD is not an edge of H.

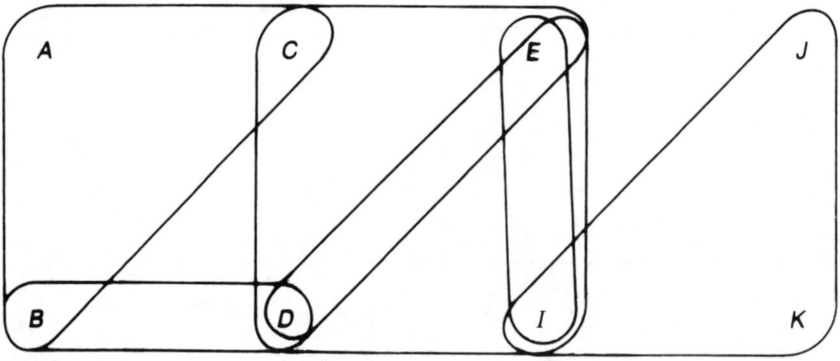

Figure 13.13

We now wish to generalize the notion of "strongly connected" from ordinary graphs to hypergraphs. Recall that a strongly connected graph is one with no articulation points.

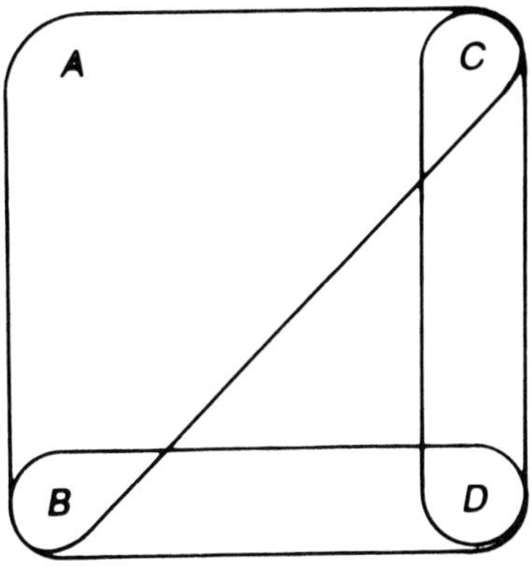

Figure 13.14

Definition 13.12 Let $H = (\mathfrak{N},\mathcal{E})$ be a hypergraph. A set $F \subseteq \mathfrak{N}$ is an *articulation set* for H if $F = E_1 \cap E_2$ for some pair of edges $E_1, E_2 \in \mathcal{E}$, and $H_{\mathfrak{N}'}$ has more connected components than H, where $\mathfrak{N}' = \mathfrak{N} - F$. That is, removing the nodes in F from H disconnects some pair of nodes that were previously connected in H.

Definition 13.13 Let $H = (\mathfrak{N},\mathcal{E})$ be a hypergraph. A *block* of H is an $\mathfrak{M}$-induced hypergraph of H with no articulation set, for some $\mathfrak{M} \subseteq \mathfrak{N}$. A block is *trivial* if it has only one edge. A reduced hypergraph is *acyclic* if it has no blocks; otherwise it is *cyclic*. An arbitrary hypergraph is cyclic or acyclic precisely when its reduction is.

Example 13.15 Let H be the hypergraph of Example 13.14. DE is an articulation set of H, since $DE = CDE \cap DEI$, and H_{ABCIJK} has two components where H had one. H_{ABCD}, shown in Figure 13.14, is a block of H, since it contains no articulation set. Since H is reduced, we conclude it is cyclic.

Example 13.16 Consider the database scheme $\mathbf{R}_a = \{ABC, BCD, CDE\}$ as a hypergraph. $\mathbf{R}_a$ is acyclic. For example, consider $(\mathbf{R}_a)_{ABDE}$, shown in Figure 13.15. It is not a block because it has B and D as articulation sets.

We now give a slightly different definition of acyclicity that only considers induced hypergraphs that are subhypergraphs.

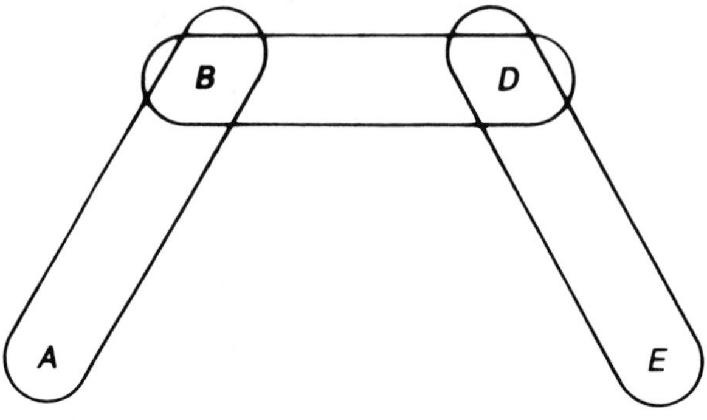

Figure 13.15

Definition 13.14 Let $H = (\mathfrak{N}, \mathcal{E})$ be a hypergraph and let $H' = (\mathfrak{N}', \mathcal{E}')$ be a subhypergraph of H. H' is *closed* relative to H if $H' = H_{\mathfrak{M}}$ for some $\mathfrak{M} \subseteq \mathfrak{N}$. Clearly if such an $\mathfrak{M}$ exists, it must be $\mathfrak{N}'$. Equivalently, H' is a closed subhypergraph of H if for any edge $E \in \mathcal{E}$ there is an edge $E' \in \mathcal{E}'$ such that $E' \supseteq \mathfrak{N}' \cap E$.

Definition 13.15 A reduced hypergraph H is *closed-acyclic* if every closed, connected subhypergraph of H with two or more edges has an articulation set; otherwise H is *closed-cyclic*. An arbitrary hypergraph is closed-acyclic and closed-cyclic exactly as its reduction is.

Example 13.17 Let H be the hypergraph of Example 13.14. $H' = (ABCD, \{ABC, BD\})$ is not closed relative to H. Consider the edge CDE of H. $CDE \cap ABCD = CD$, and CD is not contained in any edge of H'. $H'' = (ABCDE, \{ABC, BD, CDE\})$ is closed relative to H, since $H'' = H_{ABCDE}$. H'' is pictured in Figure 13.16. H'' has no articulation set, so H is closed-cyclic.

Acyclic and closed-acyclic are equivalent conditions (see Exercise 13.22). A database scheme $\mathbf{R}$ is *acyclic* if $\mathbf{R}$ considered as a hypergraph is acyclic.

13.2.2 Join Trees

Definition 13.16 Let $\mathbf{R} = \{R_1, R_2, \ldots, R_p\}$ be a database scheme over $\mathbf{U}$. The *complete intersection graph* for $\mathbf{R}$, denoted $I_{\mathbf{R}}$, is the complete undirected graph on nodes $R_1, R_2, \ldots, R_p$ and with edge labels chosen from the subsets

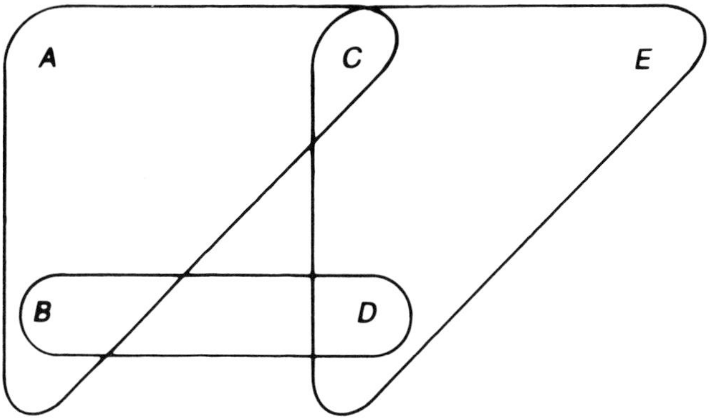

Figure 13.16

of **U**. For an edge $e = (R_i, R_j)$, the label of e, denoted $L(e)$, is $R_i \cap R_j$. An *intersection graph* for **R** is any subgraph of $I_{\mathbf{R}}$ formed by removing only edges. In drawing an intersection graph, we generally omit any edge e where $L(e) = \emptyset$.

Definition 13.17 Let $\mathbf{R} = \{R_1, R_2, \ldots, R_p\}$ be a database scheme over **U**. Let G be an intersection graph for R and let $A \in \mathbf{U}$. A path $e_1, e_2, \ldots, e_k$ from node R_i to node R_j in G is an A-*path* if $A \in L(e_i)$ for all $1 \leq i \leq k$. If $e_1, e_2, \ldots, e_k$ is an A-path, then it follows $A \in R_i$ and $A \in R_j$. In fact, A must be in every node R along the A-path.

Example 13.18 Consider the database scheme $\mathbf{R} = \{ABC, BD, CDE, DEI, IJK\}$ over $ABCDEIJK$, which corresponds to the hypergraph of Example 13.14. $I_{\mathbf{R}}$ is shown in Figure 13.17 (omitting edges with empty labels). Figure 13.18 gives an intersection graph G for **R**. G has a D-path from BD to CDE. There is no B-path in G from ABC to BD, although $I_{\mathbf{R}}$ has such a path.

Definition 13.18 Let $\mathbf{R} = \{R_1, R_2, \ldots, R_p\}$ be a database scheme over **U**. An intersection graph G for **R** is a *join graph* if for every pair of nodes R_i, R_j in G, if $A \in R_i \cap R_j$ then there is an A-path from R_i to R_j. A *join tree* is a join graph that is a tree.

Example 13.19 Let **R** be the database scheme from Example 13.18. $I_{\mathbf{R}}$ is a join graph for **R**. (The complete intersection graph is always a join graph.)

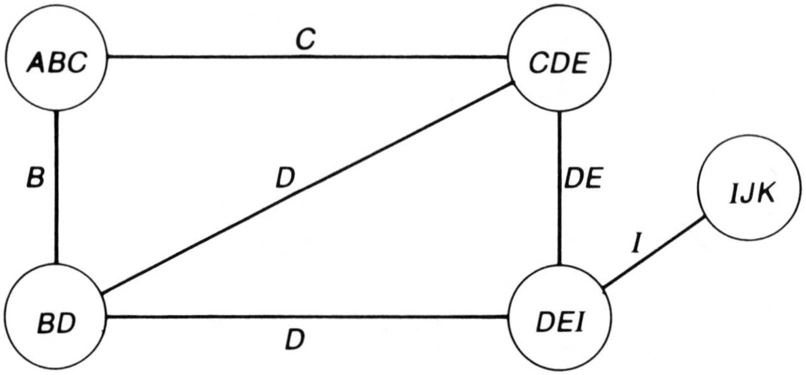

Figure 13.17

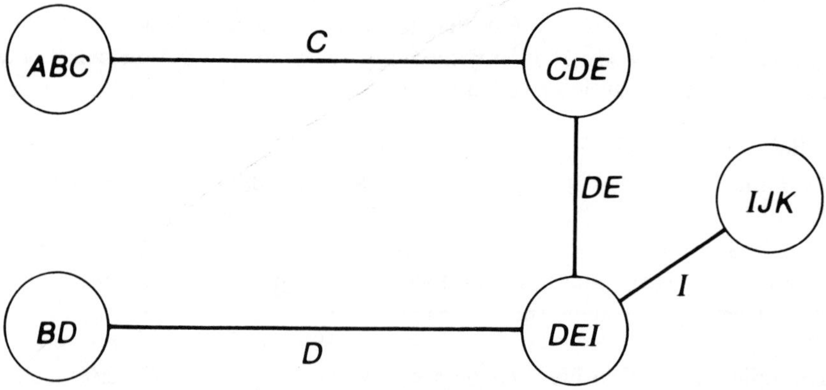

Figure 13.18

The intersection graph in Figure 13.18 is not a join graph for **R**, since there is no B-path from ABC to BD. **R** has no join trees. Any join graph G for R must have the edge (ABC,BD) to give a B-path from ABC to BD, as well as the edge (ABC,CDE) to give a C-path from ABC to CDE. Nodes BD and CDE must be connected by a D-path. The D-path cannot go through ABC, so G must contain a cycle.

We are interested in database schemes where join trees exist. We shall see later that a join tree can be used to construct monotone join plans.

Example 13.20 The database scheme $\mathbf{R}_a = \{ABC, BCD, CDE\}$ does have a join tree, as shown in Figure 13.19.

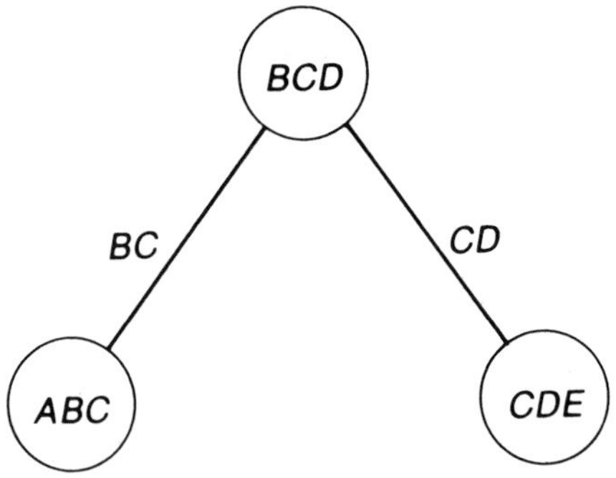

Figure 13.19

13.2.3 The Running Intersection Property

Definition 13.19 Let $\mathbf{R} = \{R_1, R_2, \ldots, R_p\}$ be a database scheme. $\mathbf{R}$ has the *running intersection property* if there is a permutation $S_1, S_2, \ldots, S_p$ of $R_1, R_2, \ldots, R_p$ such that for every $1 < i \leq p$, there exists a $j < i$ such that

$$(S_1 S_2 \cdots S_{i-1}) \cap S_i \subseteq S_j.$$

That is, the intersection of S_i with the union of all the previous schemes is contained entirely within one of those schemes.

Example 13.21 $\mathbf{R} = \{ABC, CDE, BCEI\}$ has the running intersection property, as witnessed by the ordering $BCEI$, ABC, CDE of its relation schemes.

13.3 EQUIVALENCE OF CONDITIONS

As was remarked at the beginning of the chapter, and as the running examples $\mathbf{R}_a$ and $\mathbf{R}_c$ indicate, all the properties and conditions in Sections 13.1 and 13.2 describe the same class of database schemes. Before proving the equivalences, we look at algorithms to decide whether a database scheme $\mathbf{R}$ is acyclic and whether $\mathbf{R}$ has a join tree.

13.3.1 Graham Reduction

The following algorithm on hypergraphs was introduced by Graham, although Yu and Ozsoyoglu independently gave an essentially equivalent algorithm that runs on a different data structure. The *Graham reduction algorithm* consists of repeated application of two reduction rules to hypergraphs until neither can be applied further. Let $H = (\mathcal{N}, \mathcal{E})$ be a hypergraph. The two reduction rules are

rE. (edge removal) If E and F are edges in $\mathcal{E}$ such that E is properly contained in F, remove E from $\mathcal{E}$.
rN. (node removal) If A is a node in $\mathcal{N}$, and A is contained in at most one edge in $\mathcal{E}$, remove A from $\mathcal{N}$ and also from all edges in $\mathcal{E}$ in which it appears.

Example 13.22 Figure 13.20 shows the stages in applying the Graham reduction algorithm to the hypergraph for $\mathbf{R}_a = \{ABC, BCD, CDE\}$. The labeled arrows represent applications of the corresponding reduction rule.

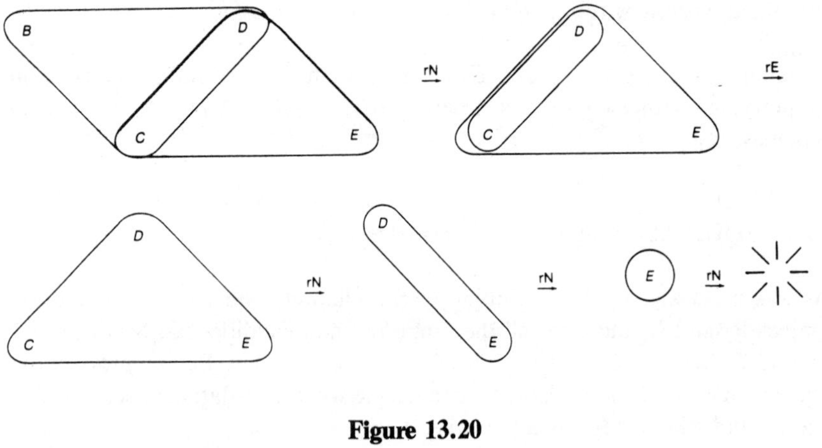

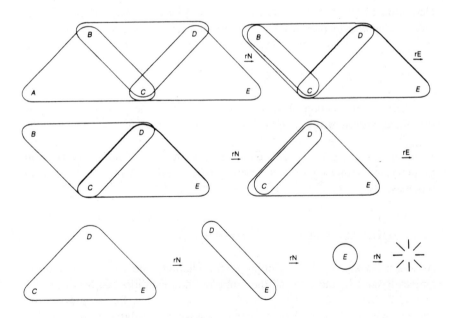

Figure 13.20

Example 13.23 Figure 13.21 shows the stages in applying Graham reduction to $\mathbf{R}_c = \{ABC, BCD, CE, DE\}$.

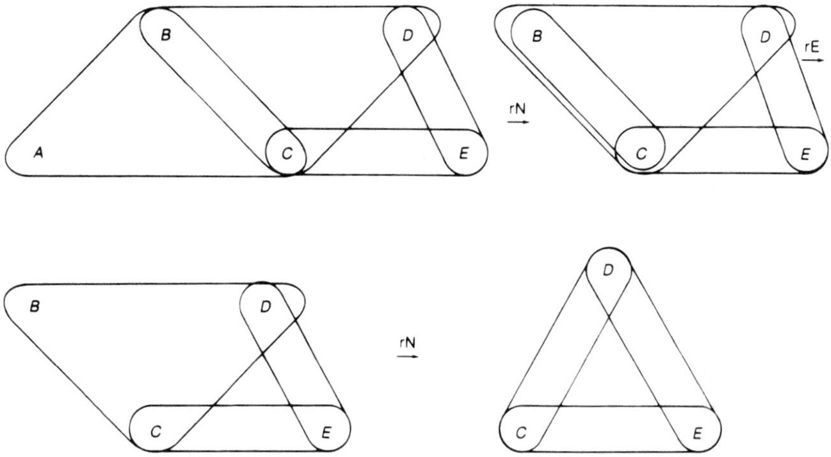

Figure 13.21

We say the Graham reduction *succeeds* on hypergraph H if the result of applying the Graham reduction algorithm to H is the empty hypergraph, as for $\mathbf{R}_a$ above.

13.3.2 Finding Join Trees

In this section we assume the reader is familiar with algorithms for finding minimum-weight spanning trees of undirected graphs with weighted edges. We shall actually be interested in finding *maximum-weight* spanning trees. Since all spanning trees for a graph have the same number of edges, an algorithm for finding a minimum-weight spanning tree can be converted to an algorithm for maximum-weight spanning trees by negating edge weights.

For the following definitions we assume a database scheme $\mathbf{R} = \{R_1, R_2, \ldots, R_p\}$ over $\mathbf{U}$ and an intersection graph G for $\mathbf{R}$.

Definition 13.20 For attribute $A \in \mathbf{U}$, the *class of* A, denoted $CLASS(A)$, is $\{R_i | A \in R_i \text{ and } R_i \in \mathbf{R}\}$. The *weight of* A, denoted $WT(A)$, is $|CLASS(A)| - 1$. The *weight of* $\mathbf{R}$, $WT(\mathbf{R})$, is

$$\sum_{A \in \mathbf{U}} WT(A).$$

Definition 13.21 The *weight of* A *in* G, denoted $WT(A,G)$ is the number of edges in G that contain A in their labels. The *weight of* G, denoted $WT(G)$, is

$$\sum_{A \in U} WT(A,G).$$

Definition 13.22 For an edge e in G, the *weight of* e, denoted $WT(e)$, is $|L(e)|$. Observe that $WT(G)$ could also be computed as

$$\sum_{e \in G} WT(e)$$

Example 13.24 Let G be the join graph in Figure 13.22 for the database scheme $\mathbf{R} = \{ABC, BD, CDE, DEI, IJK\}$. For $\mathbf{R}$,

$$\begin{array}{ll} WT(A) = 0 & WT(E) = 1 \\ WT(B) = 1 & WT(I) = 1 \\ WT(C) = 1 & WT(J) = 0 \\ WT(D) = 2 & WT(K) = 0 \end{array}$$

and so $WT(\mathbf{R}) = 6$. For G,

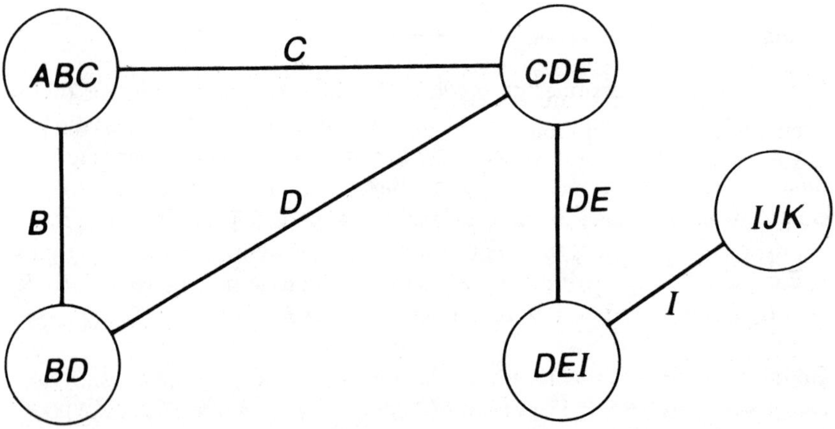

Figure 13.22

$WT(A,G) = 0$	$WT(E,G) = 1$
$WT(B,G) = 1$	$WT(I,G) = 1$
$WT(C,G) = 1$	$WT(J,G) = 0$
$WT(D,G) = 2$	$WT(K,G) = 0$

and so $WT(G) = 6$.

Theorem 13.1 If a database scheme $\mathbf{R} = \{R_1, R_2, \ldots, R_p\}$ has a join tree G, then any maximum-weight (edge weight) spanning tree for $I_{\mathbf{R}}$ is a join tree. Furthermore, G is a maximum-weight spanning tree for $I_{\mathbf{R}}$ and $WT(G) = WT(\mathbf{R})$.

Proof First, we show that in G, $WT(A)$ must equal $WT(A,G)$ for any attribute A. There are $WT(A) + 1$ nodes in G that contain A. It requires at least $WT(A)$ edges to construct A-paths between every pair. Hence, $WT(A,G) \geq WT(A)$. Any edge e with $A \in L(e)$ must connect elements of $CLASS(A)$. If G contained more than $WT(A)$ edges with A in their label, those edges would form a cycle among some set of the nodes in $CLASS(A)$. Hence $WT(A,G) \leq WT(A)$, so $WT(A,G) = WT(A)$. It follows that $WT(G) = WT(\mathbf{R})$.

G is a spanning tree for $I_{\mathbf{R}}$. Suppose there is another spanning tree G' for $I_{\mathbf{R}}$ with weight greater than G. There must be an attribute A with $WT(A,G) < WT(A,G')$. By the remarks in the last paragraph, G' must contain a cycle among some nodes in $CLASS(A)$, contradicting the choice of G'. G must be a maximum-weight spanning tree.

Finally, let G' be any maximum-weight spanning tree of $I_{\mathbf{R}}$. By previous arguments, for any attribute A, $WT(A) = WT(A,G) = WT(A,G')$. Since G' is a tree, and there are $WT(A)$ edges with A in their label in G', any two members of $CLASS(A)$ must be connected by an A-path in G'. Hence G' is a join tree.

Theorem 13.1 gives a reasonably efficient test for the existence of join trees for a database scheme R. Find $I_{\mathbf{R}}$ (only edges with non-empty labels are necessary) and then find a maximum-weight spanning tree G for $I_{\mathbf{R}}$. If G is a join tree, then, obviously, $\mathbf{R}$ has a join tree. If G is not a join tree, then $\mathbf{R}$ has no such tree.

Example 13.25 Figure 13.18 shows a maximum-weight spanning tree G for $I_{\mathbf{R}}$, where $\mathbf{R} = \{ABC, BD, CDE, DEI, IJK\}$. G is not a join tree, so $\mathbf{R}$ has no join tree, as was noted before.

Example 13.26 Figure 13.19 shows a maximum-weight spanning tree G for $I_{\mathbf{R}_a}$, where $\mathbf{R}_a = \{ABC, BCD, CDE\}$. As noted before, G is a join tree for $\mathbf{R}_a$.

13.3.3 The Equivalence Theorem for Acyclic Database Schemes

Theorem 13.2 Let **R** be a connected database scheme. The following conditions are equivalent:

1. **R** is acyclic
2. Graham reduction succeeds on **R**.
3. **R** has a join tree.
4. **R** has a full reducer.
5. PC implies TC for **R**.
6. **R** has the running intersection property.
7. **R** has the increasing join property.
8. *RED*(**R**) is a unique 4NF decomposition.
9. The maximum weight spanning tree for $I_{\mathbf{R}}$ is a join tree.
10. $MVD(\mathbf{R}) \models *[\mathbf{R}]$.

Proof The proof will proceed via a series of lemmas. The equivalence of 3 and 9 was established in Theorem 13.1. The method for the rest of the equivalence is $1 \Rightarrow 2 \Rightarrow 3 \Rightarrow 4 \Rightarrow 5 \Rightarrow 1$, $3 \Rightarrow 6 \Rightarrow 7 \Rightarrow 5$, $8 \Longleftrightarrow 1$, $3 \Rightarrow 10$. The implication of any other condition by 10 is left as Exercise 13.36. The lemmas for these implications are shown in Figure 13.23.

Lemma 13.2 If $\mathbf{R} = \{R_1, R_2, \ldots, R_p\}$ is an acyclic database scheme, then Graham reduction succeeds on **R**.

The proof of Lemma 13.2 proceeds through four propositions. The first two show that the Graham reduction algorithm neither creates nor destroys blocks. The second two show that one of the two removal rules is always applicable to an acyclic hypergraph.

Proposition 13.1 The Graham reduction algorithm preserves blocks.

Proof Let $H = (\mathcal{N}, \mathcal{E})$ be a hypergraph such that $H_{\mathcal{M}}$ is a block for some $\mathcal{M} \subseteq \mathcal{N}$. Let H' be obtained from H by one application of rE (edge removal). $H_{\mathcal{M}}$ must be the same as $H'_{\mathcal{M}}$ because reduction is applied in forming an induced hypergraph. If $E \subseteq F$ is the edge removed, then $E \cap \mathcal{M} \subseteq F \cap \mathcal{M}$, so E makes no contribution to $H_{\mathcal{M}}$.

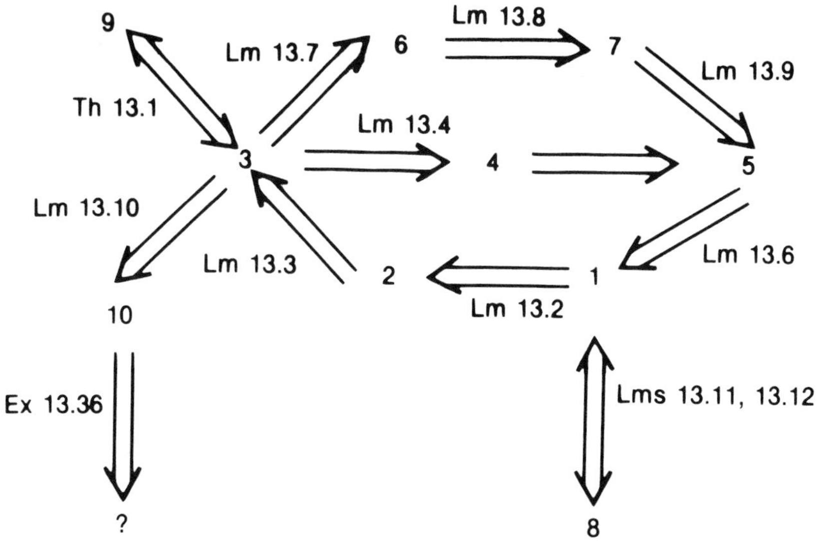

Figure 13.23

Suppose now that rule rN (node removal) was used on node A to obtain H'. If $A \notin \mathcal{M}$, and $H_{\mathcal{M}}$ is a block, then so is $H'_{\mathcal{M}}$. If $A \in \mathcal{M}$, and $H_{\mathcal{M}}$ is a block, we must show $H'_{\mathcal{M}-A}$ is a block. If $F = E_1 \cap E_2$ is an articulation set of $H'_{\mathcal{M}-A}$, then it must also be an articulation set of $H_{\mathcal{M}}$. E_1 or E_2 could be augmented by A in $H_{\mathcal{M}}$, but not both, since A appears in at most one edge of H. It follows F is the intersection of edges in $H_{\mathcal{M}}$. If removing F disconnects $H'_{\mathcal{M}-A}$, it will also disconnect H_{M}, since A cannot contribute to connectivity. We conclude that if H does not have an articulation set, neither does $H_{\mathcal{M}}$.

Application of either rE or rN preserves blocks, so Graham reduction preserves blocks.

Proposition 13.2 Graham reduction does not introduce blocks.

Proof Let $H = (\mathcal{N}, \mathcal{E})$ be a hypergraph. As noted in the last proof, if H' is obtained from H by rE, then $H_{\mathcal{M}} = H'_{\mathcal{M}}$ for any $\mathcal{M} \subseteq \mathcal{N}$. Hence, rE cannot introduce blocks.

Suppose H' is obtained from H by removing node A according to rN. Suppose $H_{\mathcal{M}}$ has an articulation set while $H'_{\mathcal{M}-A}$ is a block. $H_{\mathcal{M}-A} = H'_{\mathcal{M}-A}$, so H had a block to begin with. Since neither rE nor rN introduce blocks, Graham reduction does not introduce blocks.

If F is an articulation set of hypergraph $H = (\mathcal{N}, \mathcal{E})$, we say *F splits H* into subhypergraphs $H_1, H_2, \ldots, H_k$ if each H_i is one of the connected components in $H_{\mathcal{N}-F}$ with its partial edges augmented back to full edges by the addition of nodes from F. Note that $H_1, H_2, \ldots, H_k$ share no edges.

Example 13.27 BC is an articulation set for $H = (ABCDEIJ, \{ABC, BCD, BEI, CEJ\})$. BC splits H into

$$H_1 = (ABC, \{ABC\}),$$
$$H_2 = (BCD, \{BCD\}), \text{ and}$$
$$H_3 = (BCEIJ, \{BEI, CEJ\}).$$

Proposition 13.3 Let $H = (\mathcal{N}, \mathcal{E})$ be an acyclic hypergraph where $|\mathcal{E}| \geq 2$ and such that H is connected. H has an articulation set F that splits H into subhypergraphs $H_1, H_2, \ldots, H_k$ where each H_i contains an edge E_i with $F \subseteq E_i$. It follows that each H_i is a closed subhypergraph of H.

Proof Let H be an acyclic hypergraph with fewest nodes that violates the lemma. Let $F = E_1 \cap E_2$ be any articulation set of H that does not properly contain another articulation set. Let F split H into subhypergraphs $H_1, H_2, \ldots, H_k$. Suppose, without loss of generality, that $H_1 = (\mathcal{N}_1, \mathcal{E}_1)$ contains no edge containing F. Form a subhypergraph H' of H where $H' = (\mathcal{N}_1 \cup E_1, \mathcal{E} \cup \{E_1\})$. Any edge outside H' that intersects $\mathcal{N}_1 \cup E_1$ must do so within E_1, so H' is closed with respect to H. It follows that H' is the $(\mathcal{N}_1 \cup E_1)$-induced hypergraph for H.

Since H is acyclic, and H' is node-induced, H' must be acyclic (see Exercise 13.27). H' is smaller than H, so it has an articulation set $F' = E_3 \cap E_4$ that splits H' into subhypergraphs $H_1', H_2', \ldots, H_m'$ such that every H_i' contains an edge containing F'. We claim that F' is an articulation set for all of H. Let H_1' be the subhypergraph of H' containing E_1. If any edge E of H outside of H' touches $H_2', H_3', \ldots, H_m'$ outside of E_1, F could not have split off H_1 in the first place.

We further claim that F' splits H into $H_1'', H_2', H_3', \ldots, H_m'$, where H_1'' is H_1' plus all the nodes and edges from $H_2, H_3, \ldots, H_k$. That is, H_1'' is H_1' plus all of H outside of H_1. Certainly, F' splits $H_2', H_3', \ldots, H_m'$ from H. Can F' split the rest of H into more than one subhypergraph? All of $H_2, H_3, \ldots, H_k$ touch H_1', since they all touch E_1 in H_1'. Consider F' relative to F. If $F' \supseteq F$, then both E_3 and E_4 contain F, and H_1 would have had an edge containing F.

We must have that $F' \cap E_1 \subsetneq F$. $F' \cap E_1$ disconnects part of H outside of H_1, and $F' \cap E_1 = E_3 \cap E_1$ or $E_4 \cap E_1$, contradicting the minimality of F.

We have shown that if F does not meet the requirements of the lemma, then F' does, because each of H_1'', H_2', $\ldots$, H_m' contain an edge containing F'.

Definition 13.23 An edge E in hypergraph H is a *knob* if E contains at least one node contained in no other edge of H. Such a node is called a *solitary node*.

Example 13.28 In the hypergraph $H_1 = (ABCDE, \{ABC, BCD, CDE\})$, both ABC and CDE are knobs. A and E are solitary nodes. The hypergraph $H_2 = (ABCDE, \{ABC, BCD, CDE, ADE\})$ has no knobs.

Proposition 13.4 Any reduced, acyclic hypergraph H with two or more edges has at least two knobs.

Proof The proposition is clearly true for any reduced, acyclic hypergraph $H = (\mathcal{N}, \mathcal{E})$ where $|\mathcal{E}| = 2$. Assume the proposition holds when $|\mathcal{E}| = k - 1$ and consider the case where $|\mathcal{E}| = k$. Let F be an articulation set of H as guaranteed in Proposition 13.3. Let F split H into H_1, H_2, $\ldots$, H_k. Each H_i is closed with respect to H, hence node-induced, hence acyclic. Since H_i contains only edges from H, it is reduced.

Consider H_1. If H_1 has more than one edge, then, by induction, it has two knobs. Since some edge E_1 in H_1 contains F, at most one knob of H_1 can have all its solitary nodes contained in F. The other knob cannot intersect H_2, H_3, $\ldots$, H_k outside of F, or else F would not have split off H_1. Thus, the other knob is a knob for H. If H_1 is a single edge, that edge is a knob for H.

Since the same argument holds for H_2, H has two knobs.

Proof of Lemma 13.2 By Proposition 13.2, Graham reduction preserves acyclicity. At any point in Graham reduction of an acyclic hypergraph H, if H is not reduced, rE can be applied. If the intermediate result is reduced, Proposition 13.4 holds, or we are down to a single edge, so rN can be used to remove a solitary node. Since in Graham reduction, an application of a removal rule reduces the number of nodes or edges, the algorithm must eventually succeed in reducing H to the empty hypergraph.

Graham reduction cannot succeed on a cyclic hypergraph H. H must have at least three edges. If Graham reduction succeeded on H, there must have been an intermediate result with just two edges, which must therefore have been acyclic. Such an intermediate result contradicts Proposition 13.1.

Lemma 13.3 If Graham reduction succeeds on the hypergraph for a connected database scheme **R**, then **R** has a join tree.

Proof Let $\mathbf{R} = \{R_1, R_2, \ldots, R_p\}$. Running Graham reduction on **R** will never disconnect **R**. We build a join tree G for **R** as follows. Let $REM_j(R_i)$ be what remains of R_i before the jth step of the reduction. If the jth step applies rE to remove $REM_j(R_i)$ because it is contained in $REM_j(R_k)$, add edge (R_i, R_k) to G with label $R_i \cap R_k$.

The resulting graph G is clearly an intersection graph. G can have no cycles. Each node R_i in G is connected to at most one node R_k in G such that the remainder of R_k was removed after the remainder of R_i. Any cycle must contain an R_i connected to two nodes whose remainders were removed after the remainder of R_i in Graham reduction. G is a tree by the connectivity remark above.

Is G a join graph? Suppose not. Renumber the schemes in **R** so that there is an attribute $A \in R_1 \cap R_2$ but there is no A-path from R_1 to R_2 in G. Assume further that R_1 and R_2 were chosen so as to minimize the distance between them in the tree G. Finally, assume the remainder of R_1 was removed before the remainder of R_2. At some step j, we must have $REM_j(R_i) \subseteq REM_j(R_k)$, where $R_2 \neq R_k$. $REM_j(R_2)$ is non-empty when $REM_j(R_1)$ is removed. $A \in REM_j(R_1) \cap REM_j(R_2)$, because it could not have been a solitary node while the remainders of R_1 and R_2 are both non-empty. Therefore, $A \in REM_j(R_k)$. Pick a node of G as a root and orient G such that the remainder of any child node was removed before the remainder of its parent. In this orientation of G, R_k is the parent of R_1.

R_2 cannot be in the subtree of G headed by R_1. The path from R_1 to R_2 must go through R_k. There is a shorter path from R_k to R_2 than from R_1 to R_2. Since $A \in R_2 \cap R_k$, and by the minimum distance assumption for R_1 and R_2, there is an A-path from R_k to R_2 in G. The edge (R_1, R_k) has A in its label. We conclude there is an A-path from R_1 to R_2, a contradiction. G must be a join graph, and hence a join tree for **R**.

Lemma 13.4 Let **R** be a connected database scheme. If **R** has a join tree, then R has a full-reducer.

Before proceeding with the proof of Lemma 13.4, we need some notation.

If $\mathbf{R} = \{R_1, R_2, \ldots, R_p\}$ is a connected database scheme, and G is a join tree for **R**, let G_i represent G considered as an oriented tree with root R_i, $1 \leq i \leq p$. Let $d = \{r_1(R_1), r_2(R_2), \ldots, r_p(R_p)\}$ be a database over **R**. Consider a semijoin program $SP = sj_1, sj_2, \ldots, sj_k$ over d. Let j be a number between 1 and k. SP_j denotes the prefix $sj_1, sj_2, \ldots, sj_j$ of SP, which itself is a semijoin program. SP_0 is the semijoin program with no steps. For $R_\ell \in \mathbf{R}$, j is a *completion point for* R_ℓ *in* SP *relative to* G_i if

1. for every child R of R_ℓ in G_i, if r is the relation on R and r_ℓ is the relation on r_ℓ, SP_j contains a step $r_\ell \leftarrow r_\ell \ltimes r$, and
2. for no $j' < j$ does condition 1 hold.

That is, the completion point for R_ℓ is the step in SP at which the relation for R_ℓ has been semijoined with all the relations for children of R_ℓ. If j is the completion point (should one exist) for R_ℓ in SP relative to G_i, we write $CP_i(R_\ell) = j$. If R_ℓ has no completion point in SP relative to G_i, we let $CP_i(R_\ell)$ be undefined. If R_ℓ is a leaf of G_i, let $CP_i(R_\ell) = 0$.

Example 13.29 Let $R = \{R_1, R_2, R_3, R_4, R_5\}$ be a database scheme where

$$R_1 = ABC \qquad R_3 = CDE \qquad R_5 = DJ.$$
$$R_2 = BCD \qquad R_4 = DI$$

Figure 13.24 contains a join tree G for R, which is oriented to be G_2. Let r_1, r_2, r_3, r_4, and r_5 be relations on R_1, R_2, R_3, R_4, and R_5, respectively. For the semijoin program SP =

1. $r_3 \leftarrow r_3 \ltimes r_4$
2. $r_3 \leftarrow r_3 \ltimes r_5$
3. $r_2 \leftarrow r_2 \ltimes r_1$
4. $r_2 \leftarrow r_2 \ltimes r_3$

$CP_2(R_3) = 2$ and $CP_2(R_2) = 4$. If we consider SP relative to G_3, shown in Figure 13.25, $CP_3(R_3)$ is undefined, since $r_3 \leftarrow r_3 \ltimes r_2$ does not occur in SP.

The semijoin program SP is *complete for* **R** *relative to* G_i if

1. $CP_i(R_\ell)$ is defined for every $R_\ell \in R$, and
2. if R is a child of R_ℓ in G_i, then $CP_i(R) < CP_i(R_\ell)$.

That is, by step $CP_i(R_\ell)$ in SP, the relation for R_ℓ, has been semijoined with the relations for all its children, whose relations, in turn, have been semijoined with the relations for all their children, and so forth.

Example 13.30 Let **R** and SP be as in Example 13.29. SP is complete for **R** relative to G_2, but not relative to G_1, G_3, or G_4.

For each G_i, there is at least one complete semijoin program for **R**. For example, do a postorder traversal of G_i and when a node is visited, a semijoin of the relation for the parent of the node with the relation for the node is added

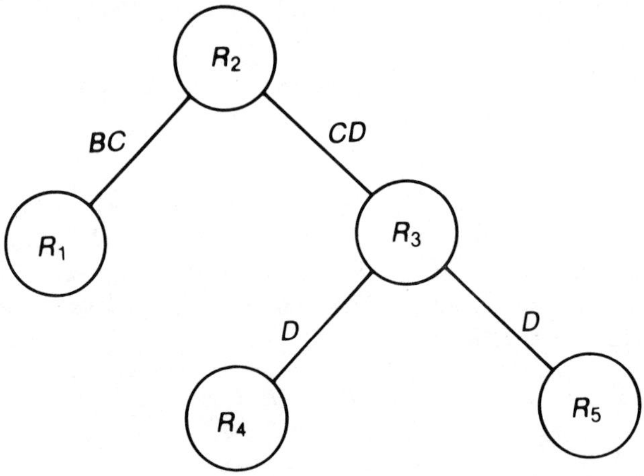

Figure 13.24

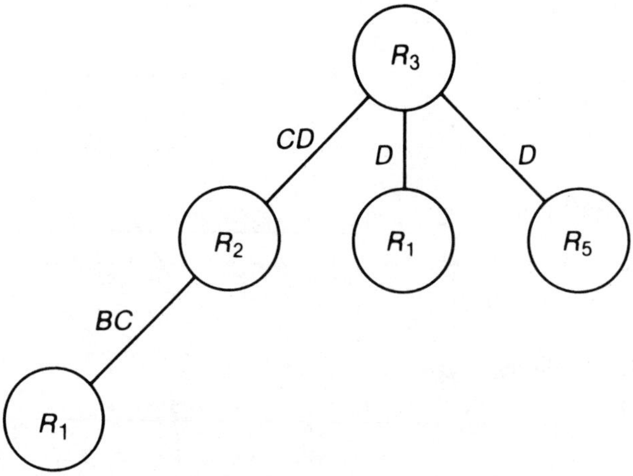

Figure 13.25

to the semijoin program. For each i, $1 \le i \le p$, let $SP(i)$ denote a minimal-length, complete semijoin program for **R** relative to G_i.

Example 13.31 Let **R** and SP be as in Example 13.29. If we use a postorder traversal of G_2, we get a complete semijoin program for **R**, $SP(2) =$

1. $r_2 \leftarrow r_2 \ltimes r_1$
2. $r_3 \leftarrow r_3 \ltimes r_4$
3. $r_3 \leftarrow r_3 \ltimes r_5$
4. $r_2 \leftarrow r_2 \ltimes r_3$.

$SP(2)$ is minimal-length.

Finally, some notation for the oriented trees $G_1, G_2, \ldots, G_p$. For $R_\ell \in \mathbf{R}$, $TREE_i(R_\ell)$ is the set of schemes in the subtree of G_i headed by R_ℓ. Note that $TREE_i(R_i) = \mathbf{R}$. The *extended scheme* of R_ℓ in G_i, $EX_i(R_\ell)$, is defined as

$$EX_i(R_\ell) = \cup \{R_j | R_j \in TREE_i(R_\ell)\}.$$

That is, $EX_i(R_\ell)$ is R_ℓ union all its descendents in G_i.

Proposition 13.5 Let $\mathbf{R} = \{R_1, R_2, \ldots, R_p\}$ be a connected database scheme and let G be a join tree for $\mathbf{R}$. Let $d = \{r_1(R_1), r_2(R_2), \ldots, r_p(R_p)\}$ be a database on $\mathbf{R}$. If SP is a complete semijoin program for $\mathbf{R}$ relative to G_i, then $SP(r_i,d) = FR(r_i,d)$.

Proof We prove a slightly stronger result. For $R_\ell \in R$, let d_ℓ be the subdatabase of d on the schemes in $TREE_i(R_\ell)$. Let $q = CP_i(R_\ell)$. We show that $SP_q(r_\ell,d) \subseteq FR(r_\ell,d_\ell)$. That is, at the completion point for R_ℓ in SP, r_ℓ is fully reduced relative to the relations for schemes in $TREE_i(R_\ell)$. Furthermore, for every tuple $t_\ell \in SP_q(r_\ell,d)$, there is a tuple $u_\ell \in \bowtie d_\ell$ such that $u_\ell(R_\ell) = t_\ell$. Note that the scheme for u_ℓ is $EX_i(R_\ell)$.

If R_ℓ is a leaf, the containment holds, for r_ℓ is fully reduced with respect to itself with no semijoins being applied. That is

$$SP_0(r_\ell,d) = FR(r_\ell, \{r_\ell\}).$$

Also $\bowtie d_\ell = r_\ell$, so for any tuple t_ℓ in r_ℓ, $\bowtie d_\ell$ contains a tuple $u_\ell(=t_\ell)$ such that $u_\ell(R_\ell) = t_\ell$.

Suppose now that R_ℓ is an interior node in G_i, with $q = CP_i(R_\ell)$ in SP. For notational convenience, assume $R_1, R_2, \ldots, R_m$ are the children of R_ℓ in G_i. We inductively assume the result holds for all of $R_1, R_2, \ldots, R_m$. Since SP is complete relative to G_i, $CP_i(R_j) < q$ for $1 \le j \le m$. At some point in SP_q, r_j was fully reduced relative to d_j. Furthermore, at that point, for every tuple $t_j \in t_j$, there is a tuple $u_j \in \bowtie d_j$ with $u_j(R_j) = t_j$. Can these properties be changed by semijoins subsequent to $CP_i(R_j)$? No. The only semijoins to worry about are those involving relations in d_j. Any semijoin that removes tuples from r_j will not change the properties. Any semijoins that remove tuples from other relations in d_j must involve only relations in d_j, which cannot remove tuples used in $\bowtie d_j$. (Why?)

Let t_ℓ be a tuple in $SP_q(r_\ell,d)$. We must exhibit a tuple u_ℓ in $\bowtie d_\ell$ such that $u_\ell(R_\ell) = t_\ell$. Since q is the completion point for R_ℓ, r_ℓ has been semijoined with all of $r_1, r_2, \ldots, r_m$ in SP_q. Each r_j, $1 \leq j \leq m$ must contain a tuple t_j that joins with t_ℓ. (Again, semijoins subsequent to $r_\ell \leftarrow r_\ell \ltimes r_j$ cannot change this fact.) In turn, for each t_j, $\bowtie d_j$ contains a tuple u_j with $u_j(R_j) = t_j$. We claim we can form u_ℓ by $t_\ell \bowtie u_1 \bowtie u_2 \bowtie \cdots \bowtie u_m$.

We must show that $t_\ell, u_1, u_2, \ldots, u_m$ are joinable. To show that t_ℓ joins with u_j, $1 \leq j \leq m$, we show that $R_\ell \cap EX_i(R_j) \subseteq R_j$. Note that $EX_i(R_j)$ is the scheme of u_j. If $A \in EX_i(R_j)$, then $A \in R$ for some $R \in TREE_i(R_j)$. If $A \in R$, then there is an A-path from R to R_ℓ in G_i. This path necessarily passes through R_j, so $A \in R_j$. A similar argument shows that for $1 \leq j_1 < j_2 \leq m$, $R_\ell \supseteq EX_i(R_{j_1}) \cap EX_i(R_{j_2})$, so u_{j_1} and u_{j_2} only overlap in R_ℓ. Since u_{j_1} and u_{j_2} both agree with t_ℓ on R, they agree with each other. Since $t_\ell, u_1, u_2, \ldots, u_m$ agree pairwise, they are joinable (see Exercise 13.3). If u_ℓ is the result of joining $t_\ell, u_1, u_2, \ldots, u_m$, obviously $u_\ell(R_\ell) = t_\ell$. We conclude $SP_p(r_\ell,d) \subseteq FR(r_\ell,d_\ell)$.

To conclude, we have, in particular, that $SP(r_i,d) = SP(r_i,d_i) \subseteq FR(r_i,d)$. Since it is always the case that $SP(r_i,d) \supseteq FR(r_i,d)$, we have $SP(r_i,d) = FR(r_i,d)$,

Proof of Lemma 13.4 Let G be a join tree for $\mathbf{R} = \{R_1, R_2, \ldots, R_p\}$. Let $SP(1)$ be a minimal length, complete semijoin program for R relative to G_1. Let $\overline{SP}(1)$ be the semijoin program obtained from $SP(1)$ by reversing the order of the steps and changing each step $r_i \leftarrow r_i \ltimes r_j$ to $r_j \leftarrow r_j \ltimes r_i$. We leave it to the reader to show that the semijoin program SP equal to $SP(1)$ followed by $\overline{SP}(1)$ is complete for $\mathbf{R}$ relative to any G_ℓ, $1 \leq \ell \leq p$ (see Exercise 13.28). Note that SP has $2p - 2$ steps; this number is necessary (see Exercise 13.29). By Proposition 13.5, $SP(r_\ell,d) = FR(r_\ell,d)$, $1 \leq \ell \leq p$, so SP is a full-reducer for $\mathbf{R}$.

Lemma 13.5 Let $\mathbf{R}$ be a connected database scheme. If $\mathbf{R}$ has a full reducer SP, then PC implies TC for $\mathbf{R}$.

Proof We show the contrapositive. Let d be a database on $\mathbf{R}$ that is PC but not TC. Any semijoin program SP for $\mathbf{R}$ leaves d unchanged, so SP cannot be a full reducer for $\mathbf{R}$.

For the next lemma, we need some additional concepts for hypergraphs. Let $H = (\mathcal{N}, \mathcal{E})$ be a connected hypergraph. An edge F in $\mathcal{E}$ is a *bottleneck* for H if $\mathcal{E} - \{F\}$ can be partitioned into two non-empty sets $\mathcal{E}_1$ and $\mathcal{E}_2$ such that for any $E_1 \in \mathcal{E}_1$ and $E_2 \in \mathcal{E}_2$, $E_1 \cap E_2 \subseteq F$. Removal of the nodes in F would disconnect H. Also, if $E_1, E_2, \ldots, E_k$ is a path in H from E_1 in $\mathcal{E}_1$ to E_k in $\mathcal{E}_2$, then for some i, $1 \leq i < k$, $E_i \cap E_{i+1} \subseteq F$. Therefore, for an edge F not to be a bottleneck, every pair of edges in $\mathcal{E} - \{F\}$ must be connected by a path that avoids F: no two consecutive edges in the path have an intersection that lies entirely within F.

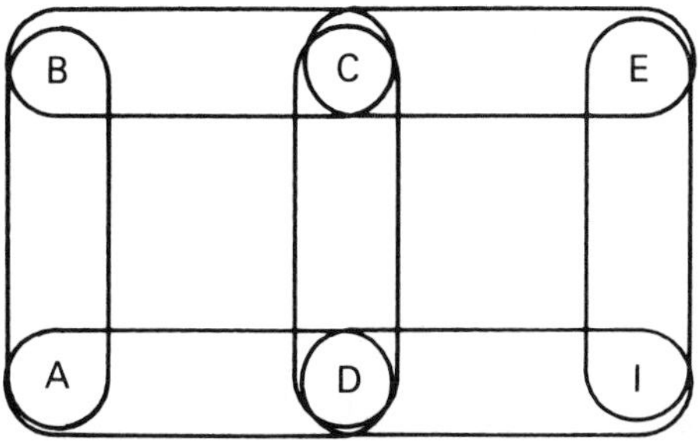

Figure 13.26

If F is a bottleneck to H relative to the sets $\mathcal{E}_1$ and $\mathcal{E}_2$, then the hypergraphs defined by $\mathcal{E}_1 \cup \{F\}$ and $\mathcal{E}_2 \cup \{F\}$ must be closed relative to H. Moreover, if H is cyclic, at least one of $\mathcal{E}_1 \cup \{F\}$ and $\mathcal{E}_2 \cup \{F\}$ is cyclic (see Exercise 13.30).

Lemma 13.6 Let **R** be a connected database scheme. If PC implies TC for **R**, then **R** is acyclic.

Proof We show the contrapositive: If **R** is cyclic then there exists a PC database d on **R** that is not TC. Let $\mathbf{R} = \{R_1, R_2, \ldots, R_p\}$ be a smallest counterexample to the contrapositive. **R** is cyclic, but every PC database d on **R** is TC. Let p be minimum among all such counterexamples, and let the number of attributes in **R** be minimum relative to p. Graham reduction leaves **R** unchanged. If Graham reduction changed **R** to **R**$'$, then **R**$'$ is smaller than **R** in attributes or schemes, and is not a counterexample. **R**$'$ thus has a PC database d' that is not TC. Database d' can be extended to a database d on **R** that is not TC, by Exercise 13.31.

Considering $\mathbf{R}$ as a hypergraph, since Graham reduction does not apply, no edge of $\mathbf{R}$ contains a solitary node, nor is that edge contained in another edge. $\mathbf{R}$ cannot contain a bottleneck. Suppose R_i is a bottleneck, and, for notational convenience, $\{R_1, R_2, \ldots, R_{i-1}\}$ and $\{R_{i+1}, R_{i+2}, \ldots, R_p\}$ are two sets of edges that R_i separates. Both $\mathbf{R}_1 = \{R_1, R_2, \ldots, R_i\}$ and $\mathbf{R}_2 = \{R_i, R_{i+1}, \ldots, R_p\}$ must define closed subhypergraphs of $\mathbf{R}$, at least one of which is cyclic. Say $\mathbf{R}_1$ is cyclic. $\mathbf{R}_1$ is smaller than $\mathbf{R}$ in number of schemes, so there is a database d_1 on $\mathbf{R}_1$ that is PC and not TC. Database d_1 can be extended into a PC database d on R by adding relations on $R_{i+1}, R_{i+2}, \ldots, R_p$ (see Exercise 13.32). Database d is not TC. (Why?) We have a contradiction to the definition of $\mathbf{R}$, so $\mathbf{R}$ must have no bottleneck.

We are now ready to construct a database on $\mathbf{R}$ that is PC but not TC. Let $A_1, A_2, \ldots, A_n$ be the attributes in R_1, and let $A_{n+1}, A_{n+2}, \ldots, A_q$ be the rest of the attributes in $\mathbf{R}$. We construct a relation $r(A_1 A_2 \cdots A_q)$ with n tuples $t_1, t_2, \ldots, t_n$, defined as

$$t_i(A_j) = \begin{cases} 1 \text{ if } i = j \\ 0 \text{ if } i \neq j \text{ and } j \leq n \\ i \text{ if } n < j \leq q. \end{cases}$$

Figure 13.27 shows relation r.

	$r(A_1$	A_2	$\ldots$	A_i	$\ldots$	A_n	A_{n+1}	A_{n+2}	$\ldots$	$A_q)$
t_1	1	0	$\ldots$	0	$\ldots$	0	1	1	$\ldots$	1
t_2	0	1	$\ldots$	0	$\ldots$	0	2	2	$\ldots$	2
$\vdots$					$\vdots$					
t_i	0	0	$\ldots$	1	$\ldots$	0	i	i	$\ldots$	i
$\vdots$					$\vdots$					
t_n	0	0	$\ldots$	0	$\ldots$	1	n	n	$\ldots$	n

Figure 13.27

Let $r_i = \pi_{R_i}(r)$ for $1 \leq i \leq p$. We claim that $r_2 \bowtie r_3 \bowtie \cdots \bowtie r_p = r$. Any two schemes in $\{R_2, R_3, \ldots, R_p\}$ are connected by a path that avoids R_1, since R_1 is not a bottleneck. Hence, any tuple $t \in r_2 \bowtie r_3 \bowtie \cdots \bowtie r_p$ must have the same value on each of $A_{n+1}, A_{n+2}, \ldots, A_q$. Suppose the value of t is i on all of these attributes. We show that $t = t_i$. Consider any scheme R_j, $2 \leq j \leq p$, that contains one or more attributes from among $A_1, A_2, \ldots, A_p$. Since $R_1 \not\supseteq R_j$, R_j also contains at least one attribute from among $A_{n+1}, A_{n+2}, \ldots, A_q$, say A_ℓ. If u_j is the tuple from r_j that contributed to t, then $u_j(A) = i$. It must be that $u_j = t_i(R_j)$. We conclude that t agrees with t_i wherever t is defined. Since no attribute in R_1 is solitary, t must be defined on all of $A_1 A_2 \cdots A_q$. We see that $r \supseteq r_2 \bowtie r_3 \bowtie \cdots \bowtie r_p$. The other containment is a direct property of project-join mappings, so $r = r_2 \bowtie r_3 \bowtie \cdots \bowtie r_p$.

Since $r_1, r_2, \ldots, r_p$ are all projections of the same relation, they are TC and hence PC. Let $s_1 = r_1 \cup \{\langle 0\,0 \ldots 0\rangle\}$. That is, s_1 is r_1 plus the tuple of all 0's. We claim that $s_1, r_2, r_3, \ldots, r_p$ are PC. For each R_j, $2 \le j \le p$,

$$\pi_{S_1 \cap S_j}(s_1) = \pi_{S_1 \cap S_j}(r_1)$$

since $S_1 \cap S_j \neq S_j$. The projection, in both cases, contains the tuple of all 0's plus every tuple with one 1 and 0's elsewhere. Thus, s_1 is consistent with each of $r_2, r_3, \ldots, r_p$, which are already known to be consistent among themselves.

The database $d = \{s_1, r_2, r_3, \ldots, r_p\}$ is a PC database on $\mathbf{R}$. However, d cannot be TC, since $r_2 \bowtie r_3 \bowtie \cdots \bowtie r_p = r$ and s_1 and r do not join completely. $\mathbf{R}$ cannot be a counterexample, and the lemma is proved.

Lemma 13.7 Let $\mathbf{R}$ be a connected database scheme. If $\mathbf{R}$ has a join tree then $\mathbf{R}$ has the running intersection property.

Proof Let $\mathbf{R} = \{R_1, R_2, \ldots, R_p\}$ and let G be a join tree for $\mathbf{R}$. Assume $R_1, R_2, \ldots, R_p$ are in preorder according to G_1. It follows that if R_j is an ancestor of R_k in G_1, then $j < k$. Consider any R_i for $2 \le i \le p$. One of $R_1, R_2, \ldots, R_{i-1}$ is the parent of R_i in G_1. Let it be R_j. None of $R_1, R_2, \ldots, R_{i-1}$ is a descendent of R_i. Let A be any attribute in $(R_1 R_2 \cdots R_{i-1}) \cap R_i$. There must be an A-path from R_i to one of $R_1, R_2, \ldots, R_{i-1}$, and this A-path necessarily passes through R_j. Hence $R_j \supseteq (R_1 R_2 \cdots R_{i-1}) \cap R_i$ and so $\mathbf{R}$ has the running intersection property.

Lemma 13.8 Let $\mathbf{R}$ be a connected database scheme. If $\mathbf{R}$ has the running intersection property then $\mathbf{R}$ has the increasing join property.

Proof Let $R_1, R_2, \ldots, R_p$ be an ordering of the schemes in R such that for $2 \le i \le p$, $(R_1 R_2 \cdots R_{i-1}) \cap R_i \subseteq R_j$ for some $1 \le j < i$. Let $d = \{r_1(R_1), r_2(R_2), \ldots, r_p(R_p)\}$ be a PC database on $\mathbf{R}$. Let JP be the join plan corresponding to the parenthesized join expression

$$(\cdots((r_1 \bowtie r_2) \bowtie r_3) \cdots \bowtie r_p).$$

We show inductively that

$$\pi_{R_j}(r_1 \bowtie r_2 \bowtie \cdots \bowtie r_i) = r_j \text{ for } 1 \le j \le i,$$

which means $r_1, r_2, \ldots, r_i$ are TC.

The basis is immediate. Since r_1 and r_2 are consistent, $\pi_{R_1}(r_1 \bowtie r_2) = r_1$ and $\pi_{R_2}(r_1 \bowtie r_2) = r_2$. Suppose the hypotheses are true for $i - 1$. Consider r_i. Let R_j be a scheme such that $j < i$

$$R_j \supseteq (R_1 R_2 \cdots R_{i-1}) \cap R_i = S.$$

Since $\pi_{R_j}(r_1 \bowtie r_2 \bowtie \cdots \bowtie r_{i-1}) = r_j$, it follows that $\pi_S(r_1 \bowtie r_2 \bowtie \cdots \bowtie r_{i-1}) = \pi_S(r_j)$. Since r_i is consistent with r_j, r_i joins completely with $\pi_S(r_j)$ and hence with $r_1 \bowtie r_2 \bowtie \cdots \bowtie r_{i-1}$. Since $r_1, r_2, \ldots, r_{i-1}$ join completely, so do $r_1, r_2, \ldots, r_i$. It follows that

$$\pi_{R_i}(r_1 \bowtie r_2 \bowtie \cdots \bowtie r_i) = r_i$$

and, more generally, that

$$\pi_{R_j}(r_1 \bowtie r_2 \bowtie \cdots \bowtie r_i) = r_j, \text{ for } 1 \le j \le i.$$

Since the joins

$$r_1 \bowtie r_2 \bowtie \cdots \bowtie r_i \text{ for } 2 \le i \le p$$

are exactly the joins corresponding to the interior nodes of join plan *JP*, we see that *JP* is a monotone join plan. Thus, **R** has the increasing join property.

Lemma 13.9 Let **R** be a connected database scheme. If **R** has the increasing join property, then PC implies TC for databases for **R**.

Proof Let *JP* be a monotone join plan for **R** and let *d* be a PC database on **R**. *JP* gives a method to join all the relations in *d* such that no tuples are lost along the way. Therefore, *d* is TC.

Lemma 13.10 Let **R** be a connected database scheme. If **R** has a join tree, then $MVD(R) \models *[\mathbf{R}]$.

Proof Let $\mathbf{R} = \{R_1, R_2, \ldots, R_p\}$ and let G be a join tree for **R**. Recall that G_1 is G viewed as an oriented tree with R_1 as the root. Choose any R_i, $2 \le$

$i \le p$, and let R_j be its parent in G_1. Let $S_i = EX_1(R_i)$. That is, S_i is the union of all the schemes in the subtree headed by $\mathbf{R}_i$. Let S_j be the union of all the rest of the schemes in $\mathbf{R}$. We claim $S_i \cap S_j = R_i \cap R_j$.

$S_i \cap S_j \supseteq R_i \cap R_j$ is immediate because $S_i \supseteq R_i$ and $S_j \supseteq R_j$. To see the other inclusion, the presence of any A in $S_i \cap S_j$ implies an A-path through R_i and R_j, so that $A \in R_i \cap R_j$. We thus have the equality.

From the remarks after Lemma 13.1, we now know that $*[\mathbf{R}] \models *[S_i, S_j]$. In MVD notation, $*[S_i, S_j]$ is $R_i \cap R_j \twoheadrightarrow S_i|S_j$. We use G_1 as a plan for chasing the tableau $T_\mathbf{R}$ so as to yield the row of all distinguished variables. We show, recursively, that for each R_i, $1 \le i \le p$, we can derive a row that is a's (distinguished variables) on exactly $EX_1(R_i)$ in computing $chase_{MVD(\mathbf{R})}(T_\mathbf{R})$. Since $EX_1(R_1) = R_1\, R_2\, \cdots\, R_p$, establishing this result proves the lemma.

If R_i is a leaf in G_1, then $EX_1(R_i) = R_i$ and we have a row distinguished exactly on R_i in $T_\mathbf{R}$ initially. If R_i is an interior node in G_1, let $Q_1, Q_2, \ldots, Q_k$ be its children. Assume that $T_\mathbf{R}$ has been chased under $MVD(\mathbf{R})$ to a tableau $T'_\mathbf{R}$ that has a row w_j distinguished on $EX_1(Q_j)$ for $1 \le j \le k$. Let v be the row that is distinguished on R_i. For each Q_j, we have that $R_i \cap Q_j \twoheadrightarrow EX_1(Q_j)$ by the initial paragraphs of this proof. Applying $R_i \cap Q_j \twoheadrightarrow EX_1(Q_j)$ to v and w_j for $1 \le j \le k$ will transform v into the row distinguished on exactly $R_i \cup EX_1(Q_1) \cup EX_1(Q_2) \cdots \cup EX_1(Q_k)$. That is, v is distinguished $EX_1(R_i)$. Note that the distinguished variables that $R_i \cap Q_j \twoheadrightarrow EX_1(Q_j)$ adds to v are not removed by $R_i \cap Q_\ell \twoheadrightarrow EX_1(Q_\ell)$, $j \ne \ell$, since $R_i \supseteq EX_1(Q_j) \cap EX_1(Q_\ell)$.

We shall shortly be looking at tight decompositions of a scheme $\mathbf{U}$ relative to a set of MVDs, where the set is $MVD(\mathbf{R})$ for a database scheme $\mathbf{R}$ over $\mathbf{U}$. If (S_1,S_2) is a tight decomposition of $\mathbf{U}$ relative to $MVD(\mathbf{R})$, there can be no MVD $*[S_1',S_2']$ in $MVD(\mathbf{R})$ such that $S_1' \cap S_2'$ is properly contained in $S_1 \cap S_2$. Since $MVD(\mathbf{R}) \models *[S_1,S_2]$, $*[S_1,S_2]$ must be in $MVD(\mathbf{R})$. Thus $\mathbf{R}$ can be partitioned into $\mathbf{R}_1$ and $\mathbf{R}_2$ such that $\cup\mathbf{R}_1 = S_1$ and $\cup\mathbf{R}_2 = S_2$. For the proof of the next lemma, we need the following proposition.

Proposition 13.6 Let $\mathbf{R}$ be a reduced, connected, acyclic database scheme over $\mathbf{U}$. Suppose (S_1,S_2) is a tight decomposition of $\mathbf{U}$ relative to $MVD(\mathbf{R})$. The set $X = S_1 \cap S_2$ is an articulation set for $\mathbf{R}$.

Proof Let $\mathbf{R}$ be partitioned into $\mathbf{R}_1$ and $\mathbf{R}_2$ such that $\cup\mathbf{R}_1 = S_1$ and $\cup\mathbf{R}_2 = S_2$. The removal of the attributes in X surely disconnects $\mathbf{R}$, so the only way X can fail to be an articulation set is by not being the intersection of two edges in $\mathbf{R}$ (treating $\mathbf{R}$ as a hypergraph).

Assume that $\mathbf{R}_1$ has no edge containing X. We assume that every pair of edges in $\mathbf{R}_1$ is connected by a path in $\mathbf{R}_1$ that avoids X. If not, pick an edge R in $\mathbf{R}_1$. Move all the edges in $\mathbf{R}_1$ that are not connected to R, by a path that avoids X, to $\mathbf{R}_2$. By the minimality of $S_1 \cap S_2$, the movement of these edges preserves the property that $(\cup \mathbf{R}_1) \cap (\cup \mathbf{R}_2) = X$.

We show a contradiction by showing that Graham reduction can never succeed on $\mathbf{R}$. In particular, we show that the nodes in X never get removed. Initially, any $A \in X$ is contained in an edge from $\mathbf{R}_1$ and an edge from $\mathbf{R}_2$, so it is not solitary. We show that Graham reduction preserves this property.

First we look at $\mathbf{R}_1$. Let $Y_1, Y_2, \ldots, Y_m$ be the maximal intersections of edges in $\mathbf{R}_1$ with X. That is, for each Y_i, $1 \leq i \leq m$, $\mathbf{R}_1$ contains an edge R_i such that $R_i \cap X = Y_i$ and for no other edge $R_j \in \mathbf{R}_1$ does $R_j \cap X$ properly contain $R_i \cap X$. For each Y_i, $1 \leq i \leq m$, there is a Y_j, $i \neq j$, with edges $R_i \supseteq Y_i$ and $R_j \supseteq Y_j$ in $\mathbf{R}_1$ such that R_i and R_j are connected by a path that avoids X. Let the path be $R_i = S_1, S_2, \ldots, S_k = R_j$. Node removal preserves this path, since no node in the intersection of successive edges can be solitary, and none of the nodes in Y_i or Y_j is solitary. If some edge S_ℓ in $S_1, S_2, \ldots, S_k$ is removed because it is contained in another edge Q, Q must be in $\mathbf{R}_1$, since S_ℓ contains a node not in X. If Q is not in the path, replace S_ℓ by Q in the path. All the properties of the path are preserved. If Q is already in the path, remove the portion of the path from S_ℓ to Q. Q cannot contain both $S_1(=R_1)$ and $S_m(=R_j)$ by the maximality of Y_i and Y_j. In this case also, all the properties of the path are preserved.

Thus, at every point in Graham reductions, Y_i is contained by an edge $R_i \subseteq \mathbf{R}_1$, and every node in X is contained in some Y_i, $1 \leq i \leq m$.

Consider the maximal intersections $Z_1, Z_2, \ldots, Z_n$ of edges in $\mathbf{R}_2$ with X. If for some Z_i, $1 \leq i \leq n$, there is a Z_j, $i \neq j$, with edges $R_i \supseteq Z_i$ and $R_j \supseteq Z_j$ with R_i and R_j connected by a path in $\mathbf{R}_2$ that avoids X, then there will always be an edge in $\mathbf{R}_2$ containing Z_i, by the argument above. If there is no such path, consider any $R_i \supseteq Z_i$ in $\mathbf{R}_2$. If R_i had nodes outside of X, then $\{R_i\}$ and $\mathbf{R} - \{R_i\}$ could have been used to form a decomposition of $\mathbf{U}$ that was "tighter" than (S_1,S_2). Hence $R_i \subseteq X$, and so $R_i = Z_i$. R_i cannot be contained in any other edge in $\mathbf{R}$, since $\mathbf{R}$ is reduced. Further, every node in R_i is contained in some edge of $\mathbf{R}_1$, so R_1 can never be reduced by node removal.

In either case, there is always an edge R_i in $\mathbf{R}_2$ containing Z_i during Graham reduction. Since every node in X is in some Y_i, $1 \leq i \leq m$, and some Z_j, $1 \leq j \leq n$, during Graham reduction, Graham reduction fails on $\mathbf{R}$, a contradiction. Both $\mathbf{R}_1$ and $\mathbf{R}_2$ must contain edges containing X, so X is an articulation set.

Lemma 13.11 Let $\mathbf{R}$ be a reduced, connected, acyclic database scheme. $\mathbf{R}$ is a unique 4NF decomposition.

Proof Let $\mathbf{R} = \{R_1, R_2, \ldots, R_p\}$ and let $\mathbf{U} = R_1 R_2 \cdots R_p$. We show that $\mathbf{R}$ is a unique decomposition for $\mathbf{U}$ under $MVD(\mathbf{R})$. We need only consider the case where $p \geq 2$. Since $\mathbf{R}$ must have articulation sets, there must be MVDs in $MVD(\mathbf{R})$ that can be used to decompose $\mathbf{U}$. By the discussion before Proposition 13.6, if (S_1, S_2) is a tight decomposition of $\mathbf{U}$ relative to $MVD(\mathbf{R})$, then $\mathbf{R}$ can be partitioned into $\mathbf{R}_1$ and $\mathbf{R}_2$ with $\bigcup \mathbf{R}_1 = S_1$ and $\bigcup \mathbf{R}_2 = S_2$. By Proposition 13.6, each of $\mathbf{R}_1$ and $\mathbf{R}_2$ includes an edge that contains $S_1 \cap S_2$. Thus, $\mathbf{R}_1$ and $\mathbf{R}_2$ are closed relative to $\mathbf{R}$.

Let M_i be the set of MVDs that $MVD(\mathbf{R})$ induces on S_i, $1 \leq i \leq 2$. We claim that M_i is equivalent to $MVD(\mathbf{R}_i)$. This claim is sufficient to prove the lemma. Since $\mathbf{R}_1$ and $\mathbf{R}_2$ are closed relative to $\mathbf{R}$, they are both reduced, connected, and acyclic. Every $R \in \mathbf{R}$ is in either S_1 or S_2. If we inductively assume that $\mathbf{R}_1$ is a unique decomposition for S_1 relative to $MVD(\mathbf{R}_1)$, and $\mathbf{R}_2$ is a unique decomposition for S_2 relative to $MVD(\mathbf{R}_2)$, then the claim allows us to conclude that $\mathbf{R}$ is a unique decomposition of $\mathbf{U}$ relative to $MVD(\mathbf{R})$.

Consider S_1 and $\mathbf{R}_1$. The claim follows from comparing chasing tableaux on S_1 under $MVD(\mathbf{R}_1)$ and chasing tableaux on $\mathbf{U}$ under $MVD(\mathbf{R})$. For a tableau T over S_1, let T *extended to* $\mathbf{U}$, denoted $T^{\mathbf{U}}$, be obtained by padding each row in T with new nondistinguished variables on $\mathbf{U} - S_1$. If w is a row in T, let $w^{\mathbf{U}}$ be the corresponding row in $T^{\mathbf{U}}$.

Suppose we are testing whether some MVD on S_1 is implied by $*[\mathbf{R}_1]$. Let T be the tableau for the MVD. Whatever changes made to T using $*[\mathbf{R}_1]$ can be mimicked on $T^{\mathbf{U}}$ using $*[\mathbf{R}]$ in such a way that $T^{\mathbf{U}}$ restricted to S_1 equals T. Suppose $\mathbf{R}_1 = \{R_1, R_2, \ldots, R_q\}$ and $\mathbf{R}_2 = \{R_{q+1}, R_{q+2}, \ldots, R_p\}$. Suppose the J-rule for $*[\mathbf{R}_1]$ is used on rows $w_1, w_2, \ldots, w_q$ in T to yield row v. For convenience, assume R_q is an edge in $\mathbf{R}_1$ containing $S_1 \cap S_2$. We can apply $*[\mathbf{R}]$ to rows $w_1^{\mathbf{U}}, w_2^{\mathbf{U}}, \ldots, w_q^{\mathbf{U}}, w_q^{\mathbf{U}}, \ldots, w_q^{\mathbf{U}}$ to yield a row $v^{\mathbf{U}}$ such that $v^{\mathbf{U}}(S_1) = v$. Therefore, if we ever arrive at the row of all distinguished variables in T, there is a row in $T^{\mathbf{U}}$ that is distinguished on S_1. Hence, any MVD on S_1 implied by $*[\mathbf{R}_1]$ is an embedded MVD on $\mathbf{U}$ implied by $*[\mathbf{R}]$. That is, the MVD is in M_1, so $MVD(\mathbf{R}_1) \subseteq M_1$.

To show the other containment, we use the following property of the chase. If the chase of a tableau is being computed under a single JD, then any row derived during the chase can be derived directly from the original rows in the tableau (see Exercise 13.33). Suppose we use the chase on a tableau T over $\mathbf{U}$ to show that $*[\mathbf{R}]$ implies an MVD embedded in S_1. The chase must have produced a row w that was distinguished on all of S_1. That row can be produced in one step from the original rows in T, by the property of the chase given above. It follows that if T' is T restricted to S_1, then the row of all distinguished variables can be produced in T' by one application of the J-rule for $*[\mathbf{R}_1]$. We conclude $M_1 \subseteq MVD(\mathbf{R}_1)$, so $M_1 = MVD(\mathbf{R}_1)$. By symmetry, $M_2 = MVD(\mathbf{R}_2)$, so the claim is established and the lemma is proved.

For the final lemma of this chapter, we need two more propositions and some definitions.

Proposition 13.7 Let M be a set of MVDs over **U**. Let $R \subseteq S \subseteq$ **U**. If M implies a nontrivial MVD $X \twoheadrightarrow Y$ embedded in R, then M implies some nontrivial MVD $X \twoheadrightarrow Z$ embedded in S.

Proof Left to the reader as Exercise 13.34.

The next lemma states that if **R** is a unique decomposition, then **R** is acyclic. We shall represent tight 4NF decompositions by trees.

Definition 13.24 Let M be a set of MVDs over **U**. A *decomposition tree* for **U** over M is a rooted binary tree with the following properties:

1. The nodes in G are labeled with subsets of **U**.
2. The root of G is labeled with **U**.
3. If a node labeled R has children labeled R_1 and R_2, then (R_1, R_2) is a tight 4NF decomposition of R relative to M.
4. If R labels a leaf of G, R is in 4NF relative to M.

Clearly, if G is a decomposition tree for **U** under M, then the labels of the leaves of G form a tight 4NF decomposition for **U** under M. If v is an interior node in G, we let $INT(v)$ be the intersection of the schemes of the children of v.

Example 13.31 Let **U** $= A\ B\ C\ D\ E$ and let $M = \{A \twoheadrightarrow B,\ D \twoheadrightarrow E\}$. Figure 13.28 shows a decomposition tree G for **U** under M. In G, $INT(v_1) = A$ and $INT(v_3) = D$.

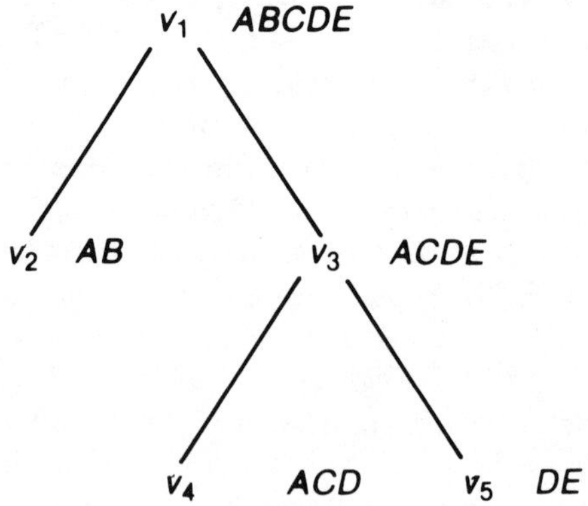

Figure 13.28

By Proposition 13.7, if v is an ancestor of w in a decomposition tree G, we cannot have $INT(v) \supsetneq INT(w)$, or else the decomposition at v was not tight. Further, the labels of nodes must be nonincreasing along every root-leaf path. That is, if v is an ancestor of w, the label of v contains the label of w. If x and y are nodes in G with labels R and S, but neither node is the ancestor of the other, then $R \not\supseteq S$. Let z be an ancestor of both x and y. $INT(z)$ must contain $R \cap S$. If $R \supseteq S$, then $R \cap S = S$. However, $S \supseteq INT(z)$, and so the decomposition at Z was trivial. It follows that no two leaves in G can be labeled with the same scheme.

Lemma 13.12 Let **R** be a connected database scheme. If **R** is a unique decomposition, then **R** is acyclic.

Proof We show that no cyclic database scheme can be a unique decomposition. First consider the case where **R** consists of a single block. Suppose **R** is a unique decomposition for **U** under a set M of MVDs. Let G be a decomposition tree for **U** under M. Consider an interior node v of G at one level up from the leaves. Let R be the label of the left child of v and S be the label of the right child, with $INT(v) = Y \cap Z = X$. Both Y and Z are schemes from **R**, since they label leaves of G. By Proposition 13.7, there must be some nontrivial MVD $X' \twoheadrightarrow W$ on **U** implied by M with $X' \subseteq X$. Assume that no nontrivial MVD on **U** implied by M has a left side contained in X'.

Construct another decomposition tree G' for **U** under M by using $X' \twoheadrightarrow W$ to decompose **U** at the first step. The other decompositions in G' are arbitrary. Since **R** is a unique decomposition relative to M, the labels on leaves of G' are the same as G, namely, all the schemes in **R**. Let $\mathbf{R}_1$ be all the labels of leaves in the left subtree of the root. Let $\mathbf{R}_2$ be the corresponding set for the right subtree. $\mathbf{R}_1$ and $\mathbf{R}_2$ are disjoint by the remarks before this lemma. The removal of X' separates $\mathbf{R}_1$ from $\mathbf{R}_2$. Since Y and Z are in **R**, and $Y \cap Z = X \supseteq X'$, **R** has an articulation set. (Note that no edge may be contained in X.)

The remainder of the proof is left to the reader as Exercise 13.35. The strategy is to show that if **R** is cyclic and is a unique decomposition, but has an articulation set, then a smaller counterexample to the lemma could be found by breaking **R** at the articulation set.

13.3.4 Conclusions

We have seen several syntactic and operational characterizations for acyclic schemes. The exercises present more characterizations. One interesting class of questions about cyclic schemes is how they may be transformed or altered to produce acyclic schemes. Some possibilities are merging schemes, adding attributes to relation schemes, deleting attributes from relation schemes, breaking the database scheme into acyclic components, and adding new relation schemes. Unfortunately, most of these modifications are NP-complete if the minimum modification is sought. Another area for further work is how to exploit local acyclicity in a database scheme that is globally cyclic. Also, much work is going on in determining how data dependencies ameliorate the effects of cyclicity.

13.4 EXERCISES

13.1 Consider the database scheme $\mathbf{R}_a = \{ABC, BCE, CDE\}$. Give a database $d(\mathbf{R}_a) = \{r_1(ABC), r_2(BCD), r_3(CDE)\}$ and two full-reducers SP_1 and SP_2 such that SP_1 is beneficial to apply to d before computing $r_1 \bowtie r_2 \bowtie r_3$, but S_2 is not. Assume that all domain values have a transmission cost of 1, the cost of $r_i \ltimes r_j$ is the cost of transmitting r_j's projection on r_i's scheme, and the join is to be computed at the site of r_1.

13.2 Can the assignment $r \leftarrow r \ltimes s$ change r if the schemes of r and s do not intersect?

13.3 Show that a database d where every relation has a single tuple can always be fully reduced with semijoins. (Alternatively, PC implies TC for d.)

13.4 Let $\mathbf{R} = \{R_1, R_2, \ldots, R_p\}$ be a database scheme. Suppose $*[\mathbf{R}] \models *[S_1, S_2]$. Show that there is a pair of relation schemes S_1', S_2' such that for some function

$$f: \{1, 2, \ldots, p\} \rightarrow \{1, 2\}$$

we have

$$S_i' = \bigcup_{f(j)=i} R_j,\ i = 1, 2$$

and $*[S_1', S_2'] \models *[S_1, S_2]$.

13.5* If $\mathbf{R}$ has p schemes, how big can $MVD(\mathbf{R})$ be?

13.6 For the database schemes $\mathbf{R}_a$ and $\mathbf{R}_c$ in Example 13.4, verify that $MVD(\mathbf{R}_a) = *[\mathbf{R}_a]$ while $MVD(\mathbf{R}_c) \not\models *[\mathbf{R}_c]$.

13.7* Show that if $MVD(\mathbf{R}) \models *[\mathbf{R}]$, then there is a set of MVDs M equivalent to $MVD(\mathbf{R})$ with no more elements than schemes in $\mathbf{R}$.

13.8 Let **R** be a database scheme over **U**. What is the time complexity of the obvious algorithm to test if a relation $r(\mathbf{U})$ satisfies $*[\mathbf{R}]$? (The obvious algorithm is computing $m_{\mathbf{R}}(r)$.) How fast can satisfaction of $*[\mathbf{R}]$ be tested if $MVD(\mathbf{R}) \models *[\mathbf{R}]$? (Use Exercise 13.7.)

13.9 Give a "non-tight" decomposition of $A\ B\ C\ D\ E\ I$ under the MVDs $\{BC \twoheadrightarrow E,\ CD \twoheadrightarrow I\}$.

13.10 Show that if **R** is a unique decomposition of **U**, then $MVD(\mathbf{R})$ uniquely decomposes **U**.

13.11 Consider the database scheme $\mathbf{R}_c = \{ABC, BCD, CE, DE\}$ from the examples.

(a) Show that $\mathbf{R}_c$ is not a unique decomposition.

(b) Show two tight 4NF database schemes for $A\ B\ C\ D\ E$ under $MVD(\mathbf{R}_c)$.

13.12 Prove that if a database d is TC it must also be PC.

13.13 Show that for any $n \geq 3$ there is a database d of n relations such that any $n - 1$ relations join completely but d is not TC.

13.14 Verify that any way of computing $r_1 \bowtie r_2 \bowtie r_3 \bowtie r_4$ using pairwise joins for the database in Figure 13.6 gives at least one intermediate result that is not the complete join of its child relations.

13.15* Let **R** be a database scheme such that for any join plan P for **R** there exists a database $d(\mathbf{R})$ such that $P(d)$ is not monotone. Show that there is a database $\hat{d}$ that is such that $P(\hat{d})$ is not monotone for *any* join plan for **R**.

13.16 Let P be the join plan of Figure 13.9 and let d be the database in Figure 13.6. Verify that $P(d)$ is not monotone.

13.17 Show that the database $\mathbf{R}_c = \{ABC, BCE, CE, DE\}$ has no monotone join plan.

13.18 Can a database scheme have a join plan P where $P(d)$ is never monotone (excluding a database of empty relations)?

13.19 Enumerate all the reduced hypergraphs on five nodes (up to isomorphism).

13.20 Let H be a non-reduced cyclic hypergraph and let H' be its reduction. Show that $H'_{\mathfrak{M}}$ could be a block while $H_{\mathfrak{M}}$ is not, for some $\mathfrak{M}$. Can H have no blocks at all?

13.21 Determine whether each of the following database schemes are cyclic or acyclic.

(a) $\{ABC, CDE, AIE, ACE\}$

(b) $\{ABC, BCD, ACD, ABD\}$

(c) $\{AB, BD, CD, CE, DE\}$

13.22 Prove that a hypergraph is acyclic if and only if it is closed-acyclic.

13.23 Find join trees for the acyclic schemes in Exercise 13.21.

13.24 Show that the acyclic schemes in Exercise 13.21 have the running intersection property.

13.25 Show that the hypergraph for a database scheme **R** consists of a single connected component if and only if every join graph for **R** is connected.

13.26 Find a join tree for each acyclic database scheme in Exercise 13.21.

13.27 Show that if $H = (\mathcal{N}, \mathcal{E})$ is an acyclic hypergraph, then so is $H_{\mathcal{M}}$ for any $\mathcal{M} \subseteq \mathcal{N}$.

13.28 Let $\mathbf{R} = \{R_1, R_2, \ldots, R_p\}$ be a connected database scheme with join tree G. Let $SP(1)$ be a complete semijoin program for R relative to G_1. Show that $SP = SP(1); \overline{SP(1)}$ is a complete semijoin program for any G_ℓ, $1 \leq \ell \leq p$, where $\overline{SP}(1)$ is $SP(1)$ reversed and with each step $r_i \leftarrow r_i \ltimes r_j$ changed to $r_j \leftarrow r_j \ltimes r_i$.

13.29* Let **R** be a database scheme. Show that if **R** has a full reducer SP, then SP must have at least $2 \cdot |\mathbf{R}| - 2$ steps.

13.30 Let $H = (\mathcal{N}, \mathcal{E})$ be a cyclic hypergraph. Let $F \in \mathcal{E}$ be a bottleneck for H relative to the partition $\mathcal{E}_1$, $\mathcal{E}_2$ of $\mathcal{E} - \{F\}$. Show that at least one of the hypergraphs defined by $\mathcal{E}_1 \cup \{F\}$ and $\mathcal{E}_2 \cup \{F\}$ is cyclic.

13.31 Let **R** be a connected database scheme and let **R**$'$ be **R** after applying Graham reduction. Show that if **R**$'$ has a PC database that is not TC, so does **R**.

13.32 Let $\mathbf{R} = \{R_1, R_2, \ldots, R_p\}$ be a connected database scheme. Suppose R_i is a bottleneck for R relative to $\{R_1, R_2, \ldots, R_{i-1}\}$ and $\{R_{i+1}, R_{i+2}, \ldots, R_p\}$. Let d' be a PC database on $\{R_1, R_2, \ldots, R_i\}$. Show that d' can be extended to a PC database on **R** by adding relations on $R_{i+1}, R_{i+2}, \ldots, R_p$.

13.33 Consider taking the chase of a tableau T under a single JD $*[R_1, R_2, \ldots, R_p]$. Let w be a row at any point in the chase. Show that for any R_i, $1 \leq i \leq p$, there is an original row v in the chase such that $w(R_i) = v(R_i)$.

13.34 Prove Proposition 13.7.

13.35 Complete the proof of Lemma 13.12.

13.36* Show that condition 10 of Theorem 13.2 implies one of the conditions 1-9.

Definition 13.25 Let $H = (\mathcal{N}, \mathcal{E})$ be a hypergraph and let $P = E_1, E_2, \ldots, E_m$ be a path in H. Define

$$F_i = E_i \cap E_{i+1},\ 1 \leq i \leq m.$$

P is *chordless* if there is no edge E in $\mathcal{E}$ that contains $F_i \cup F_j \cup F_k$ for some $1 \le i < j < k < m$. That is, no edge in $\mathcal{E}$ contains three intersections of adjacent edges in the path. P is a *cycle* if $E_1 = E_m$.

13.37 Let H be a hypergraph. Prove: H is acyclic if and only if H contains no chordless cycles of 3 or more edges (counting the first and last edge only once).

13.38 Give an example of an acyclic hypergraph with a cycle.

13.39* Let d be a database on scheme $\mathbf{R} = \{R_1, R_2, \ldots, R_p\}$. Show that if a full reducer exists for d, it must have at least $2p - 2$ semijoins.

Definition 13.26 Let d be a database on scheme $\mathbf{R}$. A semijoin program SP is a *maximal reducer* for d if for any state of d, after applying SP to d, no semijoin will further reduce d (although d need not be fully reduced after applying SP).

13.40* Show that if a database d on scheme $\mathbf{R}$ has no full reducer, then it has no maximal reducer.

13.41 Say a join plan JP is *sequential* if every right child in JP is a leaf. Show that a database scheme $\mathbf{R}$ has a monotone join plan if and only if it has a monotone, sequential join plan.

Definition 13.27 Let $H = (\mathcal{N}, \mathcal{E})$ be a hypergraph. The *graph for H*, G_H, is an ordinary, undirected graph on the nodes in $\mathcal{N}$ that contains an edge (A, B) exactly when A and B are contained in a single edge of $\mathcal{E}$.

Definition 13.28 Let G be an undirected graph. A *clique* of G is a subset of nodes of G such that every pair of nodes in the subset forms an edge in the graph. G is *chordal* if every cycle of 4 or more nodes has a *chord*: an edge in G connecting non-adjacent nodes in the cycle.

Definition 13.29 Let H be a hypergraph. H is *conformal* if every set of nodes $\mathcal{M}$ that is a clique of G_H is contained in a hyperedge of H. H is *chordal* if it is *conformal* and G_H is *chordal*.

13.42 Prove that a hypergraph H is acyclic if and only if it is chordal.

Recall that for a set of MVDs M and a set of attributes X, $DEP(X)$ is the dependency basis of X.

Definition 13.30 Let M be a set of MVDs. Let X be a *key* of M if X is the left side of an MVD in M. Two keys X and Y in M are *conflict-free* if we can write $DEP(X)$ and $DEP(Y)$ as

$$DEP(X) = \{V_1, V_2, \ldots, V_k, X_1, X_2, \ldots, X_m, Z_1 Y_1 Y_2 \cdots Y_n\}$$

and

$$DEP(Y) = \{V_1, V_2, \ldots, V_k, Y_1, Y_2, \ldots, Y_n, Z_2 X_1 X_2 \cdots X_m\}$$

such that

1. $Z_1 X = Z_2 Y$,
2. $DEP(X) \cap DEP(Y) = \{V_1, V_2, \ldots, V_k\}$, and
3. $DEP(X \cap Y) \supseteq \{V_1, V_2, \ldots, V_k\}$.

M is *conflict-free* if every pair of keys in M is conflict-free.

13.43 Prove that a database scheme R is acyclic if and only if $*[\mathbf{R}]$ is equivalent to a conflict-free set of MVDs.

13.44* Let **R** be a database scheme. Recall that $[\cdot]_{*\mathbf{R}}$ is the window function defined by total projections of $*[\mathbf{R}]$-weak instances. Give an algorithm to compute $[X]_{*\mathbf{R}}$ that is polynomial in the size of the database.

13.45 Let **R** be a cyclic database scheme.
- (a) Show that **R** can always be transformed to an acyclic scheme by the addition of a single relation scheme. (Don't think too hard.)
- (b) Give an algorithm that is polynomial in the size of **R** that determines the size of the smallest relation scheme that will make **R** acyclic.

13.5 BIBLIOGRAPHY AND COMMENTS

The first manifestations of acyclic database schemes came from work on semijoins and on comparing pairwise consistency versus total consistency. The first definition of semijoin was given by Hall, Hitchcock, and Todd [1975], who called the operation "generalized intersection." There is mention of "semijoin" about the same time, but the operation referred to has nothing to do with what we are calling semijoin. Semijoins are used extensively in the distributed query processing algorithms for SDD-1, a distributed database system developed by Rothnie, Bernstein, *et al.* [1981]. Bernstein and Chiu [1981] were the first to connect join trees with full reducers, although they handled only the case of semijoins on a single attribute. Bernstein and Goodman [1979a, 1979c] extended the theory to multiattribute semijoins. Theorem 13.1 is due to them. Several algorithms for finding minimum spanning trees may be found in Aho, Hopcroft, and Ullman [1974].

The interest in pairwise consistency and total consistency came from the problem of determining when a database is a projection of a common instance. Honeyman, Ladner, and Yannakakis [1980] showed the problem was NP-complete in general. Graham [1979] defined a large class of database schemes for which PC implies TC, but his class was a proper subset of the acyclic schemes. He gave the reduction algorithm, which was formulated independently by Yu and Ozsoyoglu [1979, 1980], although their algorithm is phrased in terms of join graphs. Honeyman [1980b] noted the connection between PC implying TC and the existence of full reducers, although his proof of equivalence is flawed.

Namibar [1979] was among the first researchers to formulate database scheme problems in terms of hypergraphs. The definition of acyclic database scheme, as well as the characterizations and equivalences not already attributed, comes from a series of papers by Fagin, Mendelzon, and Ullman [1980], Beeri, Fagin, Maier, Mendelzon, *et al.* [1981], and Beeri, Fagin, Maier, and Yannakakis [1981].

Bernstein and Goodman [1979b, 1980a] extend the theory of semijoins to involve inequality comparisons. Chiu and Ho [1980], and Chiu, Bernstein, and Ho [1980] give algorithms for finding the fastest full reducer for a given database state, provided a full reducer exists. Goodman and Shmueli [1980a, 1980b, 1981a, 1981b] examine a number of questions involving full-reducers and join trees, including reducers that use operations other than semijoins, the inapplicability of chase-type computation for determining if full reducers exist, generalizing cycles and cliques from graphs to hypergraphs and the complexity of modifying cyclic schemes to be acyclic. Chase [1981] also examines methods for eliminating acyclicity. Lien [1980] and Sciore [1981] look at sets of conflict-free MVDs, which can be used to characterize acyclic database schemes. Both argue that sets of MVDs that arise naturally from real world situations are conflict-free.

Yannakakis [1981] shows that acyclic schemes admit more efficient algorithms for some problems than cyclic schemes do. Katsuno [1981a] studies the interaction of acyclicity with FDs and MVDs. Maier and Ullman [1981] show that, in a certain sense, acyclic schemes are those where connections among sets of attributes are unique. Atzeni and Parker [1981] question the applicability of acyclic database schemes.

Exercises 13.7, 13.22, 13.41, 13.42, and 13.43 are from Beeri, Fagin, Maier, and Yannakakis [1981]. Exercise 13.13 is from Goodman and

Shmueli [1980a]. Exercise 13.28 is suggested by Bernstein and Chiu [1981]. Exercise 13.36 is answered by Fagin, Mendelzon, and Ullman [1980]. The "only if" direction of Exercise 13.37 is from Maier and Ullman [1981]. The "if" direction was noted by Kent Laver. Exercise 13.40 follows from Bernstein and Goodman [1979c]. The answer to Exercise 13.44 can be found in Yannakakis [1981]. Exercise 13.45b comes from Goodman and Shmueli [1981b].

Chapter 14

ASSORTED TOPICS

This chapter examines further topics in dependency theory, some limitations of relational algebra, and an extension of the relational model to include computed relations.

14.1 LOGIC AND DATA DEPENDENCIES

In this chapter we establish a connection between the theory of FDs and MVDs and a fragment of propositional logic. We give a way to interpret FDs and MVDs as formulas in propositional logic. For a set of dependencies **C** and a single FD or MVD c, we show that **C** implies c as dependencies if and only if **C** implies c under the logic interpretation. We first prove this result when **C** is FDs alone. We then extend the results to include MVDs, which complicates the proofs of the results considerably.

The correspondence between FDs and propositional formulas is direct. Let $X \rightarrow Y$ be an FD, where

$$X = A_1 A_2 \cdots A_m$$

and

$$Y = B_1 B_2 \cdots B_n.$$

The corresponding logical formula is

$$(A_1 \wedge A_2 \wedge \cdots \wedge A_m) \Rightarrow (B_1 \wedge B_2 \wedge \cdots \wedge B_n).$$

The A's and B's are viewed as propositional variables. The shorthand we use for this logical formula is $X \Rightarrow Y$. If X or Y is empty, we use *true* in place of the conjunction of variables. Thus, the corresponding logical formula for $X \rightarrow Y$ when $X = \emptyset$ is

$$true \Rightarrow B_1 \wedge B_2 \wedge \cdots \wedge B_n.$$

There is some easy evidence that this correspondence of FDs and formulas will give the desired equivalence of FD implication and logical implication: all the inference rules for FDs are valid inference rules for logic when the FDs are interpreted as logical formulas (see Exercise 14.1).

Example 14.1 Consider the transitivity rule for FDs:

$$X \rightarrow Y \quad \text{and} \quad Y \rightarrow Z \quad \text{imply} \quad X \rightarrow Z.$$

The corresponding rule for logical inference is

$$X \Rightarrow Y \quad \text{and} \quad Y \Rightarrow Z \quad \text{imply} \quad X \Rightarrow Z,$$

which is the transitive rule of inference for logic. If we know $A\,B \rightarrow C$ and $C \rightarrow D\,E$, we may conclude $A\,B \rightarrow D\,E$. Likewise, if we know $A \wedge B \Rightarrow C$ and $C \Rightarrow D \wedge E$, we may infer $A \wedge B \Rightarrow D \wedge E$.

14.1.1 The World of Two-Tuple Relations

In the rest of the material on dependencies and logic, we shall make extensive use of relations with only two tuples. By *the world of two-tuple relations* we mean dependency theory restricted to relations consisting of exactly two tuples. For FDs and MVDs, we shall see that implication in the world of two-tuple relations is the same as implication over unrestricted (finite) relations. The equivalence does not hold for JDs or embedded MVDs.

Let r be a relation over scheme R with exactly two tuples. Call them t_1 and t_2. Relation r can be used to define a truth assignment for the attributes in R, when they are considered as propositional variables.

Definition 14.1 Let r be a relation on scheme R. The *truth assignment for* r, denoted Ψ_r, is the function from R to $\{true, false\}$ defined by

$$\Psi_r(A) = \begin{cases} true \text{ if } t_1(A) = t_2(A) \\ false \text{ if } t_1(A) \neq t_2(A). \end{cases}$$

Example 14.2 Let $r(A\ B\ C\ D)$ be the relation in Figure 14.1. The truth assignment for r is given by

$$\Psi_r(A) = true$$
$$\Psi_r(B) = false$$
$$\Psi_r(C) = false$$
$$\Psi_r(D) = true.$$

$r(A$	B	C	$D)$
1	2	4	6
1	3	5	6

Figure 14.1

Lemma 14.1 Let $X \rightarrow Y$ be an FD over R and let r be a relation on R with two tuples, t_1 and t_2. $X \rightarrow Y$ is satisfied by r if and only if $X \Rightarrow Y$ is true under the truth assignment Ψ_r.

Proof (if) Let $X = A_1 A_2 \cdots A_m$ and let $Y = B_1 B_2 \cdots B_n$. If Ψ_r makes $X \Rightarrow Y$ true, then Ψ_r must make $A_1 \wedge A_2 \wedge \cdots \wedge A_m$ false or $B_1 \wedge B_2 \wedge \cdots \wedge B_n$ true. If $A_1 \wedge A_2 \wedge \cdots \wedge A_m$ is false, then for some i between 1 and m we have $t_1(X_i) \neq t_2(X_i)$. It follows that r satisfies $X \rightarrow Y$. If $B_1 \wedge B_2 \wedge \cdots \wedge B_n$ is made true by Ψ_r, then $t_1(Y) = t_2(Y)$, and so $X \rightarrow Y$ is again satisfied.

(only if) Left to the reader (see Exercise 14.3).

Example 14.3 Let $r(A\ B\ C\ D)$ be the relation from the last example. The FD $A \rightarrow D$ is satisfied by r, and Ψ_r makes $A \Rightarrow D$ true. Relation r does not satisfy $A \rightarrow B$, and Ψ_r makes $A \Rightarrow B$ false.

Lemma 14.2 Let $r(R)$ be a relation, let F be a set of FDs on R, and let $X \rightarrow Y$ be a single FD on R. If r satisfies F and violates $X \rightarrow Y$, then some two-tuple subrelation s of r satisfies F and violates $X \rightarrow Y$.

Proof The result is fairly immediate, and we do not include a proof. We only recall that if r satisfies F, so does any subrelation of r.

Example 14.4 Figure 14.2 shows a relation r on scheme $A\ B\ C\ D$ that satisfies the set of FDs $F = \{AB \rightarrow D,\ C \rightarrow D\}$ and violates $C \rightarrow B$. Figure 14.3 shows a two-tuple subrelation s of r that satisfies F and violates $C \rightarrow B$.

r(A	B	C	D)
1	2	4	6
1	2	5	6
1	3	5	6
1	3	4	6

Figure 14.2

s(A	B	C	D)
1	2	5	6
1	3	5	6

Figure 14.3

There is a certain set of two-tuple relations that we shall need in the proof of the next theorem. Let R be a relation scheme and let $X \subseteq R$. We let 2_X stand for the relation on R that consists of two tuples, t_1 and t_2, where t_1 is all 1's and t_2 is 1's on X and 0's elsewhere. The important point is that 2_X is a two-tuple relation where the tuples agree on exactly X.

Example 14.5 Figure 14.4 shows the relation 2_{AB} on scheme $A\ B\ C\ D$.

2_{AB}(A	B	C	D)
1	1	1	1
1	1	0	0

Figure 14.4

14.1.2 Equivalence of Implication for Logic and Functional Dependencies

Theorem 14.1 Let F be a set of FDs over scheme R and let $X \rightarrow Y$ be an FD over R. The following are equivalent.

1. F implies $X \rightarrow Y$.
2. F implies $X \rightarrow Y$ in the world of two-tuple relations.
3. F implies $X \Rightarrow Y$ as logical formulas.

Proof Obviously 1 $\Rightarrow$ 2. By Lemma 14.2, 2 $\Rightarrow$ 1. For 2 $\Rightarrow$ 3, we show the contrapositive, $\neg 3 \Rightarrow \neg 2$. Let Ψ be a truth assignment on R that makes every formula in F true, but makes $X \Rightarrow Y$ false. Let

$$Z = \{A \in R \mid \Psi(A) = \mathit{true}\}.$$

Consider the two-tuple relation 2_Z on R. By Lemma 14.1, 2_Z satisfies F (as FDs) but not $X \rightarrow Y$.

The proof is similar for 3 $\Rightarrow$ 2. Suppose F does not imply $X \rightarrow Y$ for two-tuple relations over R. Let $r(R)$ be a two-tuple relation satisfying the FDs in F and violating $X \rightarrow Y$. By Lemma 14.1, Ψ_r makes F true (as formulas), but makes $X \Rightarrow Y$ false.

14.1.3 Adding Multivalued Dependencies

In this section we add extend Lemmas 14.1 and 14.2 and Theorem 14.1 to include multivalued dependencies. Throughout this section, we shall assume that for an MVD $X \rightarrow\!\!\!\rightarrow Y$, the left and right sides are disjoint. The correspondence between MVDs and logical formulas is not quite as direct as for FDs. Let R be a relation scheme. Let $X = A_1 A_2 \cdots A_m$, $Y = B_1 B_2 \cdots B_n$, and $Z = C_1 C_2 \cdots C_p$ be a partition of R. The logical formula corresponding to $X \rightarrow\!\!\!\rightarrow Y$ is

$$(A_1 \wedge A_2 \wedge \cdots \wedge A_m) \Rightarrow ((B_1 \wedge B_2 \wedge \cdots \wedge B_n) \vee (C_1 \wedge C_2 \wedge \cdots \wedge C_p)).$$

For the cases where m, n, or p are 0, we assume the conjunction of 0 propositional variables is *true*. We abbreviate the formula above as $X \Rightarrow (Y \vee Z)$.

Example 14.6 The MVD $B \rightarrow\!\!\!\rightarrow A\ D$ on scheme $A\ B\ C\ D\ E$ corresponds to the logical formula $B \Rightarrow ((A \wedge D) \vee (C \wedge E))$.

We now introduce a few definitions for MVDs in connection with two-tuple relations. Let $X \rightarrow\!\!\!\rightarrow Y$ be an MVD on scheme R and let $r(R)$ be a two-tuple relation that satisfies $X \rightarrow\!\!\!\rightarrow Y$. We say r *actively* satisfies $X \rightarrow\!\!\!\rightarrow Y$ if the two tuples in r agree on X.

Lemma 14.3 Let R be a relation scheme, and let X, Y, and Z partition R. Let $r = \{t_1, t_2\}$ be a two-tuple relation on R. Relation r actively satisfies $X \rightarrow\!\!\!\rightarrow Y$ if and only if

1. $t_1(X) = t_2(X)$, and
2. $t_1(Y) = t_2(Y)$ or $t_1(Z) = t_2(Z)$.

Proof Left to the reader (see Exercise 14.5).

We now give the analogue of Lemma 14.1 with MVDs added.

Lemma 14.4 Let c be an FD or MVD over scheme R and let r be a two-tuple relation on R. The dependency c is satisfied by r if and only if c as a logical formula is true under the truth assignment Ψ_r.

Proof Let $r = \{t_1, t_2\}$. If c is an FD, we may appeal to Lemma 14.1, so let c be the MVD $X \twoheadrightarrow Y$, and let $Z = R - XY$.

(if) Ψ_r makes $X \Rightarrow (Y \vee Z)$ true. If Ψ_r makes X false, then $t_1(X) \neq t_2(X)$ in r. Thus r satisfies $X \twoheadrightarrow Y$. If Ψ_r makes X true, it must also make Y true or Z true. It follows that $t_1(X) = t_2(X)$ and either $t_1(Y) = t_2(Y)$ or $t_1(Z) = t_2(Z)$. Hence, by Lemma 14.3, $X \twoheadrightarrow Y$ is satisfied.

(only if) Suppose r satisfies $X \twoheadrightarrow Y$. If $t_1(X) \neq t_2(X)$, then Ψ_r makes X false, and hence makes $X \Rightarrow (Y \vee Z)$ true. If $t_1(X) = t_2(X)$, then r actively satisfies $X \twoheadrightarrow Y$. By Lemma 14.3, $t_1(Y) = t_2(Y)$ or $t_1(Z) = t_2(Z)$. It follows that Ψ_r makes Y true or Z true, so Ψ_r makes $X \Rightarrow (Y \vee Z)$ true.

Lemma 14.5 Let $r = \{t_1, t_2\}$ and $s = \{u_1, u_2\}$ be two-tuple relations over scheme R. Suppose for every attribute $A \in R$, $t_1(A) = t_2(A)$ implies $u_1(A) = u_2(A)$. If $X \twoheadrightarrow Y$ holds actively in r, it also holds actively in s.

Proof Left as Exercise 14.6.

The next lemma is the analogue of Lemma 14.2 with MVDs added. The proof is more complex than that for Lemma 14.2, since it is not the case that any subrelation of a relation satisfying an MVD also satisfies the MVD.

Lemma 14.6 Let r be a relation on scheme R, let $\mathbf{C}$ be a set of FDs and MVDs on R, and let c be a single FD or MVD on R. If r satisfies $\mathbf{C}$ and violates c, then some two-tuple subrelation s of r satisfies $\mathbf{C}$ and violates c.

Proof **Case 1** (c is an FD) Assume that c is $X \rightarrow A$. (Why is it permissible to assume that c has a single attribute on the right side?) By Lemma 14.2, there is at least one two-tuple subrelation of r that violates $X \rightarrow A$. Let s be one such relation, chosen to actively satisfy as many MVDs in $\mathbf{C}$ as any other such subrelation.

Relation s satisfies all the FDs in **C**. Let $W \twoheadrightarrow Y$ be an arbitrary MVD in **C**, where W, Y, and Z partition R. Call the two tuples in s u_1 and u_2. If $u_1(W) \neq u_2(W)$, then s satisfies $W \twoheadrightarrow Y$. Suppose $u_1(W) = u_2(W)$ but s does not actively satisfy $W \twoheadrightarrow Y$. We look at u_1 and u_2 in terms of their W, Y, and Z components. Let $u_1 = \langle w(W), y(Y), z(Z) \rangle$ and $u_2 = \langle w(W), y'(Y), z'(Z) \rangle$, where $y \neq y'$ and $z \neq z'$. Since s violates $X \rightarrow A$, u_1 and u_2 agree on X but not on A, so $A \in Y$ or $A \in Z$. Assume $A \in Y$.

Consider the relation $q(R)$ consisting of the two tuples $v_1 = \langle w, y, z \rangle$ and $v_2 = \langle w, y', z \rangle$. Relation q is a subrelation of r since r satisfies $W \twoheadrightarrow Y$. Now q violates $X \rightarrow A$ (why?), but actively satisfies $W \twoheadrightarrow Y$. By Lemma 14.5, q actively satisfies any MVD that s actively satisfies. The existence of q contradicts the choice of s, since q actively satisfies more MVDs from **C** than s does. The assumption that s violated $W \twoheadrightarrow Y$ must be incorrect. We conclude that s is the desired two-tuple relation.

Case 2 (c is an MVD) Let c be $X \twoheadrightarrow Y$, where X, Y, Z is a partition of R. We know that whatever two-tuple subrelation of r we choose will satisfy the FDs in **C**. Consider tuples in R broken into X, Y, and Z components. Since r violates $X \twoheadrightarrow Y$, there are tuples $t_1 = \langle x, y, z \rangle$ and $t_2 = \langle x, y', z' \rangle$ such that either $\langle x, y', z \rangle$ or $\langle x, y, z' \rangle$ is missing from r. Choose s to be such a pair $\{t_1, t_2\}$ where the number of MVDs that s actively satisfies is maximized.

Suppose s does not satisfy all the MVDs in **C**. Let $U \twoheadrightarrow V$ be an MVD in **C** that s does not satisfy. Let $W = R - UV$. We now look at t_1 and t_2 broken into U, V, and W components. Let $t_1 = \langle u, v, w \rangle$ and let $t_2 = \langle u, v', w' \rangle$. Define

$$V^* = \{A \in V \mid v(A) \neq v'(A)\}$$

and

$$W^* = \{A \in W \mid w(A) \neq w'(A)\}.$$

Neither V^* or W^* is empty, or else s would satisfy $U \twoheadrightarrow V$. Relation r satisfies **C**, so $t_3 = \langle u, v', w \rangle$ and $t_4 = \langle u, v, w' \rangle$ must be tuples in r. We consider two subrelations of r, $q_1 = \{t_1, t_3\}$ and $q_2 = \{t_2, t_4\}$. Since $v \neq v'$ and $w \neq w'$, q_1 and q_2 are two-tuple relations. Note that t_1 and t_3 disagree only on V^*, that t_2 and t_4 disagree only on W^*, and that t_1 and t_2 disagree on V^*W^*.

We show that q_1 and q_2 both actively satisfy more MVDs from **C** than s. The pairs t_1, t_3 and t_2, t_4 both agree in every attribute in which the pair t_1, t_2

agrees. Thus, by Lemma 14.5, q_1 and q_2 actively satisfy every MVD that s actively satisfies. Further, q_1 and q_2 both actively satisfy $U \twoheadrightarrow V$.

If either q_1 or q_2 violates $X \twoheadrightarrow Y$, we are done, for we then have a contradiction to the choice of s. Suppose q_1 and q_2 both satisfy $X \twoheadrightarrow Y$. They both must then actively satisfy $X \twoheadrightarrow Y$, since t_1, t_2, t_3, and t_4 all have the same X-value. By Lemma 14.3, since q_1 actively satisfies $X \twoheadrightarrow Y$, t_1 and t_3 agree on X, and they also agree on either Y or Z. If they agree on Y, then $V^* \subseteq Z$, since t_1 and t_3 only disagree on V^*. If t_1 and t_3 agree on Z, then $V^* \subseteq Y$. A similar argument on q_2 shows that $W^* \subseteq Z$ or $W^* \subseteq Y$.

If $V^* \subseteq Y$ and $W^* \subseteq Y$, then t_1 and t_2 agree on all of Z, which means s satisfies $X \twoheadrightarrow Y$. Thus, that combination of containments cannot hold. Similarly, $V^* \subseteq Z$ and $W^* \subseteq Z$ cannot hold simultaneously. The only remaining possibility for the combination is $V^* \subseteq Y$ and $W^* \subseteq Z$, or $V^* \subseteq Z$ and $W^* \subseteq Y$. By symmetry, we only examine the first possibility. We have $t_3 = \langle x, y', z \rangle$ and $t_4 = \langle x, y, z' \rangle$. One of $\langle x, y', z \rangle$ and $\langle x, y, z' \rangle$ was assumed missing from r in the construction of s, but t_3 and t_4 are both supposed to be in r. We have a contradiction to the supposition that q_1 and q_2 satisfy $X \twoheadrightarrow Y$.

We conclude that at least one of q_1 and q_2 violates $X \twoheadrightarrow Y$, which contradicts the choice of s. Our assumption that s violated some MVD in **C** must have been incorrect, so s is the desired two-tuple relation.

Theorem 14.2 Let **C** be a set of FDs and MVDs over scheme R and let c be a single FD or MVD over r. The following conditions are equivalent.

1. **C** implies c.
2. **C** implies c in the world of two-tuple relations.
3. **C** implies c when dependencies are interpreted as logical formulas.

Proof The proof is similar to that of Theorem 14.1. Lemmas 14.4 and 14.6 take the place of Lemmas 14.1 and 14.2. The details are left to the reader (see Exercise 14.7).

14.1.4 Nonextendibility of Results

The correspondence between logic and data dependencies cannot be extended to include JDs or embedded MVDs. This limitation is not too suprising when we note that implication for these types of dependencies is not the same in the world of two-tuple relations as it is for regular relations (see Exercise 14.9).

We show that no extension of our correspondence works for JDs; the corresponding proof for EMVDs is left as Exercise 14.10.

Suppose the correspondence between logic and data dependencies extended to JDs. Consider the JD $*[AB, BC, AC]$. Suppose that this JD has a corresponding logical formula f. Since $*[AB, BC, AC]$ follows from $A \twoheadrightarrow B$, $A \Rightarrow (B \vee C)$ should imply f. Likewise, considering $B \twoheadrightarrow C$, $B \Rightarrow (A \vee C)$ should imply f. Consider any truth assignment Ψ for $\{A, B, C\}$. If $\Psi(A) =$ *false*, then Ψ makes $A \Rightarrow (B \vee C)$ true, and so Ψ makes f true. If $\Psi(A) =$ *true*, then Ψ makes $B \Rightarrow (A \vee C)$ true, so it also makes f true. Formula f must be a tautology, since every truth assignment makes it true. However, $*[AB, BC, AC]$ does not always hold. We were in error assuming $*[AB, BC, AC]$ has a corresponding logical formula that is consistent with the logical interpretation that we gave to MVDs.

14.2 MORE DATA DEPENDENCIES

Why do we need more types of data dependencies? Are not FDs, MVDs, JDs and their embedded versions enough? There is some evidence that these dependencies do not form a natural class, that there is something missing. The class of sets of instances definable with FDs, MVDs, and JDs is not closed under projection. In Section 9.3 we saw that for a set F of FDs over scheme R, $\pi_X(SAT(F))$ cannot be described always as $SAT(F')$ for a set F' of FDs over X. We saw that a similar remark holds for MVDs. The remark also applies to JDs (see Exercise 14.11). Another problem is that there are no complete sets of inference axioms for embedded MVDs, and there is no known complete set of inference axioms for JDs. It has been shown that no such set of axioms exists for EMVDs, and there is evidence that no such rules exist for JDs. (See Bibliography and Comments at the end of this chapter.) While we do have the chase for determining implication of JDs, the fast implication algorithms for FDs and MVDs are based on inference axioms and not the chase. Also, the chase is an unwieldy tool for generating all dependencies of a given type that are implied by a set of dependencies.

The hope in studying larger classes of data dependencies is that a more general class will be found that contains FDs and JDs, and also avoids the problems mentioned above. Template dependencies and generalized functional dependencies are attempts to find such a class of more general dependencies. Template dependencies generalize JDs, and generalized functional dependencies generalize (you guessed it) FDs. These more general dependencies handle the first problem above. Sets of instances defined by satisfaction of these dependencies are closed under projection, as we shall see. These generalized dependencies do not do quite as well in solving the inference axiom problem. A complete set of inference axioms exists for template dependencies, but only for "infinite implication." That is, the axioms are complete for reasoning about implication in situations where relations are allowed to be infinite. We shall see that the inference axioms are not complete for implication where relations are restricted to be finite. We shall also see that there are an infinite number of inequivalent template dependencies over schemes of sufficiently large size, so it is generally not possible to generate all the template dependencies implied by a set of template dependencies.

The chase computation can be extended to template dependencies with a few modifications, but the tableaux that result from chasing with template dependencies can be infinite. Even though we are guaranteed to generate the "winning row" in the chase after a finite amount of time (if an implication holds), the chase cannot serve as a basis for a decision procedure for template dependency implication. One might imagine a decision procedure that simultaneously runs the chase to test a given implication and looks for counterexamples to the implication. This plan fails because there can be an infinite counterexample to a relation but no finite counterexample. It is not likely that any modification of this plan will work, for the implication problem has been shown undecidable for a slight generalization of template dependencies.

There are some subcases of the implication problem for template dependencies that are decidable. One is where we seek only implication by a single template dependency. Another case is where the template dependencies are not embedded. In both cases the chase computation terminates. In the latter case, the chase computation terminates even when generalized functional dependencies are added.

14.2.1 Template Dependencies

A template dependency is essentially a statement that a relation is invariant under a certain tableau mapping. When written down, a template dependency looks like a tableau with a special row at the bottom, somewhat like an upside-down tableau query. The special row is called the *conclusion row*; the other rows are the *hypothesis rows*. For a relation r to satisfy a template dependency, whenever there is a valuation ρ that maps the hypothesis rows to tuples in r, ρ also must map the conclusion row to a tuple in r. There is a slight complication to this informal definition, to handle variables in the conclusion row that do not appear in the hypothesis rows.

Example 14.7 Figure 14.5 shows a template dependency τ over scheme $A\ B\ C$. The hypothesis rows are w_1-w_4; w is the conclusion row. Relation r in Figure

14.6 does not satisfy τ, since the valuation ρ that maps w_i to t_i, $1 \leq i \leq 4$, does not map w to any tuple in r. Adding a tuple $t_5 = \langle 1\ 3\ 6 \rangle$ to r makes r satisfy τ, although this fact is tedious to check.

τ(	A	B	C)
w_1	a	b	c'
w_2	a	b'	c'
w_3	a	b'	c
w_4	a'	b	c
w	a	b	c

Figure 14.5

r(	A	B	C)
t_1	1	3	5
t_2	1	4	5
t_3	1	4	6
t_4	2	3	6

Figure 14.6

We now provide a formal definition for a template dependency and its satisfaction. While template dependencies are not exactly the same as tableaux, they are sufficiently similar so that tableau concepts, such as *valuation* and *containment mapping*, apply to the set of hypothesis rows in a template dependency. In the following definition, when we refer to a *row over scheme* R, we mean a tuple of abstract symbols or variables, as in tableaux. We do not make the distinguished-nondistinguished distinction on variables that we did with tableaux, however.

Definition 14.2 A *template dependency* (TD) on a relation scheme R is a pair $\tau = (T, w)$ where $T = \{w_1, w_2, \ldots, w_k\}$ is a set of rows on R, called the *hypothesis rows*, and w is a single row on R, called the *conclusion row*. A relation $r(R)$ *satisfies* TD τ if for every valuation ρ of T such that $\rho(T) \subseteq r$, ρ can be extended in such a way that $\rho(w) \in r$. TD τ is *trivial* if it is satisfied by every relation over R.

TDs are written as shown in Figure 14.5, with the conclusion row at the bottom, separated from the hypothesis rows by a line. For variables, we usually use lowercase letters corresponding to the attribute name or symbol, with the unprimed or unsubscripted version appearing in the conclusion row.

While TDs almost look like tableau mappings turned upside down, there are two differences:

1. A variable in the conclusion row need not appear in any hypothesis row.
2. Variables are not restricted to a single column.

To elaborate on point 1, a TD τ on scheme R where every variable in the conclusion row appears in some hypothesis row is called *full*. Let $w_1, w_2, \ldots, w_k$ be the hypothesis rows of τ and let w be the conclusion row. We say τ is S-*partial*, where S is the set

$$\{A \in R \mid w(A) \text{ appears in one of } w_1, w_2, \ldots, w_k\}.$$

Naturally, if $S = R$, then τ is full. If $S \neq R$, we say τ is *strictly partial.* If τ is S-partial, the conclusion row of τ specifies a tuple with certain values on the attributes in S, but it puts no restriction on the values for attributes in R-S.

Example 14.8 The TD τ on $A\ B\ C$ in Figure 14.7 is $A\ B$-partial.

τ(A	B	C)
a'	b'	c'
a'	b	c''
a	b'	c''
a	b	c

Figure 14.7

To elaborate on point 2, a TD where each variable appears in exactly one column is called a *typed* TD. If some variable appears in multiple columns, the TD is called *untyped*. The TDs in Figures 14.5 and 14.7 are typed. For the rest of our treatment of template dependencies, we shall assume that all TDs are typed, unless they are explicitly said to be untyped.

Example 14.9 Figure 14.8 shows an untyped TD τ. This TD assumes that $dom(A) = dom(B)$ and asserts that a relation is transitively closed (when considered as a binary relation in the mathematical sense).

$\tau(A$	$B)$
a	b
b	c
a	c

Figure 14.8

Any join dependency, full or embedded, can be represented as a TD (see Exercise 14.15).

Example 14.10 The MVD $A\ B \twoheadrightarrow C$ over relation scheme $A\ B\ C\ D\ E$ is equivalent to the TD τ in Figure 14.9. TD τ asserts that if a relation has two tuples t_1 and t_2 that agree on $A\ B$, it must also have a tuple t_3 such that $t_3(A\ B\ C) = t_1(A\ B\ C)$ and $t_3(A\ B\ D\ E) = t_2(A\ B\ D\ E)$, which is just a way of stating that the relation satisfies $A\ B \twoheadrightarrow C$.

$\tau(A$	B	C	D	$E)$
a	b	c	d'	e'
a	b	c'	d	e
a	b	c	d	e

Figure 14.9

Not every TD corresponds to a JD or EJD. First note that there are an infinite number of different TDs over a given relation scheme, while there are only a finite set of JDs over the same scheme. It could be that many of the TDs are equivalent, which is certainly the case for one-attribute schemes. For schemes with three or more attributes, we shall see that there are an infinite number of inequivalent TDs. Therefore, some of these TDs must not be equivalent to any JD. For schemes with two attributes, there are only three distinct TDs (see Exercise 14.19). The next example shows that one of those TDs is not equivalent to any JD.

Example 14.11 Consider the TD τ on scheme $A\ B$ in Figure 14.10. This TD is not trivial, for it is easy to construct a relation that does not satisfy τ. (Take the relation consisting of just the hypothesis rows of τ.) The only nontrivial JD over $A\ B$ is $*[A, B]$. However, τ is not equivalent to $*[A, B]$. Relation r in Figure 14.11 satisfies τ but not $*[A, B]$. To see that r satisfies τ, note that any valuation from τ to r maps w_1, w_2, and w_3 to the same tuple of r, and so maps w to that tuple.

	$\tau(A$	$B)$
w_1	a	b'
w_2	a'	b'
w_3	a'	b
w	a	b

Figure 14.10

$r(A$	$B)$
1	3
2	4

Figure 14.11

14.2.2 Examples and Counterexamples for Template Dependencies

In this section we see that there is a strongest TD over any scheme, as well as a weakest, nontrivial, full TD. We shall also exhibit a relation that obeys every strictly partial TD, but violates every full TD, thus showing that a set of strictly partial TDs cannot imply a nontrivial full TD.

Theorem 14.3 For any relation scheme R, there is a strongest TD τ on R. That is, any relation $r(R)$ that satisfies τ also satisfies any other TD τ' on R.

Proof The TD τ we want states that a relation is a column-wise Cartesian product. For example, on the scheme $A\ B\ C\ D$, the Cartesian product TD is shown in Figure 14.12. Any relation that is a Cartesian product satisfies every TD (see Exercise 14.21).

$\tau(A$	B	C	$D)$
a	b_1	c_1	d_1
a_1	b	c_2	d_2
a_2	b_2	c	d_3
a_3	b_3	c_3	d
a	b	c	d

Figure 14.12

While there is no weakest nontrivial TD in general (see Exercise 14.22b), there is a weakest full TD on any scheme with 2 or more attributes. Note that there are only trivial TDs over a scheme with a single attribute.

Theorem 14.4 For any relation scheme R with two or more attributes, there is a weakest nontrivial full TD τ on R. That is, if τ' is another nontrivial full TD on R, any relation $r(R)$ that satisfies τ' also satisfies τ.

Proof Assume $R = A_1 A_2 \cdots A_n$, where $n \geq 2$. For each A_i, τ has two variables in the A_i-column, a_i and b_i. Let $\tau = (T, w)$, where T contains every possible row of a's and b's, except the row of all a's. The conclusion row, w, is the row of all a's. Figure 14.13 shows TD τ when $R = A_1 A_2 A_3$.

Let $\tau' = (T', w')$ be another nontrivial full TD over R. The conclusion row w' cannot appear in T' (see Exercise 14.23). We show that τ' is stronger than τ by exhibiting a containment mapping ψ from τ' to τ. That is, ψ maps variables in τ' to variables in τ in such a way that $\psi(T') \subseteq T$ and $\psi(w') = w$. Thus, for any relation $r(R)$ and for any valuation mapping ρ on T such that $\rho(T) \subseteq r$, $\rho' = \rho \circ \psi$ is a valuation mapping for T' such that $\rho'(T') \subseteq r$. If r satisfies τ', then r contains $\rho'(w')$, which is the same as $\rho(w)$, so r satisfies τ.

For ease of notation while dealing with ψ, assume that the variables in τ' are renamed so that $w = w'$. For the A_i-column of τ', let ψ map a_i to a_i, and let it map any other variable to b_i. Clearly, $\psi(w') = w$. For any hypothesis row v of T', $\psi(v)$ will be a row of a's and b's (other than the row of all a's), so $\psi(v) \in T$. Therefore $\psi(T') \subseteq T$, and we are finished.

$\tau(A_1$	A_2	$A_3)$
b_1	b_2	b_3
b_1	b_2	a_3
b_1	a_2	b_3
b_1	a_2	a_3
a_1	b_2	b_3
a_1	b_2	a_3
a_1	a_2	b_3
a_1	a_2	a_3

Figure 14.13

Theorem 14.5 Let R be a relation scheme, and let **C** be a set of strictly partial TDs over R. **C** does not imply any nontrivial full TD over R.

Proof Let $R = A_1 A_2 \cdots A_n$. Consider the relation $r(R)$ that contains all tuples of n 0's and 1's, except the row of all 1's. Figure 14.14 shows r for $R = A_1 A_2 A_3$. Since the projection of r onto any proper subset of R is a Cartesian product relation, r satisfies every strictly partial TD. However, r violates the weakest nontrivial full TD, constructed in the proof of Theorem 14.3. The valuation ρ that maps a_i to 1 and b_i to 0, $1 \leq i \leq n$, maps the weakest TD into r, but ρ cannot be extended to the row of all a's. It follows that r violates any nontrivial full TD over R, and so r serves as a counterexample to any proposed implication of a full nontrivial TD by **C**.

$r(A_1$	A_2	$A_3)$
0	0	0
0	0	1
0	1	0
0	1	1
1	0	0
1	0	1
1	1	0

Figure 14.14

14.2.3 A Graphical Representation for Template Dependencies

Testing whether or not a relation r satisfies a TD τ is a tedious task at best, since it involves finding all valuations from the hypothesis rows of τ into the tuples of r. In this section we introduce a graphical representation for relations and TDs that makes finding such valuations somewhat easier, at least for small examples done by hand. Also, the graphical notation removes some extraneous details, and so gives a more concise method for expressing TDs in most cases.

The actual values in relations and the actual variables in TDs are of no importance in testing if a relation satisfies a TD. What is important is equalities among values and among variables. We use undirected graphs to represent relations and TDs. The nodes stand for tuples or rows, as the case may be; labeled edges between nodes indicate where two tuples or rows match.

Definition 14.3 Let r be a relation on scheme $R = A_1 A_2 \cdots A_n$. The *graph of* r, denoted G_r, is an undirected graph with labeled edges constructed as follows. The nodes of G_r are the tuples of r. For two tuples t_1 and t_2 in r, there is an edge (t_1, t_2) in G_r exactly when t_1 and t_2 agree on some attribute in R. The edge (t_1, t_2) is labeled by the set of attributes on which t_1 and t_2 agree.

Example 14.12 Let r be the relation in Figure 14.6. Figure 14.15 shows G_r, the graph of r. In drawing graphs of relations, we remove any edge from a node to itself (there is such an edge for every node), and sometimes omit edges that can be inferred by transitivity. Thus, we could just as well depict G_r as in Figure 14.16.

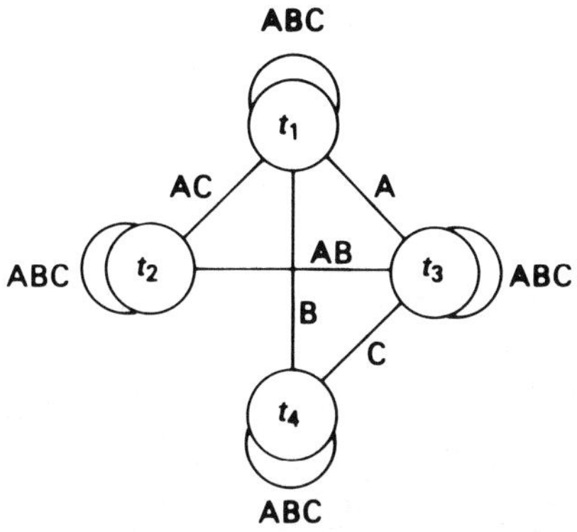

Figure 14.15

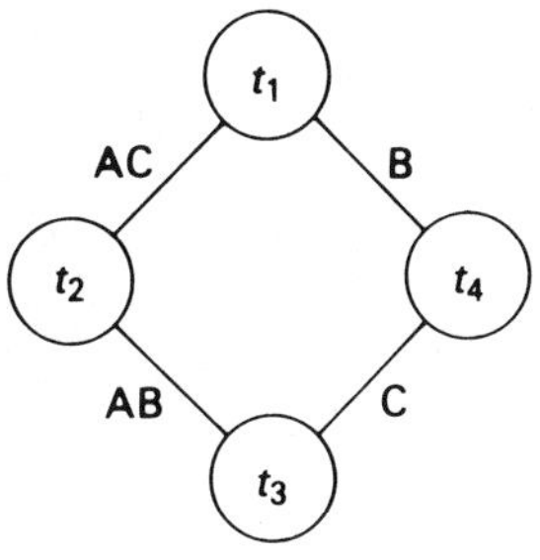

Figure 14.16

The graph for a TD τ, denoted G_τ, is defined similarly, except that we label the node for the conclusion row with a *.

Example 14.13 If τ is the TD from Figure 14.5, then G_τ is shown in Figure 14.17. Again, we omit self-loops and some edges implicit by transitivity.

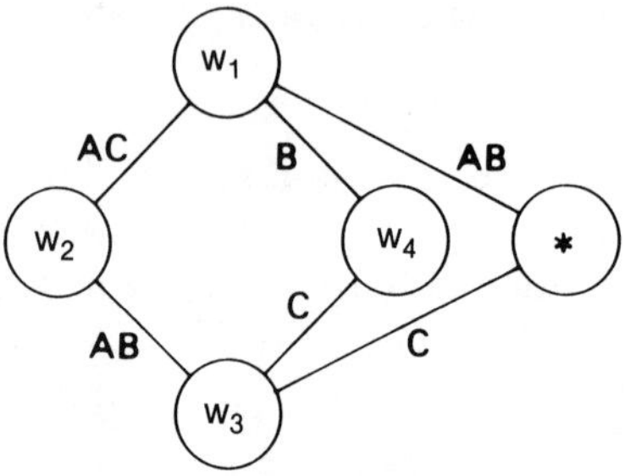

Figure 14.17

Since the order of tuples in a relation or the order of the hypothesis rows in a TD is unimportant, we shall sometimes label the nodes in the graph for a relation or TD arbitrarily. We make the proviso that the conclusion row in a TD will always be labeled *. Apart from *, we need not label the nodes at all, actually. We can also go from graphs to TDs. The transformation gives a unique TD, up to a one-to-one renaming of variables, as long as the scheme is given.

Example 14.14 The graph G in Figure 14.18 gives rise to the TD τ in Figure 14.19, when the scheme is assumed to be $A\ B\ C$.

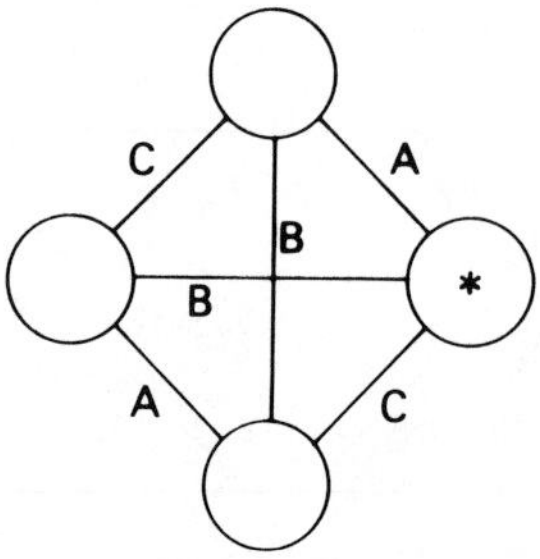

Figure 14.18

$\tau(A$	B	$C)$
a	b'	c'
a'	b	c'
a'	b'	c
a	b	c

Figure 14.19

We now define an analogue for valuation in terms of labeled graphs.

Definition 14.4 Let $G_1 = (N_1, E_1)$ and $G_2 = (N_2, E_2)$ be two undirected graphs whose edges are labeled with subsets of some set L. A mapping $h: N_1 \to N_2$ is a *label-preserving homomorphism* (lp-homomorphism) of G_1 to G_2 if for any edge $e = (v, w)$ in E_1, if L_1 is the label of e and L_2 is the label of $(h(v), h(w))$ in G_2, then $L_1 \subseteq L_2$.

Example 14.15 Let G_r be the graph in Figure 14.16 and let G_τ be the graph in Figure 14.17. The function h_1 defined as

$$\begin{aligned} h_1(w_1) &= t_1 \\ h_1(w_2) &= t_2 \\ h_1(w_3) &= t_2 \\ h_1(w_4) &= t_1 \\ h_1(*) &= t_1 \end{aligned}$$

is an lp-homomorphism from G_τ to G_r. (Recall that there are self-loops for all the nodes in G_r, although they are omitted from the figure.) The mapping h_2 defined as

$$\begin{aligned} h_1(w_1) &= t_1 \\ h_1(w_2) &= t_3 \\ h_1(w_3) &= t_3 \\ h_1(w_4) &= t_2 \\ h_1(*) &= t_2 \end{aligned}$$

is not an lp-homomorphism from G_r to G_τ, since, for example, (w_1, w_4) has label B in G_τ, but $(h(w_1), h(w_2)) = (t_1, t_2)$ has label $A\ C$.

We can express satisfaction of a TD by a relation in terms of lp-homomorphism between their graphs. In the following theorem, $G_\tau - \{*\}$ means the graph of TD τ without the node for * or its connecting edges.

Theorem 14.6 Let r be a relation over scheme R with graph G_r. Let τ be a TD over R with graph G_τ. Relation r satisfies τ if and only if for any lp-homomorphism h from $G_\tau - \{*\}$ to G_r can be extended to an lp-homomorphism from all of G_τ to G_r.

Proof Left to the reader (see Exercise 14.27).

Example 14.16 Let G_r be the graph in Figure 14.16 and let G_τ be the graph in Figure 14.17. (The same graphs as in the last example.) The mapping h defined as

$$h(w_1) = t_1$$
$$h(w_2) = t_2$$
$$h(w_3) = t_3$$
$$h(w_4) = t_4$$

is an lp-homomorphism from $G_\tau - \{*\}$ to G_r. Any extension of h to all of G_τ is not an lp-homomorphism. Suppose we extend h so that $h(*) = t_4$. This extension is not an lp-homomorphism since $(w_4, *)$ has label $A\ B$ in G_τ, but $(h(w_1), h(*)) = (t_1, t_4)$ has only label A in G_r.

We now give an application of graphical representation of TDs in proving that there are an infinite number of inequivalent full TDs over a scheme of three attributes. We first need the following lemma, which also is proved with the use of graphical representations.

Lemma 14.7 Let τ be a TD over relation scheme R. Let w' be a row over R such that if w' mentions any variable in the conclusion row of τ, some hypothesis row of τ also contains that variable. Form TD τ' by adding w' to the hypothesis rows of τ. Then τ implies τ'.

Proof By the choice of w', we can draw the graph $G_{\tau'}$ as G_τ with a node w' added such that no edges connect w' and $*$. Consider an arbitrary relation $r(R)$. Any lp-homomorphism h' from $G_{\tau'} - \{*\}$ to G_r can be restricted to an lp-homomorphism h from $G_\tau - \{*\}$ to G_r. If r satisfies τ, then h can be extended to all of G_τ. By the form of the graph $G_{\tau'}$, h' can therefore be extended to all of $G_{\tau'}$. Hence, if r satisfies τ, it also satisfies τ'.

Theorem 14.7 (progressively weaker chain) There is an infinite sequence τ_1, τ_2, τ_3, ... of full TDs such that τ_i implies τ_{i+1} for $i \geq 1$ and no two TDs in the sequence are equivalent.

Proof Consider the infinite graph G in Figure 14.20. For $i \geq 1$, let G_i be the sub-graph of G on nodes $\{*, 1, 2, \ldots, i+1\}$ and let τ_i be the TD corresponding to G_i. By Lemma 14.7, we have that τ_i implies τ_{i+1} for $i \geq 1$. To complete this proof, we need only show that no pair τ_i, τ_{i+1} of consecutive TDs are equivalent. We do so by exhibiting a relation r that violates τ_i but satisfies τ_{i+1}.

We construct r by treating the hypothesis rows of τ_i as a relation. Note that the graph G_r for r is just G restricted to the nodes $\{1, 2, \ldots, i+1\}$. Relation r is easily seen to violate τ_i. The mapping h defined as $h(j) = j$ for $1 \leq i \leq i+1$ is an lp-homomorphism from $G_i - \{*\}$ to G_r that cannot be extended to *.

We now must show that r satisfies τ_{i+1}. Let h be an arbitrary lp-homomorphism from $G_{i+1} - \{*\}$ to G_r. We prove that h can be extended to all of G_{i+1}. Since $G_{i+1} - \{*\}$ has one more node than G_r, h must map two nodes of $G_{i+1} - \{*\}$ to the same node of G_r. Suppose an odd-numbered node m and an even-numbered node n of $G_{i+1} - \{*\}$ get mapped to the same node of G_r. Node m agrees on A with all odd-numbered nodes of $G_{i+1} - \{*\}$ and n agrees on A with all even-numbered nodes. Since $h(m) = h(n)$, $h(j)$ must agree with $h(k)$ on A for any nodes j and k in $G_{i+1} - \{*\}$. In particular, $h(1)$ and $h(2)$ agree on A, so h can be extended to G_{i+1} by letting $h(*) = h(2)$.

We now show that a contradiction arises if we assume that h never maps an odd-numbered node and an even-numbered node of $G_{i+1} - \{*\}$ to the same node in G_r. Let $h(1) = j$. Consider the case where j is odd. Since $h(2)$ must agree with $h(1)$ on B and we assume $h(1) \neq h(2)$, $h(2)$ is forced to be $j+1$. For $h(3)$, since $h(2)$ and $h(3)$ must agree on C, but $h(2) \neq h(3)$, we must have $h(3) = j+2$. Continuing in this manner, we see that $h(k) = j+k-1$ for $1 \leq k \leq i+2$. However, we must then have $h(i+2) = j+i+1 \geq i+2$, which cannot happen since $i+1$ is the largest-numbered node in G_r.

In the case where j is even, we can show that $h(k) = j-k+1$ by a similar argument. We again run into a contradiction, since we must then have $h(i+2) = j-i-1$, which is less than 1 because j is no larger than $i+1$.

We see that h can always be extended to G_{i+1}. Hence, τ_{i+1} satisfies r, and we have shown τ_i and τ_{i+1} inequivalent.

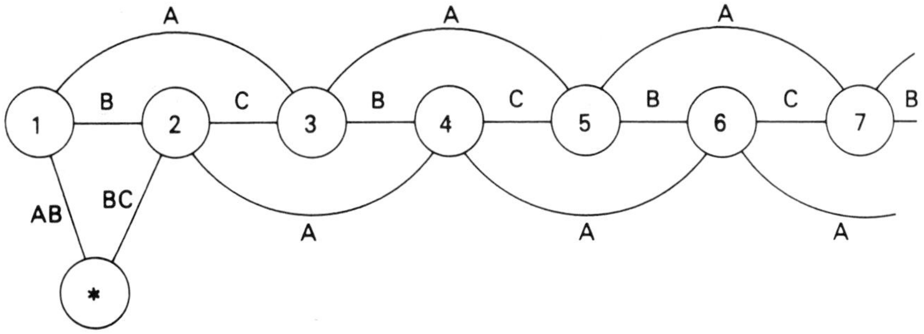

Figure 14.20

14.2.4 Testing Implication of Template Dependencies

In this section we take a short look at problems that arise in computing implications of TDs. The first problem is that certain implications holding for finite relations do not hold when relations are allowed to be infinite. Thus, it is unlikely that a complete set of TD inference axioms exists for finite relations, although such a set exists for arbitrary relations. The next theorem shows that implication is not the same for finite relations and arbitrary relations. By *arbitrary* relations we mean relations that may be finite or infinite.

Theorem 14.8 There is a set **C** of TDs and a single TD τ such that any finite relation that satisfies **C** also must satisfy τ, but there is an infinite relation that satisfies **C** yet violates τ.

Proof The proof is quite long. We sketch the proof here and leave the details to the reader (see Exercise 14.29).

Let $\mathbf{C} = \{\tau_1, \tau_2, \tau_3, \tau_4\}$ where τ_i corresponds to graph G_i, $1 \leq i \leq 4$, in Figures 14.21-24. There is a system behind the TDs in **C**. We interpret the graph G_r of a relation r as a directed graph D_r. A subgraph of G_r that matches Figure 14.25 is interpreted as the directed edge $t_1 \rightarrow t_3$ in D_r. TDs τ_1 and τ_2 together say that if D_r has an edge $u \rightarrow v$, then it also has an edge $v \rightarrow w$, for some w. That is, every node in D_r with an incoming edge also has an outgoing edge. (A node with no incoming edges is called a *sink*.) TD τ_3 basically forces D_r to be transitively closed. TD τ_4 comes into play when D_r has a self-loop edge $u \rightarrow u$. TD τ corresponds to the graph G in Figure 14.26.

The property from graph theory that is the mechanism behind this proof is that any finite directed graph that is transitively closed and has no sinks must have a self-loop. The property does not hold for infinite graphs. The proof that **C** implies τ for finite relations basically mimics the proof of the property from graph theory. First, the existence of an lp-homomorphism from $G - \{*\}$ to G_r, for some relation r, implies an edge in D_r. The presence of an edge implies a cycle in D_r reachable from the edge, otherwise, some node would be a sink (so r would violate τ_1 or τ_2). Once the cycle is established, transitivity (application of τ_3) provides the self-loop. The self-loop means τ_4 is applicable. The tuple that τ_4 requires in r is also the tuple that τ requires.

The infinite relation that satisfies **C** but violates τ is

$$r = \{\langle i\, i\, j\, 0\rangle \mid 1 \leq i < j\} \cup \{\langle 0\, i\, i\, i\rangle \mid i \geq 1\}.$$

A proof by cases shows that r satisfies each TD in **C**. However, the lp-homomorphism h from G to G_r defined by

$$h(1) = \langle 0\ 1\ 1\ 1 \rangle$$
$$h(2) = \langle 1\ 1\ 2\ 0 \rangle$$
$$h(3) = \langle 0\ 2\ 2\ 2 \rangle$$
$$h(4) = \langle 2\ 2\ 3\ 0 \rangle$$

cannot be extended to *, since we would need $h(*)(A) = h(*)(D) = 0$, and no such tuple exists in r.

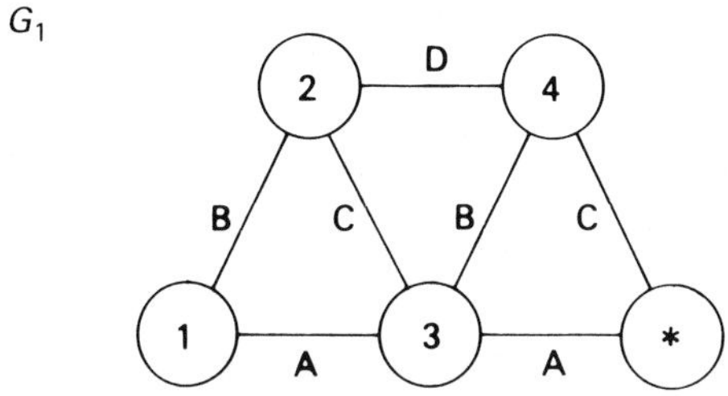

Figure 14.21

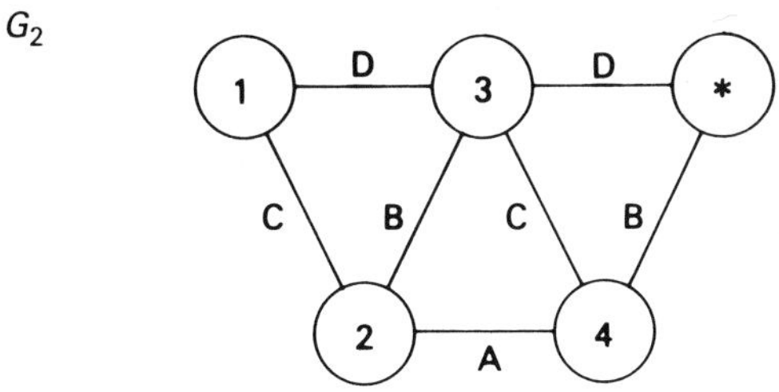

Figure 14.22

G_3

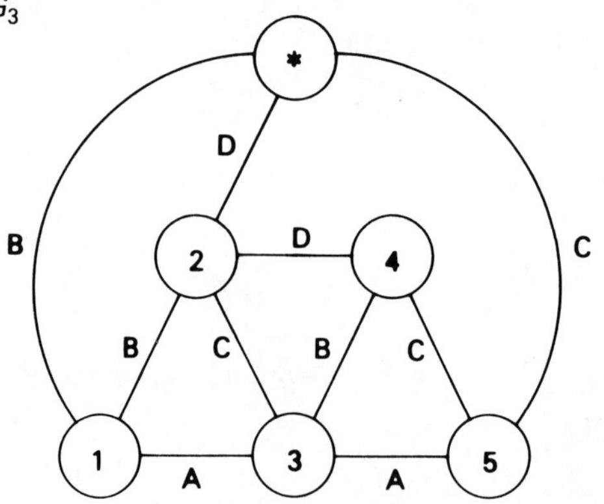

Figure 14.23

G_4

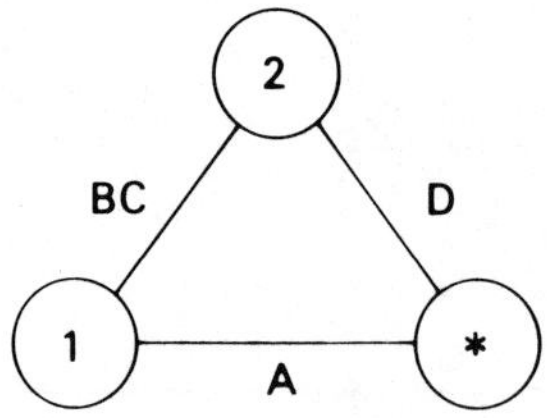

Figure 14.24

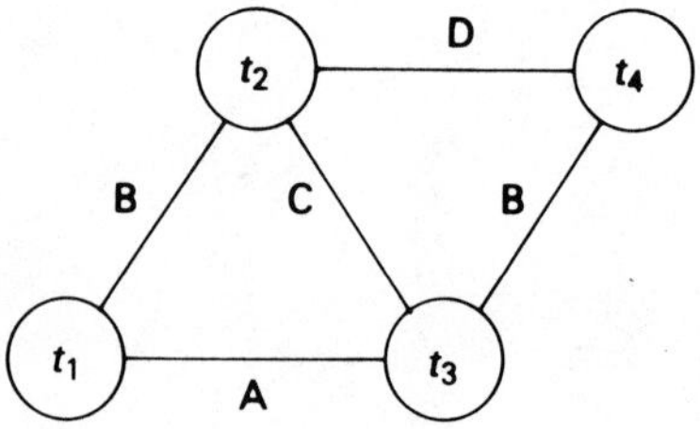

Figure 14.25

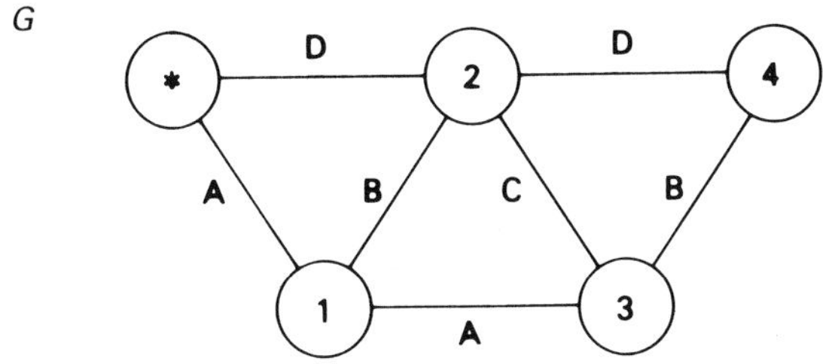

Figure 14.26

There is a special case where the set of TDs implied by a set **C** of TDs is the same for finite and arbitrary relations. If all the TDs in **C** are S-partial for the same S, then if **C** implies τ for finite relations, **C** implies τ for arbitrary relations (see Exercise 14.30). In particular, finite and arbitrary implication are the same for full TDs.

There is a complete set of inference axioms for TDs in arbitrary relations. The axioms are, of course, correct for finite relations, but not complete, by the last theorem. One inference axiom, called *augmentation*, is given by the statement of Lemma 14.7. We give another axiom here, but leave the rest of the set and the proof of completeness as Exercises 14.31 and 14.32.

Weakening If $\tau = (T, w)$ is a TD, and we obtain the row w' from w by changing some variables in w to variables that do not appear in T, then τ implies the TD $\tau' = (T, w')$.

To see that weakening is correct, let r be a relation satisfying τ. If ρ is a valuation such that $\rho(T) \subseteq r$, then $\rho(w) \in r$. We can extend ρ so that $\rho(w') = \rho(w)$, since ρ is unconstrained on any variable in w' not in w. Hence, $\rho(w') \in r$ and so r satisfies τ'.

Example 14.17 The TD τ in Figure 14.27 implies the TD τ' in Figure 14.28 by weakening.

τ(A	B	C)
a	b'	c'
a'	b'	c
a'	b	c
a	b	c

Figure 14.27

τ(A	B	C)
a	b'	c'
a'	b'	c
a'	b	c
a	b''	c

Figure 14.28

We now look at extending the chase to handle TDs. We want to use a TD $\tau_1 = (T_1, w_1)$ to chase the hypothesis rows of a TD $\tau_2 = (T_2, w_2)$ to see if w_2 can be generated. We need a *T-rule* for chasing with TDs. The definition of the T-rule is straightforward for full TDs.

T-rule Let $\tau = (T_2, w)$ be a full TD on scheme R and let T_2 be a tableau on R. If there exists a valuation ρ on T_1 such that $\rho(T_1) \subseteq T_2$, but $\rho(w)$ is not in T_2, add $\rho(w)$ to T_2.

Example 14.18 Let τ_1 be the TD in Figure 14.29. Let T be the tableau shown in Figure 14.30. To simplify the notation, we shall represent T with just the subscripts of the variables, remembering that the same number stands for different variables in different columns. The simplified version of T is shown in Figure 14.31. Using the valuation ρ from τ_1 to T such that

$$\rho(\langle a\ b'\ c'\rangle) = \langle 3\ 3\ 2\rangle$$
$$\rho(\langle a'\ b\ c'\rangle) = \langle 2\ 3\ 3\rangle$$
$$\rho(\langle a'\ b'\ c\rangle) = \langle 2\ 2\ 2\rangle,$$

we can apply the T-rule for τ_1 to T to add the row

$$\rho(\langle a\ b\ c\rangle) = \langle 3\ 3\ 2\rangle.$$

The resulting TD T' is shown in Figure 14.32.

τ_1(A	B	C)
a	b'	c'
a'	b	c'
a'	b'	c
a	b	c

Figure 14.29

T(A	B	C)
a_1	b_2	c_3
a_3	b_2	c_2
a_2	b_3	c_2
a_2	b_3	c_1
a_2	b_2	c_2

Figure 14.30

T(A	B	C)
1	2	3
3	2	2
2	3	2
2	3	1
2	2	2

Figure 14.31

T(A	B	C)
1	2	3
3	2	2
2	3	2
2	3	1
2	2	2
3	3	2

Figure 14.32

A problem arises in extending the T-rule to strictly partial TDs. We have to create new variables in the columns where the conclusion row contains a variable not in any hypothesis row. We extend the T-rule to handle partial TDs.

T-rule (revised) Let $\tau = (T_1, w)$ be an S-partial TD on scheme R, and let T_2 be a tableau on R. If there exists a valuation ρ on T_1 such that $\rho(T_1) \subseteq T_2$, and there is no row in T_2 that matches $\rho(w)$ on S, then add the row w' to T_2, where w' matches $\rho(w)$ on S and $w'(A)$ is a new variable for $A \in R - S$.

Example 14.19 Let τ_2 be the partial TD in Figure 14.33. Using the valuation ρ from τ_2 to tableau T in Figure 14.31 where

$$\rho(\langle a\ b'\ c'\rangle) = \langle 1\ 2\ 3\rangle$$
$$\rho(\langle a'\ b'\ c\rangle) = \langle 3\ 2\ 2\rangle,$$

we can apply the T-rule for τ_2 to add the row $\langle 1\ 4\ 2\rangle$ to T.

τ_2(A	B	C)
a	b'	c'
a'	b'	c
a	b	c

Figure 14.33

Since the choice of new variables is arbitrary in the revised T-rule, chasing with partial TDs does not give a unique result. There is little we can do about this problem, and it is not that serious, for we are interested in which combinations of original variables in a tableau get generated during a chase computation. A serious problem is that applying the T-rule can result in an infinite sequence of tableaux where no new combinations of original variables are being generated, but such combinations could be obtained by applying the T-rule in a different manner.

Example 14.20 Let τ_2 be the TD in Figure 14.33 and let τ_3 be the TD in Figure 14.34. Say we start chasing the tableau T in Figure 14.35 (again we show only subscripts). We can first apply the T-rule with τ_3 to generate the row $\langle 3\ 1\ 2\rangle$. We can then apply the T-rule with τ_2, using the new row, to get $\langle 3\ 4\ 1\rangle$. We can continue on indefinitely in this manner, as shown in Figure 14.36, and never generate a row that is $\langle 2\ 1\rangle$ on $B\ C$, although such a row could be generated at any time from T.

τ_3(A	B	C)
a'	b	c'
a'	b'	c
a	b	c

Figure 14.34

T(A	B	C)
1	1	1
1	2	2

Figure 14.35

$T(A$	B	$C)$	
1	1	1	
1	2	2	
3	1	2	$\cdots \tau_3$
3	4	1	$\cdots \tau_2$
5	4	2	$\cdots \tau_3$
5	6	1	$\cdots \tau_2$
7	6	2	$\cdots \tau_3$

Figure 14.36

We need to guide the chase computation when using the T-rule to insure we generate all possible combinations of original variables. It might seem we could make the restriction that the T-rule may only be applied when it will generate some new combination of original variables. While this restriction would guarantee that the chase process eventually terminates, it can prevent some combinations of original variables from being generated (see Exercise 14.33). Instead, we note that if we repeatedly apply the T-rule for a single TD τ, possibly partial, we will eventually run out of new rows to generate. This observation leads to a more comprehensive rule for chasing with TDs.

T^+-rule Let τ be a TD over scheme R and let T be a tableau on R. Use the T-rule for τ on T as long as it applies.

Example 14.21 If τ_1 is the TD in Figure 14.29 and T is the tableau in Figure 14.31, then using the T^+-rule for τ_1 on T gives the tableau T' in Figure 14.37.

$T'(A$	B	$C)$
1	2	3
3	2	2
2	3	2
2	3	1
2	2	2
3	3	2
3	3	1
3	2	1
2	2	1

Figure 14.37

When chasing under a set of TDs **C**, to ensure that every TD "gets its chance," we make the following definition.

Definition 14.5 Let $\mathbf{C} = \{\tau_1, \tau_2, \ldots, \tau_k\}$ be a set of TDs over scheme R and let T be a tableau on R. *Chasing* T *with* **C** means generating a (possibly infinite) sequence of tableaux $T_0(=T)$, T_1, T_2, ..., where T_i is obtained by applying the T$^+$-rule with each of $\tau_1, \tau_2, \ldots, \tau_k$ in sequence to T_{i-1}. The generation of T_i from T_{i-1} is a *stage* in the chase computation. The sequence is finite if it happens that $T_{i-1} = T_i$ for some $i \geq 1$.

The order that the TDs in **C** are applied at each stage in the chase computation is immaterial so far as which combinations of original variables are eventually produced (see Exercise 14.34). Note that if all the TDs in **C** are S-partial for the same S, the chase computation runs for a finite number of stages, because new variables are never introduced in the S-columns. In particular, the chase with full TDs always terminates and, moreover, the final tableau is unique (see Exercise 14.35).

Example 14.22 Let $\mathbf{C} = \{\tau_1, \tau_2\}$, where τ_1 is given in Figure 14.29 and τ_2 is given in Figure 14.31. Tableau T_1 in Figure 14.38 is the result after the first stage of chasing T with **C**.

$T_1(A$	B	$C)$
1	2	3
3	2	2
2	3	2
2	3	1
2	2	2
3	3	2
3	3	1
3	2	1
2	2	1
1	4	2
1	5	1
2	6	3
3	7	3

Figure 14.38

Testing if a set of TDs implies another TD is similar for testing implication of JDs with the chase.

Definition 14.6 Let T_0, T_1, T_2, ... be the sequence of tableaux generated when chasing T_0 with a set of TDs. The *limit* of this sequence is the tableaux

$$T^* = T_0 \cup T_1 \cup T_2 \cup \cdots.$$

Note that T^* might be infinite.

Theorem 14.9 Let **C** be a set of TDs over scheme R and let $\tau = (T, w)$ be an S-partial TD on R. Let T^* be the limit of the sequence $T_0(=T)$, T_1, T_2, ... generated in chasing T with **C**. **C** implies τ on arbitrary relations if and only if T^* contains a row w^* such that $w^*(S) = w(S)$.

Proof We give only a sketch of the proof. For the "if" direction, assume that w^* first appears after the kth stage in the chase computation. That is, w^* is in T_k but not in T_{k-1}. Let r be a relation in $SAT(\mathbf{C})$ and let ρ be a valuation such that $\rho(T) \subseteq r$. Following the chase computation leading up to T_k, we can show that r must contain a tuple t^* such that $\rho(w^*)(S) = t^*(S)$. It follows that $\rho(w)(S) = t^*(S)$ and so r satisfies τ. Notice that the theorem holds in this direction for finite relations instead of arbitrary relations.

For the "only if" direction, we first show that T^*, as a relation, satisfies **C**. If T^* does not contain a row w^* that matches w on S, then T^*, as a relation, is a counterexample to **C** implying τ. Thus, if **C** does imply τ, w^* must exist.

Example 14.23 Let τ be the $A\ C$-partial TD in Figure 14.39. Note that the hypothesis rows of τ correspond to the tableau T in Figure 14.30. If **C** is the set of TDs in the last example, we see that **C** implies τ. From that example, we know that chasing the hypothesis rows of τ with **C** gives a row that is $\langle a_1\ c_1 \rangle$ in the $A\ C$-columns.

$\tau(A$	B	$C)$
a_1	b_2	c_3
a_3	b_2	c_2
a_2	b_3	c_2
a_2	b_3	c_1
a_2	b_2	c_2
a_1	b_1	c_1

Figure 14.39

14.2.5 Generalized Functional Dependencies

In Section 9.3 we briefly examined the structure of projections of $SAT(F)$ for a set of FDs F. Projecting $SAT(\{A \rightarrow E, B \rightarrow E, CE \rightarrow D\})$ onto the scheme $A\ B\ C\ D$ we came up with the following "curious" dependency that any relation in the projection must satisfy: If t_1, t_2, and t_3 are tuples in $r(A\ B\ C\ D)$ such that

1. $t_1(A) = t_3(A)$
2. $t_1(C) = t_2(C)$
3. $t_2(B) = t_3(B)$

then

4. $t_1(D) = t_2(D)$.

This constraint is an example of a *generalized functional dependency*, which can be written in a notation similar to that for TDs, as shown in Figure 14.40. The rows above the line are again called hypothesis rows. The equality below the line is called simply the *conclusion*. A relation r satisfies this particular generalized functional dependency if any valuation ρ that maps the hypothesis rows into r necessarily has $\rho(d_1) = \rho(d_3)$. We now give a formal definition.

$\gamma($	A	B	C	$D)$
w_1	a_1	b_2	c_1	d_1
w_2	a_2	b_1	c_1	d_2
w_3	a_1	b_1	c_2	d_3
		$d_1 = d_3$		

Figure 14.40

Definition 14.7 A *generalized functional dependency* (GFD) on a relation scheme R is a pair $\gamma = (T,\ a = b)$, where T is a set of rows on R, called *hypothesis rows*, and a and b are two variables from the rows in T. The equality $a = b$ is called the *conclusion*. A relation $r(R)$ satisfies the GFD γ if for every valuation ρ of T such that $\rho(T) \subseteq r$, $\rho(a) = \rho(b)$. The GFD γ is *trivial* if it is satisfied by every relation on r; it is *typed* if no variable appears in more than one column of T and a and b come from the same column of T.

We shall assume that all GFDs are typed, henceforth. Figure 14.40 shows how GFDs are written. Not every FD is equivalent to a GFD, but only because GFDs enforce equality in only one column. Any FD with a single attribute on the right side can be expressed as a GFD, so any FD is equivalent to a set of GFDs.

Example 14.24 Consider the FD $A\ B \rightarrow C$ on scheme $A\ B\ C\ D$. Figure 14.41 shows the equivalent GFD for this FD.

γ(A	B	C	D)
a	b	c	d
a	b	c'	d'

$$c = c'$$

Figure 14.41

It is possible to give a complete set of inference axioms for GFDs, but we shall not do so, since such axioms essentially mimic the chase computation. Complete axiomatizations also exist for TDs and GFDs together, although they are for implication on arbitrary relations if partial TDs are allowed. We give one axiom for inferring TDs from FDs.

GT1 Let $X \rightarrow A$ be a nontrivial FD over relation scheme R and let $Y = R - (X\,A)$. This FD implies the TD τ shown in Figure 14.42. Note that we use a little shorthand in τ. For instance, x_1 and x_2 stand for sequences of variables over X that are distinct in every column.

	τ(X	A	Y)
w_1	x_1	a_1	y_1
w_2	x_1	a_2	y_2
w_3	x_2	a_2	y_3
w	x_2	a_1	y_3

Figure 14.42

Example 14.25 Figure 14.43 shows a TD τ implied by the FD $A\ B \rightarrow C$ on scheme $A\ B\ C\ D$.

$\tau(A$	B	C	$D)$
a_1	b_1	c_1	d_1
a_1	b_1	c_2	d_2
a_2	b_2	c_2	d_3
a_2	b_2	c_1	d_3

Figure 14.43

To see that the TD τ in GT1 follows from the FD $X \rightarrow Y$, consider the GFD γ in Figure 14.44 that is equivalent to $X \rightarrow Y$. Let r be an arbitrary relation on R. Let ρ be a valuation that maps w_1-w_3 into r. If r satisfies γ, then $\rho(a_1) = \rho(a_2)$, since the first two rows of γ are the same as the first two rows of τ. It follows that $\rho(w)$ is in τ, since $\rho(w)$ must equal $\rho(w_3)$.

	$\gamma(X$	A	$Y)$
w_1	x_1	a_1	y_1
w_2	x_1	a_2	y_2

$$a_1 = a_2$$

Figure 14.44

Axiom GT1 can be generalized from FDs to GFDs (see Exercise 14.39). The derived TD can be used in place of the FD when inferring TDs from a set **C** of FDs and TDs. That is, if we form **C**′ by replacing every FD in **C** with the TD given by GT1, **C** and **C**′ imply the same TDs (see Exercise 14.40).

Extending the chase computation to GFDs is fairly straightforward.

G-rule Let $\gamma = (T_1, a = b)$ be a GFD over scheme R. Let T_2 be a tableau over R. For any valuation ρ such that $\rho(T_1) \subseteq T_2$ and $\rho(a) \neq \rho(b)$, identify $\rho(a)$ and $\rho(b)$ in T_2.

The chase computation under a set **C** of GFDs on a tableau T is just the application of the G-rule for GFDs in **C** until no more variables in T can be equated. The computation terminates, because no new rows or variables are introduced in T. Although not proved here, the result is unique given the proper mechanism for renaming variables when identifying them (such as always choosing the one with the lower subscript to replace the other). Since the result of the chase with GFDs is unique, we may denote it as $chase_{\mathbf{C}}(T)$.

Example 14.26 Let $\mathbf{C} = \{\gamma_1, \gamma_2\}$, where γ_1 and γ_2 are as shown in Figures 14.45 and 14.46. Let T be the tableau in Figure 14.47. Again, we give only the subscripts for the variables in T for simplicity, so, for instance, "2" represents different variables in different columns. We first apply the G-rule for γ_1 to T. There is a valuation ρ_1 from the hypothesis rows of γ_1 to T such that

$$\begin{aligned}\rho(u_1) &= w_3\\ \rho(u_2) &= w_4\\ \rho(u_3) &= w_5\end{aligned}$$

Thus, we identify $\rho(c_1)$ and $\rho(c_3)$, that is, 2 and 3 in the C-column. The result is tableau T' in Figure 14.48. We adopt the rule of replacing higher subscripts with lower ones. We next apply the G-rule for γ_2 to T' using the valuation ρ_2 where

$$\begin{aligned}\rho(v_1) &= w_2\\ \rho(v_2) &= w_3\\ \rho(v_3) &= w_4\end{aligned}$$

We can equate 2 and 3 in the A-column to obtain the tableau T^* in Figure 14.49. At this point, no more variables can be identified with the G-rule, so $chase_{\mathbf{C}}(T) = T^*$.

γ_1	A	B	C
u_1	a_1	b_2	c_1
u_2	a_1	b_1	c_2
u_3	a_2	b_1	c_3

$$c_1 = c_3$$

Figure 14.45

γ_2	A	B	C
v_1	a_1	b_1	c_1
v_2	a_2	b_1	c_2
v_3	a_3	b_2	c_1

$$a_1 = a_3$$

Figure 14.46

$T(A$	B	$C)$
w_1 1	3	1
w_2 2	1	2
w_3 3	1	2
w_4 3	2	2
w_5 2	2	3

Figure 14.47

$T'(A$	B	$C)$
w_1 1	3	1
w_2 2	1	2
w_3 3	1	2
w_4 3	2	2
w_5 2	2	2

Figure 14.48

$T^*(A$	B	$C)$
w_1 1	3	1
w_2 2	1	2
w_5 2	2	2

Figure 14.49

We now give a theorem that shows how to test implication of GFDs. In the statement of the theorem, saying that two variables are equated in the chase means that one was renamed to the other, or that they both were ultimately renamed to the same third variable.

Theorem 14.10 Let **C** be a set of GFDs over scheme R and let $\gamma = (T, a = b)$ be a single GFD on R. **C** implies γ if and only if a and b are equated when computing $chase_{\mathbf{C}}(T)$.

Here implication means implication over finite relations, which is the same as implication over arbitrary relations for GFDs (see Exercise 14.41).

Proof The proof is similar to previous proofs, so we omit details. If **C** does not imply γ, then $chase_{\mathbf{C}}(T)$ serves as a counterexample. If a and b are equated during the chase computation, then, by following the steps in the computation, we can show that any valuation ρ from T into a relation r in $SAT(\mathbf{C})$ must have $\rho(a) = \rho(b)$.

Example 14.27 The GFD γ in Figure 14.50 is implied by the set of GFDs $\{\gamma_1, \gamma_2\}$ from the last example, as the chase computation given there shows.

γ	A	B	C
w_1	a_1	b_3	c_1
w_2	a_2	b_1	c_2
w_3	a_3	b_1	c_2
w_4	a_3	b_2	c_2
w_5	a_2	b_2	c_3

$$a_2 = a_3$$

Figure 14.50

When using the G-rule and T-rule together, we must exercise some care when we identify variables. The T-rule can create new variables; the G-rule might change an original variable to some new variable. Such a change makes conditions for testing implication hard to state and makes it hard to define the tableau to which the chase converges. To avoid such problems, we maintain an ordering on variables in a tableau. The original variables come first in the ordering; new variables are added to the end of the ordering as they are introduced during the chase computation. Whenever the G-rule identifies variables, the variable earlier in the ordering replaces the variable later in the ordering. In the event that the tableau we are chasing is the hypothesis rows of a TD, we assume that the variables appearing in the conclusion row of the TD occur at the very beginning of the ordering. We can then check directly if the conclusion row is ever generated during the chase, without worrying about variable replacements in the conclusion row.

Definition 14.8 Let **C** be a set of TDs and GFDs over scheme R. Let T be a tableau on R. *Chasing* T *with* **C** means generating a (possibly infinite) sequence of tableaux T_0 $(=T)$, T_1, T_2, ... where T_i is obtained by applying the T$^+$-rule for each TD in **C**, followed by applying the G-rule for GFDs in **C** as much as possible, to T_{i-1}. The sequence will be finite if it happens that $T_i = T_{i-1}$ for some $i \geq 1$.

Note that the sequence is always finite if all the TDs in **C** are S-partial for the same $S \subseteq R$. The T$^+$-rule can generate only a finite number of tuples with new combinations of variables in the S-columns. We cannot define the limit of the chase sequence as we did for TDs alone, since rows can be changed from one stage to the next. We need to identify the rows at a given stage that undergo no subsequent changes.

Definition 14.9 Let T_0, T_1, T_2, ... be the sequence of tableaux generated by chasing a tableau T with a set **C** of TDs and GFDs. Relative to this sequence, a row w in T_i is *stabilized* if w appears in T_j for $j \geq i$. Let $STABLE(T_i)$ denote all the stable rows in T_i. The *limit* of the sequence T_0, T_1, T_2, ... is the tableau

$$T^* = STABLE(T_0) \cup STABLE(T_1) \cup STABLE(T_2) \cdots.$$

(T^* may be infinite.)

An important point is that T^*, as a relation, satisfies **C**. Note that if some set of rows w_1, w_2, ..., w_k in T^* gives rise to a violation of a GFD in **C**, then at least one of them is not stabilized, since it would have the offending value changed by the G-rule.

The next Theorem summarizes implication of TDs and GFDs for arbitrary relations.

Theorem 14.11 Let **C** be a set of TDs and GFDs over scheme R and let T be a tableau on R. Let T^* be the limit of the sequence $T_0(=T)$, T_1, T_2, ... generated when chasing T with **C**. We have

1. **C** implies the S-partial TD (T, w) if and only if T^* contains a row w^* such that $w^*(S) = w(S)$, and
2. **C** implies the GFD $(T, a = b)$ if and only if a and b are equated in generating T^*.

Proof Left to the reader (see Exercise 14.43).

It follows from the theorem that TDs by themselves imply only trivial GFDs. Note that the tests for implication of FDs and JDs in Sections 8.6.3 and 8.6.4 are specializations of this theorem.

Example 14.28 Let $\mathbf{C} = \{\tau, \gamma\}$, where τ is the TD in Figure 14.51 and γ is the GFD in Figure 14.52. Let T_0 be the tableau in Figure 14.53. Again, we show only subscripts for simplicity. Consider chasing T_0 with **C**. Applying the T$^+$-rule for τ gives the tableau T' in Figure 14.54. Applying the G-rule for γ thrice to T' yields the tableau T_1 in Figure 14.55. No further applications of the T^+-rule or G-rule are possible, so T_1 is the limit of this chase computation (see Exercise 14.44). From this limit, Theorem 14.11 allows us to conclude that **C** implies the TD τ' in Figure 14.56 and the GFD γ' in Figure 14.57.

$\tau(A$	B	$C)$
a'	b	c'
a'	b'	c
a	b	c

Figure 14.51

$\gamma(A$	B	$C)$
a	b'	c
a'	b	c
a''	b	c'

$$a = a''$$

Figure 14.52

$T(A$	B	$C)$
1	1	2
1	2	3
2	1	3
2	2	1

Figure 14.53

$T'(A$	B	$C)$
1	1	2
1	2	3
2	1	3
2	2	1
3	2	2
4	1	1

Figure 14.54

$T_1(A$	B	$C)$
1	1	2
1	2	3
1	1	3
1	2	1
1	2	2
1	1	1

Figure 14.55

$\tau'(A$	B	$C)$
a_1	b_1	c_2
a_1	b_2	c_3
a_2	b_1	c_3
a_2	b_2	c_1
a_1	b_1	c_1

Figure 14.56

$\gamma'(A$	B	$C)$
a_1	b_1	c_2
a_1	b_2	c_3
a_2	b_1	c_3
a_2	b_2	c_1

$a_1 = a_2$

Figure 14.57

14.2.6 Closure of Satisfaction Classes Under Projection

Recall the notation introduced in Chapter 8 for expressing the class of all relations on a given relation scheme R that satisfy a set of constraints **C**, $SAT_R(\mathbf{C})$. Also recall that we may extend a relational operator to sets of relations in an element-wise fashion. Thus, if P is a set of relations on scheme R, and $X \subseteq R$, then

$$\pi_X(P) = \{\pi_X(r) | r \in P\}.$$

In Chapter 9 we briefly considered the question of whether $\pi_X(SAT_R(\mathbf{C}))$ necessarily can be expressed as $SAT_X(\mathbf{C}')$ for $\mathbf{C}$ and $\mathbf{C}'$ coming from given classes of dependencies. The answer was "no" if $\mathbf{C}$ and $\mathbf{C}'$ are both FDs or both MVDs.

In this section we show that if $\mathbf{C}$ is TDs and GFDs, then there is always a set $\mathbf{C}'$ of TDs and GFDs such that $\pi_X(SAT_R(\mathbf{C})) = SAT_X(\mathbf{C}')$. However, to make the equality hold, we must interpret $SAT(\mathbf{C})$ as including both finite and infinite relations satisfying $\mathbf{C}$. We shall see that if the TDs in $\mathbf{C}$ are restricted to be full, then $SAT(\mathbf{C})$ may be interpreted as only the finite relations satisfying $\mathbf{C}$.

For $\mathbf{C}$ a set of TDs and GFDs over R and $X \subseteq R$, $\pi_X(\mathbf{C})$ will mean the set of TDs and GFDs over scheme X that are satisfied by all relations in $\pi_X(SAT(\mathbf{C}))$. Clearly, $\pi_X(SAT_R(\mathbf{C})) \subseteq SAT_X(\pi_X(\mathbf{C}))$, so if there is any set $\mathbf{C}'$ such that $\pi_X(SAT_R(\mathbf{C})) = SAT_X(\mathbf{C}')$, $\pi_X(\mathbf{C})$ will also be such a set. It turns out that $\pi_X(\mathbf{C})$ can be infinite, with no equivalent finite set of TDs and GFDs (see Exercise 14.45), so there is no algorithm guaranteed to generate all of $\pi_X(\mathbf{C})$ in general. The next lemma, however, points out some of the dependencies in $\pi_X(\mathbf{C})$.

For a tableau T over scheme R and $X \subseteq R$, let $T(X)$ be the tableau over scheme X obtained by restricting the rows in T to X.

Definition 14.10 Let $\tau = (T, w)$ be a TD on scheme R. If X is a subset of R such that no two rows of T agree in any column in $R - X$, then we define the *restriction of* τ *to* X, denoted $\tau(X)$, as the TD $\tau' = (T(X), w(X))$ with scheme X.

Example 14.29 Let τ be the TD on scheme $A\ B\ C\ D$ given in Figure 14.58. Figure 14.59 shows the TD $\tau' = \tau(A\ B\ C)$.

τ(A	B	C	D)
a'	b	c'	d'
a	b'	c'	d
a	b'	c	d''
a	b	c	d

Figure 14.58

$\tau'(A$	B	$C)$
a'	b	c'
a	b'	c'
a	b'	c
a	b	c

Figure 14.59

Lemma 14.8 Let τ be a TD over scheme R such that $\tau(X)$ is defined. If r is a relation in $SAT(\tau)$, then $\pi_X(r)$ is in $SAT(\tau(X))$.

Proof Left to the reader (see Exercise 14.47).

Definition 14.11 Let $\gamma = (T, a = b)$ be a GFD on scheme R. If X is a subset of R such that no two rows of T agree in any column in $R - X$ and a and b occur in some column of X, we define the *restriction of* γ *to* X, denoted $\gamma(X)$, as the GFD $\gamma' = (T(X), a = b)$.

Lemma 14.9 Let γ be a GFD on R such that $\gamma(X)$ is defined. If r is a relation in $SAT(\gamma)$, then $\pi_X(r)$ is in $SAT(\gamma(X))$.

Proof Assume $\gamma = (T, a = b)$. Let ρ be a valuation from $T(X)$ into $\pi_X(r)$. Since no two rows of T agree outside of X, ρ can be extended to a valuation ρ' from T into r. Moreover, ρ can be extended so that $\rho(w(X)) = \rho'(w)(X)$, for every row w of T (hence for every row $w(X)$ of $T(X)$). Since r satisfies γ, $\rho'(a) = \rho'(b)$. Since a and b appear in $T(X)$, $\rho(a) = \rho(b)$, so $\pi_X(r)$ satisfies $\gamma(X)$.

Theorem 14.12 Let **C** be a set of TDs and GFDs over scheme R. If X is a subset of R, then

$$\pi_X(SAT_R(\mathbf{C})) = SAT_X(\pi_X(\mathbf{C})).$$

Proof As we remarked previously, the right set contains the left set. To show the other inclusion, let s be a relation in $SAT_X(\pi_X(\mathbf{C}))$. We exhibit a relation r in $SAT_R(\mathbf{C})$ such that $\pi_X(r) = s$. Form $s'(R)$ by extending each tuple in s to R with new values in the $(R - X)$-columns. Let r be the limit of chasing s' with **C**. In extending the chase to relations, we do allow identification of values in this instance. However, we show shortly that no identifications are made in the X-columns of s'. Since r is obtained by chasing with **C**, r is in $SAT(\mathbf{C})$. We show that $\pi_X(r) = s$.

Let t be any tuple in s and let t' be the extended version of t in s'. Suppose at some stage in the chase computation, some value in the X-columns of t' is changed by application of the G-rule. Interpreting s' as a tableau, we see that **C** implies a GFD γ that has s' as hypothesis rows and whose conclusion equates two values in the X-columns of s'. Since all the values in the $(R - X)$-columns of s' are distinct, we apply Lemma 14.9 to show that $\gamma(X)$ is in $\pi_X(\mathbf{C})$. But $\gamma(X)$ has s as its hypothesis rows, and equates two values in s. Therefore, s violates $\pi_X(\mathbf{C})$, a contradiction. We conclude that t' remains unchanged in the X-columns during the chase computation. If t'' is the tuple in r corresponding to t', then $t''(X) = t'(X) = t$. We conclude that $s \subseteq \pi_X(r)$.

Now let t'' be any tuple in r. Again interpreting s' as a tableau, we see that **C** implies the TD τ that has s' as hypothesis rows and t'' as the conclusion row. By Lemma 14.8, $\pi_X(\mathbf{C})$ contains the TD $\tau(X)$, which has s as hypothesis rows and $t''(X)$ as the conclusion row. Since s satisfies $\tau(X)$, s must contain $t''(X)$. Hence, $s \supseteq \pi_X(r)$, and so $s = \pi_X(r)$.

Theorem 14.12 is true for $SAT(\mathbf{C})$ interpreted as finite relations satisfying **C** if **C** contains only full TDs and GFDs. Looking back in the proof, the relation r generated by chasing s' with **C** will be finite if **C** meets this restriction. In particular, the "finite relation" version of the theorem is true for **C** consisting of FDs and JDs (although $\pi_X(\mathbf{C})$ may have dependencies that are not JDs or FDs).

14.3 LIMITATIONS OF RELATIONAL ALGEBRA

We have used relational algebra as the "yardstick" for a complete query system. In this section we show that this definition for complete can be disputed, since there are some natural operators on relations that cannot be expressed by relational algebra. To be exact, we show that there is no algebraic expression E that specifies the transitive closure of a two-attribute relation.

Definition 14.12 Let r be a relation on a two-attribute relation scheme, call it A_1A_2, where $dom(A_1) = dom(A_2)$. The *transitive closure of* r, denoted r^+, is the smallest relation on A_1A_2 such that $r \subseteq r^+$ and r^+ satisfies the untyped TD

$\tau(A_1$	$A_2)$
a	b
b	c
a	c

Note that this definition is symmetric in A_1 and A_2.

Example 14.30 If r is the relation in Figure 14.60, then Figure 14.61 shows r^+.

$r(A$	$B)$
1	2
2	1
2	3

Figure 14.60

$r^+(A$	$B)$
1	2
2	1
2	3
1	1
1	3

Figure 14.61

In the next theorem, we shall construct something that looks like a domain calculus expression, except we shall use a different set of atoms than usual. Assume r is a relation on scheme A_1A_2 where $dom(A_1) = dom(A_2)$. We use the atom $r^i(a\ b)$ to mean that b is i "steps away" from a in r. More precisely, for $i \geq 0$, $r^i(a\ b)$ is true when there are values $a_1, a_2, \ldots, a_{i-1}$ in $dom(A_1)$ such that $\langle a\ a_1\rangle, \langle a_1\ a_2\rangle, \langle a_2\ a_3\rangle, \ldots, \langle a_{i-1}\ b\rangle$ are all tuples in r. We let $r^0(a\ b)$ mean $a = b$ and a appears in r. That is, r^0 is equality on values in r. Finally, for $i < 0$, $r^i(a\ b)$ if and only if $r^{-i}(b\ a)$. Note that $r^i(a\ b)$ and $r^j(b\ c)$ together imply $r^{i+j}(a\ c)$ and that $r^1(a\ b)$ if and only if $\langle a\ b\rangle \in r$.

Example 14.31 For relation r in Figure 14.60, $r^0(1\ 1)$, $r^1(2\ 1)$, $r^2(1\ 1)$, and $r^2(1\ 3)$ are all true, while $r^0(4\ 4)$, $r^1(1\ 1)$, and $r^2(1\ 2)$ are all false.

Theorem 14.13 Let A_1 and A_2 be two attributes with the same domain. There is no relational algebra expression E involving a relation $r(A_1A_2)$ such that $E(r) = r^+$ for all states of r.

Proof Assume that the domain of A_1 and A_2 is the positive integers with only the comparators $=$ and $\neq$. While we do not allow inequality comparisons in selections, we shall use the order of the integers in our arguments. It suffices to show that there is some state of r for which $E(r) \neq r^+$. We restrict our attention to states of the form $\{\langle 1\ 2\rangle, \langle 2\ 3\rangle, \ldots, \langle p-1\ p\rangle\}$ for $p > 1$. We denote this state of r by $[p]$.

We begin by showing that for any relational algebra expression over r and for sufficiently large p, there is a domain calculus-like expression

$$E_p = \{b_1(B_1)\, b_2(B_2) \cdots b_m(B_m) | f(b_1, b_2, \ldots, b_m)\}$$

such that $E([p]) = E_p([p])$. The b's in E_p are assumed to range over $\{1, 2, \ldots, p\}$. Formula f is constructed of atoms of the form $r^i(a_1\ a_2)$, where a_i is a constant or one of the b's, $1 \leq i \leq 2$, and the connectives $\wedge$, $\vee$ and $\neg$. A *literal* of f is an atom or its negation and a *clause* of f is a conjunction of literals. In the remainder of the proof, b's and d's are variables, c's are constants and a's are either.

The important property that E_p will have is that the form of f will depend on E but not on p. The value of p will appear in f as a constant, but the number of literals and clauses in f is independent of p.

The proof that E_p exists is done by induction on the number of operators in E. By Theorem 3.1, we shall assume that E contains only the relation symbol r, single-attribute single-tuple constant relations, selection with a single comparison, natural join, union, difference, renaming, and projection. We further assume that any projection removes exactly one attribute.

Basis If E has no operators, then E is r or $\langle c{:}B\rangle$ for some constant c. In the first case,

$$E_p = \{b_1(A_1)\, b_2(A_2) | r^1(b_1\ b_2)\}.$$

In the second case,

$$E_p = \{b_1(A_1) | r^0(b_1\ c)\},$$

as long as p is sufficiently large that c appears in $[p]$ (that is, $p \geq c$).

Induction We consider the form of E by cases. In all the cases, we assume that E' and E'' are subexpressions of E with corresponding calculus-like expressions

$$E_p' = \{b_1(B_1)\, b_2(B_2) \cdots b_m(B_m) | f'(b_1, b_2, \ldots, b_m)\}$$

and

$$E_p'' = \{d_1(D_1)\, d_2(D_2) \cdots d_n(D_n) | f''(d_1, d_2, \ldots, d_n)\}.$$

1. *Selection* $E = \sigma_C(E')$. E_p has the form

$$\{b_1(B_1)\, b_2(B_2) \cdots b_m(B_m) | f'(b_1, b_2, \ldots, b_m) \wedge g\}$$

   where g is $r^0(b_i\, b_j)$, $\neg r^0(b_i\, b_j)$, $r^0(b_i\, c)$ or $\neg r^0(b_i\, c)$ depending on if the selection condition C is $B_i = B_j$, $B_i \neq B_j$, $B_i = c$, or $B_i \neq c$, respectively.
2. *Join* $E = E' \bowtie E''$. Assume that $B_1, B_2, \ldots, B_k$ are the same as $D_1, D_2, \ldots, D_k$ in E_p' and E_p''. E_p is then

$$\{b_1(B_1)\, b_2(B_2) \cdots b_m(B_m)\, d_{k+1}(D_{k+1}) \cdots d_n(D_n) | \\ f'(b_1, b_2, \ldots, b_m) \wedge f''(b_1, b_2, \ldots, b_k, d_{k+1}, \ldots, d_n)\}.$$

3. *Union* $E = E' \cup E''$. For E to be a legal expression, E_p'' must have the form

$$\{b_1(B_1)\, b_2(B_2) \cdots b_m(B_m) | f''(b_1, b_2, \ldots, b_m)\}.$$

   E_p is

$$\{b_1(B_1)\, b_2(B_2) \cdots b_m(B_m) | f'(b_1, b_2, \ldots, b_m) \vee \\ f''(b_1, b_2, \ldots, b_m)\}.$$

4. *Difference* $E = E' - E''$. E_p'' must be as in Case 3. E_p is

$$\{b_1(B_1)\, b_2(B_2) \cdots b_m(B_m) | f'(b_1, b_2, \ldots, b_m) \wedge \neg f''(b_1, b_2, \ldots, b_m)\}.$$

5. *Renaming* $E = \delta_{B_i \leftarrow D}(E')$. E_p is

$$\{b_1(B_1)\, b_2(B_2) \cdots b_i(D) \cdots b_m(B_m) | f'(b_1, b_2, \ldots, b_m)\}.$$

6. *Projection* $E = \pi_X(E')$, where $X = B_1 B_2 \cdots B_{m-1}$. This is the hard case to handle. Assume $m > 1$ and that $f'(b_1, b_2, \ldots, b_m)$ has the form

$$f_1(b_1, b_2, \ldots, b_m) \vee f_2(b_1, b_2, \ldots, b_m) \vee \cdots \vee f_q(b_1, b_2, \ldots, b_m),$$

where each f_i is a clause (f' is then said to be in *disjunctive normal form* or DNF). It is an elementary theorem of logic that f' can be put into DNF if it does not already have that form. E_p could be represented as

$$\{b_1(B_1)\ b_2(B_2) \cdots b_{m-1}(B_{m-1}) | \exists\, b_m(B_m) f'(b_1, b_2, \ldots, b_m)\},$$

but we do not want the existential quantifier. This expression is equivalent to

$$\begin{aligned}&\{b_1(B_1)\ b_2(B_2) \cdots b_{m-1}(B_{m-1})|\\ &\quad (\exists\, b_m(B_m) f_1(b_1, b_2, \ldots, b_m)) \vee\\ &\quad (\exists\, b_m(B_m) f_2(b_1, b_2, \ldots, b_m)) \vee \cdots \vee\\ &\quad (\exists\, b_m(B_m) f_q(b_1, b_2, \ldots, b_m))\},\end{aligned}$$

so we consider only the case where f' is itself a single clause.

Before we attempt to remove the existential quantifier, we do some manipulations of f'. For every atom that mentions b_m, we move b_m to the first slot, if it is not already there, using the identity $r^i(a\ b_m) = r^{-i}(b_m\ a)$. We can leave out any literal of the form $r^0(b_m\ b_m)$ or $\neg r^i(b_m\ b_m)$, $i \neq 0$, as they are always true for $[p]$. Likewise, $\neg r^0(b_m\ b_m)$ or $r^i(b_m\ b_m)$, $i \neq 0$, can be replaced by $\neg r^0(b_1\ b_1)$, as they are always false for $[p]$.

Two possibilities remain.

6.1 There is no literal of the form $r^i(b_m\ a)$ in f'. That is, any atom mentioning b_m is negated in f'. Let $f(b_1, b_2, \ldots, b_{m-1})$ be the conjunction of all the literals in f' that do not mention b_m. We claim that when p is sufficiently large, for any $m - 1$ constants $c_1, c_2, \ldots, c_{m-1}$ chosen from $\{1, 2, \ldots, p\}$,

$$f(c_1, c_2, \ldots, c_{m-1}) \equiv \exists\, b_m f'(c_1, c_2, \ldots, c_{m-1}, b_m).$$

The right side implies the left side, since $c_1, c_2, \ldots, c_{m-1}$ must satisfy every literal that does not mention b_m. In the other direction, if p is sufficiently large, there is always some constant c_m that makes every literal of the form $\neg r^i(b_m\ c)$ in $f(c_1, c_2, \ldots, c_{m-1}, b_m)$ true when b_m is replaced with c_m. Each such literal can prohibit only a single value for c_m. Since the number of literals in f' is fixed, but we allow p to be as large as necessary, there is always a choice for c_m. Thus, if $f(c_1, c_2, \ldots, c_{m-1})$ is true, so is $\exists\, b_m f'(c_1, c_2, \ldots, c_{m-1}, b_m)$, by the choice of c_m for b_m. In this case we have

$$E_p = \{b_1(B_1)\, b_2(B_2) \cdots b_{m-1}(B_{m-1}) | f(b_1, b_2, \ldots, b_{m-1})\}.$$

6.2 The other possibility is that there is some literal of the form $r^i(b_m\ a)$ in f'. In this case, to form f, we remove $r^i(b_m\ a)$ and make a replacement for any other atom mentioning b_m. Since we have the relative position of b_m and a, we can convert any reference to b_m to a reference to a.

If the literal that mentions b_m is $r^j(b_m\ a')$, we replace it with $r^{j-i}(a\ a')$. Certain simplifications can then be made. For example, any literal of the form $r^k(c\ c')$ can be removed if $c + k = c'$, or replaced by $\neg r^0(b_1\ b_1)$ if $c + k \neq c'$. Similarly, any literal of the form $r^k(a\ b)$ can also be replaced by $\neg r^0(b_1\ b_1)$ if $|k| \geq p$.

To finish forming f, we must add a few more literals if the a in $r^i(b_m\ a)$ is actually b_k for some $1 \leq k \leq m - 1$. If $i > 0$, we must conjoin the literals $\neg r^l(1\ b_k)$, $0 \leq l < i$. Since b_k is at least i steps away from b_m, it must be at least i steps away from 1. If $i < 0$, we conjoin $\neg r^l(b_k\ p)$, $1 \leq l \leq -i$.

We leave Exercise 14.48 to show that

$$f(b_1, b_2, \ldots, b_{m-1}) \equiv \exists b_m f'(b_1, b_2, \ldots, b_m).$$

The final expression, as in the last subcase, is

$$E_p = \{b_1(B_1)\, b_2(B_2) \cdots b_{m-1}(B_{m-1}) | f(b_1, b_2, \ldots, b_{m-1})\}.$$

We have completed the case for projection. We now know that if E is a relational algebra expression as in the hypothesis of the theorem, for a sufficiently large choice of p, there is an expression

$$E_p = \{b_1(A_1)\, b_2(A_2) | f(b_1, b_2)\}$$

such that $E_p([p]) = [p]^+$. We may assume that f is in DNF.

We now argue that E_p cannot correctly compute $[p]^+$. It is important that the form of f is the same regardless of the choice of p (as long as p is sufficiently large that we can form f correctly). In particular, the number of clauses in f is independent of p. The only place p enters the construction (other than as a constant in E) is in the literals $\neg r^l(b_m\ p)$ that we add in subcase 6.2. Thus, we can convert E_p to $E_{p'}$, $p' \geq p$, by replacing each $\neg r^l(b_m p)$ by $\neg r^l(b_m\ p')$. Another property of f is that, by our simplifications, f contains no atom of the form $r^i(a_1\ a_2)$ for $|i| \geq p$, nor any atom of the form $r^i(c_1\ c_2)$.

Suppose each clause of f contains an unnegated literal $r^i(a_1\ a_2)$ where a_i, $1 \leq i \leq 2$, is b_1, b_2, or a constant, but not both a_1 and a_2 are constants. The number of clauses in f is independent of p. Say there are k of them, so we are dealing with k unnegated literals. If p is sufficiently larger than k, then there are choices c_1 and c_2 for b_1 and b_2 such that $\langle c_1\ c_2\rangle \in [p]^+$, but replacing b_1 and b_2 by c_1 and c_2 makes each of the k unnegated literals false. For example, if $\bar{i}$ is the magnitude of the largest superscript of any of the unnegated literals, and $\bar{c}$ is the largest constant appearing in any of them, let $c_1 = \bar{i} + \bar{c} + 1$ and let $c_2 = 2\bar{i} + \bar{c} + 2$. By such a choice of c_1 and c_2, we have $f(c_1, c_2)$ is false, so $\langle c_1\ c_2\rangle$ is not in $E_p([p])$, but $\langle c_1\ c_2\rangle$ is in $[p]^+$, a contradiction.

If every clause of f does not contain an unnegated literal, then there is some clause in which every literal has the form $\neg r^i(a_1\ a_2)$, where a_i, $1 \leq i \leq 2$, is b_1, b_2 or a constant, but not both a_1 and a_2 are constants. Since there are a fixed number of literals in this clause, if p is large enough, we can choose values c_1 and c_2 for b_1 and b_2 such that $\langle c_1\ c_2\rangle$ is not in $[p]^+$, but all the atoms in the clause are false. Since all the atoms are false, all the literals are true, so the clause is true and $f(c_1, c_2)$ is true. (How do we pick c_1 and c_2?) Hence, $\langle c_1\ c_2\rangle \in E_p([p])$, a contradiction. We see that in any case, there is some p for which $E_p([p]) \neq [p]^+$. Since E_p is equivalent to E, E cannot compute transitive closures correctly for all states of r.

There have been several proposals for extending relational algebra so it can express more operations on relations. These proposals generally involve addition of programming language constructs or fixed-point operators. The query language QBE, which we cover in the next chapter, includes constructs specifically for dealing with transitive closures of relations (for relations whose closures are anti-symmetric).

14.4 COMPUTED RELATIONS

14.4.1 An Example

Consider a relation *schedule*(FLIGHT# FROM TO DEPARTS ARRIVES) containing flight information for our mythical airline. Suppose we want to create a relation *length*(FLIGHT# FLYTIME) that gives the duration of each flight. One approach is to use a database command to extract tuples from the relation, perform a calculation in some general-purpose programming language, and use another database command to insert tuples into *length*. That is, we embed calls to the database system within programs in some standard programming language. If the times in *schedule* are local, the program doing the duration calculation has to know what the time zone is for each city served. It would simplify the program if the database system could connect each city with its time zone. We can keep a relation *inzone*(CITY ZONE) giving the time zone for each city served. We can then define two virtual relations

$$fromzone = \delta_{CITY \leftarrow FROM, ZONE \leftarrow FZONE}(inzone)$$
$$tozone = \delta_{CITY \leftarrow TO, ZONE \leftarrow TZONE}(inzone)$$

and use them to define a third virtual relation

$$zonetimes = \pi_{FLIGHT\# \; DEPARTS \; FZONE \; ARRIVES \; TZONE}(schedule \bowtie fromzone \bowtie tozone).$$

The program can then access *zonetimes* to compute *length* without having to look up time zones for cities.

Suppose we want *length* to be a virtual relation, so its state is always consistent with that of *schedule*. We need to do the computation of *length* entirely within the database system. We could have a relation *lasts*(DEPARTS FZONE ARRIVES TZONE FLYTIME) that gives the duration for all combinations of departure and arrival times and zones. If we had *lasts*, we could define *length* as

$$\pi_{FLIGHT\# \; FLYTIME}(zonetimes \bowtie lasts).$$

While such an approach is conceivable, *lasts* will be a huge relation if it includes all possible combinations of times and zones. Even if we took this approach, we would probably need a program to calculate all the tuples in *lasts*.

What would be nice is if *lasts* only contained the tuples needed to correctly compute *length*. There is no way to know in advance what tuples will be needed in *lasts*, so it would be desirable to compute the proper tuples upon demand. That is, we would like to implicitly embed calls to programs within database commands. Rather than associating any stored extension with *lasts*, we instead associate a program that calculates FLYTIME, given values for DEPARTS, FZONE, ARRIVES, and TZONE, so tuples can be created upon demand when computing *length*.

We call a relation whose extension is a function a *computed* relation. To distinguish computed relations from relations with stored extensions, we call the latter *tabular* relations.

We cannot use the computed relation *lasts* in arbitrary expressions, for example

$$dtimes = \pi_{DEPARTS\ FZONE}(\sigma_{ARRIVES=1:10p, FLYTIME=2:20}(lasts)).$$

The procedure associated with *lasts* does not work in the right direction for use in computing *dtimes*. We can associate other programs with *lasts* to generate tuples when values on other sets of attributes are given. To handle *dtimes*, we would need a procedure that generates all DEPARTS FZONE TZONE-values for a given ARRIVES FLYTIME-value. While such a procedure is not unreasonable, we probably would not want to deal with a procedure that generates all DEPARTS FZONE FLYTIME-values for a given ARRIVES TZONE-value. In general, while we can associate several procedures with a computed relation to handle different sets of input attributes, it is unlikely that there will be a procedure for every set of attributes.

If we associate a procedure with *lasts* to compute an ARRIVES-value from a DEPARTS FZONE TZOME FLYTIME-value, we can evaluate the expression

$$\pi_{TO\ FROM\ ARRIVES}(\sigma_{DEPARTS=8:15a, FLYTIME=2:40}(lasts \bowtie fromzone \bowtie tozone))$$

to get the arrival times in various cities of a flight that departs at 8:14a and lasts 2 hours and 40 minutes. It may not be immediately apparent that we can evaluate this expression given the procedural extension of *lasts*, but we shall show shortly that it is possible.

The procedures associated with computed relations need not return a value for every possible value on the input attributes. For *lasts*, for any set of four attributes, there is a function that will return a value on a fifth attribute, so long as there is a legal value. However, there may not always be a legal value for the fifth attribute to go with a given value on the other four. For instance, if we have ⟨9:20a Pacific 1:20p 2:40⟩ as a value on DEPARTS FZONE ARRIVES FLYTIME, there is no value for TZONE that will form a legal tuple in *lasts*.

Sometimes we cannot evaluate a given expression involving a computed relation because certain procedures are absent from the relation's extension.

In some of those cases, however, we may still be able to test if a particular tuple is in the relation represented by the expression. Suppose the only procedures associated with *lasts* are ones that generate a fifth value, given four others. Consider again the expression

$$dtimes = \pi_{DEPARTS\ FZONE}(\sigma_{ARRIVES=\text{1:10}p, FLYTIME=\text{2:20}}(lasts)).$$

While with the specified computed extension for *lasts* we cannot evaluate *dtimes*, we can test if a particular tuple, say ⟨10:50a Eastern⟩, is in *dtimes*. We can make this test because it amounts to evaluating the expression

$$\sigma_{DEPARTS=\text{10:50}a, FZONE=\text{Eastern}}(\pi_{DEPARTS\ FZONE}$$
$$(\sigma_{ARRIVES=\text{1:10}p, FLYTIME=\text{2:20}}(lasts))),$$

for which the given procedural extension of *lasts* is adequate.

The next section examines the problem of determining, given a restricted algebraic expression involving computed relations, if the expression can be effectively evaluated, tested for membership, or neither.

14.4.2 Testing Expressions Containing Computed Relations

We shall not worry much about the exact mechanism for specifying the procedures that make up the extension of a computed relation. We are mainly concerned with which sets of attributes can be used to determine values for other attributes.

To develop the theory of computed relations, it helps to imagine that any computed relation $r(R)$ does have a tabular extension, although that extension might be infinite. We shall use simply r to denote that extension. For X, $Y \subseteq R$, we say there is a *computed dependency* (CD) of Y on X in r, written $X =: Y$, if given an X-value x, there is a procedure to compute $\pi_Y(\sigma_{X=x}(r))$. While not essential to the following discussion, it may clarify things to assume that a CD $X =: Y$ implies the FD $X \rightarrow Y$. That is, there is a function to compute a single Y-value given an X-value, so $\pi_Y(\sigma_{X=x}(r))$ contains at most one tuple. A *determining set* for r is any left side of a CD on r.

Example 14.32 If for the computed relation *lasts* in the previous section we could compute a fifth value from any four, *lasts* would satisfy the CDs

DP FZ AR TZ =: FT
DP FZ AR FT =: TZ
DP FZ TZ FT =: AR
DP AR TZ FT =: FZ
FZ AR TZ FT =: DP,

using the abbreviations DP, FZ, AR, TZ and FT for DEPARTS, FZONE, ARRIVES, TZONE and FLYTIME. To recast remarks in the previous section, it is conceivable that *lasts* could satisfy the CD

AR FT =: DP FZ TZ,

but it is unlikely that the extension of *lasts* would contain a procedure that would give rise to

AR TZ =: DP FZ FT.

We now define the terms *listable* and *decidable* for algebraic expressions involving computed relations. We limit ourselves to expressions with single-tuple constant relations, project, select on equality, and natural join. Recall that these constraints define the class of restricted algebraic expressions, for which equivalent tagged tableau queries exist. We actually define listable and decidable for tagged tableau queries. Recall the notation associated with a tagged tableau query. For a tagged tableau query Q, a database d, and a valuation ρ of Q, $\rho(Q) \subseteq d$ means that ρ maps every row w in Q to a tuple in the relation in d with scheme $tag(w)$. We then have

$$Q(d) = \{\rho(w_0) | \rho(Q) \subseteq d\},$$

where w_0 is the summary of Q. Since we imagine every computed relation to have an extension, even if we cannot effectively compute it, $Q(d)$ makes sense even when d contains computed relations.

To make our definitions, we need the algorithm MARK given in Figure 14.62. MARK marks symbols in a tableau query, succeeding if it marks all the symbols in the summary, and marks all matched symbols and a determining set for each row that is tagged with a computed relation. We assume MARK has global access to two set variables, *TABULAR* and *COMPUTED*, that give the sets of tabular and computed relations in the database.

Input: A tagged tableau query Q, and an array *CDEP* of sets of computed dependencies for each relation in *COMPUTED*.
Output: *true* if all symbols of Q get marked; *false* otherwise.
MARK(Q, *CDEP*)
begin

1. *Initialization.*
   Mark all constant symbols in Q;
   for each row $w \in Q$ **do**
     if $tag(w) \in TABULAR$
     then mark every symbol in w;

2. *Computation.*
   2.1. *Propagate Marks.*
     while changes occur **do**
       for each marked variable a in Q **do**
         mark all copies of a in Q, including those in the summary;
   2.2. *Apply CDs.*
     for each row $w \in Q$ **do**
       if $tag(w) \in COMPUTED$
       then begin
         for each CD $X =: Y$ in $CDEP(tag(w))$ **do**
           if all the symbols in the X-columns of w are marked
           then mark all the symbols in the Y-columns of w
       end;

3. *Return Results*
   if all the symbols in the summary are marked **and**
     every row tagged with a computed relation is marked on
     all its matched variables and on some determining set
   then return(*true*)
   else return(*false*)

end.

Figure 14.62

Example 14.33 Consider the tagged tableau query Q_1 in Figure 14.63, which corresponds to one of the expressions of the last section (where FR abbreviates FROM). Assume the first five CDs from the last example hold on *lasts* and that relations *fromzone* and *tozone* are tabular. Figure 16.64 shows

Q_1 after the initialization step in MARK. We use the symbol $\times$ for marks. Figure 14.65 shows Q_1 after propagation of marks. Applying the CD DR FZ TZ FT =: AR, we may mark a_5 in the first row, as shown in Figure 14.66. Finally, in the second pass through the computation step, the mark on a_5 is propagated to the summary, so MARK returns *true*.

Q_1(FR	TO	DR	FZ	AR	TZ	FT)	
a_1	a_2			a_5			
		8:14a	b_1	a_5	b_2	2:41	(*lasts*)
a_1			b_1				(*fromzone*)
	a_2				b_2		(*tozone*)

Figure 14.63

Q_1(FR	TO	DR	FZ	AR	TZ	FT)	
a_1	a_2			a_5			
		8:14a $\times$	b_1	a_5	b_2	2:41 $\times$	(*lasts*)
a_1 $\times$			b_1 $\times$				(*fromzone*)
	a_2 $\times$				b_2 $\times$		(*tozone*)

Figure 14.64

Q_1(FR	TO	DR	FZ	AR	TZ	FT)	
a_1 $\times$	a_2 $\times$			a_5			
		8:14a $\times$	b_1 $\times$	a_5	b_2 $\times$	2:41 $\times$	(*lasts*)
a_1 $\times$			b_1 $\times$				(*fromzone*)
	a_2 $\times$				b_2 $\times$		(*tozone*)

Figure 14.65

Q_1(FR	TO	DR	FZ	AR	TZ	FT)	
a_1 $\times$	a_2 $\times$			a_5			
		8:14a $\times$	b_1 $\times$	a_5 $\times$	b_2 $\times$	2:41 $\times$	(*lasts*)
a_1 $\times$			b_1 $\times$				(*fromzone*)
	a_2 $\times$				b_2 $\times$		(*tozone*)

Figure 14.66

Example 14.34 The tagged tableau query Q_2, in Figure 14.67, also corresponds to an expression given in the last section. Assume again that *lasts* has the first five CDs in Example 14.32. If we apply MARK to Q_2, the two constants in the first row get marked, but no other marks are made. Thus, MARK returns *false* for Q_2.

Q_2(DR	FZ	AR	TZ	FT)	
a_1	a_2				
a_1	a_2	1:10p	b_1	2:20	(*lasts*)

Figure 14.67

Definition 14.13 A tagged tableau query Q is *listable* relative to a set of CDs *CDEP* if MARK(Q, *CDEP*) = *true.*

Example 14.35 The query Q_1 given in Example 14.33 is listable, while the query Q_2 in Example 14.34 is not.

We have done things in a rather backwards manner. Usually we define a property, and then give an algorithm to test for it. Here we have given the algorithm, and defined the property from it. We shall now show that the term "listable" is well-chosen—that for a listable query Q and a database d, we can indeed compute $Q(d)$. We leave it to the reader to show that there is no way, in general, to evaluate $Q(d)$ if Q is not listable (see Exercise 14.51). To simplify the argument, we assume that each CD $X =: Y$ implies the corresponding FD $X \rightarrow Y$. Hence, for any relation r with CD $X =: Y$, we may assume a function f_{XY} that returns a Y-value for any X-value, or possibly a special value κ (for *kill*) that indicates r contains no tuple with the given X-value. The argument can be generalized to allow several Y-values for a given X-value (see Exercise 14.53).

To evaluate a tagged tableau query Q on a database d, we need to find every valuation ρ of Q such that $\rho(Q) \subseteq d$. Let Q_{tab} be the set of rows in Q whose tags are tabular relations and let Q_{com} be the rows with tags that are computed relations. The possibilities for ρ are limited by its value on rows in Q_{tab}. It is a straightforward enumeration to find every valuation ρ of Q_{tab} such that $\rho(w) \in tag(w)$ for every row w in Q_{tab}, that is, $\rho(Q_{tab}) \subseteq d$. We assume that we start with such a valuation ρ for Q_{tab}, and attempt to extend it to a valuation for all of Q. We know that $\rho(c)$ must equal c for every constant c, so we can extend ρ to all the constants in Q. At this point ρ is defined on the symbols that are marked after the initialization stage of running

MARK on Q. The strategy of this argument is to show that we can extend ρ to any symbol marked during that computation.

Any symbol a that is marked during the propagation step must already have $\rho(a)$ defined. If we apply a CD $X =: Y$ on a row w to mark the symbols in the Y-columns, the X-columns must already be marked. Hence, we know the value of $\rho(w(X))$. Using the function f_{XY} corresponding to the CD, we can get a Y-value $y = f_{YX}(\rho(w(X)))$. If y is actually κ, we know there is no way to extend ρ so that $\rho(w) \in tag(w)$. Also, no extension is possible if ρ is already defined on $w(A)$, $A \in Y$, and $\rho(w(A)) \neq y(A)$. If neither of these cases arises, then we may extend ρ to $w(Y)$ by letting $\rho(w(Y)) = y$.

If we continue on in this manner, we either find at some point ρ cannot be extended, or it is extended to all the symbols that get marked by MARK. The valuation ρ might not be defined on every symbol in some row $w \in Q_{com}$. Let $tag(w) = r(R)$. Even if ρ is not defined on all of w, since MARK succeeds on Q, for some determining set X of r, ρ is defined. Thus, if ρ is defined on exactly $w(Z)$, for some $Z \subseteq R$, we can determine if there is a tuple t in r such that $\rho(w(Z)) = t(Z)$. Since any variable in $w(R - Z)$ is not marked, it cannot be matched, or Q would not be listable. Theoretically, then, ρ could be extended to all of w by letting $\rho(w) = t$. We may not actually be able to determine the value of t on attributes in $R - Z$, but it is sufficient to know that appropriate values exist. Since the summary, say w_0, of Q gets marked, $\rho(w_0)$ is defined, and is a tuple in $Q(d)$.

We have argued that any valuation ρ found by the method above can be extended to all of Q in such a manner that $\rho(Q) \subseteq d$. Starting with some valuation ρ such that $\rho(Q) \subseteq d$, it is not hard to see that if we restrict ρ to Q_{tab} and then extend it by the method above, we end up with a valuation that agrees with ρ on all the marked symbols of Q, and hence has the same value on the summary. Therefore, we can find every tuple in $Q(d)$.

We now turn to the definition of decidable. Let MARK$'$ be the algorithm MARK of Figure 14.62 modified so that all the symbols in the summary of Q are marked during the initialization step.

Definition 14.14 A tagged tableau query Q is *decidable* relative to a set of CDs *CDEP* if MARK$'$(Q, *CDEP*) $=$ *true*.

Example 14.36 Referring back to Example 14.34, let Q_2 be the tagged tableau query in Figure 14.67. Running MARK$'$ on Q_2, we mark all the symbols in the summary and the constants during initialization, as shown in Figure 14.68. Propagating the marks on a_1 and a_2, and applying the CD

DR FZ AR FT =: TZ results in all the symbols of Q_2 being marked. Hence MARK′ returns *true* for Q_2 and so Q_2 is decidable.

Q_2(DR	FZ	AR	TZ	FT)	
a_1 ×	a_2 ×				
a_1 ×	a_2 ×	1:10p ×	b_1	2:20 ×	(*lasts*)

Figure 14.68

We now argue that for a decidable tagged tableau query Q and a tuple t, we can effectively decide if $t \in Q(d)$. Let R be the scheme of $Q(d)$, and assume t is a tuple on R. Deciding if $t \in Q(d)$ is the same as determining if $\sigma_{R=t}(Q(d))$ has any tuples. Let w_0 be the summary of Q. We can form a query Q' for $\sigma_{R=t}(Q(d))$ by replacing any variable a_i in the A_i-column of w_0 by the constant $t(A_i)$. If $w(A_i)$ is already a constant and not equal to $t(A_i)$, we can stop, for we know t is not in $Q(d)$. Q' is just Q with summary variables replaced by constants, so MARK succeeds on Q' exactly when MARK′ succeeds on Q. Therefore, if Q is decidable, Q' is listable, and we can effectively decide if $t \in Q(d)$ by computing $Q'(d)$.

The definitions of listable and decidable implicitly assume that domains are infinite. If a domain is finite, we can enumerate its values as part of an evaluation strategy. For example, if we had a computed relation $r(A\ B)$ with CD A =: B, and $dom(A)$ is finite, we could compute the extension of r by enumerating the domain of A. Exercise 14.55 shows how to incorporate information on finite domains into the definitions of listable and decidable.

14.5 EXERCISES

14.1 Show that all the inference rules for FDs are valid rules of inference for logic when FDs are interpreted as propositional formulas.

14.2* Choose any complete set of inference rules for FDs. Show that these rules, when interpreted as inference rules in propositional logic, are a complete set of inference rules for the subtheory of propositional logic consisting only of formulas of the form $X \Rightarrow Y$.

14.3 Complete the proof of Lemma 14.1.

14.4 Show that all the inference rules for MVDs alone and MVDs with FDs are valid rules of inference for logic when FDs and MVDs are interpreted as propositional formulas.

14.5 Prove Lemma 14.3.

14.6 Prove Lemma 14.5.

14.7 Prove Theorem 14.2.

14.8 Let F be a set of FDs, each with a single attribute on the right side. Define

$$M_F = \{X \twoheadrightarrow Y \mid X \rightarrow A \in F\}.$$

M_F is F converted to MVDs. Use Theorem 14.2 to prove the following theorem of Beeri.

Theorem 14.14 Let F be a set of FDs and let M be a set of MVDs. For an MVD $X \twoheadrightarrow Y$, $F \cup M$ implies $X \twoheadrightarrow Y$ if and only if $M_F \cup M$ implies $X \twoheadrightarrow Y$.

One consequence of this theorem is that any procedure for implication of MVDs by MVDs can easily be converted to a procedure for the inference of MVDs by FDs and MVDs.

14.9 Show that inference in the world of two-tuple relations is not the same as inference over regular relations for JDs and embedded MVDs.

14.10* Show that the correspondence of FDs and MVDs with formulas in propositional logic can not be extended to embedded MVDs in such a way as to preserve equivalence of implication.

14.11 Let J be a set of JDs over scheme R. Let X be a subset of R. Show that $\pi_X(SAT(J))$ cannot necessarily be expressed as $SAT(J')$ for a set J' of JDs over X.

14.12 Give the smallest relation containing the relation r below that satisfies the TD τ in Figure 14.5.

$r(A$	B	$C)$
1	3	5
1	3	6
1	3	7
2	3	5
2	4	5
1	4	6

14.13 Give the smallest relation containing relation r above that satisfies the TD τ in Figure 14.7.

14.14 Show that the TD τ in Figure 14.5 is not equivalent to any JD.

14.15 Prove that any JD, full or properly embedded, is equivalent to some TD.

Definition 14.15 A (typed) TD is *simple* if each column has at most one repeated variable.

14.16 (a) Prove that if a TD is simple and full, then it is equivalent to some JD.
(b) Give a simple TD that is not equivalent to any full or embedded JD.

14.17* Show that any set of full TDs over the same scheme is equivalent to a single TD.

14.18* Give a set of partial TDs over the same scheme that is not equivalent to a single TD.

14.19* Prove that there are only three distinct TDs over a relation scheme with two attributes. (They are the trivial TD, the Cartesian product TD, and the TD in Figure 14.10.)

14.20 Show that a TD can be expressed as a quantified predicate calculus formula with a single predicate symbol (for the relation). Note that if the TD is full, the formula uses no existential quantifiers.

14.21 Prove that any relation that is a column-wise Cartesian product satisfies every TD over its scheme.

14.22 (a) Consider the set of all S-partial TDs over a scheme R, where $S \subseteq R$ and S has two or more attributes. Show that there is a strongest TD and a weakest nontrivial TD in this set.
(b) Prove that there is no weakest nontrivial TD over any scheme of three or more attributes.

14.23 Prove that a full TD is trivial if and only if the conclusion row is also a hypothesis row.

14.24 Characterize those TDs that are equivalent to JDs in terms of the graphs of the TDs.

14.25 Give two different graphs for the TD τ in Figure 14.13.

14.26 Is every TD whose graph can be drawn as a triangle equivalent to an EMVD?

14.27 Prove Theorem 14.6.

14.28* Exhibit a chain of progressively stronger TDs, along the lines of Theorem 14.7. Hint: Consider cutting the graph G in Figure 14.20 at node i, and then overlaying nodes 1 and i.

14.29* Finish the proof of Theorem 14.8.

14.30 Let **C** be a set of S-partial TDs on scheme R and let τ be an arbitrary TD on R. Show that if there is an infinite relation that satisfies **C** but violates τ, then there is a finite relation with the same property.

14.31 Show that the following inference axioms for TDs are correct. Let $\tau = (T, w)$ be a TD.
(a) *Renaming* If τ' is formed from τ by a one-to-one renaming of symbols, then τ implies τ'.
(b) *Identification of variables* If τ' is formed by replacing all oc-

currences of some variable in T of τ with a variable from the same column of T, then τ implies τ'. (Note that this axiom does not allow identifying a variable that only appears in w with a variable in T.)

(c) *Transitivity* Let $\tau_1 = (T_1, w_1)$ and $\tau_2 = (T_2, w_2)$ where $T_1 \supseteq T_2 \cup \{w_2\}$. TDs τ_1 and τ_2 together imply $\tau_3 = (T_1 - \{w_2\}, w_1)$.

(d) *Reflexivity* The TD $(\{w\}, w)$ holds for any row w.

14.32* Prove that Augmentation (Lemma 14.7), Weakening (Section 14.3.4), Renaming, Identification of variables, Transitivity, and Reflexivity (from the last exercise) are a complete set of inference axioms for implication of TDs on arbitrary relations.

14.33* Show that if the T-rule is restricted to generate only rows that contain new combinations of original variables in a tableau, then some combinations of original symbols will not be obtained that would be obtained without the restriction. That is, provide an example tableau and some TDs where the T-rule cannot generate any new combination of original variables immediately, but will do so eventually.

14.34 Let **C** be a set of TDs over scheme R and let T be a tableau on R. Show that chasing T with **C** produces the same combinations of original variables no matter what the order in which the TDs in **C** are used.

14.35 Let **C** be a set of full TDs over a scheme R and let T be a tableau on R. Show that chasing T with **C** always gives a unique result for the tableau at the last stage.

14.36 Referring to Example 14.23, show that neither TD in **C** by itself implies τ.

14.37 Which of the following relations satisfies the GFD γ in Figure 14.40?

r_1

A	B	C	D
1	3	5	7
1	4	6	8
2	3	6	7

r_2

A	B	C	D
1	2	3	5
1	2	4	6

r_3

A	B	C	D
1	2	4	5
1	3	4	6

14.38 Give a syntactic characterization for when a GFD is trivial.

14.39 Find an inference axiom along the lines of GT1 that gives a nontrivial TD implied by a nontrivial GFD.

14.40 Show that axiom GT1 can be used to replace FDs with TDs when considering the TDs implied by a set of FDs and GFDs.

14.41 Prove that implication of GFDs is the same for finite and arbitrary relations.

14.42 Note that row w_1 can be removed from the GFD γ in Figure 14.50 to get an equivalent GFD. State and prove a general result about superfluous rows in TDs and GFDs.

14.43 Sketch the proof of Theorem 14.11. Be sure to indicate why our method for renaming variables when applying the G-rule is adequate.

14.44 In doing a chase computation with TDs and GFDs, show that if the sequence of tableaux generated is finite, then the last tableau in the sequence is the limit of the sequence.

14.45* Let **C** be a finite set of TDs and GFDs. Demonstrate that $\pi_X(\mathbf{C})$ can have an infinite number of dependencies, and also not be equivalent to any finite set of dependencies. What if **C** happens to contain only FDs and JDs?

14.46 (a) Prove that there is a set of GFDs equivalent to $\pi_X(\mathbf{C})$ when **C** contains only FDs.

(b) Prove that there is a set of TDs equivalent to $\pi_X(\mathbf{C})$ when **C** contains only JDs.

14.47 Prove Lemma 14.8.

14.48 In Case 6.2 of the proof of Theorem 14.13, show that

$$f(b_1, b_2, \ldots, b_{m-1}) \equiv \exists b_m\, f'(b_1, b_2, \ldots, b_m).$$

14.49 (a) Let *lasts* and *zonetimes* be as defined in Section 14.4.1. Assume *connects*(*F*#1 *F*#2) is a relation giving all pairs of connecting flights. Give an algebraic expression that defines a relation giving total duration and layover time for each pair of connecting flights.

(b) What CDs must *lasts* satisfy in order to be able to evaluate your answer to part (a)?

14.50 Let $r_1(A\ B\ C)$ and $r_2(C\ D)$ be tabular relations. Let $s_1(B\ D\ E)$ be a computed relation with CDs $B =: D\ E$ and $D\ E =: B$. Let $s_2(C\ E\ I)$ be a computed relation with CD $C\ E =: I$. Convert each of the following restricted algebraic expressions to a tagged tableau query, and say which of the resulting queries are listable.

(a) $r_1 \bowtie s_1$
(b) $r_2 \bowtie s_1$
(c) $\pi_{BC}(r_2 \bowtie s_1)$
(d) $\pi_{BE}(r_2 \bowtie s_1)$
(e) $\sigma_{E=1}(r_2 \bowtie s_1)$
(f) $r_1 \bowtie s_1 \bowtie s_2$
(g) $\pi_{ACE}(r_1 \bowtie r_2 \bowtie s_2)$
(h) $s_1 \bowtie s_2$
(i) $\pi_{BI}(s_1 \bowtie s_2)$
(j) $\pi_{DI}(s_1 \bowtie s_2)$

14.51 Show that in general there is no effective method to evaluate a query that is not listable. Assume that all domains are infinite.

14.52* Does tableau query equivalence preserve listability?

14.53 Give a method to evaluate a listable query without the assumption that a CD $X =: Y$ implies the FD $X \rightarrow Y$.

14.54 Which of the tableau queries you produced in Exercise 14.50 are decidable?

14.55 Show how information on finite domains can be brought into the theory of computed relations by using a single-attribute tabular relation $r(A)$ for every attribute A with a finite domain. The extension of r will be $dom(A)$.

14.6 BIBLIOGRAPHY AND COMMENTS

The connection between FDs and propositional formulas was first exhibited by Delobel and Casey [1973], and was fully developed by Fagin [1977b]. Sagiv [1980] showed the connection between MVDs and formulas. The material in this chapter on the connection between FDs and MVDs together and propositional formulas, particularly the material on two-tuple relations and the proof of Lemma 14.6, is from Sagiv, Delobel, Parker, and Fagin [1981]. Namibar [1979] also points out the connection between MVDs and logical formulas.

Template dependencies were introduced by Sadri and Ullman [1980a], although they deal only with the typed case. They give a complete axiomatization for TDs and also show how to extend the chase to TDs. Sadri and Ullman [1980b] also show how to include FDs with the TDs in the chase. The material on examples and counterexamples for TDs, graphical representations, and implication on finite versus infinite relations is from Fagin, Maier, Ullman, and Yannakakis [1981]. GFDs were defined by Sadri [1980a, 1980b, 1980c], who gives inference rules for TDs and GFDs together, extends the chase to GFDs, shows satisfaction classes are closed under projection, and defines a normal form with respect to TDs and GFDs.

There have been numerous dependency classes defined in attempts to overcome problems with existing classes or to produce a more expressive language of relational constraints. Nicolas [1978a, 1978b] introduced *mutual dependencies,* which are a kind of join dependency, and showed that FDs, MVDs and mutual dependencies can all be expressed in first-order logic. Maier and Mendelzon [1979] generalized mutual dependencies. Tanaka, Kambayashi, and Yajima [1979b] explore the properties of EMVDs. Parker and Parsaye-Ghomi [1980], and Sagiv and Walecka [1979] proved that there is no finite complete axiomatization of the EMVDs by themselves. Both proofs work by showing that for any k there is an inference axiom that says a certain k EMVDs imply some other EMVD τ, but any $k - 1$ of those EMVDs only imply other EMVDs that are implied by the EMVDs singly. Thus, that inference axiom cannot be derived from any set of inference axioms with $k - 1$ or less hypothesis EMVDs. The latter pair of authors define the class of *subset dependencies,* which properly include the EMVDs, and which has a finite complete axiomatization. A subset dependency is a statement of the form

$$\pi_Z(\sigma_{X=x}(r)) \subseteq \pi_Z(\sigma_{Y=y}(r)).$$

Sciore [1982], attempting to axiomatize JDs, had to generalize that class of dependencies slightly in order to do so, and conjectures there is no finite axiomatization of JDs. His dependencies were essentially TDs with the restriction that any column may contain at most two repeated variables.

Several people independently came up with classes of dependencies similar to TDs and GFDs. Fagin [1980a] used Horn clauses to define *embedded implicational dependencies* (EIDs), which are equivalent to untyped TDs and GFDs (where we consider any typed dependency to also be an untyped dependency). Among other results, he shows that any set **C** of EIDs has an Armstrong relation, that is, a relation that satisfies exactly the EIDs in **C**. Fagin also shows closure of satisfaction classes of EIDs under projection. Yannakakis and Papadimitriou [1980] give the class of *algebraic dependencies,* which are set inequalities on algebraic expressions formed with projection and equijoin. They show that algebraic dependencies are equivalent to EIDs. Grant and Jacobs [1980] use logic to define a class of dependencies that are equivalent to "full" EIDs. That is, their class is equivalent to untyped full TDs and untyped GFDs. Paredaens and Janssens [1981] define *generalized dependencies,* which are equivalent to TDs and GFDs.

Beeri and Vardi [1980a, 1980b, 1980c] define *tuple generating dependen-*

cies and *equality generating dependencies,* which correspond to untyped TDs and untyped GFDs, respectively. They prove a number of complexity and decidability results, such as finite and infinite implication are undecidable for EIDs and implication of S-partial TDs is decidable. They also show the inequivalence of finite and infinite implication for untyped dependencies. Chandra, Harel, and Makowsky [1981] show undecidability of infinite implication for typed EIDs and untyped TDs. They also show that implication of "full" EIDs is decidable, but exponential-time complete. There are recent reports from several researchers that implication for typed TDs is undecidable, but the decidability of EMVDs has yet to be resolved.

Hull [1981] explores the properties of EIDs, and proves that satisfaction classes of EIDs are closed under join.

Several types of dependencies of a flavor different from TDs and GFDs have been proposed. Lipski and Marek [1979] discuss constraints involving cardinalities. Ginsburg and Hull [1981] consider constraints involving ordered domains. Casanova [1981] presents a class of dependencies called *subset dependencies,* but they are not the same as the subset dependencies of Sagiv and Walecka. Rather, they are interrelational constraints that connect projections of two relations.

The proof that transitive closure is not expressible in relational algebra is due to Aho and Ullman [1979], and they give some proposals for extensions of the algebra. Banchilon [1978], Paredaens [1978], Chandra [1981], and Chandra and Harel [1980a, 1980b] have all proposed other notions of query language completeness. The language specification for QBE (Query-by-Example) given by Zloof [1976] includes specific constructs for dealing with transitive closures.

The section on computed relations is adapted from Maier and Warren [1981a]. The ISBL query language, presented by Hall, Hitchcock, and Todd [1975] and Todd [1975, 1976], allows some forms of computed relations.

Exercises 14.2, 14.8, and 14.10 are from Sagiv, Delobel, Parker, and Fagin [1981]. The original proof of Theorem 14.14 is by Beeri [1980]. Exercises 14.17, 14.18, 14.19, 14.28, and 14.29 are from Fagin, Maier, Ullman, and Yannakakis [1981]. Answers to Exercises 14.32 and 14.33 can be found in Sadri and Ullman [1980a]. Exercise 14.39 is from Beeri and Vardi [1980a]. Exercise 14.45 on finite specification is taken from Hull [1981]. Exercise 14.46 is from Sadri [1980a].

Chapter 15

RELATIONAL QUERY LANGUAGES

In this chapter we give a brief overview of several query languages from various relational database systems. We shall not give a complete exposition of the languages. Our point is, rather, to give the flavor of each, show how they are based on the algebra, calculus, or tableaux, and indicate where they depart from the relational model as we have defined it.

We shall look at five languages: ISBL, from the PRTV system; QUEL, from INGRES; SQL, from System R; QBE, which runs atop several database systems; and PIQUE, from the experimental PITS system. ISBL is based on relational algebra, QUEL and SQL resemble tuple calculus, and QBE is a domain calculus-like language, with a syntax similar to tableau queries. PIQUE is a tuple calculus-like language, but it presents a universal relation scheme interface through the use of window functions.

For practical reasons and usability considerations, relational query languages do not conform precisely to the relational model. They all contain features that are extensions to the model, and some have restrictions not present in the model. Nearly all relational systems have facilities for virtual relation definition. Languages based on tuple and domain calculus must allow only safe expressions. Safety is usually guaranteed by the absence of explicit quantifiers or by having variables range over relations rather than all tuples on a given scheme. Query languages often allow a limited amount of arithmetic and string computation on domain values, and sometimes handle sets of values through aggregate operators (count, average, maximum) and set comparisons. As mentioned in the last chapter, QBE contains operators for dealing with transitive closures. In the theory, order of attributes and tuples within a relation is immaterial. Query languages give control over attribute order and sort order for tuples when listing relations. In addition to output commands, query languages usually contain some form of assignment statement to store intermediate results. Some languages also give explicit control over duplicate tuple elimination after projection, so the data type they support is actually multisets of tuples. Suppression and invocation of duplicate removal are useful in connection with aggregate operators. Relational languages sometimes have special constructs or alternative syntax for use from within a regular programming language.

All the query languages we examine are as powerful as relational algebra. In some cases, however, this power may only be achieved through use of a sequence of assignment statements, and not within a single expression in the language. Sometimes, data manipulation commands must be used to get the effect of certain algebraic operators.

We shall not be exhaustive in demonstrating the features of the languages we present here. Some of the languages have facilities for data manipulation in addition to querying; we shall consider only the "query" portion of those languages. We shall not spend much time on formal syntax or semantics of the languages studied, but rather work by example. To make comparisons between the languages easy, all examples in this chapter will be based on the database in Figure 15.1, which is the same database as was used for most examples in Chapter 10.

15.1 ISBL

ISBL (Information System Base Language) is an algebra-based query language used in the PRTV (Peterlee Relational Test Vehicle) system. PRTV is an experimental, interactive database system developed at IBM's United Kingdom Scientific Centre.

ISBL expressions are built up with six operators, which correspond to algebraic operators or generalizations of them. Union, intersection, and join are denoted as +, ., and *, respectively, and behave exactly as in the algebra. Difference, denoted by −, has been generalized to be an "antijoin" operator. For relations r and s, with possibly different schemes,

$$r - s = r - (r \ltimes s),$$

where the − on the left is the one from ISBL and the one on the right is the usual one from relational algebra. Thus, in ISBL, $r - s$ is all the tuples in r that join with no tuple in s. The selection $\sigma_C(r)$ is written as $r{:}C$ in ISBL, where C is a selection condition built up from attribute names and constants with the comparators in $\{=, \neq, >, \geq, \leq, <\}$, parentheses, and the logical connectives & (and), | (or), and $\neg$ (not). Projection and renaming are combined into one operation in ISBL. The projection $\pi_{ABC}(r)$ is r % A, B, C in ISBL. To rename an attribute A_1 to be A_2 during projection, A_1 −> A_2 is used in place of A_1 to the right of %. A rename by itself is accomplished using % with all the attributes in the relation on the right. Three dots can be *pinfo*

PART#	SUBPARTOF	PARTNAME
211	0	coach seat
2114	211	seat cover
2116	211	seat belt
21163	2116	seat belt buckle
21164	2116	seat belt anchor
318	21164	funny little bolt
206	0	overhead console
2061	206	paging switch
2066	206	light switch
2068	206	air nozzle

usedon

PART#	PTYPE	NUSED
211	707	86
211	727	134
2114	707	86
2114	727	134
2116	707	244
2116	727	296
21164	707	488
21164	727	592

instock

PART#	LOCATION	QUANTITY
211	JFK	106
211	Boston	28
211	O'Hare	77
2114	JFK	6
2114	O'Hare	28
2116	Boston	341
2116	O'Hare	29
21164	Atlanta	36,391

Figure 15.1

used to stand for all unnamed attributes in a relation. Thus, if we want to rename just B in r, we would write r % B −> D, ... Expressions in ISBL are left-associative; parentheses may be used to override that associativity.

The keyword **list** is used to print the result of an expression in ISBL, and the result of an expression can be assigned to a relation using =.

To keep examples in this chapter concise, many of them will contain just an English statement of a query and the corresponding query language statement, with the result of evaluating the query included sometimes.

Example 15.1 What are the names of subparts of part 2116?

> **list** *pinfo* : *PART#* = 2116 % *PARTNAME*

(PARTNAME)
seat belt buckle
seat belt anchor

Example 15.2 How many seat belts are at Boston?

> **list** *pinfo* * *instock* : *PARTNAME* = "seat belt" &
> *LOCATION* = "Boston"% *QUANTITY*

(QUANTITY)
341

Example 15.3 Which parts are not in stock at either Boston or O'Hare?

> **list** *pinfo* − (*instock* : *LOCATION* = "Boston"|
> *LOCATION* = "O'Hare")% *PART#*

(PART#)
21163
21164
318
206
2061
2066
2068

Example 15.4 What are all the subparts of subparts of seat belts?

> **list** *pinfo* % *PART#*− >*SUBSUBPART*, *SUBPARTOF*− >*PART#**
> pinfo : *PARTNAME* = "seat belt" % *SUBSUBPART*

(SUBSUBPART)
21163
21164

Example 15.5 Which parts used on a 707 are in stock at Atlanta?

> **list** *usedon* : *PTYPE* = "707" % *PART#*
> (*instock* : *LOCATION* = "Atlanta" % *PART#*)

(PART#)
21164

We could also perform the same query by assigning intermediate results to relations.

> *r*1 = *usedon* : *PTYPE* = "707" % *PART#*
> *r*2 = *instock* : *LOCATION* = "Atlanta" % *PART#*
> *r*3 = *r*1 . *r*2
> **list** *r*3

ISBL can support virtual relations through use of a delayed evaluation feature. No expression is evaluated in ISBL until its result is needed. Relation names in expressions are normally bound to the current value of the relation. Prefixing a relation name with N! indicates that the value of the relation to be used is the current value at the time of evaluation.

Example 15.6 Suppose we want a virtual relation *stock*707 that gives part number, number used, location, and quantity for all parts used in a 707. If we make the assignment

> *stock*707 = N!*usedon* * N!*instock* : *PTYPE* = "707" %
> *PART#, NUSED, LOCATION, QUANTITY*

then any time we write **list** *stock*707 or *stock*707 occurs in an expression being evaluated, the current values of *usedon* and *instock* are used. If the N! is removed in both places, *stock*707's value will depend on the state of *usedon* and *instock* at the point when *stock*707 is defined.

ISBL does not have any operators within itself to perform computation on values. However, computed relations, whose extensions are functions or procedures in a general-purpose programming language, can be used to provide computation. The extension of a computed relation in ISBL takes one of two forms. One is a Boolean-valued function that recognizes those tuples that are in the relation, which is a slight departure from what we saw in Section 14.4.

The other form is a procedure that takes some values in a tuple as inputs and returns others as output.

Example 15.7 Let *adequate*(a, b) be a function that returns *true* exactly when $a \geq .5b$. The ISBL statement

> **list** *usedon * instock * adequate(QUANTITY, NUSED)* %
> *PART#, PTYPE, LOCATION*

gives the locations that have at least half the number of a part used on a given aircraft:

(PART#	PTYPE	LOCATION)
211	707	JFK
211	727	JFK
211	707	O'Hare
211	727	O'Hare
2116	707	Boston
2116	727	Boston
21164	707	Atlanta
21164	727	Atlanta

Example 15.8 Let *needed*(a, b, c) be a procedure that takes a and b as input and returns $c = max(.5b - a, 0)$. The statement

> **list** *usedon * instock * needed(QUANTITY, NUSED* |
> *AMT:ORDER)* : *PTYPE* = "727" & *ORDER* > 0 % *PART#,*
> *LOCATION, ORDER*

gives the number of each part to order at each location to bring the supply up to half the number used on a 727 (provided that the location already stocks the part):

(PART#	LOCATION	ORDER)
211	Boston	39
2114	JFK	61
2114	O'Hare	39
2116	O'Hare	119

In the call to *needed*, the vertical bar separates input parameters from output parameters, and *AMT*:*ORDER* indicates that the output parameter is supposed to be a new attribute *ORDER* with domain *AMT*.

ISBL also contains features for passing entire relations to and from procedures for updating, computing aggregates, and formatting output.

15.2 QUEL

QUEL (QUEry Language) is the data manipulation language for the INGRES (INteractive Graphics and REtrieval System) database system. INGRES is a fairly complete relational system that was developed at the University of California at Berkeley, and it is still being revised and extended. QUEL, in addition to retrieval functions, contains commands for update, authorization, integrity, and view definition. We shall only cover the retrieval aspects of QUEL.

QUEL is based on the tuple relational calculus. Tuple variables are all existentially quantified and bound to relations. Tuple variables are declared and bound with a statement of the form,

range of ⟨tuple variable⟩ **is** ⟨relation name⟩.

The *A*-component of a tuple variable *x* is denoted as *x.A*.

Example 15.9 For subsequent examples in this section, we shall assume the following bindings:

range of *p* **is** *pinfo*
range of *p*1 **is** *pinfo*
range of *u* **is** *usedon*
range of *i* **is** *instock*

With these bindings, *p.PART#*, *u.NUSED* and *i.PART#* are all proper references to tuple variable components.

The basic form of a retrieval in QUEL is

retrieve (⟨target list⟩) **where** ⟨condition⟩.

The condition corresponds to the formula in a tuple calculus expression. The target list is a sequence of tuple variable components, which resembles the portion of of a domain-calculus expression to the left of the bar.

Example 15.10 What is the name of part 2116?

retrieve (*p.PARTNAME*) **where** *p.PART#* = 2116

(PARTNAME)
seat belt

Example 15.11 What are the names and quantities of parts at O'Hare?

retrieve (*p.PARTNAME, i.QUANTITY*)
where *p.PART#* = *i.PART#* and *i.LOCATION* = "O'Hare"

(PARTNAME	QUANTITY)
coach seat	77
seat cover	28
seat belt	29

The comparators =, !=, >, >=, <= and < are allowed in comparisons, and the logical connectives **and**, **or**, and **not** can be used to combine comparisons. The attributes for the result of a retrieval are taken from the corresponding tuple variable components. The attributes in the result relation can be changed by using *NEWNAME* = *x.OLDNAME* in the target list. Renaming must be done if the resulting relation would have the same attribute twice.

Example 15.12 Which parts are subparts of the same part?

retrieve (*SUBPART*1 = *p.PART#*, *SUBPART*2 = *p*1*.PART#*)
where *p.SUBPARTOF* = *p*1*.SUBPARTOF* **and**
p.SUBPARTOF != 0 **and** *p.PART#* < *p*1*.PART#*

(SUBPART1	SUBPART2)
2114	2116
21163	21164
2061	2066
2061	2068
2066	2068

The condition *p.PART#* < *p*1*.PART#* is included to prevent an extra tuple for each pair of parts and to eliminate pairing a part with itself.

The condition part of a query is optional. The keyword **all** can be used to represent all components of a tuple variable in the target list. Thus,

retrieve *u*.**all**

returns the entire *usedon* relation. Computational expressions can appear most places that a tuple variable component would be appropriate. If an expression appears in the target list, it must be renamed.

Example 15.13 Which locations have at least half the number of a part used in a given aircraft?

retrieve (*u.PART#, u.PTYPE, i.LOCATION*)
  where *u.PART#* = *i.PART#* **and** *u.NUSED* * 0.5
    <= *i.QUANTITY*

Example 15.14 What proportion of the number of coach seats used on a 707 does each location have?

retrieve (*i.LOCATION, PROPORTION* =
  (*i.QUANTITY/u.NUSED*))
  where *p.PART#* = *u.PART#* **and** *p.PARTNAME*
    = "coach seat" **and** *u.PART#* = *i.PART#* **and**
    u.PTYPE = "707"

(LOCATION	PROPORTION)
JFK	1.233
Boston	.326
O'Hare	.894

Assignment of the result of a retrieval to a relation is achieved via the notation **into** ⟨relation⟩ after **retrieve.**

Example 15.15

retrieve into *used*727 (*u*.**all**) **where** *u.PTYPE* = "727"

makes *used*727 a relation with the same scheme as *usedon*, but consisting only of 727 information.

QUEL provides the aggregation operators **count**, **min**, **max**, **avg**, and **sum**, which can be used in expressions.

Example 15.16 How many different parts are there?

retrieve (*NUMPARTS* = **count**(*p.PART#*))

(NUMPARTS)
10

Example 15.17 Which part has the most in stock and which part has the least in stock at any one location?

retrieve (*i.PART#, i.LOCATION*)
where *i.QUANTITY* = **max**(*i.QUANTITY*) **or** *i.QUANTITY* =
min(*i.QUANTITY*)

(PART#	LOCATION)
2114	JFK
21164	Atlanta

The aggregate operators **count**, **avg**, and **sum** have "unique" versions, distinguished by a "**u**" on the end, that eliminate duplicates before applying the operator.

Example 15.18 How many locations have parts?

retrieve (*NUMLOCS* = **countu**(*i.LOCATION*))

(NUMLOCS)
4

Using **count** in place of **countu** in this query would produce the answer 8.

The component to which an aggregate operator is applied can be qualified. However, the qualification is local, and is not affected by the rest of the query.

Example 15.19 How many of part 211 are in stock?

retrieve (*TOTAL* = **sum**(*i.QUANTITY* **where** *i.PART#* = 211))

(TOTAL)
211

Example 15.20 The following query does *not* answer the question: How many seat belts are in stock?

retrieve (*NUMBELTS* = **sum**(*i.QUANTITY*))
where *p.PART#* = *i.PART#* **and** *p.PARTNAME* = "seat belt"

The **sum** is computed independently of the rest of the query.

QUEL has a grouping feature for aggregates, invoked with the keyword **by** within the argument to an aggregate operator. The component following the **by** is linked to the rest of the query.

Example 15.21 How many of each part are there?

retrieve (*i.PART#*, *TOTAL* = **sum**(*i.QUANTITY* **by** *i.PART#*))

(PART#	TOTAL)
211	211
2114	34
2116	370
21164	36,391

Example 15.22 How many seat belts are there in stock?

retrieve (*NUMBELTS* = **sum**(*i.QUANTITY* **by** *i.PART#*))
where *p.PART#* = *i.PART#* **and** *p.PARTNAME* = "seat belt"

(NUMBELTS)
370

Example 15.23 How many of each part over the maximum needed by any aircraft does each location have in stock?

retrieve ($u.PART\#$, $i.LOCATION$, $OVERSTOCK$ =
  ($i.QUANTITY$ − **max**($u.NUSED$ **by** $u.PART\#$))
 where $u.PART\# = i.PART\#$ **and**
  ($i.QUANTITY$ − **max**($u.NUSED$ **by** $u.PART\#$)) > 0

(PART#	LOCATION	OVERSTOCK)
2116	Boston	45
21164	Atlanta	35,799

15.3 SQL

SQL (Structured Query Language) is the data manipulation language for the System R database system. System R is a prototype relational database system developed at the IBM San Jose Research Laboratory. A commercial IBM product, SQL/Data System, is based on the System R prototype. While SQL is a complete data manipulation language, we cover only its retrieval capabilities.

SQL's syntax resembles tuple calculus, though not so closely as that of QUEL. SQL's precursor is SQUARE, which resembles relational algebra in some aspects and tuple calculus in others. The main operator in SQUARE is the *mapping*, which is a selection followed by a projection. The mapping is carried over into the basic syntax of SQL, which is

select ⟨attribute list⟩
from ⟨relation⟩
where ⟨condition⟩

Example 15.24 What are the names and numbers of subparts of part 211?

select *PARTNAME, PART#*
from *pinfo*
where *SUBPARTOF* = 211

(PARTNAME	PART#)
seat cover	2114
seat belt	2116

Example 15.25 What parts are at Boston or O'Hare?

> **select** *PART#*
> **from** *instock*
> **where** *LOCATION* = "Boston" **or** *LOCATION* = "O'Hare"

(PART#)
211
211
2114
2116
2116

The logical connectives **and**, **or**, and **not** can be used to combine comparisons. As we see from the last example, SQL does not automatically eliminate duplicates. Duplicates can be removed by including the keyword **unique** after **select**.

Example 15.26 To get rid of duplicate entries in the last example, we can use the query

> **select unique** *PART#*
> **from** *instock*
> **where** *LOCATION* = "Boston" **or** *LOCATION* = "O'Hare"

(PART#)
211
2114
2116

SQL has constructs for tests involving sets of values and sets of tuples. A set can be listed explicitly, or it can be the result of a subquery. Tests can be made for membership, emptiness, inclusion, and comparison with members of a set, one at a time.

Example 15.27 What parts are at Boston or O'Hare?

> **select unique** *PART#*
> **from** *instock*
> **where** *LOCATION* **in** ("Boston", "O'Hare")

Example 15.28 What are the names of parts at JFK?

```
select PARTNAME
from pinfo
where PART# in
    (select PART#
     from instock
     where LOCATION = "JFK")
```

(PARTNAME)
coach seat
seat cover

Example 15.29 Which location has the fewest of part 211?

```
select LOCATION
from instock
where QUANTITY <=all
    (select QUANTITY
     from instock
     where PART# = 211)
```

(LOCATION)
Boston

Example 15.30 Which locations stock all the parts that Boston does?

```
select LOCATION
from instock
where set(PART#) contains
    (select PART#
     from instock
     where LOCATION = "Boston")
```

(LOCATION)
Boston
O'Hare

The notation **set**(*PART#*) refers to the set of all *PART#*-values occurring with a *LOCATION*-value. It is possible for a subquery to reference fields from the relation in the containing query. If there are identical field names in the containing query and subquery, they are qualified with the relation name. In essence, the relation name serves as a tuple variable bound to the relation.

Example 15.31 Which locations have at least as many of a part as are used on a 707?

> **select** *PART#, LOCATION*
> **from** *instock*
> **where** *PART#* **in**
>   (**select** *PART#*
>   **from** *usedon*
>   **where** *PTYPE* = "707" **and** *NUSED* <= *QUANTITY*)

Note that *QUANTITY* refers to *instock*.

(PART#	LOCATION)
211	JFK
2116	Boston
21164	Atlanta

Another formulation of this question is

> **select** *PART#, LOCATION*
> **from** *instock*
> **where** *QUANTITY* >= **any**
>   (**select** *NUSED*
>   **from** *usedon*
>   **where** *PTYPE* = "707" **and** *instock.PART#* = *usedon.PART#*)

usedon.PART#)

When two copies of a relation are used in a query, the fields of each cannot be distinguished by prefixing the relation name. In these cases, an alternate qualifier may be listed after the relation name in the **from**-clause.

Example 15.32 What parts are available at more than one location?

select unique *PART#*
from *instock i*
where *PART#* **in**
  (**select** *PART#*
   from *instock*
   where *LOCATION* ¬= *i.LOCATION*)

(PART#)
211
2114
2116

In previous examples, we have been specifying joins by the use of **in**. This method for taking joins will not work if the answer to the query involves fields from more than one relation. In that case, multiple relations are used in the **from**-clause.

Example 15.33 What are the names and quantities of parts at JFK?

select *PARTNAME, QUANTITY*
from *pinfo, instock*
where *pinfo. PART#* = *instock.PART#* **and** *LOCATION* = "JFK"

(PARTNAME	QUANTITY)
coach seat	106
seat cover	6

Example 15.34 What parts are subparts of the same part?

select *p*1.*PART#*, *p*2.*PART#*
from *pinfo p*1, *pinfo p*2
where *p*1.*SUBPARTOF* = *p*2.*SUBPARTOF* **and**
  *p*1.*SUBPARTOF* ¬= 0 **and** *p*1.*PART#* < *p*2.*PART#*

(*p*1.PART#	*p*2.PART#)
2114	2116
21163	21164
2061	2066
2061	2068
2066	2068

SQL allows queries to be combined with the set operators **union**, **intersect**, and **minus**. Duplicates are removed after computing **union**.

Example 15.35 Which parts are not stocked by any location?

> **select** *PART#*
> **from** *pinfo*
> **minus**
> **select** *PART#*
> **from** *instock*

(PART#)
21163
318
206
2061
2066
2068

The order of columns in the result of a query is taken from the order of the attributes in the **select**-clause. The order of the tuples can be controlled with an **order by**-clause, which contains a list of attributes from the result of the query, each followed by **asc** or **desc**, for ascending or descending order. Another feature of SQL, demonstrated in the next example, is the use of * to stand for all the attributes in a relation.

Example 15.36 The following query lists the *instock* relation by decreasing quantity and increasing part number.

> **select** *
> **from** *instock*
> **order by** *QUANTITY* **desc**, *PART#* **asc**

(PART#	LOCATION	QUANTITY)
21164	Atlanta	36,391
2116	Boston	341
211	JFK	106
211	O'Hare	77
2116	O'Hare	29
211	Boston	28
2114	O'Hare	28
2114	JFK	6

SQL allows arithmetic expressions and provides the aggregate operators **avg**, **min**, **max**, **sum**, and **count**.

Example 15.37 Which locations have at least half the number of a part used in a given aircraft?

> **select** *usedon.PART#, PTYPE, LOCATION*
> **from** *usedon, instock*
> **where** *usedon.PART#* = *instock.PART#* **and**
>   *NUSED* * 0.5 <= *QUANTITY*

Example 15.38 How many coach seats are in stock?

> **select sum** (*QUANTITY*)
> **from** *instock*
> **where** *PART#* **in**
>   (**select** *PART#*
>   **from** *pinfo*
>   **where** *PARTNAME* = "coach seat")

( )
211

SQL does not name columns corresponding to aggregates or expressions. If an **order by**-clause must refer to such a column, it uses an integer denoting the position of the column.

SQL uses a **group by**-clause to partition the tuples in a result before application of an aggregate operator. A **having** clause may be included to remove some groups of tuples.

Example 15.39 How many of each part are there?

> **select** *PART#*, **sum**(*QUANTITY*)
> **from** *instock*
> **group by** *PART#*

Example 15.40 For which parts is the total in stock at least the number used by a 707, and by what amount does the total exceed the number used?

> **select** *usedon.PART#, NUSED* − **sum**(*QUANTITY*)
> **from** *usedon, instock*
> **where** *usedon.PART#* = *instock.PART#* **and** *PTYPE* = "707"
> **group by** *usedon.PART#*
> **having** *NUSED* − **sum**(*QUANTITY*) >= 0

(PART#	)
211	125
2116	136
21164	35,903

15.4 QBE

QBE (Query-By-Example) is a relational data manipulation language designed by M. M. Zloof at IBM's Watson Research Center. A subset of the language has been implemented to run with various IBM systems. We cover the retrieval aspects of QBE. QBE also has update operations, authorization and integrity mechanisms, domain declarations, and view definition facilities.

The syntax of QBE is two-dimensional. Queries are formed by filling in a *skeleton*, which contains a relation name and its attributes, such as

pinfo	PART#	SUBPARTOF	PARTNAME

The skeleton is filled in with rows of constants and variables. A filled-in skeleton has a syntax and semantics reminiscent of tableau queries. Tableau queries, in turn, can be readily described in domain calculus. A row in a QBE query, such as

pinfo	PART#	SUBPARTOF	PARTNAME
	a	*b*	*c*

corresponds to the atom *pinfo*(a b c) in domain calculus.

Variables in QBE are existentially quantified, and are represented by underlined strings. The particular name given a variable in no way affects the interpretation of a query, although it is usual to use example values from the domain of an attribute as names. Strings without underlines are constants. The operator **P.**, for *print*, is prefixed to any variable or constant to appear in the result of the query. **P.** is essentially a mechanism to form the equivalent of a summary in a tableau query, without having to write a separate row.

Example 15.41 Which locations stock part 211?

instock	PART#	LOCATION	QUANTITY
	211	**P.** Chicago	25

Result:

instock	LOCATION
	JFK
	Boston
	O'Hare

Note that the name Chicago for a variable has no effect on the values ultimately retrieved.

If a variable is mentioned in only one place, it may be omitted. QBE assumes each blank slot in a row contains a unique variable.

Example 15.42 The query in the last example could be written

instock	PART#	LOCATION	QUANTITY
	211	**P.**	

Selections with comparators other than equality are done by prefixing a constant or variable with the comparator. Essentially, θa, for comparator θ, represents the subset of the domain of the column equal to $\{c \mid c\ \theta\ a\}$.

Example 15.43 Which parts have more than 50 in stock at some location?

instock	PART#	LOCATION	QUANTITY
	P.		>=50

Result:

instock	PART#
	211
	2116
	21164

Note that QBE does eliminate duplicates.

Example 15.44 For which parts are more than 100 used on an aircraft other than a 727?

usedon	PART#	PTYPE	NUSED
	P.	¬= 727	>= 100

Result:

usedon	PART#
	2116
	21164

Queries are not limited to one row. Multiple rows may be used.

Example 15.45 Which parts are in stock at Boston and O'Hare?

instock	PART#	LOCATION	QUANTITY
	P. <u>100</u>	Boston	
	<u>100</u>	O'Hare	

Result:

instock	PART#
	211
	2116

Using the print operator in multiple rows gives the union of the results specified by each row.

Example 15.46 What parts are in stock at Boston or O'Hare?

instock	PART#	LOCATION	QUANTITY
	P. <u>100</u>	Boston	
	P. <u>101</u>	O'Hare	

Result:

instock	PART#
	211
	2114
	2116

Example 15.47 The following query retrieves information on part 211.

pinfo	PART#	SUBPARTOF	PARTNAME
	P. 211	**P.**	**P.**
	P.	**P.** 211	**P.**

Result:

pinfo	PART#	SUBPARTOF	PARTNAME
	211	0	coach seat
	2114	211	seat cover
	2116	211	seat belt

The print operator can be applied to an entire row by placing it at the left end of the row.

Example 15.48 The query in the last example can be written as follows.

pinfo	PART#	SUBPARTOF	PARTNAME
P.	211		
P.		211	

As part of a condition, it is possible to specify that no tuple matching a certain row may appear in a relation. No portion of such a row may be printed, however. The ability to test for the absence of a tuple is not available with tableau queries.

Example 15.49 Which locations have parts that Boston does not, and what are the parts?

instock	PART#	LOCATION	QUANTITY
	P. 100	**P.** Chicago	
	100	Boston	

Result:

instock	PART#	LOCATION
	2114	JFK
	2114	O'Hare
	21164	Atlanta

QBE also has the facility for matching substrings of string values by concatenating variables and constants.

Example 15.50 The query

pinfo	PART#	SUBPARTOF	PARTNAME
	P.		**P.** seatbelt

finds all parts where the partname begins with "seat."
Result:

pinfo	PART#	PARTNAME
	2114	seat cover
	2116	seat belt
	21163	seat belt buckle
	21164	seat belt anchor

With tableau queries, rows are bound to various relations with tags. In QBE, a separate skeleton is used for each relation involved in a query.

Example 15.51 What are the names of parts at JFK?

pinfo	PART#	SUBPARTOF	PARTNAME
	100		**P.** bolt

instock	PART#	LOCATION	QUANTITY
	100	JFK	

Example 15.52 Which locations have at least as many of a part as are used on a 707?

usedon	PART#	PTYPE	NUSED
	100	707	50

instock	PART#	LOCATION	QUANTITY
	P. 100	**P.** Chicago	>= 50

If values from multiple relations must be combined, variables in the same column of one relation are to appear in different columns, or a column must be renamed, it is necessary to specify an additional relation for the result.

Example 15.53 What are the names and quantities of parts at JFK?

pinfo	PART#	SUBPARTOF	PARTNAME
	100		bolt

instock	PART#	LOCATION	QUANTITY
	100	JFK	50

jfkparts	PARTNAME	QUANTITY
P.	bolt	50

Result:

jfkparts	PARTNAME	QUANTITY
	coach seat	106
	seat cover	6

Sometimes it is impossible or inconvenient to specify all the constraints among variables with a skeleton. QBE provides an auxiliary condition box to hold additional constraints.

Example 15.54 Which parts are subparts of the same part?

pinfo	PART#	SUBPARTOF	PARTNAME
	100	200	
	101	200	

CONDITIONS
200 ¬= 0
100 < 101

subparts	SUBPART1	SUBPART2
P.	100	101

Result:

subparts	SUBPART1	SUBPART2
	2114	2116
	21163	21164
	2061	2066
	2061	2068
	2066	2068

The order of tuples in a result can be controlled by the prefixes **AO.** (ascending order) and **DO.** (descending order) in the appropriate columns. When specifying orders on multiple columns, a number in parentheses after **AO.** or **DO.** specifies the precedence of the columns.

Example 15.55 The following query lists the *instock* relation by decreasing quantity and increasing part number.

instock	PART#	LOCATION	QUANTITY
P.	**AO**(2).		**DO**(1).

Arithmetic expressions may appear in QBE skeletons and the condition box.

Example 15.56 Which locations have at least half the number of a part used on a given aircraft?

usedon	PART#	PTYPE	NUSED
	100	DC10	25

instock	PART#	LOCATION	QUANTITY
	100	Chicago	>= 0.5 * 25

hashalf	PART#	PTYPE	LOCATION
P.	100	DC10	Chicago

Example 15.57 What proportion of the number of coach seats used on a 707 does each location have?

pinfo	PART#	SUBPARTOF	PARTNAME
	100		coach seat

usedon	PART#	PTYPE	NUSED
	100	707	25

instock	PART#	LOCATION	QUANTITY
	100	Chicago	30

seats	LOCATION	PROPORTION
P.	Chicago	30/25

QBE has the aggregate operators **CNT.**, **SUM.**, **AVG.**, **MAX.**, and **MIN.** that can be applied to an entry in a row. The entry must be prefixed with **ALL.** to indicate that all values for the entry are to be collected and treated as a set.

Example 15.58 How many of part 211 are in stock?

instock	PART#	LOCATION	QUANTITY
	211		**P. SUM. ALL.** 50

Result:

instock	QUANTITY Sum
	211

QBE appends the word "Sum" (and appropriate words for other aggregate operators) to the column heading to indicate that the value in the result is an aggregate rather than a directly-retrieved value.

To eliminate duplicates in a set formed by **ALL.**, the operator **UNQ.** is used.

Example 15.59 How many locations have parts?

instock	PART#	LOCATION	QUANTITY
		P. CNT. UNQ. ALL.	

Grouping before application of aggregate operators is accomplished by the operator **G.** in the columns on which the grouping is to take place.

Example 15.60 Which parts have the number needed on a 727 in at least one location?

usedon	PART#	PTYPE	NUSED
	$\underline{100}$	727	$\underline{50}$

instock	PART#	LOCATION	QUANTITY
	P. G. $\underline{100}$		**MAX. ALL.** $\underline{25}$

CONDITIONS
MAX. ALL. $\underline{25}$ >= $\underline{50}$

Result:

instock	PART#
	2116 21164

Example 15.61 How many of each part are there?

instock	PART#	LOCATION	QUANTITY
	P. G.		**P. SUM. ALL.**

Example 15.62 At how many locations is each part stocked?

instock	PART#	LOCATION	QUANTITY
	P. G.	**P. CNT. ALL.**	

Result:

instock	PART#	LOCATION Count
	211	3
	2114	2
	2116	2
	21164	1

We look finally at a feature of QBE, access to the transitive closure of a relation, that is unique among relational query languages. (However, the feature is not available in current implementations.) The transitive closure mechanism assumes a pair of attributes in a relation for which the transitive closure of the projection of the relation on those two attributes is tree-structured. *PART#* and *SUBPARTOF* in *pinfo* form such a pair. No part is a subpart of itself, at any level, and no part is a subpart of more than one part. (The last restriction may not seem likely in general, but it holds in the current state of *pinfo*.) The structure described by the transitive closure on *PART#* and *SUBPARTOF* in *pinfo* is shown in Figure 15.2.

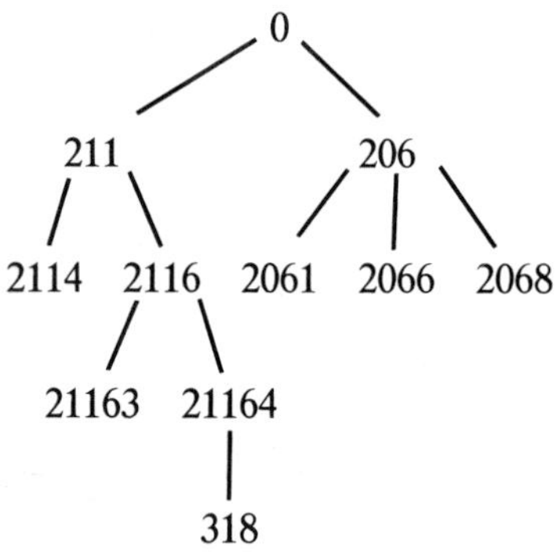

Figure 15.2

If we wanted to answer the question "What are the subparts of subparts of part 211?", we could use the following QBE query.

pinfo	PART#	SUBPARTOF
	100	211
	P. 101	100

(QBE queries need not list all the attributes in a relation.) However, with the features of QBE outlined so far, there is no query to answer the question "What parts are subparts of part 211 at all levels?", unless there is an a priori bound on the number of levels of subparts there can be.

QBE allows direct reference to the transitive closure of a projection of a relation through the notation (*n***L**) after an entry. The *n* can be either a positive integer constant or a variable. If *n* is a constant, it refers to the number of levels up or down the tree to go.

Example 15.63 What are the subparts of subparts of part 211?

pinfo	PART#	SUBPARTOF
	P. 100(2**L**)	211

Result:

pinfo	PART#
	2114(2**L**) 2116(2**L**)

Note that level information is incorporated in the answer to the query.

Example 15.64 What part contains part 318 as a third-level subpart?

pinfo	PART#	SUBPARTOF
	318	**P.** 200(3**L**)

pinfo	SUBPARTOF
	211(3**L**)

The level operator, **L**, may be preceded by a variable to indicate a search up or down the tree by an indeterminate number of levels.

Example 15.65 At what level is part 21164 a subpart of part 211?

pinfo	PART#	SUBPARTOF
	P. 21164(4**L**)	211

Result:

pinfo	PART#
	21164(2**L**)

Example 15.66 What are the subparts of part 211 at all levels?

pinfo	PART#	SUBPARTOF
	P. 100(4**L**)	211

Result:

pinfo	PART#
	2114(1**L**)
	2116(1**L**)
	21163(2**L**)
	21164(2**L**)
	318(3**L**)

There are two operators, **MAX.** and **LAST.**, that can be used with **L** to refer to items at the lowest level in the tree and items that are leaves in the tree, respectively.

Example 15.67 What are the lowest level subparts?

pinfo	PART#	SUBPARTOF
	P. 100(**MAX. L**)	0

Result:

pinfo	PART#
	318(4**L**)

Example 15.68 What subparts of part 211, at any level, themselves have no subparts?

pinfo	PART#	SUBPARTOF
	P. 100(**LAST. L**)	211

Result:

pinfo	PART#
	2114(1**L**) 21163(2**L**) 318(3**L**)

15.5 PIQUE

PIQUE (PIts QUEry language) is an experimental data retrieval language for the PITS (Pie-In-The-Sky) database system under development at the State University of New York at Stony Brook and the Oregon Graduate Center. PIQUE has a QUEL-like syntax. However, tuple variables are implicitly bound to windows, rather than explicitly bound to relations, thus removing range statements and join conditions. A QUEL query to answer the question "Which locations have as many coach seats as are used on a 707?" is

> **range of** *p* **is** *pinfo*
> **range of** *u* **is** *usedon*
> **range of** *i* **is** *instock*
> **retrieve** (*i.LOCATION*)
> **where** *p.PART#* = *u.PART#* **and** *p.PART#* = *i.PART#* **and**
> *u.PTYPE* = "707" **and** *u.NUSED* <= *i.QUANTITY*

The same question can be answered in PIQUE with

> **retrieve** *LOCATION where* (*PTYPE* = "707") *
> (*NUSED* <= *QUANTITY*).

The semantics of PIQUE is defined relative to some window function. The only assumption PIQUE makes is that the window function obeys the containment condition. For examples in this section, we use an object-based window function $[\,]_{\mathbf{R},\mathbf{O}}$, where

$$\mathbf{R} = \{PART\#\ SUBPARTOF,\ PART\#\ PARTNAME,\ PART\#\ PTYPE\ USEDON,\ PART\#\ LOCATION\ NUSED\}$$

and **O** consists of all nonempty unions of schemes in **R**, as shown in Figure 15.3.

O = **R** ∪
{*PART# SUBPARTOF PARTNAME,*
PART# SUBPARTOF PTYPE NUSED,
PART# PARTNAME PTYPE NUSED,
PART# SUBPARTOF PARTNAME PTYPE NUSED,
PART# SUBPARTOF LOCATION QUANTITY,
PART# PARTNAME LOCATION QUANTITY,
PART# SUBPARTOF PARTNAME LOCATION QUANTITY,
PART# PTYPE NUSED LOCATION QUANTITY,
PART# SUBPARTOF PTYPE NUSED LOCATION QUANTITY,
PART# PARTNAME PTYPE NUSED LOCATION QUANTITY,
PART# SUBPARTOF PARTNAME PTYPE NUSED LOCATION QUANTITY}

Figure 15.3

As we see from the objects, all two-, three-, and four-way joins of relations are permitted. For a database on **R** we use *usedon* and *instock* for *PART# PTYPE NUSED* and *PART# LOCATION QUANTITY*. For *PART# SUB-PARTOF* and *PART# PARTNAME* we use

$$pinfo1 = \pi_{PART\#\ SUBPARTOF}(\sigma_{SUBPARTOF \neq 0}(pinfo))$$

and

$$pinfo2 = \pi_{PART\#\ PARTNAME}(pinfo).$$

The relations *pinfo*1 and *pinfo*2 are shown in Figure 15.4. By splitting *pinfo* in this way, we avoid using a special value for *SUBPARTOF* when a part is not a subpart of any part. We could have made the same decomposition for previous examples, but at the expense of complicating some queries. In PIQUE, there is no added complexity in queries for making this decomposition.

*pinfo*1(PART#	SUBPARTOF)
2114	211
2116	211
21163	2116
21164	2116
318	21164
2061	206
2066	206
2068	206

*pinfo*2(PART#	PARTNAME)
211	coach seat
2114	seat cover
2116	seat belt
21163	seat belt buckle
21164	seat belt anchor
318	funny little bolt
206	overhead console
2061	paging switch
2066	light switch
2068	air nozzle

Figure 15.4

For each tuple variable x in a PIQUE query, the *mention set* of x, denoted $men(x)$, is the set of attributes that appear with x in the query. In evaluating the query, x is bound to $[men(x)]$. Thus, if x appears with *PARTNAME* and *LOCATION*, it will be bound to [*PARTNAME LOCATION*], which is

$$\pi_{PARTNAME\ LOCATION}(pinfo2 \bowtie instock).$$

The simplest PIQUE queries have a retrieve list and a sequence of selection conditions connected with *'s.

Example 15.69 Which locations have coach seats?

retrieve *x.LOCATION* **where** (*x.PARTNAME* = "coach seat")

(LOCATION)
JFK
Boston
O'Hare

Example 15.70 Which locations have at least as many of a part as are used on a 707?

retrieve *x.PART#, x.LOCATION* **where** (*PTYPE* = "707")
 * (*x.QUANTITY* >= *x.NUSED*)

Here x is bound to [*PART# LOCATION PTYPE QUANTITY*].

Example 15.71 Which parts are subparts of the same part?

retrieve *x.PART#* −> *SUBPART1*, *y.PART#* −> *SUBPART2*
 where (*x.SUBPARTOF* = *y.SUBPARTOF*)
 * (*x.PART#* < *y.PART#*)

Here x and y are bound to separate copies of [*PART# SUBPARTOF*]. The symbol −> is used for renaming attributes.

(SUBPART1	SUBPART2)
2114	2116
21163	21164
2061	2066
2061	2068
2066	2068

A syntactic simplification allowed in PIQUE is the use of a "blank" tuple variable. Any attributes not preceded by a tuple variable are assumed to be qualified by a special tuple variable "blank."

Example 15.72 The queries in the last three examples can be written as

> **retrieve** *LOCATION* **where** (*PARTNAME* = "coach seat")

> **retrieve** *PART#, LOCATION* **where** (*PTYPE* = "707")
> * (*QUANTITY* >= *NUSED*)

> **retrieve** *PART#* −> *SUBPART*1, *y.PART#* −> *SUBPART*2
> **where** (*SUBPARTOF* = *y.SUBPARTOF*) * (*PART#* < *y.PART#*)

In the last query, one explicit tuple variable is still needed.

The types of selection conditions seen so far are *simple conditions*: sequences of comparisons connected with *'s. *Compound conditions* are formed from simple conditions with the connectives **and**, **or**, and **not**. The semantics of queries with compound conditions is given by the following equivalences.

> **retrieve** ⟨list⟩ **where** ⟨condition1⟩ **and** ⟨condition2⟩ ≡
> (**retrieve** ⟨list⟩ **where** ⟨condition1⟩) ∩
> (**retrieve** ⟨list⟩ **where** ⟨condition2⟩)

> **retrieve** ⟨list⟩ **where** ⟨condition1⟩ **or** ⟨condition2⟩ ≡
> (**retrieve** ⟨list⟩ **where** ⟨condition1⟩) ∪
> (**retrieve** ⟨list⟩ **where** ⟨condition2⟩)

> **retrieve** ⟨list⟩ **where not** ⟨condition⟩ ≡
> (**retrieve** ⟨list⟩) − (**retrieve** ⟨list⟩ **where** ⟨condition⟩)

Example 15.73 Which parts are in stock at both Boston and O'Hare?

> **retrieve** *PART#* **where** (*LOCATION* = "Boston") **and**
> (*LOCATION* = "O'Hare")

(PART#)
211
2116

Example 15.74 Which parts are not in stock at Boston?

retrieve *PART#* **where not** (*LOCATION* = "Boston")

(PART#)
2114
21163
21164
318
206
2061
2066
2068

The difference between * and **and** is important. Using * means that the conditions connected will be enforced on the same window, while **and** enforces the conditions on two windows and intersects the results, possible after projection. The connectives **and**, **or**, and **not** are essentially shorthand for writing certain two-variable queries with one variable. Referring back to Example 15.73, if we instead wrote

retrieve *PART#* **where** (*LOCATION* = "Boston")
 * (*LOCATION* = "O'Hare"),

the result would be an empty relation, since no tuple t has both $t(LOCATION)$ = Boston and $t(LOCATION)$ = O'Hare. Another consideration is that **and** can be used when no object spans all the attributes mentioned.

Example 15.75 For this example, assume that all objects that mention both *PTYPE* and *LOCATION* are removed from **O**. The query

retrieve *PART#* **where** (*PTYPE* = "707")
 * (*LOCATION* = "Boston")

cannot be used, while

retrieve *PART#* **where** (*PTYPE* = "707") **and**
 (*LOCATION* = "Boston")

would work.

Another important distinction is between a negated condition and the condition with the comparator complemented, such as **not** (*LOCATION* = "Boston") and (*LOCATION* ≠ "Boston").

Example 15.76 The query

retrieve *PART#* **where not** (*LOCATION* = "Boston")

from Example 15.74 is asking for any part not stocked at Boston, while

retrieve *PART#* **where** (*LOCATION* ≠ "Boston")

asks for parts stocked at some location besides Boston. The answer to the second query is

(PART#)
211
2114
2116
21164

To get parts not stocked at Boston, but stocked at some location, we write

retrieve *PART#*
where (*LOCATION* = *LOCATION*) **and not**
(*LOCATION* = "Boston")

(PART#)
2114
21164

The last query in the preceding example contains the condition (*LOCATION* = *LOCATION*). At first sight, that condition may seem superfluous, since it is always true. However, it affects the answer to the query, since it changes the mention set of the tuple variable. A condition such as (*LOCATION* = *LOCATION*) can be abbreviated to (*LOCATION*), and is called a *name drop*. The purpose of a name drop is to include an attribute in the realm of discourse, with no condition other than that it be present.

Example 15.77 What parts are there?

retrieve *PART#*

(PART#)
211
2114
2116
21163
21164
318
206
2061
2066
2068

Example 15.78 Which parts are stocked at some location?

retrieve *PART#* **where** *LOCATION*

(PART#)
211
2114
2116
21164

Example 15.79 Which parts are not subparts of any part?

retrieve *PART#* **where not** (*SUBPARTOF*)

(PART#)
211
206

PIQUE allows references to subqueries via the keyword **in**, which specifies a semijoin of the window for a tuple variable with the result of the subquery. Thus, **in** denotes set membership of a tuple (or parts of it) in the set of tuples resulting from the subquery. The tuple variables in the subquery are local to the subquery, and are not connected with tuple variables by the same name in the containing query.

Example 15.80 Which locations stock some part that Boston stocks?

> **retrieve** *PART#, LOCATION*
> **where** (*LOCATION* ≠ "Boston") * (*PART#* **in**
> **retrieve** *PART#* **where** (*LOCATION* = "Boston"))

(PART#	LOCATION)
211	JFK
211	O'Hare
2116	O'Hare

15.6 BIBLIOGRAPHY AND COMMENTS

ISBL and the PRTV system are described by Todd [1975, 1976]. Stonebraker, Wong, *et al.* [1976] present QUEL and the INGRES system. Astrahan, Blasgen, *et al.* [1976, 1980], Blasgen, Astrahan, *et al.* [1981] and Chamberlin, Astrahan, *et al.* [1981] report on System R. Boyce, Chamberlin, *et al.* [1975] introduce SQUARE and an early version of SQL. SQL is covered in more detail by Astrahan and Chamberlin [1975] and Astrahan, Chamberlin, *et al.* [1976]. SEQUEL and SEQUEL2 are names of earlier versions of SQL. QBE is described in a series of papers by Zloof [1976, 1977, 1981]. PIQUE is presented by Maier, Rozenshtein, *et al.* [1981]. PIQUE is based heavily upon a similar language, System/U, under development at Stanford. Korth [1981] and Korth and Ullman [1980] describe that language.

Chamberlin [1976] and Kim [1979] both give surveys of relational database management systems. Pirotte [1979] classifies relational query languages by whether their underlying structure is relational algebra, tuple calculus, or domain calculus. Cooper [1980] compares the expressive power of various relational query languages.

BIBLIOGRAPHY

Aho, A.V., Beeri, C., and Ullman, J.D. [1979]. The Theory of Joins in Relational Databases. *ACM TODS* 4:3, September 1979, 297-314.

Aho, A.V., Hopcroft, J.E, and Ullman, J.D. [1974]. *The Design and Analysis of Computer Algorithms.* Reading, MA: Addison-Wesley.

Aho, A.V., Sagiv, Y., Szymanski, T.G., Ullman, J.D. [1979]. Inferring a Tree from Lowest Common Ancestors with an Application to the Optimization of Relational Expressions. *SIAM J. on Computing* 10:3, August 1981, 405-421.

Aho, A.V., Sagiv, Y., and Ullman, J.D. [1979a]. Efficient Optimization of a Class of Relational Expressions. *ACM TODS* 4:4, December 1979, 435-454.

Aho, A.V., Sagiv, Y., and Ullman, J.D. [1979b]. Equivalences Among Relational Expressions. *SIAM J. on Computing* 8:2, May 1979, 218-246.

Aho, A.V., and Ullman, J.D. [1979]. Universality of Data Retrieval Languages. *ACM Symp. on Principles of Prog. Lang.* 1979, 110-120.

ANS1/X3/SPARC [1975]. Study group on data base management systems: interim report. *FDT* 7:2 (Bulletin of ACM SIGFIDET), February 1975.

Armstrong, W.W. [1974]. Dependency Structures of Data Base Relationships. 1974 *IFIP Cong.,* Geneva, Switzerland, 580-583.

Armstrong, W.W., and Delobel, C. [1980]. Decompositions and Functional Dependencies in Relations. *ACM TODS* 5:4, December 1980, 404-430.

Arora, A.K., and Carlson, C.R. [1978]. The Information Preserving Properties of Relational Databases Transformations. *VLDB IV,* West Berlin, Germany. ACM, IEEE. 352-359.

Astrahan, M.M., Blasgen, M.W., Chamberlin, D.D., Gray, N.J., King, W.F., Lindsay, B.G., Lorie, R., Mehl, J.W., Price, T.G., Putzolu, F., Selinger, P.C., Schkolnick, M., Slutz, D.R., Traiger, I.L., Wade, B.W., Yost, R.A. A History and Evaluation of System R. *IBM Report* RJ2843, San Jose, CA, June 1980.

Astrahan, M.M., Blasgen, M.W., Chamberlin, D.D., Eswaran, K.P., Gray, J.N., Griffiths, P.P., King, W.F., Lorie, R.A., McJones, P.R., Mehl, J.W., Putzolu, G.R., Traiger, I.L., Wade, B.W., Watson, V. System R: A Relational Approach to Database Management. *ACM TODS* 1:2, June 1976, 97-137.

Astrahan, M.M., and Chamberlin, D.D. [1975]. Implementation of a Structured English Query Language. *CACM* 18:10, October 1975, 580-587.

Atzeni, P., and Parker, D.S. [1981]. Properties of Acyclic Database Schemes: An Analysis. *XP2 Workshop on Relational Database Theory,* Pennsylvania State Univ., University Park, PA, June 1981.

Bachman, C.W., and Daya, M. [1977]. The Role Concept in Data Models. *VLDB III*, Tokyo, Japan. ACM, IEEE. 464–476.

Banchilon, F. [1978]. On the Completeness of Query Languages for Relational Databases. *Proc. Seventh Symp. on Math. Found. of Computing.* New York: Springer-Verlag, 112–123.

Beck, L.L. [1978]. On Minimal Sets of Operations for Relational Data Sublanguages. *Computer Science Report* 7802, Southern Methodist Univ., Dallas, TX, February 1978.

Beeri, C. [1980]. On the Membership Problem for Functional and Multivalued Dependencies in Relational Databases. *ACM TODS* 5:3, September 1980, 241–259.

Beeri, C. [1979]. On the Role of Data Dependencies in the Construction of Relational Database Schemas. *Computer Science Report* 43, Hebrew Univ., Jerusalem, Israel, January 1979.

Beeri, C., and Bernstein, P.A. [1979]. Computational Problems Related to the Design of Normal Form Relational Schemas. *ACM TODS* 4:1, March 1979, 30–59.

Beeri, C., Bernstein, P.A., and Goodman, N. [1978]. A Sophisticate's Introduction to Database Normalization Theory. *VLDB IV*, West Berlin, Germany. ACM, IEEE. 113–124.

Beeri, C., Dowd, M., Fagin, R., Statman, R. [1980]. On the Structure of Armstrong Relations for Functional Dependencies. *IBM Report* RJ2901, San Jose, CA, September 1980.

Beeri, C., Fagin, R., and Howard, J.H. [1977]. A Complete Axiomatization for Functional and Multivalued Dependencies in Database Relations. *ACM SIGMOD Conf.* 1977, 47–61.

Beeri, C., Fagin, R., Maier, D., Mendelzon, A., Ullman, J., Yannakakis, M. [1981]. Properties of Acyclic Database Schemes. *ACM Symp. on Theory of Computing* 1981, 355–362.

Beeri, C., Fagin, R. Maier, D., Yannakakis, M. [1981]. On the Desirability of Acyclic Database Schemes. *IBM Report* RJ3131, San Jose, CA, May 1981.

Beeri, C., and Honeyman, P. [1981]. Preserving Functional Dependencies. *SIAM J. on Computing* 10:3, August 1981, 647–656.

Beeri, C., Mendelzon, A.O., Sagiv, Y., Ullman, J.D. [1979]. Equivalence of Relational Database Schemes. *SIAM J. on Computing* 10:2, May 1981, 352–370.

Beeri, C., and Rissanen, J. [1980]. Faithful Representations of Relational Database Schemes. *IBM Report* RJ2722, San Jose, CA, January 1981.

Beeri, C., and Vardi, M.Y. [1980a]. The Implication Problem for Data Dependencies. *Computer Science Report*, Hebrew Univ., Jerusalem, Israel, May 1980.

Beeri, C., and Vardi, M.Y. [1981a]. A Note on Decompositions of Relational Databases. *Unpublished manuscript* (Hebrew Univ., Jerusalem, Israel), January 1981.

Beeri, C., and Vardi, M. [1980b]. On the Complexity of Testing Implications of Data Dependencies. *Computer Science Report,* Hebrew Univ., Jerusalem, Israel, December 1980.

Beeri, C., and Vardi, M.Y. [1981b]. On the Properties of Join Dependencies. In Gallaire, Minker, and Nicolas [1981], New York: Plenum Publ. Co., 25–72.

Beeri, C., and Vardi, M.Y. [1980c]. A Proof Procedure for Data Dependencies. *Computer Science Report,* Hebrew Univ., Jerusalem, Israel, December 1980.

Békéssy, A., and Demetrovics, J. [1979]. Contribution to the Theory of Database Relations. *Discrete Mathematics* 27, Amsterdam, Netherlands: North-Holland, 1–10.

Békéssy, A., Demetrovics, J., Hannak, L., Frankl, P., Katona, Gy. [1980]. On the Number of Maximal Dependencies in a Database Relation of Fixed Order. *Discrete Mathematics* 30, Amsterdam, Netherlands: North-Holland, 83–88.

Bernstein, P.A. [1976a]. Comment on 'Segment Synthesis in Logical Database Design.' *IBM J. of Research and Development* 20:4, Armonk, NY, July 1976, 412.

Bernstein, P.A. [1976b]. Synthesizing Third Normal Form Relations from Functional Dependencies. *ACM TODS* 1:4, December 1976, 277–298.

Bernstein, P.A., Blaustein, B.T., and Clarke, E.M. [1980]. Fast Maintenance of Semantic Integrity Assertions Using Redundant Aggregate Data. *VLDB VI,* Montreal, Canada. ACM, IEEE. 126–136.

Bernstein, P.A., and Chiu, D.-M. [1981]. Using Semi-joins to Solve Relational Queries. *JACM* 28:1, January 1981, 25–40.

Bernstein, P.A., and Goodman, N. [1979a]. Full Reducers for Relational Queries Using Multi-attribute Semi-joins. *IEEE Computer Network Symp.* 1979.

Bernstein, P.A., and Goodman, N. [1979b]. Inequality Semi-joins. *Computer Corp. of America Report* 79–28, Cambridge, MA, December 1979.

Bernstein, P.A., and Goodman, N. [1980a]. The Power of Inequality Semijoins. *Aiken Computation Lab. Report* 12–80, Harvard Univ., Cambridge, MA, August 1980.

Bernstein, P.A., and Goodman, N. [1979c]. The Theory of Semijoins. *Computer Corp. of America Report* 79–27, Cambridge, MA, November 1979.

Bernstein, P.A., and Goodman, N. [1980b]. What Does Boyce-Codd Normal Form Do? *VLDB VI,* Montreal, Canada. ACM, IEEE. 245–259.

Biskup, J. [1980a]. A Formal Approach to Null Values in Database Relations. In Gallaire, Minker, and Nicolas [1981], New York: Plenum Publ. Co., 299–342.

Biskup, J. [1981]. A Foundation of Codd's Relational Maybe-operations. *XP2 Workshop on Relational Database Theory,* Pennsylvania State Univ., University Park, PA, June 1981.

Biskup, J. [1980b]. Inferences of Multivalued Dependencies in Fixed and Undetermined Universes. *Theoretical Computer Science* 10:1, Amsterdam, Netherlands: North-Holland, January 1981, 93–106.

Biskup, J. [1978]. On the Complementation Rule for Multivalued Dependencies on Database Relations. *Acta Informatica* 10:3, New York: Springer-Verlag, 297–305.

Biskup, J., Dayal, U., and Bernstein, P.A. [1979]. Synthesizing Independent Database Schemas. *ACM SIGMOD Conf.* 1979, 143–152.

Blasgen, M.W. Astrahan, M.M., Chamberlin, D.D., Gray, N.J., King, W.F., Lindsay, B.G., Lorie, R.A., Mehl, J.W., Price, T.G., Putzolu, G.R., Schkolnick, M., Selinger, P.C., Slutz, D.R., Strong, H.R., Traiger, I.L., Wade, B.W., Yost, R.A. [1981]. System R: An Architectural Overview. *IBM Systems J.* 20:1, Armonk, NY, February 1981, 41–62.

Blasgen, M., and Eswaren, M.K. [1977]. Storage and Access in Relational Database Systems. *IBM Systems J.* 16:4, Armonk, NY. December 1977, 363–377.

Boyce, R.F. Chamberlin, D.D., King, W.F., Hammer, M.M. [1975]. Specifying Queries as Relational Expressions: The SQUARE Data Sublanguage. *CACM* 18:11, November 1975, 621–628.

Brodie, M.L. [1978]. Specification and Verification of Database Semantic Integrity. *Computer Systems Research Group Report* 91, Univ. of Toronto, Canada. April 1978.

Cardenas, A.F. [1979]. *Data Base Management Systems.* Boston, MA: Allyn and Bacon.

Carlson, C.R., and Kaplan, R.S. [1976]. A Generalized Access Path Model and its Application to a Relational Database System. *ACM SIGMOD Conf.* 1976, 143–154.

Casanova, M.A. [1981]. The Theory of Functional and Subset Dependencies over Relational Expressions. *Dep. de Informatica Report* 3/81, Pontificia Universidade Catolica, Rio de Janiero, Brazil, January 1981.

Ceri, S., and Pelagatti, G. [1980]. Correctness of Execution Strategies of Read-only Transactions in Distributed Databases. *Inst. di Elettrotecnica ed Elletronica Politecnico di Milano Report* 80–16, Milan, Italy.

Chamberlin, D.D. [1976]. Relational Database Management Systems. *ACM Computing Surveys* 8:1, March 1976, 43–66.

Chamberlin, D.D., Astrahan, M.M., King, W.F., Lorie, R.A., Mehl, J.W., Price, T.G., Schkolnick, M., Selinger, P.G., Slutz, D.R., Wade, B.W., Yost, R.A. [1981]. Support for Repetitive Transactions and Ad-hoc Queries in System R. *ACM TODS* 6:1, March 1981, 70–94.

Chamberlin, D.D., Astrahan, M.M., Eswaran, K.P., Griffiths, P.P., Lorie, R.A., Mehl, J.W., Reisner, P., Wade, B.W. [1976]. SEQUEL 2: A Unified Approach to Data Definition, Manipulation and Control. *IBM J. of Research and Development* 20:6, Armonk, NY, November 1976, 560-575.

Chandra, A.K. [1981]. Programming Primitives for Database Languages. *ACM Symp. on Principles of Prog. Lang.*, 1981, 50-62.

Chandra, A.K., and Harel, D. [1980a]. Computable Queries for Relational Databases. *J. of Computer and System Sciences* 21:2, October 1980, 156-178.

Chandra, A.K., and Harel, D. [1980b]. Structure and Complexity of Relational Queries. *XP1 Workshop on Relational Database Theory,* SUNY at Stony Brook, NY, June-July 1981.

Chandra, A.K., Lewis, H.R., and Makowsky, J.A. [1981]. Embedded Implicational Dependencies and Their Inference Problem. *ACM Symp. on Theory of Computing* 1981, 342-354.

Chandra, A.K., and Merlin, P.M. [1976]. Optimal Implementation of Conjunctive Queries in Relational Databases. *ACM Symp. on Theory of Computing* 1976, 77-90.

Chase, K. [1981]. Join Graphs and Acyclic Database Schemes. *VLDB VII,* Cannes, France. ACM, IEEE. 95-100.

Chen, P.P.-S. [1976]. The Entity-Relationship Model—Toward a Unified View of Data. *ACM TODS* 1:1, March 1976, 9-36.

Childs, D.L. [1968]. Feasibility of a Set-Theoretic Data Structure——A General Structure Based on a Reconstituted Definition of Relation. 1968 *IFIP Cong.,* Geneva, Switzerland, 162-172.

Chiu, D.-M., Bernstein, P.A., and Ho, Y.-C. [1981]. Optimizing Chain Queries in a Distributed Database System. *Aiken Computation Lab. Report* 01-81, Harvard Univ., Cambridge, MA, January 1981.

Chiu, D.-M., and Ho., Y.-C. [1980]. A Methodology for Interpreting Tree Queries into Optimal Semijoin Expressions. *ACM SIGMOD Conf.* 1980, 169-178.

Clifford, J., and Warren, D.S. [1981]. Formal Semantics for Time in Databases. *XP2 Workshop on Relational Database Theory,* Pennsylvania State Univ., University Park, PA, June 1981.

Codd, E.F. [1971a]. A Database Sublanguage Founded on the Relational Calculus. *ACM SIGFIDET Workshop on Data Description, Access and Control,* November 1971, 35-61.

Codd, E.F. [1979]. Extending the Database Relational Model to Capture More Meaning. *ACM TODS* 4:4, December 1979, 397-434.

Codd, E.F. [1972a]. Further Normalization of the Database Relational Model. In Rustin [1972]. Englewood Cliffs, NJ: Prentice-Hall, 33-64.

Codd, E.F. [1971b]. Normalized Database Structure: A Brief Tutorial. *ACM SIGFIDET Workshop on Data Description, Access and Control,* November 1971, 1-17.

Codd, E.F. [1974]. Recent Investigations in Relational Database Systems. 1974 *IFIP Conf.* 1017-1021.

Codd, E.F. [1972b]. Relational Completeness of Database Sublanguages. In Rustin [1972], Englewood Cliffs, NJ: Prentice-Hall, 65-98.

Codd, E.F. [1970]. A Relational Model of Data for Large Shared Data Banks. *CACM* 13:6, June 1970, 377-387.

Codd, E.F. [1975]. Understanding Relations (Installment #7). *FDT* 7:3-4 (Bulletin of ACM SIGMOD), December 1975, 23-28.

Connors, T., and Vianu, V. [1981]. Tableaux Which Define Expression Mappings. *XP2 Workshop on Relational Database Theory,* Pennsylvania State Univ., University Park, PA, June 1981.

Cooper, E.C. [1980]. On the Expressive Power of Query Languages for Relational Databases. *Aiken Computation Lab. Report* 14-80, Harvard Univ., Cambridge, MA.

Date, C.J. [1981]. *An Introduction to Data Base Systems.* 3rd ed. Reading, MA: Addison-Wesley.

Dayal, U., and Bernstein, P.A. [1978a]. The Fragmentation Problem: Lossless Decomposition of Relations in Files. *Computer Corp. of America Report* CCA-78-13, Cambridge, MA, November 1978.

Dayal, U., and Bernstein, P.A. [1978b]. On the Updatability of Relational Views. *VLDB IV,* West Berlin, Germany. ACM, IEEE. 368-377.

Delobel, C. [1978]. Normalization and Hierarchical Dependencies in the Relational Data Model. *ACM TODS* 3:3, September 1978, 201-222. Based partly on work from Contributions Theoretiques a la Conception d'un Systeme d'Informations, *doctoral diss.,* Univ. of Grenoble, Switzerland, 1973.

Delobel, C., and Casey, R.G. [1973]. Decomposition of a Data Base and the Theory of Boolean Switching functions. *IBM J. of Research and Development* 17:5, Armonk, NY, September 1973, 374-386.

Delobel, C., Casey, R.G., and Bernstein, P.A. [1977]. Comment on 'Decompositions of a Data Base and the Theory of Boolean Switching Functions.' *IBM J. of Research and Development 21:5,* Armonk, NY, September 1977, 484-485.

Demetrovics, J. [1979]. On the Equivalence of Candidate Keys with Sperner Systems. *Acta Cybernetica* 4:3, Szeged, Hungary, 247-252.

Demetrovics, J. [1978]. On the Number of Candidate Keys. *Information Processing Letters* 7:6, Amsterdam, Netherlands: North-Holland, October 1978, 226-269.

Downey, P.J., Sethi, R., and Tarjan, R.E. [1980]. Variations on the Common Subexpression Problem. *JACM* 27:4, October 1980, 758-771.

Epstein, R., Stonebraker, M.R., and Wong, E. [1978]. Distributed Query Processing in a Relational Database System. *ACM SIGMOD Conf.* 1978, 169-180.

Fagin, R. [1977a]. The Decomposition Versus the Synthetic Approach to Relational Database Design. *VLDB III,* Tokyo, Japan. ACM, IEEE. 441-446.

Fagin, R. [1977b]. Functional Dependencies in a Relational Database and Propor- tional Logic. *IBM J. of Research and Development* 21:6, Armonk, NY, November 1977, 534-544.

Fagin, R. [1980a]. Horn Clauses and Database Dependencies. *ACM Symp. on Theory of Computing* 1980, 123-134.

Fagin, R. [1977c]. Multivalued Dependencies and a New Normal Form for Relational Databases. *ACM TODS* 2:3, September 1977, 262-278.

Fagin, R. [1980b]. A Normal Form for Relational Databases that is Based on Do- mains and Keys. *ACM TODS* 6:3, September 1981, 387-415.

Fagin, R. [1979]. Normal Forms and Relational Database Operators. *ACM SIG- MOD Conf.* 1979, 153-160.

Fagin, R., Maier, D., Ullman, J.D., Yannakakis, M. [1981]. Tools for Template Dependencies. *IBM Report* RJ3030, San Jose, CA, May 1981.

Fagin, R., Mendelzon, A.O., and Ullman, J.D. [1980]. A Simplified Universal Re- lation Assumption and its Properties. *IBM Report* RJ2900, San Jose, CA, November 1980.

Fischer, P.C., Jou, J.H., and Tsou, D.-M. [1981]. Succinctness in Dependency Sys- tems. *XP2 Workshop on Relational Database Theory,* Pennsylvania State Univ., University Park, PA, June 1981.

Forsyth, J., and Fadous, R. [1975]. Finding Candidate Keys for Relational Data- bases. *ACM SIGMOD Conf.* 1975, 203-210.

Galil, Z. [1979]. An Almost Linear Time Algorithm for Computing a Dependency Basis in a Relational Database. *IBM Report* RJ2656, San Jose, CA, October 1979.

Gallaire, H., and Minker, J. eds. [1979]. *Logic and Databases.* New York: Plenum Publ. Co.

Gallaire, H., Minker, J., and Nicolas J.-M. eds. [1980]. *Advances in Data Base Theory*, vol. 1. New York: Plenum Publ. Co.

Garey, M.R., and Johnson, D.S. [1979]. *Computers and Intractability: A Guide to the Theory of NP-Completeness.* San Francisco, CA: Freeman.

Gewirtz, W.L. [1979]. The Universal Relation Assumption and Decomposition Strategies for Schema Design. *IEEE Computer Applications and Software Conf.* 1979 (COMPSAC '79), 136-140.

Ginsburg, S., and Hull, R. [1980]. Characterization for Functional Dependency and Boyce-Codd Normal Form Databases. *Unpublished manuscript,* December 1980.

Ginsburg, S., and Hull, R. [1981]. Ordered Attribute Domains in the Relational

Model. *XP2 Workshop on Relational Database Theory,* Pennsylvania State Univ., University Park, PA, June 1981.

Ginsburg, S., and Zaiddan, S.M. [1981]. Properties of Functional Dependency Databases. *Computer Science Report,* Univ. of So. California, Los Angeles, CA, January 1981.

Goldstein, B.S. [1981a]. Constraining Values in a Relational Database. *XP2 Workshop on Relational Database Theory,* Pennsylvania State Univ., University Park, PA, June 1981.

Goldstein, B.S. [1981b]. Constraints on Null Values in Relational Databases. *VLDB VII,* Cannes, France. ACM, IEEE. 101–111.

Goldstein, B.S. [1980]. Formal Properties of Constraints on Null Values in Relational Databases. *Computer Science Report* 80-013, SUNY at Stony Brook, NY, December 1980.

Goodman, N., Bernstein, P.A., Wong, E., Reeve, C.L., Rothnie, J.B. [1979]. Query Processing in SDD-1: A System for Distributed Databases. *Computer Corp. of America Report* 79-06, Cambridge, MA, October 1979.

Goodman, N., and Shmueli, O. [1980a]. Hierarchies of Database State Reductions. *Aiken Computation Lab. Report* 18-80, Harvard Univ., Cambridge, MA, November 1980.

Goodman, N., and Shmueli, O. [1981]. Limitations of the Chase, *Aiken Computation Lab. Report* 02-81, Harvard Univ., Cambridge, MA, January 1981.

Goodman, N., and Shmueli, O. [1980b]. Nonreducible Database States for Cyclic Queries. *Aiken Computation Lab. Report* 15-80, Harvard Univ., Cambridge, MA, July 1980.

Goodman, N., and Shmueli, O. [1981b]. Syntactic Characterizations of Tree Database Schemas. *XP2 Workshop on Relational Database Theory,* Pennsylvania State Univ., University Park, PA, June 1981.

Gotlieb, L.R. [1975]. Computing Joins of Relations. *ACM SIGMOD Conf.* 1975, 55–63.

Graham, M.H. [1981a]. Functions in Databases. *Computer Systems Research Group Report,* Univ. of Toronto, Canada, June 1981.

Graham, M.H. [1981b]. Independence (Preliminary Results). *XP2 Workshop on Relational Database Theory,* Pennsylvania State Univ., University Park, PA. June 1981.

Graham, M.H. [1979]. On the Universal Relation. *Computer Systems Research Group Report,* Univ. of Toronto, Canada, December 1979.

Graham, M.H. [1980]. A New Proof that the Chase is a Church-Rosser Replacement System. *XP1 Workshop on Relational Database Theory,* SUNY at Stony Brook, NY, June-July 1980.

Grant, J. [1977]. Null Values in a Relational Database. *Information Processing Letters* 6:5, Amsterdam, Netherlands: North-Holland, October 1977, 156–157.

Grant, J. [1979]. Partial Values in a Tabular Database Model. *Information Processing Letters* 9:2, Amsterdam, Netherlands: North-Holland, August 1979, 97–99.

Grant, J., and Jacobs, B. [1980]. On Generalized Dependency Statements. *Unpublished manuscript.*

Hagihara, K., Ito, M., Taniguchi, K., Kasami, T. [1979]. Decision Problems for Multivalued Dependencies in Relational Databases. *SIAM J. on Computing* 8:2, May 1979, 247–264.

Hall, P.A.V. [1976]. Optimization of a Single Relational Expression in a Relational Database System. *IBM J. of Research and Development* 20:3, Armonk, NY, May 1976, 244–257.

Hall, P., Hitchcock, P., and Todd, S. [1975]. An Algebra of Relations for Machine Computation. *ACM Symp. on Principles of Prog. Lang.* 1975, 225–232.

Hammer, M., and McLeod, D. [1981]. Database Description with SDM: A Semantic Database Model. *ACM TODS* 6:3, September 1981, 351–386.

Hammer, M., and McLeod, D. [1978]. The Semantic Data Model: A Modelling Mechanism for Database Applications. *ACM SIGMOD Conf.* 1978, 26–36.

Heath, I.J. [1971]. Unacceptable File Operations in a Relational Data Base. *ACM SIGFIDET Workshop on Data Description, Access and Control,* November 1971, 19–33.

Honeyman, P. [1980a]. Extension Joins. *VLDB VI,* Montreal, Canada. ACM, IEEE. 239–244.

Honeyman, P. [1980b]. Functional Dependencies and the Universal Instance Property in the Relational Model of Database Systems. *Doctoral diss.,* Princeton Univ., Princeton, NJ, October 1980.

Honeyman, P. [1980c]. Testing Satisfaction of Functional Dependencies. *Unpublished manuscript,* March 1980 (to appear in *JACM*).

Honeyman, P., Ladner, R.E., and Yannakakis, M. [1980]. Testing the Universal Instance Assumption. *Information Processing Letters* 10:1, Amsterdam, Netherlands: North-Holland, February 1980, 14–19.

Housel, B.C., Waddle, V., and Yao, S.B. [1979]. The Functional Dependency Model for Logical Database Design. *VLDB V,* Rio de Janeiro, Brazil. ACM, IEEE. 194–208.

Hull, R. [1981]. Implicational Dependency and Finite Specification. *Computer Science Report,* Univ. of So. California, Los Angeles, CA.

Jacobs, B.E. [1980]. Applications of Database Logic to Automatic Program Conversion. *Computer Science Report,* Univ. of Maryland, College Park, MD, May 1980.

Jacobs, B.E., [1980]. A Generalized Algebraic Data Manipulation Language and the

Automatic Conversion of Its Programs. *XP1 Workshop on Relational Database Theory,* SUNY at Stony Brook, NY, June–July 1980.

Jacobs, B.E. [1979]. On Queries Definable in Database Structures. *Computer Science Report* 757, Univ. of Maryland, College Park, MD, April 1979.

Jou, J.H. [1980]. Theory of Functional Relation Schemes in Relational Databases. *Doctoral diss.,* Pennsylvania State Univ., University Park, PA, October 1980.

Kambayashi, Y. [1979]. A New Synthetic Approach for Relational Database Design. *AFIPS National Computer Conf.,* session 42. Also, *Yajima Lab. Report* ER78–02, Kyoto Univ., Japan, November 1978.

Kambayashi, Y. [1978]. An Efficient Algorithm for Processing Multirelation Queries in Relational Databases. *Information Sciences Report* 78–01, Kyoto Univ., Japan.

Kanellakis, P.C. [1980]. On the Computational Complexity of Cardinality Constraints in Relational Databases. *Lab. for Computer Science Report* 160, MIT, Cambridge, MA, March 1980.

Katsuno, H. [1981a]. On an Extended Conflict-Free Set of Functional Dependencies and Multivalued Dependencies. *Unpublished manuscript,* July 1981.

Katsuno, H. [1981b]. On Two Different Meanings of Multivalued Dependencies in a Conceptual Schema. *Trans. of the IECE of Japan* E64:6, June 1981, 383–389.

Kent, W. [1979a]. The Entity Join. *VLDB V,* Rio de Janeiro, Brazil. ACM, IEEE. 232–238.

Kent, W. [1973]. A Primer of Normal Forms (In a Relational Database). *IBM Report* 02.600, San Jose, CA, December 1973.

Kent, W. [1979b]. Limitations of Record-Based Information Models. *ACM TODS* 4:1, March 1979, 107–131.

Kim, W. [1980]. A New Way to Compute the Product and Join of Relations. *ACM SIGMOD Conf.* 1980, 178–187.

Kim, W. [1981a]. On Optimizing a SQL-Like Nested Query. *IBM Report* RJ3063, San Jose, CA, February 1981.

Kim. W. [1981b]. Query Optimation for Relational Database Systems. *IBM Report* RJ3081, San Jose, CA, March 1981.

Kim, W. [1979]. Relational Database Systems. *ACM Computing Surveys* 11:3, September 1979, 185–212.

Klug, A. [1980a]. Calculating Constraints on Relational Expressions. *ACM TODS* 5:3, September 1980, 260–290.

Klug, A. [1980b]. Locking Expressions for Increased Database Concurrency. *Computer Science Report* 400, Univ. of Wisconsin, Madison, WI, October 1980.

Klug, A. [1980c]. On Inequality Tableaux. *Computer Science Report* 403, Univ. of Wisconsin, Madison, WI, November 1980.

Klug, A., and Price, R. [1980]. Determining View Dependencies Using Tableaux. *Computer Science Report* 386. Univ. of Wisconsin, Madison, WI.

Korth, H. [1981]. System/U: Progress Report. *XP2 Workshop on Relational Database Theory*, Pennsylvania State Univ., University Park, PA, June 1981.

Korth, H.F., and Ullman, J.D. [1980]. System/U: A Database System Based on the Universal Relation Assumption. *XP1 Workshop on Relational Database Theory*, SUNY at Stony Brook, NY, June-July 1980.

LaCroix, M., and Pirotte, A. [1976]. Generalized Joins. *ACM SIGMOD Record* 8:3, September 1976, 14-15.

LeDoux, C.H., and Parker, D.S. [1980]. A New Algorithm for Testing Boyce-Codd Normal Form. *Unpublished manuscript*.

LeViet, C., Kambayashi, Y., Tanaka, K., Yajima, S. [1979]. Use of Abstracted Characteristics of Data in Relational Databases. *IEEE Computer Software and Applications Conf.* 1979 (COMPSAC '79), 409-414.

Lewis, E.A., Sekino, L.C., and Ting, P.D. [1977]. A Canonical Representation for the Relational Schema and Logical Data Independence. *IEEE Computer Software and Applications Conf.* (COMPSAC '77), 276-280.

Lien, Y.E. [1981]. Hierarchical Schemata for Relational Database Schemata. *ACM TODS* 6:1, March 1981, 48-69.

Lien, Y.E. [1979]. Multivalued Dependencies With Null Values in Relational Databases. *VLDB V*, Rio de Janeiro, Brazil. ACM, IEEE. 61-66.

Lien, Y.E. [1980]. On the Equivalence of Database Models. *Unpublished manuscript*, June 1980.

Ling, T.W., Tompa, F.W., and Kameda, T. [1981]. An Improved Third Normal Form for Relational Databases. *ACM TODS* 6:2, June 1981, 329-346.

Lipski, W. [1981]. On Databases With Incomplete Information. *JACM* 28:1, January 1981, 41-47.

Lipski, W. [1979b]. On Semantic Issues Connected With Incomplete Information Databases. *ACM TODS* 4:3, September 1979, 262-296.

Lipski, W., and Marek, W. [1979]. Information Systems: On Queries Involving Cardinalities. *Information Systems* 4:3, Elmsford, NY: Pergamon Press, Inc., 241-246.

Liu, L., and Demers, A. [1978]. An Efficient Algorithm for Testing Lossless Joins in Relational Databases. *Computer Science Report* 78-351, Cornell Univ., Ithaca, NY.

Lozinskii, E.L. [1980]. Construction of Relations in Relational Databases. *ACM TODS* 5:2, June 1980, 208-224.

Lozinskii, E.L. [1978]. Performance Considerations in Relational Database Design. In Shneiderman [1978], New York: Academic Press, Inc., 272-294.

Lucchesi, C.L., and Osborn, S.L. [1978]. Candidate Keys for Relations, *J. of Computer and System Sciences* 17:2, October 1978, 270–279.

Maier, D. [1980a]. Discarding the Universal Instance Assumption: Preliminary Results. *XP1 Workshop on Relational Database Theory*, SUNY at Stony Brook, NY, June–July 1980.

Maier, D. [1980b]. Minimum Covers in the Relational Database Model. *JACM* 27:4, October 1980, 664–674.

Maier, D., Mendelzon, A.O., Sadri, F., Ullman, J.D. [1980]. Adequacy of Decompositions of Relational Databases. *J. of Computer and System Sciences* 21:3, December 1980, 368–379.

Maier, D., Mendelzon, A.O., and Sagiv, Y. [1979]. Testing Implications of Data Dependencies. *ACM TODS* 4:4, December 1979, 455–469.

Maier, D., Rozenshtein, D., Salveter, S., Stein, J., Warren, D. [1981]. Semantic Problems in an Association-Object Query Language. *Unpublished manuscript*, October 1981.

Maier, D., Sagiv, Y., and Yannakakis, M. [1981]. On the Complexity of Testing Implications of Functional and Join Dependencies. *JACM* 28:4, October 1981, 680–695.

Maier, D., and Ullman, J.D. [1981a]. Connections in Acyclic Hypergraphs. *Computer Science Report* 81–853, Stanford Univ., Stanford, CA, May 1981.

Maier, D., and Ullman, J.D. [1981b]. Fragments of Relations: First Hack. *XP2 Workshop on Relational Database Theory*, Pennsylvania State Univ., University Park, PA, June 1981.

Maier, D., and Ullman, J.D. [1980]. Maximal Objects and the Semantics of Universal Relation Databases. *Computer Science Report* 80–016, SUNY at Stony Brook, NY, November 1980.

Maier, D., and Warren, D.S. [1981a]. Incorporating Computed Relations in Relational Databases. *ACM SIGMOD Conf.* 1981, 176–187.

Maier, D., and Warren, D.S. [1981b]. Specifying Connections for a Universal Relation Scheme Database. *Unpublished manuscript*, October 1981.

Mendelzon, A.O. [1981]. Database States and Their Tableaux. *XP2 Workshop on Relational Database Theory*, Pennsylvania State Univ., University Park, PA, June 1981.

Mendelzon, A.O. [1979]. On Axiomatizing Multivalued Dependencies in Relational Databases. *JACM* 26:1, January 1979, 37–44.

Mendelzon, A.O., and Maier, D. [1979]. Generalized Mutual Dependencies and the Decomposition of Database Relations. *VLDB V*, Rio de Janeiro, Brazil. ACM, IEEE. 75–82.

Minker, J. [1975a]. Performing Inferences over Relational Databases. *ACM SIGMOD Conf.* 1975, 79–91.

Minker, J. [1978]. Search Strategy and Selection Function for an Inferential Relational System. *ACM TODS* 3:1, March 1978, 1-31.

Minker, J. [1975b]. Set Operations and Inferences over Relational Databases. *Computer Science Report* 427, Univ. of Maryland, College Park, MD, December 1975.

Namibar, K.K. [1979]. Some Analytic Tools for the Design of Relational Database Systems. *VLDB V*, Rio de Janeiro, Brazil. ACM, IEEE. 417-428.

Nicolas, J.-M. [1978a]. First Order Logic Formalization for Functional, Multivalued and Mutual Dependencies. *ACM SIGMOD Conf.* 1978, 40-46.

Nicolas, J.-M. [1978b]. Mutual Dependencies and Some Results on Undecomposable Relations. *VLDB IV*, West Berlin, Germany. ACM, IEEE. 360-367.

Nijssen, G.M. ed. [1979]. *Architecture and Models in Data Base Management Systems*. Amsterdam, Netherlands: North-Holland.

Nijssen, G.M. ed. [1976]. *Modelling in Data Base Management Systems*. Amsterdam, Netherlands: North-Holland.

Osborn, S.L. [1977]. Normal Forms for Relational Databases. *Doctoral diss.*, Univ. of Waterloo, Canada.

Osborn, S.L. [1979a]. Testing for Existence of a Covering Boyce-Codd Normal Form. *Information Processing Letters* 8:1, Amsterdam, Netherlands: North-Holland. January 1979, 11-14.

Osborn, S.L. [1979b]. Towards a Universal Relation Interface. *VLDB V*, Rio de Janeiro, Brazil. ACM, IEEE. 52-60.

Palermo, F.P. [1974]. A Database Search Problem. In Tou [1974], New York: Plenum Publ. Co. 67-101.

Paolini, P., and Pelagatti, G. [1977]. Formal Definitions of Mappings in a Data Base. *ACM SIGMOD Conf.* 1977, 40-46.

Paredaens, J. [1977]. About Functional Dependencies in a Database Structure and Their Coverings. *Philips MBLE Lab. Report* 342, Brussels, Belgium, March 1977.

Paredaens, J. [1980]. Horizontal and Vertical Decompositions. *XP1 Workshop on Relational Database Theory*, SUNY at Stony Brook, NY, June-July 1980.

Paredaens, J. [1978]. On the Expressive Power of Relational Algebra. *Information Processing Letters* 7:2, Amsterdam, Netherlands: North-Holland, February 1978, 44-49.

Paredaens, J., and De Bra, P. [1981]. On Horizontal Decompositions. *XP2 Workshop on Relational Database Theory*, Pennsylvania State Univ., University Park, PA, June 1981.

Paredaens, J., and Janssens, D. [1981]. Decompositions of Relations: A Comprehensive Approach. In Gallaire, Minker, and Nicolas [1981], New York: Plenum Publ. Co., 73-100.

Parker, D.S., and Parsaye-Ghomi, K. [1980]. Inferences Involving Embedded Multivalued Dependencies and Transitive Dependencies. *ACM SIGMOD Conf.* 1980, 52–57.

Pecherer, R.M., [1975]. Efficient Evaluation of Expressions in a Relational Algebra. *ACM Pacific Conf.* 1975, 44–49.

Pichat, E., and Delobel, C. [1979]. Designing Third Normal Form Relational Database Schema. *Mathematiques Appliquées et Informatique Report* 149, Univ. Scientifique et Medicale et Institut National Polytechnique de Grenoble, France, January 1979.

Pirotte, A. [1979]. High Level Database Query Languages. In Gallaire and Minker [1979], New York: Plenum Publ. Co., 409–436.

Reiter, R. [1978]. On Closed World Databases. In Gallaire and Minker [1979], New York: Plenum Publ. Co., 55–76.

Rissanen, J. [1977]. Independent Components of Relations. *ACM TODS* 2:4, December 1977, 317–325.

Rothnie, J.B., Bernstein, P.A., Fox, S., Goodman, N., Hammer, M., Landers, T.A., Reeve, G., Shipman, D.W., Wong, E. [1981]. Introduction to a System for Distributed Databases (SDD-1). *ACM TODS* 5:1, March 1981, 1–17.

Rozenshtein, D. [1981]. Implementing Null Values in Relations. *Unpublished manuscript,* May 1981.

Rustin, R. ed. [1972]. *Data Base Systems.* Courant Inst. Computer Science Symp. 6, Englewood Cliffs, NJ: Prentice-Hall.

Sadri, F. [1980a]. Characterization of Projections of Legal Instances: An Application of GFD's and TD's. *Unpublished manuscript.*

Sadri, F. [1980b]. Data Dependencies in the Relational Model of Data: A Generalization. *Doctoral diss.*, Princeton Univ., Princeton, NJ, October 1980.

Sadri, F. [1980c]. A Normal Form with Respect to GFD's and TD's and New Conditions for Decomposition of Relational Databases. *Unpublished manuscript.*

Sadri, F., and Ullman, J.D. [1980a]. A Complete Axiomatization for a Large Class of Dependencies in Relational Databases. *ACM Symp. on Theory of Computing* 1980, 117–122.

Sadri, F., and Ullman, J.D. [1980b]. The Interaction Between Functional Dependencies and Template Dependencies. *ACM SIGMOD Conf.* 1980, 45–51.

Sagiv, Y. [1980]. An Algorithm for Inferring Multivalued Dependencies With an Application to Propositional Logic. *JACM* 27:2, April 1980, 250–262.

Sagiv, Y. [1981a]. Can We Use the Universal Instance Assumption Without Using Nulls? *ACM SIGMOD Conf.* 1981, 108–120.

Sagiv, Y. [1981b]. A Characterization of Globally Consistent Databases and Their Correct Access Paths. *Computer Science Report*, Univ. of Illinois, Urbana, IL, July 1981.

Sagiv, Y., Delobel, C., Parker, D.S., Fagin, R. [1981]. An Equivalence Between Relational Database Dependencies and a Fragment of Propositional Logic. *JACM* 28:3, July 1981, 435-453.

Sagiv, Y., and Walecka, S. [1979]. Subset Dependencies as an Alternative to Embedded Multivalued Dependencies. *Computer Science Report* 79-080, Univ. of Illinois, Urbana, IL, July 1979.

Sagiv, Y., and Yannakakis, M. [1980]. Equivalence Among Relational Expressions With the Union and Difference Operators. *JACM* 27:4, October 1980, 633-655.

Schenk, K.L., and Pinkert, J.R. [1977]. An Algorithm for Servicing Multirelational Queries. *ACM SIGMOD Conf.* 1977, 10-20.

Schkolnick, M., and Sorenson, P. [1981]. The Effects of Denormalization on Database Performance. *IBM Report* RJ3082, San Jose, CA, March 1981.

Schmid, H.A., and Swenson, J.R. [1975]. On the Semantics of the Relational Data Model. *ACM SIGMOD Conf.* 1975, 221-223.

Sciore, E. [1982]. A Complete Axiomatization for Full Join Dependencies. To appear in *JACM*.

Sciore, E. [1979]. Improving Semantic Specification in a Relational Database. *ACM SIGMOD Conf.* 1979, 170-178.

Sciore, E. [1980a]. The Inclusion of Role-Playing in Relational Databases. *Unpublished manuscript*, March 1980.

Sciore, E. [1981]. Real-World MVD's. *ACM SIGMOD Conf.* 1981, 121-132.

Sciore, E. [1980b]. The Universal Instance and Database Design. *Doctoral diss.*, Princeton Univ., Princeton, NJ, October 1980.

Selinger, P.G., Astrahan, M.M., Chamberlin, D.D., Lorie, R.A., Price, T.C. [1979]. Access Path Selection in a Relational Database Management System. *ACM SIGMOD Conf.* 1979, 23-34.

Sethi, R. [1974]. Testing for the Church-Rosser Property. *JACM* 21:4, October, 1974, 671-679.

Shneiderman, B. ed. [1978]. *Databases: Improving Usability and Responsiveness*. New York: Academic Press, Inc.

Shopiro, J.E. [1979]. Theseus—A Programming Language for Relational Databases. *ACM TODS* 4:4, December 1979, 493-517.

Smith, J.M., and Chang. P.Y.-T. [1975]. Optimizing the Performance of a Relational Database Interface. *CACM* 18:10, October 1975, 568-579.

Smith, J.M., and Smith, D.C.P. [1977a]. Database Abstraction: Aggregation. *CACM* 20:6, June 1977, 405-413.

Smith, J.M., and Smith, D.C.P. [1977b]. Database Abstraction: Aggregation and Generalization. *ACM TODS* 2:2, June 1977, 105-133.

Sowa, J.F. [1976]. Conceptual Graphs for a Database Interface. *IBM J. of Research and Development* 20:4, Armonk, NY, July 1976, 336-357.

Stein, J.H. [1981]. Enforcing the Modified Foreign Key Constraint. *Unpublished manuscript*, July 1981.

Steiner, H.-G. [1981]. Functional Flow Graphs (Extended Abstract). *XP2 Workshop on Relational Database Theory*, Pennsylvania State Univ., University Park, PA, June 1981.

Stockmeyer, L.H., and Wong, C.K. [1979]. On the Number of Comparisons to Find the Intersection of Two Relations. *SIAM J. on Computing* 8:3, August 1979, 388–404.

Stonebraker, M. [1975]. Implementation of Integrity Constraints and Views by Query Modification. *ACM SIGMOD Conf.* 1975, 65–78.

Stonebraker, B., and Rubenstein, P. [1976]. The INGRES Protection System. *ACM National Conf.* 1976, 80–84.

Stonebraker, M., and Wong, E. [1974]. Access Control in a Relational Database Management System by Query Modification. *ACM National Conf.* 1974, 180–187.

Stonebraker, M., Wong, E., Kreps, P., Held, G. [1976]. The Design and Implementation of INGRES. *ACM TODS* 1:3, September 1976, 189–222.

Sundgren, B. [1975]. *Theory of Databases*. New York: Mason/Charter.

Tanaka, K., and Kambayashi, Y. [1980]. Preservability of Data Dependencies for Update Operations in Relational Databases. *Yajima Laboratory Report* 80–02, Kyoto Univ., Japan, February 1980.

Tanaka, K., Kambayashi, Y., and Yajima, S. [1979a]. On the Representability of Decompositional Schema Design with Multivalued Dependencies. *Yajima Laboratory Report* 79–01, Kyoto Univ., Japan, January 1979.

Tanaka, K., Kambayashi, Y., and Yajima, S. [1979b]. Properties of Embedded Multivalued Dependencies in Relational Databases. *J. IECE of Japan* E62:8, August 1979, 536–543.

Tanaka, Y., and Tsuda, T. [1977]. Decomposition and Composition of a Relational Data Base. *VLDB III*, Tokyo, Japan. ACM, IEEE. 454–461.

Todd, S.J.P. [1976]. The Peterlee Relational Test Vehicle—A System Overview. *IBM Systems J.* 15:4, Armonk, NY, December 1976, 285–308.

Todd, S. [1975]. PRTV, An Efficient Implementation for Large Relational Databases. *VLDB I*, Framingham, MA. ACM. 554–556.

Tou, J.T. ed. [1974]. *Information Systems COINS IV*. New York: Plenum Publ. Co.

Tsichritzis, D.C., and Lochovsky, F.H. [1977]. *Data Base Management Systems*. New York: Academic Press, Inc.

Tsou, D.-M. [1980]. Analysis of the Logical Design in Relational Databases. *Doctoral diss.*, Pennsylvania State Univ., University Park, PA, October 1980.

Tsou, D.-M., and Fischer, P.C. [1980]. Decomposition of a Relation Scheme into Boyce-Codd Normal Form. *Computer Science Report* 80-04, Vanderbilt Univ., Nashville, TN, July 1980.

Ullman, J.D. [1980]. *Principles of Database Systems*. Rockville, MD: Computer Science Press.

Vardi, M.Y. [1980a]. Axiomatization of Functional and Join Dependencies in the Relational Model. *M. Sc. thesis*, Weizman Institute, Rehovot, Israel, April 1980.

Vardi, M.Y. [1980b]. Inferring Multivalued Dependencies from Functional and Join Dependencies. *Unpublished manuscript*, March 1980.

Vassiliou, Y. [1980a]. Functional Dependencies and Incomplete Information. *VLDB VI*, Montreal, Canada. ACM, IEEE. 260-269.

Vassiliou, Y. [1979]. Null Values in Database Management—A Denotational Semantics Approach. *ACM SIGMOD Conf.* 1979, 162-169.

Vassiliou, Y. [1980b]. Testing Satisfaction of FDs on a Multi-Relation Database "Fast". *XP1 Workshop on Relational Database Theory*, SUNY at Stony Brook, NY, June-July 1980.

Walker, A. [1980a]. On Retrieval from a Small Version of a Large Database. *VLDB VI*, Montreal, Canada. ACM, IEEE. 47-54.

Walker, A. [1980b]. Time and Space in a Lattice of Universal Relations with Blank Entries. *XP1 Workshop on Relational Database Theory*, SUNY at Stony Brook, NY, June-July 1980.

Walker, A. [1979]. A Universal Table Relational Database Model with Blank Entries. *Unpublished manuscript*.

Wang, C.P., and Wedekind, H.H. [1975]. Segment Synthesis in Logical Database Design. *IBM J. of Research and Development*, Armonk, NY, January 1975, 71-77.

Wiederhold, G. [1977]. *Database Design*. New York: McGraw-Hill.

Wong, E., and Youssefi, K. [1976]. Decomposition—A Strategy for Query Processing. *ACM TODS* 1:3, September 1976, 223-241.

Yannakakis, M. [1981]. Algorithms for Acyclic Database Schemes. *VLDB VII*, Cannes, France. ACM, IEEE. 82-94.

Yannakakis, M., and Papadimitriou, C.H. [1980]. Algebraic Dependencies. *IEEE Foundations of Computer Science Conf.* 1980, 328-332.

Yao, S.B. [1979]. Optimization of Query Evaluation Algorithms. *ACM TODS* 4:2, June 1979, 133-155.

Yu, C.T., and Ozsoyoglu, M.Z. [1979]. An Algorithm for Tree-Query Membership of a Distributed Query. *IEEE Computer Software and Applications Conf.* 1979 (COMPSAC '79), 306-312.

Yu, C.T., and Ozsoyoglu, M. [1980]. On Determining Tree-Query Membership of a

Distributed Query. *Computer Science Report* 80-1, Univ. of Alberta, Edmonton, Canada, January 1980.

Zaniolo, C. [1976]. Analysis and Design of Relational Schemata for Database Systems. *Doctoral diss.*, UCLA, Los Angeles, CA, July 1976.

Zaniolo, C. [1979]. Mixed Transitivity for Functional and Multivalued Dependencies in Database Relations. *Information Processing Letters* 8:1, Amsterdam, Netherlands: North-Holland, January 1979, 11-14.

Zaniolo, C. [1977]. Relational Views in a Database System: Support for Queries. *IEEE Computer Software and Applications Conf.* 1977 (COMPSAC '77), 267-275.

Zaniolo, C., and Melkanoff, M.A. [1982]. A Formal Approach to the Definition and the Design of Conceptual Schemata for Database Systems. To appear in *ACM TODS*.

Zaniolo, C., and Melkanoff, M.A. [1981]. On the Design of Relational Database Schemata. *ACM TODS* 6:1, March 1981, 1-47.

Zloof, M.M. [1977]. Query-by-Example: A Database Language. *IBM Systems J.* 16:4, Armonk, NY, December 1977, 324-343.

Zloof, M.M. [1981]. Query-by-Example Language Specifications. *Unpublished manuscript*.

Zloof, M.M. [1976]. Query-by-Example: Operations on the Transitive Closure. *IBM Report* RC5526, Yorktown Heights, NY, October 1976.

INDEX